Reader Series
in Library and Information Science

Reader in
Research Methods
for Librarianship

edited by

Mary Lee Bundy and Paul Wasserman

with

Gayle Araghi

 **MICROCARD® EDITIONS**
901 TWENTY-SIXTH STREET, N.W., WASHINGTON, D. C. 20037, 202/333-6393
INDUSTRIAL PRODUCTS DIVISION, THE NATIONAL CASH REGISTER COMPANY

Copyright © 1970 by the National Cash Register Company, Dayton, Ohio, United States of America. All Rights Reserved. Printed in the U.S.A. Published by Microcard Editions, 901 26th St. N.W., Washington, D.C. 20037, a part of the Industrial Products Division, The National Cash Register Company.

Library of Congress Catalog Card Number 70-86858

Contents

VI
THE ENVIRONMENT OF RESEARCH

APPENDICES

Introduction

The fundamental purpose of this volume is to assist its reader to genuinely perceive the nature of scholarship and its relationship to the goals of librarianship. Viewed in this way, and perhaps as antidote to the more rigidly formalistic treatments of the technical matters of research, the editors' concern here has been less with the rituals and far more with the fundamental nature of intellectual inquiry and its societal contribution, with the modes of analysis, the habits of thought and expression which characterize scholarship and the scholar.

Another primary purpose has been to put research into a context which clearly depicts the task of the researcher, and so illuminates realistically not only the rigor and the discipline, but the human triumphs and joys which derive from its accomplishment. Seen thus, as a dynamic field fit for the adventurer of the mind, perhaps it may succeed in enticing more to its fold from among those in librarianship with imaginative and creative capacity, who have not before held this perspective of research.

The urgent need to develop a systematized and organized body of knowledge relevant to librarianship's most essential issues provided the impetus for this effort. For the library field is viewed by the editors to be at a decisive stage in its evolution. It will go forward or it will sink lower. Scholarship into its fundamental issues is seen both as the most hopeful and the most viable instrument for its advance. In order to exploit the potential of research to its fullest, problems must be generalized, conceived in their broadest context, and removed from the technical limits imposed by a narrow view of practice.

A variety of approaches to exploring key issues and basic processes are incorporated within the volume's framework—academic treatments of various aspects of research, illustrative examples of theory, field research accounts, and actual research instruments. To find the most provocative and insightful contributions, a wide range of the literature on research methods was screened. Seen as relevant were articles concerned with not only the design and conduct of research, but also its philosophical and social implications and relationships.

A quick overview of content will reveal that very few selections dealing directly with library research have been included. This imbalance reflects the editors' view that the more basic and sophisticated social science contributions better illuminate the nature of the problems and the methods of attack upon them than would material from the heavily method-oriented and less sophisticated literature of library research. Because this is so, an important element of the editorial task has been to identify the relevance of the selections to librarianship and to specify how the concerns of the library field might most profit from the methods of analysis detailed.

The emphasis of this book is upon the theoretical basis of research. A number of the selections are concerned in whole or in part with conceptual issues and a section of the volume is devoted in its entirety to the presentation of illustrative conceptual formulations. In the editors' view, a decided limit of the field's development has been the essentially weak or non-existent conceptual basis for its practice. If this is so, the limits of library research may be seen to stem less from lack of methodological rigor and more from theoretical weakness. Yet, the theoretical limitations may not be clearly perceived even by those who conduct investigations in librarianship. Perhaps this is why the basic theoretical development of the field has come more nearly from social scientists, rather than from library researchers. The capacity of a field to advance as an intellectual discipline, and ultimately as a field of practice, is not extended until its research contribution is constructed upon theoretical bases and is less a successive stream of descriptive, unrelated studies. In important part, this book will explain why this is so.

The distillation from the inordinately large body of significant publication, of those contributions which would comprise an organized and orderly orientation for the student of research methods in librarianship has been the prime task of the editors. Many other selections might have been included. To delimit, to choose and so to exclude, is excruciatingly difficult. The items chosen have been measured thoughtfully against an evaluative yardstick of genuine relevance in the present context.

This volume's content is not at a beginning level; some choices are highly advanced treatments. Selections are drawn from the work of some of the most distinguished contributors to the knowledge base of the social sciences. The reader is thus immersed in the fundamental concerns to which social research is addressing itself. One consequence is that some readers may find it useful to supplement this work with more detailed explanations provided in basic textbooks in research methods. To facilitate such selection, a bibliography has been appended to the volume's content.

This volume is intended for use by the individual who is attempting to better understand how research provides the capacity for a field to move forward. Such a book might be read in or out of formal courses in library education. The work may be used by those with differing levels of sophistication and applied variously—as general orientation to research methods, as the basis for study and discussion in seminar, and as introduction to the issues around which a more scholarly basis for librarianship may be constructed. It would serve then as accompaniment to a formal course, as focus for seminar discussion, or as orientation to the independent reader who seeks to advance his understanding outside the formal academic framework.

If the book succeeds, it will provide its reader with a genuine grasp of what research is all about. It should help to clarify how research happens and what it is like to function in a research context as individual or as group member. It should also clarify the way in which a scholar thinks, convey a sense of the frustrations and the satisfactions of his role. If the book succeeds, it will attract some to the banner of library research, or at least lure some on beyond the extracts included here to a fuller reading in the rich literature from which they have been drawn. If the work achieves these ends, even in part, it will have fulfilled the most optimistic expectation of its compilers.

I

INTRODUCTION TO RESEARCH

These introductory selections have been drawn together in order to state the nature and the premises of scientific inquiry. They are designed also to identify in the behavioral movement of the social sciences the broad conceptual setting for library research and to orient the reader to the scholarly issues in the social sciences which are relevant to library research. The Riesman selection introduces basic reservations about the potential contribution of research in a volume otherwise fully committed to the research process and to its tenets. Through the Potter piece, the efficacy of most of historical research in librarianship may be seen from a penetratingly questioning perspective.

A number of other issues not treated in the selections, yet germane to the interests of the student of research methods, deserve special mention. Students of librarianship, particularly those drawn from humanistic disciplines, often question fundamentally the validity and sometimes even the propriety of research into the personal, the human realm. They doubt that there is order or regularity in the human universe which may be observed and understood as in the physical universe. And, given the present limited capacity of the social sciences to predict behavior, they would call into question the basic validity of theoretical generalization. Another issue which calls forth skepticism is the applicability of scientific method to the study of human behavior. Intrinsic to the study of physical science is the experiment, the manipulation of physical ingredients in such a way as to establish control over variables. Some fields of behavioral research, certain branches of psychology in particular, have adopted the experimental approach almost entirely. Others have concerned themselves with other means of control and other forms of proof. This objection may be answered by what is implicit in many of the articles contained in this volume: that while the social sciences may embrace the overall method and philosophy of science, the particular methods employed may be different. Yet, these are legitimate issues which require further discussion and analysis, both as to the general issues and as to the specific approaches used in the various disciplines and for various ends.

The study of human beings engenders unique problems seldom precisely specified or understood. In the process of studying people, the researcher may often himself influence change in their behavior so that they are no longer representative. For the fact of being studied, either during the process or afterward, does influence behavior (voting behavior studies are a good case in point). Another complication arises in library research when the researcher is not only another human being with his own orientation and values, but is often himself a member of a profession with a personal stake and point of view about librarianship. However much he may try to be value neutral, his orientation and his outlook can enter into his choice of problem, and in design and analysis. The consequences of these issues also deserve careful consideration by the serious student of the research process.

Many other subtle issues will be identified in the selections which follow. For students of librarianship, drawn predominantly from the humanities, to view human behavior in analytical, in problem-solving terms, often calls for a traumatic reorientation of perspective. But, perhaps the main lesson is to understand that the careful objective analysis of human beings and of their behavior is not to be equated with coldness, lack of sympathy or unconcern with human values. For behavioral research may also be viewed to be spawned out of the desire to influence the course of human events for the better.

What is Scientific Method?

by Morris Cohen and Ernest Nagel

The last chapter of this classic volume captures the essence of scientific inquiry. Such an idealized and abstract view of science may seem far removed from the average library research project. Yet, this profession needs as never before the commitment to truth and the process by which it is obtained to be clear and unambiguous. In librarianship, operating philosophy and theory are frequently conditioned more by history and tradition, than by the rigor of intellectual analysis. "When we are asked to treat our cherished beliefs as mere hypotheses, we rebel as violently as when those dear to us are insulted." Perhaps here is the basis for the hostility to rational scientific procedure so frequently encountered in librarianship.

In a time requiring radical change, research can reduce the uncertainty which surrounds the future, provide the basis for rational decision-making, help to replace convention and dogma by an orderly change process which avoids succumbing to expediency or to fads of the moment. But, without genuine understanding of the potential, the commitments or the ethics of research, by those who sponsor it, such library research as is done will remain inextricably tied to immediate practical ends. Or, it will be misused in order to simply bolster the status quo. Above all, those who conduct research and share in its legitimate aspirations, must override the pressures and short-term outcomes so often sought by pragmatists and beleaguered administrators. Social science legitimately tests and challenges the tenets of the "establishment," and those engaged in library research must be clear about the difference between serving as hired hands and conducting scholarship oriented toward scientific ends.

Anyone contemplating a career in research must then assess its requirements in personal terms and the authors of this selection provide a basis for such self-evaluation. The essential ingredient is curiosity, the desire to know. This may be expressed as a compulsion to find order and meaning in a world otherwise composed of miscellaneous accidental or capricious occurrences. Skepticism and doubt, the willingness to challenge conventional wisdom, and to venture into areas often forbidden by dogma and tradition, are its concomitants. Then, there is discipline—the capacity to suspend judgment until all the facts are in, and the cool impersonal detachment so much easier to assume in the physical than in the social sciences.

These requirements do not easily blend with the real world of funding and action and the mitigating influences which they inspire. Nor is every personality suited to a life-style of inquiry. A conformist society produces only a relative few who maintain their early child-like interest in exploring the world around them. Yet, the fundamental problems in librarianship, as in other fields, require assault through a means more scientifically sound than those which simply provide ad hoc answers. To take a stance for scientific method in a field which seldom honors or understands the difference is less easy than acceptance of the world as it is and conforming to it. Still, those who teach and conduct research must somehow ponder the why and whether of every issue they address. For, to raise the questions and to derive genuinely scientific solutions is to forge ahead. There is no alternate route.

SOURCE: From *An Introduction to Logic and Scientific Method* by Morris R. Cohen, copyright, 1934, by Harcourt, Brace & World, Inc.; renewed, 1962, by Ernest Nagel and Leonora Cohen Rosenfield. Reprinted by permission of the publisher.

We asserted earlier that the method of science is free from the limitations and willfulness of the alternative methods for settling doubt which we there rejected. Scientific method, we declared, is the most assured technique man has yet devised for controlling the flux of things and establishing stable beliefs. What are the fundamental features of this method? We have already examined in some detail different constituent parts of it. Let us bring together here the more important threads of our discussions.

Facts and Scientific Method

The method of science does not seek to impose the desires and hopes of men upon the flux of things in a capricious manner. It may indeed be employed to satisfy the desires of men. But its successful use depends upon seeking, in a deliberate manner, and irrespective of what men's desires are, to recognize, as well as to take advantage of, the structure which the flux possesses.

1. Consequently, scientific method aims to discover what the facts truly are, and the use of the method must be guided by the discovered facts. But, as we have repeatedly pointed out, what the facts are cannot be discovered without reflection. Knowledge of the facts cannot be equated to the brute immediacy of our sensations. When our skin comes into contact with objects having high temperatures or with liquid air, the immediate experiences may be similar. We cannot, however, conclude without error that the temperatures of the substances touched are the same. Sensory experience sets the *problem* for knowledge, and just because such experience is immediate and final it must become informed by reflective analysis before knowledge can be said to take place.

2. Every inquiry arises from some felt problem, so that no inquiry can even get under way unless some selection or sifting of the subject matter has taken place. Such selection requires, we have been urging all along, some hypothesis, preconception, prejudice, which guides the research as well as delimits the subject matter of inquiry. Every inquiry is specific in the sense that it has a definite problem to solve, and such solution terminates the inquiry. It is idle to collect "facts" unless there is a problem upon which they are supposed to bear.

3. The ability to formulate problems whose solution may also help solve other problems is a rare gift, requiring extraordinary genius. The problems which meet us in daily life can be solved, if they can be solved at all, by the application of scientific method. But such problems do not, as a

rule, raise far-reaching issues. The most striking applications of scientific method are to be found in the various natural and social sciences.

4. The "facts" for which every inquiry reaches out are propositions for whose truth there is considerable evidence. Consequently what the "facts" are must be determined by inquiry, and cannot be determined antecedently to inquiry. Moreover, what we believe to be the facts clearly depends upon the stage of our inquiry. There is therfore no sharp line dividing facts from guesses or hypotheses. During any inquiry the status of a proposition may change from that of hypothesis to that of fact, or from that of fact to that of hypothesis. Every so-called fact, therefore, *may* be challenged for the evidence upon which it is asserted to be a fact, even though no such challenge is actually made.

Hypotheses and Scientific Method

The method of science would be impossible if the hypotheses which are suggested as solutions could not be elaborated to reveal what they imply. The full meaning of a hypothesis is to be discovered in its implications.

1. Hypotheses are suggested to an inquirer by something in the subject matter under investigation, and by his previous knowledge of other subject matters. No rules can be offered for obtaining fruitful hypotheses, any more than rules can be given for discovering significant problems.

2. Hypotheses are required at every stage of an inquiry. It must not be forgotten that what are called general principles or laws (which may have been confirmed in a previous inquiry) can be applied to a present, still unterminated inquiry only with some risk. For they may not in fact be applicable. The general laws of any science function as hypotheses, which guide the inquiry in all its phases.

3. Hypotheses can be regarded as suggestions of possible connections between actual facts or imagined ones. The question of the truth of hypotheses need not, therefore, always be raised. The necessary feature of a hypothesis, from this point of view, is that it should be statable in a determinate form, so that its implications can be discovered by logical means.

4. The number of hypotheses which may occur to an inquirer is without limit, and is a function of the character of his imagination. There is a need, therefore, for a technique to choose between the alternative suggestions, and to make sure that the alternatives are in fact, and not only in appear-

ance, *different* theories. Perhaps the most important and best explored part of such a technique is the technique of formal inference. For this reason, the structure of formal logic has been examined at some length. The object of that examination has been to give the reader an adequate sense of what formal validity means, as well as to provide him with a synoptic view of the power and range of formal logic.

5. It is convenient to have on hand—in storage, so to speak—different hypotheses whose consequences have been carefully explored. It is the task of mathematics to provide and explore alternative hypotheses. Mathematics receives hints concerning what hypotheses to study from the natural sciences; and the natural sciences are indebted to mathematics for suggestions concerning the type of order which their subject matter embodies.

6. The deductive elaboration of hypotheses is not the sole task of scientific method. Since there is a plurality of possible hypotheses, it is the task of inquiry to determine which of the possible explanations or solutions of the problem is in best agreement with the facts. Formal considerations are therefore never sufficient to establish the material truth of any theory.

7. No hypothesis which states a general proposition can be demonstrated as absolutely true. We have seen that all inquiry which deals with matters of fact employs probable inference. The task of such investigations is to select that hypothesis which is the most probable on the factual evidence; and it is the task of further inquiry to find other factual evidence which will increase or decrease the probability of such a theory.

Evidence and Scientific Method

Scientific method pursues the road of systematic doubt. It does not doubt *all* things, for this is clearly impossible. But it does question whatever lacks adequate evidence in its support.

1. Science is not satisfied with psychological certitude, for the mere intensity with which a belief is held is no guarantee of its truth. Science demands and looks for logically adequate grounds for the propositions it advances.

2. No single proposition dealing with matters of fact is beyond every significant doubt. No proposition is so well supported by evidence that other evidence may not increase or decrease its probability. However, while no single proposition is indubitable, the body of knowledge which supports it, and of which it is itself a part, is better grounded than any alternative body of knowledge.

3. Science is thus always ready to abandon a theory when the facts so demand. But the facts must really demand it. It is not unusual for a theory to be modified so that it may be retained in substance even though "facts" contradicted an earlier formulation of it. Scientific procedure is therefore a mixture of a willingness to change, and an obstinacy in holding on to, theories apparently incompatible with facts.

4. The verification of theories is only approximate. Verification simply shows that, within the margin of experimental error, the experiment is *compatible* with the verified hypothesis.

System in the Ideal of Science

The ideal of science is to achieve a systematic interconnection of facts. Isolated propositions do not constitute a science. Such propositions serve merely as an opportunity to find the logical connection between them and other propositions.

1. "Common sense" is content with a miscellaneous collection of information. As a consequence, the propositions it asserts are frequently vague, the range of their application is unknown, and their mutual compatibility is generally very questionable. The advantages of discovering a system among facts is therefore obvious. A condition for achieving a system is the introduction of accuracy in the assertions made. The limit within which propositions are true is then clearly defined. Moreover, inconsistencies between propositions asserted become eliminated gradually because propositions which are part of a system must support and correct one another. The extent and accuracy of our information is thus increased. In fact, scientific method differs from other methods in the accuracy and number of facts it studies.

2. When, as frequently happens, a science abandons one theory for another, it is a mistake to suppose that science has become "bankrupt" and that it is incapable of discovering the structure of the subject matter it studies. Such changes indicate rather that the science is progressively realizing its ideal. For such changes arise from correcting previous observations or reasoning, and such correction means that we are in possession of more reliable facts.

3. The ideal of system requires that the propositions asserted to be true should be connected without the introduction of further propositions for which the evidence is small or nonexistent. In a system the number of unconnected propositions and the number of propositions for which there is

no evidence are at a minimum. Consequently, in a system the requirements of simplicity, as expressed in the principle of Occam's razor, are satisfied in a high degree. For that principle declares that entities should not be multiplied beyond necessity. This may be interpreted as a demand that whatever is capable of proof should be proved. But the ideal of system requires just that.

4. The evidence for propositions which are elements in a system accumulates more rapidly than that for isolated propositions. The evidence for a proposition may come from its own verifying instances, or from the verifying instances of *other* propositions which are connected with the first in a system. It is this systematic character of scientific theories which gives such high probabilities to the various individual propositions of a science.

The Self-Corrective Nature of Scientific Method

Science does not desire to obtain conviction for its propositions in *any* manner and at *any* price. Propositions must be supported by logically acceptable evidence, which must be weighed carefully and tested by the well-known canons of necessary and probable inference. It follows that the *method* of science is more stable, and more important to men of science, than any particular result achieved by its means.

1. In virtue of its method, the enterprise of science is a self-corrective process. It appeals to no special revelation or authority whose deliverances are indubitable and final. It claims no infallibility, but relies upon the methods of developing and testing hypotheses for assured conclusions. The canons of inquiry are themselves discovered in the process of reflection, and may themselves become modified in the course of study. The method makes possible the noting and correction of errors by continued application of itself.

2. General propositions can be established only by the method of repeated sampling. Consequently, the propositions which a science puts forward for study are either confirmed in all possible experiments or modified in accordance with the evidence. It is this self-corrective nature of the method which allows us to challenge any proposition, but which also assures us that the theories which science accepts are more probable than any alternative theories. By not claiming more certainty than the evidence warrants, scientific method succeeds in obtaining more logical certainty than any other method yet devised.

3. In the process of gathering and weighing evidence, there is a continuous appeal from facts to theories or principles, and from principles to facts. For there is nothing intrinsically indubitable, there are no absolutely first principles, in the sense of principles which are self-evident or which must be known prior to everything else.

4. The method of science is thus essentially circular. We obtain evidence for principles by appealing to empirical material, to what is alleged to be "fact"; and we select, analyze, and interpret empirical material on the basis of principles. In virtue of such give and take between facts and principles, everything that is dubitable falls under careful scrutiny at one time or another.

The Abstract Nature of Scientific Theories

No theory asserts *everything* that can possibly be asserted about a subject matter. Every theory selects certain aspects of it and excludes others. Unless it were possible to do this—either because such other aspects are irrelevant or because their influence on those selected is very minute—science as we know it would be impossible.

1. All theories involve abstraction from concrete subject matter. No rule can be given as to which aspects of a subject matter should be abstracted and so studied independently of other aspects. But in virtue of the goal of science—the achievement of a systematic interconnection of phenomena—in general those aspects will be abstracted which make a realization of this goal possible. Certain common elements in the phenomenon studied must be found, so that the endless variety of phenomena may be viewed as a system in which their structure is exhibited.

2. Because of the abstractness of theories, science often seems in patent contradiction with "common sense." In "common sense" the unique character and the pervasive character of things are not distinguished, so that the attempt by science to disclose the invariant features often gives the appearance of artificiality. Theories are then frequently regarded as "convenient fictions" or as "unreal." However, such criticisms overlook the fact that it is just certain *selected invariant relations* of things in which science is interested, so that many familiar properties of things are necessarily neglected by the sciences. Moreover, they forget that "common sense" itself operates in terms of abstractions, which are familiar and often confused, and which are inadequate to express the complex structure of the flux of things.

Types of Scientific Theories

Scientific explanation consists in subsuming under some rule or law which expresses an invariant character of a group of events, the particular events it is said to explain. Laws themselves may be explained, and in the same manner, by showing that they are consequences of more comprehensive theories. The effect of such progressive explanation of events by laws, laws by wider laws or theories, is to reveal the interconnection of many apparently isolated propositions.

1. It is clear, however, that the process of explanation must come to a halt at some point. Theories which cannot be shown to be special consequences from a wider connection of facts must be left unexplained, and accepted as a part of the brute fact of existence. Material considerations, in the form of contingent matters of fact, must be recognized in at least two places. There is contingency at the level of sense: just *this* and not *that* is given in sense experience. And there is contingency at the level of explanation: a definite system, although not the only possible one from the point of view of formal logic, is found to be exemplified in the flux of things.

2. In a previous chapter we have enumerated several kinds of "laws" which frequently serve as explanations of phenomena. There is, however, another interesting distinction between theories. Some theories appeal to an easily imagined *hidden mechanism* which will explain the observable phenomena; other theories eschew all reference to such hidden mechanisms, and make use of *relations* abstracted from the phenomena actually observable. The former are called *physical* theories; the latter are called *mathematical* or *abstractive* theories.

It is important to be aware of the difference between these two kinds of theories, and to understand that some minds are especially attracted to one kind, while others are comfortable only with the other kind. But it is also essential not to suppose that either kind of theory is more fundamental or more valid than the other. In the history of science there is a constant oscillation between theories of these two types; sometimes both types of theories are used successfully on the same subject matter. Let us, however, make clear the difference between them.

The English physicist Rankine explained the distinction as follows: There are two methods of framing a theory. In a mathematical or abstractive theory, "a class of objects or phenomena is defined . . . by describing . . . that assemblage of properties which is common to all the objects or phenomena composing the class, as perceived by the senses, without introducing anything hypothetical." In a physical theory "a class of objects is defined . . . as being constituted, in a manner not apparent to the senses, by a modification of some other class of objects or phenomena whose laws are already known."[1]

In the second kind of theory, some visualizable model is made the pattern for a mechanism hidden from the senses. Some physicists, like Kelvin, cannot be satisfied with anything less than a mechanical explanation of observable phenomena, no matter how complex such a mechanism may be. Examples of this kind of theory are the atomic theory of chemistry, the kinetic theory of matter as developed in thermodynamics and the behavior of gases, the theory of the gene in studies on heredity, the theory of lines of force in electrostatics, and the recent Bohr model of the atom in spectroscopy.

In the mathematical type of theory, the appeal to hidden mechanisms is eliminated, or at any rate is at a minimum. How this may be done is graphically described by Henri Poincaré: "Suppose we have before us any machine; the initial wheel work and the final wheel work alone are visible, but the transmission, the intermediary machinery by which the movement is communicated from one to the other, is hidden in the interior and escapes our view; we do not know whether the communication is made by gearing or by belts, by connecting-rods or by other contrivances. Do we say that it is impossible for us to understand anything about this machine so long as we are not permitted to take it to pieces? You know well we do not, and that the principle of the conservation of energy suffices to determine for us the most interesting point. We easily ascertain that the final wheel turns ten times less quickly than the initial wheel, since these two wheels are visible; we are able thence to conclude that a couple applied to the one will be balanced by a couple ten times greater applied to the other. For that there is no need to penetrate the mechanism of this equilibrium and to know how the forces compensate each other in the interior of the machine."[2] Examples of such theories are the theory of gravitation, Galileo's laws of falling bodies, the theory of the flow of heat, the theory of organic evolution, and the theory of relativity.

As we suggested, it is useless to quarrel as to which type of theory is the more fundamental and which type should be universally adopted. Both kinds of theories have been successful in coördinating vast domains of phenomena, and fertile in making discoveries of the most important kind. At some periods in the history of a science, there is a tendency to mechanical models and atomicity;

at others, to general principles connecting characteristics abstracted from directly observable phenomena; at still others, to a fusion or synthesis of these two points of view. Some scientists, like Kelvin, Faraday, Lodge, Maxwell, show an exclusive preference for "model" theories; other scientists, like Rankine, Ostwald, Duhem, can work best with the abstractive theories; and still others, like Einstein, have the unusual gift of being equally at home with both kinds.

THE LIMITS AND THE VALUE OF SCIENTIFIC METHOD

The desire for knowledge for its own sake is more widespread than is generally recognized by anti-intellectualists. It has its roots in the animal curiosity which shows itself in the cosmological questions of children and in the gossip of adults. No ulterior utilitarian motive makes people want to know about the private lives of their neighbors, the great, or the notorious. There is also a certain zest which makes people engage in various intellectual games or exercises in which one is required to find out something. But while the desire to know is wide, it is seldom strong enough to overcome the more powerful organic desires, and few indeed have both the inclination and the ability to face the arduous difficulties of scientific method in more than one special field. The desire to know is not often strong enough to sustain critical inquiry. Men generally are interested in the results, in the story or romance of science, not in the technical methods whereby these results are obtained and their truth continually is tested and qualified. Our first impulse is to accept the plausible as true and to reject the uncongenial as false. We have not the time, inclination, or energy to investigate everything. Indeed, the call to do so is often felt as irksome and joy-killing. And when we are asked to treat our cherished beliefs as mere hypotheses, we rebel as violently as when those dear to us are insulted. This provides the ground for various movements that are hostile to rational scientific procedure (though their promoters do not often admit that it is science to which they are hostile).

Mystics, intuitionists, authoritarians, voluntarists, and fictionalists are all trying to undermine respect for the rational methods of science. These attacks have always met with wide acclaim and are bound to continue to do so, for they strike a responsive note in human nature. Unfortunately they do not offer any reliable alternative method for obtaining verifiable knowledge.

The great French writer Pascal opposed to logic the spirit of subtlety or finesse (*esprit géometrique* and *esprit de finesse*) and urged that the heart has its reasons as well as the mind, reasons that cannot be accurately formulated but which subtle spirits apprehend none the less. Men as diverse as James Russell Lowell and George Santayana are agreed that:

"The soul is oracular still,"

and

"It is wisdom to trust the heart . . .
To trust the soul's invincible surmise."

Now it is true that in the absence of omniscience we must trust our soul's surmise; and great men are those whose surmises or intuitions are deep or penetrating. It is only by acting on our surmise that we can procure the evidence in its favor. But only havoc can result from confusing a surmise with a proposition for which there is already evidence. Are all the reasons of the heart sound? Do all oracles tell the truth? The sad history of human experience is distinctly discouraging to any such claim. Mystic intuition may give men absolute subjective certainty, but can give no proof that contrary intuitions are erroneous. It is obvious that when authorities conflict we must weigh the evidence in their favor logically if we are to make a rational choice. Certainly, when a truth is questioned it is no answer to say, "I am convinced," or, "I prefer to rely on this rather than on another authority." The view that physical science is no guide to proof, but is a mere fiction, fails to explain why it has enabled us to anticipate phenomena of nature and to control them. These attacks on scientific method receive a certain color of plausibility because of some indefensible claims made by uncritical enthusiasts. But it is of the essence of scientific method to limit its own pretension. Recognizing that we do not know everything, it does not claim the ability to solve all of our practical problems. It is an error to suppose, as is often done, that science denies the truth of all unverified propositions. For that which is unverified today may be verified tomorrow. We may get at truth by guessing or in other ways. Scientific method, however, is concerned with verification. Admittedly the wisdom of those engaged in this process has not been popularly ranked as high as that of the sage, the prophet, or the poet. Admittedly, also, we know of no way of supplying creative intelligence to those who lack it. Scientists, like all other human beings, may get into ruts and apply their techniques regardless of varying circumstances.

There will always be formal procedures which are fruitless. Definitions and formal distinctions may be a sharpening of tools without the wit to use them properly, and statistical information may conform to the highest technical standards and yet be irrelevant and inconclusive. Nevertheless, scientific method is the only way to increase the general body of tested and verified truth and to eliminate arbitrary opinion. It is well to clarify our ideas by asking for the precise meaning of our words, and to try to check our favorite ideas by applying them to accurately formulated propositions.

In raising the question as to the social need for scientific method, it is well to recognize that the suspension of judgment which is essential to that method is difficult or impossible when we are pressed by the demands of immediate action. When my house is on fire, I must act quickly and promptly—I cannot stop to consider the possible causes, nor even to estimate the exact probabilities involved in the various alternative ways of reacting. For this reason, those who are bent upon some specific course of action often despise those devoted to reflection; and certain ultramodernists seem to argue as if the need for action guaranteed the truth of our decision. But the fact that I must either vote for candidate X or refrain from doing so does not of itself give me adequate knowledge. The frequency of our regrets makes this obvious. Wisely ordered society is therefore provided with means for deliberation and reflection *before* the pressure of action becomes irresistible. In order to assure the most thorough investigation, all possible views must be canvassed, and this means toleration of views that are *prima facie* most repugnant to us.

In general the chief social condition of scientific method is a widespread desire for truth that is strong enough to withstand the powerful forces which make us cling tenaciously to old views or else embrace every novelty because it is a change. Those who are engaged in scientific work need not only leisure for reflection and material for their experiments, but also a community that respects the pursuit of truth and allows freedom for the expression of intellectual doubt as to its most sacred or established institutions. Fear of offending established dogmas has been an obstacle to the growth of astronomy and geology and other physical sciences; and the fear of offending patriotic or respected sentiment is perhaps one of the strongest hindrances to scholarly history and social science. On the other hand, when a community indiscriminately acclaims every new doctrine the love of truth becomes subordinated to the desire for novel formulations.

On the whole it may be said that the safety of science depends on there being men who care more for the justice of their methods than for any results obtained by their use. For this reason it is unfortunate when scientific research in the social field is largely in the hands of those not in a favorable position to oppose established or popular opinion.

We may put it the other way by saying that the physical sciences can be more liberal because we are sure that foolish opinions will be readily eliminated by the shock of facts. In the social field, however, no one can tell what harm may come of foolish ideas before the foolishness is finally, if ever, demonstrated. None of the precautions of scientific method can prevent human life from being an adventure, and no scientific investigator knows whether he will reach his goal. But scientific method does enable large numbers to walk with surer step. By analyzing the possibilities of any step or plan, it becomes possible to anticipate the future and adjust ourselves to it in advance. Scientific method thus minimizes the shock of novelty and the uncertainty of life. It enables us to frame policies of action and of moral judgment fit for a wider outlook than those of immediate physical stimulus or organic response.

Scientific method is the only effective way of strengthening the love of truth. It develops the intellectual courage to face difficulties and to overcome illusions that are pleasant temporarily but destructive ultimately. It settles differences without any external force by appealing to our common rational nature. The way of science, even if it is up a steep mountain, is open to all. Hence, while sectarian and partisan faiths are based on personal choice or temperament and divide men, scientific procedure unites men in something nobly devoid of all pettiness. Because it requires detachment, disinterestedness, it is the finest flower and test of a liberal civilization.

FOOTNOTES

[1] W. J. M. Rankine, *Miscellaneous Scientific Papers*, 1881, p. 210.
[2] *Op. cit.*, pp. 290–91.

The Current Meaning of Behavioralism

by David Easton

The utility of this contribution for librarianship may seem remote. But, the parallels with librarianship are pronounced. David Easton, himself an important contributor to the behavioral movement in political science, characterizes behavioralism and assesses its status and impact. The piece serves both as orientation for those whose background in the social sciences may be in the classical tradition and as encouragement to explore the rich and abundant research possibilities within this mainstream of the social sciences.

Part of the excitement of behavioral research is, as Easton suggests, that its theory has been closely tied to empirical research. Ideal models of state, the traditional concern of classical political science, were discarded in favor of studying the political process as it actually occurs. In place of descriptive, legalistic tracts, dynamic studies bring the political process to life by following its path in and out of the formal process of government.

Similarly, the study of administration took on a wholly new perspective as its underlying assumptions were challenged. This was achieved as social scientists, attracted to the study of organizational research, brought with them social values and behavioral perspectives at variance with traditional managerial views. Librarianship can exercise the same option. Instead of reinforcing prevailing managerial modes and organizational structure, the goals of research can be shifted toward better understanding of how human beings function and interact in organizational life. Through the use of the conceptual framework of behavioralism, understanding of the political and the organizational issues of libraries would be enhanced and thereby the capacity of librarianship to be more responsive and relevant might be improved in significant ways.

Periodically, waves of concern pass over American political science as we contemplate the creature, called political behavior, to which we have given birth in the last two decades. The now not-so-young Turks who a decade ago were speaking in loud, strident, and sometimes rude voices about the dire need for scientific method in political research have begun to feel that they have finally acquired the garments of legitimacy. But, no sooner do they dare to comfort themselves with this thought than another panel at a professional meeting stirs up new and stormy conflict over the parentage of this latest offspring, its respectability, and its future. No sooner does the profession settle down and seem to accept it, as testified by the growing feeling that no department of political science is complete without at least one representative of this point of view, than a new book or article again challenges its assumptions, meaning, and intent. It may be, as a recent advocate has announced,[1] that the battle for acceptance

has really been won, but, if so, it is by no means over as yet and not everyone has been willing to give credence to the good news. There are some who would say that we are mistaking a series of continuous preliminary skirmishes for the main engagement.

The truth probably lies somewhere between these two points of view. But, regardless of where the discipline now finds itself with regard to the reception of the behavioral approach, before we can even begin to explore its meaning, there is some sense in outlining in bold relief the nature of the creature about which we shall be talking. Because at least its adversaries are prone to identify this approach as political *behaviorism*, we might well begin by asking whether this is indeed the correct name for the offspring or whether, on the contrary, it is just a sly way of calling it a rude name, hoping thereby to keep it out of the front parlor. That there is some genuine doubt about its paternity, however, is

SOURCE: Reprinted from David Easton, "Introduction: The Current Meaning of 'Behavioralism' in Political Science," *The Limits of Behavioralism in Political Science*, ed. James C. Charlesworth (Philadelphia: American Academy of Political and Social Science, 1962), pp. 1–25, by permission of the publisher.

attested to by the fact that it is just as often described as behavioristic, not only by its least hospitable critics but by neutral bystanders as well. What validity is there in thus labeling it behavioristic?

I am quite puzzled by the use of this adjective. As far as I know, there is probably no one in political science who would consider himself a behaviorist, however elastic his imagination, or who would wish to be so designated, at least if the term is used in its rigorous and proper sense. In origin, as associated with J. B. Watson, it is a psychological concept which was adopted to help exorcise from scientific research all reference to such subjective data as purposes, intentions, desires, or ideas. Only those observations obtained through the use of the sense organs or mechanical equipment were to be admitted as data. Observable behavior generated by external stimuli rather than inferences about the subjective state of mind of the person being observed were to constitute the subject matter of research.

In the intervening years since behaviorism was first enunciated, most psychologists have come to recognize that, between external stimulus and observable response, subjective experiences occur that influence the interpretation and effect of the stimulus and, thereby, the nature of the response. The original behavioristic paradigm, S-R (stimulus-response), has yielded to the more intelligible one of S-O-R (stimulus-organism-response) in which feelings, motivations, and all the other aspects of the subjective awareness and reaction of the organism are taken into account as potentially useful data. This has, of course, spelled the doom of pristine behaviorism, and as a term, although not necessarily as a point of view, it has just about disappeared from psychology.

Until recently, political science has borrowed little from psychology, so that, even to the extent that behaviorism has been adopted by psychologists, there could have been slight opportunity for it to seep in. It has been even less likely that this would happen in the case of a theoretical position so indefensible to most psychologists themselves. Aside from a rather quaint, not entirely consistent, and, for that matter, not too intelligible formal adoption of Watsonian behaviorism by A. F. Bentley in his *Process of Government*, I know of no one associated with political research who has advocated a position that even begins to approximate so rigid an exclusion of subjective data. Ideas, motives, feelings, attitudes, all appear as important variables. By design at least, students

of political behavior have given no indication of intending to adopt a behavioristic posture.

In the eyes of some, it is true, behavioral research may indeed be viewed as behavioristic in its outcome. We must, however, look upon this as problematic, a matter of interpretation. To describe this kind of research as "political behaviorism" is to be guilty either of a very loose usage of words or of prejudging an issue that ought to be a subject for thorough discussion. There is perhaps still another alternative, however, which may help to explain the misuse of the term. In part, it may arise out of the polemics surrounding the behavioral movement in political science. As part of a critical counterideology, a behavioristic interpretation is one that those opposed to the assumptions and procedures of the behavioral approach might well seek to keep alive. If this is so, there is even greater reason for abandoning the term in our search for clarity about the correct meaning to attribute to research in political behavior.

To summarize, I shall assume that the term political behavior is not necessarily equivalent to political behaviorism and that the latter description is improperly used except as a conclusion to a relevant argument. The concept of which I am undertaking to discuss the meaning is that of political "behavior," the adjective being "behavioral" as in the phrase "behavioral sciences," not "behavioristic." Support for the clear distinction and difference between the terms is lent by its use in such institutional titles as the Center for Advanced Study in the Behavioral Sciences at Stanford, the section of the Ford Foundation, now liquidated, that was known as the Behavioral Sciences Division, and the Institute of Behavioral Science at the University of Colorado, as well as the journals of *Behavioral Science* and the *American Behavioral Scientist*. Substitution of "behavioristic" in these names would be entirely confusing and misleading about the scope and direction of interest of the institution or publication involved. The generic noun referring to this whole approach in the various social sciences would probably be "behavioralism," but it is such an awkward neologism that most people sensibly avoid it where possible.

TENDENCY AND MOVEMENT

Political behavior stands for both an intellectual tendency and a concrete academic movement. As a tendency, it is an intellectual current that may be found among many students of politics, in some minor degree at least; as a movement, it has many fewer outright adherents and advocates. So much is clear and, with respect to it, we could probably obtain agreement from those more or less associated with this point of view. But, beyond this, the approach is still so new and its limits so poorly defined that it is doubtful whether we could arrive at a consensus on its positive aspects. We would find it extremely difficult to come to terms, first, about who among political scientists ought to be identified as pursuing behavioral research; that is, who are the authentic members of the movement or its valid practitioners. Second, we would also find sharp disagreement on where the emphasis in this research ought to lie, that is, on its nature as an intellectual enterprise.

To consider the first point, aside from the prestige that inclusion in the movement might carry with it for some or the embarrassment it might occasion others, the criteria for membership are as loose and ambiguous as the boundaries are vague and arguable. As in most social movements, membership is not a matter of belonging to a formal organization but of possessing a sense of belonging together, sharing similar assumptions and ideals, respecting one another's interests, seeking reciprocal aid and sustenance, or accepting a common leadership.

In addition, however, there are some physical symbols and behavior patterns that distinguish the movement. Its adherents have tended to publish through a limited number of periodicals such as the *Public Opinion Quarterly, World Politics,* the *American Behavioral Scientist*, and *Behavioral Science*, and, unexpectedly, the movement has even evoked a limited degree of specialization in the choice of book publishers. Although the movement has never crystallized in a formal sense, there are structures such as the Social Science Research Council's Committee on Political Behavior and the Committee on Comparative Politics that provide some institutional focus in at least these two fields. Furthermore, some time ago, the strength or feeling of the adherents was sufficiently strong to stimulate discussion of separatist institutions, such as a special journal.[2] But, unlike the fields of psychology, psychiatry, and other sciences where splinter associations have emerged, in spite of some talk at one time, a special subdivision of the American Political Science Association providing institutional expression for the new approach never did hive off. The Association has proved sufficiently flexible to adapt with the necessary speed to the changing character of the field.[3]

But these material symbols have provided too informal a connection with the behavioral approach, and they have been too fragmented and limited in scope to offer a major or satisfying central focus for the movement. The result is that it has remained quite rudimentary, unable to generate a true sense of orthodoxy or of inviolable tenets. The political science profession has thereby been spared the trauma of institutional schisms. But, the other side of the coin is that card-carriers in the behavioral movement are not easy to distinguish from fellow-travelers, tolerant sympathizers, occasional supporters, or ambivalent critics. One and the same person may be seen by traditionalists as belonging to opposing camps or may well be disowned by both for diametrically opposite reasons.

Perhaps some of the ambiguity also stems from the nature of the commitment required of a behavioralist. It is such that a devotee is not automatically prohibited or incapacitated from continuing traditional research where it seems necessary and appropriate, as in the study of the relationship among institutions. The behavioral approach has shown its greatest strength in research on individuals, especially in a face-to-face relationship, or with respect to a type of aggregative behavior such as voting. Small groups and organizations in their internal structure and processes and certain aspects of well-defined communities represent the maximal scope for which there have been contrived research techniques entirely harmonious with the assumptions of behavioralism. The techniques become less reliable and their results less valid when applied to the interrelationships of institutions such as party systems and legislatures, or electoral systems and parties, or the effect of alternative types of institutional arrangements on recruitment to positions of leadership and authority.[4]

Criticism to the contrary notwithstanding, it is the rare student of political behavior who overcommits himself to the limits of research as defined by his rigorous techniques. In practice, we find most behavioralists prepared to use the best available technical resources, even if it means that the traditional approach alone is feasible. The behavioralist is, in effect, a product mix of the traditional and the behavioral, weighted on the side of the latter. But it is the particular mixture that frequently leads to difficulty in identifying those who constitute authentic behavioralists.

If our first point is that political behavior has

many of the qualities of an inchoate social movement, our second one is that, just because the movement is so ill defined, it is far more easily described by reference to its intellectual content than to its membership. Most students of politics, even those unwilling to accept classification as behavioralists, would probably agree about the general nature of its assumptions and objectives, although strong differences might well arise concerning the precise emphasis to be given to any one of these.

What is the nature of these assumptions and objectives, the intellectual foundation stones on which this movement has been constructed? No single way of characterizing them is satisfactory to everyone, but the following itemized list provides a tolerably accurate and reasonably exhaustive account of them.[5]

(1) Regularities: There are discoverable uniformities in political behavior. These can be expressed in generalizations or theories with explanatory and predictive value.

(2) Verification: The validity of such generalizations must be testable, in principle, by reference to relevant behavior.

(3) Techniques: Means for acquiring and interpreting data cannot be taken for granted. They are problematic and need to be examined self-consciously, refined, and validated so that rigorous means can be found for observing, recording, and analyzing behavior.

(4) Quantification: Precision in the recording of data and the statement of findings require measurement and quantification, not for their own sake, but only where possible, relevant, and meaningful in the light of other objectives.

(5) Values: Ethical evaluation and empirical explanation involve two different kinds of propositions that, for the sake of clarity, should be kept analytically distinct. However, a student of political behavior is not prohibited from asserting propositions of either kind separately or in combination as long as he does not mistake one for the other.

(6) Systematization: Research ought to be systematic; that is to say, theory and research are to be seen as closely intertwined parts of a coherent and orderly body of knowledge. Research untutored by theory may prove trivial, and theory unsupportable by data, futile.

(7) Pure science: The application of knowledge is as much a part of the scientific enterprise as theoretical understanding. But the understanding and explanation of political behavior logically precede and provide the basis for efforts to utilize political knowledge in the solution of urgent practical problems of society.

(8) Integration: Because the social sciences deal with the whole human situation, political research can ignore the findings of other disciplines only at the peril of weakening the validity and undermining the generality of its own results. Recognition of this interrelationship will help to bring political science back to its status of earlier centuries and return it to the main fold of the social sciences.

This list probably includes all the major tenets of the behavioral credo and represents the major differences between the behavioral and traditional modes of research. As such, we have a purely formal statement of the meaning of behavioralism, one that helps us less in understanding its meaning than in appreciating the nature of the kind of questions we must begin to ask. For, even if we were to have little difficulty in obtaining formal agreement to this list, there can be no doubt that major differences would immediately well to the surface, not necessarily about the composition of the behavioral credo itself, but about the relative prominence of one or another of the articles.

As we review the varied explanations offered by behavioralists themselves, and I include my own writings among them, we find that, within the broad limits set by the credo, the behavioral approach has come to mean about as many things as there are commentators. Every man puts in his own emphasis and thereby becomes his own behavioralist. Is it exclusively the use of scientific method or just a mood favoring that method?[6] Does it represent the use of kinds of data hitherto absent from political research, especially the findings from such "hard core" sciences as psychology, sociology, and anthropology,[7] or does it stand largely for a return to the individual as the focal point for political research?[8] May we interpret behavioralism even more broadly and flexibly and view it as a virtually empty bottle into which one pours any kind of wine, new or old, as long, presumably, as it is aromatic of science?[9] Whatever our point of view, we have authorities to whom we can turn to press out interpretation.

But complete interpretive anomie does not exist. Even though the relative emphases bring different aspects of the landscape into prominence and, momentarily, may even leave the impression that the authorities are geographically far apart, closer inspection does reveal that they are all looking ahead towards the same region in space—a science of politics modeled after the methodological assumptions of the natural sciences, as the well-worn cliché has it.

As I have suggested, this conclusion leaves us with a fundamental question still unanswered. If this is all that the revolt against tradition has really meant, if all that behavioralists are arguing for is the introduction of scientific method and nothing more, why are we not content with calling a spade a spade? Why has it been necessary or useful to mint and distribute a new conceptual currency, political behavior? After all, science is still an honored and prestigious ideal in the United States. Indeed, during the 1920's and 1930's, the phrase "science of politics" was the preferred way for referring to the newer tendencies of the period out of which the modern revolt has sprung. Need we call the rose by any other name?

If we were satisfied to accept the explanation of political behavior as just the continued application of scientific method to politics begun in the 1920's and 1930's, we could quickly brush aside this change in terminology by attributing it to caprice, to the inexplicable alternations brought about by the fads and fashions of language, or to the need for a distinctive symbol of self-identification in the battles with established orthodoxy. Undoubtedly, such factors as these have played a part in the diffusion of the behavioral label. But, if we stopped here and concluded that this is all that the new name conveys, we would be neglecting some essential substantive implications of the contemporary movement in political science, implications of a kind that show our discipline to be an integral part of a deeper shift taking place in the social sciences as a whole in our age. To appreciate the full and rich meaning of the behavioral trend in political research, we must broaden our horizons momentarily. We must pause to see this development as a reaction to and reflection of the fact that all the social sciences are together advancing to a new stage, one of increased scientific maturity, I am tempted to say.

CAVEATS

If we are content to accept the behavioral approach as just another way of signifying that we are proposing to use the most advanced methods of social science and nothing more, we saddle ourselves with the following real problem. A number of other social sciences, such as the so-called hardcore sciences we have already mentioned, have for many years, well before World War II, looked upon themselves as devotees of the scientific method.

Much of their labor has gone into clarifying and elaborating the methodological premises of the social sciences and developing sophisticated and rigorous techniques for accumulating, interpreting, and analyzing data. The striking point here is that, even though these disciplines so conceived of themselves in the interval between the wars, it is only in the last decade that they too have come to describe themselves and to be designated by others as behavioral sciences.

As in the case of political science itself, we might argue that there is really nothing in a name, that the oscillation in nomenclature between social sciences and behavioral sciences today is inconsequential and irrelevant. But, if ordinary common sense tells us little else, it does sensitize us to the fact that names reflect and, often in anticipation, reinforce changes already taking place in the objects to which they refer. It is my argument that the name changes have precisely this meaning in the social sciences.

The inclusion of the study of political life as part of the behavioral sciences, if it has indeed got its foot in the door of this privileged club, similarly hints that, regardless for the moment of the nature of the transformation that has taken place, it must involve more than just the importation into political science of the scientific method. It is for this reason that we cannot hope to understand the full connotations of the term "political behavior" unless we see it as part of the evolution of the social disciplines as a whole. It is just too deceptively easy to interpret it either as a synonym for what is virtuous in research or for scientific method; it is only partly correct to see in it an ideological weapon lending color and vigor to the movement of a diffuse and informal group of academic rebels against traditions.

Furthermore, aside from anything else, it sells this new movement quite short. Such simplistic interpretations inadvertently lend credence to the very point that the most impassioned critics of political behavior have advanced. These critics have accused students of political behavior of selecting their problems not in the light of theoretical or ethical relevance but largely on grounds of the accidental availability of technically adequate means for research. If a reliable technique is not at hand, the subject is not considered researchable. As a result of the admittedly early stages in the development of technical means of social research, the argument runs, the behavioral approach is able to deliver reliable knowledge only with regard to political commonplaces or trivia.

The really significant problems of political life cannot be challenged by these means, the argument continues, hence, insistence upon the priority of technical competence manages to squeeze out the free play of insight and imagination.

This is not the chapter in which the merits of this criticism can be weighed. But, from the point of view of the meaning of political behavior, if we were to concede that it conveys nothing more than the tried and true phrase "scientific method," we could not help but leave the impression that its critics were not too far wrong. It would represent basically a change in mood in favor of scientific methodology, methods, and techniques, with the emphasis on the latter.

No one could argue that it does not represent these things, and if it did nothing else, it would be a significant enough contribution. But we cannot stop at this point if we seek to do full justice to this tendency. It would lead us to neglect or ignore entirely an equally crucial contribution of a substantive kind, one that helps to build a major bridge between ourselves as political scientists and our neighboring disciplines on the one side and the future of political research on the other.

HISTORICAL PERSPECTIVE

To appreciate how far the emergence of a behavioral approach goes beyond a methodological or mere technical reorientation, we have to put recent trends in political research into the context of the whole historical movement of the social sciences. The quickest way of doing this, without becoming enmeshed in the intracacies of their history, is to trace out lightly the evolution in names used to identify what today we are coming to call the behavioral sciences. These names mirror the essence of the historical transformations relevant to our immediate purposes.

Historically, as we know, all social knowledge was originally one and indivisible; the intellectual specialization of labor appears late upon the scholarly scene in the Western world. For almost two thousand years, from the early classical Greek period to somewhere in the eighteenth century, men basically saw each other not as specialists but as general seekers after wisdom and knowledge, as philosophers in the original sense of the word. It is true, as early as the Middle Ages, law, theology, and medicine stood as separate and co-ordinate fields of learning and teaching in the universities: but philosophy still embraced the bulk of human knowledge about man in society.

With the increasing weight and differential rate and direction of the development of knowledge in the modern historical periods, however, this general corpus gradually began to break up into specialized segments. By the eighteenth century, for example, we can already distinguish what came to be called natural philosophy from moral philosophy, and, as knowledge in both these fields increased remarkably during that century, their names underwent a further subtle modification. Under the heightening prestige of chemistry, physics, and biology, they acquired the names natural and moral sciences. With further elaboration during the nineteenth century, especially under the impetus of Saint-Simon and August Comte with their sharp focus on human relationships in society, the moral sciences finally became known by the contemporary phrase, social sciences. Of course, ethical inquiry and philosophy persisted throughout all of what is a very complicated evolution of social knowledge. But, from a repository for almost all knowledge, philosophy has been left as a residual category which until today has continued to shrink in scope and of necessity to redefine its tasks periodically.

If this light survey of names associated with social knowledge at its various stages does nothing else, it alerts us to the fact that the emergence of a new name today is not unique and occurs at a particular point in a history that has been under way for thousands of years and will undoubtedly continue. Each transition, from philosophy to natural and moral philosophy, to moral and natural sciences, then to the social sciences, and now to behavioral sciences, signals a stage in a truly linear movement in the nature and assumptions about our understanding of man in society. We may well suspect that some fundamental transformations have taken place today or are in mid-process.

RECENT DEVELOPMENT

We are left with the problem, therefore, of seeking to understand why, at this particular moment in its history, a significant part of the social sciences has come to be called the behavioral sciences. In its origins, it may well be that the concept can be laid at the door of accident. At the time a Senate committee was exploring the need for a national science foundation to stimulate and provide funds for scholarly research, representatives of the social sciences worked hard for the inclusion of their disciplines within the scope of the proposed legislation. Whether through genuine

error or design, there were some disapproving sena-
tors who, from the floor of the Senate, insisted upon
talking of social science as socialist science. To
abort the growth of further confusion, the phrase
"behavioral sciences" is said to have been coined
to refer to all living systems of behavior, biological
as well as social, an underlying idea being that it
would serve to identify those aspects of the social
sciences that might come under the aegis of a
foundation devoted to the support of hard
science.[10] At about the same time, the Ford
Foundation was being organized, and, in looking
around for an appropriate title for the section
devoted to the encouragement of the scientific
development of social knowledge, the decision
was made to call it the Behavioral Sciences Division. Hence, these two accidental forces converged
to popularize the new name.

Whether or not the story about its origin is
apocryphal, and however interesting speculation
about the source of an idea may be, it is, of course,
not decisive. Many ideas are born; only a few survive and spread. The task is to try to understand
what there is in the nature of the present historical
situation in research that has led social scientists
to seize upon the new name in place of the much
older and more familiar one.

We can see that, in the adoption of this name
by the various foundations, institutes, and departmental programs at universities, the idea of behavioral science is applied to any social research
concerned with a scientific understanding of man
in society, regardless of the disciplinary umbrella
under which it may find shelter. We hear talk
about the study of religious behavior, economic
behavior, political behavior, psychological behavior,
and so on. The concept applies well beyond the
boundaries of the three so-called hard-core disciplines. But, as we have seen, at least from the
point of view of helping to move these disciplines
more quickly or surely in a scientific direction,
the use of the concept would be superfluous. They
were and are well known for their scientific commitments and have given little evidence of changing course. We might ask, therefore, whether, in
the broad sweep of the history of social knowledge, the idea of the behavioral sciences does not
foreshadow a new turning in the road, the beginning of a fundamentally new direction of development?

The answer is clearly in the affirmative. This
new terminology reflects the fact that two new ingredients have been added to contemporary social
research that will help to set it apart from all past
eras. In the first place, never before has there

been so great a demand for self-conscious attention
to empirical theory at all levels of generality—
middle range as well as general—that, in principle,
can be reduced to testable propositions. In the
second place, as part of this, the social sciences
have been compelled to face up to the problem of
locating stable units of analysis which might
possibly play the role in social research that the
particles of matter do in the physical sciences.[11]

In part, this turn towards empirical theory has
been related to a hope that has never been completely lost from sight in the whole history of increasing specialization of knowledge and which appeared again in particularly strong form in the
1930's and 1940's. This was the idea that the
understanding of man in society would be immeasurably enriched if some way could be found
to draw the social sciences together into a basic
unity. For a time, integration of the social
sciences became something of an academic
will-o'-the-wisp and, although today it has lost
its initial momentum, it has left a vital residue
behind.

It turned out that scholars could conceive of
intergration of the disciplines as occurring at several different levels.[12] At the applied level, one
could bring the data of the social sciences together
for the solution of whole social problems. Unification was to take place on the job, as it were.
Housing, employment, peace, and the like were
not to be seen as sociological or economic or political matters exclusively; adequate consideration
of these would include the use of knowledge from
a whole range of disciplines. Teams of specialists
working together for practical purposes might
thereby provide one kind of disciplinary integration.

A second kind might emerge through programs
of research training. Students would be expected
to address themselves not to a discipline but to
social problems in the hope that they would learn
to bring to bear on them the modes of analysis
and data from any area of knowledge and research
that seemed relevant and appropriate. The student
was supposed to ignore the walls between the disciplines and to consider himself simply a social
scientist. In such programs, reference to the formal name of a discipline might be strictly taboo.

Related to but nonetheless different from this
approach was a third kind in which it was felt that
thorough training of a person in two or three disciplines might bring about a limited integration in
the mind of a single individual, or at least encourage it within the limits of the capacity of a
single person to absorb and independently to syn-

thesize a number of social fields. Here, training was to be disciplinary in its orientation, but, in the outcome, two or more disciplines would be fused.

Each of these three levels had something to commend it, each has left its mark on curricula for the training of social scientists today, and each has helped to create a new self-image of the social sciences, at least with respect to their intrinsic interconnections. But none of these paths led towards any integral unification of the disciplines; at most, what was proposed was some kind of cross-fertilization or exchange of knowledge. They left the way open to search for a means of genuinely synthesizing the disciplines, and this has come to form a possible fourth level of integration.

The key idea behind this approach has been the conviction that there are certain fundamental units of analysis relating to human behavior out of which generalizations can be formed and that these generalizations might provide a common base on which the specialized sciences of man in society could be built. In place of some mechanical combination of the social sciences, this substituted an underlying basic science of behavior. Although, in reductionist vein, some have argued for psychology as the already existing basic science and others have put in a plea for sociology or anthropology or even political science, the main effort has gone towards the search for an entirely new foundation.

The expectation and hope that it will be possible to develop a common underlying social theory impels research in certain inescapable directions.[13] The most significant of these for our purposes is that it has led to the search for a common unit of analysis that could easily feed into the special subject-matters of each of the disciplines. Ideally, the units would be repetitious, ubiquitous, and uniform, molecular rather than molar. In this way they would constitute the particles, as it were, out of which all social behavior is formed and which manifest themselves through different institutions, structures, and processes.

We can concretize the meaning of this conviction if we glance at the way it has worked itself out to this point. As an example, in the case of Talcott Parsons, the Weberian derived notion of *action* seemed to provide the most fruitful unit out of which a common macrotheory might be constructed, one that would be serviceable to all of the social disciplines. Although the action frame of reference can thus be easily associated with the name of one scholar, there are other units of analysis that have been proposed but of which the paternity is multiple, diffuse, and converging.

For some who have been strongly influenced by social psychology, the *decision*, or choice, among alternatives has seemed to be the most promising unit. It even infected economics, which is the one social science that seemed invulnerable to change in this direction, so tightly knit and self-contained a theory did it already have. For others deriving from anthropology, *functions* of varying kinds supplied a rather broad and different kind of unit, somewhat slippery to handle, to be sure, but nevertheless a unit that could be discovered and utilized in all of the disciplines.[14]

Most recently, *systems* have made their appearance as a possible focus, beginning with the smallest cell in the human body as a system and working up through ever more inclusive systems such as the human being as an organism, the human personality, small groups, broader institutions, societies, and collections of societies, such as the international system. The assumption is that behavior in these systems may be governed by homologous processes. General systems analysis is perhaps an even more ambitious effort than action theory to draw disciplines into a common framework, for it spreads its net over all of the sciences, physical and biological as well as social, and views them all as behaving systems.[15]

Let us disregard for the moment the particular answers designed to form the bridgework of a general theory. In its broadest sweep, adoption of the label "behavioral sciences" symbolizes the hope that, ultimately, some common variables may be discovered, variables of a kind that will stand at the core of a theory useful for the better understanding of human behavior in all fields. In some vague way, there has been added to this the feeling that psychology, sociology, and anthropology are the core sciences out of which such a theory may well spring.

This approach, it is clear, reaffirms a commitment to the assumptions and methods of empirical science, especially for those disciplines such as political science that have hitherto been reluctant to adopt them. But it goes further. It enriches this method by stressing the hitherto quite neglected theoretical component. Out of the whole scientific credo presented earlier, it is the theoretical tenet that is becoming magnified in our present historical period and that gives the scientific enterprise in the social disciplines the special character implied in the idea of behavioral sciences.

RELEVANCE TO POLITICAL SCIENCE

At this point, we may well ask: This is all very well for the current historical position of the social sciences as a whole, but what relevance for the meaning of the behavioral approach in political science can we attach to these trends? Bearing in mind the broader context in which we have been placing our discussion, we can now begin to draw together the threads so that we may more clearly see the source of some of the ambiguity about the meaning of behavioralism in political science.

As I have already pointed out, the literature on the subject insists upon interpreting the behavioral approach in politics as the symbol of scientific method, the introduction of new kinds of data from the hard-core social sciences, and the like, each interpreter providing his own favorite emphasis. At the risk of laying myself open to the accusation of adding still another special plea and emphasis, I am now going to argue the following. What all of these points of view fail to take into account in any serious way is the connection between the behavioral approach in political science and the current trends towards theory in the general body of the social sciences, sparked as this new theoretical tendency has been by a strong interest in the integration of the disciplines. The behavioral aspect of the new movement in political research involves more than method; it reflects the inception in our discipline of a theoretical search for stable units for understanding human behavior in its political aspects.

How does it come about that current interpretations of the behavioral movement in our discipline have failed to appreciate this theoretical aspect? Our neglect is understandable; it flows from the peculiar historical conditions under which political science finds itself today.

If we look again for a moment at the so-called hard-core sciences, especially psychology and sociology, we can see that, in them, the techniques of empirical research had been slowly maturing long before World War II. In fact, these disciplines had even had plenty of time to become overcommitted to the bare technical skills associated with a scientific approach. They had fallen into the bad habits of crude empiricism, that is, the accumulation of data for the sake of the data themselves with relatively little consideration to matters of relevance and broader significance of the findings. It was only late in the interval between the two world wars that they began to respond seriously to the idea that crude empiricism is not enough and to rediscover what some few had been long insisting upon, that relevance and understanding could be achieved only through the development of broad theory. But the reception of scientific method

took place long before the term behavioral science was ever heard of. Commitment to and engagement in scientific research was therefore antecedent to the relatively recent reawakening to the need for general theory relevant to human behavior. These disciplines, therefore, had experienced a two-stage effect: first came scientific method and considerably later, through behavioralism, theoretical concerns.

But, in political science, there has been no such orderly sequence of exposure to the different aspects of scientific method. From the point of view of the experiences of other social sciences, our discipline has been undergoing two revolutions simultaneously. We have come to scientific method at about the same time as the social sciences as a whole have been shifting their emphasis from the methods of research alone to theory as well. In effect, we have jumped a stage experienced by the so-called core disciplines, or, alternately, we can say that we have combined two stages in one. We are in the process of absorbing the basic assumptions of scientific method at the same time as we proceed to the equally trying task of giving meaning to the behavior we study by relating it to some empirical theoretical context.

At the risk of adding to the complexity of an already sufficiently involved analysis, I would suggest that what has been happening in political science is as follows. We have been adopting the assumptions and technical means associated with a science of society and at the same time we have been moving toward a behavioral approach. There is a danger to this formulation. It implies that behavioralism is different from scientific method, whereas it is only this method with a shift in emphasis to the substantive problems of concept formation and theory construction. But, because the behavioral emphasis is extremely visible in other social sciences today, we have adopted this label to apply to both kinds of changes that happen to be taking place simultaneously in political science. If we temporarily keep the technical imperatives of scientific method separate from the behavioral approach, we shall have a much better opportunity to understand the true character of the dual revolution currently under way in political science. By any logical criteria, of course, both these aspects, the technical and theoretical, are part and parcel of scientific method.

With regard to the reception of the technical aspect, surely little has to be said. Its origin lies in the early part of this century with the development by the 1920's of a series of conferences devoted to the new science of politics. But the full invasion did not occur until after World War II. The increasing prevalence in political research of the use of carefully devised interviews, survey research, technical methods for measurement, and the formalization of analysis in logical and mathematical symbols testify to the growing inroads that rigorous techniques are making. These have been fortified by the widespread introduction of instruction on the scope and method of political science and training in the use of mechanized procedures for recording and analyzing data. It is becoming increasingly difficult to keep up with political research unless one has at least a reading familiarity with the techniques being used. There can be little doubt about the nature and prevalence of this segment of the dual revolution.

Although, as I have indicated, we may include this technical change as part of the behavioral movement, it seems to me sensible to do so only if, at the same time, we are equally conscious of the second revolution that has been concurrently under way and which much more faithfully reflects pressures that have transformed other social sciences into behavioral disciplines. As we saw, this revolution has involved the sharp consciousness in recent years that, without far more concentrated effort on empirical theory, our technical resources would be squandered.

In political science, we may not always be conscious of the progress we have slowly been making with respect to the search for useful theoretical orientations under the very broad and poorly outlined behavioral umbrella. Perhaps this is due to the fact that we have been concentrating on the difficult and time-consuming task of refashioning our tools of research, learning new languages of analysis, and familiarizing ourselves with the methods, data, and findings of related disciplines. But, the long traditional pre-occupation of political science with theory has left us peculiarly sensitive to the theoretical implications of the behavioral tendencies and, without being overly conscious about it, we have been responding to these tendencies. In fact, when we pause to look at our inventory of empirically oriented theoretical ideas, it is slight, as we might expect. But, given the very short time that the behavioral approach has been persuasive in political research, it may come as a pleasant surprise to discover that we have a respectable number of alternative conceptual approaches for the study of political life

or some of its major segments. Not that these conceptual structures are fully developed or close to any ideal form. But they do constitute a beginning and a promise for the future.

As in the case of the purely technical revolution, not all theoretical innovations have been confined to the postwar period. In a few instances, during the interval between the wars, empirical frameworks of analysis were proposed and elaborated. Catlin, for example, had turned to the "will" as his basic unit of analysis,[16] Merriam and others in the Chicago School had focused on power, and the group had been elevated to a central position. But, in recent decades, many important additions have been offered, and these have helped to broaden our range of choice, to link us to the main currents of research in other disciplines, and to enrich our theoretical insights. Undoubtedly, this search for adequate units of analysis—whatever the degree of awareness present—is preparing the ground out of which, in the none too distant future, may well emerge some minimal consensus.

We can get a better sense of the theoretical ferment that is accompanying the behavioral tendency and which forms a central part of it if we look somewhat more closely at the kinds of units that have emerged. Until the 1940's Lasswell, virtually alone, had carried the burden of seeking to weave together theory and empirical research. But, with the end of the war, he was joined by Herbert Simon. Although little recognition has been given to the fact, in retrospect there can be little doubt that to Simon is due major credit for awakening postwar political scholarship to the role of empirical theory. The very title of his ground-breaking volume, *Administrative Behavior*, showed how closely the new behavioral movement was linked with theory, in this case, in administration. At the same time, it introduced the profession to the theoretical and empirical potency of his main unit of analysis, the decision.

The use of this variable as a central unit quickly spread to other areas of political science, aided as it was by its prevalence in other fields of social research as well. Today, decision-making has become the most generalized new concept in political research. It has been seriously and systematically adopted for research in community political-structure and processes, in the empirical understanding of international relations,[17] and, at the formal level, in the logic of choice as expressed in game theories.[18] Simultaneously, research on voting, under the stimulus of social psychology, discovered a theoretical matrix for itself in the decisional concept.[19] The vote now came to be interpreted not just as a rather unique kind of act in a democratic system but as one that brought to a head a special kind of decision that persons are expected to make in any number of contexts, such as committees and the economic market place as well as elections. The integrative quality of the decisional approach is most apparent at this level.

Furthermore, in a vague and general way, it has been adopted by large numbers of political scientists in their research on general political processes; these tend to be described as the processes through which political decisions or public policies are made. The result is that, at the present time, it may be that the decisional orientation has begun to lose its original impetus, not because it has proved unequal to its tasks but rather because its points of major value may now be largely absorbed into the mainstream of political research.

Units of analysis other than the decision have been proposed or elaborated for the study of political behavior. For example, although the concept of the group had been prominent in the interval between the wars, Truman elevated it to a new level of refinement and thereby made it eminently more usable for theoretical purposes.[20] In the last few years, Almond has sought to weave together the ideas of system, culture, function, structure, and action into a conceptual scheme designed particularly for comparative analysis and research.[21] Deutsch has organized a conceptual structure around the message and its networks as the major unit for a kind of analysis that leads towards a theory of political communications.[22] In my own work, I have been exploring the utility of the system as the major unit, focusing on political life as a system of behavior operating within and responding to its social environment as it makes binding allocations of values.[23] And, for many others associated with the behavioral movement, the major unit has been at least some undefined but nonetheless real "behaving individual" in relationship with other behaving individuals, all of whom have determinable attitudes, motivations, knowledge, and values and who thereby constitute the universal "particles" of political life.

Although this list may not be exhaustive, it does illustrate the increasing attention to empirically or behaviorally oriented concepts in political research. Entirely aside from the merits of any one conceptual perspective, we cannot easily separate from a behavioral approach the fact that we now have a considerable variety of alternative units from which to select and that we are sharply aware of the need to articulate and to question critically the theoretical premises of empirical work.

Hence, too, we can better understand the efforts to redefine or describe the limits of political science as a field of relatively self-contained phenomena. What some have felt to be fruitless and wasteful inquiries into the theoretical boundaries of our discipline have simply represented a groping toward at least the gross units in terms of which political life can be identified, observed, and analyzed; power, policy- or decision-making, groups, systems, political communications, functions are all such units. Slay the dragon of disciplinary redefinition as we may, it insists upon rearing its head in a new form each time and to higher levels of conceptual sophistication.

SUMMARY

Behavioral research thus stands for a new departure in social research as a whole; it is the most recent development in a long line of changing approaches to the understanding of society. It means more than scientific techniques, more than rigor. This alone would indeed mean *rigor mortis* as its critics from the traditional points of view, both classical and institutional, have been so quick and correct to point out. The behavioral approach testifies to the coming of age of theory in the social sciences as a whole, wedded, however, to a commitment to the assumptions and methods of empirical science. Unlike the great traditional theories of past political thought, new theory tends to be analytic, not substantive, general rather than particular, and explanatory rather than ethical. That portion of political research which shares these commitments to both the new theory and the technical means of analysis and verification thereby links political science to broader behavioral tendencies in the social sciences and, hence, its description as political behavior. This is the full meaning and significance of the behavioral approach in political science today.

FOOTNOTES

[1] R. A. Dahl, "The Behavioral Approach," *American Political Science Review*, Vol. 55 (1961), pp. 763–772.
[2] I think that it is fair to say that it was in the atmosphere of these discussions that the *American Behavioral Scientist* (formerly PROD) was founded, on the initiative and responsibility of its present editor, Alfred de Grazia.

[3] This in itself has a history which it would be interesting to explore if we are to understand the way in which a discipline successfully copes with changes in its intellectual objectives and methods, an adaptation that cannot by any means be taken for granted. In this history, the roles of Evron M. Kirkpatrick, executive director of the American Political Science Association, and of Pendleton Herring, through his leadership as President of the Social Science Research Council, would loom very large.

[4] See M. Sherif and B. L. Koslin, *Theoretical and Research Reports: The "Institutional" vs. "Behavioral" Controversy in Social Science with Special Reference to Political Science* (Norman, Oklahoma: Institute of Group Relations, University of Oklahoma, 1960). The authors of this work, looking at political research from the perspectives of social psychology, loudly applaud the insistence on an institutional approach that we find in political science.

[5] Most of the items can be distilled from what is said about the behavioral approach in the following sources: B. Crick, *The American Science of Politics, Its Origins and Conditions* (London: Routledge and Kegan Paul, 1959); R. A. Dahl, *op. Cit.;* M. Duverger, *Méthodes de la Science Politique* (Paris: Presses Universitaries de France, 1959); D. Easton, *The Political System* (New York: Knopf, 1953); and "Traditional and Behavioral Research in American Political Science" in *Administrative Science Quarterly*, Vol. 2 (1957), pp. 110–115; C. S. Hyneman, *The Study of Politics* (Urbana: University of Illinois Press, 1959); D. B Truman, "The Impact on Political Science of the Revolution in the Behavioral Sciences" in *Research Frontiers in Politics and Government* (Washington: The Brookings Institution, 1955), pp. 202–232, and "The Implications of Political Behavior Research," *Items*, Vol. 5 (1951), pp. 37–39; V. Van Dyke, *Political Science, A Philosophical Analysis* (Stanford: Stanford University Press, 1960); D. Waldo, *Political Science in the United States of America* (Paris: Unesco, 1956); *A Report of the Behavioral Sciences at the University of Chicago* (Chicago: Self-Study Committee, 1954); Editorial—"What is Political Behavior," PROD, Vol. 1 (1958), pp. 42–43; and papers presented at the panels on "The Contribution of Studies of Political Behavior" at the Fifth World Congress of the International Political Science Association, Paris, September 26–30, 1961.

[6] R. A. Dahl, *op. cit.*

[7] D. B. Truman, *op. cit.*

[8] D. Easton, *op. cit.*

[9] PROD, *op. cit.*

[10] J. G. Miller, "Toward a General Theory for the Behavioral Sciences," in L. D. White, *The State of the Social Sciences* (Chicago: University of Chicago Press, 1956), pp. 29–65.

[11] For the analogy to physics, see T. Parsons, "The Point of View of the Author" in M. Black (ed.), *The Social Theories of Talcott Parsons, A Critical Examination* (Englewood Cliffs, N. J.: Prentice-Hall, 1961).

[12] For some suggestions along these lines: L. Wirth (ed.), *Eleven Twenty-Six, A Decade of Social Science Research* (Chicago: University of Chicago Press, 1940); C. Dollard, "A Middleman Looks at Social Science," in *American Sociological Review*, Vol. 15 (1950), pp. 16–20; B. F. Hoselitz, "The Social Sciences in the Last Two Hundred Years," in *The Journal of General Education*, Vol. 4 (1950), pp. 85–103; E. R. A. Seligman, "What Are the Social Sciences," in *Encyclopaedia of the Social Sciences* (New York: Macmillan, 1930), Vol. 1, pp. 3–8; W. Gee (ed.), *Research in the Social Sciences* (New York: Macmillan, 1929).

[13] Some of these directions are indicated in R. G. Grinker (ed.), *Toward a Unified Theory of Human Behavior* (New York: Basic Books, 1956).

[14] R. K. Merton, *Social Theory and Social Structure* (Glencoe, Ill.: Free Press, 1949); M. J. Levy, *Structure of Society* (Princeton: Princeton University Press, 1952); K. Davis, "The Myth of Functional Analysis as a Special Method in Sociology and Anthropology," *American Sociological Review*, Vol. 24 (1959), pp. 757–773.

[15] A. R. Radcliffe-Brown, *A Natural Science of Society* (Glencoe, Ill.: The Free Press and Falcon's Wing Press, 1957); various articles in *General Systems*, Yearbook of the Society for General Systems Research, especially those by L. von Bertalanffy and K. Boulding in volume 1, 1956; R. G. Grinker, *op. cit.*

[16] G. Catlin, *A Study of the Principles of Politics* (New York: Macmillan, 1930).

[17] Particularly in the works of Richard Snyder.

[18] See the writings of M. Kaplan, Arthur L. Burns, and R. E. Quandt and the symposium in *World Politics*, Vol. 14, 1961.

[19] See the prevalence of this orientation in B. R. Berelson, P. F. Lazarsfeld, and W. N. McPhee, *Voting* (Chicago: University of Chicago Press, 1954); there is a brief comment on this in D. Easton and R. D. Hess, "Youth and the Political System" in S. M. Lipset and L. Lowenthal, *Culture and Social Character* (New York: The Free Press of Glencoe, 1961), pp. 226–251, esp. at p. 232.

[20] D. B. Truman, *The Governmental Process* (New York: Knopf, 1951). In this respect the brief remarks by A. de Grazia should be examined in "Research on Voters and Elections," *Research Frontiers in Politics and Government*, pp. 104–134, esp. at p. 121.

[21] G. A. Almond, "Introduction: A Functional Approach to Comparative Politics," in G. A. Almond and J. S. Coleman (eds.), *The Politics of Developing Areas* (Princeton: Princeton University Press, 1960). For a greater structural emphasis, see the writings of David Apter.

[22] K. W. Deutsch, *National and Social Communication* (New York: Wiley, 1953).

[23] D. Easton, "An Approach to the Analysis of Political Systems" in *World Politics* (1957), pp. 383–400 and a forthcoming volume elaborating more fully the basic approach and concepts of this article.

Some Observations on Social Science Research[1]

by David Riesman

Riesman stands in the middle here. His mission is to draw together those who concede only the utility of theory with those who focus solely upon data. He embraces it all. Moreover, he reasons that theory is often abstracted from observations on the culture, the media, the societal system, and therefore that the work of the artist, the journalist, the novelist, remains significant to the development of an emergent social science.

The lesson which Riesman relates is that there is not one source of truth in advancing knowledge, but many, and that each deserves a fair hearing. Particularly is this true in those social disciplines which may be characterized as being at the handicraft stage. Seen thus, librarianship requires theorists and philosophers as well as disciplined research. It has already enjoyed the benefit of good journalistic reporting which serves in lieu of research in such areas as censorship. It now requires basic grounding, analytic insight committed to purpose and scope and to explorations and explanations of the variables operative under different conditions. Concepts, theory and philosophy, matched with empirical effort, will then provide mutual reinforcement. In turn, the product of research effort might be more imaginatively and insightfully presented by utilizing journalistic and other literary forms as an alternative to the standardized form and style of the research report.

When theory inspires empirical observation, the prospects may be greatest, and when data is perceived, not simply in order to compile and contribute numbers or facts, but rather to reinforce the capacity of the field to understand, then progress is more assured. Perhaps Garceau's volume* best epitomizes the congruence of theory and data. By utilizing data drawn from field study to reinforce his theoretical political base, more meaningful intelligence was generated than if there were only theoretical design or only statistical evidence. This will explain why such a volume remains a classic contribution and how it may still be used to understand some of the fundamental problems of one type of library long after the time when it was written. When library research sees its commitment more nearly as the construction of a bridge leading from theory to data, and back, only then will it be approaching maturity.

Every work of social science today establishes itself on a scale whose two ends are "theory" and "data": that is, the great theoretical structures by which we attempt to understand our age at one end, and the relatively minuscule experiments and data which we collect as practicing social scientists at the other. In between are smaller schemes of generalization as well as larger and less precise observations. The relationship of the two ends of the scale to each other has never been completely clear, and all efforts simply to resolve the problem by comparisons with the natural sciences, or by drastic rejections of one or the other end of the scale, have failed to achieve general acceptance. Social scientists in pursuit of professionalization of their craft and of status as "scientists" are disturbed by this state of affairs, and are hopeful that, if not now, then soon the theory-data tension can be reconciled by some "operational" formula, and that there will then be no doubt as to what is social science. In this paper, I propose to indicate some reasons for skepticism as to these hopes, and some reasons for thinking that the tension is a productive one in the present state of the art, one we might as well enjoy.

To be sure, some deny there is any problem of

SOURCE: Reprinted from David Riesman, "Some Observations on Social Science Research," *Antioch Review*, 11 (Sept., 1951), pp. 259-278, by permission of the publisher.

*Oliver Garceau, *The Public Library in the Political Process: A Report of the Public Library Inquiry* (New York: Columbia University Press, 1949).

reconciliation by arguing that only experiments and data are science while all the rest, though it may be produced by people who call themselves social scientists, is art or polemics, journalism or whatnot. Still others escape the problem of reconciliation by the opposite denial: they reject as pettyfogging make-work the meticulous technical operations of social science, and they use the club of late great essayistic thinkers to beat live field-workers into humiliation. Their trade-mark: did it take all this foundation money and all these IBM machines to tell us this, which Toqueville already knew a hundred years ago!

What is today the most influential group of social scientists espouses neither of these extreme polarities. Rather, it hopes that the large visions of the "fathers"—of such thinkers as Marx, Simmel, Durkheim, Weber, Freud—can be broken down into smaller-scale parcels that could be subjected to empirical verification by contemporary researchers. In this way, it is thought, we should eventually be able to work our way from research projects testing rather small bits of generalization to large theoretical structures, no less illuminating than those of the past, but in their relation to data more closely parallel to the theories of natural science.[2] As yet, the hope that one can thus ascend from the twigs of research projects to the main trunk of social science theory remains only a hope—though one pursued with ingenuity and devotion by some of the most competent and gifted workers.

II

The sharpness of the polarity between theory and data varies with the age: we live in a third period, succeeding one in which theory reigned supreme, and another, data. Since the gospel of data is connected by personal, if not by inevitable intellectual ties to the concept of a value-free social science, its supremacy has fallen with the present self-consciousness of social scientists concerning values, and their desire to be useful in the formation of public policy; if we had to set a date for this development, we could set it in 1939, when World War II began and when Robert Lynd published his influential *Knowledge for What?* In this third period, each side in the theory-data conflict has strong defenders and the issue is joined with an exigent sense of mission. Moreover, it is part of the conflict that ambitious philosophies of history, past and present, should be sent tumbling down before some inconvenient facts energetically marshalled by the "data"—wing. But it is no less a

mark of the intellectual history of our age that new philosophers of history, reacting against the slavery to fact of most contemporary historians and many contemporary social scientists, should be constantly exasperated by the paucity of data and tempted to stretch their theories over larger ground than those data allow. And in its turn this recrudescent temerity, especially when as with Toynbee it attracts a large lay audience, distresses many of the workers who prefer the data end of the scale, and then seek to arm themselves with still more data, first, to demolish the new philosophy of history, and second, to build the pile of data high enough to compete with it.

In this climate of opinion, the theorist—and I speak here of the scholar who theorizes, who tries to pull together many facts in a large scheme of understanding, not of the person who is concerned with the problem of theory as a methodological specialty—can hope, at best, to be considered "stimulating," but irrelevant to the main course of social science. His "intuitions," as they are half-enviously, half-patronizingly, called, if they are not exploded out of hand by facts, may be considered worthy of processing by other social scientists—we have thus arrived at the strange position where the most seminal works in the social sciences, if they were published today, would probably be denounced in many professional quarters as sheer talk, though talk which might, under a particularly broad-minded thesis committee, be considered as a quarry for graduate students seeking a topic. That is, works of the type that in the past were most significant for the development of social science would today be considered, charitably, as plausible and interesting, but not as starting points for serious intellectual discussion among social scientists trying to evaluate their meaning and value and even validity.

It is argued, of course, that with the rise of empirical techniques social science has outgrown the need to rely on the type of "impressionistic" work of its early formative years. And we cannot dismiss this view as sheer error, for contrary to what many of the "theory"-wing suppose, these techniques have an unexampled richness and promise. Any kind of formal use of interviews, for instance, was not known in the social sciences even thirty years ago; the projective psychological tests are for the most part still younger; the formal, systematic effort at controlled observation that we find in the community survey or the professional ethnographic monograph is less than sixty years old, and in this period works in this genre have become increasingly more precise and many-skilled in method. In their general form and in their possibilities for technical validation and for mathematical treatment, these methods suggest a new vision of social science: superseding social science as an only moderately specialized development out of history and common observation, the goal now looms of a systematically organized body of observation and strict generalization as taut and impressive as the structure of natural science. In my judgment, attainment of the goal is still a long way off, for reasons that I shall come to in a moment; but the impatience of those to whom the goal seems close at hand, with any social science enterprise which does not appear to move directly towards it, is understandable.

Indeed, there is one problem which no amount of improvement in research methods will ever permit us to overcome, namely the limitation of our knowledge of the past imposed by the unfortunate fact that we cannot interview or test the dead. Historiography and archeology can do remarkable jobs of reconstruction, but they can seldom satisfy the ambitious social scientist in search of quantitative comparisons—a point well made in Paul Lazarsfeld's presidential address to the American Association for Public Opinion Research on "The Obligation of the 1950 Pollster to the 1984 Historian." Thus, if we are comparing, let us say, religious affects today with those of a generation ago, there is no need to be markedly more precise at the near than at the far end. Frequently the consequence is, however, that social scientists bemused by the richness of contemporary method confine their studies to the contemporary scene. And they do so not only when they deal with preliterate cultures where historical materials are scanty (though, if one is not perfectionist, less scanty than sometimes supposed), but also when they deal with civilizations where historical materials are abundant but frustrating. Yet it hardly needs argument in these pages that we cannot assay the weight of any prevailing pattern of attitudes and institutions without appreciating their historical development, and that if we do not study permanence and change in a time dimension we might as well surrender altogether the effort to understand society.

This, then, is the dilemma created by the development of our new tools: that they suggest to us a strict form of social science, in which every generalization refers directly or by a process of unassailable deduction to objectively available bodies of data—these generalizations being as meaningful, useful, and interesting as those of natural science; but for the present—possibly, indeed, for the foreseeable future—such generalizations are impoverished and hobbled by these self-same scientific forms, and consequently social science becomes less interesting, meaningful, and useful—as far as permitting us to understand a sequence of development goes—and less attractive altogether as an intellectual enterprise.

III

In the present state of controversy, there is tremendous pressure on students of social science (including especially sociology, social anthropology, psychology, and political science) to take sides either in the "theory" or in the "data" camp; this is easy to observe at such an institution as my own, the University of Chicago, or at Columbia, where both camps are well-armed but hungry for more arms, and where both can call on the support of a great tradition. When these students in their own research discover the really extraordinary difficulties of linking any important generalization to measurable data, and thereby closing the gap between the camps, they are apt to conclude, not that there is something wrong with the warfare, but that they are themselves lacking in what it takes to be warriors. The students would be much better off if they could take a stand against taking a stand: if they could realize that the dilemma is at present irresolvable, and nobody's "fault," and accept it as such; that it makes no sense, on the one hand, to reject the new techniques as grubby and inartistic, or, on the other hand, to discard the humanly valuable essence of social science: its power, as seen in the impact of certain great works in the past, to illuminate and describe in some larger framework the experienced details of social life.

Yet I know how difficult it is to convince anyone that one has not, even surreptitiously, taken a stand for "data" or for "theory." Margaret Mead can publish Samoan house-descriptions and genealogies, or cooperate in a wartime study of food habits using the most advanced techniques, and still be dismissed by many professional colleagues as "intuitive," or belabored by the even more fearsome term "insightful." The late W. I. Thomas would today perhaps be startled to see his work viewed as a storehouse of social-psychological theory, when his own much greater preoccupation was with the facts and forms of social reportage. On a much smaller scale, I find similar misunderstanding of my own teaching and writing. *The*

Lonely Crowd, which lies towards the theory end of the scale, aroused misplaced enthusiasm from some historians and humanists because of its lack of graphs and tables, and perhaps misplaced animadversions from some social scientists who viewed it as more biased towards the "theory" end than was intended. For the book is full of data, mainly but not entirely in the traditional form of observation from everyday life: I speak there of movies, comic books, magazines; of progressive schools and traditional schools; of the way parents think of children, and vice versa; of the way executives think of workers, and vice versa. Many humanists fail to realize that such data require supporting data, and a more formal and systematic effort to demonstrate that what they and the author refer to as matters of common knowledge are really so. Conversely, many social scientists, prematurely dazzled by the new techniques, fail to realize how far we still are from being able to prove what we "know" by them.

To put matters another way, I do not believe that one is surrendering the strict demands of science to a human but unscientific desire for understanding if one accepts the theory-data dilemma and works within its limitations, while recognizing that at some future date those limitations will greatly change. For science itself arises out of the desire to explain, to understand: the technical operations are subsidiary to this. If the natural sciences did not satisfy this desire by real accomplishments, it is unlikely that they would enlist creative minds to serve the hard discipline of the techniques—though as a paying and going concern they can enlist many unadventurous minds drawn by motivations other than those of the pioneers. So, too, social scientists who insist that we must serve the machines and the techniques regardless of the quality of understanding that emerges from that service—for that service alone is real science—fail to appreciate not only the history of science in general but also that social science is still too untried to enlist and retain large-scale support without large-scale accomplishment.

Undoubtedly, science requires sacrifices of its acolytes, but the nature of those sacrifices differs with the age. By and large, American social science no longer requires of its personnel the humiliation, poverty, lack of recognition that were the fate of Marx, Comte, Freud, and, to a degree, of Sumner, Sorel, Veblen. But field-work is still arduous and heart-breaking, research still filled with disappointments, blind alleys, and want of adequate resources.[3] It is a sacrifice of vanity to realize that one will never even approximate the glorious achievements of the fathers, nor perhaps live to see the edifice constructed by the technical adeptness of the great-grandsons. It is a sacrifice of impatience to be charitable both to one's work and that of others when this work has the status of "pilot projects," as social scientists overoptimistically dub most of their present enterprises—overoptimistically, because they assume that there will soon be a whole plant engaged in the production of results. In this situation, the claim that we should make the sacrifices of scientific work without the hope of gaining a better understanding of society—indeed while ridiculing whatever understanding is achieved, for instance by novelists, without training and technique—is to make vain demands on our willingness to wait for "production miracles."

I am quite aware that this formulation does not solve the question of how we know that an understanding not established directly or by strict reasoning on a sufficient volume of empirical data is a true understanding. I don't propose to unravel this epistemological mystery here: it is enough to observe that the acceptance of the position that only the generalizations founded on irrefutable data are true leaves us to conclude that all understanding of society (other than in economics, the social science with the greatest achievements to its credit) established up till now is pure illusion; and that all sociology is simply hypothesis awaiting proof, for I believe it can be shown that with rare exceptions even the most up-to-date data support the most up-to-date generalization only as example, not as proof in any (even probability-theory) scientific sense. Yet at the same time, only a data-extremist would insist that the study of Weber, Durkheim, Simmel and other great turn-of-the-century founders is irrelevant to our understanding of social processes: some light emerges.

And the reason for this is that we are ourselves men living in society; and, as the saying goes, we were not born yesterday. Many social scientists, worried about bias and struck by what natural scientists have achieved in studying stars and atoms, being neither one nor the other, feel that when they approach work in their field they should cultivate a complete skepticism, at least until the not far distant day when theories will be buttressed at every point by data; ironically, this wanton innocence is itself the cultural product of some of the very thinkers whose writings they would reject as unscientific. Natural science deserves tremendous credit for having achieved so much when so inevitably distant from its objects; social scientists, rather than trying to impose on themselves similar handicaps, should take full advantage of the fact that they are themselves part of their universe of study, and heirs to a long and not utterly noncumulative tradition of thinking about man.[4]

IV

Doubtless, more social scientists will agree that the problem is to proceed from one end of the theory-data scale to the other, so as to encompass a suitable combination of thought and fact, than will agree on which end should be taken as the starting-point. My own belief, already indicated, is that there is no "right" end, no royal road, but that one can fruitfully begin at either end, or anywhere between. One must be willing to take seriously theories which are not established, and even theories which are, in some formal sense, "refuted," when they offer a real illumination and insight, which will undoubtedly turn out to be a partial illumination. Thus, it makes not very fruitful use of Weber's book on the Protestant ethic to ask whether it is true or false. To be sure, the book evoked a whole historiography of disproof, but the book still helps us understand our world and our place in it. Certainly, no theory can have this success if it is in plain opposition to many facts, for the theory itself is an effort to explain and order facts; yet agreement with some large and crucial facts may be more important than contradiction by them in details.

At the same time, social scientists should be more willing than many of the ablest are, to begin at the "data" end of the scale, though without the illusion that they can move immediately therefrom to the grist of theory. Our obsession with our image of the natural sciences tends to make us think of data as only verification, as supporting a theory or destroying it. Yet the value of data as simple reporting on the quality and details of social life has been a most significant part of social science: Booth's *Life and Labour of the People in London,* Thomas and Znaniecki's *The Polish Peasant in Europe and America,* the Lynds' *Middletown* volumes, the Allison Davis and John Dollard studies of the Deep South, and many other works that present full pictures of some social phenomenon, partake of many of the qualities of good reporting. The theoretical schemes which the reporting supports usually seem less and less important with the passage of time: the data remain valuable and

stimulating, and as useful in support of the theoretical schemes of the future as of those of the original authors.[5] Important branches of social science are even more clearly reporting rather than theory: this has been true, at least until recently, of most public opinion research: the poll data gathered in the public opinion journals, in the recent Cantril-Strunk volume, and in the *American Soldier,* form a rich body of materials, which we would never have had if we had had to wait for a structure of the theory-hypothesis-data-new-theory sort to justify gathering it.

Likewise, the scorn so frequently heaped on "gadgeteers," from without as well as within the ranks of social science, fails to grasp how much we owe, in all the sciences, to sheer fooling around with methods and techniques, more or less for their own sakes. In many ways, Freud was a gadgeteer, first in his work on the staining of cells for histological purposes, later in his experiments with hypnosis and other therapies; we forget this, since he also used his techniques to make brilliant discoveries. True, "gadgeteer" is often applied to those who see in a device or machine a panacea for all ills, or at the very least a solvent for hitherto intractable problems, and here certainly scorn is justifiable. But scorn is also levelled at gadgeteers who make no such grandiose claims, and here it seems to reflect attitudes of a very widespread sort: our hierarchy of skill and learning snobberies, our gnawing uneasiness about "materialism" and mechanical know-how, our ambivalence towards those aspects of American life that John A. Kouwenhoven, in his book *Made in America,* sums up as the "vernacular." Science suffers, however, when the gadgeteer must justify himself by association with some immediate and high-flown purpose, whether drawn from the realm of theory or of social action.

In sum, whatever end of the scale one begins at, one is likely to be under pressure to move rapidly towards the other end—"to link theory and data" as the phrase goes—by people who have insufficient respect for either end in its own terms, and who fail to appreciate all the intermediate and frequently indirect and unplannable steps in between. This leads to the most paradoxical results: on the one hand, scholars think they have "proved" their case scientifically when they are very far from it—for if their case were not, to their own satisfaction, demonstrated, they could have no respect for themselves; and, on the other hand, other scholars are reduced to despair when they discover that the petty data they have accumulated in a stretch of painstaking and mayhap costly work bears little relation to the grand hypothesis with which they began. In this situation, work which is very far from technical validation, let alone from proving anything important about society, is often desperately seized upon by the promoters and defenders of social science in order to convince themselves and others that they are in a good line of work, and, beyond that, that they could produce far more if they got the funds and the go-ahead orders. As the design engineers in an industry feel harried by the demands and expectations of the product engineers who want to produce, and the sales engineers who want to sell, so the design engineers of social science are under the pressures just indicated from the production and sales staff who insist on putting on the social science assembly line what is still necessarily in the handicraft and mock-up stage.[6] In many quarters, the promoters of social science have aroused such unfulfillable expectations as to risk a disillusioning bust of the whole enterprise. Thus, while at an earlier time social scientists may have been over-timid, "ivory-towerish," and afraid of responsibility, they seem today more endangered by check-kiting (in terms of reports leading to "pilot studies," to more reports, and so on endlessly) than by reticence.

V

One can imagine the relief with which some promoters of social science have greeted a few recent very successful efforts to link theory and data. I shall discuss briefly two such major efforts —The Authoritarian Personality, by T. W. Adorno, Else Frenkel-Brunswik, Daniel J. Levinson, and R. Nevitt Sanford; and the Yankee City series by W. Lloyd Warner and his coworkers—in order to show that the difficulties we have been discussing arise even on the highest and most sophisticated level of research, and to show some of the risks one runs in taking such studies as models for slavish imitation.

The Authoritarian Personality is perhaps the most impressive attempt in recent American social psychology and sociology to link a large-scale and important theory to data which would support and demonstrate it. This thousand-page volume is the outgrowth of many years of study, first by members of the (Frankfort) Institute for Social Research, later by an able and energetic group at Berkeley that worked for another period of years: it was not a project set up to pay quick dividends

out of capital to attract further capital, but rather one which took its time about the study of the authoritarian personality and its role in modern industrial society—a large order, indeed. The thinking at the "theory" end began in the late '20's and early '30's in Germany; a large volume dealing with many facets of the problem—Autorität und Familie—appeared in the mid-'30's, at which time empirical research projects had already begun; the research work that The Authoritarian Personality itself reports was carried out over a span of five years or more in Berkeley, and incorporates the use of the most subtle and advanced of psychological techniques. Time to work and think and experiment is essential for serious investigation, and this long period of maturation makes The Authoritarian Personality as good and significant as it is.

But there is just the rub. Society does not stand still—American society perhaps least of all—and the problem of twenty years ago is not the problem of today, and the problem of Germany then is not the problem of America now. Events continually outdistance our attempts to understand them; social scientists, no less than other people, must structure the world while at the same time keeping up with it. Economists kept talking about our economy as if its problems were those of under-employment for years after this problem had disappeared, and under circumstances that made its recrudescence unlikely for years to come, if ever.[7] The Authoritarian Personality rests on the equally irrelevant fundamental premise—as it appears to me—that European-style fascism is the great danger hanging over America, as well as on the minor premise—to me not important for America, and dubious even for Germany—that authoritarianism in character structure breeds and is bred by authoritarianism in social structure. As to fascism: there is no room here to set out all my reasons for believing that this is not the principal American menace—among them, is the position, developed in The Lonely Crowd, that virtually all sectors of American life (including would-be fascists) have an "in" on the political and social scene which would be disturbed by a coup d'état; moreover, that American big business is not as unified, ruthless, or conspiratorial as the authors of the book suppose; finally, if there exists a danger of internal repression in America today, it ensues more from the threat of totalitarian Soviet expansion than from sources in American "authoritarian personality."[8] As to the minor premise linking character and society, I suggest that, in

America and England, the Puritan character, which qualifies in many ways as "authoritarian," actually helped foster a democratic social structure under given conditions of seventeenth-century life; conversely, the pliable "democratic" personality can be molded and made use of, under other social conditions and institutions, in developing a rigid and authoritarian society.

These may seem like drastic criticisms, and they certainly go to the heart of the authors' aims and conclusions. Yet the by-products of the study are invaluable: never, for instance, have we had, on such a large scale, such brilliant and brilliantly-validated use of "diagnostic" questions arranged in scales to test underlying attitudes, nor such grasp of nuances of verbal expression as clues to character, nor such an interesting discussion of the political attitudes of criminals, nor so capable an appraisal of the possibilities of typological treatment in social research. Nor is the study of fascism itself all waste effort by any means: there are undoubtedly some millions of fascist-minded people in the United States, and we now have an un-exampled look at many sides of their outlooks and personalities. Nevertheless, the study itself, as an effort to understand America, does not carry us far; the very gift and social concern of the planners of the work, which led them to the problem of fascism, led them off on what turned out, two decades later, to be a false scent; and if the study contributes, as I think likely, to the understanding of society, it will be indirectly, through its by-products.

Other examples of the complexities introduced by the necessarily long process of data-gathering and publishing are the studies of social class directed and inspired by Lloyd Warner. His first work in this field was done in a New England town at the beginning of the depression; the same techniques and concerns that were used in "Yankee City" in the early '30's have been carried over, with minor systematizations and modifications, to "Deep South" and to "Elmtown" ("Jonesville"), with way stations in between. But in these later studies the question is not raised whether class remains the most fruitful concept for understanding American culture and personality in 1951; or whether people today are as concerned with social mobility as they were twenty years ago, and as the technique then devised nearly inevitably makes it appear that they still are—for the technique tends to confuse membership in a social class, as symbolized by a brilliant variety of indices, with consciousness of that membership and of its implica-

tions, honorific and otherwise. The technique is not neutral—no technique is; it was devised at a time when certain problems relating to class were pre-eminent, and when Warner's insistence on their importance was stimulating and heretical; the technique took years to perfect, but now that it is perfected (a much-debated point among experts), and relatively easy for students to apply, it must be asked whether other problems—divisions within social classes, for instance, or cutting across classes —may not have become more significant, even though class is still of great and obvious significance. Professor Warner himself, in fact, not being committed to a large and expensive apparatus, seems in his most recent work to be as interested in comparing the fantasy life of people on what he calls the "common man" level with that of the "uncommon man" as he is with new applications of the Yankee City scheme.

We must conclude, then, that the effort to link theory and data, at the present pace of work, runs into a most important set of logistical problems. It is hard enough to modify one's own conceptions to take account of a changing world, and perhaps to help change it; it is harder, much harder, to overhaul a huge research project, planned over the many years required for work, evaluation, and publication, so as to fit these changing conceptions. In answer to such dejections, it is often argued that money is the only bottleneck to the spectacular advance of social science—and that, if only a quarter as much were made available as was put at the disposal of atomic scientists, there would be no important areas of ignorance left about the world, let alone the United States! Conceivably, if there were *enough* money, and *enough* personnel, monopolistic competition among even large-scale research enterprises would tend to keep them flexible and fast on their feet to a degree— yet even here the logistical problem would remain, for a country that could be brought to devote such enormous resources to its own self-scrutiny would obviously be a very different land from the present U.S.A., so different perhaps that social science would no longer appear as inviting or necessary! One is almost awe-struck with the lack of humor, if not of humility, on the part of those social scientists who feel their trade so all-important that they can make such requests of the national income and the national manpower, and one could greatly admire the implicit utopian faith so displayed, if one did not feel an underlying insecurity prompting the frequent use of the nuclear physicists as a reference group.

It is evident, moreover, that the large-scale the-ory-testing operation runs the risks of encouraging mere discipleship which are always present in in-tellectual and artistic enterprise. The easiest way to do research is to apply the beautifully-engi-neered models supplied by such work as that of the Berkeley group and Warner—though actually, partly because this work has many complexities and is highly controversial, much inferior models are usually chosen. But while a proved sire may be the best bet in cattle-breeding, proved pater-nities in the social sciences are filled with ambi-guities. The disciple has much less chance, gen-erally, of adapting his conceptions to the rapidly changing course of social development than the originator—but even the latter may be trapped by fear of disappointing, or "disemploying," his disciples.

Since I am myself a practitioner of social sci-ence, as well as a critic thereof, I must guard against the possible implication that I consider my own writing and teaching to have escaped these pitfalls—on the contrary, it is from falling in that I have learned to locate some of them. But I do sug-gest that certain aspects of my work which appear to some contemporary social scientists to be sim-ply defects—a somewhat casual and unsystematic approach, and a refusal to set up the grand money- and time- and man-consuming research projects that would demonstrate my hypotheses—are not only defects, and certainly not unintended ones: if what I have said hitherto is sound, there are also virtues in the handicraft approach which, not en-tirely committed to a major course of action, is able to shift and turn with the development of the thought of the researcher, as well as with the course of social development. Without any ques-tion, however, this unmethodical method is sub-ject to its own hazards, most of which have been examined at length in the social science literature of the recent, method-conscious decades.

VI

It is interesting to speculate about what Ameri-can social science would look like today if journal-ism had had as much prestige in the late nineteenth and early twentieth centuries as natural science, though perhaps the drive towards professionaliza-tion has been more important in shaping social science than the fact that the professional model chosen has generally been physics or biology. In England an organization has grown up in the last fifteen years—Mass Observation, or MO for short—

which deserves to be better known in this country, for in conception it is a frontal attack both on the natural science model and on professionalization. It consists of a group of animated and amateur so-cial observers who are encouraged to send in re-ports on assigned topics—and to suggest topics—to a central office run by social scientists: they have studied such British institutions as the pub, church-going, the last Coronation Day, and what happens at "all-in" wrestling. MO attempts to reduce the distance between observers and observed by allowing the latter to participate in the processes of social study—to bring to it what they have in the way of gifts of observation and to receive in return instruction and information based on others' observation. In intention, though not in its rather sloppy execution, it is an adult education venture in the social sciences.[9]

American (and British) public opinion specialists have heaped scorn on the MO sampling methods or lack of them; and one could also criticize the raw empiricism of such a book as *May the Twelfth*, which reports, without interpretation or selection or preliminary training of the reporters, what ob-servers noticed on Coronation Day in 1938; there MO forgot that the first duty of a reporter is to be interesting, a duty which demands both selection and interpretation.[10]

In the United States there have been a few de-velopments similar to MO but, significantly enough, all of them appear to have been motivated by immediate problems of social policy rather than, as in the case of the British organization, by this coupled with "idle curiosity" about the society. During World War II the OWI ran what were called Correspondence Panels: men and women throughout the country who sent in re-ports on such assigned topics as how the draft was going, the effect of price control, and morale, receiving in return instructions and commentary; under the direction of Elizabeth Herzog, many small businessmen, housewives, and others learned for the first time to look at their communities with the detached and inquiring air which is the hall-mark of the good reporter and the good social science observer. (With the end of the war, the program, like so much else that had been painfully built up, was hastily demolished.) More widely known is the "action-research" approach of the late Kurt Lewin and a group of his followers; their idea was that it might be possible to enlist ordinary citizens to study their own community problems; more than that, this self-study, they believed, would help in the solution of these problems, while the very effort at solution would in turn invigorate research. Under the influence of this approach there have been, for example, a number of "community self-audits," in which citizens, under the direction of social scientists, have examined their community from the point of view of its failings and fulfillments, particularly as to race relations. The method has much to be said for it, both as adult education and as social action, but I have some misgivings about its usefulness for research and deeper understanding: usually the social scientists in charge already know, in a rough way, that they will find anti-Negro bias in housing in Montclair or discrimination in employment in Northfield (two cities where successful audits were made), and "self-audit" can become, despite the democratic sympathies of the leaders, little more than a new gimmick to spur community activity.

At any rate, America, much more than England, seems to me to need both the reporting technique and the enlistment of the amateur observer that characterize MO—to need them for the basic job of finding out what goes on, apart from any question as to what can be done about it. This country is so big, so varied, so almost if not quite unencompassable, that social research cannot have enough observers who will break down its momentary generalizations and open up new views. Something like MO would permit what might be called "research by exception," where a researcher would count on his "far-flung correspondents" to tell him where something he had taken for granted was not so. Indeed, there are many fields of social research which simply cannot be handled by existing techniques. If we want to know, for example, the reactions of movie audiences to a nationally-exhibited film, as this varies from showing to showing, we cannot learn this at present, nor can sampling methods tell us how an audience, a group en masse, responds; the whole wide field of American popular culture needs mass explorers and mass observers; for sports events, dance-halls, bookie joints, fairs, and countless other pastimes. By bringing these observers into our research organizations, moreover, we are likely greatly to amplify our conception both of the complexity of our country and of its newly emerging problems, for there will be no want of stimulating queries and reports.[11]

Certainly, a social science militia of this type would go far to complement, and perhaps to check, the social science army of professionals envisaged by the logistics discussed earlier. We would be overwhelmed with data: our poor schemes would have to be sturdy indeed to stand up to it—perhaps, afraid of drowning in data, we would become fonder of theory! We would also have to focus on questions that interested our militia—and work on the problem of easy communication with them—for they would be bound to us, not by professional ties, but by mutual needs for understanding. We may perhaps not be prepared for the new functions that would be forced upon us. But at the same time, accepting our function as reporters as well as systematizers, we might continue to be happy even where we were unsuccessful.

VII

In a thought-provoking essay on "The Art of Social Science," Robert Redfield has called attention to some of the ambiguities of current emphasis on method in social research, pointing out that Tocqueville and other great and gifted observers had added much to our knowledge while ignorant of or violating the rules laid down by men who have added much less. If what I have said in this paper makes sense, we may draw a further analogy with contemporary problems of art, especially literary art. For it would seem that social scientists, too, have their "New Critics" who have been laying down a canon which, in the minds of some, operates to intimidate creative work. The canon is actually more perfectionist than its literary analogue, since it is based, not on actual work, but on often brilliant extrapolation from our old friends, the "pilot studies." And whereas the new critics in literature frequently have a verve and elegance in writing, and a depth in understanding, which compensates for much that may be lacking in creative writing, the new critics in social science—while they would hardly agree with William F. Ogburn's paper on "The Folklore of Social Science" that the social scientists of the future will not be gifted with wit or originality but will publish merely statistical reports—seem to feel that their ascetic laboriousness and lugubriousness in the content of criticism should also be reflected in its style.

Both developments, moreover, in literature and in social science, are in part the outcome of the tremendous advance in university teaching in the humanities and in the social sciences in the last several decades. At many institutions, large and small, there has been a heightening of critical standards, and students are confronted, not with easy-going teachers using casual texts, but with able and energetic new critics, who can discover the flaws in the finest poetry and fiction, or in the most heralded works of social science. And in both areas, as a price for this advance, there is a temptation for students to become easily discouraged about what they could contribute to creative work; they have to bear in mind so many injunctions, each of them "correct," that they can no more start their own enterprises than could a businessman in a completely regimented state—for their vanity and ambition are already low, as the result of other social developments than the rise of the new critics.

In the art world at least, the battle of artists and critics is an old one. But it is a battle of a noncumulative sort, which must be fought over in every era, because of changes in the division of labor, and in the strength and self-confidence of the several sides. In American writing, those seem to fare best who pay no attention to critics—symbolized by William Faulkner calling himself aggressively a farmer, and not a literary man. In American social science, many of the best contributions have been made by journalists and others who were out of the circle of academic life and criticism. But surely this is not an optimum solution, for it lowers the intellectual level of creative writing, and leaves critics as the audience for other critics. And while in art there is an inexhaustible storehouse for the critics to draw upon, in social science there is not enough good work to occupy many critics for a full-time day. Marx was right when he wrote in *The German Ideology* that it should be "possible for one to do one thing today and another tomorrow—to hunt in the morning, to fish in the evening, to criticize after dinner just as I have in mind, without ever becoming hunter, fisherman, shepherd, or critic."

FOOTNOTES

[1]In collaboration with Nathan Glazer.

[2]It goes without saying that the "natural science" that thus serves as a model is itself often a mirage: not natural science as it is actually practiced by its best contemporaries, but an ideology often based on Newtonian models.

[3]The scientific workers in the field of "culture and personality" must endure a particular kind of sacrifice, namely to have to live with heightened self-consciousness of all personal relations and cultural phenomena, making it hard for them to separate their professional work from the rest of their lives. Cf. my article, "Some Problems of a Course in 'Culture and Personality'," *Journal of General Education*: V (1951), 122–136.

[4]Crane Brinton, in *Ideas and Men*, sees social science as largely noncumulative—having to be learned over again for each worker and each generation—while natural science is largely cumulative. And there can be no doubt that the truths of social interaction—of psychoanalysis, let us say—have to be experienced by each individual before he can make important use of them in research; yet there is a cumulative tradition which makes it possible to learn noncumulative truths, helping new field workers, for example, to face the ineluctable hardships of their initiation.

[5]In the middle '30's a type of reporting developed which had much in common with social science: in those days, reporters took to crossing the country and asking questions of various people they ran into (James Rorty, Benjamin Appel, John Dos Passos, Samuel Grafton, and others), presenting pictures which can support a number of different interpretations. At the same time, *Fortune* began to give large scope to reporters—some of whom have become very interested in social science and its problems—who developed a new kind of "story" which often surpasses the work of professional social scientists in information and even, though perhaps without intending it, in "theory."

My understanding of the origins and present importance of the reportorial tradition in social science has profited greatly from discussions with my colleague Everett Hughes.

[6]It should be added that this is often done in the friendliest spirit. At times, the production engineer will show an overgreat deference to the design engineer—as the result of snobberies already touched upon—leading the former to premature attempts to use and sell the work of the latter to raise his own status. Obviously enough, novelists and other artists are subjected to analogous briberies and temptations, and in the relation between highbrow and middlebrow art one can find similar tensions.

[7]We run here, among other things, into the matter of the "self-confirming prophecy" discussed by Robert K. Merton in this *Review*. Since people on all levels of our society believe that depressions are controllable (some, as the result of the Keynesians; others, as a result of their interpretation of our war experience), while they do not believe wars are controllable, the government will be under great if not irresistible pressure to live up to these expectations—by a war economy if necessary. This seemed evident to a number of observers before economists became concerned with the problems of full employment.

[8]For a similar view, see Paul Kecskemeti, "Prejudice in the Catastrophic Perspective," *Commentary* (March, 1951).

[9]There is, of course, a tradition of local history studies, and also of local linguistics and folk culture studies, which goes back a long way in Europe, and to a lesser degree in this country.

[10]Fortunately, Robert E. Park never got over his training as a Sunday Supplement feature writer for the Detroit press; he never managed, in his late career as a sociologist, to stay away from interest or "human interest" for very long at a time. See his "Autobiographical Note" in *Race and Culture*.

[11]Thanks to the cooperation of the National Opinion Research Center, I once had the opportunity to go over many reports sent in by interviewers to accompany their formal schedules—letters, really, rather than reports, which touched on how hard the interviewing had gone or how easy, on what types of questions made for trouble or interest, and on many of the day-to-day events and encounters in the interviewers' rounds. Often, these reports were more stimulating than the content of the schedules, which dealt with ephemeral opinions: what do you think of the UN, of Truman, of Palestine partition, or whatever else were the "issues" of 1948.

History, the Behavioral Studies and the Science of Man

by David M. Potter

Potter suggests that perhaps historians, not unlike administrators, become so bogged down with the need to gather the facts and detail them that their perceptions and contributions have been more of the practical, concrete variety than of the philosophical or theoretical. Here in the main is the indictment of most of what passes for historical research in librarianship—exhaustive fact gathering, monumental accretions of accounts of little consequence, seldom ordered into the fabric of understanding of the time or the place or the correlation between libraries and the cultures which give rise to them.

Historical research into librarianship legitimately needs to seek out underlying explanations for events, to try to understand the forces which have acted to bring libraries into being and to shape their direction and their course. Indeed, it seems impossible even to begin the selection of pertinent facts to be collected without some initial thought as to the explanations to be sought or the broad questions to be answered.

To criticize library history is not to dismiss it. History has an invaluable contribution to make, for it introduces the important dimension of time into the study of institutions. Without this long term perspective, we can never hope truly to understand libraries as social institutions. Prototypes for this kind of work may be found in the studies of Shera* and Ditzion.** Out of the evidence of the past, there can be distilled the lessons for tomorrow, but only if library scholars concern themselves with questions of "why" as well as "what" and "when," and only if they will derive their explanations from more sophisticated conceptual bases than from their own personal and intuitive view of the world.

In the summer of 1950, under the stimulus of an invitation from the Walgreen Foundation, I embarked upon the seemingly innocent task of writing six lectures on the American character, and especially on the influence of American economic abundance upon this character. The theme itself was certainly a wide-open one, and nobody capable of arranging words on paper has ever been required to show any further credentials before offering vast generalizations on the American, this "new man," as Crèvecœur called him. My original purpose, therefore, was only to join the mixed lot of scholars, maiden ladies, itinerant lecturers, professional pundits, and overnight experts whose writings have adorned this subject. As I moved into the inquiry, however, I was assailed by misgivings as to the validity of the whole concept of "national character," and, as I burrowed into the literature relating to it, I was embarrassed, as a historian, to discover that the most telling contributions, in my opinion, came from cultural anthropologists and social psychologists rather than from my fellow-historians.

After a while, the problems of establishing a valid concept of national character and of seeking some possible links between the work done by historians and by behavioral scientists in this field began to seem more important than the specific problem of the influence of economic abundance upon the American character. Yet, at the same time, it remained true that my primary purpose was to examine the operation of this economic factor in the development of American life. First one aspect has seemed to predominate and then the other, and I am at last left in uncertainty as to which side is heads and which side tails on my own

*Jesse H. Shera, *Foundations of the Public Library: The Origins of the Public Library Movement in New England, 1629-1855* (Hamden, Conn.: Shoe String Press, 1965).

**Sidney Ditzion, *Arsenals of a Democratic Culture: A Social History of the American Public Library Movement in New England and the Middle States from 1850 to 1900* (Chicago: American Library Association, 1947).

coin. One can read this volume as a theoretical study of the conceptual problem of national character and of the relationships between history and the behavioral sciences, regarding the chapters on abundance and its influence in America as merely illustrative; or one can read it as the concrete study of the impact of one tangible factor upon the character of the American people, regarding the opening sections on historical and behavioral approaches to national character simply as a framework necessary for fixing the material on America in its proper logical place in the literature of the subject. I am keenly aware that by thus writing a book of a dualistic nature I expose myself to the inevitable gambit of the reviewer: that the portion on which he is expert really will not do at all but that the other part appears rather interesting. Perhaps I will be fortunate if each part is not compared unfavorably with the other.

In any event, it seems valid to begin by recognizing that generalization about national character is only a special case of the larger practice of generalization about human groups of any kind. There are just a few branches of learning which attempt this kind of generalization, and history was, for many centuries, the only one. But today there are several, and it may be well to start with a consideration of the way in which these various disciplines have approached this part of their responsibility in the study of man.

Of all the branches of learning cultivated by man, there is probably none which deals with a greater body of data than does history. The task of history, to record all that is significant in human experience, for many centuries and many lands, has implied such an immense responsibility, and one of such immediacy, that it has engendered in historians an almost obsessive drive to get on with the job, to start marshaling the data, to begin straightening out the detailed and complex factual questions with which the record abounds. Consequently, history has become pre-eminently a concrete and "practical" subject, with but little attention to philosophical or theoretical aspects. Occasionally, some aberrant historian has paused to consider the philosophy of history, the problem of historical causation, the existence of laws of history, or the like, but the rank and file of historians have never paid very patient attention to these speculations. With mutterings about "work to do," they have quickly turned back to their busyness with deeds and events. As for historical interpretation, they have often disclaimed any such function, insisting that the facts alone would answer the historian's questions and never recognizing that these questions themselves, like fishers' nets, might profoundly influence the character of the facts which would be caught in the haul.

This preoccupation with fact, coupled as it was with a rough-and-ready willingness to tackle the most profound problems of society, has been the principal glory and, at the same time, the major weakness of history as a branch of learning. The glory, because history has dared to seek the answers to questions which other disciplines would have declined for the lack of an adequate method. History has never held itself aloof from life or guarded its own purity by confining itself to topics for which it possessed a fully tested methodological and conceptual apparatus of attack. It has never permitted the tyranny of method to dictate the subjects which it would investigate and has never shifted its attention from men to mice because of the seductive fact that mice lend themselves to precise investigation more readily than do men. It has also been the glory of history that its professional devotees have never entirely lost communication with the intelligent layman, as the practitioners of the social sciences have almost universally done. The language of history has never become divorced from the common speech, and the historian has scarcely been touched by the baneful belief that it would lower his professional standards to write in plain terms which any man might understand. In a democracy which depends upon men of learning to provide the ordinary man with sound information for dealing with public affairs, the historian is almost the only kind of scholar who has fulfilled the responsibility of speaking directly to the people.

But if history may claim these glories, it must also admit the serious defects implicit in its merits. In its headlong, *ad hoc* assault upon the record of human experience, history has built its narrative upon an extraordinary mélange of unstated premises, random assumptions, untested hypotheses, and miscellaneous notions about the nature of man, the workings of society, and the causation of historical change. The anomalous nature of this conceptual foundation has scarcely been recognized by historians, much less confronted by them, and thus they have written with assurance about the distinctive character of individual persons or groups of men, without having reached any agreement as to the nature of man in general; they have traced the course of history as a fight for human freedom, although no one has ever proved that humanity really prefers freedom to security;

they have enumerated the "causes" of countless wars, without ever coming to an understanding about the causation of war in general; and they have described the process by which nationalism reshaped the modern world, without being sure what they mean by "nationalism."[1]

Unfortunately, this lack of precision in evaluating or defining the basic elements betrayed itself most glaringly in connection with the one factor which remains central throughout all history— namely, the human factor. The very term "history" means, in fact, human history, and the whole record of history is, in a sense, an account of dynamic external forces operating upon men and of the reactions and responses of men to these forces. For such an account, therefore, it would seem obviously necessary to take an analytical view both of the dynamic factors which have operated and of the human receptors—either individual men or individual societies—upon which these factors have had their impact. Yet it is a curious fact that the same analytical standards were not applied on both sides of the equation, and scholars who would never have dreamed of discussing the influence of geography upon man without taking a scientific approach to geography apparently felt no obligation to take a scientific approach to man. This has been conspicuously true, for instance, in the literature dealing with the American frontier, where fairly refined study has been given to the precise nature of the different attractions which drew men to the frontier at various stages, but little attention has been accorded to the differential character of diverse human groups— the French as contrasted with the Anglo-Americans, or twentieth-century Americans as contrasted with nineteenth-century Americans—which made some groups highly responsive and some relatively unresponsive to frontier attractions.

At times it has even appeared that historians could not arrive at a settled conception as to the nature of man, for at various times they have harbored a wide range of unstated and unconsidered assumptions about the human creature. Orthodox historians regarded him as a being made in the image of God and endowed with an immortal soul; materialistic ones regarded him as a mammal tortured by the attempt to transcend his own animal nature. Democrats postulated his capacity to think for himself and his equality with other men. Economists accepted as an axiom the belief that he would always be guided by enlightened self-interest. Liberals pictured the yearning for freedom as one of his basic drives. Calvinists be-

lieved him to be born sinful but liable to regeneration through God's grace, while romantics believed him to be born virtuous but liable to corruption through the evils of society. The mid-nineteenth century, as Ralph H. Gabriel has remarked, confidently explained him in terms of a double triad: "He was body, mind, and soul, and his mind consisted of emotions, intellect, and will." When historians wrote about the history of man, they seldom paused to specify whether the protagonist of their tale was one of the types named above or was some other fellow altogether.[2]

If history failed to grapple effectively with the problem of man and his nature, this was very largely because the study of man requires the derivation of general or abstract conclusions from a mass of concrete human data, and history for nearly twenty-five centuries after the time of Herodotus simply did not deal in generalization. It dealt with unique events, such as the conduct of a particular battle or the negotiation of a particular treaty, and all of the much-vaunted "historical method" was a method for determining specific events by means of rigorous textual criticism and severe rules for the evaluation of evidence. The arts or techniques of broad interpretation or of generalization from a mass of specific data were not part of the "historical method," even though historians might engage freely in interpretations and generalizations based on their personal judgment as individuals. In recent decades, as history has turned increasingly to the treatment of social and economic themes, such as changes in ideas or morals, the relations between diverse social classes, or the operation of economic forces upon society, the historian's lack of systematic procedure in the practice of generalization has become a serious liability. But the force of tradition is so strong that this deficiency has scarcely even been recognized by writers on historical method, and certainly no serious steps have been taken to correct it. This observation, however, is somewhat aside from the point, and all that needs to be said for purposes of this discussion is that although history has constantly made all sorts of assumptions about the nature of man, it has never possessed any systematic method for checking these assumptions. In a sense, this is equivalent to saying that historical method has not included any means for analysis of the chief factor with which history deals.

In making these observations upon the increasingly conspicuous deficiencies of historical scholarship, I do not by any means intend to suggest that historians have failed in their task as recorders of human experience. On the contrary, historical analysis and historical writing have improved immeasurably over the last two centuries and also over the last two decades. But I do mean to suggest that the achievements of historians have been made largely through the exercise of common sense and individual sagacity, in spite of the defective methodological and conceptual foundation upon which their work has been erected. And I mean especially to argue that this deficiency has shown itself most acutely in the historian's failure to take an analytical view of the one factor which is present in all history—namely, the human factor, both in its singular manifestation, where it involves the individual man, or in its group manifestation, where it involves society.

For many centuries historians held almost exclusive jurisdiction over the applied study of man. It is not without significance that in ancient times, when the nine Muses presided over the arts and sciences, Clio, and Clio alone, held sway in the area where the social sciences now flourish. This remained true until very recent times, and even when economics and political science developed, they did not scrutinize human behavior but instead assumed the existence of an "economic man" or a "political animal" or an individual in a state of "nature" (the state of nature most favored by economists was a desert island occupied by economic men in a number not greater than could be counted on the fingers of one hand). These creatures, it was supposed, would act automatically in accordance with the laws of economic or political reason rather than in accordance with the uncharted workings of human psychology. Therefore, the actual conduct of the human creature was left almost entirely to be recorded by history, and one might say that history retained this monopoly for two and a half millenniums—from Herodotus to Sigmund Freud.

So long as history retained sole custody of the study of human conduct, the extent of its omissions was the measure of what remained neglected. But the past few decades have witnessed the rapid growth of a group of behavioral sciences which have moved in to fill the vacuum, and these new sciences have developed so rapidly that the late Ralph Linton felt justified in declaring in 1943 that "it seems safe to say that the next few years will witness the emergence of a science of human behavior."[3]

The branches of learning which Linton visualized as converging to produce a science of human behavior and which are now customarily designated as the "behavioral sciences" are three in number. First, psychology, with a focus primarily upon the individual, concerns itself with human drives, motivation, and conditioning and contributes insight into the way in which "the deeper levels of personality are conditioned by environmental factors." Second, sociology, with a focus primarily upon the group, concerns itself with the complex structure of society and provides a basis for the understanding of interpersonal relations, which are vital in the formation of personality and which cannot be understood "except with reference to the positions which the individuals involved occupy in the structural system of their society." Third, anthropology, through its scrutiny of diverse societies, gives a certain perspective to the study of human behavior, and, through its concept of culture—"the way of life of any society," the pattern of "organized repetitive responses of a society's members"—it provides a key to the continuity of society, to the socializing of the individual, and to the differentiation of personality patterns and group behavior in diverse societies.

The development of the behavioral sciences and their convergence in a science of human behavior hold great potential importance for history. These new studies displace history as the primary study of man. They are moving, perhaps imperfectly, but certainly purposefully, to resolve those basic questions about the nature of man and his society which history has not only failed to answer but has often failed even to recognize or to define. They are formulating concepts, such as that of "culture," which the historian may on occasion use with great advantage. Of these facts we may be sure.

But as to the broader relationship between history and the behavioral sciences, there is no such assurance. Certainly history has not been, and cannot and should not be, regarded as one of the cluster which make up the behavioral group. Probably it cannot even operate in close relationship with them. But the contiguity of the two in dealing, perhaps at different levels, with aspects of human experience, must hold important implications for each which have not been explored on either side. Linton offered a clue to the meaning of history for the study of culture when he declared that "culture is the precipitate of history"; but, on the whole, he left this suggestion undeveloped. Caroline Ware has broken ground for a consideration of the meaning of the culture concept to the study of history in her symposium on *The Cultural Approach to History* (1949), which grew out of a session at the meeting of the American Historical Association in 1948. But historians, generally, failed to take their cues from her study.

Even in advance of specific efforts to bring history and the behavioral sciences into conjunction, however, one can anticipate certain valuable results. History can learn much about the nature of man and society from the behavioral sciences; the behavioral sciences can learn much about what may be called the "external forces impinging upon man," and about the nature of social change, from history. The value to history of a more precise understanding of the nature of man is too obvious to require elaboration, but it may be noted that historians at present attempt to treat the history of particular ideas, without any adequate recognition of the individual personalities and the cultural contexts within which these ideas are rooted; they constantly attempt to assess the motivation of men in such specific acts as going to war or initiating economic aggression, without possessing adequate knowledge of the general principles and complexities of human motivation; and they attempt to account for the rise and fall of civilizations without any systematic inquiry into what conditions are requisite for the effective operation of society and what ones are detrimental. The potential value to the behavioral sciences, on the other hand, of a more active awareness of historical forces, is suggested by the fact that the behavioral sciences, and especially cultural anthropology, have scored their greatest successes in dealing with so-called "primitive" societies and have encountered storms of controversy when they turned their focus upon Western man, in America or elsewhere. There are, no doubt, several reasons for this, including our own reluctance to be clinically dissected by the cultural anthropologist; but certainly one of the foremost reasons is that primitive societies present relatively static cultures, and the existence of these cultures in a state of equilibrium makes it possible to explain the society in terms of the culture, without reference to historic forces. Modern Western society, however, presents a culture or cultures in a state of fairly rapid change; therefore, society cannot be explained except in terms of the process of change, and the concept of culture provides no means for such an explanation, without the aid of history. It is not the "simplicity," as one might loosely suppose, of primitive societies which has made them easier for the anthropologist to explain, for they are, in fact, not simple, as he will be the first to agree. It is the absence of rapid or significant change, and the consequent opportunity to work without using the one study that deals with social change, which is history. Indeed, if there is any one subject with which history is concerned, that subject is change —how things ceased to be as they had been before, how they became what they had not been.

But though one might hope to obtain fairly ready agreement to these observations, it still remains for scholars from both sides to explore this highly important and seldom-crossed frontier between history and the behavioral sciences.

FOOTNOTES

[1] Karl W. Deutsch, *Nationalism and Social Communication* (Boston: Technology Press of the Massachusetts Institute of Technology; New York: John Wiley & Sons, Inc., 1953), pp. 3-14.

[2] "The study of history and politics is primarily the study of men, and . . . all political theory and political science must begin with a clear view of the psychology of man, at least in certain aspects of his behaviour. All the great and effective political theorists have recognised this. Hobbes began his political theory with a psychological theory—his mechanical, despotic state was devised for a mechanical, fear-driven humanity. John Locke and his eighteenth-century followers advocated political freedom—*i.e.* non-intervention by government—on the assumption that man was naturally good and self-improving and that his economic activities were naturally helpful to society; while the seventeenth-century philosophers whom he challenged had proceeded from an opposite assumption. The same point can be made indefinitely. Political theory which does not start from a theory of man is in my view quite worthless" (Hugh Trevor-Roper, "Human Nature in Politics," *The Listener,* December 10, 1953), pp. 993-94.

[3] *The Cultural Background of Personality* (New York: D. Appleton-Century Co., 1945), p. 5. The quoted passages in the paragraph that follows are from this volume (pp. xvi, xvii, 5, 19).

II
RESEARCH DESIGN

Except for the Stouffer piece which directs attention to other design aspects, this section concentrates on conceptual elements. Goode and Hatt add to Merton's discussion of the role of theory in empirical research a particular examination of the hypothesis. These two articles and Mills' essay orient the reader to the way in which problems are conceived and how, unless they are linked up with theoretical bases, they may be the wrong or the irrelevant questions to study. In the process, the reader becomes more adroit himself in exercising discrimination in the choice of problems worthy of investigation by testing their fit within a conceptual framework.

The concern here then is not with the formal elements of proposal design. Rather, it is with how one identifies the research questions to be answered. This is neither to down-grade the expertise involved in study design or the role of technique and instruments in exposing or limiting the questions to be studied. The value of preliminary field study, particularly in developing fields like librarianship with little prior empirical research from which to draw problems, seems apparent. The case study approach can be particularly fruitful in identifying variables and in exposing their inter-relationships. A field like librarianship, precisely because it enjoys such an unstructured research terrain, can offer both challenge and excitement to those of a pioneering cast of mind. Some have been drawn into the information sciences for this reason, but fewer into the behavioral realm.

Another important way to view the research project is as an excellent opportunity to learn. Once focused upon a problem, and given such point and purpose, the scholar can grasp and see the significance of and learn from almost everything he reads and hears. Students motivated by the incentive of a research problem, proceed more rapidly in assimilating and correlating subject matter than they do within a formal course structure removed from such application. Such success in genuinely reaching students through the application of the problem-solving mode of learning has important implications for professional instruction generally. While the research process for the practicing scholar affords the one tested medium to assure his intellectual growth and the learning and insight necessary to provide fresh perspectives for his courses and his student relationships.

The Bearing of Sociological Theory on Empirical Research

by Robert K. Merton

Merton offers the basic primer in which theory is linked to research. But, unlike the typical primer, here is the most sophisticated analysis raised to the highest level of abstraction. Not only does he perceive the stage or state of methodological development in behavioral inquiry, but Merton characterizes across the broadest possible continuum the several elements of work which in composite form the basis for sociological inquiry. In essence, the role of theory is to provide the broad context for empirical study. Out of this context, the variables to be examined and their possible relationships are generated. The findings of the investigation can then be set back into the theoretical system from which they were derived. Only in this manner is a systematized body of knowledge developed for a field.

Merton cautions against the rationalization into theory of empirical observation after the fact. Plausibility is not synonymous with verifiability. The lack of a theoretical base is the essential limit of library research. This limitation is a paramount shortcoming, not only of scholarship, but actually can and does distort the perception of the field and those who practice it by failing to orient the field to the realities of its situation.

How policy makers could have been misled is illustrated by a study conducted by one of the editors into why library elections in rural areas of Illinois following a demonstration service were failing.* In the absence of a theoretical orientation, the study would have concentrated primarily on aspects of the demonstration bookmobile service. To have done so would have been to ignore other key variables in the situation—the informal as well as formal means by which people formed their opinions on this issue, the part played by rural leaders, the interest groups which were identified with this issue. The library service provided rural residents was only one force influencing the outcome of the election. To have focused entirely upon it would have been to fail to perceive why rural voters were rejecting tax-supported library service in Illinois—and library leaders could have been lulled into thinking that with adaptation in their service, they could win a library election.

The recent history of sociological theory can in large measure be written in terms of an alternation between two contrasting emphases. On the one hand, we observe those sociologists who seek above all to generalize, to find their way as rapidly as possible to the formulation of sociological laws. Tending to assess the significance of sociological work in terms of scope rather than the demonstrability of generalizations, they eschew the "triviality" of detailed, small-scale observation and seek the grandeur of global summaries. At the other extreme stands a hardy band who do not hunt too closely the implications of their research but who remain confident and assured that what they report is so. To be sure, their reports of facts are verifiable and often verified, but they are somewhat at a loss to relate these facts to one another or even to explain why these, rather than other, observations have been made. For the first group the identifying motto would at times seem to be: "We do not know whether what we say is true, but it is at least significant." And for the radical empiricist the motto may read: "This is demonstrably so, but we cannot indicate its significance."

Whatever the bases of adherence to the one or the other of these camps—different but not neces-

*Mary Lee Bundy, *An Analysis of Voter Reaction to a Proposal to Form a Library District in LaSalle and Bureau Counties, Illinois* (Research Series No. 1; Springfield: Illinois State Library, December, 1960).

sarily contradictory accountings would be provided by psychologists, sociologists of knowledge, and historians of science—it is abundantly clear that there is no logical basis for their being ranged *against* each other. Generalizations can be tempered, if not with mercy, at least with disciplined observation; close, detailed observations need not be rendered trivial by avoidance of their theoretical pertinence and implications.

With all this there will doubtless be widespread if, indeed, not unanimous agreement. But this very unanimity suggests that these remarks are platitudinous. If, however, one function of theory is to explore the implications of the seemingly self-evident, it may not be amiss to look into what is entailed by such programmatic statements about the relations of sociological theory and empirical research. In doing so, every effort should be made to avoid dwelling upon illustrations drawn from the "more mature" sciences—such as physics and biology—not because these do not exhibit the logical problems involved but because their very maturity permits these disciplines to deal *fruitfully* with abstractions of a high order to a degree which, it is submitted, is not yet the case with sociology. An indefinitely large number of discussions of scientific method have set forth the logical prerequisites of scientific theory, but, it would seem, they have often done so on such a high level of abstraction that the prospect of translating these precepts into current sociological research becomes utopian. Ultimately, sociological research must meet the canons of scientific method; immediately, the task is so to express these requirements that they may have more direct bearing on the analytical work which is at present feasible.

The term "sociological theory" has been widely used to refer to the products of several related but distinct activites carried on by members of a professional group called sociologists. But since these several types of activity have significantly different bearings upon empirical social research—since they differ in their scientific functions—they should be distinguished for purposes of discussion. Moreover, such discriminations provide a basis for assessing the contributions and limitations characteristic of each of the following six types of work which are often lumped together as comprising sociological theory: (1) methodology; (2) general sociological orientations; (3) analysis of sociological concepts; (4) *post factum* sociological interpretations; (5) empirical generalizations in sociology and (6) sociological theory.

METHODOLOGY

At the outset we should distinguish clearly between sociological theory, which has for its subject matter certain aspects and results of the interaction of men and is therefore substantive, and methodology, or the logic of scientific procedure. The problems of methodology transcend those found in any one discipline, dealing either with those common to groups of disciplines[1] or, in more generalized form, with those common to all scientific inquiry. Methodology is not peculiarly bound up with sociological problems, and, though there is a plenitude of methodological discussions in books and journals of sociology, they are not thereby rendered sociological in character. Sociologists, in company with all others who essay scientific work, must be methodologically wise; they must be aware of the design of investigation, the nature of inference, the requirements of a theoretic system. But such knowledge does not contain or imply the particular *content* of sociological theory. There is, in short, a clear and decisive difference between *knowing how to test* a battery of hypotheses and *knowing the theory* from which to derive hypotheses to be tested.[2] It is my impression that current sociological training is more largely designed to make students understand the first than the second.

As Poincaré observed a half-century ago, sociologists have long been hierophants of methodology, thus, perhaps, diverting talents and energies from the task of building substantive theory. This focus of attention upon the logics of procedure has its patent scientific function, since such inventories serve a critical purpose in guiding and assessing theoretical and empirical inquiries. It also reflects the growing-pains of an immature discipline. Just as the apprentice who acquires new skills self-consciously examines each element of these skills in contrast to the master who habitually practices them with seeming indifference to their explicit formulation, so the exponents of a discipline haltingly moving toward scientific status laboriously spell out the logical grounds of their procedure. The slim books on methodology which proliferate in the fields of sociology, economics, and psychology do not find many counterparts among the technical works in the sciences which have long since come of age. Whatever their intellectual function, these methodological writings imply the perspectives of a fledgling discipline, anxiously presenting its credentials for full status in the fraternity of the sciences. But, significantly enough, the instances of adequate scientific method utilized by sociologists for illustrative or expository purposes are usually drawn from disciplines other than sociology itself. Twentieth-century, not sixteenth-century, physics and chemistry are taken as methodological prototypes or exemplars for twentieth-century sociology, with little explicit recognition that between sociology and these other sciences is a difference of centuries of cumulating scientific research. These comparisons are inevitably programmatic rather than realistic. More appropriate methodological demands would result in a gap between methodological aspiration and actual sociological attainment at once less conspicuous and less invidious.

GENERAL SOCIOLOGICAL ORIENTATIONS

Much of what is described in textbooks as sociological theory consists of general orientations toward substantive materials. Such orientations involve broad postulates which indicate *types* of variables which are somehow to be taken into account rather than specifying determinate relationships between particular variables. Indispensable though these orientations are, they provide only the broadest framework for empirical inquiry. This is the case with Durkheim's generic hypothesis, which holds that the "determining cause of a social fact should be sought among the social facts preceding it" and identifies the "social" factor as institutional norms toward which behavior is oriented.[3] Or, again, it is said that "to a certain approximation it is useful to regard society as an integrated system of mutually interrelated and functionally interdependent parts."[4] So, too, the importance of the "humanistic coefficient" in cultural data as expounded by Znaniecki and Sorokin, among others, belongs to this category. Such general orientations may be paraphrased as saying in effect that the investigator ignores this *order of fact* at his peril. They do not set forth specific hypotheses.

The chief function of these orientations is to provide a general context for inquiry; they facilitate the process of arriving at determinate hypotheses. To take a case in point: Malinowski was led to re-examine the Freudian notion of the Oedipus complex on the basis of a general sociological orientation, which viewed sentiment formation as patterned by social structure. This generic view clearly underlay his exploration of a specific "psychological" complex in its relation to a system of status relationships in a society differing in structure from that of western Europe. The

specific hypotheses which he utilized in this inquiry were all congruent with the generic orientation but were not prescribed by it. Otherwise put, the general orientation indicated the relevance of *some* structural variables, but there still remained the task of ferreting out the particular variables to be included.

Though such general theoretic outlooks have a more inclusive and profound effect on the development of scientific inquiry than do specific hypotheses—they constitute the matrix from which, in the words of Maurice Arthus, "new hypotheses follow one another in breathless succession and a harvest of facts follow closely the blossoming of these hypotheses"—though this is the case, they constitute only the point of departure for the theorist. It is his task to develop specific, interrelated hypotheses by reformulating empirical generalizations in the light of these generic orientations.

It should be noted, furthermore, that the growing contributions of sociological theory to its sister-disciplines lie more in the realm of general sociological orientations than in that of specific confirmed hypotheses. The development of social history, of institutional economics, and the importation of sociological perspectives into psychoanalytic theory involve recognition of the sociological dimensions of the data rather than incorporation of specific confirmed theories. Social scientists have been led to detect sociological gaps in the application of their theory to concrete social behavior. They do not so often exhibit sociological naiveté in their interpretations. The economist, the political scientist, and the psychologist have increasingly come to recognize that what they have systematically taken as given, as data, may be sociologically problematical. But this receptivity to a sociological outlook is often dissipated by the paucity of adequately *tested specific theories* of, say, the determinants of human wants or of the social processes involved in the distribution and exercise of social power. Pressures deriving from the respective theoretic gaps of the several social sciences may serve, in time, to bring about an increasing formulation of specific and systematic sociological theories appropriate to the problems implied by these gaps. General orientations do not suffice. Presumably this is the context for the complaint voiced by an economist:

[The economist always seeks to refer his analysis of a problem] back to some "datum," that is to say, to something which is extra-economic. This something may be apparently very remote from the problem which was first taken up, for the chains of economic causation are often very long. But he always wants to hand over the problem in the end to some sociologist or other—*if there is a sociologist waiting for him. Very often there isn't.*[5]

ANALYSIS OF SOCIOLOGICAL CONCEPTS

It is at times held that theory is comprised of concepts, an assertion which, being incomplete, is neither true nor false but vague. To be sure, conceptual analysis, which is confined to the specification and clarification of key concepts, is an indispensable phase of theoretic work. But an array of concepts—status, role, *Gemeinschaft,* social interaction, social distance, *anomie*—does not constitute theory, though it may enter into a theoretic system. It may be conjectured that, in so far as an antitheoretic bias occurs among sociologists, it is in protest against those who identify theory with clarification of definitions, who mistakenly take the part for the whole of theoretic analysis. It is only when such concepts are interrelated in the form of a scheme that a theory begins to emerge. Concepts, then, constitute the definitions (or prescriptions) of what is to be observed; they are the variables between which empirical relationships are to be sought. When propositions are logically interrelated, a theory has been instituted.

The choice of concepts guiding the collection and analysis of data is, of course, crucial to empirical inquiry. For, to state an important truism, if concepts are selected such that no relationships between them obtain, the research will be sterile, no matter how meticulous the subsequent observations and inferences. The importance of this truism lies in its implication that truly trial-and-error procedures in empirical inquiry are likely to be comparatively unfruitful, since the number of variables which are not significantly connected is indefinitely large.

It is, then, one function of conceptual clarification to make explicit the character of data subsumed under a concept.[6] It thus serves to reduce the likelihood that spurious empirical findings will be couched in terms of given concepts. Thus, Sutherland's re-examination of the received concept of "crime" provides an instructive instance of how such clarification induces a revision of hypotheses concerning the data organized in terms of the concept.[7] He demonstrates an equivocation implicit in criminological theories which seek to account for the fact that there is a much higher rate of crime, as "offically measured," in the lower than in the upper social classes. These crime "data" (organized in terms of a particular operational concept or measure of crime) have led to a series of hypotheses which view poverty, slum conditions, feeble-mindedness, and other characteristics held to be highly associated with low-class status as the "causes" of criminal behavior. Once the concept of crime is clarified to refer to the violation of criminal law and is thus extended to include "white-collar criminality" in business and professions—violations which are less often reflected in official crime statistics than are lower-call violations—the presumptive high association between low social status and crime may no longer obtain. We need not pursue Sutherland's analysis further to detect the function of conceptual clarification in this instance. It provides for a *reconstruction of data* by indicating more precisely just what they include and what they exclude. In doing so, it leads to a liquidation of hypotheses set up to account for spurious data by questioning the assumptions on which the initial statistical data were based. By hanging a question mark on an implicit assumption underlying the research definition of crime—the assumption that violations of the criminal code by members of the several social classes are representatively registered in the official statistics—this conceptual clarification had direct implications for a nucleus of theories.

In similar fashion, conceptual analysis may often resolve apparent antinomies in empirical findings by indicating that such contradictions are more apparent than real. This familiar phrase refers, in part, to the fact that initially crudely defined concepts have tacitly included significantly different elements so that data organized in terms of these concepts differ materially and thus exhibit apparently contradictory tendencies.[8] The function of conceptual analysis in this instance is to maximize the likelihood of the comparability, in significant respects, of data which are to be included in a research.

The instance drawn from Sutherland merely illustrates the more general fact that in research, as in less disciplined activities, our conceptual language tends to fix our perceptions and, derivatively, our thought and behavior. The concept defines the situation, and the research worker responds accordingly. Explicit conceptual analysis helps him recognize to what he is responding and which (possibly significant) elements he is ignoring. The findings of Whorf on this matter are, with appropriate modifications, applicable to empirical research.[9] He found that behavior was oriented toward linguistic or conceptual meanings connoted by the terms applied to a situation. Thus, in the presence of objects which are conceptually described as "gasoline drums," behavior will tend modally toward a particular type: great care will be exercised. But when people are confronted with what are called "*empty* gasoline drums," behavior is different: it is careless, with little control over smoking and the disposition of cigarette stubs. Yet the "empty" drums are the more hazardous, since they contain explosive vapor. Response is not to the physical but to the conceptualized situation. The concept "empty" is here used equivocally: as a synonym for "null and void, negative, inert," and as a term applied to physical situations without regard to such "irrelevancies" as vapor and liquid vestiges in the container. The situation is conceptualized in the second sense, and the concept is then responded to in the first sense, with the result that "empty" gasoline drums become the occasion for fires. Clarification of just what "empty" means in the universe of discourse would have a profound effect on behavior. This case may serve as a paradigm of the functional effect of conceptual clarification upon research behavior: it makes clear just what the research worker is doing when he deals with conceptualized data. He draws different consequences for empirical research as his conceptual apparatus changes.

This is not to say, however, that the vocabulary of concepts fixes perceptions, thought and associated behavior once and for all. Even less is it to say that such instances of misleading terminology are embedded in one or another language (as Whorf tended to imply in this theory of linguistic behaviorism). Men are not permanently imprisoned in the framework of the (often inherited) concepts they use; they can not only break out of this framework but can create a new one, better suited to the needs of the occasion. Yet, at any particular time, one should be prepared to find that the governing concepts can, and often do, lag behind the behavioral requirements of the case. During these sometimes prolonged periods of lag, misapplied concepts do their damage. However, this very inaptness of concept to situation, recognized through painful experience, will often evoke self-correcting and more appropriate formulations. The job is to identify conceptual lag and to liberate ourselves from the patterns of cognitive misbehavior which it tends to produce.[9a]

A further task of conceptual analysis is to institute observable indices of the social data with which empirical research is concerned. Early efforts in this direction were manifest in the works of Durkheim (and constitute one of his most significant contributions to sociology). Though his formalized conceptions along these lines do not approach the sophistication of more recent formulations, he was patently utilizing "intervening variables," as lately described by Tolman and Hull, and seeking to establish indices for these variables.[10] The problem, as far as it need be stated for our immediate purposes, consists in devising indices of unobservables or symbolic constructs (*e.g.,* social cohesion)—indices which are theoretically supportable. Conceptual analysis thus enters as one basis for an initial and periodic critical appraisal of the extent to which assumed signs and symbols are an adequate index of the social substratum. Such analysis suggests clues for determining whether in fact the index (or measuring instrument) proves adequate to the occasion.[11]

POST FACTUM SOCIOLOGICAL INTERPRETATIONS

It is often the case in empirical social research that data are collected and only then subjected to interpretative comment. This procedure in which the observations are at hand and the interpretations are subsequently applied to the data has the logical structure of clinical inquiry. The observations may be case-history or statistical in character. The defining characteristic of this procedure is the introduction of an interpretation *after* the observations have been made rather than the empirical testing of a predesignated hypothesis. The implicit assumption is that a body of generalized propositions has been so fully established that it can be approximately applied to the data in hand.

Such *post factum* explanations, designed to "explain" observations, differ in logical function from speciously similar procedures where the observational materials are utilized in order to *derive* fresh hypotheses to be confirmed by *new* observations.

A disarming characteristic of the procedure is that the explanations are indeed consistent with the given set of observations. This is scarcely surprising, in as much as only those *post factum* hypotheses are selected which do accord with these observations. If the basic assumption holds—namely, that the *post factum* interpretation utilizes abundantly confirmed theories—then this type of explanation indeed "shoots arrowy light into the dark chaos of materials." But if, as is more often the case in sociological interpretation, the *post factum* hypotheses are also *ad hoc* or, at the least, have but a slight degree of prior confirmation, then such "precocious explanations," as H. S. Sullivan called them, produce a spurious sense of adequacy at the expense of instigating further inquiry.

Post factum explanations remain at the level of *plausibility* (low evidential value) rather than leading to "compelling evidence" (a high degree of confirmation). Plausibility, in distinction to compelling evidence, is found when an interpretation is consistent with one set of data (which typically has, indeed, given rise to the decision to utilize one, rather than another, interpretation). It also implies that alternative interpretations equally consistent with these data have not been systematically explored and that inferences drawn from the interpretation have not been tested by new observations.

The logical fallacy underlying the *post factum* explanation rests in the fact that there is available a variety of crude hypotheses, each with some measure of confirmation but designed to account for quite contradictory sets of affairs. The method of *post factum* explanation does not lend itself to nullifiability, if only because it is so completely flexible. For example, it may be reported that "the unemployed tend to read fewer books than they did previously." This is "explained" by the hypothesis that anxiety increases as a consequence of unemployment and, therefore, that any activity requiring concentration, such as reading, becomes difficult. This type of accounting is plausible, since there is some evidence that increased anxiety *may* occur in such situations and since a state of morbid preoccupation does interfere with organized activity. If, however, it is now reported that the original data were erroneous and it is a fact "the unemployed read more than previously" a new *post factum* explanation can at once be invoked. The explanation now holds that the unemployed have more leisure or that they engage in activity intended to increase their personal skills. Consequently, they read more than before. Thus, whatever the observations, a new interpretation can be found to "fit the facts."[12] This example may be sufficient to indicate that such reconstructions serve only as illustrations and not as tests. It is this logical inadequacy of the *post factum* construction that led Peirce to observe:

It is of the essence of induction that the consequence of the theory should be drawn first in regard to the unknown, or virtually unknown, result of experiment; and

that this should virtually be only ascertained afterward. For if we look over the phenomena to find agreements with the theory, it is a mere question of ingenuity and industry how many we shall find.[13]

These reconstructions typically by-pass an explicit formulation of the conditions under which the hypotheses will be found to hold true. In order to meet this logical requirement, such interpretations would necessarily be predictive rather than postdictive.

As a case in point, we may quote the frequency with which Blumer asserts that the Thomas-Znaniecki analyses of documents "merely seem to be plausible."[14] The basis for plausibility rests in the consistency between the interpretation and the data; the absence of compelling evidence stems from the failure to provide distinctive tests of the interpretations apart from their consistency with the initial observations. The analysis is fitted to the facts, and there is no indication of just which data would be taken to contravene the interpretations. As a consequence, the documentary evidence merely illustrates rather than tests the theory.[15]

EMPIRICAL GENERALIZATIONS IN SOCIOLOGY

Not infrequently it is said that the object of sociological theory is to arrive at statements of social uniformities. This is an elliptical assertion and hence requires clarification. For there are two types of statements of sociological uniformities which differ significantly in their bearing on theory. The first of these is the empirical generalization: an isolated proposition summarizing observed uniformities of relationships between two or more variables.[16] The sociological literature abounds with such generalizations which have not been assimilated to sociological theory. Thus, Engel's "laws" of consumption may be cited as examples. So, too, the Halbwachs finding that laborers spend more per adult unit for food than white-collar employees of the same income class.[17] Such generalizations may be of greater or less precision, but this does not affect their logical place in the structure of inquiry. The Groves-Ogburn finding, for a sample of American cities, that "cities with a larger percentage engaged in manufacturing also have, on the average, slightly larger percentages of young persons married" has been expressed in an equation indicating the degree of this relationship. Although propositions of this order are essential in empirical research, a miscellany of such propositions only provides the raw materials for sociology as a discipline. The theoretic task, and the orientation of empirical research toward theory, first begins when the bearing of such uniformities on a set of interrelated propositions is tentatively established. The notion of directed research implies that, in part,[18] empirical inquiry is so organized that if and when empirical uniformities are discovered, they have direct consequences for a theoretic system. In so far as the research is directed, the rationale of findings is set forth before the findings are obtained.

SOCIOLOGICAL THEORY

The second type of sociological generalization, the so-called scientific law, differs from the foregoing in as much as it is a statement of invariance *derivable* from a theory. The paucity of such laws in the sociological field perhaps reflects the prevailing bifurcation of theory and empirical research. Despite the many volumes dealing with the history of sociological theory and despite the plethora of empirical investigations, sociologists (including the writer) may discuss the logical criteria of sociological laws without citing a single instance which fully satisfies these criteria.[19]

Approximations to these criteria are not entirely wanting. To exhibit the relations of empirical generalizations to theory and to set forth the functions of theory, it may be useful to examine a familiar case in which such generalizations were incorporated into a body of substantive theory. Thus, it has long been established as a statistical uniformity that in a variety of populations, Catholics have a lower suicide rate than Protestants.[20] In this form the uniformity posed a theoretical problem. It merely constituted an empirical regularity which would become significant for theory only if it could be derived from a set of other propositions, a task which Durkheim set himself. If we restate his theoretic assumptions in formal fashion, the paradigm of his theoretic analysis becomes clear:

1. Social cohesion provides psychic support to group members subjected to acute stresses and anxieties.
2. Suicide rates are functions of *unrelieved* anxieties and stresses to which persons are subjected.
3. Catholics have greater social cohesion than Protestants.
4. Therefore, lower suicide rates should be anticipated among Catholics than among Protestants.[21]

This case serves to locate the place of empirical generalizations in relation to theory and to illustrate the several functions of theory.

1. It indicates that theoretic pertinence is not inherently present or absent in empirical generalizations but appears when the generalization is conceptualized in abstractions of higher order (Catholicism—social cohesion—relieved anxieties—suicide rate) which are embodied in more general statements of relationships.[22] What was initially taken as an isolated uniformity is restated as a relation, not between religious affiliation and behavior, but between groups with certain conceptualized attributes (social cohesion) and the behavior. The *scope* of the original empirical finding is considerably extended, and several seemingly disparate uniformities are seen to be interrelated (thus differentials in suicide rates between married and single persons can be derived from the same theory).

2. Once having established the theoretic pertinence of a uniformity by deriving it from a set of interrelated propositions, we provide for the *cumulation* both of theory and of research findings. The differentials-in-suicide-rate uniformities add confirmation to the set of propositions from which they—and other uniformities—have been derived. This is a major function of *systematic theory*.

3. Whereas the empirical uniformity did not lend itself to the drawing of diverse consequences, the reformulation gives rise to various consequences in fields of conduct quite remote from that of suicidal behavior. For example, inquiries into obsessive behavior, morbid preoccupations, and other maladaptive behavior have found these also to be related to inadequacies of group cohesion.[23] The conversion of empirical uniformities into theoretic statements thus increases the *fruitfulness* of research through the successive exploration of implications.

4. By providing a rationale, the theory introduces a *ground for prediction* which is more secure than mere empirical extrapolation from previously observed trends. Thus, should independent measures indicate a decrease of social cohesion among Catholics, the theorist would predict a tendency toward increased rates of suicide in this group. The atheoretic empiricist would have no alternative, however, but to predict on the basis of extrapolation.

5. The foregoing list of functions presupposes one further attribute of theory which is not altogether true of the Durkheim formulation and which gives rise to a general problem that has peculiarly beset sociological theory, at least, up to the present. If theory is to be productive, it must be sufficiently *precise* to be *determinate*.

Precision is an integral element of the criterion of *testability*. The prevailing pressure toward the utilization of statistical data in sociology, whenever possible, to control and test theoretic inferences has a justifiable basis, when we consider the logical place of precision in disciplined inquiry.

The more precise the inferences (predictions) which can be drawn from a theory, the less the likelihood of *alternative* hypotheses which will be adequate to these predictions. In other words, precise predictions and data serve to reduce the *empirical* bearing upon research of the *logical* fallacy of affirming the consequent.[24] It is well known that verified predictions derived from a theory do not prove or demonstrate that theory; they merely supply a measure of confirmation, for it is always possible that alternative hypotheses drawn from different theoretic systems can also account for the predicted phenomena.[25] But those theories which admit of precise predictions confirmed by observation take on strategic importance since they provide an initial basis for choice between competing hypotheses. In other words, precision enhances the likelihood of approximating a "crucial" observation or experiment.

The internal coherence of a theory has much the same function, for if a variety of empirically confirmed consequences are drawn from one theoretic system, this reduces the likelihood that competing theories can adequately account for the same data. The integrated theory sustains a larger measure of confirmation than is the case with distinct and unrelated hypotheses, thus accumulating a greater weight of evidence.

Both pressures—toward precision and logical coherence—can lead to unproductive activity, particularly in the social sciences. Any procedure can be abused as well as used. A premature insistence on precision at all costs may sterilize imaginative hypotheses. It may lead to a reformulation of the scientific problem in order to permit measurement with, at times, the result that the subsequent materials do not bear on the initial problem in hand.[26] In the search for precision, care must be taken to see that significant problems are not thus inadvertently blotted from view. Similarly, the pressure for logical consistency has at times invited logomachy and sterile theorizing, in as much as the assumptions contained in the system of analysis are so far removed from empirical referents or involve such high abstractions as not to permit of empirical inquiry.[27] But the warrant for these criteria of inquiry is not vitiated by such abuses.

FORMAL DERIVATIONS AND CODIFICATION

This limited account has, at the very least, pointed to the need for a closer connection between theory and empirical research. The prevailing division of the two is manifested in marked *discontinuities* of empirical research, on the one hand, and systematic theorizing unsustained by empirical test, on the other.[27a] There are conspicuously few instances of consecutive research which have cumulatively investigated a succession of hypotheses derived from a given theory. Rather, there tends to be a marked dispersion of empirical inquiries, oriented toward a concrete field of human behavior, but lacking a central theoretic orientation. The plethora of discrete empirical generalizations and of *post factum* interpretations reflect this pattern of research. The large bulk of general orientations and conceptual analyses, as distinct from sets of interrelated hypotheses, in turn reflect the tendency to separate theoretic activity from empirical research. It is a commonplace that continuity, rather than dispersion, can be achieved only if empirical studies are theory-oriented and if theory is empirically confirmable. However, it is possible to go beyond such affirmations and to suggest certain conventions for sociological research which might well facilitate this process. These conventions may be termed "formalized derivation" and "codifications."[28]

Both in the design and in the reporting of empirical research, it might be made a definite convention that hypotheses and, whenever possible, the theoretic grounds (assumptions and postulates) of these hypotheses be explicitly set forth. The report of data would be in terms of their immediate pertinence for the hypotheses and, derivatively, the underlying theory. Attention should be called specifically to the introduction of interpretative variables other than those entailed in the original formulation of hypotheses and the bearing of these upon the theory should be indicated. *Post factum* interpretations which will inevitably arise when new and unexpected relationships are discovered should be so stated that the direction of further probative research becomes evident. The conclusions of the research might well include not only a statement of the findings with respect to the initial hypotheses but, when this is in point, an indication of the order of observations needed to test anew the further implications of the investigation. Formal derivation of this character has had a salutary effect in psychology and economics, leading, in the one case, to sequential experiments[29] and, in the other, to an articulated series of investigations. One consequence of such formalization is that it serves as a control over the introduction of unrelated, undisciplined, and diffuse interpretations. It does not impose upon the reader the task of ferreting out the relations between the interpretations embodied in the text.[30] Above all, it prepares the way for consecutive and cumulative research rather than a buckshot array of dispersed investigations.

The correlative process which seems called for is that which Lazarsfeld terms "codification." Whereas formal derivation focuses our attention upon the implications of a theory, codification seeks to systematize available empirical generalizations in *apparently different* spheres of behavior. Rather than permitting such separate empirical findings to lie fallow or to be referred to distinctive areas of behavior, the deliberate attempt to institute relevant provisional hypotheses promises to extend existing theory, subject to further empirical inquiry. Thus, an abundance of empirical findings in such fields as propaganda and public opinion, reactions to unemployment, and family responses to crises suggest that when persons are confronted with an "objective stimulus-pattern" which would be expected to elicit responses counter to their "initial predispositions," their actual behavior can be more successfully predicted on the basis of predispositions than of the stimulus-pattern. This is implied by "boomerang effects" in propaganda,[31] by findings on adjustive and maladjustive responses to unemployment,[32] and by research on the stability of families confronted with severe reductions in income.[33] A codified formulation, even as crude as this, gives rise to theoretic problems which would be readily overlooked if the several empirical findings were not re-examined within a single context. It is submitted that codification, as a procedure complementing the formal derivation of hypotheses to be tested, will facilitate the codevelopment of viable sociological theory and pertinent empirical research.

FOOTNOTES

[1] Consider several volumes which set forth methodological as distinct from procedural concerns of sociology: Florian Znaniecki, *The Method of Sociology* (New York: Farrar & Rinehart, 1934); R. M. MacIver, *Social Causation* (Boston: Ginn & Co., 1942); G. A. Lundberg, *Foundations of Sociology* (New York: Macmillan Co., 1939); Felix Kaufmann, *Methodology of the Social Sciences* (New York: Oxford University Press, 1944); P. F. Lazarsfeld and M. Rosenberg, (eds.) *The Language of Social Research* (Glencoe: The Free Press, 1955), esp. the Introductions to sections.

[2] However, it should be noted not only that instruments and procedures used in sociological (or other scientific) inquiry must meet methodological criteria but that they also logically presuppose substantive theories. As Pierre Duhem observed in this connection, the instrument as well as the experimental results obtained in science are shot through with specific assumptions and theories of a substantive order. *La théorie physique* (Paris: Chevalier et Rivière, 1906), 278.

[3] Durkheim, *The Rules of Sociological Method,* 110; *L'Education morale* (Paris: Félix Alcan, 1925), 9-45, *passim.*

[4] Conrad M. Arensberg and Solon Kimball, *Family and Community in Ireland* (Cambridge: Harvard University Press, 1940), xxvi.

[5] J. R. Hicks, "Economic theory and the social sciences," *The Social Sciences: Their Relations in Theory and in Teaching* (London: Le Play Press, 1936), p. 135. (Italics mine.)

[6] As Schumpeter remarks about the role of "analytic apparatus": "If we are to speak about price levels and to devise methods of measuring them, we must know what a price level is. If we are to observe demand, we must have a precise concept of its elasticity. If we speak about productivity of labor, we must know what propositions hold true about total product per man-hour and what other propositions hold true about the partial differential coefficient of total product with respect to man-hours. No hypotheses enter into such concepts, which simply embody methods of description and measurement, nor into the propositions defining their relation (so-called theorems), and yet their framing is the chief task of theory, in economics as elsewhere. This is what we mean by *tools of analysis*." Joseph A. Schumpeter, *Business Cycles* (New York: McGraw-Hill Book Co., 1939), I, 31.

[7] Edwin H. Sutherland, "White-collar criminality," *American Sociological Review,* 1940, 5, 1-12.

[8] Elaborate formulations of this type of analysis are to be found in Corrado Gini, *Prime linee di patologia economica* (Milan: Giuffre, 1935); for a brief discussion see C. Gini, "Un tentativo di armonizarre teorie disparate e osservazioni contrastanti nel campo dei fenomeni sociali," *Rivista di politica economica*, 1935, 12, 1-24.

[9] B. L. Whorf, "Relation of habitual thought and behavior to language," in L. Spier, A. I. Hallowell, and S. S. Newman (eds.), *Language, Culture, and Personality* (Menasha: Sapir Memorial Fund Publication, 1941), 75-93.

[9a] For an extended discussion, see the posthumously published volume of selected writings by B. L. Whorf, *Language, Thought and Reality* (Cambridge: Technology Press of M.I.T., 1956). It is the extreme Whorfian position which Joshua Whatmough attacks in his *Language: A Modern Synthesis* (New York: St Martin's Press, 1956), 85, 186-7, 227-34. Yet Whatmough's well-placed salvoes do not entirely destroy Whorf's position but only compel a retreat to a more limited and defensible position. Socially entrenched concepts do affect perception, thought and behavior but the structure of language

provides sufficient scope for inappropriate concepts to be replaced by more suitable concepts. An appreciative review of Whorf's ideas will be found in Franklin Fearing, "An examination of the conceptions of Benjamin Whorf in the light of theories of perception and cognition," Harry Hoijer, ed. *Language in Culture* (University of Chicago Press, 1954), 47-81.

[10] Durkheim's basic formulation, variously repeated in each of his monographs, reads as follows: "It is necessary . . . to substitute for the internal fact which escapes us an external fact that symbolizes it and to study the former through the latter." See his *Rules of Sociological Method,* chap. ii; *Le Suicide* (Paris: F. Alcan, 1930), 22ff. Most detailed consideration of Durkheim's views on social indices is provided by Harry Alpert, *Emile Durkheim and His Sociology* (New York: Columbia University Press, 1939), 120 ff. On the general problem see C. L. Hull, "The problem of Intervening Variables in molar behavior theory," *Psychological Review,* 1943, 50, 273-91.

[11] Among the many functions of conceptual analysis at this point is that of instituting inquiry into the question of whether or not the index is "neutral" to its environment. By searching out the assumptions underlying the selection (and validation for a given population) of observables as indices (e.g., religious affiliation, an attitude scale), conceptual analysis initiates appropriate tests of the possibility that the index has become dissociated from its substratum. For a clear statement of this point see Louis Guttman, "A basis for scaling qualitative data," *American Sociological Review,* 1944, 9, 139-50, esp. 149-50.

[12] The pertinent data have not been assembled. But, on the plausibility of the second interpretation, see Douglas Waples, *People and Print: Social Aspects of Reading in the Depression* (Chicago: University of Chicago Press, 1937), 198.

[13] Charles Sanders Peirce, *Collected Papers*, ed. Charles Hartshorne and Paul Weiss (Cambridge: Harvard University Press, 1932), II, 496.

[14] Herbert Blumer, *An Appraisal of Thomas and Znaniecki's "The Polish Peasant in Europe and America"* (New York: Social Science Research Council, 1939), 38, see also *ibid.,* 39, 44, 46, 49, 50, 75.

[15] It is difficult to see on what grounds Blumer asserts that these interpretations cannot be mere cases of illustration of a theory. His comment that the materials "acquire significance and understanding that they did not have" would apply to *post factum* explanations generally.

[16] This usage of the term "empirical" is common, as Dewey notes. In this context, "*empirical* means that the subject-matter of a given proposition which has existential inference, represents merely a set of uniform conjunctions of traits repeatedly observed to exist, without any understanding of *why* the conjunction occurs; without a theory which states its rationale." John Dewey, *Logic: The Theory of Inquiry* (New York: Henry Holt & Co., 1938), 305.

[17] See a considerable collection of such uniformities summarized by C. C. Zimmerman, *Consumption and Standards of Living* (New York: D. Van Nostrand Co., 1936), 51 ff.

[18] "In part," if only because it stultifies the possibilities of obtaining fertile new findings to confine researches *wholly* to the test of predetermined hypotheses. Hunches originating in the course of the inquiry which may not have immediately obvious implications for a broader theoretic system may eventuate in the discovery of empirical uniformities which can later be incorporated into a theory. For example, in the sociology of political behavior, it has been recently established that the larger the number of social cross-pressures to which voters are subjected, the less interest they exhibit in a presidential election (P. F. Lazarsfeld, Bernard Berelson, and Hazel Gaudet, *The People's Choice* [New York: Duell, Sloan & Pearce, 1944], 56-64). This finding, which was wholly unanticipated when the research was first formulated, may well initiate new lines of systematic inquiry into political behavior, even though it is not yet integrated into a generalized theory. Fruitful empirical research not only tests theoretically derived hypotheses; it also originates new hypotheses. This might be termed the "serendipity" component of research, i.e., the discovery, by chance or sagacity, of valid results which were not sought for.

[19] E.g., see the discussion by George A. Lundberg, "The concept of law in the social sciences," *Philosophy of Science,* 1938, 5, 189-203, which affirms the possibility of such laws without including any case in point. The book by K. D. Har, *Social Laws* (Chapel Hill: University of North Carolina Press, 1930), does not fulfil the promise implicit in the title. A panel of social scientists discussing the possibility of obtaining social laws finds it difficult to instance cases (Blumer, *op. cit.,* 142-50).

[20] It need hardly be said that this statement assumes that education, income, nationality, rural-urban residence, and other factors which might render this finding spurious have been held constant.

[21] We need not examine further aspects of this illustration, e.g., (1) the extent to which we have adequately stated the premises implicit in Durkheim's interpretation; (2) the supplementary theoretic analysis which would take these premises not as given but as problematic; (3) the grounds on which the potentially infinite regression of theoretic interpretations is halted at one rather than another point; (4) the problems involved in the introduction of such intervening variables as social cohesion which are not directly measured; (5) the extent to which the premises have been empirically confirmed; (6) the comparatively low order of abstraction represented by this illustration and (7) the fact that Durkheim derived several empirical generalizations from this same set of hypotheses.

[22] Thorstein Veblen has put this with typical cogency: "All this may seem like taking pains about trivialities. But the data with which any scientific inquiry has to do are trivialities in some other bearing than that one in which they are of account." *The Place of Science in Modern Civilization* (New York: Viking Press, 1932), 42.

[23] See, e.g., Elton Mayo, *Human Problems of an Industrial Civilization* (New York: Macmillan Co., 1933), 113 *et passim*. The theoretical framework utilized in the studies of industrial morale by Whitehead, Roethlisberger, and Dickson stemmed appreciably from the Durkheim formulations, as the authors testify.

[24] The paradigm of "proof through prediction" is, of course, logically fallacious:

If *A* (hypothesis), then *B* (prediction).

B is observed.

Therefore, *A* is true.

This is not overdisturbing for scientific research, in as much as other than formal criteria are involved.

[25] As a case in point, consider that different theorists had predicted war and internecine conflict on a large scale at mid-century. Sorokin and some Marxists, for example, set forth this prediction on the basis of quite distinct theoretic systems. The actual outbreak of large-scale conflicts does not in itself enable us to choose between these schemes of analysis, if only because the observed fact is consistent with both. Only if the predictions had been so *specified,* had been so precise, that the actual occurrences coincided with the one prediction and not with the other, would a determinate test have been instituted.

[26] Stuart A. Rice comments on this tendency in public opinion research; see *Eleven Twenty-six: A Decade of Social Science Research,* ed. Louis Wirth (Chicago: University of Chicago Press, 1940), 167.

[27] It is this practice to which E. Ronald Walker refers, in the field of economics, as "theoretic blight." *From Economic Theory to Policy* (Chicago: University of Chicago Press, 1943), chap. iv.

[27a] See in this connection the dramatic example of such *discontinuity* cited in Chapter I (i.e., the recent rediscovery of the primary group within formal associations some decades after this had been elaborately treated by Thomas and Znaniecki).

[28] To be sure, these conventions are deduction and induction, respectively. Our sole interest at this point is to translate these logical procedures into terms appropriate to current sociological theory and research.

[29] The work of Clark Hull and associates is preeminent in this respect. See, e.g., Hull, *Principles of Behavior* (New York: D. Appleton-Century Co., 1943); also comparable efforts toward formalization in the writings of Kurt Lewin (e.g., Kurt Lewin, Ronald Lippitt, and S. K. Escalona, *Studies in Topological and Vector Psychology I* ["University of Iowa Studies in Child Welfare," Vol. XVI (Iowa City, 1940)], 9-42).

[30] A book such as John Dollard's *Caste and Class in a Southern Town* teems with suggestiveness, but it is an enormous task for the reader to work out explicitly the theoretic problems which are being attacked, the interpretative variables, and the implicit assumptions of the interpretations. Yet all this needs to be done if a sequence of studies building upon Dollard's work is proposed.

[31] Paul F. Lazarsfeld and Robert K. Merton, "Studies in radio and film propaganda," *Transactions of the New York Academy of Sciences, Series II,* 1943, 6, 58-79.

[32] O. M. Hall, "Attitudes and unemployment," *Archives of Psychology,* No. 165 (March, 1934); E. W. Bakke, *The Unemployed Worker* (New Haven: Yale University Press, 1940).

[33] Mirra Komarovsky, *The Unemployed Man and His Family* (New York: Dryden Press, 1940); R. C. Angell, *The Family Encounters the Depression* (New York: Charles Scribner's Sons, 1936); E. W. Burgess, R. K. Merton, *et al., Restudy of the Documents Analyzed by Angell in The Family Encounters the Depression* (New York: Social Science Research Council, 1942).

Basic Elements of the Scientific Method: Hypotheses

by William J. Goode and Paul K. Hatt

This is the best statement we know of the hypothesis. It is valuable, both for the sources of hypotheses which it suggests and for its set of criteria for evaluating the hypothesis. A salient point is the need of social research to confirm the obvious since not infrequently what is commonly viewed to be obvious may simply be a wholly incorrect assumption. The more tradition-bound a field, the more uncommon is its disposition to raise fundamental questions. Yet, failure to ask the simplest questions, the ones whose answers seem so obvious that they are never challenged, may be precisely why or when an institution is most vulnerable. To question is not to labor the obvious, but only to confirm that it is so or not so. The library faith stands in need of such skepticism.

A time of change, far more than a stable period, furnishes cues and insights into possible problem areas. The rise of new types of information service calls into question the relatively passive form of the conventional library and the disposition of libraries to adapt or modify their programs. Similarly, as efforts are made to adapt libraries to other than traditional middle class clienteles, basic questions of role and mission and social impact of the library as a public institution are raised.

The proclivity of a pragmatic field, unschooled in and impatient with theory, is to study problems close to what they see as possible practical solutions. The disposition is to deal with the problem as it appears on its surface. And, this forcloses the possibility of deeper analysis, more susceptible of clearer insight. The manpower shortage in librarianship, for example, suggests investigating the use of technicians. Yet, such an approach would overlook the entire range of political, social, economic and psychological forces which influence the problem in fundamental ways. Goode and Hatt help to sort out the differences in discriminating the superficial from the genuine problem.

THE FUNCTION OF THE HYPOTHESIS

Facts, as has been shown, are dependent upon a theoretical framework for their meaning. They are also statements of relationships between concepts. A basic requirement in the application of the scientific method, the clear definition of concepts, has just been discussed. The next step, how to ask the questions which lead to new scientific propositions, must now be considered.

Chapter 2 has shown how theory serves to order and give meaning to facts. It also pointed out that theory can give direction to the search for facts. A hypothesis states what we are looking for. When facts are assembled, ordered, and seen in a relationship, they constitute a theory. The theory is not speculation, but is built upon fact. Now, the various facts in a theory may be logically analyzed, and relationships other than those stated in the theory can be deduced. At this point there is no knowledge as to whether such deductions are correct. *The formulation of the deduction,* however, constitutes a hypothesis; if verified it becomes part of a future theoretical construction. It is thus clear that the relation between the hypothesis and theory is very close indeed. One scientist, in this connection, has stated: "In practice a theory is an elaborate hypothesis which deals with more types of facts than does the simple hypothesis. . . . The distinction . . . is not clearly defined." [1] While it is true that the two can never be satisfactorily separated, it is useful to think of them as two aspects of the way in which science adds to knowledge. Thus a theory states a logical relationship between facts. From this theory other propositions can be deduced that *should* be true, if the first relationship holds. These deduced propositions are hypotheses.

A hypothesis looks forward. It is a proposition which can be put to a test to determine its validity.

It may seem contrary to, or in accord with, common sense. It may prove to be correct or incorrect. In any event, however, *it leads to an empirical test.* Whatever the outcome, the hypothesis is a question put in such a way that an answer of some kind can be forthcoming. It is an example of the organized skepticism of science, the refusal to accept any statement without empirical verification.

Every worth-while theory, then, permits the formulation of additional hypotheses. These, when tested, are either proved or disproved and in turn constitute further tests of the original theory. In either case they may be of use to existing theory and may make possible the formulation of still other hypotheses. Such a simple outline, unfortunately, fails to indicate that the formulation of useful hypotheses is one of the most difficult steps in scientific method.

PROBLEMS IN FORMULATING THE HYPOTHESIS

As difficult as the process may be, it is necessary for the student to see the fundamental need of a hypothesis to guide sound research. Without it, research is unfocused, a random empirical wandering. The results cannot even be stated as facts with a clear meaning. The hypothesis is the necessary link between theory and the investigation which leads to the discovery of additions to knowledge.

The chief difficulties in the road to the formulation of useful hypotheses are three. First among these is the absence of (or the absence of knowledge of) a clear theoretical framework. Second is the lack of ability to utilize that theoretical framework logically. Third is the failure to be acquainted with available research techniques so as to be able to phrase the hypothesis properly. These obstacles will be treated later in the chapter, but at the moment it is possible to stop and consider the question, "Just how difficult is it to ask an important, testable question?"

Let the student answer this question himself. By the time he completes this course, he will have had several sociology courses. If he happens to be a superior student, he has also read several monographs in sociology. With this knowledge of sociological theory at hand, let him formulate one good, definite, testable hypothesis.

Many students will completely fail such a test. If so, they should not be discouraged, for this is not a simple task. In any case, one of the functions of this course is to improve the ability to formulate good hypotheses. If the student is able to formulate propositions at all, closer investigation will show many of them not to be hypotheses. Some students will have merely selected an *area* of study: the socialization of the child, juvenile delinquency, white-collar crime, or courtship behavior. Such formulations, of course, are not hypotheses; they do not formulate precise and testable questions.

Somewhat closer to the mark will be some who might suggest the *replication* of previous studies. That is, some may think it useful to repeat a previous piece of scientific work, duplicating the conditions exactly. This is useful work and does in one sense state a hypothesis, *i.e.,* that the results will be the same. But the utility of this procedure does not go beyond checking findings and it is likely to make no contribution to new knowledge.

Still closer to the formulation of a hypothesis would be those few who might suggest the study of *empirical regularities.* This type of research would be represented by the study of such things as the ecological distribution of mental disorders, the acceptance of contraceptive practices in Latin America, or the marital adjustment of rural Southerners. Such questions do suggest the *type of data* to be gathered, but they are hypotheses of a low level of abstraction; they merely predict that *some* type of patterning will appear without predicting *what* that pattern will be.

On the other hand, if we actually begin with a broad theory, and by deduction predict a social regularity as a relationship between two or more factors, we may develop a hypothesis. We might then obtain such formulations as the following, although space does not allow a statement of the entire chain of theoretical reasoning upon which they are based, or the detailed definitions necessary:

(1) *Principle:* A socially recognized relationship in which there are strains built into the situation will also be surrounded by institutionalized controls, to ensure conformity of the participants with implicit or explicit norms.

Deduction: We therefore predict that in those professions (such as psychiatry and psychotherapy generally, medicine, and law to a lesser degree) which deal with the more intimate aspects of clients' lives there are (*a*) more emotional strains in the client-practitioner relationship, and (*b*) more internalized and external controls upon both participants than is the case in other professions (such as engineering, architecture, dentistry). Of course, such a hypothesis can and must be broken down into sub-hypotheses. These would take these forms: (*a*) specification of the *degree* of difference; (*b*) specification of profession and problem, to separate criminal law from corporation law, types of contacts between profession and client, and types of strain-producing problems; and (c) specification of kinds of controls.

(2) *Principle:* Rather extensive, but relatively unsystematized, data show that members of the upper occupational-class strata experience less unhappiness and worry and are subject to more formal controls than members of lower strata.

Deduction: Our hypothesis would then predict that this comparison also applies to the marital relationships of members of these strata and would predict that such differential pressures could be observed through divorce rates. There should be an inverse correlation between class position and divorce rates. Again, we would have to define our terms carefully and show the systematic connection between our original premises and our deduction, but the result can be tested by the degree of our correlation.

The above examples indicate not only the difficulty of formulating a hypothesis, but also the need to do so. Early in any investigation a definite hypothesis should be formed. At first this may not be very specific. In such an instance it is referred to as a "working hypothesis," which will be subject to modification as the investigation proceeds. The utilization of a hypothesis, however, is necessary for any useful research results.

TYPES OF HYPOTHESES

What are the *kinds* of hypotheses with which the sociologist deals? There are many ways of classifying hypotheses. For the purpose of this book, however, it seems adequate to separate them on the basis of the level of abstraction. Three broad levels may be distinguished. These will be discussed in the order of increasing abstractness.

Some hypotheses state the existence of empirical uniformities. These hypotheses frequently, though not always, represent the scientific examination of common-sense propositions. Thus, we might make a survey of some area that seems to represent a "problem" in common-sense terms. It usually represents, also, a problem about which some "common-sense" observations already exist. There are many types of such empirical uniformities which are common in sociological research. These studies may show regularities in the distribution of business establishments in a city, the ethnic backgrounds of workers in an industry, the size of families on relief, or the distribution of Negroes in the nation.

Or, they may describe the behavior patterns of specific groups—for example, the students at a particular college in their freshman year. Here we might tabulate conformity and nonconformity to customary usage; the wearing of the "dink," the submission to "initiation" rites, or the pledging to a fraternity. From research of this type the tabulations will yield expressions of the *degree of uniformity* in social behavior. They may be symbolized by graphs, figures, or maps. In any event, their end product is a simple description of group activities.

It may be protested, of course, that these investigations do not involve the *testing* of a hypothesis at all, but are merely adding up the facts. Such a charge may have merit in a particular case, but the line is difficult to draw. Certainly, many such studies have actually sought to test common-sense statements about these phenomena, using such statements as hypotheses.

It may be further objected that these are not useful hypotheses, on the grounds that they merely represent what everyone already knows. There are two answers to this objection. First, "what everyone knows" is not put in precise terms nor is it integrated into the framework of science. The importance of these deficiencies has been discussed in Chapters 4 and 5. Second, "what everyone knows" may well be incorrect. To put common-sense ideas into precisely defined concepts and subject the proposition to test is an important task of science.

These statements are particularly true for sociology at its present, early stage of development. Folk knowledge of social relations is abundant, but it is often a confused mixture of clichés and moral judgments. Sociology thus has a large-scale job in transforming and testing these so that they can become useful knowledge. This requires that three tasks be performed: first, the removal of value judgments; second, the clarification of terms; and third, the application of validity tests.

For example, such statements as "Bad children are born that way" or its reverse, "Bad parents produce bad children," or "Wealthy people have a high divorce rate because they lead such self-indulgent lives" are the kinds of generalizations which, though commonplace, cannot be tested. As they stand, they merely express sentiment rather than describe fact, and the concepts are unclear. They could be made into adequate hypotheses, however, if cleared of moral overtones and put into carefully defined terms.

Not only sociology, as noted previously, but all science has found such common-sense knowledge fruitful for study—even when it has been wrong. "Everybody knew" that the sun revolved around the earth, that horsehairs in a watering trough would turn to worms, that a bag of asafetida hung around the neck would prevent colds (this last, at least, may have been true, since the smell kept others at a distance!). All those beliefs have been exploded by patient, plodding empirical checking of the facts, so that we now know that horsehairs do not turn into worms and asafetida has no effect on colds.

In social relations, too, there are many clichés which are not correct. The objection that it "elaborates the obvious" has been made by a good number of critics against the monumental work *The American Soldier* (Princeton, N.J.: Princeton University Press, 1949–1950; 4 vols.). It would seem, for example, that there was no need for the social researchers to prove the following hypotheses, since they were known already:

1. Soldiers from white-collar jobs were somewhat less adjusted in the Army, since they had sacrificed more than lower class men by going into the service.

2. Negro soldiers, knowing that the barriers against promotion were rigid, did not work for promotion so hard as did white soldiers.

3. Soldiers in units with high promotion rates had a more optimistic view of promotion chances and were more satisfied about promotion policies than were soldiers in units with low promotion rates.

Nevertheless, these were among the hypotheses tested—with the result that all three were proved to be *incorrect*. Often, we believe that "everybody knows that," but we make the statement *after* the investigation. We could not have predicted the result. We believe that the result is only common sense, since *some* of our experience fits the result. However, if the result had turned out differently, we would have found still other experiences, of a contrary order, to fit the different results. As a consequence, many supposedly obvious facts must actually be tested.[2] It hardly needs to be added, moreover, that even when we know in general that a given relationship exists, we do not know to what degree or in what proportions it exists. Science demands a higher precision than "in general."

In any case it is certain that "what everybody knows" is not known until it has been tested. The simple level of hypothesis that seeks empirical generalization plays an important role in the growth of science.

Some hypotheses are concerned with complex ideal types. These hypotheses aim at testing the existence of logically derived relationships between empirical uniformities. If this test sounds difficult to understand, an example may help to make it

clearer. Human ecology early described a large number of empirical uniformities. Land values, industrial concentrations, types of businesses, ethnic groups, mental disorders, and many other phenomena appeared to show unquestionable uniformities in distribution. Further study and logical analysis of these and other related findings led to the formulation of various hypotheses concerning the way in which these were related. One such hypothesis was Ernest W. Burgess's statement of the concentric growth circles that characterize the city.

This hypothesis was then tested against a variety of variables in a number of cities. That this ideal type does represent the actual pattern of city growth is not accepted by all ecologists, however, and so this formulation remains a hypothesis until a more crucial test of it is made.

Another hypothesis concerning an ideal type resulted from these same ecological empirical uniformities. This was the notion that areas tend to represent certain characteristics in a series of predictable patterns. This was called the hypothesis of "the natural area." Much research has been done on this hypothesis, and the results, although they have modified the original statement somewhat, have generally supported it. With the growth of supporting evidence, notions about natural areas have become a part of sociological theory rather than remaining hypotheses.

A similar type of hypothesis in another area resulted from the analysis of minority groups. Many studies revealed empirical uniformities in the behavior of members of a wide variety of minorities. Logical analysis then led to the hypothesis that these uniformities produced an ideal type. This was at first called by H. A. Miller the "oppression psychosis," but it was subsequently modified to the "marginal man" by E. W. Stonequist and others. Empirical evidence supported the hypothesis, and thus the "marginal man" is today also a part of sociological theory.

It is important to see here that this level of hypothesizing moves beyond the expectations of simple empirical uniformity, by *creating* a complex referent in society. Not *all* areas must be natural areas, not *all* members of minority groups must be marginal men, not *all* cities must show perfect concentric circles, for these hypotheses to be useful. They must, of course, be verified in that under *certain conditions* of maximum opportunity such instances will occur, but in reality such hypotheses are purposeful distortions of empiric exactness. Because of their removal from empirical reality these constructs are termed "ideal types." The function of such hypotheses is to create tools and problems for further research in otherwise very complex areas of investigation.

Some hypotheses are concerned with the relation of analytic variables. These hypotheses occur at a level of abstraction beyond that of ideal types. Whereas the hypotheses of empirical uniformities lead to the observation of simple differences, and those dealing with ideal types lead to specific coincidences of observations, the study of *analytic variables* requires the formulation of a relationship between changes in one property and changes in another.

To take an example from sociology, the study of human fertility might show empirical regularities by wealth, region, size of community, and religion. If this were then raised to the level of ideal type formulation, one result might be the hypothesis that there are two high-fertility population segments in the United States. One would be the low-income Southern, rural Protestant, and the other the low-income, Northern, urban Catholic. At a still higher level of abstraction the *qualities* of region, size of community, and religion might be abstracted and controlled; that is, their effects on fertility held constant. This would allow a better measurement of the relation between the *variables* of wealth and fertility. Similarly, the problem could be stated in such a way that any three could be controlled so as to allow the fourth to vary and hence to measure its relation to fertility. It is clear that this is a very abstract way to handle the problem because *there are no people* whose fertility is not affected by *all* the variables. Of course, not all the characteristics mentioned are as yet expressed as variables.

This level of hypothesizing is not only more abstract than the others; it is also the most sophisticated and the most flexible mode of formulation. At this level, the number of variables which can be abstracted and studied is limited only by theory; and since theory grows by the process itself, opportunities for new research are constantly being created.

In the event that it should appear that any of these types of hypotheses is "better" than another, a word of explanation may be needed. The function of the ideal-type method, it will be recalled, is to provide constructs for use in further hypothesizing. This is also one function of studies of empirical uniformities. Without the painstaking, grubbing labor which characterizes this type of investigation, none of the "brilliant" theories of a

more abstract nature could have ever appeared. Particularly in sociology is it necessary for the student to learn that at whatever the level of abstraction the hypothesis lies, the need for careful work does not vary, nor is the significance of the findings automatically apparent.

Thus far in the chapter, three major points have been made: (1) that a hypothesis is a necessary condition for successful research; (2) that formulation of the hypothesis must be given considerable attention, to clarify its relation to theory, remove vague or value-judgmental terms, and specify the test to be applied; and (3) that hypotheses may be formulated on different levels of abstraction. At various points in the discussion, more or less casual references have been made to the question of the *origins* of hypotheses. At this point it seems useful, then, to look at this matter in greater detail and somewhat more systematically. It seems possible to distinguish four such sources more or less clearly.

The general culture in which a science develops furnishes many of its basic hypotheses. This point has been mentioned several times before in the discussions of science and values, pure and applied science, and the simplest hypotheses which state empirical regularities. It has been pointed out that science has developed in Western society and that this is no mere accident but is a function of the culture itself.

The fact that sociology is so new and that its growth has taken place very largely in the United States, England, Germany, and France means that the hypotheses which have been put forth and tested have been related to a particular cultural complex. To oversimplify the situation, let us assume that the American variant of Western European culture emphasizes individual happiness, mobility, and competition. This is in contrast, let us say, to the Zuñi type of Pueblo culture in which there is more emphasis upon the group, an avoidance of personal competition and achievement, and less concern about individual happiness. Flowing from this, certain hypotheses could be expected to occupy the attention of American sociologists. To say that these hypotheses are the product of the cultural values does not make them scientifically less important than others, but it does at least indicate that attention has been called to them by the culture itself.

For example, the American emphasis upon personal happiness has had considerable effect upon social science in this country. Not only is there an excellent market for books explaining "how to be happy," but the phenomenon itself has been studied in great detail. Much of textbook economics is based upon a theory of human action which is predicated upon personal happiness as the central motivation. There have been many studies of the factors which make for marital happiness. Even the term "adjustment" used by sociologists and psychologists customarily means happiness and is the focus of innumerable studies. Happiness in one way or another has been correlated with income, education, occupation, ethnic origin, social class, and parental happiness. The factors contributing to adjustment in sexual relations, marital relations, on the job, and in other social groups have been analyzed in detail. From all this it is at least clear that the cultural emphasis upon happiness has been productive of an almost limitless range of hypotheses for American social science.

Not only do the major cultural values serve to direct research interests, but folk wisdom serves as another source of hypotheses. In Western society, in varying degrees, race is thought to be an important determinant of human behavior. This is perhaps most widely and extremely held in the United States and in South Africa. The sociologist in this cultural setting cannot accept such a folk belief as fact but must test it scientifically. It would be very simple to think of an almost limitless number of similar common-sense propositions which have served or could serve as a source of hypotheses.

This raises still another point. It is not merely that the existence of such propositions is productive of hypotheses but also that social change increases the value of the culture as a source of scientific questions. Common-sense propositions are usually unquestioned. Ideas and behavior often seem so obvious as to call for no serious study. It is, in these cases, a real test of the investigator's ingenuity to see a question in such truisms. Social change, however, may call these into question, thus providing a hypothesis for study. Thus, doctrines of both "liberalism" and "progressivism" have played important roles in social science. The latter, by embracing change, challenges the old assumptions; and the former, by emphasizing the importance of the individual, insists that he not be prejudged. In either case there is present the kind of skepticism which is productive of hypotheses.

For example, the folk notions about race were called into question on *moral* grounds. The progressive and liberal ideology held the old notion of the racial determination of behavior to be

false. Careful analysis of the Army Alpha tests of World War I, studies of the IQs of Negroes and whites, anthropological evidence about the learning ability of "primitives," and many other studies piled up scientific evidence opposed to the older folk beliefs. Similar results occurred in other areas, such as the inherent lack of capabilities in the lower classes. Alcoholism is no longer considered to be the result of weak moral fiber but is regarded as a disease. These examples could be multiplied almost indefinitely, but enough have already been given to indicate the role of "equalitarian" thought patterns and of social change, in the generation of hypotheses.

Hypotheses originate in the science itself. Mention has already been made of the fact that this operates in two ways. First, in the discussion on theory and fact it was pointed out that theory gives direction to research by stating what is known. Logical deduction from this leads to new problems. Second, in the treatment of values and science it was pointed out that science is a social relation and that the scientist must acquire the folkways of his discipline.

As an example of the way the first effect comes about, a development in communications research may be cited. It was first established in theory and fact that there existed people who could be considered as "opinion leaders." It was further seen that these were prestigeful people, that is, that they possessed high status in the community. Since it was also known that high status is a function of a number of variables, it was logical to hypothesize the existence of an ideal type, "the influential person." However, in an actual study, the influential persons did not seem to have many characteristics in common. This led to still further questioning and the development of two major categories, which Merton termed "cosmopolitan" and "local" influentials, each with its own set of characteristics. Thus, what was known led to the asking of still another question or, in other words, to the formulation of a new hypothesis.[3] Indeed, the student will find a number of suggested readings at the end of this chapter, which deal with hypotheses whose origins lay in the *deviant* cases.

The "socialization" process in learning a science also affects the hypotheses which will be developed by the scientist. First of all the student learns from his teachers which are the promising areas, which methods are adequate, which scholars are superior, and, of course, which are "inferior." Thus, the range of hypotheses open to him is limited by the direction of his learning experience.

Later in his life, the scientist is affected by a similar process—the approval of his colleagues. Formally and informally, scientists continually discuss current research, both orally and in print. In this way consensus is reached as to which areas and problems are thought to be important. Through this constant interaction in the area, "fashionable" modes of thought, terminology, concepts, and problems develop. These, in turn, of course, operate to suggest further hypotheses.

Analogies are often a source of useful hypotheses. Julian Huxley has pointed out that casual observations in nature or in the framework of another science may be a fertile source of hypotheses. The hypotheses that resulted in the development of human ecology, for example, were an application of established theory in the fields of plant and animal ecology. Thus, the hypothesis that similar human types or activities may be found occupying the same territory came from plant ecology, where the phenomenon is known as segregation. When the hypothesis was borne out by social observation, the same term was taken into sociology where it has become an important idea in sociological theory.

Similarly, the observation that the behavior of human groups seems to exhibit some of the same patterns as found in gravitational and electric fields led to the basic hypothesis of what is called social physics. This hypothesis is that if people are related in some way similar to the structure of such a physical field then human behavior should show reliable correlation with the values secured by such a field analysis. John Q. Stewart has now published much evidence to indicate that the application of this analogy might be interesting.

The use of analogy as a source of hypotheses is not without its dangers, of course. There is reason to suspect any analogy from another science, since the models to be applied are clearly understood in their own theoretical framework but are not related to the new frame of reference. Thus, it is dangerous to assume that natural areas in human society are a product of symbiosis as is true in biology. We have no empirical method of applying the concept to human beings. Similarly, it is dangerous to assume, as in social physics, that "demographic potential" is the same phenomenon as "gravitational potential" in physics. In short, analogy may be very suggestive, but care must be taken not to accept models for sociology from other disciplines without careful examination of the concepts which make up the models.

Hypotheses are also the consequence of per-

sonal, idiosyncratic experience. Not only do culture, science, and analogy affect the formulation of hypotheses. The way in which an *individual* reacts to each of these is also a factor in the statement of hypotheses. Therefore, the individual experience of the scientist contributes to the type and the form of the questions he asks.

In just the same way that perception has been shown to be structured by experience, producing odd and interesting illusions, some persons will perceive an interesting pattern from what may merely seem a jumble of facts to another. The history of science is full of instances of discoveries made because the "right" individual happened to make the "right" observation because of his particular life history.

Thomas Henry Huxley is reported to have exclaimed, on reading Darwin's *Origin of Species*, "Oh, what an ass I was not to have thought of that!" Even if the story is apocryphal, it is pertinent, for Darwin had assembled many facts which had been known for at least two generations. In addition he had added many observations on his famous 4-year voyage on H.M.S. *Beagle*. Nevertheless, this enormous body of data did not take on any systematic order until a fortuitous event occurred. Darwin was pondering the problem of understanding what caused species to change when he happened to read Thomas Malthus's notion that a population tended, in the absence of certain other checks, to overwhelm the resources for the sustenance of that population. In other words, the physical environment itself was always snapping at the heels of any species. If individuals change in certain directions they will be at an advantage; if they change in other directions, at a disadvantage. This, then, combined with Darwin's other information, resulted in the notion of the struggle for survival of the species. After its public expression and in spite of the fierce theological controversy it aroused, this explanation was quickly accepted by scientists. Huxley was simply exclaiming, because "anyone could have seen it." This was indeed the "right" man at the "right" time.

This should not be construed that certain ideas will be observable only by one particular man. In fact, Wallace independently worked out the same idea as Darwin but decided the latter's greater body of data justified publication by him. All discoveries are made not once but many times. It is merely that personal life histories are a factor in determining the kinds of perception and conception. These factors may, in turn, direct one person to certain hypotheses more quickly. Often, of course, these persons were not seeking the particular observation or hypothesis. They were simply trained to understand and use the strategic fact when it appeared. The story of Newton and the falling apple, however untrue, illustrates this individual, accidental process. Similar occurrences are by no means unknown in the scientific laboratory.

An illustration of individual perspective in the social sciences may be seen in the work of Thorstein Veblen. The product of an isolated Norwegian community in Minnesota, Veblen lived at a time when the capitalistic system was not usually called into question except by "radicals." His own community background, however, was replete with negative experiences concerning the working of the economic system, and he was himself a kind of outsider or "marginal man," able to look at the capitalist system objectively. He was thus in an excellent position to attack the fundamental concepts and postulates of classical economics. In a very real sense he was an alien who could bring a different experience to bear upon the economic world. As a result he made penetrating analyses of our society which have profoundly influenced social science since his time.

All these sources of hypotheses—value orientations of the culture, folk wisdom and cliché, rebellion against common-sense ideas, observation of deviant cases (the cases which "don't fit the rule"), social experience within the science, the application of analogies, and personal experience—provide a wealth of hypotheses. In fact it is an almost embarrassing profusion. The problem which this raises is how to select those ideas which may actually prove useful.

THE CHARACTERISTICS OF USABLE HYPOTHESES

In the privacy of the scientist's mind, alone or in social gatherings, in odd moments or in the press of business, many hypotheses are entertained. Most of them, having appeared, are fortunately left to die alone. A few survive, however, to be exhibited in "bull sessions" or to be tried out on sleepy undergraduates at eight o'clock on a wintry morning. Most are not destined to play any significant role in the growth of science. Some of these would seem to be the product of the fact, as the philosopher Suzanne Langer has argued, that man's mind, like his body, is often active without any immediate goal. It is only by the imposition of firm standards that it is possible to winnow out the good ideas from the bad.

Let us now look at some criteria for judging hypotheses.

The hypotheses must be conceptually clear. Enough emphasis upon this requirement was made in the preceding chapter to require little further elaboration. It should be repeated, however, that this involves two things. The concepts should be clearly defined, operationally if possible. Moreover, they should be definitions which are commonly accepted and communicable rather than the products of a "private world."

What to do: One simple device for clarifying concepts is to write out a list of the concepts used in the research outline. Then try to define them (*a*) in words, (*b*) in terms or particular operations (index calculations, types of observations, etc.), and (*c*) with reference to other concepts to be found in previous research. Talk over each concept with fellow students and other researchers in the field. It will often be found that supposedly simple concepts contain many meanings. Then it is possible to decide which is the desired referent. For systematic conceptual clarification, perform all the operations suggested in Chapter 5.

Hypotheses should have empirical referents. It has also been previously pointed out that scientific concepts must have an ultimate empirical referent. No usable hypotheses can embody moral judgments. Such statements as "criminals are no worse than businessmen," "women should pursue a career," or "capitalists exploit their workers," are no more usable hypotheses than is the familiar proposition that "pigs are well named because they are so dirty" or the classical question, "How many yards of buttermilk are required to make a pair of breeches for a black bull?" In other words, while a hypothesis may study value judgments, such a goal must be separated from a moral preachment or a plea for acceptance of one's values.

What to do: First, analyze the concepts which express attitudes rather than describing or referring to empirical phenomena. Watch for key words such as "ought," "should," "bad," etc. Then transform the notions into more useful concepts. "Bad parents" is a value term, but the researcher may have a definite description in mind: parents who follow such practices as whimsical and arbitrary authoritarianism, inducing psychic insecurity in the child, failure to give love, etc. "Should" is also a value term, but the student may simply mean, "If women do not pursue a career, we can predict emotional difficulties when the children leave home, or we can predict that the society will not be able to produce as much goods," etc. When, instead, we find that our referent is simply a vague feeling, and we cannot define the operations needed to observe it, we should study the problem further and discover what it is that we really wish to investigate.

The hypotheses must be specific. That is, all the operations and predictions indicated by it should be spelled out. The possibility of actually testing the hypothesis can thus be appraised. Often hypotheses are expressed in such general terms, and with so grandiose a scope, that they are simply not testable. Because of their magnitude, such grand ideas are tempting because they seem impressive and important. It is better for the student to avoid such problems and instead develop his skills upon more tangible notions.

By making all the concepts and operations explicit is meant not only conceptual clarity but a description of any *indexes* to be used. Thus, to hypothesize that the degree of vertical social mobility is decreasing in the United States requires the use of indexes. At present there is no satisfactory operational definition of the status levels which define mobility. Therefore, the hypothesis must include a statement of the indexes which are to be used; that is, political office, occupation, effective income, education, etc.

Such specific formulations have the advantage of assuring that research is practicable and significant, in advance of the expenditure of effort. It furthermore increases the validity of the results, since the broader the terms the easier it is to fall into the trap of using *selective evidence*. The fame of most prophets and fortunetellers lies in their ability to state predictions so that almost any occurrence can be interpreted as a fulfillment. We can express this in almost statistical terms: the more specific the prediction, the smaller the chance that the prediction will actually be borne out as a result of mere accident. Scientific predictions or hypotheses must, then, avoid the trap of selective evidence by being as definite and specific as possible.

What to do: Never be satisfied with a general prediction, if it can be broken into more precise subhypotheses. The general prediction of war is not enough, for example: we must specify time, place, and participants. Predicting the general decline of a civilization is not a hypothesis for testing a theory. Again, we must be able to specify and measure the forces, specify the meaning and time of decline, the population segments involved, etc. Often this can be done by conceptual analysis and the formation of related hypotheses; *e.g.*, we may predict that urbanization is accompanied by a decline in fertility. However, we gain in precision if we attempt to define our indexes of urbanization; specify which segments will be affected, and how much (since in the United States the various ethnic and religious segments are affected differently); specify the amount of fertility decline, and the type (percentage childless, net reproduction rate, etc.). Forming sub-hypotheses (1) clarifies the relationship between the data sought and the conclusions; and (2) makes the specific research task more manageable.

Hypotheses should be related to available techniques. In earlier chapters the point was repeat-

edly made that theory and method are not opposites. The theorist who does not know what techniques are available to test his hypotheses is in a poor way to formulate usable questions.

This is not to be taken as an absolute injunction against the formulation of hypotheses which at present are too complex to be handled by contemporary technique. It is merely a sensible requirement to apply to any problem in its early stages in order to judge its researchability.

There are some aspects of the impossible hypothesis which may make its formulation worthwhile. If the problem is significant enough as a possible frame of reference it may be useful whether or not it can be tested at the time. The socioeconomic hypotheses of Marx, for example, were not proved by his data. The necessary techniques were not available either then or now. Nevertheless, Marxian frameworks are an important source of more precise, smaller, verifiable propositions. This is true for much of Émile Durkheim's work on suicide. His related formulations concerning social cohesion have also been useful. The work of both men has been of paramount importance to sociology, even though at the time their larger ideas were not capable of being handled by available techniques.

Furthermore, posing the impossible question may *stimulate* the growth of technique. Certainly some of the impetus toward modern developments in technique has come from criticisms against significant studies which were considered inadequate because of technical limitations. In any serious sociological discussion, research frontiers are continuously challenged by the assertion that various problems "ought" to be investigated even though the investigations are presently impossible.

What to do: Look for research articles on the subject being investigated. Make a list of the various techniques which have been used to measure the factors of importance in the study. If you are unable to locate any discussions of technique, you may find it wiser to do a research *on the necessary research techniques*. You may, instead, decide that this lack of techniques means your problem is too large and general for your present resources.

Some items, such as stratification or race attitudes, have been studied by many techniques. Try to discover why one technique is used in one case and not in another. Note how refinements in technique have been made, and see whether one of these may be more useful for your purposes. Look for criticisms of previous research, so as to understand the weaknesses in the procedures followed.

Again, other problems may have been studied with few attempts at precise measurement. Study the literature to see why this is the case. Ascertain whether some subareas (for example, of religious behavior) may be attacked with techniques used in other areas (for example, attitude measurement, stratification measures, research on choice making, etc.).

The hypothesis should be related to a body of theory. This criterion is one which is often overlooked by the beginning student. He is more likely to select subject matter which is "interesting," without finding out whether the research will really help to refute, qualify, or support any existing theories of social relations. A science, however, can be cumulative only by building on an existing body of fact and theory. It cannot develop if each study is an isolated survey.

Although it is true that the clearest examples of crescive theoretical development are to be found in the physical and biological sciences, the process can also be seen in the social sciences. One such case is the development of a set of generalizations concerning the social character of intelligence. The anthropological investigations at the end of the nineteenth century uncovered the amazing variety of social customs in various societies, while demonstrating conclusively that there were a number of common elements in social life: family systems, religious patterns, an organization of the socialization process, etc.

The French school of sociology, including Lucien Lévy-Bruhl, Émile Durkheim, Marcel Mauss, Henri Hubert, and others, formulated a series of propositions, at the turn of the century, which suggested that the intellectual structure of the human mind is determined by the structure of the society. That is, perception and thought are determined by society, not alone by the anatomical structure of our eyes, ears, and other senses. Modes of thought vary from society to society. Some of these formulations were phrased in an extreme form which need not concern us now, and they were often vague. Nevertheless, the idea was growing that the intelligence of a Polynesian native could not be judged by European standards; his thinking was qualitatively, not merely quantitatively, different.

At the same time, however, better techniques were being evolved for measuring "intelligence," which came to be standardized in the form of scores on various IQ tests. When these were applied to different groups it became clear that the variation in IQ was great; children of Italian immigrants made lower grades on such tests, as did Negroes. Northern Negroes made higher grades than whites from many Southern states. American children of Chinese and Japanese parents made rather high scores. Since it was generally assumed that these tests measured "innate intelligence," these data were sometimes generalized to suggest that certain "racial" groups were by nature inferior and others superior.

However, such conclusions were opposed on rational grounds, and liberal sentiments suggested that they be put to the test. There were, then, two major sets of conclusions, one suggesting that intelligence is in the main determined by social experience, the other suggesting that the IQ is innately determined. To test such opposing generalizations, a research design was needed for testing logical expectations in more specific situations. If, for example, it is true that the intelligence of individuals who are members of "inferior" groups is really determined biologically, then changes in their environments should not change their IQ. If, on the other hand, the social experience is crucial, we should expect that such changes in social experience would result in definite patterns of IQ change.

Further deductions are possible. If identical twins are separated and are placed in radically different social experiences at an early age, we might expect significant differences in IQ. Or, if a group of rural Negro children moves from the poor school and social experience of the South, to the somewhat more stimulating environment of the North, the group averages would be expected to change somewhat. Otto Klineberg, in a classic study, carried out the latter research. He traced Negro children of various ages after they had moved to the North and found that, in general, the earlier the move to the North occurred, the greater the average rise in the IQ. The later the move, the smaller the increase. Even if one assumes that the "better," more able, and more daring adult Negroes made this move, this does not explain the differences by time of movement. Besides, of course, the subjects were children at the time of the migration.[4]

In this research design a particular result was predicted by a series of deductions from a larger set of generalizations. Further, the prediction was actually validated. In justice to the great number of scholars who have been engaged in refining and developing IQ tests, it should be mentioned that other tests and investigations of a similar order have been carried out by many anthropologists, sociologists, and social psychologists. They do not invalidate the notion that IQ is based in part on "innate" abilities, but they do indicate that to a great extent these abilities must be stimulated by certain types of experience in order to achieve high scores on such tests.

From even so sketchy an outline of a theoretical development as the foregoing is, it can be seen that when research is systematically based upon a body of existing theory, a genuine contribution in knowledge is more likely to result. In other words, to be worth doing, a hypothesis must not only be carefully stated, but it should possess theoretical relevance.

What to do: First, of course, cover the literature relating to your subject. If it is impossible to do so, then your hypothesis probably covers too much ground. Second, try to abstract from the literature the way in which various propositions and sets of propositions relate to one another (for example, the literature relating to Sutherland's theory of differential association in criminology, the conditions for maximum morale in factories, or the studies of prediction of marital adjustment). Third, ascertain whether you can deduce any of the propositions, including your own hypothesis, from one another or from a small set of major statements. Fourth, test it by some theoretical model, such as Merton's "Paradigm for Functional Analysis in Sociology" (*Social Theory and Social Structure,* pp. 50–54), to see whether you have left out major propositions and determinants. Fifth, especially compare your own set of related propositions with those of some classic author, such as Weber on bureaucracy or Durkheim on suicide. If you find this task of abstraction difficult, compare instead with the propositions of these men as explained by a systematic interpreter such as Talcott Parsons in his *Structure of Social Action.* What is important is that, whatever the *source* of your hypothesis, it must be *logically* derivable from and based upon a set of related sociological propositions.

SUMMARY

The formulation of the hypothesis is a central step in good research, and it is important to give it a great deal of thought. Because of this significance, we have looked at the hypothesis from several points of view.

1. We have shown why it is so crucial a step to take, and how it functions in a research. It is the question which we put to the empirical world, in such a form that an answer can be obtained.

2. We have also looked at some of the problems which occur when we attempt to formulate hypotheses. It is clear that the formulation of hypotheses does not occur automatically but is usually preceded by many false starts, evaluational propositions, vague statements, etc.

3. As an aid in understanding hypotheses, we noted that they may be developed at different levels of concreteness, from fairly common-sense statements to the relationships between complex, abstract variables.

4. Making hypotheses is a creative act, but we can study such acts. We saw that hypotheses come from many sources, from the general emphases of our culture to the most individual of experiences.

5. Finally, we sketched a few criteria for *selecting* the more useful hypotheses and offered a few suggestions for improving those hypotheses which seem to be weak.

Such an outline at least offers the student a set of preliminary but useful notions for thinking fruitfully about research problems. Many studies fail at precisely this point, the development of a good hypothesis. On the other hand, the history of science gives innumerable examples to prove that great strides were made when someone asked the right question.

SUGGESTED READINGS

Campbell, Norman, *What Is Science?* (London: Methuen, 1921), Chaps. 3, 4, and 5.

Cohen, Morris R., and Ernest Nagel, *An Introduction to Logic and Scientific Method* (New York: Harcourt, Brace, 1934), Chap. 11.

Marx, Melvin H., "Hypothesis and Construct" in Melvin H. Marx, *Psychological Theory* (New York: Macmillan, 1951), pp. 112–128.

Waller, Willard, "Insight and Scientific Method," *American Journal of Sociology,* Vol. XL (1934), pp. 285–297.

FOOTNOTES

[1] William H. George, *The Scientist in Action* (London: Williams & Norgate, 1936), p. 220.

[2] Paul F. Lazarsfeld, *"The American Soldier*—an Expository Review," *Public Opinion Quarterly,* Vol. XIII (1949), pp. 377–404.

[3] Robert K. Merton, "Patterns of Influence: A Study of Interpersonal Influence and of Communications Behavior in a Local Community," *Communications Research, 1948-1949,* Paul F. Lazarsfeld and Frank Stanton, eds. (New York: Harper, 1949), pp. 180–219.

[4] Otto Klineberg, *Negro Intelligence and Selective Migration* (New York: Columbia University Press, 1935).

On Intellectual Craftsmanship

by C. Wright Mills

Seldom does the literature illuminate the sheer joy and intellectual adventure of research. By detailing the nature of his own imaginative work procedures, Mills does exactly this. He swiftly puts method and theory in perspective as devices pure and simple, to aid in understanding something about what goes on in the world. He describes how the scholar is formed. He specifies that the genuine issues, the problems of the culture and not abstract irrelevant, ideas ordered to serve irrelevant ends, are the social scientist's legitimate testing ground. Here is the coupling of imagination and intellect in the exciting quest of what is yet unknown. What Mills is describing is not only the program of a life's work, but an intellectual life style in which the world of the scholar is a whole and all of his experiences, observations, and intakes are relevant elements.

When Mills speaks of the sociological imagination and the limits of training, he identifies the dysfunctions of too precise a preparation for work when new entrants are indoctrinated only in what is known. When the problems call for habits of mind which see the potential of new relationships and the blending of ingredients in such a way as to introduce the possibility of new order, something more is needed. This, of course, is what innovation, in practice as well as in scholarship, is all about. If one can learn from the clear and unambiguous words of the scholar about how to proceed in research and how to communicate what he has learned, then one can receive such perception by reading Mills. The challenge to library research is not only to close the distance between its scholarship and that of other disciplines, not merely by following proven practice in librarianship or even a comparable path in the social sciences, but to carve out wholly new ways of looking at problems and where necessary, to fashion new tools to study them.

What are some concrete examples of how the imagination is stimulated? For insight into the phenomenon of change, the writers recently found themselves going back to classics in administration. Even though the issue of change was largely unnoticed at first reading, these works offer more insight than many later works devoted specifically to organizational change. Mills suggests history and biography as fertile ground. And for the writers, the study of declining industries (the American circus is a case in point) helps to sort out and derive hypotheses on a seemingly unrelated phenomenon—the contemporary library.

Sometimes, as Mills suggests, insight is drawn from observing extremes, as for example, the library which seems habitually to say "no," compared to one which seems genuinely to try to serve. What organizational and other factors distinguish them from each other? Students might well construct imaginative typologies of users which go beyond the beginning level by which they are categorized as users and non-users. For, users might be sorted into other potentially interesting classes according to their motivations. An evening spent in careful observation of human behavior in any busy public library would be productive of a "user-type" typology.

Any problem can be viewed more imaginatively when it is appraised from different perspectives. Simply to invite perception from different disciplines is to broaden its scope and to come closer to understanding. The same issue (the role of libraries in poverty areas) is seen variously. For the philosopher, the issues may be ethical or moral—should libraries help citizen groups work against police brutality? The political scientist sees information service related to the consequences of giving or withholding information to groups in community power terms.

The essential task of research is to set the imagination free of constraints, and only later to bring discipline and order to the process.
Far too frequently rigidity is its prevailing characteristic.

ONE

Useful discussions of method and of theory usually arise as marginal notes on work-in-progress or work about to get under way. "Method" has to do with how to ask and to answer questions with some assurance that the answers are more or less durable. "Theory" has to do with paying close attention to the words one is using, especially their degree of generality and their logical relations. What both method and theory amount to is clarity of conception and economy of procedure, and, most importantly just now, the release rather than the restriction of the sociological imagination.

To have mastered "theory" and "method" is to have become a self-conscious thinker, a man at work and aware of the assumptions and the implications of whatever he is about. To be mastered by "method" or "theory" is simply to be kept from working, from trying, that is, to find out about something that is going on in the world. Without insight into the way it is done, the results of study are infirm; without a determination that study shall come to significant results, all method is meaningless pretense.

For the working social scientist, neither method nor theory is an autonomous domain. Methods are methods for some range of problem; theories are theories of some range of phenomena. They are like the language of the country you live in: having the ability to speak the language is nothing to brag about, but it is a disgrace, as well as an inconvenience, if you cannot speak it.

Method and theory must not only occur at the beginning of study, but also in the middle and at the end. They are built-in parts of the process of study itself. Of course, it is possible, and sometimes useful, to interrupt your work and to examine how several others have gone about theirs. As one begins his studies of some problem, he naturally turns first to studies that have already been done, and as he examines them, he certainly notices the methods their authors have used. He would be a fool if he did not do so. But once he goes beyond such an examination of the methods used in one area or another, and once he tries to transform methods into "methodology," he often becomes quite abstracted. He loses firm connec-

tion with the kinds of problems for which given methods have been devised, and, in the end, makes quite formal, and often even useless, his examination of methods. Although not necessarily the case, this is surely a very real danger.

In view of it, there are several cautions which might well be observed in any general attempts to "codify procedures." One must always keep uppermost a full sense of the problem at hand. This obviously means that one must be very well acquainted in a substantive way with the state of knowledge of the area with which the studies being examined are concerned. It also means, to an extent which I do not think can be made explicit, that such work is best done when the several studies examined are concerned with a similar area of study. Finally, such work is not best done as the sole speciality of any one person, much less of a young man who has in fact done little if any actual work, or who may have taken part only in studies done in one or another particular style.

When we pause in our studies to reflect on theory and method, the greatest yield is a restatement of our problems. Perhaps that is why, ultimately, in actual practice, every working social scientist must be his own methodologist and his own theorist, which means only that he must be an intellectual craftsman. Every craftsman can of course learn something from over-all attempts to codify methods, but it is often not much more than a general kind of awareness. That is why "crash programs" in methodology are not likely to help social science to develop. Really useful accounts of methods cannot evolve from a slapdash attack. If such accounts are not firmly anchored in the actual working of social study, the sense of a significant problem and the passion to solve it cannot be allowed full play in the mind of the working social scientist.

Advance in methods, then, is most likely to occur as modest generalizations out of actual work in progress. Accordingly, we should maintain in our individual practice, and in the organization of our discipline, a close state of interaction between method and work. Serious attention should be paid to general discussions of methodology only when they are in such reference to actual work. Such discussions of method do occur among social scientists; and I shall presently try to demonstrate one way in which they may be carried on, I hope, usefully.

If all students of man and society practiced this obvious and straightforward statement, how much further along the work of social science would be! At least all of us would then be at work on the problems of these disciplines. But everyone, alas, does not agree, not really. That other views of method and other views of theory are mistaken alleyways to curious destinations does not remove our need to examine them, because, for sundry reasons—mainly philosophical, academic, and temperamental—they are wordily proclaimed; often, I am afraid, they disturb people who are at work.

Statements of method and arguments about them—distinctions of concept and further distinctions—may all be very stimulating and even entertaining. But surely there will be no disagreement that by themselves they are merely promises. Statements of method promise to guide us to better ways of studying something, often in fact to studying almost anything. Elaborations of concepts, systematic and unsystematic, promise to alert us to distinctions in what we may see, or of what we may make of it, when we come to interpret it. Neither by itself can be taken as part of the actual work of the social studies.

In fact, both are often just the opposite: they are statesmanlike withdrawals from the problems of social science. Usually, they are based on some grand model of inquiry with which other people are beaten on the head. That this grand model is not capable of altogether full use is not, perhaps, too important, for it may still be used ritualistically. Usually, it is made up out of some philosophy of natural science, and quite usually, of all things, from a philosophical gloss on physics, perhaps always necessarily somewhat out of date. This little game, and others having similar rules, leads less to further work than to what may be called the methodological inhibition.

In a quite general way nowadays, such a philosophy serves to rationalize a kind of scientific know-nothingism, of which Max Horkheimer has written: "The constant warning against premature conclusions and foggy generalities implies, unless properly qualified, a possible taboo against all thinking. If every thought has to be held in abeyance until it has been completely corroborated, no basic approach seems possible and we would limit ourselves to the level of mere symptoms."[1] The young, it has frequently been noticed, are often corruptible, but in addi-

tion to them, it is curious to see older scholars of social science made uneasy by the pretensions of certain methodologists among us. How much more sensible and enlightening than the loud proclamations of some American sociologists is the conversational statement of a Swiss and an English economist: "Many authors instinctively set about tackling these problems in the right way. But after studying the methodology they become conscious of the numerous pitfalls and other dangers which are waiting for them. The result is that they lose their former sure touch, and are led astray or in unsuitable directions. Scholars of this type are warned off methodology and advised especially not to read the following treatise."[2]

Of method-and-theory-in-general, I do not here need to say any more. Frankly, I am nowadays quickly made weary by it; so much discussion of it interrupts our proper studies. I feel the need to say that I should much rather have one account by a working student of how he is going about his work than a dozen "codifications of procedure" by specialists who as often as not have never done much work of consequence. Better still: if sometimes in our professional forum we wish to discuss method and theory rather than the substance of our studies, let us ask each man whom we believe to be doing good or superior work to give us a detailed account of his ways of work.

Only by conversations in which experienced thinkers exchange information about their actual ways of working can a useful sense of method and theory be imparted to the beginning student. Since I do believe this, I want to continue practicing it. Accordingly, it is proper that I try to contribute to the kind of conversation of which I have spoken. That is why I am now going to report something of how I have gone about my studies. I know that to do this is to run the risk of failing in modesty and perhaps even to claim some peculiar virtue for my working habits. But no matter. Any attentive reader of what I have written above will surely know that I intend no such claims. It happens, at this writing, that the studies I am going to discuss are completed, and the books I have made out of them published, but I am going to write from notes made during the course of this work, and as if I were still in the middle of it.

Here, then, is a letter to a man just beginning independent work in social science:[3]

TWO

You will know that this letter is neither a statement of formal method nor an attempt to inspire. There are already too many formal discourses on method, and certainly too many inspirational pieces on how to think. Neither would seem to be of much use to you. The first does not usually touch the realities of your most urgent problems; the second is usually vulgar and often nonsense.

It is best to begin, I think, by talking to you just a bit about how your choice of intellectual work is linked with the kind of life you are going to have. This is important because the intellectual and the human context of work in social science are inevitably of one piece of cloth. Moreover, presumption and verbiage are the two major vices of your chosen field, and no intellectual technique alone can cause you to avoid them completely, for they are human as well as intellectual qualities. To conceal that, out of politeness to my colleagues, would be of no service to you. Presumption and verbiage are indeed such powerful currents that they can only be overwhelmed by firm possession of one seminal quality: the passion for confronting problems of importance. And that too is a human as well as an intellectual quality.

You must have already discovered this, for in joining the scholarly community you must have realized that the most admirable thinkers within it do not split their work from their lives. They seem to take both too seriously to allow such dissociation, and they want to use each for the enrichment of the other. Of course, such a split is the prevailing convention among men in general, deriving, I suppose, from the hollowness of the work which men in general now do. But you will have recognized that as a scholar you have the exceptional opportunity of designing a way of living which will encourage the habits of good workmanship. Scholarship is a choice of how to live as well as a choice of career; whether he knows it or not, the intellectual workman forms his own self as he works toward the perfection of his craft; to realize his own potentialities and any opportunities that come his way, he constructs a character which has as its core the qualities of the good workman.

What this means is that you must learn to use your life experience in your intellectual work. In this sense, craftsmanship is the center of yourself, and you are personally involved in every intellectual product upon which you may work. To say that you can "have experience," means, for one thing, that the past plays into and affects the present, and that it limits the capacity for future experience. As a social scientist, you have to control this rather elaborate interplay, to capture experience and sort it out; only thus can you hope to use it to guide and test your reflection and in the process shape yourself as an intellectual craftsman. But how can you do this? One answer is: you must set up a file.

A personal file increases the continuity between life and work. It permits a continuity in the work itself, and in the planning of the work. In such a file as I am going to describe, personal experience, professional activities, and actual work all come together. In this file, as an intellectual craftsman, you will try to get together what you are doing intellectually and what you are experiencing as a person. Here you will not be afraid to use your experience and directly to relate it to various projects which you have under way. In such a file, life and work become one.

By serving as a check on repetitious work, your file also enables you to conserve whatever energy you have. It also encourages you to capture "fringe-thoughts": various ideas occur, which may be by-products of everyday experience, snatches of conversation overheard on the street, or, for that matter, dreams. Once noted, these may lead to more systematic thinking, as well as lend intellectual relevance to more directed experience.

You will have often noticed how carefully accomplished thinkers treat their own minds, how closely they observe their development and organize their experience. They treasure their smallest experiences because, in the course of a lifetime, a modern man has so very little personal experience, and they recognize that experience is indispensable as a source of original intellectual work. To be able to trust your own experience even if it often turns out to be inadequate, I have come to believe, is one mark of the mature workman. Without such confidence, there can be little originality in an intellectual pursuit, and the file is one tool by which you can develop and justify this necessary assurance.

If the intellectual workman is a man who has become self-confidently aware of himself as a center of experience and reflection, the keeping of a file is one way of stabilizing, as it were, this confidence. By the keeping of an adequate file and through the self-reflective habits it fosters, you learn how to keep awake your inner world. Whenever you feel strongly about events or ideas, you must try not to let them pass from your mind. Instead, formulate them for your files. In so doing, draw out their implications, and show yourself either how foolish these feelings or ideas are, or how they might be articulated into productive shape. The file also maintains the habit of writing. You cannot "keep you hand in" if you do not write something at least every week. In the file, you can experiment as a writer and thus, as they say, develop your powers of expression.

Under various topics in your file there are ideas, personal notes, and excerpts from books; there are bibliographical items and outlines of projects. It is, I suppose, a matter of arbitrary habit, but I think you will find it best to sort all these items into a master file of "projects," with many subdivisions. The topics, of course, change. In fact, they sometimes change quite frequently. For instance, as a student working toward the preliminary examination while you are writing a thesis and, at the same time, doing term papers, your files will be arranged in these three areas of endeavor. But, after a year or so of graduate work, you will begin to reorganize the whole file in relation to the main project of your thesis. Then, as you pursue your work you will notice that no one project ever dominates it, or ever sets the master categories in which it is arranged. In fact, the use of this file encourages an expansion of the categories with which you are actively thinking. And the way in which these categories change—some being dropped out and others being added—is an index of your intellectual progress and breadth. Eventually, the file will come to be arranged according to several larger projects, having many subprojects, which change from year to year.

All this involves the taking of notes. You will have to acquire the habit of taking a very large volume of notes from any worth-while book which you read, although I have to say you often get better stuff out of yourself when you read really bad books. But enough of this. The first step in translating experience, either of other men's symbols, or of your own life, into the intellectual sphere, is to give it form. Merely to name an item of experience often invites you to explain it; the mere taking of a note from a book is often a prod to reflection. At the same time, of course, the taking of a note is a great aid in comprehending what you are reading.

Your notes may turn out, as mine do, to be of two sorts: in reading certain very important books you try to grasp the structure of the writer's argument, and take notes accordingly. But more frequently, and after a few years of independent

work, rather than reading entire books, you will very often read parts of many books, from the point of view of some particular theme or topic in which you are interested, and concerning which you have plans in your file. Therefore, you will take notes which do not fairly represent the books you read. You are *using* this particular idea, this particular fact, for the realization of your own projects.

THREE

But how is this file, which so far must seem to you more like a curious sort of journal, used in intellectual production? The maintenance of such a file *is* intellectual production, one step removed from daily speculation, and one step removed from the library and "the field." It is a continually growing store of facts and ideas, from the most vague to the most finished.

For example, the first thing I did upon deciding on a study of the elite was to make a crude outline based on a listing of the types of people which I wished to understand.[4] The next step was to examine my entire file, not only those parts of it which obviously bore on the topic but also other portions which seemed to have no relevance whatsoever. Imagination and "the structuring of an idea" are often exercised by putting together hithertofore isolated items. This leads to the discovery of unsuspected connections. I made new units in the file for this particular range of problems, which, of course, led to a new arrangement of other parts of the file.

As you rearrange a filing system, you often find that you are, as it were, loosening your imagination. Apparently this occurs as a result of your attempt to combine various ideas and to correlate notes on different topics. It is a sort of logic of combination, and "chance" sometimes plays a curiously large part in it. In a relaxed way, you apply your intellectual resources, as exemplified in the file, to the new themes.

In the present case, I also began to use my observations and daily experiences. I thought first of experiences I had had which bore upon such problems, and then I went and talked with those who might have experienced or considered the issues. As a matter of fact, I began now to alter the character of my routine so as to include in it (1) people who *were* among those whom I wanted to study (for example, I accepted invitations to lecture to such groups as "The American Management Association" and "The

Air War College"), (2) people in close contact with them (for example, servants) and (3) people interested in them (usually in some professional way; for example, lawyers). I do not know the full social conditions of the best intellectual workmanship, but certainly surrounding oneself by a circle of people who will listen and talk—and at times they have to be imaginary characters—is one of them. At any rate I try to surround myself with all the relevant environment which I think might lead me into thinking well along the lines of my work. That is one meaning of my remarks above about the fusion of personal and intellectual life.

Good work in social science today is not, and cannot usually be, made up of one clear-cut empirical "research." It is, rather, composed of a good many studies which at key points anchor general statements about the shape and the trend of the subject. So the decision—what are these anchor points?—cannot be made until existing materials are reworked and general hypothetical statements constructed.

Now, of "existing materials," I found in the files three relevant types: several theories having to do with the topic; materials already worked up by others as evidence for *those* theories; and materials already gathered and in various stages of accessible centralization, but not yet made theoretically relevant. Only after completing a first draft of a theory with the aid of such existing materials as these can I efficiently locate my own pivotal assertions and hunches and design researches to test them—and maybe I will not have to, although of course I know I will later have to shuttle back and forth between existing materials and my own research.

I make it a rule—picked up, I suppose, from early philosophical reading which led me into the sociology of knowledge—that any final statement must not only "cover the data" so far as the data is available and known to me, but also in some way, positively or negatively, take into account the available theories. (This is of course one of the active meanings, if you'll forgive me please, of "the methodological consequences of the sociology of knowledge.") Sometimes this "taking into account" of an idea is easily done by a simple confrontation of the idea with overturning or supporting fact; sometimes a detailed analysis or qualification is needed. Sometimes I can arrange the available theories systematically as a range of alternatives, and so allow their range to organize the problem itself.[5] But sometimes I allow such

theories to come up only in my own arrangement, and in various contexts. At any rate, in the book on the elite I will have to take into account the work of such men as Mosca, Schumpeter, Veblen, Marx, Lasswell, Michel, and Pareto. I am now at work on them.

In looking over some of the notes on these writers, I find that they fall into three general types of statement: (*a*) I learn directly, by restating systematically, what the man says on given points or as a whole. (*b*) I accept or refute these statements, giving reasons and arguments. (*c*) I also use the book as a source of suggestions for my own elaborations and projects. This involves grasping a point and then asking: How can I put this into testable shape and how can I test it? How can I use this as a center from which to elaborate, or use it as a perspective from which descriptive details will become relevant? It is in this handling of existing ideas, of course, that you feel yourself in continuity with previous work. Here are two excerpts from preliminary notes on Mosca, which may illustrate what I have been trying to describe:

In addition to these historical anecdotes, Mosca backs up his thesis with this assertion: It's the power of organization that enables the minority always to rule. There are organized minorities and they run things and men. There are unorganized majorities and they are run.[6] But: why not also consider the apparent opposite? In fact, why not the full scale of possibilities, as shown in the following chart?

	Elite (Minority)	Mass (Majority)	
Organized	1	2	1 the organized minority
			2 the organized majority
Unorganized	3	4	3 the unorganized minority
			4 the unorganized majority

This is worth full-scale exploration. The first thing has to be straightened out: just what is the meaning of "organized"? I think Mosca means: capable of more or less continuous and co-ordinated policies and actions. If so, his thesis is right by definition. He would also say, I believe, that an "organized majority" is impossible because all it would amount to is that new leaders, new elites, would be on top of these majority organizations, and he is quite ready to pick up these leaders in his "The Ruling Class." He calls them "directing minorities," all of which is pretty flimsy stuff alongside his big statement.

One thing that occurs to me is the use of the chart (I think it is the core of the problems of definition

Mosca presents to us) as a model for trend analysis: Try this: from the nineteenth to the twentieth century, we have witnessed a shift from a society organized as 1 and 4 to a society established *more* in terms of 3 and 2. We have moved from an elite state to an organization state, in which the elite is no longer so organized or so unilaterally powerful, and the mass is more organized and more powerful. Some power has been made in the streets, and around it whole social structures and their "elites" have pivoted. And what selection of the ruling class is more organized than the farm bloc? That's not a rhetorical question: I can answer it either way at this time; it's a matter of degree; all I want now is to get it out in the open.

Mosca makes one point that seems to me excellent and worth elaborating further. There is often in "the ruling class," according to him, a top clique and there is this second and larger stratum, with which (*a*) the top is in continuous and immediate contact, and with which (*b*) it shares ideas and sentiments and hence, he believes, policies. (page 430) Check and see if anywhere else in the book he makes other points of connection. Is the clique recruited largely from the second level? Is the top, in some way, responsible for, or at least sensitive to, this second stratum?

Now forget Mosca: in another vocabulary, we have, (*a*) the elite, by which we here mean that top clique, (*b*) those who count, and (*c*) all the others. Membership in the second and third, in this scheme, is defined by the first, and the second may be quite varied in its size and composition and relations with the first and the third. (What, by the way, is the range of variations of the relations of *b* to *a* and to *c*? Examine Mosca for hints and further extend this by considering it systematically.)

This scheme may enable me more neatly to take into account the different elites, which are elites according to the several dimensions of stratification. Also, of course, to pick up in a neat and meaningful way the Paretian distinction of governing and non-governing elites, in a way less formal than Pareto. Certainly many top status people would at least be in the second. So would the big rich. The Clique or The Elite would refer to power, or to authority, as the case may be. The elite in this vocabulary would always mean the power elite. The other top people would be the upper classes or the upper circles.

So in a way, maybe, we can use this in connection with two major problems: the structure of the elite; and the conceptual—later perhaps, the substantive—relations of stratification and elite theories. (Work this out.)

From the standpoint of power, it is easier to pick out those who count than those who rule. When we try to do the first we select the top levels as a sort of loose aggregate and we are guided by position. But when we attempt the second, we must indicate in clear detail how they wield power and just how they are related to the social instrumentalities through which power is exercised. Also we deal more with persons than positions, or we at least have to take persons into account.

Now power in the U. S. involves more than one elite. How can we judge the relative positions of these several elites? Depends upon the issue and decisions being made. One elite sees another as among those

who count. There is this mutual recognition among the elite, that other elites count; in one way or another they are important people to one another. Project: select 3 or 4 key decisions of last decade—to drop the atom, to cut or raise steel production, the G. M. strike of '45—and trace in detail the personnel involved in each of them. Might use "decisions" and decision-making as interview pegs when you go out for intensives.

FOUR

There comes a time in the course of your work when you are through with other books. Whatever you want from them is down in your notes and abstracts. On the margin of these notes, as well as in a separate file, are still further ideas for empirical studies.

Now I do not like to do empirical work if I can possibly avoid it. It means a great deal of trouble if one has no staff, and, if one does employ a staff, then the staff is often more trouble than the work itself. Moreover, and quite properly, members of the staff often leave as soon as they have been trained and made useful. Besides, and more seriously, in the social sciences there is so much to do by way of initial "structuring" (let the word stand for the kind of work I am describing) that much "empirical research" is bound to be thin and uninteresting.

In our situation, empirical work as such is for beginning students and for those who aren't able to handle the complexities of big problems; it is also for highly formal men who do not care what they study so long as it appears to be orderly. All these types have a right to do as they please or as they must; they have no right to impose in the name of science such narrow limits on others. Anyway, you ought not to let them bother you.

Although you will never be able to get the money to finance all the empirical studies you design, it is necessary that you continue designing them. For once you lay out an empirical study, even if you do not follow it through, it leads you to a new search for data which often turns out to have unsuspected relevance to your problems. Just as it is foolish to design a field study if the answer can be got from a library, so it is foolish to think you have exhausted the books before you have translated them into appropriate empirical studies, which means merely into questions of what facts are needed.

Empirical projects necessary to my kind of work must promise: First, to have relevance for the first draft, of which I wrote above; they have to anchor it in its original form or they have to cause its modification, or to put it more pretentiously they must have implications for theoretical constructions. Second: the projects must be efficient and neat and, if possible, ingenious. By this, I mean that they must promise to yield a great deal of material in proportion to the time and effort they involve.

Now, I have not decided upon the studies necessary for the present job, but here is the beginning of a larger design within which various small-scale studies have begun to arise. Again I excerpt from the files:

I am not yet in a position to study the upper circles as a whole in a systematic and empirical way. So what I do is set forth some definitions and procedures that form a sort of ideal design for such a study. I can then attempt, *first,* to gather existing materials that approximate this design; *second,* to think of convenient ways of gathering materials, given the existing indices, that satisfy it as crucial points; and *third,* as I proceed, to make more specific the full-scale, empirical researches that would in the end be necessary.

(1) The upper circles must, of course, be defined systematically in terms of specific variables. Formally —and this is more or less Pareto's way—they are the people who "have" the most of whatever is available of any given value or set of values. So I have to make two decisions: What variables shall I take as the criteria, and what do I mean by "the most"? After I've decided on my variables, I must construct the best indices I can, if possible, quantifiable indices, in order to distribute the population in terms of them; only then can I begin to decide what I mean by "the most." For this should, in part, be left for determination by empirical inspection of the various distributions, and their overlaps.

My key variables should, at first, be general enough to give me some latitude in the choice of indices, yet specific enough to invite the search for empirical indices. As I go along, I'll have to shuttle between conceptions and indices, guided by the desire not to lose intended meanings and yet to be quite specific about them. Here are the four Weberian variables with which I will begin:

I. Class refers to sources and amounts of income. So I'll need property distributions and income distributions. The ideal material here (which is very scarce, and unfortunately dated) is a cross-tabulation of source and amount of annual income. Thus, we know that X per cent of the population received during 1936 Y millions or over, and that Z per cent of all this money was from property, W per cent from entrepreneurial withdrawal, Q per cent from wages and salaries. Along this class dimension, I can define the upper circles—those who have the most—either as those who receive given amounts of income during a given time—or, as those who make up the upper 2 per cent of the income pyramid. Look into treasury records and lists of big taxpayers. See if TNEC tables on source and amount of income can be brought up to date.

II. Status refers to the amounts of deference received. For this, there are no simple or quantifiable indices. Existing indices require personal interviews for their application, are limited so far to local community studies, and are mostly no good anyway. There is the further problem that, unlike class, status involves social relations: at least one to receive and one to bestow the deference.

It is easy to confuse publicity with deference—or rather, we do not yet know whether or not volume of publicity should be used as an index to status position, although it is the most easily available: (For example: On one of three successive days in mid-March 1952, the following categories of people were mentioned by name in the *New York Times*—or on selected pages— work this out).

III. Power refers to the realization of one's will even if others resist. Like status, this has not been well indexed. I don't think I can keep it a single dimension, but will have to talk (*a*) of formal authority —defined by rights and powers of positions in various institutions, especially military, political, and economic. And (*b*) power known informally to be exercised but not formally instituted—pressure group leaders, propagandists with extensive media at their disposal, and so on.

IV. Occupation refers to activities that are paid for. Here, again, I must choose just which feature of occupation I should seize upon. (*a*) If I use the average incomes of various occupations, to rank them, I am of course, using occupation as an index, and as a basis of, class. In like manner, (*b*) if I use the status or the power typically attached to different occupations, then I am using occupations as indices, and bases, of power and skill of talent. But this is by no means an easy way to classify people. Skill—no more than status—is not a homogeneous something of which there is more or less. Attempts to treat it as such have usually been put in terms of the length of time required to acquire various skills, and maybe that will have to do, although I hope I can think of something better.

Those are the types of problems I will have to solve in order to define analytically and empirically the upper circles, in terms of these four key variables. For purposes of design, assume I have solved them to my satisfaction, and that I have distributed the population in terms of each of them. I would then have four sets of people: those at the top in class, status, power, and skill. Suppose further, that I had singled out the top 2 per cent of each distribution, as an upper circle. I then confront this empirically answerable question: How much, if any, overlap is there among each of these four distributions? One range of possibilities can be located within this simple chart: (+ = top 2%; − = lower 98%):

			Class			
			+		−	
			Status		Status	
			+	−	+	−
+ Skill	+		1	2	3	4
Power	−		5	6	7	8
− Skill	+		9	10	11	12
	−		13	14	15	16

This diagram, if I had the materials to fill it, would contain major data and many important problems for a study of the upper circles. It would provide keys to many definitional and substantive questions.

I don't have the data, and I shan't be able to get it—which makes all the more important that I speculate about it, for in the course of such reflection, if it is guided by the desire to approximate the empirical requirements of an ideal design, I'll come upon important areas, on which I might be able to get materials that are relevant as anchor points and guides to further imaginative reflection.

There are two additional points which I must add to this general model in order to make it formally complete. Full conceptions of upper strata require attention to duration and mobility. The task here is to determine positions (1-16) between which there is typical movement of individuals and groups—within the present generation, and between the last two or three generations.

This introduces the temporal dimension of biography or career-lines, and of history into the scheme. These are not merely further empirical questions; they are also definitionally relevant. For (a) we want to leave open whether or not in classifying people in terms of any of our key variables, we should define our categories in terms of how long they, or their families, have occupied the position in question. For example, I might want to decide that the upper 2 per cent of status—or at least one important type of status rank—consists of those up there for at least two generations. Also (b), I want to leave open the question of whether or not I should construct "a stratum" not only in terms of an intersection of several variables, but also, in line with Weber's neglected definition of "social class," as composed of those positions between which there is "typical and easy mobility." Thus, the lower white-collar occupations and middle- and upper-wage worker jobs in certain industries seem to be forming, in this sense, a stratum.

In the course of the reading and analysis of others' theories, the design of ideal research, and the perusal of the files, you will begin to draw up a list of special studies. Some of them are too big to handle, and will in time be regretfully given up; some will end as materials for a paragraph, a section, a sentence, a chapter; some will become pervading themes to be woven into the entire book. Here again are initial notes for several such special projects:

(1) A time-budget analysis of a typical working day of ten top executives of large corporations, and the same for ten federal administrators. These observations will be combined with detailed "life history" interviews. The aim here is to describe the major routines and decisions, partly at least in terms of time devoted to them, and to gain an insight into the factors relevant to the decisions made. The procedure will naturally vary with the degree of co-operation secured, but ideally will involve first, an interview in which the life history and present situation of the man are made clear; second, observations of the day, actually sitting in a corner of the man's office, and following him around; third, a longish interview that evening or the next day in which we go over the whole day and probe the subjective processes involved in the external behavior we've observed.

(2) An analysis of upper-class weekends, in which the routines are closely observed and followed by probing interviews with the man and other members of the family on the Monday following.

For both these tasks I've fairly good contacts and of course good contacts, if handled properly, lead to better ones. (Added 1957: this turned out to be an illusion.)

(3) A study of the expense account and other privileges which, along with salaries and other incomes, form the standard and the style of living of the top levels. The idea here is to get something concrete on "the bureaucratization of consumption," the transfer of private expenses to business accounts.

(4) Bring up to date the type of information contained in such books as Lundberg's *America's Sixty Families*, which is dated as of the tax returns for 1923.

(5) Gather and systematize, from treasury records and other government sources, the distribution of various types of private property by amounts held.

(6) A career line study of the Presidents, all cabinet members, and all members of the Supreme Court. This I already have on IBM cards from the Constitutional period through Truman's second term, but I want to expand the items used and analyze it afresh.

There are other—some 35 so far—"projects" of this sort (for example, comparison of the amounts of money spent in the presidential elections of 1896 and 1952, detailed comparison of Morgan of 1910 and Kaiser of 1950, and something concrete on the careers of "Admirals and Generals"). But, as I go along, I must of course adjust my aim to what is accessible. I hope that the above list will make clear the kind of thing I want to do.

My sense of form—unskilled though it is—begins to tempt me into concealment. I feel the tendency to leave my fragmentary notes and to round all this out, so as to make my ways of working seem more effective than they are. In short, I am tempted to draw your attention away from my limited discoveries and toward the ways in which I try to persuade. I want to guard against doing this. So I must tell you that during the last several months I have been doing a great deal of writing; to be sure it has been writing along the general lines of the big model and in terms of the theories examined, but still it has at times seemed entirely free of all that. I cannot say for sure whether my imagination has been prompted by having these larger designs before me, although I am aware that I can easily make it look that way. Maybe these designs are a sort of professional ritual I go through; maybe they are more than that, more than psychologically necessary. At any rate, some of this writing leads me to feel uneasy about the assumption that all the skills required to do social research and to put a book together are explicit and teachable, as are the deadbeat methods of much orthodox social science today.

Anyway, after these designs were written down, I began, with a clearer conscience, and I must say considerable zest, to read historical works on top groups, taking random (and unfiled) notes and interpreting the reading. You do not really have to *study* a topic you are working on; for, as I have said, once you are into it, it is everywhere. You are sensible to its themes; you see and hear them everywhere in your experience, especially, it always seems to me, in apparently unrelated areas. Even the mass media, especially bad movies and cheap novels and picture magazines and daytime radio, are disclosed in fresh importance to you.

From existing sources as well as those that you have fashioned, trying to remain open, as it were, on all sides, you slowly go forward, continually outlining and reoutlining the whole, specifying and elaborating and getting on with the anchor projects, refining and trying to index parts of the master design, writing this and editing that, bringing intellectual neatness for a day or a week or a month to this section or to that part.

FIVE

But, you may ask, how do ideas come? How is the imagination spurred to put all the images and facts together, to make images relevant and lend meaning to facts? I do not think I can really answer that; all I can do is talk about the general conditions and a few simple techniques which have seemed to increase my chances to come out with something.

When it is all read and some of it is being used, the social-science tradition of the last hundred years amounts to this: in the mind that has hold of it, in the mind that has been formed by it, there sometimes comes about a kind of sociological imagination. In brief, it is the capacity to shift from one perspective to another, and in the process to build up an adequate view of a total society and of its several components. I suppose it is this imagination that sets off the social scientist from the mere technician. I make no apologies for the "mere": adequate techniques can be trained in a few years. The sociological imagination can also be trained; certainly it seldom

occurs without a great deal of work. Yet there is an unexpected quality about it, perhaps because its essence is the combination of ideas that no one expected were combinable. We might consider, for example, a mess of ideas from German philosophy and British economics. There is a playfulness of mind back of such combining, as well as a truly fierce drive to make a sense of the world, which the technician as such usually lacks. Perhaps he is too well trained, too precisely trained. Since one can be *trained* only in what is already known, training sometimes means that one is incapacitated by it from learning new ways. His training rebels against what is bound to be at first loose and even sloppy. I feel the need to say that I at least have rarely had an idea that later seemed to turn out rather well which was not in its beginning more than quite foggy and tenuous. Often ideas have at first seemed almost like nonsense, and fleeting nonsense at that; certainly they were often embarrassing to discuss with anyone who was not a proven colleague and friend. But you must cling to such vague images and notions, if they are yours, and you must work them out. For it is in such forms that original ideas almost always first appear.

I hope that you do not feel that what I have said means that the sociological imagination is something given to one as a gift of grace. I do not pretend to understand how it comes about as a capacity of an individual mind, but I do believe that you have got to work in order to call it forth. When you are really in the middle of some set of problems, you are working for it all the time, even when you do not realize it. You have to develop and nurse it, and you must live as well as work in such a way as to allow it to occur.

I believe that there are definite ways of stimulating it. Although I do not want to acquire or promulgate any technique of work that might limit the play of individual fancy, there are several ways I should like to tell you about that I have found useful to invite the sociological imagination:

I. Let me begin on the most concrete level. The rearranging of the file, as I have already said, is one way to invite imagination. You simply dump out heretofore disconnected folders, mixing up their contents, and then re-sort them. You try to do it in a more or less relaxed way, and I have always found a glass of Irish whiskey quite helpful. How often and how extensively you rearrange the files will of course vary with different problems and with how well they are developing. But the mechanics of it are as simple as that. Your own file is only a little one; the library is much larger. And part of the intellectual workman's way of life consists of a kind of relaxed browsing in libraries, letting his mind play over books and periodicals and encyclopedias. Of course, you will have in mind the several problems on which you are actively working, but you will also try to be passively receptive to unforeseen and unplanned linkages. A library, you know, is an enormously exciting place.

II. An attitude of playfulness toward the phrases and words with which various issues are defined often loosens the imagination. Look up synonyms for each of your key terms in dictionaries as well as in technical books, in order to know the full range of their connotations. This simple procedure will prod you to elaborate the terms of the problem and hence to define them less wordily and more precisely. For only if you know the several meanings which might be given to terms or phrases can you select the exact ones with which you want to work. But such an interest in words goes further than that.

In all work, but especially in examining more theoretical statements, you will try to keep close watch on the level of generality of every key term, and you will often find it useful to take a high-level statement and break it down to more concrete meanings. When that is done, the statement often falls into two or three components, each lying along different dimensions. You will also try to move up the level of generality; to remove the specific qualifiers and examine the re-formed statement or inference more abstractly, to see if you can stretch it or elaborate it. So from above and from below, you will try to probe, in search of clarified meaning, into every aspect and implication of the theory.

III. Many general ideas you come upon will, as you think about them, be cast into some sort of types. A new classification is the usual beginning of fruitful developments. The skill required to make up types and then to search for the conditions and consequences of each type will, in short, become an automatic procedure with you. Rather than rest content with existing classifications, you will search for their common denominators and for differentiating factors within and between them. For good types require that the criteria of classifications be explicit and systematic. To make them so you must develop the habit of cross-classification.

The technique of "cross-classifying" is of course not limited to quantitative materials; as a matter of fact, it is the best way to imagine and to get hold of *new* types as well as to criticize and clarify old ones. Charts, tables, and diagrams of a qualitative sort are not only ways to display work already done: they are very often genuine tools of production. They clarify the "dimensions" of the types which they also help you imagine and build. As a matter of fact, in the past fifteen years, I do not believe I have written more than a dozen pages first-draft without some little cross-classification, although, of course, I do not always or even usually display them. Most of them flop, in which case you have still learned something. When they work, they help you to think more clearly and to write more explicitly. They enable you to unfold the range and the full relationships of the very terms with which you are thinking and of the facts with which you are dealing.

For a working sociologist, cross-classification is what making the sign of the cross is for a good Catholic, or diagramming a sentence is for a diligent grammarian. In many ways, the cross-classification is the very grammar of the sociological imagination.

I want to give a silly little example, for in this way perhaps you will come to see how really deep-going this habit of mind can become. Yesterday afternoon I was very depressed. Someone had left a recent copy of a certain magazine in the house and I had thumbed it. As it always does, the thing disgusted me so that I came to the edge of melancholy. I took a little walk and overhead someone on a street corner say, "Well, things are not always as bad as they seem." Immediately I heard myself saying, "Yes, sometimes they are not so bad as they always seem." That's a confused piece of a cross-classification. I took out a notebook and played with the thing: "Always vs. sometimes vs. never," I wrote. "Is vs. seems," "bad vs. not bad." Those are the dimensions, which yield of course nine statements:

Seems 'bad':	Is 'bad'		
	Always	Sometimes	Never
Always	1	2	3
Sometimes	4	5	6
Never	7	8	9

Isn't that a fascinating little business? It is a way "to objectify" some moods. In playing with it, I got over the slump and began to write an essay on that magazine for the files. I called the piece "Seeing Is Not Believing." So now you understand that cross-classification, as a persistent habit of mind, is, among other things, a prime means of personal therapy.

IV. You will find that you often get the best insights by considering extreme types, or from thinking of the opposite of that with which you are directly concerned. If you think about despair, then also think about elation; if you study the miser, then also the spendthrift. That is also a general characteristic of anchor projects, which, if it is possible, ought to be designed in terms of "polar types." The hardest thing in the world is to study one object, but when you try to contrast objects, you get a sort of grip on the materials and you can then sort out the dimensions in terms of which the comparisons are made. You will find that the shuttling between attention to these dimensions and to the concrete types is very illuminating. This technique is also logically sound, for without a sample, you can only guess about statistical frequencies anyway: what you can do is to give the range and the major types of some phenomenon, and for that it is more economical to begin by constructing "polar types," opposites along various dimensions. This does not mean of course that you will not strive to gain and to maintain a sense of proportion, with the hope of obtaining some lead on the frequencies of given types. One continually tries, in fact, to combine this quest with the search for indices for which one might find or collect statistics.

The idea is to use a variety of perspectives: you will, for instance, ask yourself how would a political scientist whom you have recently read approach this, and how would that experimental psychologist or this historian? You try to think in terms of a variety of perspectives which, as an example, are represented here by different specialties. You will try in this way to let your mind become a moving prism catching light from as many angles as possible. In this connection, the writing of dialogues is often useful.

You will frequently find yourself opposing an idea or an opinion. In trying to understand a new intellectual field, you might first isolate the major arguments and examine them closely. One of the things meant by "being soaked in the literature" is being able to locate the opponents and the friends of every available viewpoint.[7]

V. The fact that in cross-classification you first work, for simplicity, in terms of yes-or-no encourages you to think of extreme opposites. And that is generally good, for qualitative analysis cannot of course provide you with frequencies or magnitudes. Its technique and its end is to give you the range of types. For many purposes, you need no more than that, although for some of course you do need to get a more precise idea of the proportions involved.

The release of imagination can sometimes be achieved by deliberately inverting your sense of proportion.[8] If something seems minute, imagine it to be enormous, then ask yourself: what difference might that make? And vice-versa, for gigantic phenomena. Nowadays, at least, I would never think of actually counting or measuring anything before I had played with each of its elements, conditions, and consequences in a make-believe world in which I control the scale of everything. This is one thing statisticians ought to mean, but never seem to mean, by that horrible little phrase about "knowing the universe before you sample it."

VI. On almost any problem with which you are concerned, you will try to get a *comparative* grip on the materials. The search for comparable cases either in one civilization or in several historical periods gives you leads. You would never think of describing an institution in twentieth-century America without trying to bear in mind similar institutions in other types of structure and epoch. And that is so even if you do not make explicit comparisons. In time, you will also come almost automatically to put historical depth into your reflection. One reason for doing so is that often what you are examining is limited in number, so to get a comparative grip on it, you have got to place it inside a frame with historical depth. To put it another way, the contrasting type approach often requires the examination of historical cases. This sometimes results in points useful for a trend analysis, or it leads to a typology of stages. You will use historical materials, then, because of the desire for a fuller range, or for a more convenient range of some phenomena, by which I mean one that includes the variations along some known set of dimensions. Some knowledge of world history is indispensable to the sociologist. Without such knowledge, no matter what else he knows, he is simply crippled.

VII. There is, finally, a point which has more to do with the craft of putting a book together than with the release of the imagination. Yet these two are often one: how you go about arrangements of materials for presentation always affects the content of your work. The idea I have in mind I learned from a great editor, Lambert Davis, who, I suppose, after seeing what I have done with it, would not want to acknowledge it as his child. It is the distinction of theme and topic.

A topic is of course a subject, like "the careers of corporation executives," or "the increased power of military officials," or "the decline of society matrons." Usually, most of what you have to say about a topic can readily be put into one chapter or into a section of a chapter. But the order in which all your topics are arranged often brings you into the realm of themes.

A theme is an idea, usually of some signal trend or of some master conception. In working out the construction of a book, you will know that you are on top of the job when you come to realize the two or three, or as the case may be, the six or seven, themes. You will recognize these themes because they insist upon being dragged into all sorts of topics. Perhaps you will feel they are mere repetitions, and sometimes that is all they are. They often show up in badly written sections of your manuscript, breaking your flow of words and detracting from the clarity of your prose.

What you must do is sort them out and state them in a general way as clearly and briefly as you can. Then, quite systematically you must cross-classify them with the full range of your topics. All this means that you will ask of each topic: just how is it affected by each of these themes? And again: just what, if any, is the meaning for each of these themes of each of the topics?

Sometimes a theme requires a chapter or a section for itself, perhaps when it is first introduced or perhaps in an accumulation towards the end. In general, most writers, as well as most systematic thinkers, would agree, I believe, that at some point all the themes ought to appear together, in relation to one another. Often, it is possible to do this at the beginning of a book. But it must usually be done near the end in any well-constructed book. And, of course, all the way through one should attempt to relate the themes to each topic. It is easier to write about this than to do it, for it is ordinarily not so mechanical a matter as it might appear. But sometimes it is, at least after the themes are properly sorted out and clarified. Of course, that is the rub. For what I have here called themes, in the context of literary craftsmanship, is referred to as ideas, in the context of intellectual work.

Sometimes, you may find that a book you are reading does not really have any themes. It is just a string of topics. Such a string of topics is indeed indispensable to the writing of books by men without ideas. So is lack of intelligibility.

SIX

I know you will agree that you should present your work in as clear and simple a language as your subject matter and your thought permit. But, as you may have noticed, a turgid and polysyllabic prose does seem curiously to prevail in the social sciences. It has in fact been said with authority that there is "a serious crisis in literacy"—a crisis in which social scientists are very much involved.[9] Is this peculiar language due to the fact that profound and subtle issues, concepts, and methods are being discussed? If not, then what are the reasons for what Mr. Malcolm Cowley aptly calls "socspeak"?[10] Is it really necessary to your proper work? If it is, there is nothing you can do about it; if it is not, then how can you avoid it?

Such lack of ready intelligibility, I believe, has little or nothing to do with the complexity of subject matter; certainly, nothing at all with profundity of thought. It has to do almost entirely with certain confusions of the academic writer about his own status.

In many academic circles today, anyone who tries to write in a widely intelligible way is liable to be condemned as a "mere literary man" or, worse still, a "mere journalist." Perhaps you have already learned that, as commonly used, these phrases mean: superficial because readable. The academic man in America is trying to carry on a serious intellectual life in a social context that often seems firmly set against it. His prestige must make up for many of the dominant values he has sacrificed by choosing an academic career. And his claims for prestige readily become tied to his self-image as a "Scientist." To be called a "mere journalist" makes him feel undignified and shallow. It is, I think, this situation that is often at the bottom of the elaborate vocabulary and the involved manner of speaking and writing. It is less difficult to learn this manner than to avoid learning it. For it has become a convention: those who do not use it are subject to moral disapproval. And to more than that. Since there is a premium upon its use, those who avoid it do so at their own risk. It may also be that it is the result of an academic closing of the ranks on the part of the mediocre, who understandably wish to exclude those who win the attention of academic men in other fields, as well as of intelligent people in general.[11]

To write is to raise a claim for the attention of readers. That is part of *any* style. To write is also to claim for oneself at least status enough to be read. The young academic man is very much involved in both claims, and because he feels his lack of public position, he often puts the claim *for* his own status before his claim for the attention of the reader *to* what he is saying. In fact, in America, even the most accomplished men of knowledge do not have much status among wide circles and publics. That is one reason why academic men slip so readily into unintelligibility. In turn, this very intelligibility is another explanation for why they lack the status they desire. This is truly a vicious circle, but one from which any individual scholar can attempt to escape. For here indeed: "style is the man."

To overcome the academic *prose*, if you will forgive me, you have first to overcome the academic *pose*. And to do so, it is much less important to study grammar and Anglo-Saxon roots than to get clear your own answers to these three questions: (1) How difficult and complex after all is my subject? (2) When I write, what status am I claiming for myself? (3) For whom am I trying to write?

The usual answer to the first question is: not so difficult and complex as the way in which you are writing about it. Proof of that is everywhere available, and is revealed by the ease with which ninety-five per cent of the books of social science can be translated into English. Sometimes it takes more space to say it plainly: usually it takes much less.[12]

But, you may ask, do we not sometimes need technical terms?[13] Of course we do, but "technical" does not necessarily mean "difficult." If such terms are really necessary and also clear and precise, which is what "technical" means, it is not difficult to slip them into a context of plain English and thus introduce them to the reader.

Perhaps you may object that the ordinary words of common use are often loaded with feelings and values and that accordingly it might be well to avoid them in favor of newly made-up words or technical terms. Here is my answer: it is true that ordinary words are often so loaded. To write clearly is to control these loads, to say exactly what you mean in such a way that this meaning and only this meaning will be understood by others. Assume that your intended meaning is circumscribed by a six-foot circle in which you are standing; assume that the meaning understood by your reader is another such circle, in which he is standing. The circles, let us hope, do overlap. The extent of that overlap is the extent of your communication. The part of the reader's circle that does not overlap is an area of uncontrolled meaning. In your circle, the part that does not overlap is a token of your failure. You fail to put the meaning across. The skill of writing is to get the reader's circle of meaning to coincide exactly with yours. You should write in such a way that both you and the reader stand in the same circle of controlled meaning.

Remember these horrible circles the next time you are writing. Remember too: the reader is free to run away. All this is why writing and talking are such unnatural things for a man to do. Better that he should go into a cave and remain silent. But do not technical words give us a better chance to make the circles coincide, at least among the scientific fraternity? The answer, I think, must be a flat no. Most of the technical terms in common use in social science are as value loaded, if not more so, as the words in good English usage. Apart from mathematical symbols, of which I am ignorant, any words (technical or not) used in attempted communication set up those two circles, and those two circles very seldom if ever perfectly coincide. That, I suppose, is what puts the tension in writing.

My first point, then, is that by far the most of "socspeak" is in no way due to any complexity of subject matter or of thought. It certainly cannot reasonably be due to any attempt to secure attention to what is being said. It is due, almost entirely, I believe, to claims for one's academic self. To write in this way is to say to the reader, often perhaps without knowing it: "I know something that is so difficult you can understand it only if you first learn my difficult language. In the meantime, you are merely a journalist, a layman, or some other sort of underdeveloped type, and so to hell with you." The first sentence is usually rubbish; the second always a silly impertinence. But "socspeak" rests, in the first place, upon just such claims. It rests, in the second place, upon confusions about: who one really might be.

Let us now consider the second question—the question of status.

Two ways of presenting the work of social science may be distinguished according to the idea the writer has of himself: (1) One is the idea that he is a man, who may shout, whisper, or chuckle, but who is always there. It is also clear what sort of a man he is: he is a confident center of experience and reasoning; he has found out something, and now he is telling us about it and how he has found it out. This is the voice behind the best expositions available in the English language.

(2) The other idea is not that of any voice of any man. In fact it is not a "voice" at all. It is an autonomous sound. It is a prose manufactured by a machine turned god. That it is full of jargon is not as important a feature of it as that it is very strongly mannered: it is not only impersonal; it is pretentiously impersonal. Government bulletins are sometimes written in this way. So are business letters, and a great deal of social science. Any writing (I do not see how it can be denied) not

imaginable as human speech is bad writing.

But, thirdly, there is not only the voice or its absence; there are also those who are to hear it. That, too, leads to characteristics of style. It is very important for any writer to have in mind just what kinds of people he is trying to speak to—and also what he really thinks of them. To try to write well, it now seems to me, I must know who I am and to whom I am speaking. I feel the need to confess that for a long time—far too long after I had begun to publish—I did not know the answer to either question; in fact I did not really know of either question. Nowadays, I am usually aware of the questions and of their importance, but often I do not know their proper answers, or I forget them. They are not easy questions: to answer them well requires decisions about oneself, as well as knowledge of reading publics. To write is to raise a claim to be read, but by whom?

One answer has been given by my colleague, Mr. Lionel Trilling, who has given me permission to pass it on. You are to assume that you have been asked to give a lecture on some subject you know well before an audience of students, university faculty members, and interested people from a nearby city. It is as simple as this: assume that such an audience is before you and that they have a right to know; assume that you want to let them know. Now write.

Such a choice of public by a social scientist assumes that anything he is doing and anything he finds out by doing it can be presented in an intelligible English, with no loss of meaning. The ease of translation makes this assumption, nine times out of ten, the only reasonable one. To write plainly may of course require more space, although I do not think that is usually so, and I am certain that it requires less space than the standard sociological prose.

Are there not some four broad possibilities available to the social scientist as a writer? (1) If he recognizes himself as a voice and assumes that he is speaking to some such public, as I have indicated, he will try to produce a readable prose. (2) If he assumes he is a voice but is not altogether aware of any public, he may easily fall into unintelligible ravings. Such a man had better be careful. (3) If he considers himself less a voice than an agent of some impersonal sound, then his public, should he find one, will most likely be a cult-like grouping of people who are hardly specialists of anything beyond this language, for to maintain it is surely a full-time job. (4) If without knowing his own voice, he should not find any public, but

speaks solely for some record kept by no one, then I suppose we have to admit that he is a true manufacturer of the standardized prose: an autonomous sound in a great empty hall. It is all rather frightening, as in a Kafka novel, and it ought to be: we have been talking about the edge of reason.

The line between profundity and verbiage is often delicate, even perilous. No one should deny the curious charm of those who, like Whitman, beginning their studies, are so pleased and awed by the first step that they hardly wish to go further. Of itself, language does form a wonderful world, but, entangled in that world, we must not mistake the confusion of beginnings with the profundity of finished results. As a member of the academic community, you should think of yourself as a representative of a truly great language, and you should expect and demand of yourself the ability to carry on the discourse of civilized men when you speak and when you write.

There is one last point, which has to do with the interplay of writing and thinking. If you write solely with reference to the context of discovery, you will be understood by very few people; moreover, you will tend to be quite subjective in statement. To make more objective whatever you think, you must work in the context of presentation. At first, you "present" your argument or dissertation to yourself, which is often called "thinking clearly." Then when you think you have got it straight, you present it to others, and often discover that you have not been as logical and as articulate as you had assumed. Now you are in the context of presentation. Sometimes you will notice that as you try to present your subject, you will modify it, not only in form of statement but often in its content as well. You will get new ideas as you work in the context of presentation. In short, it will become a new context of discovery, different from the original one, and on a higher level, I think, because it will become more socially presentable and more objective. Here again: you cannot divorce how you think from how you write. You have to move back and forth between these two contexts, and whenever you move, it is well to know where you might be going. You need a signpost. Perhaps this will do:

In the end try to make your context of presentation reveal your context of discovery. Do not believe that you can ever do this fully and yet be understood. It is as much a mannerism, an art, a style, as is the most complete hiding of the context of discovery. But the ideal of presentation for expository writing is the clear revelation of what you have found out in terms of how you have found it out, and hence why you think it is so.

I wish I had known of this ideal ten years ago and had been practicing it. I have only got hold of it firmly this year (1956-57), and I have not worked with it long enough to know what kinds of exceptions, if any, must be made.

SEVEN

From what I have said, you will understand that in a way you never "start working on a project"; you are already "working," either in a more personal vein, in the files, in taking notes after browsing, or in more guided endeavors. Following this way of living and working, you will always have many topics which you want to work out further. After you decide on some "release," you will try to use your entire file, your browsing in libraries, your conversation, your selections of people—all for this topic. You are trying, you see, to build a little world containing all the key elements which enter into the work at hand, to put each in its place in a systematic way, to readjust continually this framework around developments in each part of it. Merely to live in such a little world is to know what is needed: ideas, facts, ideas, figures, ideas.

So you will discover and describe, setting up types for the ordering of what you have found out focusing and organizing experience by distinguishing items by name. This search for order will caus you to seek patterns and trends, to find relations that may be typical and causal. You will search, in short, for the meanings of what you come upon for what may be interpreted as visible tokens of something else that is not visible. You will make an inventory of everything that seems involved in whatever you are trying to understand; you will pare it down to essentials; then carefully and systematically you will relate these items to one another in order to form a sort of working model. And then, you will relate this model to whatever it is you are trying to explain. Sometimes it is tha easy; often it just will not come.

But always, among all the details, you will be searching for indicators that might point to the main drift, to the underlying forms and tendencies of the range of society in the middle of the Twentieth Century. For, in the end, that is what you are always writing about.

Thinking is of course a struggle for order and at the same time for comprehensiveness. You must not close it up too soon, or you will fail to see all that you should; you cannot leave it open forever, or you yourself will burst. Perhaps it is this dilemma that makes reflection, on those rare occasions when it is more or less successful, the most passionate endeavor of which the human being is capable.

FOOTNOTES

[1] Hadley Cantril, ed. *Tensions That Cause Wars* (Urbana: University of Illinois Press, 1950), p. 297.

[2] W. A. Johr and H. W. Singer, *The Role of the Economist as Official Adviser* (London: George Allen & Unwin, 1955), pp. 3-4. This book, by the way, is a model of the proper way of going about discussions of method in social science. Sig nificantly, it was written out of a kind of conversation between two experienced craftsmen.

[3] First drafted spring 1952; rewritten spring 1956.

[4] Just how and why I decided to do such a study does not seem altogether relevant here, but for what it may be worth forget how I became technically concerned with "stratification," but I think it must have been by reading Veblen. He ha always seemed to me very loose, even vague about his "business" and "industrial" employments, which are a kind of tran lation of Marx for the academic American public. Marx himself, I think you must agree, is quite unfinished and much to simple about classes; he did not write a theory of classes, although Max Weber finished one version which I believe Marx would have liked. Anyway, I wrote a book on labor organizations and labor leaders, a politically motivated task; then a book on the middle classes, a task primarily motivated by the desire to articulate my own experience in New York City since 1945. It was thereupon suggested by friends that I ought to round out a trilogy by writing a book on the upper classes. I think the possibility had been in my mind; my plans have always run far ahead of my energies; I had read Balza off and on, especially during the 'forties, and had been much taken with his self-appointed task of "covering" all the maj classes and types in the society of the era he wished to make his own. I had also written a paper on "The Business Elite," and had collected and arranged statistics about the careers of the topmost men in American politics since the Constitutio These two tasks were primarily inspired by seminar work in American history.

In doing these several articles and books and in preparing courses in stratification, I uncovered, of course, a residue of ideas and facts about the upper classes. Especially in the study of social stratification is it difficult to avoid going beyond one's immediate subject, because "the reality" of any one stratum is in large parts its relations to the rest. Accordingly, began to think of a book on the elite.

And yet that is not "really" how "the project" arose; what really happened is (1) that the idea and the plan came out my files, for all projects with me begin and end with them, and books are simply organized releases from the continuous work that goes into them; (2) that after a little while, the whole set of problems involved came to dominate me. When you keep waking up in the middle of the night to scribble a note, always about one topic, you may as well realize it: you are writing a book.

[5] See, for example, *White collar,* ch. 13. I am now trying to do this with Lederer and Gasset vs. "elite theorists" as two reactions to 18th and 19th century democratic doctrine.

[6] There are also statements in Mosca about psychological laws supposed to support his view. Watch his use of the word "natural." But this isn't central, and, in addition, it's not worth considering.

[7] On this point, see, for instance, the book on John Dewey's technique of thought by Bogoslovsky: *The Logic of Controversy* (New York: Harcourt Brace & Co., 1928).

[8] By the way, some of this is what Kenneth Burke, in discussing Nietzsche, has called "perspective by incongruity." See, by all means, Burke: *Permanence and Change* (New York: New Republic Book, 1936).

[9] By Edmund Wilson, widely regarded as the best critic in the English-speaking world, who writes: "As for my experience with articles by experts in anthropology and sociology, it has led me to conclude that the requirement, in my ideal university, of having the papers in every department passed by a professor of English might result in revolutionizing these subjects –if indeed the second of them survived at all." *A Piece of My Mind* (New York: Farrar, Straus and Cudahy, 1956), p. 164.

[10] Malcolm Cowley, "Sociological Habit Patterns in Linguistic Transmogrification," *The Reporter* (September 20, 1956), pp. 41 ff.

[11] Cf. Robert Lekachman, "Economics for Everybody?" *Commentary* (January 1956) pp. 76 ff., who I think confuses the clarity of John Galbraith's prose with such inadequacies as may mark his analysis.

[12] By the way, on various techniques of writing, the best book of which I know is: Robert Graves and Alan Hodge, *The Reader Over Your Shoulder* (New York: The Macmillan Company, 1944). See also G. E. Montague, *A Writer's Notes on His Trade* (London: Pelican Books, 1930–1949) and Bonamy Dobrée, *Modern Prose Style* (Oxford, England: The Clarendon Press, 1934–1950).

[13] Mathematical language, by the way, is of course not "socspeak": on the contrary, those who understand it tell me that it is precise, economical, clear. That is why I am so suspicious of many social scientists who claim a central place for mathematics among the methods of social study but who write prose imprecisely, uneconomically, and unclearly. They should take a lesson from Professor Paul Lazarsfeld, who believes in mathematics, very much indeed, *and* whose prose, while not at all "literary," always reveals, even in first draft, the mathematical qualities indicated. When I cannot understand his mathematics, I know that it is because I am too ignorant; when I disagree with what he writes in nonmathematical language, I know it is because he is mistaken, for one always knows just what he is saying and hence just where he has gone wrong.

Some Observations on Study Design

by Samuel A. Stouffer

Stouffer's chief point, like so many other keen insights, is so simple as to be almost not worth the mention—careful study design before undertaking research will result later in evidence less likely to be capable of innumerable alternative explanations. Stouffer pleads for the controlled experiment, and if not the completely controlled experiment, then at least that which most nearly conforms to its method. And, he raises the basic questions of what constitutes proof in the scientific sense. Essentially, he reasons for far more experimental design in the prosecution of social science research.

In spite of knowing as one proceeds in research that unanticipated factors will arise and necessitate change, the most careful process of working through all the elements of the design remains inescapable. As a consequence of defining method, the variables are inevitably refined as well, and limits are put on what is to be attempted. This agonizing preliminary process of limiting oneself helps avoid the trap of the overly ambitious project and prevents amateurish floundering in the field. Another beneficial measure likely to reduce later anguish comes from critical analysis of the study plan by experts and peers, prior to launching a study.

Initial field exploration to test method and preliminary results rewards the scholar by clarifying more precisely what can be done and by opening possibilities not originally calculated. Similarly, actual work on questionnaire construction, interview schedule, or sample strategy will inevitably assist in placing the overall design in clearer perspective.

Stouffer's wry tongue-in-cheek stricture that too much time in social science is spent in speculative discussion of research rather than its conduct is notable. Getting on with the work calls for self-discipline, an agenda of priorities, the organization of time, and control of the mundane elements without which no task is ever done or done well. For those who are not so disposed, or committed, speculative and ideological writing is an alternative. Since the editors of this volume are adding still one more entry in this genre, even at the risk of being presumptuous, one is led to suggest that librarianship has doubtless had more than its full share of such prescriptions.

As a youth I read a series of vigorous essays in the *Century Magazine* by its editor, the late Glenn Frank. His theme was that the natural sciences had remade the face of the earth; now had arrived the age of the social sciences. The same techniques which had worked their miracles in physics, chemistry, and biology should, in competent hands, achieve equally dazzling miracles in economics, political science, and sociology. That was a long time ago. The disconcerting fact is that people are writing essays just like that today. Of course, the last two decades have seen considerable progress in social science—in theory, in technique, and in the accumulation of data. It is true that the number of practitioners is pitifully few; only a few hundred research studies are reported annually in sociology, for example, as compared with more than twenty thousand studies summarized annually in *Biological Abstracts*. But the bright promise of the period when Frank was writing has not been fulfilled.

Two of the most common reasons alleged for slow progress are cogent, indeed.

The data of social science are awfully complex, it is said. And they involve values which sometimes put a strain on the objectivity of the investigator even when they do not incur resistance from the vested interests of our society. However, an important part of the trouble has very little to do with the subject matter of social science as such but, rather, is a product of our own bad work habits. That is why this paper on the subject of

SOURCE: Samuel A. Stouffer, "Some Observations on Study Design," *American Journal of Sociology*, 55 (Jan., 1950), pp. 355–361. Reprinted from *American Journal of Sociology* by permission of The University of Chicago Press.

study design may be relevant. So much has been spoken and written on this topic that I make no pretense to originality. But in the course of a little experience, especially in an effort during the war to apply social psychology to military problems, and in an undertaking to nurture a new program of research in my university, I have encountered some frustrations which perhaps can be examined with profit.

A basic problem—perhaps *the* basic problem—lies deeply imbedded in the thoughtways of our culture. This is the implicit assumption that anybody with a little common sense and a few facts can come up at once with the correct answer on any subject. Thus the newspaper editor or columnist, faced with a column of empty space to fill with readable English in an hour, can speak with finality and authority on any social topic, however complex. He might not attempt to diagnose what is wrong with his sick cat; he would call a veterinarian. But he knows precisely what is wrong with any social institution and the remedies.

In a society which rewards quick and confident answers and does not worry about how the answers are arrived at, the social scientist is hardly to be blamed if he conforms to the norms. Hence, much social science is merely rather dull and obscure journalism; a few data and a lot of "interpretation." The fact that the so-called "interpretation" bears little or no relation to the data is often obscured by academic jargon. If the stuff is hard to read, it has a chance of being acclaimed as profound. The rewards are for the answers, however tediously expressed, and not for rigorously marshaled evidence.

In the army no one would think of adopting a new type of weapon without trying it out exhaustively on the firing range. But a new idea about handling personnel fared very differently. The last thing anybody ever thought about was trying out the idea experimentally. I recall several times when we had schemes for running an experimental tryout of an idea in the sociopsychological field. Usually one of two things would happen: the idea would be rejected as stupid without a tryout (it may have been stupid, too) or it would be seized on and applied generally and at once. When the provost marshal wanted us to look into the very low morale of the MP's, our attitude surveys suggested that there was room for very much better selectivity in job assignment. There were routine jobs like guarding prisoners which could be given to the duller MP's, and there

were a good many jobs calling for intelligence, discretion, and skill in public relations. We thought that the smarter men might be assigned to these jobs and that the prestige of these jobs would be raised further if a sprinkling of returned veterans with plenty of ribbons and no current assignment could be included among them. We proposed a trial program of a reassignment system in a dozen MP outfits for the purpose of comparing the resulting morale with that in a dozen matched outfits which were left untouched. Did we get anywhere? No. Instead, several of our ideas were put into effect immediately throughout the army without any prior testing at all.

The army cannot be blamed for behavior like that. In social relations it is not the habit in our culture to demand evidence for an idea; plausibility is enough.

To alter the folkways, social science itself must take the initiative. We must be clear in our own minds what proof consists of, and we must, if possible, provide dramatic examples of the advantages of relying on something more than plausibility. And the heart of our problem lies in study design *in advance*, such that the evidence is not capable of a dozen alternative interpretations.

Basically, I think it is essential that we always keep in mind the model of a controlled experiment, even if in practice we may have to deviate from an ideal model. Take the simple accompanying diagram.

	Before	After	After−Before
Experimental group	x_1	x_2	$d = x_2 - x_1$
Control group	x'_1	x'_2	$d' = x'_2 - x'_1$

The test of whether a difference d is attributable to what we think it is attributable to is whether d is significantly larger than d'.

We used this model over and over again during the war to measure the effectivensss of orientation films in changing soldiers' attitudes. These experiences are described in Volume III of our *Studies in Social Psychology in World War II.*[1]

One of the troubles with using this careful design was that the effectiveness of a single film when thus measured turned out to be so slight. If, instead of using the complete experimental design, we simply took an unselected sample of men and compared the attitudes of those who said they had seen a film with those who said they had not, we got much more impressive differences. This was more rewarding to us, too, for the management wanted to believe the films were powerful medicine. The gimmick was the selective fallibility of memory. Men who correctly remembered seeing the films were likely to be those most sensitized to their message. Men who were bored or indifferent may have actually seen them but slept through them or just forgot.

Most of the time we are not able or not patient enough to design studies containing all four cells as in the diagram above. Sometimes we have only the top two cells, as in the accompanying diagram. In this situation

$$\boxed{x_1 \quad x_2} \qquad d = x_2 - x_1$$

we have two observations of the same individuals or groups taken at different times. This is often a very useful design. In the army, for example, we would take a group of recruits, ascertain their attitudes, and restudy the same men later. From this we could tell whose attitudes changed and in what direction (it was almost always for the worse, which did not endear us to the army!). But exactly what factors in the early training period were most responsible for deterioration of attitudes could only be inferred indirectly.

The panel study is usually more informative than a more frequent design, which might be pictured thus:

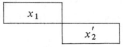

Here at one point in time we have one sample, and at a later point in time we have another sample. We observe that our measure, say, the mean, is greater for the recent sample than for the earlier one. But we are precluded from observing which men or what type of men shifted. Moreover, there is always the disturbing possibility that the populations in our two samples were initially different; hence the differences might not be attributable to conditions taking place in the time interval between the two observations. Thus we would study a group of soldiers in the United States and later ask the same questions of a group of soldiers overseas. Having matched the two groups of men carefully by branch of service, length of time in the army, rank, etc., we hoped that the results of the study would approximate what would be found if the same men could have been studied twice. But this could be no more than a hope. Some important factors could not be adequately controlled, for example, physical conditions. Men who went overseas were initially in better shape on the average than men who had

been kept behind; but, if the follow-up study was in the tropics, there was a chance that unfavorable climate already had begun to take its toll. And so it went. How much men overseas changed called for a panel study as a minimum if we were to have much confidence in the findings.

A very common attempt to get the results of a controlled experiment without paying the price is with the design that might be as shown in the accompanying diagram. This

$$\boxed{\begin{array}{c} x_2 \\ \hline x_2' \end{array}}$$

is usually what we get with correlation analysis. We have two or more groups of men whom we study at the same point in time. Thus we have men in the infantry and men in the air corps and compare their attitudes. How much of the difference between x_2' and x_2 we can attribute to experience in a given branch of service and how much is a function of attributes of the men selected for each branch we cannot know assuredly. True, we can try to rule out various possibilities by matching; we can compare men from the two branches with the same age and education, for example. But there is all too often a wide-open gate through which other uncontrolled variables can march.

Sometimes, believe it or not, we have only one cell:

$$\boxed{x_2}$$

When this happens, we do not know much of anything. But we can still fill pages of social science journals with "brilliant analysis" if we use plausible conjecture in supplying missing cells from our imagination. Thus we may find that the adolescent today has wild ideas and conclude that society is going to the dogs. We fill in the dotted cell representing our own yesterdays with hypothetical data, where x_1 represents us and x_2 our off-

$$\boxed{x_1 \quad x_2}$$

spring. The tragicomic part is that most of the public, including, I fear, many social scientists, are so acculturated that they ask for no better data.

I do not intend to disparage all research not conforming to the canons of the controlled experiment. I think that we will see more of full experimental design in sociology and social psychology in the future than in the past. But I am well aware of the practical difficulties of its execution, and I know that there are numberless important situations in which it is not feasible at all. What I am arguing for is awareness of the limitations of a design in which crucial cells are missing.

Sometimes by forethought and patchwork we can get approximations which are useful if we are careful to avoid overinterpretation. Let me cite an example:

In Europe during the war the army tested the idea of putting an entire platoon of Negro soldiers into a white infantry outfit. This was done in several companies. The Negroes fought beside white soldiers. After several months we were asked to find out what the white troops thought about the innovation. We found that only 7 per cent of the white soldiers in companies with Negro platoons said that they disliked the idea very much, whereas 62 per cent of the white soldiers in divisions without Negro troops said they would dislike the idea very much if it were tried in their outfits. We have:

	Before	After
Experimental		7%
Control		62%

Now, were these white soldiers who fought beside Negroes men who were naturally more favorable to Negroes than the cross-section of white infantrymen? We did not think so, since, for example, they contained about the same proportion of southerners. The point was of some importance, however, if we were to make the inference that actual experience with Negroes reduced hostility from 62 to 7 per cent. As a second-best substitute, we asked the white soldiers in companies with Negro platoons if they could recall how they felt when the innovation was first proposed. It happens that 67 per cent said they were initially opposed to the idea. Thus we could tentatively fill in a missing cell and conclude that, under the conditions obtaining, there probably had been a marked change in attitude.

Even if this had been a perfectly controlled experiment, there was still plenty of chance to draw erroneous inferences. The conclusions apply only to situations closely approximating those of the study. It happens, for example, that the Negroes involved were men who volunteered to leave rear-area jobs for combat duty. If other Negroes had been involved, the situation might have been different. Moreover, they had white officers. One army colonel who saw this study and whom I expected to ridicule it because he usually opposed innovations, surprised me by offering congratulations. "This proves," he said, "what I have been arguing in all my thirty years in the army—that niggers will do all right if you give 'em white officers!" Moreover, the study applied only to combat experience. Other studies would be needed to justify extending the findings to non-combat or garrison duty. In other words, one lone study, however well designed, can be a very dangerous thing if it is exploited beyond its immediate implications.

Now experiments take time and money, and there is no use denying that we in social science cannot be as prodigal with the replications as the biologist who can run a hundred experiments simultaneously by growing plants in all kinds of soils and conditions. The relative ease of experimentation in much—not all— of natural science goes far to account for the difference in quality of proof demanded by physical and biological sciences, on the one hand, and social scientists, on the other.

Though we cannot always design neat experiments when we want to, we can at least keep the experimental model in front of our eyes and behave cautiously when we fill in missing cells with dotted lines. But there is a further and even more important operation we can perform in the interest of economy. That lies in our choice of the initial problem.

Professor W. F. Ogburn always told his students to apply to a reported research conclusion the test, "How do you know it?" To this wise advice I should like to add a further question: "What of it?" I suspect that if before designing a study we asked ourselves, more conscientiously than we do, whether or not the study really is important, we would economize our energies for the few studies which are worth the expense and trouble of the kind of design I have been discussing.

Can anything be said about guides for selecting problems? I certainly think so. That is where theory comes in and where we social scientists have gone woefully astray.

Theory has not often been designed with research operations in mind. Theory as we have it in social science serves indispensably as a very broad frame of reference or general orientation. Thus modern theories of culture tell us that it is usually more profitable to focus on the learning process and the content of what is learned rather than on innate or hereditary traits. But they do not provide us with sets of interrelated propositions which can be put in the form: If x_1, given x_2 and x_3, then there is strong probability that we get x_4. Most of our propositions of that form, sometimes called "theory," are likely to be *ad hoc* common-sense observations which are not deducible from more general considerations and which are of the same quality as the observation, "If you stick your hand in a fire and hold it there, you will get burned."

Now in view of the tremendous cost in time and money of the ideal kind of strict empirical research operations, it is obvious that we cannot afford the luxury of conducting them as isolated fact-finding enterprises. Each should seek to be some sort of *experimentum crucis*, and, with rare exceptions, that will only happen if we see its place *beforehand* in a more general scheme of things. Especially, we need to look for situations where two equally plausible hypotheses deducible from more general theory lead to the expectation of different consequences. Then, if our evidence supports one and knocks out the other, we have accomplished something.

The best work of this sort in our field is probably being done today in laboratory studies of learning and of perception. I do not know of very good sociological examples. Yet in sociology experiments are possible. One of the most exciting, for example, was that initiated long before the war by Shaw and McKay to see whether co-operative effort by adult role models within a delinquent neighborhood would reduce juvenile delinquency. So many variables are involved in a single study like that that it is not easy to determine which were crucial. But there was theory behind the study, and the experimental design provided for controlling at least some variables.

It may be that in sociology we will need much more thinking and many more descriptive studies involving random ratlike movements on the part of the researcher before we can even begin to state our problems so that they are in decent shape for fitting into an ideal design. However, I think that we can reduce to some extent the waste motion of the exploratory period if we try to act as if we have some a priori ideas and keep our eyes on the possible relevance of data to these ideas. This is easier said than done. So many interesting rabbit tracks are likely to be uncovered in the exploratory stages of research that one is tempted to chase rabbits all over the woods and forget what his initial quarry was.

Exploratory research is of necessity fumbling, but I think that the waste motion can be reduced by the self-denying ordinance of deliberately limiting ourselves to a few variables at a time. Recently two of my colleagues and myself have been doing a little exploratory work on a problem in the general area of social mobility. We started by tabulating some school records of fifty boys in the ninth grade of one junior high school and then having members of our seminar conduct three or four interviews with each boy and his parents. We had all the interviews written up in detail, and we had enough data to fill a book—with rather interesting reading, too. But it was a very wasteful process because there were just too many intriguing ideas. We took a couple of ideas which were deducible from current general theory and tried to make some simple fourfold tables. It was obvious that, with a dozen variables uncontrolled, such tables meant little or nothing. But that led us to a second step. Now we are trying to collect school records and a short questionnaire on two thousand boys. We will not interview all these boys and their parents in detail. But, with two thousand cases to start with, we hope to take a variable in which we are interested and find fifty boys who are plus on it and fifty who are minus, yet who are approximately alike on a lot of other things. A table based on such matched comparisons should be relatively unambigous. We can take off from there and interview those selected cases intensively to push further our exploration of the nexus between theory and observation. This, we think, will be economical, though still exploratory. Experimental manipulation is far in the future in our problem, but we do hope we can conclude the first stage with a statement of some hypotheses susceptible to experimental verification.

I am not in the least deprecating exploratory work. But I do think that some orderliness is indicated even in the bright dawn of a youthful enterprise.

One reason why we are not more orderly in our exploratory work is that all too often what is missing is a sharp definition of a given variable, such that, if we wanted to take a number of cases and even throw them into a simple fourfold table, we could.

Suppose we are studying a problem in which one of the variables we are looking for is over-protection or overindulgence of a child by his mother. We have a number of case histories or questionnaires. Now how do we know whether we are sorting them according to this variable or not? The first step, it would seem, is to have some way of knowing whether we are sorting them along any single continuum, applying the same criteria to each case. But to know this we need to have built into the study the ingredients of a scale. Unless we have some such ingredients in our data, we are defeated from the start. This is why I think the new interest social scientists are taking in scaling techniques is so crucially important to progress. In particular, the latent-structure theory developed by Paul F. Lazarsfeld, which derives Louis Guttman's scale as an important special case, is likely to be exceedingly useful, for it offers criteria by which we can make a small amount of information go a long way in telling us the logical structure of a supposed variable we are eager to identify. The details of Guttman's and Lazarsfeld's work[2] are likely to promote a good deal of attack and controversy. Our hope is that this will stimulate others to think such problems out still better and thus make their work obsolete as rapidly as possible.

Trying to conduct a social science investigation without good criteria for knowing whether a particular variable may be treated as a single dimension is like trying to fly without a motor in the plane. Students of the history of invention point out that one reason why the airplane, whose properties had been pretty well thought out by Leonardo da Vinci, was so late in development was the unavailability of a light-weight power plant, which had to await the invention of the internal combustion motor. We are learning more and more how to make our light-weight motors in social science, and that augurs well for the future. But much work is ahead of us. In particular, we desperately need better projective techniques and better ways of getting respondents to reveal attitudes which are too emotionally charged to be accessible to direct questioning. Schemes like the latent-structure theory of Lazarsfeld should speed up the process of developing such tests.

I have tried to set forth the model of the controlled experiment as an ideal to keep in the forefront of our minds even when by necessity some cells are missing from our design. I have also tried to suggest that more economy and orderliness are made possible, even in designing the exploratory stages of a piece of research—by using theory in advance to help us decide whether a particular inquiry would be important if we made it; by narrowing down the number of variables; and by making sure that we can classsify our data along a particular continuum, even if only provisionally. And a central, brooding hope is that we will have the modesty to recognize the difference between a promising idea and proof.

Oh, how we need that modesty! The public expects us to deal with great problems like international peace, full employment, maximization of industrial efficiency. As pundits we can pronounce on such matters; as citizens we have a duty to be concerned with them; but as social scientists our greatest achievement now will be to provide a few small dramatic examples that hypotheses in our field can be stated operationally and tested crucially. And we will not accomplish that by spending most of our time writing or reading papers like this one. We will accomplish it best by rolling up our sleeves and working at the intricacies of design of studies which, though scientifically strategic, seem to laymen trivial compared with the global concerns of the atomic age. Thereby, and only thereby, I believe, can we some day have the thrilling sense of having contributed to the structure of a social science which is cumulative.

FOOTNOTES

[1] Carl I. Hovland, Arthur A. Lumsdaine, and Fred D. Sheffield, *Experiments in Mass Communication* (Princeton: Princeton University Press, 1949).

[2] Samuel A. Stouffer, Louis Guttman, Edward A. Suchman, Paul F. Lazarsfeld, Shirley A. Star, and John A. Clausen, *Measurement and Prediction* (Princeton: Princeton University Press, 1949).

III

CONCEPTUAL APPROACHES

The need for theory building in librarianship is so compelling as to warrant a separate section dealing with and giving concrete examples of conceptualization. James Thompson describes the advantages and ingredients of theory in a comparable field—administration. Richard Snyder's decision-making approach is an example of a broad theoretical scheme. Coming closer to librarianship are the selections by Ennis and Paisley, concerned with conceptualizing the study of information need and use, while Taylor, in constructing a framework for study of reference activity, strikes to the core of librarianship.

Two avenues of theoretical development are possible: borrowing or adapting conceptual models from other disciplines, and deriving of theory unique to the discipline of librarianship. A number of studies have exploited the first approach and several library research reports listed in the appendix fit within the theoretical setting of one or another of the social sciences. Theoretical construction, unique to librarianship, is exceedingly limited. Perhaps many library problems need not be studied apart from a larger social discipline. Thompson's observations are particularly relevant to this point. Yet, there is no reason, other than perhaps capacity or sophistication in conceptualizing, why library research could not contribute to the broader theoretical development of the behavioral sciences. When there is no theory to support the design or the assumptions of his study, the library scholar can himself work this out. No matter what the level of abstraction, with such a conceptual base he is then obligated to undertake the most sophisticated explanation of his findings of which he is capable.

To provide a setting for identifying research areas with students, the editors have employed the following very broad framework. The library is viewed as one institution in interaction with its environment, and its key relationships have been identified. Relationships exist with control and support groups—such as library boards and city governments. Potential or actual relationships with community groups or "interests" are also an element. It is these which may act to influence formal legislative or governmental decision-making or public opinion about a library. The continuum of groups is very broad. In the public setting, for example, they range from the Friends of the Library to the John Birch Society to parents' organizations and regional planning councils. How community power is wielded, by whom, and in what ways is a determinant of the patterns of influence bearing upon library issues.

The second key relationship is with the clients or potential clients of library services. As with its political relationships, the analyses of libraries in their service role can usefully employ the concept of interest groups or elements. External groups beyond the immediate community also act upon and influence the library and its functioning as well. Professional organizations, educational programs in the field, publishers and suppliers, competitive information services and institutions, all directly or indirectly influence the library's capability and its performance. The key internal relationship is within the working group. And it may be conceived in a variety of ways including, for example, in terms of small group behavior, authority relationships and other ways of perceiving bureaucracy.

The synthesizing notion is that to understand how libraries function, one must first understand the internal and external forces which influence behavior regarding libraries. And this brings into play the research strategies and insights of political science, organization theory, social psychology, sociology and other sub-disciplines. Insight and understanding, stemming from such research exploration, permit librarianship to take a positive stance. By putting the library in a behavioral context, less focused upon technical or procedural issues, not only are many new avenues open to fresh analysis, but policy choices for librarianship will ultimately be more securely rooted in knowledge based upon evidence.

Modern Approaches to Theory in Administration

by James D. Thompson

This author speaks of administration, but might as well be talking of libraries and librarianship. For, he sees the dependence of practice upon a theoretical structure which explains why and how practice is as it is. Librarianship has much to learn from those fields of study which have outdistanced it in their evolution. Essentially, Thompson reconstructs points already made by other writers in this volume, but by translating them into a disciplinary context (in this case, administration) he perceives precisely how a field advances through scholarship and research from descriptive lore on further to conceptual insight. This selection identifies the fact that in the exploitation of models from other disciplines, an applied field can be enlarged and further its own conceptual base. Here in essence is the rationale for the choice and inclusion of many of the selections of the present volume. Thompson's reasoning about the dysfunctions of a field's research agenda and priorities arising solely out of the concerns of the practitioner are as cogent for librarianship as they are for administration–perhaps more so. For the embryo library scholar there is a lifetime of challenge in Thompson's closing remark, "Eventually we may lead practice rather than follow it and in time may contribute significantly to the behavioral sciences."

Gradually we in our culture are coming to understand that distinctions between theory and practice are artificial distinctions. Men of action as well as scholars entertain notions of cause-and-effect relations–notions which are generalized out of series of specific events and which are employed in new and similar situations. Some of these theories –these notions of cause and effect–may be generated from the personal experiences and insights of the actor, but many are incorporated in what his particular culture and generation consider common sense.

The common-sense basis of our theories does not make them less theoretical, but it may well make them less useful than we would hope. It seems characteristic of common sense that it does not make explicit the conditions under which the relationships it asserts actually hold. When these unknown conditions change, common sense becomes a misleading guide to further action.[1]

In setting about to train students for administration, we assume that there exists generalized or generalizable knowledge about administration which can be imparted. There is the further assumption that common sense does not contain all of that knowledge; otherwise, the student would be wasting his time. Thus theory is a basic aspect

of our training programs, even while the courses labeled "theory" occupy minor roles in our curricula.

Theory per se faces an uphill battle in programs which train future administrators. The situation is different, of course, where future scientists are being trained; here theory is recognized as the core of training. This distinction, I think, reflects the fact that administrators and scientists use theory in opposite ways. The administrator uses theory as a basis for deriving answers or approaches to specific situations; he seeks principles capable of guiding the application of general notions to specific situations.[2] The scientist uses specific situations as a basis for arriving at improved theory. Hence, the same specific situation may have quite a different meaning to the scientist and to the administrator, and it may call forth quite different motivations.

These differing uses for theory do not mean, however, that the theory which the scientist seeks to build and that which the administrator seeks to use must be different theories. Indeed, unless they are basically the same, the accumulated knowledge contained in basic theory must be rediscovered by the administrator–and he lacks both the time and the training to do so. In the more mature fields of

SOURCE: Reprinted from James D. Thompson, "Modern Approaches to Theory in Administration," *Administrative Theory in Education,* ed. Andrew W. Halpin (Chicago: The Midwest Administration Center, University of Chicago, 1958), Chap. 2, pp. 20–39, by permission of the publisher.

applied science, advances have come precisely because teachers and practitioners have learned to employ the systematic theories developed by rigorous science.

We who staff professional training programs have dual needs for theory. We are obligated to equip our students with the best available theory as a guide to their practice. We also need theory to guide our search for better understanding. At this stage in our development these needs are equally pressing.

On the assumption that an adequate theory would serve both purposes, I will attempt to discuss modern approaches to theory in administration from both viewpoints. I will not attempt to judge specific formulations or "models." If these meet the test of internal logic, I know of no other test than that of empirical trial. My remarks will be on a more general level, for it seems reasonable to ask: (1) What do we hope to achieve through the use of theory? (2) What are the sources of traditional theory? (3) What are the criteria for administrative theory? (4) Are we approaching an adequate theory?

WHAT DO WE HOPE TO ACHIEVE THROUGH THEORY?

Much has been written about the uses of theory in research, less about the potential contributions of theory to the training of future administrators. In my opinion, an adequate theory of administration would go a long way toward preparing students for change. It would condition them to think of the administrative process as a complex of simultaneously variable factors rather than as a set of specific techniques. We cannot expect techniques of administration for 1977 to have much resemblance to those current today. Nor can we predict, with any degree of confidence, the nature of the techniques which will be available and current in 1977. An adequate theory would equip the future administrator to alter the values of those variables subject to his control as other variables beyond his control change in value. Rather than describing currently accepted practices, an adequate theory would explain *why* such practices work and why they might not work, if and when the surrounding context changes.

Perhaps this point can be illustrated by two examples of changing concepts of authority. "Good supervision" of the 1920 variety in America was rooted in a firm paternalism in which fear-inspired discipline had a large role. The same

supervisory behavior today is "bad supervision."[3] Why? In part, I think, because the individuals being supervised have more education, are better organized, and place higher value on human dignity.

The military provides another example of changing patterns of authority. Our Air Force grew out of an army where rank and authority were intricately connected. The traditional basis of military authority was appropriate under conditions where work was repetitive and easily divided. Individuals were practically interchangeable, and the supervisor was the one who could do everything other members of his unit did—but could do it all a little better. Each rank was occupied by people who had become experts in the activities they supervised; the various echelons differed primarily in the *scope* of their concern rather than in the *kinds* of work done. The modern Air Force, however, has very complicated equipment and missions, and it employs quite complex processes carried on by a great variety of technical specialists. In such units the supervisor can no longer be an expert in more than one or two specialized processes. Despite assignment rotations, then, it is no longer possible to assume that "any" captain is necessarily competent to exercise authority over "any" corporal. Here, I think, technology is the primary variable undermining what was once an accepted view of authority. Air Force administrators have certainly felt the impact of the changes.

A second advantage which an adequate theory of administration might offer is a system of thinking which would allow the administrator to incorporate knowledge produced by the several disciplines. Even if we could provide the administrator with the most up-to-date knowledge from all related disciplines, this would be woefully out of date long before he left active administration. We do our students a disservice if we lead them to believe that today's psychology, sociology, history, economics, or political science provides him with irrefutable facts. I mentioned above one probable reason for the change in supervisory standards; a second reason, I am confident, is that new knowledge about human motivation challenged older notions about behavior based on fear.

Somehow, in the future, our students must be alerted to the results of new discoveries and interpretations. But it is not enough to bombard them with leaflets or to call them back for "refresher" sessions. We must equip them to trace through the implications and ramifications of forthcoming knowledge about human beings and behavioral processes; we must equip them to alter their own behavior accordingly.

We are learning, for example, new things about the triad and its instability, and game theory predicts that under certain conditions triads resort to coalition behavior. As these lines of inquiry develop, the administrator must see them as more than merely "interesting" new findings. He needs a *systematic* way of thinking which will lead him to re-examine his use of competition and his methods of allocating rewards and resources among groups in his organization.

An adequate theory would also prepare students for further growth through their own later experiences by providing them with economical ways of ordering that experience. By emphasizing the interrelatedness of phenomena, such a theory would help them remain alert to the unanticipated consequences of their actions; it would help them avoid oversimplified explanations of those actions which were successful; and it would caution them to be aware of changing conditions which might call for changed behavior patterns.

If administrators are to profit from their experiences, they must have systems for ordering and generalizing specific events. The more explicit and rigorous the system for ordering experience, the greater the facility in learning.

In short, an adequate theory would direct the student's attention to processes and relationships rather than to techniques. It would provide him with a framework into which he could place both the future findings of the social sciences and his own experiences in administration.

WHAT ARE THE SOURCES OF TRADITIONAL THEORY?

There appear to be four primary sources of theory for administration: the comments and reports made by practicing administrators, the survey research of teachers, the deductive reasoning of teachers, and the adaptation of models from other disciplines. These are listed in the order in which they have appeared on the scene. The first two are long established and traditional; the last two reflect newer developments. Because my assignment is to discuss "modern approaches to theory in administration," I would like to comment first on the more traditional sources of theory—to establish some sort of base line for comparing, afterward, the more recent developments.

I have suggested that every administrator uses more or less rigorous theory in meeting specific situations. These theories become of importance to educators only when they are verbalized and, eventually, written—when they can be passed on to others. Perhaps this stating of theory is not central to the role of the administrator, but I think it is evident that much of the reading we now assign to students (and much of our lecturing) is based upon statements of theory made by practicing administrators.

We have a vast machinery for encouraging, facilitating, and disseminating such statements. We hold conferences and training institutes where administrators generalize from their experience. Our trade and professional magazines and journals vie in presenting the views of distinguished administrators; publishers compete for text manuscripts written (or ghosted) by men who "really know" because they do it every day.

These people undoubtedly have much to tell us; we have much to learn from them. Yet they are not necessarily adept at verbalizing their own behavior for purposes of systematic theory. It is not uncommon to find a real discrepancy between what they do and what they tell us they do. On many occasions, I am convinced, our students would do better to "do as they do, not as they say."

We are perhaps handicapped in the behavioral studies, as compared with the biological and physical, by the fact that the things we study—people—are "verbal." The atom and the virus cannot talk, and those who study the behavior of atoms and viruses are forced to learn about that behavior through observation by the investigator. We tend to be content to let the administrator tell us how he behaves, and we are lulled into believing that he has perceived and articulated accurately.[4] In effect, we rely on him to be not only his own philosopher but also his own psychologist, sociologist, anthropologist, historian, political scientist, and economist. The day has long passed when even a full-time scholar can master more than one or two of these disciplines.

This is not to deny that men of action have useful insights. To the contrary, their ingenuity and creativity often would put the academician to shame. I am suggesting, however, that the really creative insights of these people seldom are incorporated into our recorded theory because: (1) They lack the time to record and develop such insights.[5] (2) They tend to force their theoretical thinking into the concepts we have taught them and which we constantly reinforce in our writings and speeches. Our teachings act as blinders. (3) The platforms we afford them are not conducive to reflective critical thought, but rather to the use of journalistic or visual-aid "gimmicks"—three well-illustrated points, seven rules to success, or simple diagrams understandable at the flicker of an eye.

I suspect that in the early development of the various areas of professional training the voice of the practitioner quickly becomes the "voice of authority." Nevertheless, there also develops a pattern of research by faculty members who find it necessary to supplement the pronouncements of practitioners or to systematize their various pronouncements. We now have an extensive literature of the results of such research. With a few notable exceptions, it has been of the descriptive, survey variety. When our teaching materials have lacked details or have appeared out of date, we have interviewed practitioners or have given them questionnaires. From their replies we have developed "modal models"—models which are based on the most common way of handling administrative problems. Our journals and magazines of administration are filled with reports of this type of research.

On occasion we also do "scholarly" research in the libraries. Here we survey, collate, and compare the terminology of the distinguished writers on administration, reducing these materials to their common denominators in order to extract the essentials, or we develop an expanded list of categories which is "all inclusive," or we reorganize the list of categories into memorable slogans such as POSD-CORB. Incidentally, this can be great fun. I have always found POSDCORB easy to remember but hard to pronounce, and I would like to suggest my own arrangement, which contains all of the letters but is easier said: P-S-C-O-B-O-R-D, pronounced with the *P* silent.

I repeat, this can be fun; but where does it get us? Whether we have relied on the visiting dignitary or on our own survey efforts, we have seldom produced new knowledge. Rather, we seem to have periodically produced new packages for the same old product. Any honest appraisal of the theoretical literature of administration will reveal the vast bulk of it is of this "grass roots" variety—a mixture of common sense, descriptive categories one (and only one) step removed from common sense, and slogans and catch phrases which have dramatic appeal but little else.

Within our lifetimes there have been tremendous changes in administrative behavior. Presumably

the fundamental process has been constant, but there is no denying that the behavior through which that process operates has changed considerably. Many administrators have responded to new situations, new conditions, and new opportunities by adjusting or adapting their behavior. These responses have not always been consistent or successful, but could we expect otherwise when administrators are forced to rely on hunch and ingenuity, trial and error? These are expensive tools.

The economy of theory has been missing because we have tended to build grass roots theories which "explain" what has been done; we have not examined the outcomes of all possible permutations and combinations of variables and have not generalized the relationships into systematic theories. Our grass roots theories have described the past, but they have not faced the future. In contrast, the abstract theories of physics have had profound effects on human life; they have done more than merely reflect an aspect of reality.

Probably the most damaging criticism that can be made of any theory is that it does not generate new knowledge; I have indicated my belief that this criticism applies to traditional theories of administration. Why? A major reason, I feel, is that we have focused on descriptive categories as pigeon holes for data (for pedagogical neatness), but we have neglected the dynamic relationships among these categories. We have provided, in effect, for electric light sockets and for wall switches, but we have failed to provide the wiring which relates them, and we remain in the dark.

Typically, I think, when we decide to do research, we set aside our verbalized theories of administration and draw on common sense as the source of our research problems. More often than not, it is the common sense of practicing administrators; hence, we do research on the topics which they label as most urgent.

When industrial administrators are vexed by the changing role of foremen, we get a rash of research on this topic; and when these same administrators begin to puzzle over resistance to change, we flood the market with research and theories designed to overcome resistance to change. When the competition for skilled personnel increases employee turnover rates, we shift our research attention to matters of inducements and loyalties. We usually approach these "urgent" topics with the variables stated by the practitioner, hoping that by more careful collection of data and more minute analysis we will find answers for him. In short, I think that we only infrequently undertake research because our theories say a topic is important.

But do our grass roots theories point to strategic topics? Do they in themselves raise new questions to be answered? Do they suggest that since such-and-such relationship holds, we should also be able to find X—or be forced to revise the theory? I think not. Our traditional theories lack this self-correcting feature because they are weak in stating relationships.

My remarks have, of course, been exaggerated. To some extent our theories of administration do pose relationships, at least implicitly. Our theories indicate, for example, that "planning" or "communication" have a positive relationship with performance. Yet, a reading of such theoretical discussions usually leaves the strong impression that the relationship is linear—that twice as much planning (or communication) will double performance —and, of course, we know from experience that this is not necessarily true.

The poverty of our thinking about relationships is indicated by the fact that often we can explain the outcomes of administrative behavior only by value-loaded adjectives—that more or better communication was present, that organization was inadequate, or that planning was democratic. These "principles by adjective" are no better than rules of thumb.

A second serious indictment of our grass roots theories is that they do not facilitate the accumulation and incorporation of new knowledge. As forces from without have changed administrative behavior, have our theories been generalized and expanded to incorporate these new phenomena? Usually, we have added new courses and kept our "theory" or "principles" course intact, with the result that we now offer our students a variety of part-theories but no theory. We have added courses in human relations, operations research, group dynamics, organization and methods, and so on. Our students find a wide assortment in our curriculum cafeteria, but they get no guide to a balanced diet.

A third weakness of our grass roots theories is that they tend to be special theories of administration rather than general theories. By using the language and concepts of practitioners and by trying to see through their spectacles, we have developed theories of business administration, military administration, educational administration, hospital administration, and public administration. As Litchfield has noted:

The most serious indictment which must be made of present thought is that it has failed to achieve a level of generalization enabling it to systematize and explain administrative phenomena which occur in related fields . . . . We seem to be saying that there is business administration and hospital administration and public administration; that there is military administration, hotel administration, and school administration. But there is no administration.[6]

Of course there are differences between school systems and industrial organizations, and these differences lead to variations in administrative behavior. But there are similarities of administration which we do not observe when we use grass roots frameworks. Each of these areas has its special concerns, its pressing problems, and its distinctive jargon. When we try to approach administration as the practitioner of a particular area approaches it, we focus on the unique or distinctive, and we join him in taking for granted the underlying bases of administration which are not unique.

WHAT ARE THE CRITERIA FOR ADMINISTRATIVE THEORY?

I have tried to suggest some of the advantages to be expected of an adequate theory and some of the weaknesses of traditional approaches to theory in administration. Now I will climb further out on the limb and suggest at least a minimum set of criteria for a really usable theory. These are predictions of the characteristics an adequate theory will display when we have it.

The variables and constants for such a theory will be selected for their logical and operational properties rather than for their congruence with common sense. Common-sense terms and concepts gain currency because they are convenient for dealing with frequent events which must be acted upon. To the extent that such terms and concepts are also useful for systematic theory, it would be wasteful to discard them. But where common-sense terms lack precision or clarity, or where common-sense concepts do not order experience in the ways required by systematic theory, then new terms must be invented or adopted. Chemistry did not really begin until it stopped regarding fire, water, earth, and air as the four basic elements. These were "obvious" and "real"; hence, it was common sense to work with them. But what kind of chemistry would we have today if those concepts had not been set aside?

Perhaps I can give an example a little closer to our field. One frequent distinction between "line" and "staff" in complex organizations is that the "line" gives orders while the "staff" gives advice. Now we all know the difference between orders and advice. Or do we? When a staff assistant to my boss indicates that I am doing something inefficiently, have I received advice or an order? In many cases, I am convinced, advice has been given (or intended), but orders have been received (or perceived). The line-staff distinction is common sense to a great many administrators, but, in my opinion, it has seriously interfered with the development of administrative theory.

The selection of variables for logical and operational properties rather than for common-sense properties means that we will face charges of uttering meaningless jargon, but I believe this is an occupational hazard for those seeking new and more useful ways of looking at the world. If we cannot develop thick skins, I doubt if we can develop more useful theory.

An adequate theory will be generalizable, hence abstract. The broader the range of specific events it explains, the more powerful the theory. To regard educational administration as unique is to deny prematurely the relevance of that which is known about business administration, or military, or church administration. The inescapable conclusion in that case would be that the entire task of building a theory of educational administration falls entirely to a pitifully small number of individuals. The only hope, I think, is to approach educational administration as a variety of administration and to incorporate into the theory a variable which will encompass first one, then another, such purpose or task. If relevant knowledge from other types of administration is to be applied to education, then educational administration must be considered as only one special case. Similarly, public school administration, military training education, religious education, adult education, and so on must be considered special cases of education, and a theory adequate for educational administration must be able to encompass them all.

Another reason for abstraction is that an adequate theory of administration cannot be limited by time or place. We cannot afford to be content with a theory of educational administration for America and another for Indonesia, or with a theory of education administration for America in 1950 and another for 1970. The theory should enable us to deal with different times and places, but again as variables and not as limits to the theory.

The values capable of being attached to education and to administration will not be incorporated into the theoretical system itself; instead, the system will treat such values as variables. The values of "democracy" undoubtedly color both education and administration in twentieth-century America. But if we sincerely want to understand educational (or any other type of) administration, we must not attempt to build a theory of democratic administration into education. Instead, our theory must account for administrative behavior and processes in cases where democracy is highly valued *and* where other political ideals are highly valued. Similarly, we cannot afford a separate theory of profit-oriented administration, although our general theory must be capable of explaining administration where profit is an important concern. Values must be treated as variables, for purposes of theory, rather than as limits to the theory.

An adequate theory of administration will be rooted in the basic social and behavioral sciences. Administration is accomplished through the behavior of administrators in interaction with others. Hence, basic understanding of human behavior must be included in our theory of administration. We cannot hope to start from scratch and develop a psychology of administration, a political science of administration, or an economics or sociology of administration. Yet the subject matters of all of those fields have manifestations in administration. Psychology deals, for example, with motivation, learning, and decision processes, all of which are important in administration. The political scientist's understanding of federalism or of bilateral negotiations, for instance, is pertinent to administration. The administrator in any field has problems of resource allocation and opportunity costs; these are intensively studied by the economist. The sociologist's considerations of bureaucracy and small group processes also are clearly pertinent.

To the extent that such disciplines do not focus on behavioral processes in *administrative* situations, we face the task of extending them. But unless we build on the foundations being laid so painfully by these disciplines we face a hopeless task.

The focus of an adequate theory will be on processes rather than on correlations. Admittedly a theory is valuable only if it simplifies. Still there are limits beyond which simplification is misleading. It seems to me that administration as a self-conscious, definable activity occurs only when the activities to be administered are themselves highly complicated; and, therefore, the behavior which contributes to administration involves chain-like reactions more often than simple cause-and-effect relationships. It helps to know that A leads to B, but if the reality of administration is complex, our theory must eventually not only show that A is associated with H but also show the relations between B, C, and so on to H. In other words, it is not enough to show that a particular pattern is correlated with performance; we must eventually be able to explain how the relationship occurs.

This means, I believe, that we cannot be content with structural concepts—which tell us "what." We must also have "how" concepts.[7] The structural concept "role," for example, gives us guide lines regarding the future behavior of a supervisor, but it does not explain how members of the work group gain understanding of the supervisor's role or how various roles articulate and operate within the work group or how roles change. Structural concepts seem to be indispensible but are not sufficient for a really useful theory.

ARE WE APPROACHING AN ADEQUATE THEORY?

A decade is a short time for which to reckon the development of a body of knowledge; for the immediately preceding decade we do not have sufficient perspective in time to make a firm evaluation of what has been accomplished. Yet I believe that since World War II we have witnessed developments which will turn out to be especially significant. I will have been greatly mistaken if this flurry of activity in theories of administration becomes merely a passing fad.[8]

The war probably had much to do with this increased interest in administration. Thousands of men and women with administrative experience discovered that at least some of it was applicable in new and quite different kinds of organizations, even as they discovered that their administrative behavior also had to be adapted in some respects. War, as any crisis, placed a new urgency on problems and questions which had only occasionally crossed our minds in more "normal" times. The more mature students who returned to our campuses following the war had experienced this urgency. They were less ready to accept clichés and slogans and were often more eager to disregard traditional boundaries between bodies of knowledge. Their questions challenged complacency, stimulated multi-disciplinary study, and on occasion underscored the need for research.

Whatever the sources, research and theoretical activities increased after World War II in most of the fields of professional administrative training: business, public, educational, social work, hospital, and so on. In each of these fields, more honest-to-goodness field research is going on than ever before, and still more is demanded. New blood in the form of new disciplinary backgrounds has been injected into these fields to the point where we can no longer identify a man's training by his title or his location in the university. Admittedly, interdisciplinary collaboration is difficult, and frequently its results are disappointing. Yet in the overview, I think, the signs are clear that hypotheses are being borrowed back and forth among schools which formerly were isolated. Generalizations and concepts generated by one school turn up a year later in another. Sometimes they are embraced, or they may be bitterly challenged, but they cross boundaries more frequently.

An adequate theory has not yet come out of all this, but there have been several promising starts. The sources of these modern developments, as indicated above, have been two: the deductive reasoning of scholars and the adaptation of models from other disciplines. I doubt that it is possible to identify theories which have been derived exclusively from only one of these sources, but we can identify examples characterized by the predominance of one or the other of these approaches.

There have been a number of deductive approaches to theory—attempts to postulate a few general ideas which for one reason or another appear to be "true," or "plausible" and important, and to arrive by logical steps at more specific propositions. Two approaches of this kind have influenced a great many of us; I refer to the formulations by Chester I. Barnard and Herbert A. Simon. Both men produced books which are as instructive on the second or third reading as on the first, and both have had an influence that extends far beyond the recognized boundaries of administration as a subject.[9] Students usually find these books difficult to read, perhaps because the authors' ideas are more sophisticated and their terms more precise than those we encounter in common-sense language and in textbooks on administration, but readers who exert the necessary effort invariably find these writings extremely challenging.

Also, in the last decade several attempts have been made to formulate administrative theory on the basis of models derived from a number of different sources: learning models, decision-making models, group dynamics models, leadership models, social system models, game models, and so on. Some of these have been more deeply rooted in empirical observation than others; each has

started from unique premises. The very proliferation of these models suggests that we are dis-
satisfied with traditional approaches and are
motivated to do something about them. Probably
all these models contain some "truth," although
my impression is that they are helpful primarily in
broadening the scope of our inquiry. Two examples may be briefly noted. Parsons' approach via
social system concepts has pointed to the importance of the organization acquiring "legiti-
mization."[10] I think this calls for an expansion of
our concept of authority beyond the boundaries of
the organization. Game theory, by explicitly calling our attention to the interaction conditions
between two or more "organizations" seeking the
same or competing goals, forces us to recognize the
importance of strategies for dealing with outside
forces.

None of these approaches in its present formulation is adequate. Perhaps none can be expanded
into an adequate formulation. Yet despite their
differences, most of them reveal similar underlying
themes, and this convergence is encouraging. One
of these common themes is the serious consideration of definitions and of making them operational. There is nothing magic in definitions, and
we could bog down in them. On the other hand,
when we seek new concepts to be used in logical
systems, those concepts must be given labels and
precise descriptions. There is much confusion in
our current literature over definitions; "role,"
"status," and "authority," for example, are three
terms for which there are conflicting definitions
and which therefore confront us with conflicts
about how data should be classified. But perhaps
confusion is inescapable in moving from an old
way of ordering ideas to a new way. At least, I
think, the concern over precision and operational-
ism reflects a search for something more powerful
than common-sense concepts.

A second common theme in these modern approaches is that they are *explicitly* relational regarding human behavior. Whether they draw on
deductive reasoning or stem from the more empirically based models of the behavioral sciences,
these approaches attempt to predict human behavior under stated conditions. Sometimes we
complain that the conditions stated are not very
lifelike—but it seems to me that we need to observe behavior under all conceivable conditions.
The predictions made by the several models may
turn out to be incorrect, but if these predictions
are explicit enough to be matched against actual
human behavior, then the models can be revised
accordingly.

Moreover, the predictions contained in the
several models are based upon recognition of the
fact that human behavior flows out of persons in
situations. Some models, as opposed to others,
elaborate more on the person and less on the situation. There is a great unevenness here, and each
model analyzes its major variables in different
ways. One may posit "rational man" and try to
determine how the situation interferes with his
rationality. Another may posit "robot man" and
try to explain how environment prevents his automatic responses. A third may seek group uniformities irrespective of personal idiosyncrasies,
thus placing emphasis on the individual's social
environment. This is another way of saying that
each model tends to be based primarily on one
discipline and to include others in subordinate
ways. Here again there is confusion and very little
uniformity. Nevertheless, I believe that this confusion reflects a searching for ways of incorporat-
ing the various disciplines; competing suggestions
at this point can protect us from complacency.

A third common theme is that all of these
models are or attempt to be generalizable. They
differ in degree of abstractness, but they are hypothesized as potentially capable of explaining
administrative behavior in a great variety of specific situations and in the several types of administration. Whether the models stress learning, decisions, leadership, group dynamics, games, or
something else, they are dealing with phenomena
which are not confined to one or two levels in a
hierarchical organization; and they are not confined to phenomena unique to the school system,
the hospital, or the business firm.

A fourth common theme is the attempt to free
these models from culturally defined values, while
permitting us to use values as data. The models
do not tell us how to be "democratic" administrators or how to be "economically-rational" administrators so much as they predict how administrators will behave if they happen to be committed
to one or another of these values. My personal
belief is that our models are remiss in not explaining how such values enter the administrative
system, but this is correctable by extension, provided that values are used as variables in the
models rather than as assumptions upon which the
models themselves are predicated.

Thus on four of the five suggested criteria, I
think, modern approaches appear to be progres-
sing. On the fifth—the explanation of long chain-
like processes—there is less encouraging evidence.
We still are fumbling for process concepts, and
our models are better at dealing with relations be-

tween two variables—with perhaps one intervening variable—than with long sequences. Probably this is largely because these models tend to emphasize a few aspects of administration or behavior in selected types of administrative situations. But it is in the long sequences that complicated "switching" takes place and that outcomes of administrative activities are determined. My personal belief, also, is that we tend to stress internal relations and structures to the point where we fail to see the significance of external relations or the interaction between internal and external activities. There, perhaps, is where we will find the source of the values held by administrators and the impetus for administrative change.

In brief, modern approaches to theory in administration appear to me to be developing more promising concepts of variables which can be defined operationally; they are seeking generalizability and freedom from value-limitations; they are focusing on the sources and the consequences of human behavior. The ultimate criterion of a scientific theory, of course, is its utility in adding to our understanding. Few of these models can yet claim to have made much of a contribution in this respect, but I think there is reason to believe that they are laying the foundation for an adequate theory.

SUMMARY

I believe we are seeing in schools of education, business, public administration, hospital administration, and social work the growing pains and confusion that attend moving from infancy through adolescence. The more mature (but I trust not senile) professional schools—medicine, law, engineering—probably exhibited the same sorts of bewilderment and fumbling at an earlier stage in their development.

Professional schools, however much nurtured and protected by the university, are sired by a clientele of practitioners. They are elaborations of an apprenticeship system and are close to the grass roots.[11] Their first faculties are chosen for demonstrated success and reputation in the professional field regardless of the usual trappings of academic qualifications. Despite their popularity with students and practitioners, however, these people are considered by the rest of the university community as poor relations. They are forced to defend themselves against charges that they are operating trade schools. Under pressure to attain recognized status as a profession and to achieve academic respectability, they therefore raise the academic standards for faculty members. Gradually this encourages them to think that there are other useful approaches to their subject and reduces their subservience to their immediate clientele. Eventually, at least in the cases of medicine and engineering, the professional school incorporates into its own structure representatives of related basic disciplines and seeks to make fundamental contributions to knowledge.

In these terms, we in the fields of administration are not yet mature. But we are fighting back against the trade school charges; we are raising our standards for faculty members; we are considering more abstract materials and de-emphasizing techniques. We have even begun to incorporate into our faculties representatives from the social sciences, although we are not quite certain whether we want the facts they command, the research techniques they have mastered, or the theory in which they are disciplined.

Having presented my own "model" of professional school development, I will climb to the end of the limb and assert that we are on the way toward fashioning a bridge between the basic disciplines of human behavior and the field of administration, similar to those bridges which link medicine to the biological sciences and engineering to the physical sciences. Eventually our theories of administration may lead practice rather than follow it, and in time we may contribute significantly to the behavioral sciences.

FOOTNOTES

[1] For an interesting elaboration of this, see Bernard Barber, *Science and the Social Order* (Glencoe, Ill.: Free Press, 1952).

[2] This matter is thoughtfully treated by Harold Guetzkow, "Three Cognitive Barriers in Utilization of the Social Sciences," April, 1957 (privately circulated). See also Philip Selznick, *Leadership in Administration* (Evanston, Ill.: Row Peterson, 1957), and Alvin Gouldner, "Theoretical Requirements of the Applied Social Sciences," *American Sociological Review*, XXII (February, 1957), 92–102.

[3] American industry spent vast amounts retraining foremen to the newer concepts and replacing those on whom the training did not "take."

[4]Few of us would rely on the centenarian for a prescription on living to a ripe old age.

[5]Chester Barnard is a notable exception; he wrote while president of a large corporation.

[6]Edward H. Litchfield, "Notes on a General Theory of Administration," *Administrative Science Quarterly*, I (June, 1956), 7.

[7]This point is adapted from James D. Thompson, William J. McEwen, and Frederick L. Bates, "Sounding Out as a Relating Process" (paper read at the annual meeting of the Eastern Sociological Society), April, 1957.

[8]A recent survey of administrative courses in the field of business illustrates the "boom" in this area since 1945, as well as the newer emphasis on behavioral models. See Charles E. Sumner, Jr., *Factors in Effective Administration* (New York: Columbia University, Graduate School of Business, 1956).

[9]See Chester I. Barnard, *The Functions of the Executive* (Cambridge: Harvard University Press, 1938), and Herbert A. Simon, *Administrative Behavior* (New York: Macmillan, 1957). Many social psychologists studying small groups have derived their hypotheses from Barnard and Simon; many sociologists studying formal organizations have done likewise. Both writers are referred to frequently by political scientists.

[10]Talcott Parsons, "Suggestions for a Sociological Approach to the Theory of Organizations," *Administrative Science Quarterly*, I (1956), 63–85, 225–39.

[11]An interesting set of parallels among various aspects of professional school history and current problems is discussed by Lloyd E. Blauch (ed.) in *Education for the Professions* (Washington: Government Printing Office, 1955). The generalizations made in these closing paragraphs, however, are mine.

A Decision-Making Approach to the Study of Political Phenomena

by Richard C. Snyder

Here is a challenge to library research and to library researchers. For, it demonstrates how in another discipline one group of scholars broke out of the traditional mold and modes, saw the issues in fresh conceptual ways, and applied this view to scholarship. Snyder categorizes the limits of political science and demonstrates the utility of a decision-making orientation as potentially fruitful to both research and pedagogy. Tentative as is the conceptual design, it offers insight into the decision analysis mechanism, and so faces up more squarely to the issues of not only how, but why events transpire in organizations as they do. And here is a central analytic method for students of the policy sciences.

As a construct, the philosophical and theoretical propositions provided here offer a rich base for not only the prosecution of empirical effort in political science (which is this author's main concern) but in comparable fields like librarianship as well. It may serve equally well as guide to applied scholarship and to classroom analysis, and is prelude to the refinement and sharpening of hypotheses which may then be tested in the real world.

I shall omit the usual disclaimers concerning the tentativeness and crudeness of the focus for political analysis suggested in this paper. At this stage in the development of political science those who take a flying leap toward more ambitious targets are bound to leave portions of their intellectual anatomy exposed or awkwardly posed. Nor should it be necessary to deny any intention to argue that the decision-making approach is *the* white hope of a more systematic political science. I believe this approach has never been fully explored and I am convinced that its rigorous development will substantially aid the search for unifying concepts.

My own feeling—indeed it is one of the assumptions upon which my interest in decision-making rests—is that the major areas of future growth in political science will be: community political analysis (not· "local government" in the usual sense), the formulation and execution of public policy, the description and comparision of political systems on a high level of generalization, and the theory of complex administrative organizations. Even if we only agree that these are *some* of the directions of potential intellectual progress in our discipline, the question arises: What kinds of analytical tools and skills will be required? That the Northwestern experiment should lead ultimately to an inquiry into the nature of political science and to the quest for unifying concepts illustrates the depth and breadth of our needs provided one is courageous and skillful enough to face up to the $64 questions.

Any scheme of analysis ought to be evaluated according to two sets of criteria: first, its internal properties—assumptions, definitions, categories, logical consistency, operational qualities and so on; second, its possible contribution to the critical problems of the particular intellectual enterprise to which it is dedicated—in this case political science.

SOME MAJOR PROBLEMS OF CONTEMPORARY POLITICAL ANALYSIS

No blanket dismissal of the contributions of all of our contemporary colleagues and of the great works of the past is necessary to justify the assertion that there is currently manifest among many of us a mixed feeling of inadequacy and optimism. Whether we make real progress depends in part on how successful we are in identifying our basic difficulties. It would indeed be presumptuous of me to imply any glib grasp of these difficulties, but I

SOURCE: Reprinted from Richard C. Snyder, "A Decision-Making Approach to the Study of Political Phenomena," *Approaches to the Study of Politics*, ed. Roland Young (Evanston, Ill.: Northwestern University Press, 1958), pp. 3-38, and "Notes," pp. ix-xiii, by permission of the publisher.

should like to note several briefly, even at the risk of underestimating the reader.

1) *The Boundary Problem.* Using the term boundary somewhat loosely here, there appear to be at least three sources of confusion. First, when the question: what is political science? is raised, the troublesome line between political and non-political phenomena emerges and claims attention. With a very few exceptions,[1] those political scientists who write for their colleagues as well as for students have hardly clarified this problem, to say nothing of offering alternative solutions. Moreover, the different bases or criteria which might govern this division (a division only for purposes of analysis, of course) are rarely made explicit. Closely linked to the boundary between political science and, say, economics, is a second source of confusion: within any society how is the political realm to be distinguished? how is politics to be defined? Finally, within political science, there are boundary problems with respect to courses and subjects. This is not simply a matter of division of labor or different approaches in the usual sense.[2] Do all political science courses deal with the same kind of social phenomena having an agreed set of purposes in mind? Evidence suggests a negative answer.

2) *The Problem of Undergeneralization.* It would appear that a notable part of the complexity and confusion prevailing in the study of politics is due less to the phenomena than to shortcomings of observation and analysis. Some of our difficulty—particularly the "overwhelmingness" of the data—is artificial, and, hopefully, remediable. We have not paid enough attention to more inclusive categories and to the removal of untenable or trivial distinctions and dichotomies. One pathway toward economy (and this includes written words and class hours) and manageability is consciously and explicitly to analyze phenomena in terms of *common properties*. The heavy empiricism (healthy on many counts) which has historically characterized political science has tended to overemphasize the unique at the expense of the general. One of the unfortunate lacks—the more serious because of our interest in creating more convenient "handles" for political analysis—is simple, useful typologies.[3] Another way of stating this point is to say that political science has been partially imprisoned by a low level of generalization. One result has been to confuse the sheer number of data and variables with the relative complexity of possible analytical operations.

3) *The Problem of Interdisciplinary Synthesis.* It is unfortunate that there seems to be a greater amount of bad temper, ignorance, and intolerance on this matter than there is reliable knowledge and a willingness to experiment. However, my judgment here may be warped in view of my own personal experience, which has been rewarding indeed. Among others, I would cite two reasons for the apparently limited success of interdisciplinary collaboration so far. First, in the absence of a general framework of political analysis it is very difficult to select from the data and techniques of other disciplines those most appropriate and useful for our purposes. Most political scientists are not adequately trained as analysts of social behavior and thus further risks are added. Legitimate caution or indiscriminate sampling may interfere with the building of bridges between various branches of learning. Second, we have not been able for the most part to ask meaningful questions of our colleagues in social psychology or anthropology—questions which can be answered reliably in terms of their own intellectual operations. There has been a strong tendency to ask global questions which either cannot be operationalized sufficiently or cannot be given answers transferable to political science subjects as defined.

I suggest therefore that some of our trouble in cross-disciplinary communication and problem-solving is due to our relative lack of success in minimizing the disadvantages which flow from other weaknesses already noted: under-sized concepts, limited vocabulary, and low level of generalization. The recent Dahl-Lindblom volume shows clearly the productive results which can be attained when skill and thoroughness establish a common scheme for integrating two or more social sciences.[4]

Often the possible contributions of other specialists are not fully exploited because we reject the substantive knowledge as irrelevant and do not look into the usefulness of analytical techniques. Many of our colleagues in the other social sciences have been confronted—and not entirely defeated—by some of the same kind of tough problems of observation and explanation which confront us.

One further point: those who venture into other disciplines on foraging expeditions often come back with superficially attractive loot, in some cases exemplified by a shiny new vocabulary ripped from its theoretical context and disciplinary home. In the absence of an agreed and powerful vocabulary of political analysis this is tempting, but it also opens us to those valid and accurate charges of "jargon" which give comfort to those who employ the charge essentially as insulation against any re-examination of the intellectual foundations of their own work. I have heard some political scientists reject Parsons and Shils—which they have never read—on the basis of terms used carelessly by other political scientists who never really understood the underlying system of action analysis.[5]

Admittedly I have oversimplified the problems of interdisciplinary research, but I would argue strongly that we have fumbled these problems without fully comprehending the stakes involved or the causes of our failures. If we can push political analysis to a high level of generalization and if we are careful with out unifying concepts (including their vocabularies) we may at least clarify our difficulties. One test of unifying concepts ought to be: do they permit an intellectually responsible and scientifically respectable use of the contributions of other disciplines?

4) *The Problem of an Adequate Vocabulary.* I am sure that all of us would agree that in a broad sense the tools of our trade are words and combinations of words. For the most part, we must carry out our functions on a symbolic level. Perhaps this has led some of us to assume too easily that we could treat words as they are treated in daily life—as all-purpose items of exchange and as deliberately ambiguous communicative signs. Those who feel uneasy about this will usually go on to admit that the admonition: "define your terms" is a good starting point for discussion. Often at this point something unfortunate develops: namely, that definitions—*à la* Alice in Wonderland—are regarded as a kind of subjective game in which the one who deals controls all the rules. There are available tested rules of definition which any rigorous social analyst ought to try to employ. Sloppiness on this score has cost us dearly, not only in the obvious ways, but because even in our professional discourses words become "facilitators" (*i.e.,* of understanding or compromise) rather than genuine analytic tools.[6] The problem of vocabulary obviously cannot be separated from concept formation. When we are searching for unifying concepts, we ought to face up to the necessity for construction of the specialized vocabularies to which we—if we hope to be good scientists—are entitled. I use the plural deliberately because I think we need a basic vocabulary of terms which refer to our purposes, interests, and methods and, possibly, a set of vocabularies related to a cluster of unifying concepts. If and when we develop a general theory, we shall presumably have a single, economical, coherent vocabulary. It seems strange that not until after 1950 did such works as Lasswell and Kaplan's *Power and Society*

and T. H. Weldon's *The Vocabulary of Politics* appear. The first suffers from serious logical difficulties; in the second the author does not quite follow through on his early promises. However, both stand as significant and useful efforts. Regardless of one's posture toward political phenomena, it can hardly be denied that at the moment such words and terms as *power, group, organization, policy, objective, rationality, ideology, political process, informal, personality,* and *political behavior* are not all clear—either in meaning or analytical function. Nor are we clear on why the confusion exists.[7]

I hesitate to bring up the awkward business of "technical jargon." I do so because if we stick to the avowed purposes of this conference we shall have to be careful of selling ourselves short or of yielding to the substantial pressures against system-building in our field.[8] There are seven factors here which can be listed briefly:

i) Professional scholars have been guilty of using words for purposes which have little to do with observation and interpretation of social phenomena: to engage in no-decision verbal contests with colleagues; to provide old wine in new bottles; and to draw attention to one's existence and (hopefully) competence.

ii) Through carelessness and faulty intellectual operations we have been caught with false dichotomies, mere labels, empirically meaningless terms, and many other defects.

iii) The few who are capable of really sophisticated analysis make just enough mistakes—usually minor if one leaves out of account value-judgments on the worthwhileness of particular scholarly purposes—to condemn their total work in the eyes of critics; instead of being shrugged off as the inevitable results of risk-taking in the scientific enterprise such imperfections are alleged to prove the case.

iv) Metaphors have an overwhelming attraction both in professional writing and in teaching; the rigorous teacher or writer sacrifices most of the major techniques for spellbinding an audience; furthermore, one can easily slip from metaphor as felicity of expression to metaphor as disguised conceptualization without having to face up to logical and other requirements.

v) Those of us who have tried (albeit by small steps) to improve the conceptualization and theoretical work in political science have added to the enemy's ammunition by not always—or often—taking care to make clear "the difference it makes" to be explicit and rigorous about concepts; this is not easy but it is both a test and a good communicative strategy.

vi) Under pressure of verbal combat, we often allow the anti-generalizers and the metaphorists to destroy confidence in our claims to more effective analysis by succumbing to this gambit: "what you're really saying is . . . Right?" Upon answering "yes" we often allow a mere illustration to pass for an explanation of a concept.

vii) One of the toughest handicaps is the pressure to reduce the level of professional analysis to the lowest student denominator; there seems little doubt that many, many teachers become so accustomed to the successful communicative strategies of the classroom that these become, in subtle fashion, an intellectual way of life.

These are familiar enough to all of us. I mention them in order to suggest that in our search for unifying concepts we must keep separate the criteria for deciding what methods will enhance our knowledge, from the criteria for deciding on how our knowledge is to be transmitted or packaged. I do not minimize the translation problem or the interest-arousal problem. But our professional life—our life as scholars—ought not to be governed by whether the *technical apparatus* we employ can or should be wheeled into the class room. The notion that the scholar who has an explicit scheme of analysis is forcing jargon or propaganda or theory (in its "irrelevant" sense) is firmly entrenched, and it will not be dislodged easily. Perhaps students can be led to see that the teachers who openly disavow systematic analysis are in fact theorists of a sort—especially the ones who "let the facts speak for themselves." There are two possible by-products of this kind of conference: one is that the jargon problem may be clarified—perhaps mainly by an explicit attempt to keep ourselves intellectually honest; the other is that some encouragement may be lent to textwriters in our field who will introduce their books with a clear invitation to the reader to assume a certain posture toward the human behavior to be studied—to wear temporarily the hat of the amateur analyst, not the participant in the everyday world.

5) *The Problem of "Real" People, the "Real" World, and "Concrete Entities."* [9] While it may be carrying coals to Newcastle to continue doing so, I wish to suggest another characteristic of political science which bears on this conference and on the approach discussed in this paper. We may have imposed an unnecessary handicap on ourselves by virtually imprisoning much of our analysis within the framework of the common-sense world: *i.e.,* we have been impaled on *reality* experienced as ordinary humans, not as observers—on "real" persons and "real" entities. This opens up a bundle of problems which cannot be explored here, but the point worth emphasizing is that unifying concepts, if they are designed to help reconstruct and explain political behavior, cannot be chained to everyday concepts. The distinction between the observer and his operations on the one hand, and the social world he reconstitutes on the other, is simple yet basic. A host of confusions arise from the failure to be self-conscious about this distinction. For example, there is often evident a subtle tendency to impose the observer's rationality (either his rules of investigative procedures or his standards for conduct generally) upon persons who are being observed. At any rate, there are two portraits of the social world: one given by intuition and direct description, the other made by systematic and experimental analysis of the conditions correlated with the events initially described. The first is very close to the common-sense world, the second results from an entirely different order —the rules under which the common-sense world is to be reconstituted. These are clearly not the same. Conceptualization is, I take it, concerned with the second portrait.

Now if we were to be sound generalizers about human behavior we could not, obviously, always talk in terms of *whole, real persons;* nor should we try (even if this were possible) to recapture the complete detail, *i.e.,* the *uniqueness* of particular events and situations. So far we have neglected to explore on any noticeable scale such analytical devices as *actor, role, system, unit,* and so on—all of which are artificial creations endowed with certain properties which can, presumably, be checked against empirical evidence. The use of such devices should enable us to isolate the common elements upon which generalization can be based. No one "saw" or will "see" an actor. However, since the actor is an analytic dummy, we can build into him properties and characteristics which may be remarkably like but not identical with real persons. What this comes down to is this: analytical models of this type enable us to focus on behavioral aspects of interest to us without having to deal with whole people and reality in the usual sense. We are therefore relieved—and *explicitly* so—from some of the insurmountable analytical barriers imposed by those who insist on realism.

There are, of course, limitations—or penalties—which accompany the attempt to use models in the description and explanation of behavior. Our statements about how real persons will behave, based upon what our model predicts, will be limited to the properties built into the model in the first place. In return, however, we have a chance to do simulated, controlled experiments of the kind social science is allegedly not capable of doing.

A related point here I shall only mention briefly because it will be covered by Marion Levy's paper. One very important—and useful—distinction in social research is that between *analytic* and *concrete structures*. A crude explanation of the difference would be this: suppose we imagine six members of the State Department sitting around a table discussing a foreign policy problem—this would be a concrete structure. But if we decided we wanted to concentrate on one aspect of the relationships among them, say, the *authority relationships,* the structure of authority relationships, either postulated or discovered, would be an analytic structure. Here again liberation from the welter of actual relationships is possible—at a price. If we speak of the political structure (or structures) of a society and the nonpolitical structures are viewed as analytic structures, we cannot say anything about causal relationships.

6) *The Problem of Comparability.* Finally, a word on comparison, which is a hallmark of any science. It would be pretentious of me to imply that I can represent the sentiments of the competent scholars who specialize in something called comparative government. Evidence suggests, however, that there is dissatisfaction and re-examination at present. A casual perusal of textbooks and articles reveals that genuine comparability (*i.e.,* comparison with the purpose of throwing light on a general class of phenomena rather than simply revealing differences) is relatively scarce. No single volume or even several volumes offer the student a conceptual basis on which the political systems of the United States, Great Britain, France, China, and the Soviet Union can be analyzed on even a moderately high level of generalization. Descriptive materials are fortunately abundant yet explanations of contrasting features is notoriously weak.

There are several other rather obvious comments which are pertinent to the purposes of this paper. First, there has been—at least it appears so—a disproportionate emphasis on *differences* with a consequent neglect of *uniformities.* Superficially it is a lot easier to detect differences and it requires no elaborate conceptual scheme to establish simple classifications of differences. Cultural bias reinforces this tendency because if the observer is not confronted by familiar symbols and institutional expressions he may *assume* fundamental differences. The structure and function, or patterns and consequences, stands out in this respect. Second, much writing in the comparative government wing of political science tends to focus on concrete structures. Thus a complete and fruitful comparative analysis of, say, Congress and Parliament is unlikely or is extremely difficult. But, to take one example, an analysis of Congress and Parliament as information systems might yield some interesting insights.

Third, the categorization of governments as "free," "totalitarian," "socialistic" and so on, while perfectly proper for some purposes (*e.g.,* for applying criteria of goodness or badness, or rightness or wrongness), may have slowed up the development of categories intended to point toward differences and uniformities of political phenomena generally. Fourth, it is somewhat puzzling that very little attention has been paid to comparative analysis within a single society. Would a comparison between a large urban council and one house of a state legislature be entirely fruitless? Or comparison between policy-making bodies at various levels of government? Comparison within the executive branch has not been carried very far. One would expect that once categories, types, concepts and other apparatus are available the potential comparability of political phenomena within a single over-all system will be ascertainable.

Summary. I have attempted to state briefly six weaknesses or sources of difficulty which we ought to keep in mind as we discuss unifying concepts. The selective nature of my comment under each heading has undoubtedly skewed the total picture somewhat. Nevertheless, if I have directly or indirectly called attention to the fact that political science is not self-conscious enough about its major analytical problems, I shall be satisfied.

THE LOCATION OF THE DECISION-MAKING APPROACH

In order that the reader may gain some perspective on the kind of scheme outlined here, I should like to locate decision-making in terms of (*a*) its place among various types of social analysis and some of its analytic properties; (*b*) its relation to existing interests and approaches in political science; and (*c*) its relation to work going on in other disciplines.

Decision-Making and Social Analysis Generally.
The decision-making approach to the study of politics clearly belongs in the category of *dynamic,* as distinct from static, analysis. I hesitate to introduce this distinction because the words are ambiguous and because the line is much fuzzier than the words suggest. Relatively speaking, dynamic analysis is *process* analysis. By process is meant here, briefly, *time* plus *change*—change in relationships and conditions. Process analysis concerns a *sequence of events,*[10] *i.e.,* behavioral events. In general, static analysis is a snapshot at one point in time. One basic difference between the two types is in the way (or ways) the time factor is handled. An important brand of static analysis[11] (namely structural-functional analysis), can yield information on the nature of change between two periods in time and on the conditions under which change took place but not on the reasons for change or how it actually unfolded.

In turn, there are two kinds of process analysis: *interaction* and *decision-making.* So far as I can see, there are only two ways of scientifically studying process in the sense employed here: the making and executing of decisions and the patterns of interaction between individuals, states, organizations, groups, jurisdictions, and so on. Interaction analysis does not and cannot yield answers to "why" questions. Thus interactions can be described and measured but the explanation of the patterns—why they evolved as they did—must rest on decision-making analysis.[12]

These distinctions are neither intended to prejudice the case for or against decision-making analysis, nor are they intended to reflect favorably or unfavorably on static and dynamic analysis. As a matter of fact, I believe these types can and should supplement each other. I do not believe they are rivals (except for the energy and attention of scholars) because there are certain things each can and cannot do.[13] Requisite analysis, for example, can aid decision-making analysis though time does not permit me to discuss the point here.

C. Wright Mills[14] has made a related and also useful distinction between what he calls macroscopic and molecular social research. This distinction, too, is one of degree and emphasis. The former embraces such things as the total social structure, global forces, great sweeps of history, and gross patterns of relationship. The latter embraces the actions and reactions of social beings in particular situations and under particular conditions. Obviously, decision-making belongs more in the latter category than in the former. It is worth

noting that, as Mills says, we have as yet found no satisfactory way of relating these two types of research.

Thus decision-making is one phase or form of social action analysis. The term action has a technical meaning, not a commonsense meaning. Analytically, action depends on the empirical existence of the following components: actor (or actors), goals, means, and situation. While this formulation is borrowed from Parsons and Shils,[15] the conceptualization outlined below owes more of an intellectual debt to the writings of Alfred Schuetz.[16] Although the two schools overlap and agree in many particulars, there are fundamental differences in the observer's relationship to the actor. One such difference is that under the Parsonian scheme, a rational model of action is assumed: the observer's criteria of rationality are imposed on the actor. My own feeling is that, on balance, decision-making needs a phenomenological approach.[17] Hence no rational actor[18] is assumed in the present scheme and the observer's criteria are not imposed on the actor.

Decision-Making and Political Science. Many will probably resist the assertion that the systematic analysis of decision-making has been slighted. Yet a careful examination of the literature—particularly, of course, in public administration—reveals that this is true. Now it should be said at once that there is much discussion concerning decisions, *i.e.,* cases, administrative structure (*e.g.,* authority) and the factors which decision-makers take into account. As a matter of fact, it might be said this is what administration is about. Nonetheless, despite centuries of interest in public policy and despite the development of theory and systematic analysis in the public administration field, we have no really fruitful concept of decision-making (*i.e.,* policy-formation).[19]

Much of the conceptualization—if any—is implicit. As already noted, key words like *policy, objective, decision,* and *decision-making* remain for the most part inadequately defined or are assumed to have agreed meaning.[20] Barnard[21] and Simon[22] were among the first to insist on the primary significance of decisions in administrative organizations. Yet neither of these trail-blazers nor their contemporaries and successors have given us an answer to a very important question: if we wish to describe and explain decision-making behavior scientifically what kinds of intellectual operations are required? It is in this sense that the literature is somewhat barren. Pages and pages are available on the *substance* of decisions and *on the formal structure within which decision-making takes place,* but very few pages on *how to analyze* decisions and decision-making.[23] Problems of analysis per se are only beginning to be probed and the chief initiative has come from outside political science.[24] Although again I cannot speak as an expert in public administration, it appears to me that systematization is somewhat handicapped by implicitly different models of organization.[25]

Specifically, while in Barnard's words decision-making has been recognized "as the search for strategic factors"[26] on the part of decision-makers, no explicit categories have been established for probing why the search for these factors takes place and why it takes the forms it does. No economical set of variables has been developed for analyzing decision-making behavior. In the absence of any kind of conceptual scheme, it is difficult if not logically impossible to generalize from the abundance of case material such as is contained in Harold Stein's *Public Administration and Policy Development.* To beg all these questions is to block off interesting areas of research and to surrender too easily to "enigmas." Perhaps we ought to insist upon holding more matters problematical in political analysis. To assume is not to explain, though making assumptions is an aid to research.

At any rate, in addition to the public administration literature (I am omitting business administration for the moment), decision-making enters into the study of international politics.[27] As is true of public administration generally, there is much writing on foreign policy-making but it concerns the structural machinery (not the process) and individual cases[28] with relatively no attempt to establish categories and employ the action approach. The literature of international politics offers very fertile ground for the exploration of the decision-making approach, and some of the basic "why" questions of national behavior cannot be answered without it. American foreign policy materials lie virtually un-mined at present.[29] Closely related is the field of diplomatic history[30] where materials on particular cases, on procedures, on personalities, on precedent and so on definitely tie in with any emphasis on policy-formation.

Another paradox in political science is the lack—or so it would seem from the literature—of any systematic attention to the analysis of the decision-making behavior of judges.[31] Again there is case material and much on what judges *say* they do. Decision-making in regulatory agencies is also pertinent.[32] The third element in the triumvirate is, of course, the legislative process. Here we are somewhat better off because of the step-by-step procedures and because of some excellent case studies.[33] Nevertheless, we learn more about *what* happened (and we may learn the why of a particular bill) than about basic determinants of congressional choice. Another area of political science which relates to decision-making is personality theory—which perhaps ought to be regarded as a subhead under leadership. Increasing interest has been shown in personality traits and leadership capacity (one aspect of which is formulating alternatives) in personality types as analytic devices for explaining political responses and for demonstrating political institutional impacts on the individual, and in the social background of political decision-makers.[34] A close kin to these interests is the biographical approach, *i.e.,* case studies of individual decision-makers.

A very significant area of research and analysis is the behavior of nongovernmental groups. As David Truman has amply demonstrated,[35] it is necessary to know more than what these groups do in their attempts to influence public opinion, each other, and the various levels of government. Their organization is important and equally so is the decision-making process which in effect produces their strategies. Interactional analysis alone will not provide this. Finally, choice looms large in individual political responses. Voting behavior, group membership, and other political actions usually result from conscious decisions.

I shall omit here any reference to political theory in the sense of lore, doctrine, or values. My inclination is to believe that decision-making analysis, if it can be tested empirically, ought to throw many propositions current in our discipline into unflattering relief.

Decision-Making and Non-political Science Disciplines. Clearly there is not time to discuss all the other research (using the term broadly to include concept-formation) currently going on even if it were given to one man to know and grasp it. Only the major connections will be mentioned. An imposing and related cluster of activities can be grouped under the heading of "organizational behavior." For the most part this seems to include students of public administration,[36] sociology, business administration, economics, and social psychology. Most of the attempted synthesis and construction of analytical tools can be found reflected in the journal articles and books of non-political scientists.[37] Synthesis is seen in such collections as: Merton, *Reader in Bureaucracy;*[38]

Dubin, *Human Relations in Administration;*[39] and Gouldner, *Studies in Leadership.*[40] Sociologists have been groping toward a more orderly theoretical basis for organizational analysis.[41] Lately there has been a revival of interest in the works of Max Weber who seems, incidentally, not to be a seminal writer for political scientists. The interests, and to a certain extent the researches, of students in business administration are closely related—in particular the Harvard Business School.[42] There seems little doubt that business itself has come to show greater interest in decision-making.[43] If carefully read and with explicit concepts in mind, the business administration materials can, I feel, be profitable to the political scientist.[44] Occasionally, aid comes from the strangest places. Thus what appears to be a "how-to" volume— Irwin Bross, *Design for Decision* (Macmillan, 1953)—turns out in Chapter 1 to have rather more than the normal insights into decisions and decision-making. Again, the Entrepreneurial History Project at Harvard has done some conceptual work on decisions.[45]

Psychologists and social psychologists have done substantial research in group problem-solving and in group behavior generally.[46] I believe this work is of great potential value to political science but as I tried to say earlier, it has to be handled with care. Since we are speaking here of organizational behavior, one word of caution can be suggested. Some of the small-group experiments, though actually conducted within a business or other type organization, are nonetheless ripped out of any organization context. That is, the organizational roles and motives of the individuals observed are not under investigation; therefore, transferability of findings should remain problematical.

Turning aside from organization behavior per se, the relevant work of other groups of scholars must be noted. At the community level, tentative efforts to case social analysis in a decision-making mold are evident in Floyd Hunter's *Community Power Structure.*[47] Professional philosophers have also been concerned with decisions, but rather at the level of individual behavior.[48] As I have already mentioned, the essays of Alfred Schuetz[49] seem to me to be valuable on a number of grounds including his incisive comments on the relationship between common sense and scientific constructs. In the field of economic analysis, there are several developments bearing on decision-making. Introduction of psychological variables has opened up the whole question of motivation in economic decisions.[50] Black[51] and others have explored the possibilities of mathematically analyzing the nature of committee decisions—particularly majority decisions. Arrow has attempted to establish a basis for discovering the "system of preferences" prevailing among a group of decision-makers.[52] The theories of Black and Arrow give special attention to the committee or small group as a decision-making body, thus suggesting, of course, a particular relevance to policy-making. Finally mention must be made of game theory.[53] There is not space here to go into the possible insights a nonmathematician can derive from the theory of games.[54] My impression is that the lines of communication are as yet too feeble to warrant political scientists rejecting game theory summarily. Karl Deutsch has made an interesting attempt to apply game theory to the study of international politics.[55] Among other things, game theory points to the central importance of information in decision-making—a point to which we will return below.

Summary. I have begged the reader's indulgence for this rather rudimentary excursion in order to make four points: (1) whether one is a specialist in public administration or whether one "buys" the decision-making approach, there is exciting work going on which the student of public policy ought to sample; (2) despite the materials cited— and these are only representative—we still lack a conceptual scheme for analyzing decision-making; (3) research and theorizing in decision-making is on the whole valuable but not integrated to any extent; (4) any decision-making scheme in political science not only has a storehouse of experience to draw on but can justify itself because of its integrative value for a wide variety of efforts. I shall argue that if a sound conceptual framework can be constructed, decision-making analysis will be appropriate for *any* area of political science where there is an interest in policy-formation or judgment of some kind.[56]

THE DECISION-MAKING APPROACH[57]

I cannot hope to say all there is to say about the decision-making concept even at this crude stage in its development. Perhaps enough will be said to enable the reader to decide whether he wishes to hear more and to stimulate discussion. I shall deliberately simplify and assume that questions lead to an expansion—or perhaps exposure—of some facets. What follows is at most a frame of reference—not a general theory.[58]

There are two fundamental purposes of the

decision-making approach: to help identify and isolate the "crucial structures" in the political realm where change takes place—where action is initiated and carried out, where decisions must be made; and to help analyze systematically the decision-making behavior which leads to action and which sustains action.

Some Postulates. (1) The decision-making approach herein formulated focuses inquiry on a class of actors called decision-makers. On the assumption that *authoritative (i.e.,* binding on the whole society viewed as a political association or on some segment thereof also viewed as a political association, such as states, counties, and cities) action can be decided upon and initiated by *public officials,* who are formally or actually responsible for decisions and who engage in the making of decisions, our actors are official actors. These officials comprise a *reservoir* of decision-makers from which particular groups are drawn for particular decision-making purposes. We are concerned, then, primarily with the behavior of members of the total governmental organization in any society. And we are concerned therefore only with decisions made *within* that structure.[59] From past experience, I am aware that many will gag on this assumption. Without attempting to argue the case fully, let me anticipate some of the difficulty. An insistence upon a clear distinction between the governmental and nongovernmental realms for purposes of decision-making analysis *appears* to imply a narrowing of the definition of *political.*[60] This runs counter to the prevailing doctrine among behavioral political scientists and those who have been promoting "political process" research.[61] Also it seems to be a retreat from the discovery that noninstitutional social factors are basic to an understanding of political life. To focus on the behavior of official decision-makers seems to omit those powerful nongovernmental (but political by the broad definition) figures who (allegedly) *really* make the decisions.

To clarify, let it be said that this postulate does *not* imply that *all* politically important decisions are made *within* the governmental structure. I do insist that only decisions actually made by public officials are politically *authoritative.* A decision by a corporation or an organized group may be very significant politically and it may affect or be binding on certain persons, but it is not binding on the community politically organized. Furthermore, I know of no way that such nongovernmental decisions can be shown to have consequences for governmental decisions without accounting for the behavior of official decision-makers.

Earlier I made a distinction between two kinds of process analysis: *interaction* and *decision-making.* This may save some misunderstanding on the present point. Interaction process analysis does not require—and indeed would be handicapped by—a separation of decision-makers into official and nonofficial groups or a boundary line between governmental and nongovernmental decision-making. But the limitation here is that interaction analysis per se cannot answer "why" questions of decision-making activity. To reiterate, if one wants to analyze the "why" of governmental decisions, some other conceptual scheme is required.

I have become convinced that when one shifts to decision-making analysis, it is far less troublesome methodologically to *account* only for the behavior of official decision-makers and to relate them to decision-makers outside of government by some other scheme than one which required that *both* groups be regarded as actors *in the same social system*—which means accounting for the behavior of both according to formal rules of action analysis.

2) The behavior of official decision-makers should be described and explained in terms of action analysis. This means treating the decision-maker as an "actor in a situation." In turn, this means we make a basic choice to take as our prime analytical objective the recreation of the "social world" of the decision-makers as *they* view it. Our task is to devise a conceptual scheme which will help us to reconstruct the situation as defined by the decision-makers. The key to political action lies in the way decision-makers as actors define their situation. Definition of the situation is built around the projected action as well as the reasons for the action. Therefore, it is necessary to analyze the decision-makers in the following terms:

a) their *discrimination* and *relating* of objects, conditions, and other actors—various things are perceived or expected in a relational context;

b) the existence, establishment, or definiton of *goals*—various things are wanted from the situation;

c) attachment of significance to various courses of action suggested by the situation according to some criteria of estimation;

d) application of "standards of acceptability" which (1) narrow the range of perceptions; (2) narrow the range of objects wanted; and (3) narrow the number of alternatives.

Three features of all orientations emerge: *perception, choice,* and *expectation.*

Perhaps a translation of the vocabulary of action theory will be useful. We are saying that the actors' orientations to the action are reconstructed when the following kinds of questions are answered: What did the decision-makers think was relevant in a particular situation? How did they determine this? How were the relevant factors related to each other—what connections did the decision-makers see between diverse elements in the situation? How did they establish the connections? What wants and needs were deemed involved in or affected by the situation? What were the sources of these wants and needs? How were they related to the situation? What specific or general goals were considered and selected? What courses of action were deemed fitting and effective? How were fitness and effectiveness decided?

In other words, the actor-situation approach to social analysis alerts the observer to the *discrimination of relevancies*—to the *selection and valuation* of objects, events, symbols, conditions, and other actors. These relevancies are, so to speak, carved from a total number of phenomena present in the over-all setting.[62] Of the phenomena which might have been relevant, the actors (decision-makers) finally endow only some with *significance*. Relevancies may be "given" for the actors (*i.e.,* not open to their independent judgment, and among the "givens" will be certain cues to the determination of other relevancies). The situation—as defined—arises from selective perception: it is abstracted from a larger setting.

3) "Situation" is an analytical concept pointing to a pattern of relationship among events, objects, conditions, and other actors organized around a focus (objective, problem, course of action) which is the center of interest for the decision-makers.[63] As noted above, typologies are important to unifying concepts. A decision-making frame of reference will require several, among them a typology of kinds of situations. Only a crude formulation is possible here:

a) *Structured* vs. *unstructured situations*—pointing to the relative degree of ambiguity and stability; a situation for which the decision-makers find it difficult to establish meaning may be characterized by change as well as intrinsic obscurity.

b) Situations having different degrees of *requiredness, i.e.,* the amount of pressure to act and its source (from within the decisional system or from the setting).

c) The *cruciality* of situations—their relatedness to, and importance for, the basic purposes and values of the decision-makers.

d) *Kinds* of affect with which the situation is endowed by the decision-makers—threatening, hostile, avoidance-inducing, favorable, unfavorable, and so on.

e) How the problem is interpreted and how its *major functional characteristic* is assigned—political, moral, economic, military, or a combination of these.

f) The *time* dimension—the degree of permanence attributed to various situations.

g) The degree *to which objective factors impose* themselves on the decision-makers—the number of uncontrollable factors and imponderables.

Perhaps the chief advantage of such a breakdown is to remind us of the fact that certain objective properties of a situation will be partly responsible for the reactions and orientations of the decision-makers and that the assignment of properties to a situation by the decision-makers is indicative of clues to the rules which may have governed their particular responses.

The Organizational Context. All political decisions (as defined), on whatever level of government or wherever in the total structure of government, are formulated and executed in an organizational context. Having said that we will concentrate on decision-makers and how they orient to action, it is necessary to consider them as participants in a system of action. The concept of system is essentially an ordering device implying certain defined types of relationships among the decision-makers and patterns of activities which they engage in. Major characteristics of the system determine to a considerable extent the manner in which the decision-makers relate themselves to the setting. The type of social system with which we are primarily concerned is an organization. Many studies of politics ignore or merely assume the fact that decision-makers operate in a highly particular and specific context. To ignore this context omits a range of factors which significantly influence the behavior of decision-makers and omit not only the critical problem of how choices are made but also the conditions under which choices are made. I am convinced that many of the difficulties surrounding the attempt to apply personality theory, culture theory, and small-group theory have been due to a failure to consider the peculiar social system in which decision-makers function. Emphasis on personality and so-called informal factors[64] has tended to minimize the importance of formal factors. Combined with some of the consequences of the "political process" approach, the individual policy-maker has been regarded as operating in a vacuum.

Since we are interested in process analysis we shall take for granted many of the commonly recognized structural features of organization. In other words, such factors as personnel, internal specialization, authority and control, routinized relationships, professionalized positions and careers, and so on will be considered as given prerequisites.

Organizational Decision-Making.[65] Here is a tentative definition plus a commentary: *Decision-making results in the selection from a socially defined, limited number of problematical, alternative projects (i.e., courses of action) of one project to bring about the particular future state of affairs envisaged by the decision-makers.*

Explanation and Assumptions. (1) Decision-making leads to a *course of action* based on the project. *Project* is employed here to include both objectives and techniques. The course of action moves along a *path* toward the outcome envisaged. Adoption of the project signifies that the decision-makers were motivated by an intention to accomplish something. The means included in the project are also socially defined.

2) Organizational decision-making is a *sequence of activities.* The particular sequence is an *event* which for purposes of analysis may be isolated. The event chosen determines in good part what is or is not relevant. To illustrate: if the event in which the observer is interested is the making of the Japanese Peace Treaty, then the focus of attention is the system that produced the treaty and the various factors influencing the decision-making in that system. NATO, EDC, ERP, the Technical Assistance Program, etc., are not relevant. If, on the other hand, the over-all cluster of policy decisions with respect to the policy of containment is the focus, the Japanese Peace Treaty and NATO, EDC, ERP, the Technical Assistance Program and a number of other factors all become a part of the strategies of implementation.

3) The event can be considered a unified whole or it can be separated into its constituent elements. A suggested breakdown might be in terms of the sequence of activities: (*a*) pre-decisional activities, (*b*) choice, and (*c*) implementation.

4) Some choices are made at every stage of the decision-making process. The *point of decision* is that stage in the sequence at which decision-makers having the authority choose a specific course of action to be implemented and assume responsibility for it. The weeding out of information, condensation of memoranda, etc., all involve decisions which must be recognized as such by the observer.

5) Choice involves *evaluation* in terms of a *frame of reference.* *Weights* and *priorities* are then assigned to alternative projects.

6) The *occasion for decision* arises from uncertainty. Some aspect of the situation is no longer taken for granted and becomes problematical in terms of the decision-maker's frame of reference.

7) The problem requiring decision may originate within the decisional system or it may originate in a change in the internal or external setting.

8) The *range of alternative projects* which the decision-makers consider is limited. Limitations exist both as to means and ends. Limitations on the range of alternative projects are due in large part to the following factors: the individual decision-maker's past experience and values, the amount of available and utilized information, situational elements, the characteristics of the organizational system, and the known available resources.

Definition of the Decisional Unit and of the Decision-Makers. It is necessary to establish boundaries which encompass the actors and activities to be observed and explained. Here we specify that the organizational system within which the decision-making event takes place is the decisional *unit* which becomes the focal point of observation. The unit embraces, analytically, the actors and the system of activities which results in decision.

By what criteria is the decisional unit to be isolated and differentiated? The single criterion which seems at the moment to be most useful is the objective or mission. Objective or mission is taken to mean a particular desired future state of affairs having a specific referent. Specificity is most crucial because it is only possible to speak of the unit (or organization or system) with respect to a specified objective. In other words, regardless of the level of government or the size of the unit, it is constituted by the observer in terms of the decision-makers responsible for, and activities geared to, a particular policy, problem, or other specific assignment. With respect to any objective or mission, there is an organizational unit so constituted as to be able to select a course of action for that objective.

In passing, it might be noted that as the concept of decision-making is refined, two other typologies will be useful: a typology of kinds of political objectives and a typology of decisional units.[66]

Immediately, a two-headed question will be asked: how can the observer be sure he has all the actors in the unit who were involved in a decision and how is "involved" to be interpreted? This is mostly a matter for empirical investigation in the particular case. Very often there are established, well defined units. In some cases it may be necessary to do some detective work to reconstruct the unit. Undoubtedly, the observer will have awkward choices to make occasionally as to whether an actor or a function is to be included or excluded. When this is true, the observer will have to choose on the basis of his analytical purposes. The one great advantage of establishing the unit on the basis of the purposes of its activities is that we can avoid having to be content only with high level abstractions such as the State Department or the city government or the company, and when several agencies or other concrete structures are engaged in policy-making, only the relevant actors and functions need be considered.

The Unit as Organization. The constituent elements of *any* decisional unit will be suggested below. Here we shall only indicate that all units will be organizational in the sense that activities and relationships will be the outcome of the operation of formal rules governing the allocation of power and responsibility, motivation, communication, performance of function, problem-solving, and so on. Each unit will have its own organization in this sense. Obviously, the particular organizational form which a unit takes will depend on how and why the unit was established, who the members are, and what its specific task is. A unit may be a one-shot affair—as in the case of the Japanese Peace Treaty or an ad hoc investigating committee in Congress. Or, a unit may represent a typical decisional system for dealing with typical objectives as in the case of an interdepartmental committee at the federal level or the city council.

The Origins of Units. I have argued that the unit is an analytical tool—a device to aid the observer in reconstituting the decision-making universe and in establishing boundaries. However, as hinted above, the empirical question underlying the concept of the unit is: who becomes involved in a decision, how, and why? How does the group of officials (actors, decision-makers) whose deliberations result in decision become assembled? Often, of course, the answer to this question is essential to an explanation of why the decision-makers decided the way they did. Two methods of unit construction may be suggested: *automatic assignment* and *negotiation.* Sometimes the selection of decision-makers from the total number who might in any substructure of government become involved is based on a simple classification of problems or decisions. The formal roles of the actors provide the clue as to whether they will be part of the unit. Also, as already noted, there are standing units (*i.e.,* committees or groups) who are ex-

pected to act on given matters. A quite different method of selection is negotiation in cases where no routine procedures exist or where new conditions require special procedure. Negotiation may be simply a matter of springing the right officials loose for a particular task or it may represent basic disagreement over the location of authority and power. Thus everywhere in government the decisions on who will decide are extremely important.

In the case of complex governmental institutions in which a great many activities and a great many officials are involved, often the unit may be created by default. That is, the unit is constituted empirically by the actors, who, in effect, select themselves into it.

The Unit and the Setting. Every group of decision-makers functions in a larger setting. Setting is felt, analytically, to be more satisfactory than environment, which has certain explicit connotations in psychology and has ambiguous connotations otherwise. Setting refers to a set of categories of *potentially relevant factors and conditions* which may affect the action of decision-makers. Relevance of particular kinds of factors and conditions *in general* and *in particular situations* will depend on the attitudes, perceptions, judgments, and purposes of particular groups of decision-makers, *i.e.,* how they react to various stimuli. Setting thus is an analytical device to suggest certain enduring kinds of relevance and to limit the number of nongovernmental factors with which the student of politics must be concerned. The setting, empirically, is constantly changing and will be composed of *what the decision-makers decide is important* or *what is "given" as important.*

Two aspects of the setting of any decisional unit deserve mention: the social setting and the political institutional setting. Normally and familiarly, social setting designates public opinion, including the possible reactions of veto-groups. For bureaucracy, this means the general public *and* the specific clientele—either for regular government services or "attentive publics"[67] or an ad hoc interest grouping based on particular issues. However, an adequate concept of decision-making will include in the social setting much more fundamental categories: major common-value orientations, major characteristics of social organization, group structures and function, major institutional patterns, social processes (adult socialization and opinion formation), and social differentiation and specialization. From these can be derived conditions and forces of immediate impact on decision-makers.

Several of these can be noted briefly. First, every action taken by the decision-makers has consequences in the society at large. One kind of feedback is that the society experiences its own decisions. Possible effects can range from redistribution of social power to specific complaints, from puzzlement to understanding, from acceptance to rejection. Second, policies are usually accompanied by official interpretations which may or may not agree with nongovernmental interpretations. The strategies of *legitimation* chosen by decision-makers have a very crucial effect on the way policy results are viewed. Third, the society provides decision-makers with a wide range of means—technical services in which government must rely on private sources. Fourth, the social system has an important bearing on *who* gets recruited into decision-making posts and *how*. This raises the whole question of support for the governmental structure and this question leads to the internal adjustments in response to the social setting. In particular, this point subsumes the number of private agencies and individuals which can hold the decision-makers responsible.

The political institutional setting is perhaps a much more immediate factor. This consists of what might be called the total organizational reservoir from which the constituent elements are drawn, including constitutional prerogatives, rules of the game, responsibility equations, general purposes, concrete membership groups, roles, functions, pools of information, communication links, and so on. These are the items of traditional concern in government—government in general. Basically, the institutional setting viewed in this light is a vast pool of rules, personnel, and information for the decisional units. Within this pool, certain specialized activities—*not* concerned directly with decision-making and execution—are carried on day by day. The decision-making approach does not ignore or render unnecessary structural institutional analysis. On the contrary, it requires more and more thorough analyses of this sort, and, hopefully, it can add to their usefulness.

Unless the particular substructure is very small (*e.g.*, a village or town) any decisional unit is likely to exist simultaneously with other units. These units will be analytically connected because of the following kinds of factors: (*a*) overlapping membership; (*b*) a common set of givens—rules and precedents; (*c*) common objectives throughout the total system; (*d*) overlapping jurisdictions; (*e*) reciprocal impact of courses of action adopted.

To return to the notion of definition of the situation: the line between what is included in the definition and what is not is not just a boundary between relevance and nonrelevance. Two types of relationship appear within the defined situation. On the one hand, there will be relationships among factors within the social setting and the institutional setting and between these two aspects of setting. On the other hand, there will be relationships between the setting *and* the plans, purposes, and programs of the decision-makers.

Limitations on Decision-Making. The concept of limitations constitutes a set of assumptions about *any* decisional system. The assumptions concern the factors or conditions which limit (*a*) alternative objectives; (*b*) alternative techniques; (*c*) the combination of *a* plus *b* into strategies or projects; (*d*) decision-making resources—time, energy, skills, information; and (*e*) degree of control of external setting. In accordance with our our general phenomenological approach, we feel that the range and impact of limitations should be considered from the decision-maker's point of view, although many such assessments will be objectively verifiable. The main categories of limitations in terms of their sources are: those arising from *outside* the decisional system, those arising from the nature and functioning of the decisional system, and those arising from a combination of both of these.

Limitations Internal to the Decision-Making System. For purposes of illustration, let us list briefly some major limitations of this kind. It must be emphasized that the limitations traceable to bureaucratic pathology are perhaps the most dramatic but certainly not the only ones.

1) Information.—The decision-makers may lack information or may act on inaccurate information; in either case, the range of alternatives considered may be affected. It would appear to be a permanent liability of the decision-making process that relevant information is almost never completely adequate and testable. The necessity to adopt and employ interpretive schemes and compensatory devices such as simplification of phenomena provide a related source of limitation.

2) Communication Failures.—Reasonably full information may be present in the decisional unit but not circuláte to all the decision-makers who need it to perform their roles satisfactorily. A decisonal unit may be resistant to *new* information or the significance of new information may be lost because of the way messages are labeled and stored.

3) Precedent.—Previous actions and policy rules (the givens for any unit) may automatically nar-

row the deliberations of the decision-makers. Previous action may prohibit serious consideration of a whole range of projects. Reversal of policies is difficult in a vast organization.

4) Perception.—The selection discrimination of the setting may effectively limit action. What the decision-makers "see" is what they act upon. Through perception—and judgment—external limitations gain their significance.

5) Scarce Resources.—The fact that any unit is limited in the time, energy, and skills (and sometimes money) at its disposal also tends to limit the thoroughness of deliberation and the effectiveness with which certain related functions are performed. Time pressures may seriously restrict the number of possible courses of action which can be explored.

THE DETERMINANTS OF DECISION-MAKING BEHAVIOR

Having said that the actions of decision-makers can be conveniently analyzed in terms of a particular kind of social system which functions in an organizational unit, we come now to the factors which determine the choices of these decision-makers. I propose that any such system or unit— be it a congressional committee, a school board, the National Security Council, the Republican National Committee, a city council, or the Supreme Court—can be analyzed fruitfully in terms of three significant variables: *spheres of competence; communication and information;* and *motivation.* Discussion of these variables should be followed with the view of the literature of decision-making in mind.

Two things must be said at once. First, these variables must stand only as assumptions until empirical evidence sustains or refutes them—meanwhile I argue their logical capacity to account for *all* factors which influence decision-making. Second, one reason why this whole scheme is not a theory is that the three variables deal with decision-making from two fundamentally different perspectives: the properties of the *system* (structure and process) and the *actor* (individual decision-maker). The nature of these three variables can only be suggested briefly here.

Spheres of Competence.[68] Competence includes not only the structure of relationships and activities which results from the operation of formal rules but also the conventional methods of action necessary to achieve the organizational mission. In brief, this means the explicitly prescribed

job specifications *plus* supplementary patterns of action established and sanctioned by precedent and habit. Together, the prescribed rules and the conventional rules make up what we may call the formal characteristics of the organization. Prescribed rules and conventional rules together may be viewed as a set of guides to the conduct of the decision-maker. The rules thus comprise a normative order—a legitimate normative order—to which the actor is bound and which he must interpret.

For any decisional unit, there will be a considerable amount of information generally available to the observer concerning the division of work, structure of authority, flow of information, and so on which provide the framework within which the decision-maker operates. Evidence of this kind would be sought in statutes, directives, charters, and organizational manuals. In addition, other rules—equally necessary to the system—must be sought in routine responses, precedents, and presuppositions which comprise a set of implicit understandings.

The structure of competences within the decisional unit will determine the behavior of the actor in terms of: the specific functions assigned to him and what these mean; the command or subordinate relationships between himself and other decision-makers; the horizontal relationships with other decision-makers on the same level of authority; and the expectation he has of how his action will be received by others in the system and how others act. Viewed from the standpoint of the actor, then, his competence involves his qualifications to act, his authority to act, and the expectation that he will act and his action will be received in a certain way. The structure consists of the interrelation of numerous individual competences.

Both prescribed rules and conventional rules governing the actor's orientation toward his competence inevitably allow room for the actor's own interpretation. His job description, his powers, and the expectations concerning him cannot be perfectly appropriate for all conditions and circumstances and therefore he still has choices to make. Regardless of how simplified a model of the actor we employ, it must include at least some elements of his value system, his prior experience, and his learned behavior in order to explain his discretionary behavior within the formal structure. Latitude in interpretation will also be related to the actor's position in the hierarchy and to his expertness. Any concept of decision-making must allow for the interaction between the actor and his competence. Thus the sphere of competence must be regarded as flexible. We are handicapped here because organization theory has rarely dealt with the problem. One thing we can say is that an interpretative scale-of-competence is needed, ranging from the extreme in latitude to what might be called completely strict construction. The theoretical limits would seem to be fairly clear: at the extreme of greatest latitude, the organizational system would cease to exist or change into another unit; at the other extreme, obedience of the "letter of the law" would also cause destruction of the system.

This brief discussion of sphere of competence directs our attention to several crucial factors:

1) Decisional units may be distinguished on the basis of the tightness or looseness of the structure of competence—the latter being characterized by relatively wide opportunity for discretionary behavior.

2) Not all relationships will be necessarily "authority" relationships and therefore it will be necessary to ask whether the decision-makers equally share decision-making responsibility.

3) It will also be important to inquire under what conditions there is a discrepancy between the authority component of competence and the expectational and functional components and what the behavioral consequences are.

4) Given the interpretation of his competency by the individual actor and the fact that different missions may be assigned to the same unit, it follows that the decisional unit does not have *one* and *only* one structure of competences. Rather each unit has a number of possible structures, though each decision can only have one associated with it. The structure which emerges may result from internal negotiation or from expectations.

5) The negotiation leading to the formation of the unit may importantly determine the structure of competences by determining which actors (and hence what functions, authority, and expectations) are included in the membership.

6) Any decisional unit will have responsibility relationships to other units and/or to the total governmental structure or a substructure which will be related to its structure of competences— particularly to assigned duties, degree of authority, and normative rules binding the actors.

7) Tension points and conflicts may be linked to different functional bases of competence (line *vs.* staff; areas *vs.* subject matter expert) and to different satisfactions with the legitimate order.

8) Bureaucratization would appear to result from a process whereby more of the rules, precedents, and methods of operation are no longer easily subject to challenge, questioning, or amendment—in other words, a narrowing of choice through conventionalization.

9) Bureaucratization may simply mean a relatively great degree of efficient routinization of decision-making activities or it can mean that the institutionalization has been undermined by the persistent behavior of the actors.

Advisory vs. *Representational Roles.*[69] Competences in the decisional system are differentiated not only by the nature of authority attached to them and by specialized functions but also by the basis of participation in decision-making. Here I can only suggest briefly what is involved. Some decision-makers are automatically members of an organizational unit because of the competence they occupy. This is fairly simple and straightforward. But it is also true that in many complex systems of action, decisional units are so constituted that *claims*, or the *basis* of claims, to participation may exist and be honored. Thus some official individuals, groups, or other institutions can or may claim participation as a matter of *right*, whether this is given explicit expression or exists as a matter of general consensus. Federal interdepartmental committees are examples of participation (by some decision-makers at least) on the basis of something more than job description or expertness; namely, as representatives of agencies which have an interest in the particular organizational mission.

The advisory basis for participation involves neither claims nor authority-responsibility relationships. Such actors are brought into the system because of the need for special skills and information. Much more is implied here than expert recommendations since experts in subtle fashion may help to establish the bases of decision. Naturally, the line between advisory and representational is often blurred and one very significant organizational phenomenon is this: through time the advisory type becomes, through subtle transformation, representational.

Communication and Information. Thus far, we have analyzed certain of the structural features of the unit in terms of a set of relationships derived from spheres of competence, by which we mean: function, authority, and expectation as normatively ordered by prescribed and conventional rules. By implication at least, it was assumed that the members of the unit could communicate with one another and with others outside the unit. Ordinarily, political analysis has assumed or neglected this vital aspect of decision-making, but I am convinced that one of the most promising tools of analysis lies in the explicit recognition of this twin-factor as a key variable.[70]

Coterminous with any decisional system will be a communication system which will also be a structural feature of the unit. The communication system will consist of *channels* which are links between points in the system—really between actors and competences. The sum total of channels will constitute the communications *net*. Among the prescribed and conventional rules discussed under spheres of competence will be those governing *who communicate with whom* among the decision-makers and *how* as well as communicative links between the unit and the setting (social and institutional). As is well-known, communications take a number of forms—telephone calls, memoranda, recommendations, personal conversation, conference procedures, and so on. It is unfortunate that we know so little about the socio-psychological impact of different communicative techniques. I would venture a prediction that ultimately social analysis will be more and more cast in terms of communicative acts and strategies.[71]

Several rather basic functions are served by the communications net: to support and confirm the structure of authority; to make possible the circulation of orders and directives; to activate particular patterns of predecisional and decisional activity; and to make possible uniform definitions of the situation among decision-makers.

If we think for a moment of a decisional system as a communication net, perhaps the familiar notion of "access"—employed to analyze some relationships between private groups and the policy-making process—can be given a somewhat different twist. Three factors may be suggested. First, any net will have different *kinds* of entrances and exits so to speak. Thus, there is a *prescribed* type of communication access such as hearings and formal petitions. In addition, there are conventional points of access such as private conversations and the personal knowledge of the decision-maker. We might also find useful a distinction between face to face and *mediated* communicative acts. Second, outside the net there will be at least several *pools of information* "available" to the decision-makers. Some or all

of these may be tapped. They will exist in the social setting and the institutional setting. They may be blocked off for some reason or other. The choices as to which will be tapped will depend in part on the structure of competence, on the situation, on the mission, and on personality factors. These choices are among the crucial pre-decisional decisions. Third, one fruitful way of looking at access—including its existence and success from the outside group's point of view—is to analyze the competing kinds of information (*i.e.*, not only in terms of sources but content as well) which in effect compete to get into the net and once in compete for status. How are conflicting messages resolved? How are they checked? Are messages from the social setting "stronger" when confirmed by messages from the institutional setting? This, of course, opens up a whole range of questions.

We should note certain major kinds of consequences which may flow from the structure of a particular communications net. One of the important characteristics of a decisional unit or a governmental structure in general is the *monitoring* function—both from the standpoint of internal operations and from the standpoint of feedback from the unfolding of action decided upon. How effective is each or is there even provision for each? Again, does the net provide "easy" access to *new* information inside or outside the net? Or is there "hardening of the arteries"? Assuming full information inside the net, what are the limits on reinterpretation of old information? Finally, does the net undermine the structure of competence? Are some actors virtually rendered ineffective because channels of communication are closed to them?

Informational Analysis. A few words must be said about information itself. There are *two kinds* of information (regardless of source) which are of particular concern: information about the setting of the unit; and information about the consequences of projects already under way. Together, these may be viewed as a feedback for the decisional system. Another distinction seems useful: *primary* and *secondary* messages. It is, of course, commonplace knowledge that information in any system is *classified* and *coded*. A primary message contains raw information, *i.e.*, its contents have not been summarized or interpreted—as for example in the case of a telegram from a diplomatic officer in the field. A secondary message occurs when the telegram is stamped "urgent" or "file" or "circulate" or some other symbol is attached. Classification and coding result in *selection* and *rejection* of information and also routing.

Two considerations follow. In any system information is stored—either in files or in the heads of the actors. Thus the organization has a *memory*. Information on past activities may be "lost" in the files or it may become precedent through the remembrances of the actors. Usually one actor in any decisional unit is the walking repository of the unit's past conduct. Secondly, since information circulates through the structure of communication on the basis of choices (*i.e.*, classification, coding, routing) the question of the access of the decision-makers to all information in the net at one time arises. The distribution of this information may have a significant effect on images the decision-makers have of a situation or problem. The participation of an actor is conditioned in part by how much he knows, and withholding of information is one of the strategies employed by the actors to influence each other.

Clearly the pervasive problem or phenomenon of secrecy is pertinent here. Kinds of information can be classified according to how many people do know it, should know it, and are prohibited from knowing it. In the area of atomic weapons or other sensitive policy issues, the size of the unit may bear a direct relationship to the kind of information in this sense. The larger the unit, the larger the number of potential leaks. This would hold for any level of government. Finally, we should mention the *shutoff point*—the point at which the decision-makers refuse to consider any new information in reaching an agreement on a course of action.

The Leavening Capacity of the Decisional Unit. Organizational pathology is usually viewed in terms of structural weaknesses or the subversion of the "formal" structure by the "informal" or the unanticipated consequences of rational procedures—all of which involve communication to a certain extent. The communication and information analysis suggested might broaden this considerably. I have a hunch that the analogy of the homing weapon—as Karl Deutsch has argued—is not too far-fetched. Organizational weakness might be analyzed from the standpoint of the readjustment of responses in order to enhance goal-seeking effectiveness, inflexibility of intake of new information—particularly concerning policy consequences, and unwillingness or inability to reinterpret old information.

Motivation. We come now to the third variable. In all candor, the question of motivation has been—for reasons good and bad—a ball of snakes for most social analysts. There are many who deny any possibility of systematic investigation of the motives of political actors. Yet motivational propositions are scattered all through the literature of our discipline. One of the crudest and most misleading examples of implicit and erroneous motivational assumptions in political science is found in the field of international politics, which is my so-called specialty. Leaving this aside, I feel strongly that before anyone decides that motivational questions are ruled out as interesting but unmanageable, a few basic considerations should be laid on the table.

To begin with, I venture to reiterate again that to *assume* motivation begs many of the significant questions which arise in political analysis. To the extent that we can do *anything* with this variable, we may be able to spotlight certain aspects of decision-making which might otherwise be neglected—and have in fact been neglected because motivation has remained implicit in various conceptual schemes. If properly conceived, motivational analysis ought to provide a much more satisfactory foundation for linking the *setting* and the *unit*—one of the more troublesome areas of research. Such concepts as personality, values, learning, and attitudes have increasingly become part of the terminology which refers to the behavior of decision-makers. And motivation may possibly offer a way of synthesizing all of them.

Some Analytic Aids. One unfortunate pitfall in motivational analysis can be avoided if we understand clearly that motivation is only *one* component of action. Furthermore, if we keep in mind our actor-analytical dummy, we can assume that we are only interested in the motivational factors which may help us to account for their behavior in a particular system of activities. We are not, fortunately, interested in whole, real, discrete persons. Since the motives we are concerned with—*i.e.*, those relevant to human behavior in complex organizations—we can avoid worrying about "innate drives." The motives we are basically concerned with are *acquired*, not structurally determined (inherent in the physiology of the organism).

Our task can be rendered easier—and less dangerous—in other ways. One is to draw a very important distinction between *because of* and *in order to* motives. If we had to trace every act

back to an ultimate cause all would be lost indeed. Were we required to account for "because
of" motivation, we should have to explain a particular act in terms of a sequence of past behaviors, something which would necessitate
almost a psychoanalytic approach, whereas in
the case of "in order to" motivation, we are concerned with the future consequence of an act—its
relationship to an ultimate end from which motive can be inferred. In the first case, there is
always the problem of whether one has fully reconstructed the antecedents of an act. Explanation would entail dealing with the organism and
its psychic structure. One would need a full
medical and psychiatric case history of the Secretary of State to account for why he lost his temper at a conference or why he yielded a point
to an adversary.

I believe that we can further simplify our
analysis by employing a concept of a *vocabulary
of motives*. With Gerth and Mills[72] we can consider motives as terms which persons use in their
interpersonal relations. Fortunately—some will
say unfortunately—people talk about their motives and attribute motives to others. In a sociological sense, motive statements (concerning the
actor's or others) serve a function and have consequences in any social system. Politics is a
social realm where, par excellence, the participants pay a great deal of attention to the reasons
they give for their actions and to arguing with
others about the reasons for their action. Much
of the action which results from decision-making
is verbal. Political acts are verbal acts (oral or
written). Much political discussion is noted by
Lasswell[73] and others. Gerth and Mills argue
that it is in precisely those social situations in
which purposes are vocalized and carried out
with close reference to the speech and actions of
others where motive avowals and imputations
seem to arise most prominently.

Motives, from this standpoint, are words which
are adequate (in the eyes of an observer and/or
other actors) explanations of conduct. An adequate motive is one which satisfies those who
question an act (including the decision-maker
himself and his colleagues). Motive statements
thus function to coordinate social action by per-
suading participants to *accept* an act or acts.
Motives are *acceptable justifications* for programs of action—past, present and future. However, it should be emphasized that is not *mere
justification* because motive statements serve important social functions. A noteworthy point

emerges: *the decision to perform or not to perform a given act may be taken on the basis of
the socially adequate answers to the question:
what will be said concerning the motives of the
decision-makers*? In short, what acceptable motive can be attached to a contemplated act? We
have paid so much attention to the common-
sense interpretations of political motivation, to
the substance of motives and to proving or
disproving *real* motives, that we have neglected
the social consequences and functions of motives—particularly in those systems of action
where they are articulated and made explicit. It
follows from the foregoing that in political decisions motives are often *chosen* in the sense that
the decision-makers will be more concerned
about how a particular act (in a set of alternatives) can be motivated for others than about its
other consequences.

By this time, the word "rationalization" has
doubtless crossed the reader's mind. Can vocabularies be taken for *real* motives? Do politicians
really mean what they say? If as serious researchers into the "why" of behavior we assume
in advance that politics is a vast shell game, we
are, to repeat, lost. First, much political behavior
is verbal. The discrepancies frequently noted between alleged real motives and motive statements
may be discrepancies between two kinds of
action, verbal and non-verbal. Second, it is a
well-known principle of behavior that an actor
may influence himself by his own declarations.
Motive statements originally not reflective of
true motives may become guides to the action.
Third, motive statements do not just describe or
offer reasons—they affect other actors. It is also
a principle of behavior that an actor's motive
statements may and usually will alter the situation
through impact on other actors. Even if a decision-maker lied about his motives, we would
also have to take note that many would believe
his lie and act on it. The notion that a decision-
maker can consistently falsify his motives without consequences for ensuing decisions is misleading indeed. Fourth, we are interested in the
imputations and confession of motives among
the decision-makers themselves. It seems highly
unlikely that a decisional unit could survive constant falsifications of motives.

A Brief Definition of Motivation. Without
entering into a detailed analysis here, we can
suggest that motives refer to why questions—why
does the actor (or why do the actors) *act, i.e.,*
why does a decision get made at all, or not made?

Why does action take the *particular form* that it does *in a particular* situation? Why do *patterns* of action evolve from decision-making? Motivation refers to a psychological state of the actor in which energy is mobilized and selectively directed toward aspects of the setting. This state is characterized by a *disposition* toward certain actions and reactions. Since there will be more than one disposition we shall speak of a set of *tendencies* (limited to the particular social system): to *respond* in uniform ways to certain stimuli in the setting; to *select* certain conditions and factors as relevant; to *value* certain objectives; to make *evaluations* of alternative courses of action; to *allocate energy* to various projects and so on.

Motivation, Attitudes, and *Frames of Reference.* Clearly such tendencies are related to familiar questions: what is the *attitude* of the decision-makers toward this kind of situation or condition? What do the decision-makers *think* about this range of problems? *How* do they think about these problems? Behind questions of this type lie complicated behavioral phenomena. To probe these further, derived components of motivational analysis must be suggested.

Attitudes, as the term is used here, are the *readiness of individual decision-makers to be motivated*—in effect, the readiness to have the tendencies noted to be *activated.* Thus the structure of official attitudes constitutes a generalized potential of responses which are triggered by some stimuli. Since we cannot assume a uniform set of attitudes shared equally by all decision-makers, we would want to investigate the *content* of the various clusters likely to be present. We would also want to inquire into the *sources* of these attitudes *and* their behavioral consequences.

These generalized potential responses leave us still one step short. For example, why does a hostile attitude take the form it does? Surely there is more than one possible specific response, and readiness must be mobilized with respect to some particular situation or problem. This brings us to a second component, *frames of reference,* which will determine the specific responses of decision-makers. In turn, frame of reference has several analytical components: *perception, valuation,* and *evaluation.* Psychologists seem generally agreed that perception involves three processes: *omitting, supplementing,* and *structuring.* Perception, then, refers to the selective aspect of motivation—the actor is in a sense pre-

pared by the tendencies referred to, tendencies learned from experience and training which govern recognition and appraisal of events, objects, conditions, and so on. Knowledge and information will enter into recognition and relating of selected elements in the setting. Valuation refers to the nature and range of objectives which will be injected into the situation by the actors. The values brought to a problem as part of the motivational equipment of the decision-maker will include preferred paths or strategies which direct specific acts toward the objectives chosen. I have confined valuation to the general direction of the motive pattern as action unfolds. Evaluation refers to the appraisal of the relationship between specific acts and the objective envisaged. The combination of perception, valuation, and evaluation can be looked upon as embracing thinking or problem-solving. Actually, the separation of motive, attitude, and frame of reference is for analytical purposes only.

Motivational Data. I shall conclude the discussion of motivation as a basic determinant of decision-making behavior by indicating some of the major kinds of data which may be motivationally relevant:

1) *Functions and Objectives of the Total Decision-making Organization or Suborganizations.* The members of any decisional unit will be motivated in part by the responsibilities and missions of the particular governmental structure or substructure of which the unit is a part. Functions will range from the most general (national security) to the more and more specific (intelligence reports). Objectives refer to the existence of a set of strategies (containment of Soviet power) or a collection of prevailing plans and projects (action contemplated or under way).

2) *The Missions of Particular Units.* Decision-makers will be motivated not only by general objectives but by the purposes for which a unit was established. For example, a committee in whatever political institution will be at least partially influenced by the directive which established it.

3) *Socially defined[74] Norms and Values Internal to the Decisional Units.* Decision-makers have a membership in a total governmental organization or suborganization. In addition, membership in the unit itself usually carries a formal assignment. Decision-makers *may* be motivated by factors which have nothing to do with the purposes of the total organization or the unit. Thus competence expectations, unwillingness to appear unorthodox, a desire not to impair

communications outside the unit, these and
others may operate. Especially to be noted
are the traditions and loyalties with respect to
particular suborganization—an example would
be the Foreign Service.

4) *Socially Defined Norms and Values External to the Total Decision-Making Structure and
Internalized in the Decision-Maker.* From what
has been said under previous categories, it is
clear that when a person becomes a decision-
maker, he enters a system of purposes, preferences, and rules and becomes a group member.
Yet the decision-maker comes from a larger social
setting. He comes as a "culture bearer." Any
conceptual scheme for analyzing political decision-making must attempt to account for the
impact of cultural patterns. Of particular interest
are the major common value orientations shared
by most members of a given culture. These are
of interest on two counts: first, the effects on
the ways in which decision-makers perceive the
social world with which they deal and the un-
problematic (*i.e.*, not open to doubt or choice)
ends which they bring to their deliberations;
second, the verbal formulations which decision-
makers employ to render official policies acceptable to the society (only those relating to shared
values). It must also be noted that some decision-
makers will be affected by subsystems of cultural values (of a region or a social role).

5) *Material Needs and Values of the Society or
Community or Any Segment Thereof Not Internalized in the Decision-Maker.* The norms and
values referred to under item 4 are second nature
to the decision-maker and their pursuit is in his
self-interest so to speak. These are brought in by
the actor as part of his "preparation." The factors referred to here are "accepted" or "learned"
by the actor *after* his entrance into a decision-
making capacity. These needs or values enter
into the motivation of decision-makers in *two*
ways:

(*a*) Through *estimates* made by the decision-
makers—either independent calculations of the
importance, significance, or compellingness of
material needs and values or calculations accepted by the decision-makers as accurate (in
which case they become the calculations of
the decision-makers). Calculations will include
general and particular needs and values.

(*b*) Through *expectations* of rewards and
sanctions which the decision-makers feel might
be the consequence of deciding to maintain or
not maintain certain general conditions in the
society or to accept or reject certain demands
by particular groups.

6) *Personality of the Decision-Maker.* Two
kinds of data are pertinent here:

(*a*) *The intellectual skills* of the decision-
maker and their *application.* This can be re-
searched in terms of the following information:
(1) training and professional or technical experience inside or outside the decision-making
organization; (2) continued professional affiliations; (3) working theories of knowledge—
the ideas, concepts, formulas, and proverbs
concerning human nature and behavior which
circulate in any given culture and not necessarily inculcated through specialized training.

(*b*) *Interpretation of competence*—an assumption can be made that in the case of any
competence it is possible to isolate dimensions
which would persist regardless of the particular occupant. Beyond this, it is largely (apparently) a matter of individual interpretation
or adjustment. The activities "added" or
"subtracted" to or from a competence by
interpretation of a given competence may be
due to ego-oriented factors (*i.e.*, purely personal need-dispositions of the actors). However, there are two basic sources of pressure
for changes in competence interpretation:
(1) an organizational decision; (2) a crisis situation. Neither of these has anything to do
with idiosyncratic factors.

Personality and Decision-Making. It is necessary to say a further word concerning personality—another Pandora's Box. Normally, personality factors constitute a huge residual
category—anything which cannot be explained
by chosen variables is due to *kismet* or purely
personal factors. I have implicitly argued here
for facing up to the personality problem which is
necessary on both common sense and theoretical
grounds. Many students of politics—amateur and
professional—have been attracted by the "great
man approach" to historical explanation. Analyze the motives of Churchill and you have the
motives of Great Britain. Recent developments
in personality theory and psychoanalytic theory
make it tempting to analyze decision-makers in
terms of tension-reduction mechanisms and
Oedipus complexes. In both cases, organizational
factors are left out of account. On the other
hand, we need a method of bridging the analytical gap between those portions of the scheme
based on a system or structure. A personality
construct, devised especially for this purpose, is

needed. To repeat, if the task is defined as trying to ascertain which facets of a decision-maker's total personality structure made him behave in a certain way on a given day, we are up against a hopeless search.

We should note that analytically there is a threefold division of character structure; the physiological organism, the psychic structure, and the person, *i.e.*, the social being. What is required for our purposes is a sociological conception of personality, not a psychological. This scheme places the individual decision-maker (actor) in a special kind of social organization. Therefore, I believe we must think of a social person whose "personality" is shaped also by his interactions with other actors and by his place in the system. This does not mean that the influence of ego-related needs and tensions is rejected, but only that the behavior of the actor be explained *first* in terms of personality factors relevant to his membership and participation in the decision-making system. Thus the influence of idiosyncratic factor is isolated, and hopefully, narrowed.

THE ESSENCE OF DECISION-MAKING

I have argued that three key variables can be employed fruitfully in describing and explaining decision-making behavior: *spheres of competence* (specialized functions, authority relations, basis of participation, and reciprocal expectations); *communication and information*; and *motivation* (including personality). The six kinds of data specified as relevant imply a general concept of multiple membership for the individual actor: (1) membership in a culture and society; (2) membership in a total institutional (political) structure, (3) membership in a decisional unit, and (4) membership in noninstitutional social groupings such as professional, class, or friendship.

The analysis so far has concerned the interaction of the decision-maker with the various elements of his situation and to point to some of the consequences of this interaction. Earlier, I referred to work in economics, philosophy, and psychology dealing with the Theory of Choice.[75] The models all have two things in common (regardless of differences in mathematical or other formulation); first, the actor or decision-maker is represented by *a scale of preferences*—from the most to the least highly regarded; second, *a set of rules* governs the actions of the decision-makers—specifying the manner in which alternative choices

shall be presented, the procedure of voting, etc.

Decision-makers have preferences, though the scale may not be as highly ordered in the theories noted. What is the nature of these preferences? What are the factors influencing them? In general, these preferences are *not* entirely individual but derive in part from rules of the organizational system. Precedent may structure the scale. Shared organizational experiences and similarities and differences of biography (*i.e.*, training, experience, group membership) of the actors also can be presumed to operate. Information enters in—assessed selectively in terms of the decision-maker's frame of reference.

Two meanings of "rules" should be clarified. We have used rules in connection with structural and other properties of the decisional unit. Now with respect to choice, rules refer to the methods for determining which preferences shall prevail, such as majority vote, the will of the leader of a unit, "sense of the meeting," and so on.

In sum, information is selectively perceived and evaluated in terms of the decision-maker's frame of reference. Choices are made on the basis of preferences which are in part situationally and in part biographically determined.

UNFINISHED BUSINESS: SUPPLEMENTARY ANALYTICAL TOOLS

I had intended originally to attempt to offer briefly a definition of such terms as *objective* and *policy* and to deal with such analytical problems as *chance* in the political arena—particularly as it affects the setting of decision-making, and the *simultaneity* of operations of many decision-making units in most substructures of the total governmental structure. In particular, I wanted to develop the concept of a *path of action* which carries the scheme beyond the actual decision point. I have spoken of the need for typologies in political science generally and in the decision-making approach. In the case of *situations* I did suggest, for purposes of illustration, a crude set of typical situations. But space does not permit similar illustrations for *units, decisions,* and *decision-making personalities.* Finally, I have omitted mention of the *stages* in the decision-making process which opens up possibilities of dissecting analytically otherwise inseparable factors and phenomena. Decision-making, of course, takes place *within* units and also, often, from *unit to unit*.

I should emphasize something which is implicit in my argument, namely, that the observer has many, many choices. I fear that in trying to say a lot in a short space I have given a false impression of rigidity. Nearly all phases of this scheme represent analytical devices—something like the multi-purpose household tool. At the same time, I hope the more durable properties are evident.

Two derived concepts emerge from the decision-making approach which must await later development. First, the concept of *intellectual process*—an abstraction from the unit or system of certain elements which constitute the kinds of operations which the decision-makers as a collective group went through to reach their agreed course of action. This might provide a means of exploring more systematically such intuitive notions as "military mind," the "bureaucratic mind," and so on. Second, the concept of *policy attention* which highlights the distribution of energy and resources within the unit and within a total governmental substructure with respect to problems or issues. This might provide some cues as to the conditions under which problems get lost or neglected.

CONCLUSION

I hope my capacities as an analyst can be kept separate from the possible objective (*i.e.*, intersubjective) merit my proposal might have. Inevitably, the two have fused in this paper. I should also like to make it clear that until this scheme is tested—not only in the specific sense of empirical verification but as an exploratory, organizing, and teaching device—it must be re-

garded with skepticism. In the course of presenting the concept of decision-making in abbreviated form, I trust that I have not by implication or otherwise indicated that I regard this concept as anything more than one of several major complementary approaches to the study of politics.

If previous experience is any guide, readers will think of many exceptions, examples, and research problems which appear to offer difficulties. I would only plead that I have tried to indicate both the research possibilities and the more general organizing (*i.e.*, interpretive and teaching) functions. Sooner or later, when pushed to more specific applications, the two part company.

In general, I would argue that the criteria mentioned earlier should be applied rigorously to the decision-making approach. After several years of work, I am convinced it offers sufficient aid to some of the major analytical problems of political science to justify a substantial investment of intellectual energy on the part of some scholars.

Finally, I should like to conclude with two kinds of questions. First, does this approach offer any possible help on problems of *training* at the graduate level, both for policy-oriented positions and teaching? on problems of the *setting* of decision-making (opened up by Charles Hyneman's provocative book)? on the unexplored role of *experts* and *consultants* in complex organizations? Second, is it fruitful to ask for re-examination of certain difficult questions of political analysis which have, in effect, been in mothballs for a long time and despite hardheaded insistence that such questions are unanswerable?

AUTHOR'S NOTE: Because this paper was not in any way revised for publication, the bibliographical references are three or more years old. The literature on various kinds and facets of decision-making analysis is already very extensive and is growing rapidly. The following more recent items represent only a small sample of relevant materials and are presented as a supplement to the writings cited in the text and end notes: James Bates "A Model for the Science of Decision," *Philosophy of Science*, XXI (1954), 326–339; Anthony Downs, *An Economic Theory of Government Decision-Making in a Democracy*, Ph.D. Thesis, Department of Economics, Stanford University, 1957; Ward Edwards, "The Theory of Decision-Making," *Psychological Bulletin*, LI (1954), 380–417; Thrall, Coombs, and Davis, *Decision Processes* (New York, 1954); Harold Guetzkow and John Gyr, "An Analysis of Conflict in Decision-making Groups," *Human Relations*, VII (1954), 367–382; James March, "An Introduction to the Theory and Measurement of Influence," *American Political Science Review*, XLIX (1955), 431–451; Peter Rossi, "Community Decision-Making," elsewhere in this volume; Harold Lasswell, "Current Studies of the Decision Process: Automation Versus Creativity," *Western Political Quarterly*, VIII (1955), 381–400; Editors of *Fortune, The Executive Life* (New York, 1956), ch. 10; Jacob Marschak, "Probability in the Social Sciences," in Lazarsfeld, *Mathematical Thinking in the Social Sciences* (Glencoe, 1954), pp. 166–216; James Buchanan, "Social Choice, Democracy, and Free Markets," *Journal of Political Economy* LXII (1954), 114–123; J. Block and P. Petersen, "Some Personality Correlates of Confidence, Caution, and Speech in a Decision Situation," *Journal of Abnormal and Social Psychology*, LI (1955), 34–41; Nicholas Smith, *et al.*, "The Theory of Value and the Science of Decision," *Journal of the Operational Research Society of America*. I (1953), 103–113; Kurt Riezler, "Political Decisions in Modern Society," *Ethics*, LXV (supplement to January 1954 issue); Paul Diesing, "Noneconomic Decision-making," *Ethics*, LXVI (1955), 18–35; Donald Davidson and Patrick Suppes in collaboration with Sidney Siegle, *Decision-making—An Experimental Approach* (Stanford, 1957); Herbert Simon, "Rational Choice and the Structure of the Environments," *Psychologi-*

cal Review, LXIII (1956), 129–138; Herbert Simon, "Some Strategic Considerations in the Construction of Social Science Models," in Lazarsfeld, ed., *Mathematical Thinking in the Social Sciences* (Glencoe, 1954), pp. 388–416; Herbert Simon, "Recent Advances in Organization Theory" in *Research Frontiers in Politics and Government* (Washington, D.C., 1955), pp. 23–45; Robert A. Dahl, "Hierarchy, Democracy, and Bargaining in Politics and Economics," *Research Frontiers in Politics and Government*, pp. 45–70; R. C. Snyder, "Game Theory and the Analysis of Political Behavior," *Research Frontiers in Politics and Government*, pp. 70–104; Donald Matthews, *Social Background of Political Decision-makers* (Doubleday Short Studies in Political Science, 1954); Walter Crockett, "Emergent Leadership in Small Decision-making Groups," *Journal of Abnormal and Social Psychology*, LI (1955), 378–383; J. C. Harsanyi, "Approaches to the Bargaining Problem Before the After the Theory of Games," *Econometrika*, XXIV (1956), 144–157); W. D. Oliver, "Rational Choice and Political Control," *Ethics*, LXVI (1956), 92–97; M. Flood, "Management Science Today and Tomorrow: Decision-making," *Management Science*, VI (1955), 167–170; J. Marschak, "Probability in the Social Sciences," in Lazarsfeld, ed., *Mathematical Thinking in the Social Sciences*, pp. 166–216; R. Cyert, "Observation of a Business Decision," *Journal of Business*, October, 1956; W. J. Harris, "Decision," *Military Review*, XXXVI (1956), 33; M. H. Jones, *Executive Decision-making*; (R. D. Irwin, 1957); Harold Lasswell, *The Decision Process*, Bureau of Government Research, College of Business and Public Administration; and Karl Deutsch, "Mass Communications and the Loss of Freedom in National Decision-making: a Possible Research Approach to Interstate Conflicts," *Journal of Conflict Resolution*, I (June, 1957), 200–211.

FOOTNOTES

[1] See, for example, David Easton, *The Political System* (1953), chapters 1-5 particularly; also Lasswell and Kaplan, *Power and Society* (1950). It might be useful for many political scientists to examine Marion Levy's *Structure of Society* (1952) on this point–chapter 10. Levy's "Some Basic Methodological Difficulties in the Social Sciences," *Philosophy of Science*, XVII (1950), 287-301, is also very useful.

[2] Interestingly enough, there appears to be little clear understanding of what an "approach" consists of, or of how and why "approaches" differ. For example, the differences between an institutional and a behavioral approach may appear on the surface to be clear, but such is not the case.

[3] I shall return to this point later on. Again, exceptions would be Dahl and Lindblom, *Politics, Economics, and Welfare* (1953), and Riesman, *The Lonely Crowd* (1950).

[4] *Politics, Economics, and Welfare* (1953).

[5] The reader can obtain a reliable introduction to the general nature of action analysis in Talcott Parson's essay elsewhere in this volume.

[6] McLeod, "The Place of Phenomenological Analysis in Social Psychological Theory," in Rohrer and Sherif, *Social Psychology at the Crossroads* (1951), p. 225.

[7] However, see Easton, *op. cit.*, and Dahl-Lindblom, *op. cit.*

[8] It is highly instructive to observe the reactions of some social scientists to the Parson-Shils volume. Apart from scientifically responsible criticism, at least a few reputable critics appear to feel threatened by the implications of general theories for their own lifetime intellectual framework.

[9] Consult Schuetz, "Multiple Realities," *Philosophy and Phenomenological Research*, XV (1945), 523 *ff.*

[10] Event here is used as an analytic term, not as meaning a discrete occurrence.

[11] Other forms of static analysis are: requisite analysis (a modification of structural-functional analysis), equilibrium analysis, head-counting, and description of structure in the formal sense.

[12] It may be true that analysis and investigation will show that social change can take place without conscious choice–if so, it will be necessary to take this into account.

[13] For example, see David Easton, "Limits of the Equilibrium Model in Social Research," *Chicago Behavioral Science Publications*, Number 1, pp. 26 *ff.*

[14] "Two Types of Social Analysis," *Philosophy of Science* (October, 1953), 266-275.

[15] *Op. cit.*, pp. 3-30.

[16] See especially, "Choosing Among Projects of Action," *Philosophy and Phenomenological Research*, XII (1951), 161-184.

[17] I also hesitate to introduce this troublesome term but it points to an important quality of my analysis. See Roher and Sherif, *Social Psychology at the Crossroads* (1951), pp. 215-242.

[18] This problem of rationality is more troublesome than we have recognized. I cannot go into the matter here. However, I do not deny that rationality may be a useful concept for some purposes. Cf., Schuetz, "The Problems of Rationality in the Social World," *Economics* (N.S.), X (1943), 130-149.

[19] One of the first efforts at explicit conceptualization is James McCamy's "Analysis of the Process of Decision-Making," *Public Administration Review*, VII (1947), 41-48. See also the clear and helpful exposition in Irwin Bross, *Design for Decision* (New York, 1953).

[20] There are naturally exceptions to such a broad statement. For example, see Paul Appleby, *Policy and Administration* 1949), pp. 1-26, 47-65; Carl Friedrich, ed., *Public Policy*, IV (1953), pp. 271 *ff.*, and Simon, Smithburg, and Thompson, *Public Administration*, (1950), pp. 261-271. However, a very suggestive recent book on business administration says, for example, that "policies are simply guiding principles. . . ." See C. Redfield, *Communication in Management* (1953), p. 17.

[21] *Functions of the Executive* (1938).

[22] *Administrative Behavior* (2nd ed., 1957).

[23] For example, a recent work, E. Gladden, *The Essentials of Public Administration* (1953); ch. 1 on definitions is not

concerned with phenomena of administrative behavior and ch. 5 entitled the "Policy-maker" exhibits no conceptualization.

[24] For an exception see Waldo, *Ideas and Issues in Public Administration* (1953), ch. 1-5, 9, 14, 16; Simon, "Comments on a Theory of Organizations," *American Political Science Review,* XLVI (1952), 1130-39. See also, Feely, "An Analysis of Administrative Purpose," *American Political Science Review,* XLV (1951), 1069-1080.

[25] *Cf.* Snyder and Moore, "The Conference on Theory of Organization," *Items* (SSRC) (December, 1952), p. 41.

[26] *Op. cit.,* p. 202.

[27] Snyder, Bruck and Sapin, *Decision-making as an Approach to the Study of International Politics* (Foreign Policy Analysis Series No. 3) (1954), where it is argued that decision-making analysis offers a fruitful method of organizing the study of state behavior.

[28] Valuable case studies are exemplified by Feis, *The China Tangle* (1953), and Sapin, *The Role of the Military in the Formulation of the Japanese Peace Treaty* (Foreign Policy Analysis Series No. 1) (1954); Almond, *The American People and Foreign Policy* (1950), and Dahl, *Congress and Foreign Policy* (1950), certainly represent long strides forward.

[29] For example, the supporting papers of the Hoover Commission and the hearings on the removal of General MacArthur and on the Marshall Plan.

[30] *Cf.* Craig and Gilbert, *The Diplomats* (1953). Memoirs naturally should be included.

[31] See however Jerome Frank, *Courts on Trial* (1949), ch. 3, 10-12, 19, 20, 25. As usual, Harold Lasswell turns up with a pertinent essay: "Self-Analysis and Judicial Thinking," *International Journal of Ethics,* XL (1928-30), 354-62.

[32] *Cf.* Landis, *The Administrative Process* (1938), ch. 2.

[33] Bailey, *Congress Makes a Law* (1950); Cheever and Haviland, *American Foreign Policy and the Separation of Powers* (1952).

[34] Numerous works might be cited here. Outstanding, however, are Merriam, *Political Power* (1934); Lasswell, *Power and Personality* (1948); Riesman, *The Lonely Crowd* (1950) and *Faces in the Crowd* (1952); see also Salter, *Personality in Politics* (1948); Stanton and Perry, *Personality and Political Crisis* (1951); Millett and Macmahon, *Federal Administrators* (1939). Some social background theories and researches are reviewed in Matthews, *The Social Background of Political Decision-Makers* (1954).

[35] *The Governmental Process* (1951).

[36] Apparently some writers and teachers in public administration who are interested in non-governmental administration and who recognize the usefulness of what they regard as psychology and sociology do not necessarily believe in organizational theories or in the search for concepts relevant to complex organizations in *general.*

[37] *Cf.* Grodzins, "Public Administration and the Science of Human Relations," *Public Administration Review,* XI (Spring, 1951) 88-102.

[38] Pages dealing more specifically with decision-making are: 185-194; 202-221; 233-241.

[39] See especially pp. 199-228.

[40] Pages 100-117, 330-341, 644-679. See also his newer work, *Patterns of Industrial Bureaucracy* (1954).

[41] For example: Selznick, "Foundations of the Theory of Organization," XIII, *American Sociological Review* (February, 1948), 25-35; Bendix, "Bureaucracy: The Problem and Its Setting," *American Sociological Review,* XII (October, 1947), 493-506.

[42] For example: Copeland, *The Executive at Work* (1952); and Learned, *et al., Executive Action* (1951).

[43] *Fundamental Research in Administration,* Graduate School of Business Administration, Carnegie Institute of Technology (Pittsburgh, 1953), especially pp. 70-74; also Andrews, *The Case Method of Teaching Human Relations and Administration* (1951), Introductory Note and pp. 3-34. See also Dale, "New Perspectives in Managerial Decision-Making" *Journal of Business* (January, 1953), 1-8.

[44] To take one example: Paul Pigors, "The Symbolic Significance of Management Decisions," in Bryson, *et al., 13th Symposium of the Conference on Science, Philosophy and Religion* (1954), pp. 733-744. To take another: C. Redfield, *Communication in Management* (1953), ch. 14, on the conference process.

[45] Hugh Aitken, "The Analysis of Decisions," *Exploration in Entrepreneurial History,* I (February, 1949), 17; also Deutsch, "A Note on the History of Entrepreneurship, Innovation, and Decision-making," *ibid.* (May, 1949), 8-16.

[46] Cartwright and Zander, eds., *Group Dynamics: Research and Theory* (1953), chs. 12-14, 16, 21-22, 26, 31, 33, 34, 38; especially Jennings, "The Significance of Choice in Human Behavior," pp. 62-72, and Lewin, "Studies in Group Decision," pp. 287-304. Guetzkow, *Groups, Leadership and Men,* pp. 55-67. Guetzkow, "An Exploratory Empirical Study of the Role of Conflict in Decision-making Conferences," *International Social Science Bulletin,* V (1953), pp. 286-300. Cartwright and Festinger, "A Quantitative Theory of Decision," *Psychological Review,* L (1943), 595-621.

[47] See also Paul Miller, "The Process of Decision-making Within the Context of Community Organization," *Rural Sociology,* XVII (1952), 153-161. An excellent essay is that of Green and Mayo, "Framework for Research in the Actions of Community," *Social Forces* (May, 1953), 320-26.

[48] Oppenheim, "Rational Choice," *Journal of Philosophy* (June, 1953), 341-350; Cerf, "Value Decisions," *Philosophy of Science* (January, 1951), 26-34.

[49] *Op. cit.;* also "Multiple Realities," *Philosophy and Phenomenological Research,* V (1945), 533 *ff.*

[50] Katona, *The Psychological Analysis of Economic Behavior* (1951), chs. 1-5; also chs. 10 and 11 on business decisions.

[51] Black and Newing, *Committee Decisions with Complementary Valuation* (1951).

[52] *Social Choice and Individual Values* (1951), pp. 1-22, 61-92; see also Little's review in *Journal of Political Economy,* LX (1952), 422-432. See also Black's "The Unity of Political and Economic Science," *The Economic Journal,* LX (1950), 506 *ff.*

[53] Von Neumann and Morgenstern, *Theory of Games and Economic Behavior* (1947); Blackwell and Girschick, *Theory of Games and Statistical Decisions* (1954).

[54] Mathematical analysis of social behavioral phenomena is not completely synonymous with game theory which is only one possible application. See for example Bales, *Interaction Process Analysis* (1953).

[55] "Game Theory and International Politics" in Martin Shubik, *Game Theory and Political Behavior* (1954).

[56] Some modifications would have to be made to fit in the decisions of the individual in a non-organizational (in the sense used here) setting.

[57] I owe a great debt for many ideas and formulations to the Organizational Behavior Project at Princeton under the direction of Wilbert E. Moore and to my colleagues Henry Bruck and Burton Sapin of the Foreign Policy Analysis Project at Princeton.

[58] See Snyder, Bruck and Sapin, *op. cit.*, p. 7 *ff.* This is an important distinction. It implies no bias against general theories. Hopefully, the frame of reference may grow into a sound basis for a general theory.

[59] Contrast this with the position taken by Lasswell in *Studies in the Scope and Method of "The Authoritarian Personality,"* (R. Christie, ed., 1954) "The Selective Effort of Personality of Political Participation," pp. 197 *ff.*

[60] *Ibid.* Lasswell makes a distinction between a *conventional* definition of political decision and a functional one which makes *all* "important" decisions political. He goes on to say that in order to locate functional elite, it is necessary to locate those making "actual" decisions (pp. 203-204). This implies that there is a difference between actual and nominal decisions.

[61] For example: Garceau, "Research in the Political Process," *American Political Science Review,* XLV (1951), 69-85.

[62] To be explained below.

[63] Situational analysis is discussed in Easton, *The Political System* (1953), pp. 149-170; Carr, *Situational Analysis* (1948), pp. 1-38, 45-61, 90-100; Cole, *Human Behavior* (1953), pp. 357-388; Cartwright, ed., *Lewin's Field Theory in Social Science* (1951), pp. 30-60, 238-304. Compare the first chapter of Arthur Macmahon's excellent little book, *Administration in Foreign Affairs* (1953). This chapter is entitled the "Concept of Judgment" and should be compared with my concept of definition of the situation.

[64] I have reservations on the formal-informal dichotomy, but I shall here let conventional meaning prevail.

[65] The lack of a commonly accepted, general concept of decision-making or decision-making process has already been commented on. However, that there are theories of decision-making is clear from the previous section.

[66] Typologies would not be as necessary for historical studies as they would be for prediction.

[67] The phrase is Gabriel Almond's, *op. cit.,* ch. 1.

[68] Adoption of "competence" in preference to "office" or "authority" or "role" is due partly to ambiguities and misleading usages and partly because a more inclusive term was necessary.

[69] See Sapin and Snyder, *The Role of the Military in American Foreign Policy* (1954), pp. 35-39; *cf.* Sapin, Snyder, and Bruck, *An Appropriate Role for the Military in American Foreign Policy-making: A Research Note* (1954).

[70] See for example: Deutsch, "On Communication Models in the Social Sciences," *Public Opinion Quarterly* (Fall, 1952); Deutsch, "Self-Referent Symbols and Self-Referent Communication Patterns: A Note on Some Pessimistic Theories of Politics," in Bryson, et al., *13th Symposium of Conference on Science, Philosophy and Religion* (1954), p. 619; C. Redfield, *Communication in Management* (1953); Newcomb, "An Approach to the Study of Communicative Acts," *Psychological Review,* LX (1953), 393-404. See also Special Issue on International Communications Research, *Public Opinion Quarterly,* XVI (Winter, 1952-53).

[71] Newcomb, *op. cit. Cf.* Hartley and Hartley, *Social Psychology* (1952)—a text cast in terms of communication analyses.

[72] *Character and Social Structure,* ch. 5.

[73] Lasswell and Leites, *Languages of Politics* (1949).

[74] That is, as defined by the actors not by the observer.

[75] Black and Newing, *op. cit.;* Arrow, *op. cit.,* Oppenheim, *op. cit.* See also, Black, "The Rationale of Group Decision-making," *Journal of Political Economy,* LVI (1948), 23-24.

Question-Negotiation and Information Seeking in Libraries

by Robert S. Taylor

One serious limit in library education and research is the pragmatic base. Taylor offers here broad conceptual generalizations amenable to research in a preliminary theoretical model derived from the reference process. In this way, he has restructured and given the student a perspective formerly absent. While not explicitly written for research purposes, the design does lend itself to elaboration, testing and further amplification. It seems especially well suited as a framework for instruction in reference work as a more appealing intellectual alternative to conventional approaches. While the library field has few behavioral students of the reference process, the exploitation in reference study of such a model would appear infinitely more promising as productive of understanding and insight into the phenomenon, than all the books which describe the content of reference sources.

DELBRUCK'S PRINCIPLE OF LIMITED SLOPPINESS

You should be sloppy enough so that the unexpected happens, yet not so sloppy that you cannot figure out what happens after it has happened—in Eiduson, Bernice T. *Scientists: Their Psychological World* (1962), p. 126.

The major problem facing libraries, and similar information systems, is how to proceed from "things as they are now" to "things as they may be." It is an illuminating exercise to extrapolate from present technology to describe the library of the future. However, such exercises have little to say as to how to proceed from "now" to "then."[1]

There are two possible alternatives to this process of change, with a whole range of options.[2] First the revolutionary concept: libraries will wither away and their place in the communications network will be taken by some new institutional form, probably imposed from the outside. The second one, an evolutionary development, is that libraries themselves will gradually make the transition.

The work described here is based on the second alternative. The objective was to examine and analyze certain relationships between library system and library user. It is hoped that this paper develops sufficiently fruitful generalizations, so that further investigations can start at a different level, with new assumptions. It is further hoped that, as a result of future investigations in this

area, the evolution of libraries from passive warehouses to dynamic communication centers will be less traumatic and more effective.

This paper is not concerned with the usual library automation, although the effect that automation may have on the interface between user and system is recognized. In time, the automation of routine processes, *i.e.*, order, catalog, and circulation control, after the bugs are worked out, will allow a different level of interaction. But routine automation is merely an extension of the control and warehousing functions of libraries. The work described here is an early effort to understand better the communications functions of libraries and similar types of information centers, *because this is what libraries are all about.*

Consequently this paper is concerned with two phases of this interface, which revolve around the process of negotiating the question. This act of negotiation usually takes one or both of these forms: (*a*) working through a human intermediary, *i.e.* the reference librarian; (*b*) self-help, by which the user himself attempts, often unsuccessfully, to sharpen his question by interacting with the library and its contents.

Reference librarians and information specialists have developed, both consciously and unconsciously, rather sophisticated methods of interrogating users. These methods are difficult to describe, indeed some believe they are indescribable. No such assumption is made here, in the belief that there *are* gross categories or levels of informa-

SOURCE: Reprinted from Robert S. Taylor, "Question-Negotiation and Information Seeking in Libraries," *College & Research Libraries*, 29 (May, 1968), pp. 178–194, by permission of the publisher.

tion which are consciously sought and received by the librarian in the negotiation process. We are dealing here of course with a very subtle problem—how one person tries to find out what another person wants to know, when the latter cannot describe his need precisely. There are a few good but unsystematic papers on the reference functions, but very little has been done of an analytical nature.[3]

In the self-help process, the user depends upon his own knowledge, frequently incomplete, of the system. It appears that there are a large number of users of information systems who, for a variety of reasons, will not ask a librarian for assistance. They develop their own search strategy, neither very sure of what it is they want nor fully cognizant of the alternatives open to them.

Both of these processes have some things in common: the development of a strategy of search, and frequently a change in the type of answer anticipated or acceptable as the search or negotiation continues. There is an implicit assumption in this paper, which intuitively seems valid. Most experimental work with retrieval systems and most attitudes toward reference questions look upon the inquiry and the relevance of answers as single events. This is mistaken. An inquiry is merely a micro-event in a shifting non-linear adaptive mechanism.[4] Consequently, in this paper an inquiry is looked upon not as a command, as in conventional search strategy, but rather as a description of an area of doubt in which the question is open-ended, negotiable, and dynamic.[5]

The first part of the paper discusses and analyzes the negotiation process as practiced by reference librarians and information specialists. The author is indebted to a number of professionals who subjected themselves to taped interviews ranging in length from sixty to ninety minutes. The interviews were limited to special librarians and information specialists for several reasons.[6] First, they are usually concerned with substantive questions. Second, their inquiries usually come from highly motivated and critical people who have an idea of what is acceptable as an answer. Third, to find material, the librarian must understand and therefore must negotiate the question. In contrast, public and academic librarians, because of the nature of their clientele and institutions, have educational responsibilities and staff restrictions which limit their response to inquiry. One special librarian pointed out:

The levels of frustration in using libraries are awfully high for most people. It's amazing, as hard as we work at making ourselves popular with these people, we still have them come in and stand diffidently at our desk and say, "Well, I don't want to interrupt, but . . ." To which I reply, "If you don't interrupt me I don't have a job." But it's amazing how people can't get over this. I think it would be a study in itself, that we grow up in school libraries, public libraries, and college libraries, generally where this kind of service is not provided. Consequently you are conditioned to feeling that the library is a place you almost have to drag something out of. The library is almost the last place they want to go, because they've been conditioned.[7]

The interviews were open-ended and unstructured.[8] They were designed to elicit three things, described in the librarian's own words:
1. What categories of information does a librarian attempt to obtain from an inquirer?
2. What is the role of system file organization in the negotiation process?
3. What kinds of answers will inquirers accept and what influence might this have on the negotiation process?

QUESTION NEGOTIATION BY LIBRARIANS

Without doubt, the negotiation of reference questions is one of the most complex acts of human communication.[9] In this act, one person tries to describe for another person not something he knows, but rather something he does not know. Quantitative data about this process is nonexistent. In spite of its complexity, however, it is possible to say certain things about it and to form a gross classification of the process. This is a first necessary step toward a basis for valid observation and the statement of testable hypotheses.

It is worthwhile in this consideration of the negotiation process to attempt to understand what a question is. Although reference librarians and other "question negotiators" count what are called "questions," this is not really what this paper is concerned with. Let us attempt to reconstruct in general terms this negotiation process, that is, as it pertains to the interaction between an inquirer and an information specialist.

The inquirer has what D. M. Mackay calls "a certain incompleteness in his picture of the world—an inadequacy in what we might call his 'state of readiness' to interact purposefully with the world around him,"[10] in terms of a particular area of interest. He comes to the library or information center as one of several possible alternatives, for information to fill out "his picture of the world."

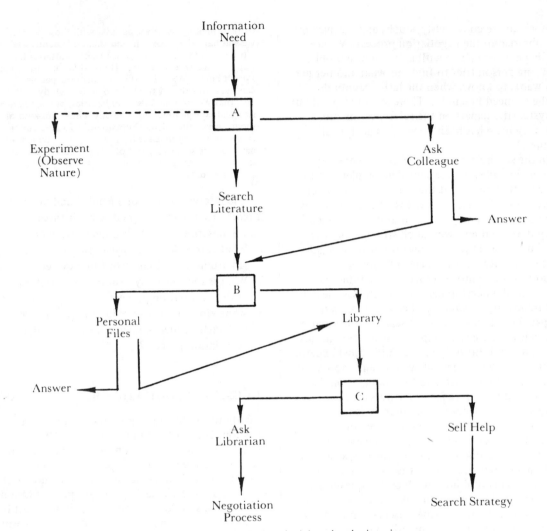

Fig. 1.   Prenegotiation decisions by the inquirer.

These alternatives themselves pose an important problem, illustrated in Figure 1.

In Figure 1, at decision point A, the inquirer decides whether to discuss his problem with a colleague or to go to whatever literature or information center may be available. Before he disturbs a busy colleague, he is likely to make a minimum search of his own files. This will happen only, however, if he has analyzed his "inadequacy" sufficiently to be able even to look through his own files.

He also makes a second decision (B in Figure 1): to go to the library or information center. This is an important choice and reflects a number of factors: previous experience, environment (is this an accepted procedure in his activity?), and ease of access. Studies of information-seeking behavior

indicate, for example, that "ease of access" to an information system is more significant than "amount or quality of information" retrievable.[11]

At decision point C he makes another choice of paths: (*a*) to ask an information specialist; or (*b*) to help himself. Most important in this decision is the inquirer's image of the personnel, their effectiveness, and his previous experience with this or any other library and librarian.

All three of these decisions will have an influence, largely undetermined, on the negotiation process. It is not the intent of this paper to do more than list these prenegotiation choices as forming part of the context and background for the process itself.

Assuming that the inquirer has made these choices and has arrived at the desk of the information specialist, he then specifies in some form what it is he hopes to find out. "Arrived" can mean any of several communication modes: by letter, by telephone, or by direct face-to-face interview. It is at this point that negotiation begins. Before consideration of this process, it is first necessary to discuss various levels of questions. In general we can describe four levels of information need and the configuration of question which represents each level.[12]

1. First of all, there is the conscious or even unconscious need for information not existing in the remembered experience of the inquirer. It may be only a vague sort of dissatisfaction. It is probably inexpressible in linguistic terms. This need (it really is not a question yet) will change in form, quality, concreteness, and criteria as information is added, as it is influenced by analogy, or as its importance grows with the investigation.

2. At the second level there is a conscious mental description of an ill-defined area of indecision. It will probably be an ambiguous and rambling statement. The inquirer may, at this stage, talk to someone else to sharpen his focus. He presumably hopes that two things will happen in this process: (a) his colleague will understand the ambiguities; and (b) these ambiguities will gradually disappear in the course of the dialogue.

3. At this level an inquirer can form a qualified and rational statement of his question. Here he is describing his area of doubt in concrete terms and he may or may not be thinking within the context or constraints of the system from which he wants information. By the way, he may view the librarian as part of the system at this level, rather than as a colleague. This distinction is important. As one interviewed librarian said: "For most people, I am the information system."

4. At the fourth level the question is recast in anticipation of what the files can deliver. The searcher must think in terms of the organization of particular files and of the discrete packages available—such as books, reports, papers, drawings, or tables.

These four levels of question formation shade into one another along the question spectrum. They are stated here only as convenient points along a continuum. They may be outlined as follows:

Q_1—the actual, but unexpressed need for information (the *visceral* need);

Q_2—the conscious, within-brain description of the need (the *conscious* need);

Q_3—the formal statement of the need (the *formalized* need);

Q_4—the question as presented to the information system (the *compromised* need).

Unless the inquirer knows the information specialist well, he is inclined to pose his first question in positive and well-defined terms, even to the point of specifying a particular package (Q_4). If the specialist is accepted as a colleague, the negotiation process can start earlier and be much more fruitful. An important necessity for such acceptance appears to be subject knowledge. As one information specialist put it: "A person with a technical background will handle a technical subject in less than half the time and with more competent and thorough results." This is where the process of negotiation starts. The compromised question (Q_4) is the information specialist's business, the representation of the inquirer's need within the constraints of the system and its files. The skill of the reference librarian is to work with the inquirer back to the formalized need (Q_3), possibly even to the conscious need (Q_2), and *then* to translate these needs into a useful search strategy.

This is a directed and structured process, although there are of course many different styles and many levels of competence and knowledge on the part of both librarian and inquirer. There are certain obvious traits which will help the librarian: empathy, sense of analogy, subject knowledge, and knowledge of files, collection, and clientele.[13]

Fig. 2.   Schematic representation of communications between two friends over time.

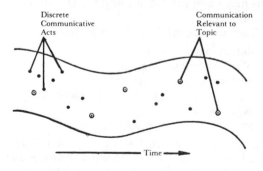

The negotiation process is a form of communication. It is illuminating to contrast it with normal conversation, in which one person finds out in random fashion about another's interest. Figure 2 shows the stream of communicative acts on a variety of subjects between friends over a period of time. However, embedded in this conversation are elements of a subject of interest, which one person is communicating randomly to his friend. Communicative acts are shown by a dot; those which are relevant to the subject are circled.

In contrast, the negotiation process must compress both the boundaries of the interview and the time span. More information must be communicated in less time. This requires both direction and structure on the part of the information specialist. Figure 3 illustrates this compression, where relevant communicative acts are much more frequent.

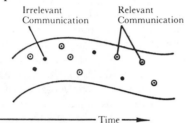

Fig. 3. Schematic representation of communication between inquirer and librarian during negotiation process.

From the interviews with librarians and information specialists there appear to be five filters through which a question passes, and from which the librarian selects significant data to aid him in his search. It is the structure of these filters, modified for the specific inquiry, that provides the compression of subject and time illustrated in Figure 3. These five general types of information necessary for the search definition are not mutually exclusive categories. The listing is approximately in order of occurrence, although they may occur simultaneously, *i.e.*, relevant data for several filters may be embedded in a single statement by the inquirer.

They may be briefly stated as follows:

1. determination of subject;
2. objective and motivation;
3. personal characteristics of inquirer;
4. relationship of inquiry description to file organization;
5. anticipated or acceptable answers.

The problems associated with these "filters" are well known, even obvious, to active librarians and information specialists. They have not been put together in rational form before.

DETERMINATION OF SUBJECT

Determination of the *limits and structure of the subject* of the inquiry comprise the content and aim of the first filter. The information culled at this level of negotiation is of course closely in-

tertwined with that of the second filter (the objective and motivation behind the inquiry). However, the two filters appear to have a sufficiently different function and necessary style of negotiation to require separate consideration for each.

At the first pass the primary purpose of negotiated subject definition is to provide some general delineation of the area: from biomedicine to genetics to the genetic code in DNA. Continued dialogue on the ramifications and structure of the subject will define, expand, narrow, and qualify the inquiry.

> X said he was interested in "contact terminals." Well, that's rather a vague term, and it probably took me a few minutes to find out what he meant by that. He might not even have started with that terminology. He meant "binding post" type of terminals. I probably asked him a question like; "Do you mean the type of spring terminals that are used in jacks, plugs and jacks?" He said, "No," and probably then said something about "binding posts." And I remarked "Oh, you mean soldered terminals." He probably replied, "No, that's where the contact comes into it, I mean the wrapped type." And so after a few exchanges like that, I would have gotten a picture in my mind as to what he was talking about. This is where my practical experience in radio engineering is helpful, because I can visualize these things.

At some stage, depending on the state of other relevant categories of information, it may be necessary to call a halt to this initial phase, in order to allow the librarian to make a brief search to determine the extent of the subject. He can then come back to the inquirer with "Is this what you mean?" or "Is this in the ball park?" From discussion in answer to these questions, the subject is further limited and qualified. This form of dynamic interaction may continue for some time, until the librarian is satisfied he knows what is wanted.

> Engineer X will come in and say "Gee, I have these three references on subject A. I've got all the ones I know about. Are there any more?" He may just stop in passing. This may develop into a major project, just because the man is so busy, he is not aware of the vast amount of information available to him. Once the subject is defined, we define the peripheral areas that may bear upon this. We inform him of our basic search strategies so he feels he is part of the effort. And we inform him how he in turn can interact with us, depending on the time constraints. If it is a long term project, he will receive in the normal course of his work material we may not be aware of. In turn we ask that he input these data to us. And if it becomes necessary for one of our people to go to his office and physically go over and read some of the more important papers on the sub-

ject, we will do this. So there is a continuous interaction between the people in the information research group and the scientist and engineer asking for the material.

The fact that they write the question doesn't help one bit. We think if it's written it's clear. You know "put it in writing." But you get no feedback with writing. It's the dialogue, the feedback, that is the important thing. For the librarian, the important thing is this awareness of the fact that you will need feedback in order to make sure of what you've got. You have to have this suspicion—a sensing of when it is you know what it is the inquirer wants, and when it is you are sure he has got it clear and when it is you are not sure.

MOTIVATION AND OBJECTIVE
OF THE INQUIRER

The second filter or category of information negotiated is probably the most critical: Why does the inquirer want this information? What is his objective? What is his motivation? This requires subtlety in negotiation, but usually has a high payoff in subject definition. It further qualifies the subject, or may even alter the entire inquiry. It also offers an opportunity to ascertain the point of view and influence the size, shape, and form of possible answers. Most of the librarians interviewed felt strongly that this type of question was critical to the success of any negotiation and consequent search. In those instances where this is not the case, the librarian's approach is that the inquirer (a) knows what he wants, (b) knows more than the librarian, and (c) is aware of the search strategies necessary to satisfy his *need*. None of these assumptions appear to be wholly valid.

Unless you are sure what the why is, you can never be sure what it is the person really wants. What's he going to do with the information . . . We can't help him unless we understand his needs as well as he does.

It is an obvious truism to every librarian who works at an information or reference desk that inquirers seldom ask at first for what they want. When they reach the point of confessing, "But this is really what I want to know . . . ," the acute librarian knows he is over a major hurdle.

Inquirers frequently cannot define what they want, but they can discuss why they need it. Consequently they are inclined to ask very specific questions, as if they were ashamed to hold up their ignorance for everyone to see. These may include an innocent and unambiguous request for a directory address, which develops into a search on molds; a request for a copy of *Aviation Week* which turns into a basic and broad company pro-

posal on commercial aviation; an inquiry to verify if there is a place called P   , which turns into a search for information on rat repellants. In these cases, as one interviewee pointed out, "My function is to help him decide what it is he wants."

The first step is to be eternally suspicious and the realization that in most cases they simply don't tell you what it is they really need. I think this is a matter of human communication—that we need the dialogue to frame up what we are after. I find this is true even in the simplest questions. There is that eternal suspicion that what they ask is probably not what they really want.

PERSONAL BACKGROUND
OF THE INQUIRER

The third level or category of information necessary in the negotiation process has to do with the personal background of the inquirer. What is his status in the organization? Has he been in the library before? What is his background? What relationship does his inquiry have to what he knows? What is his level of critical awareness? Answers to these types of questions have relevance to the total negotiation process. It may well determine the urgency, the strategy of the negotiation, the level of any dialogue, and the critical acceptance of search results. In short, it is the context, the environment for the negotiation process. It determines what questions should and may be asked.

Because we get to know our clientele personally, we know the type of response they need and require. We know whether a person is a thorough individual, or a less thorough one. In the latter case, it may be somewhat frustrating at times when you know you haven't gone far enough, yet they are satisfied.

Have I worked with him before? This makes a great deal of difference. If he is an old timer and I've worked with him before, I know pretty well what steps I can take in negotiating the question. If he is a stranger, or relative stranger to the information service, it presents a problem to me. Some of the questions I might ask are: What group are you working with? Who is your leader? Where he is situated in the organization is important. His status. Whether he is at ease or not. Sometimes we get people who feel very inadequate in coming to the library. They may come to us as a last resort, not knowing what they are getting into. They may feel that they are exposing themselves to someone looking over their shoulder. That is a position we don't want them to feel in.

There are many problems in this facet of negotiation. An instance cited by one interviewee is when an inquirer, who may be in his own right a highly competent researcher, is used as a high level messenger by, for example, the vice president for research. It is at this point, as the librarian pointed out, that experience and personal knowledge of the organization and people become important. The "messenger" frequently may not know the background and motivation for the inquiry. It is here that the librarian must make some educated guesses and associations based on experience. He must in some way bring the vice president into the dialogue, without undermining the reputation of the "messenger."

RELATIONSHIP OF INQUIRY DESCRIPTION TO FILE ORGANIZATION

An information specialist or a reference librarian is an intermediary, an interlocutor, between the inquirer and the system. As such, the negotiation process not only provides him with a substantive description of the inquiry, but also supplies him clues for devising his search strategy. He becomes a translator, interpreting and restructuring the inquiry so it fits the files as they are organized in his library.[14] In the symbolism discussed earlier, he must construct a Q_4, or a set of Q_4's, so that the total system can be searched efficiently.

> The inquirer will state briefly his problem over the phone. This is not enough so we go to him. We very likely do not discuss the specific problem but rather the relationship of the problem to the work he is doing. How does it tie in? We work from the general to the specific. He will often use a blackboard. What are the limits of the problem? In many cases we redefine the approach because he isn't familiar with the search strategy. So we redefine the problem to match the search strategy necessary. The inquirer is usually not aware of the sources available to him.

If we view the negotiation process as a "game of chess" as one librarian suggested, the librarian has a tremendous advantage. He is the one who knows the rules of the game; the inquirer doesn't. The "rules of the game" are the organization, structure, associations, and specific peculiarities of the files. The quotation above hints this: "We redefine the problem to match the search strategy." *The implications of such a statement, if taken at face value, can have the effect of redefining librarianship*.

It should be understood that the "files" refer not only to the catalogs, indexes, abstracts, and other standard files of the library. There is also the "who knows what" file, not on cards but in the librarian's memory. There are special files: previous requests, news notes, recent items read, the unstructured notes (or pieces of paper nap-kins) in the librarian's desk drawer. There is the sense, or activity, of building the inquiry into the system—the system including the information specialist and all the relevant files.

> Referring people to other people is one of the methods we use. But before referring them, we ask "Whom have you talked to? Are you working by yourself or with others? Do you know X? Do you want to talk to X, or should we?" You see, we don't want to go charging off in all directions, duplicating effort.

As much as possible, the librarians interviewed also tried to elicit from the inquirer any stray bits of information from his specialized knowledge that would give clues in support of a search strategy.

> One of the standard questions we ask: "To your knowledge what will probably be the most fruitful area in which to search?" This opens up some leads . . . often, he will say something like, "Well, I think there was a Proceedings of the IEEE about 1963 and I thought I saw something in there. Maybe that will give you a lead." In this particular case his hint was sufficient to open up the problem for us.

What the inquirer is saying is "Here is a paper. I'd like ones similar to it, or similar to it in this specific way."

WHAT KIND OF ANSWER WILL THE INQUIRER ACCEPT?

When an inquirer approaches the reference desk, he has some picture in mind as to what he expects his answer to look like, *i.e.* format, data, size, etc.[15] The problem of the inquirer's acceptability of an answer is an important filter in the process of answering inquiries. One of the results of the negotiation process is to alter the inquirer's *a priori* picture of what it is he expects. This picture is altered as the inquirer changes his question in response to feedback, as he becomes aware of the capabilities of both the library *and* the librarian, as he changes his search strategy in the negotiation process, and as he is forced in the negotiation process to place limits of time and size on his inquiry.

The sense of urgency in the inquiry definitely has an influence on the type of answer expected.

> The inquirer may say "I need this in 30 minutes." By doing so he has pretty well determined what form he will accept and what questions I can ask.

Whether or not the inquirer is asking for information in his own specialty will shape the kind of answer useful to him.

If a person is asking for a search in his own field, then you can sit down and talk to him. If he is asking in a field peripheral to his interest, then he has probably been asked to express an opinion on something. He doesn't want a search, but rather something limited, for example a review or a state-of-the-art paper.

Undoubtedly the subject field of the library and its clientele has a bearing on the type of answer expected, in ways we do not even know about yet. For example, in the law[16] it appears that the questions are very precise, but the answers are less precise. This is due to the nature of precedence in the law, in which a law, a court ruling, or an administrative regulation *might* be pertinent to a specific case, and are the only answers available. They don't however answer the question. Training in the law appears to make a difference. As one librarian put it: "I can almost tell the law school by the type of question."

One of the nagging problems in the delivery of answers seems to be the degree of evaluation the information staff can and should make. There are of course a variety of factors at work here: the librarian's own capability; the inquirer's attitude; and the available time. One interviewed librarian described the problem as follows:

Now the next level beyond this is one in which we have hardly done anything at all, primarily because we don't have the manpower. But I think it is probably the most important . . . . That is to make an evaluation of these materials. Just to hand someone a batch of raw abstracts is not enough; or even a list of numbers; paper A says the property equals this, paper B says it's that, and so on. Well, if they don't agree, shouldn't someone read the papers, and decide what were the experimental techniques, and give these a weight? That is, this is the most significant number, or the most valid number, or this is a significant average. We have just not been able to do it except in a few rare instances. Now the hope had been—when I say "hope" I don't mean only ours, but from the top of the Research and Engineering Department down—that, if we gave the individual chemist or engineer these other materials, he would do this evaluation. The evidence is that he doesn't do it. I would say only 1% actually do it. The others will take the first number at the top of the pile, some will average all the numbers, some will apparently take the number that fits their number best. You know, it's the human problem.

Perhaps the most important obstacle to evaluation by the librarian is the sense of puritanism on the part of both librarians and management who believe, for ethical rather than economic reasons, that everyone should do his own work. Such an ethos is at odds with the sense of service in librarianship, with the requirements of management for the best information as soon as possible, and with the growing complexity of libraries in a "data-rich civilization."

THE INFORMATION SEEKING STRATEGIES OF USERS

This paper makes an assumption which seems intuitively valid. In the self-help process, *i.e.* when an inquirer attempts to find information in his own way, we view the inquiry not as a command, but rather as an adaptive self-organizing system in which the question is open-ended and dynamic. In fact, as will be illustrated, the inquirer's original question may change during the search, as he adapts to the feedback of the search process.

Let us discuss briefly *commands* and *questions*, for an understanding of the difference between them is critical for the development of truly interactive systems.[17] A *command* basically denotes the request for a specific item or specific subject combination which the inquirer has already assumed will satisfy his need. Whether his assumption is valid or not has been discussed before. For the moment we accept its validity. In response to his command, the inquirer is delivered, or he locates, a specific package. Here the process ends, and he is satisfied (by definition).

Libraries and other information systems have been developed and operated on these premises. However, one may suspect that the rise of reference services—historically, a rather recent development—and the care lavished upon indexing, cataloging, and classification schemes indicates a feeling that traditional "command" systems must have some form of feedback built into them.

There are of course many mechanisms by which classificationists, index designers, and other information system developers have attempted to develop strategies and alternatives for the inquirer. For the inquirer, however, these are frequently oversophisticated, *at least in the display forms in which they presently exist*. The inquirer is only concerned with getting an answer, not with system niceties. Nor is he interested in learning and maintaining currency with a system in which only a very minor part has relevance to him. An analogy may be made to the myriads of directional signs on an urban freeway. The signs seem to be designed for the benefit of natives and not strangers. Though the principle remains the same, the results of a wrong decision in the latter case are apt to be somewhat more catastrophic in the immediate sense at least.

There really has been little empathy for the unsophisticated (*i.e.* non-native) user. Within the conventional information system, the signs offered the inquirer pose too many alternatives without specification as to where each may lead or what each will do for the inquirer. It may be that better forms of display and interrogation by the system, in an interactive sense, can provide more adaptive interfaces.

The concept of the interface, in this context, must be extended beyond its usual meaning of a physical surface or panel of control buttons and knobs. It includes here not only the physical problems, *e.g.* ease of use, but also the subtle and personal interrelationship, however primitive this knowledge may be at present, between user and recorded knowledge.

Within this context, the *question*, as contrasted to the command, can be better understood. In the symbolism developed above, the command is Q_4, the question compromised by the rigidities of the system *and* by the specific need assumed by the inquirer. However the *question* moves back toward Q_3 and even toward Q_2. It is ambiguous, imprecise, and requires feedback from the system, or from a colleague, in order to provide an acceptable answer. This approach, without intruding on epistemological grounds, may also give clues to a better understanding of the differences between information and knowledge.

As a first pass at understanding information-seeking, approximately twenty undergraduate students in a course, "The Information Sciences" at Lehigh University were asked to report on the process resulting from a self-generated information need. Four of these searches are discussed here. The project had two purposes. First, from a pedagogical standpoint, it was intended to create an awareness in the students of themselves as information-seekers: the decisions they make; the sources they use; the complexities and failures of the systems they encounter; and the ambiguities and strategies of their question-asking processes. Second, it was hoped that some gross generalizations could be made of this process, notwithstanding the open-endedness and uncontrolled nature of the project.

The students were first asked to read the section on "Human Search Strategies," from the report of the Advanced Information Systems Company.[18] This was done to give them some feel for the scope and nature of the problem. They were then asked, following class discussion, to write a description of their search for specific information in any topic of interest to them at that time. This approach was felt to be better than one based on artificially generated searches, because (a) they could draw on their own experience and interests, and (b) they could determine when they had an acceptable answer. They were allowed to use any sources they wished and to ask advice from anyone. They were instructed to conduct the search in whatever way seemed easiest and most efficient. They were not restricted to the library, although they were requested to use the library somewhere in their search.

The following instructions were given orally and were briefly discussed:

1. Do not attempt to describe *every* motion or *every* decision in full detail. However, please pick out what, in your judgment, are some of the more important or significant decision points and record those completely.

2. In the beginning analyze your question: What do I know already? What will I accept as an answer? Note that your question, and your criteria of answer acceptability, may change as the search progresses.

3. Analyze possible search strategies and estimate probability of success. Note that new strategies may appear in the search process, or may be altered in a variety of ways.

4. The following activities are significant:
   a. the original question and any re-evaluation of it;
   b. interrogation of a source, both human and printed or graphic;
   c. decisions to try a new strategy or to re-evaluate the strategy;
   d. significant results of an interrogation, including important clues;
   e. memory or store, *i.e.* partial data thought pertinent to the search, which you hold in "memory," or record in some fashion.
   f. "dead end" of a search path, in which you could (1) go to new strategy, (2) re-evaluate question, or (3) consider the whole question not worth the trouble.

There are several observations and a few generalizations that can be extracted from the resulting search strategies.

1. All searchers used some human intermediaries, fellow students, or reference librarians, to give them clues or guidance.

2. No student thought in terms of a library strategy, that is, to view the total collection as a source and then devise one or several approaches to it. All of them however used certain library mechanisms of a strategic nature:

a. To use the classification schedule as a means of searching:

None of the books indicated looks promising. However they all have the same catalog number (510.7834). I'll look in the stacks at that number and see if any of the books are promising.

b. To use the Subject Catalog (the library used a divided catalog).

c. To search the Subject Catalog beyond the original subject heading for phrases, etc.

Under CURVES there were nine books. . . . So I was about to look at SURFACES when I noticed a card saying CURVES ON SURFACES.

3. Most of the inquiries posed could not be answered by any single book or paper. They represent, however, questions of the type that users (in this case, engineers) wish to have answered:

No. 1: What is the relationship for the rate of gaseous molecular bombardment of the walls of the gases container?
No. 2: What is micro-programming?
No. 3: What is a concise definition of "Gaussian Curvature?"
No. 4: How does the Philco F_{10} differential amplifier operate in the model 228 digital memory unit?[19]

4. The searchers generally made good use of tables of contents and indexes of single books examined. When they did not, they made poor judgments as to the usefulness of specific chapters to their inquiry.

5. Answers usually do not come in neat little packages in answer to a specific question of the type posed here. One, for example, had to put his answer together from seven different sources, albeit in a single book.

6. When available information sources do not provide enough information for an acceptable answer, it is necessary to alter the question. As the student with Question No. 4 found out:

The question will have to be generalized because specific data supply is exhausted. How is a general transistor differential amplifier analyzed?

7. For the type of questions posed, there is a great deal of noise in library catalogs, particularly in the Subject section. This *may* be characteristic of academic libraries, whose collections are based on quantity rather than quality.

The results seem to support the belief that the inquirer's interaction with a library or information system has certain similarities to the negotiation process. If this belief has validity, it means that libraries are very frustrating to use and that library systems need considerably more experimental work to enhance this interface between user and library.

SUMMARY AND CONCLUSIONS

What has been gained by this investigation? Or does it merely reiterate what is already known? Is this, as someone has said about psychology, an elaboration of the obvious? In part, it certainly has been an elaboration of the obvious. But it has been more. It has attempted, by restructuring the obvious, to open up new ways of looking at libraries. The whole purpose has been, by organization and structure, to allow the reference and searching processes to be seen from a point closer to actual fact. This was done in the hope that a more intensive study of this process will result, and that elements could be isolated for fruitful analysis and eventual improvement of services.

NEGOTIATION

It has been shown in this report that the *negotiation process*, in its best form, is structured and can be analyzed. However, the five filters discussed above are neither absolute nor fixed. They provide a first pass at structuring a complex process. They appear to be valid at this state of investigation. Each filter, however, requires data, analysis, and testing. They could be, for example, further broken down, if it appears fruitful to do so, so that the more important elements could be better understood and utilized by information specialists in the future.

This approach to the negotiation process suggests ways by which library schools could reexamine course content in reference work. Is it possible, for example, to orient these courses more toward the dynamism of communication, *i.e.* negotiation, rather than concentrating solely on the static content of reference collections and classification systems? The former has been slighted, if considered at all, in the emphasis on the latter, the static approach. A newer approach should mean, for example, more attention to the social dynamics of definable parts of the population of library users, both actual and potential. This approach is already included in the training of children's librarians. It implies the total pattern of publishing, formal and informal communication, sociology, dissemination and professional education, if any, at whatever level of society a course is presumed relevant, from the "culturally deprived" to the "scientifically sophisticated."

A third result of this concern with the negotiation process is an understanding of the difference between a command and a question. A command assumes either (or both) of two things on the part of the inquirer. First, he knows exactly what he wants and can describe its form (book, paper, etc.) and its label (author and title). The second assumption is that the inquirer knows the functional organization of the system, the "rules of the game." It has been the argument of this paper that only the first assumption may be valid. The second assumption, with some exceptions, is not valid.

SELF-HELP

It is obvious that librarians and information specialists are unable, physically, to handle the present demands on their services, let alone potential user demand. It is equally obvious that, as a communication channel, libraries are frustrating and complex systems to use. The previous section implied that a different type of education for librarians might make them more efficient in serving their various publics. That is, they could help more people. Such a course would by no means be sufficient to nullify the self-help process, even if we wanted to. Do we then wish to duplicate reference negotiation? Duplication of such a complex process is obviously impossible now. In spite of the glittering but distant potential of artificial intelligence, problem solving, and theorem-proving systems, the nature of print and other media may in fact require different approaches than those of human negotiation. There do appear to be several elements of the negotiation process worth investigating to see if mechanical systems might be feasible and useful.

Certainly *substantive definition* is one of these processes. Present subject naming systems however appear to be more concerned with the description of physical objects (books, papers, etc.), than assistance to the user in defining his subject. This is an important and critical differentiation, for present systems are object-oriented (static) rather than inquiry-oriented (dynamic). This is related directly to the concept of *feedback*—presentation to the user of various levels of display

requiring a response from him. The inquirer's response in turn guides, alters, or limits future displays, searches, and answers by the system. However, most important in the process of subject definition is the display to the inquirer of alternatives, with specification of what these alternatives mean, where they lead to.

A second element or negotiation filter relevant to self-help is the inquirer's description of what he anticipates as an answer. Is it quantitative? descriptive? review? What is the level of sophistication? The very brief dialogue reported by one student in describing his search illustrates this process.

> She began to look in a book of mathematical tables and I explained to her that she would not find "Gaussian Curvature" there. I told her it was a theory, not a measurement. Whereupon she gave me a mathematical dictionary which looked as if it would help.

The important part of this process is that the user must be presented with choices, which match his type of anticipated answer with the forms available in the system.[20]

A third relevant filter is the process of *translating from the inquirer's terminology to system terminology*. The idea here of course is to allow the inquirer as much latitude as possible in describing his need (Q_3 or even Q_2), and then funneling these into system terms (Q_4).

The remaining two elements of the negotiation process probably cannot at present be built into the self-help process. However it may be possible at a primitive level to interrogate the user about the *objective* of his inquiry, what the information is to be used for. Using the ELIZA program developed by Project MAC[21] or a related system presently being devised by James Green of Lehigh University,[22] it is possible to extract from such questions as "What do you intend to do with this information?" additional concepts, phrases, and terms which would aid in specifying the subject. As such it may have a therapeutic effect on the inquirer, forcing him to define, limit, and analyze his inquiry, even though the system itself is not sophisticated enough to do much with the information in response to such questions.

The *background or status* of the inquirer does not appear to have much relevance to the self-help process, except as it may serve to determine a level of sophistication in the displays presented to him or in the answer delivered.

POSSIBLE SYSTEMS AND DEVICES

All present systems have forms and elements intended to aid the inquirer: *see also* and *see* references; broader term, related term, and narrower term; form division in classification; generic relationships in classification. As more research goes into these sophisticated and often intricate mechanisms, the more the inquirer must turn to the information specialist. As was implied earlier, these are librarian's tools and appear to have little relevance—*in their present form*—for the inquirer. The system that is best able to display itself in a useful and functional way for the inquirer will be the most effective. Like information itself, the system that provides ease of access, specifically physical convenience, will be more effective than those concerned only with the quality of the scheme of subject organization. Video, film, microform, and computer media offer a tremendous array of possibilities hardly touched for interactive systems at the operating, *i.e.* public, level. Even at the elementary level of description of collection and its physical arrangement, very little has been done to direct the user to areas of concern to him.

General instruction in the use of library and information systems is presently normally accomplished by tours, formal instruction, and handbooks, none of which are available when the user actually has an inquiry. One of the more interesting systems presently under development is the Videosonic system at Mt. San Antonio College.[23] Controlled experiment with these devices indicates that students who utilized the system used the library more effectively and sought services from the staff less frequently than those not exposed.

The Recordak Lodestar Microfilm Reader-Printer with an Image Control Keyboard offers several possibilities for a programed learning and interrogating system relevant to the library. Each of approximately twenty-five hundred frames on a reel are available by dialing, or otherwise signifying an address on the keyboard. Michael B. Liebowitz of Lehigh University has done a preliminary design study[24] for such a microfilm system in the field of metallurgy. In the system the user moves from index frames to subject network frames, then to bibliography, tables of contents, or data, as his needs indicate. The important part of this process is that the user is led through the system not in serial fashion, but by his area of interest as he responds to questions. He can also obtain hard copy as he moves along. There are some grave limitations in such microfilm systems. Updating for example becomes difficult, without redesigning an entire reel. However, the display of subject maps may allow a user a much better understanding of the relationship of his inquiry to terms within the system and to the interrelationships among terms. The presentation of tables of contents in this form may allow a user to scan quickly a summary of the contents of a specialized reference collection.

The study now underway at the graduate library school of the University of Chicago on the format, information, and public use of data on catalog cards[25] may indicate more effective display of bibliographic information. The augmented catalog, now being experimented on by Project INTREX (21), will include such important forms of display as reviews and tables of contents. Although both of these developments will influence the display of information, they appear to be related more to command rather than to question. The work by Engelbart and others at the Stanford Research Institute[26] on the augmentation of human intellect by computers may generate interesting systems sometime in the future, but appears to have little pertinence at this time to the problems under consideration here.

If nothing else it is hoped that this first pass at the analysis of negotiation, both by human intermediaries and by self-help, may induce libraries and librarians to become critically aware of their role in this process. The advent of the MARC project, commercial processing of library materials, and the gradual disappearance of local cataloging operations will have a profound influence on operating libraries. It will become increasingly important for librarians to become interpreters and guides, developing both negotiation skills and displays for users of all levels of sophistication.

The contrast between the "wholesaler" and "retailer" of information may serve as an analogy here. However much they like to think otherwise, most libraries are "wholesalers" of knowledge, and the library is a warehouse (however grand the Gothic windows or beautiful the new carpeting) from which gobs of knowledge are indiscriminately doled out to whomever happens to be captive of the system at that moment. There are exceptions—and they are noble ones. Certainly most of the librarians who gave their time for this study are helping to make their libraries "retailers." This is the difference between the supermarket or discount house and the local dealer who takes pride in serving his customers, *i.e.* public. He is not pushing merchandise. He is matching a customer and his merchandise.

If libraries, at any level of service, are going to grow and evolve (and indeed exist) as integral parts of our urban technico-scientific culture, then they must know themselves. They must know themselves both as local and rather special institutions and as parts of very large, very dynamic, and very complex information and communications networks, which operate on both a formal and an informal level.

It may be, as someone has said of formal education, that the storage media which libraries handle are noise in the system. The real education and communication may take place outside or on the periphery of libraries and formal education. Indeed it may be that the reference interview, the negotiation of questions is the *only* process in libraries that is not noise. For it is through negotiation that an inquirer presumably resolves his problem, begins to understand what he means, and begins to adjust his question to both system and substantive noise in the store of recorded knowledge called the library.

FOOTNOTES

[1] J. C. R. Licklider, *Libraries of the Future* (Cambridge: The M.I.T. Press, 1965).

[2] Philip H. Ennis, "Technological Change and the Professions: Neither Luddite nor Technocrat," *Library Quarterly*, XXXII (July 1962), 189-98.

[3] M. Francillon, "Information Retrieval: A View from the Reference Desk," *Journal of Documentation*, XV (December 1959), 187-98; Margaret K. Goggin, ed., "Current Trends in Reference Services," *Library Trends*, XII (January 1964); Ellis Mount, "Communication Barriers and the Reference Question," *Special Libraries*, LVII (October 1966), 575-78.

[4] D. M. Mackay, "Operational Aspects of Some Fundamental Concepts of Human Communication," *Synthese*, IX (Issue 3, No. 3-5, 1954), 182-98.

[5] L. B. Doyle, "Is Relevance an Adequate Criterion in Retrieval System Evaluation," in American Documentation Institute, 26th Annual Meeting, October 1963, *Automation and Scientific Communication*, Part II, 199-200; R. S. Taylor, "The Process of Asking Questions," *American Documentation*, XIII (October 1962), 391-96.

[6] In this report, the designations "reference librarian," "librarian," "information specialist," and "subject specialist" are used interchangeably. There are differences. In this report, however, these terms are used merely to identify the person negotiating the question, in contrast to the "inquirer," who poses the questions and requires information in some form as an answer.

[7] Unacknowledged quotations in this paper are from the taped interviews with reference librarians and information specialists. It was mutually agreed that such quotations would be anonymous. Minor editing has been done for clarity only.

[8] Stanley L. Payne, *The Art of Asking Questions* (Princeton, N.J.: Princeton University Press, 1951); Stephen A. Richardson, et al., *Interviewing, Its Forms and Functions* (New York: Basic Books, 1965).

[9] N. D. Belnap, Jr., *An Analysis of Questions: Preliminary Report.* Document TM-1287 (Santa Monica, California, 1963); R. F. Simmons, "Answering English Questions by Computer: A Survey," *ACM Communications*, VIII (January 1966), 53-70.

[10] D. M. Mackay, "What Makes a Question," *The Listener*, LXIII (May 5, 1960), 789-90.

[11] Victor Rosenberg, "The Application of Psychometric Techniques to Determine the Attitudes of Individuals Toward Information Seeking," *Report No. 2*, Studies in the Man-System Interface in Libraries (Bethlehem, Pennsylvania: Center for the Information Sciences, Lehigh University, July 1966).

[12] James W. Perry, *Defining the Query Spectrum—The Basis for Designing and Evaluating Retrieval Methods* (n.p., 1961 [mimeo.]); Taylor, *op. cit.*

[13] Francillon, *op. cit.*

[14] Susan Artandi, "The Searchers—Links Between Inquirers and Indexes," *Special Libraries*, LVII (October 1966), 571-74.

[15] Caroline E. Hieber, "An Analysis of Questions and Answers in Libraries," *Report No. 1*, Studies in the Man-System Interface in Libraries (Bethlehem, Pennsylvania: Center for Information Sciences, Lehigh University, June 1966).

[16] Lord Radcliffe, "How a Lawyer Thinks," *Lancet*, CCLXX (January 1956), 1-5.

[17] D. M. Mackay, "Informational Analysis of Questions and Commands," in *Information Theory*, C. Cherry, ed. (London: Butterworths, 1961), pp. 469-76.

[18] Advanced Information Systems Co. *Report on the Organization of Large Files with Self-Organizing Capability* (Los Angeles: 1961).

[19] J. S. Green, "GRINS, an On-Line Structure for the Negotiation of Inquiries," *Report No. 4*, Studies in the Man-System Interface in Libraries (Bethlehem, Pennsylvania: Center for Information Sciences, Lehigh University, June 1966).

[20] It is worth noting that the form divisions in the Dewey Classification anticipated this kind of approach.

[21] J. Weizenbaum, "ELIZA, a Computer Program for the Study of Natural Language Communication," *ACM Communications*, IX (January 1966), 36-45.

[22] J. S. Green, *op. cit.*

[23] Harriet Genung, "Can Machines Teach the Use of the Library?" *CRL*, XXVIII (January 1967), 25-30.

[24] Michael B. Leibowitz, *A Proposed System for Displaying Accessing Techniques to Library Users in the Field of Metallurgy* (M.S. Thesis, Lehigh University, 1967).

[25] University of Chicago. Graduate Library School. *Requirements Study for Future Catalogs*, Progress Report No. 1, October 1966.

[26] R. S. Taylor, *op. cit.*

The Study of the Use and Users of Recorded Knowledge[1]

by Philip H. Ennis

Ennis offers a framework for shifting certain types of library research beyond the relatively low level around which most studies have clustered. He details and explains how limited has been the scale of research by libraries and by librarianship into the technical information community and identifies most of the work as being centered upon in-library issues and upon more generalized fields of concern, rather than the technical and specialized ones. He thus provides a convenient handle for taking hold of differences between study method in general purpose library situations as against more specialized services and settings. He then goes on to conceptualize a number of issues and problems which seem relevant to furthering understanding of those who use or do not use libraries and why or how this may be so. Here then is a good deal of raw material and a wide ranging research perspective for students who would employ social science research methods in advancing the understanding of this field.

The word "knowledge" in the title of this paper will gradually transmute to the word "information," because the emphasis of this conference is on professional and scientific uses of knowledge and the word "information" is associatively more at home in this context. It is important, however, to note that man's printed record carries other associations; moral instruction and sustenance, imaginative release and recreation, individual and social solace and satire. The use and users of these aspects of recorded knowledge have not as yet been studied as intensively as have "information users"; they should not be forgotten, however.

Before we can discuss how to *study* use and users, some boundaries and distinctions are necessary. Otherwise practically all of library science would be subsumed into this field, which is large and untidy enough. The first distinction is a cautionary note for us not to fall into a total concern with the needs of the present users of libraries, for the classical responsibility of the library to collect and preserve a body of recorded materials implies that the future users should be considered. Since their needs are likely to be different from those of the present users, flexibility of all library functions is imperative.

Next, two apparently fragmentary ancedotes introduce a tentative architecture for this area of user studies.

The first story is about a scientist friend of mine who was talking with me about books and reading. He observed, in a moment of self-discovery, that his professional reading was quite different from his recreational reading. For the latter he read in the traditional way, from the beginning through to the end. In his professional reading, however, he often read backward, turning first to the conclusions of an article, then working back to the data, then finally back to the introductory statement of the problem. I have done this myself and recognized immediately the differences in these two ways of reading. It is not entirely or simply a matter of speed, but different purposes are being served.

The second story is the paradox that, at the same time great sums of money are being spent to develop more efficient abstracting services which condense information into short bundles, the *New York Review of Books* has become a considerable success—and its most outstanding feature is the *long* review.

Both these observations point to a decisive distinction between *general audiences* for books on the one hand and *specialized* audiences for particu-

SOURCE: Philip H. Ennis, "The Study of the Use and Users of Recorded Knowledge," *Library Quarterly*, 34 (Oct., 1964), pp. 305-314. Reprinted from *Library Quarterly* by permission of The University of Chicago Press. Copyright 1964 by the University of Chicago Press.

lar types of recorded information on the other. The general audience is comprised of an unknown number of individuals, scattered invisibly across the entire landscape of the country. Their reading serves a variety of purposes and is comprised of many disparate patterns.

In contradistinction, the audiences for specialized communication can generally be bounded by familiar occupational or institutional labels, within the scientific communities, the medicine and health field, education, engineering, and so forth. There are other kinds of specialized audiences as well, those, for example, defined by religious or ethnic boundaries or those created by specialized leisure interests.

TABLE 1

SCHEMATIC ARCHITECTURE OF USE STUDIES

PERSPECTIVE OF STUDY	TYPE OF AUDIENCE	
	General	Specialized
"Inside" the library.	1	2
"Outside" the library	3	4

There is a multiplicity of general audiences and a multiplicity of specialized audiences which overlap within and between each other in an unraveled tangle. Nevertheless, the *conceptual* separation of the two types, though certainly not new, is vital, for the two types of audience invite a different kind of question, each of which in turn relates to a different and basic sociological problem.

A second distinction, of comparable importance, is that which differentiates research primarily oriented to problems *inside* the library from those concerned mainly with those *outside* or beyond the library. Researches "inside" the library deal with problems of contact between users and a library function, be it acquisition, reference service, the use of the catalog, or circulation. Studies "outside" the libraries have to do with the broader issues of identifying the characteristics of readers, describing their communications practices, and sources of information, including the library as but one source among many.

If we put these two dimensions together, we have four basic types of user studies, shown in Table 1.

It should be clear that these four kinds of studies do not specify anything about methods of research, types of libraries, or sources of data. In fact, a variety of libraries, methods, and data is used in each of the four kinds of studies. I am not sure that all of the many kinds of studies of library use and users can be fitted into this scheme, but a surprisingly large number do. To illustrate the kinds of studies that fall in each of the cells, cell 1, the studies of general audiences inside the library, would contain research into catalog use, or analyses of reference questions. In cell 2 are studies which describe how specialists of one kind or other (e.g., physicians, engineers, scientists, or scholars) use various library services or facilities. In cell 3 are the familiar studies which ask who is reading what kinds of books and where do they come from, and in cell 4 are several different kinds of studies, the most familiar type being the study, through interview, diary, or observation, aimed at describing the communications patterns and information needs of different kinds of specialists. It is these latter studies that have, I think, most often been called "use or user" studies. At least two other kinds of studies also fall into cell 4; they are, first, "readership studies" wherein the specialist's response to a particular publication is analyzed, and, second, citation studies, in which specialist journals, typically in some field of science, are analyzed for the references cited in their articles. Later I will have more to say about the distribution of studies in these cells and about user-research problems generally.

For most of the paper, however, I would like to discuss this fourfold table, identify its intellectual roots, and draw some implications for the study of the use of recorded knowledge.

First, let us consider the distinction between general and specialized audiences. As noted above each has generated a typical kind of question which, in turn, has shaped its research traditions. For general audiences the studies have been designed mainly to arm librarians, educators, and publishers in the perennial struggle to create and maintain an adult audience of readers. A key element in that struggle was the instilling and sustaining of motivation to read. Thus, a good deal of inquiry was devoted to discovering the techniques to get people to read and to evaluating the efficacy of those techniques.

For specialized audiences, on the other hand, motivation to read has been pretty much taken for granted. It is assumed that a specialized audience, in seeking information, is carrying out some well-motivated performance of an occupational role, for example, scientist, physician. Being informed and keeping up with the literature are part of that role.

The basic problem of the specialized audience, instead, becomes a diffusion-decision problem—

that is, a description of the communication structure of a specialized audience, a tracing of recorded messages proceeding through that structure, and an evaluation of the impact of these messages on the decisions that are made in the course of performing the specialized functions of the particular audience.

There is another way to describe the difference between a general and a special audience. It is in the relations—quantitative and qualitative—between their readers and writers. Quantitatively, the difference may be described in terms of the ratio of writers to readers. One can define the degree of specialization of an audience partly by its absolute size and partly by the extent to which the number of writers approaches the number of readers.

Qualitatively, the difference between a general and a special audience is the kind and amount of feed-back from reader to writer. In the special audience there is more of the tendency for a member to be, at alternate times, reader *and* writer, with the channel of recorded knowledge being part of mutual communication. In the general audience the reader simply tends to say yea or nay (accept or reject), to various items transmitted. In brief this is the difference between two-way communication and one-way communication. This means one- or two-way communication through that channel only. The exchange of money for words indicates that there are feed-back processes in general audiences as well, but they are different and have different consequences for the system. And above all, they involve the librarian in different ways for each system.

So to continue the logic of the previously mentioned fourfold table, it should be noted that the research question asked of each type of audience can be answered either from the point of view of the *library's contribution* or from the point of view of the *audience as a whole*.

Now these two different ways of formulating problems have historically grown from the library's practical concerns and from its professional ideology, some key elements of which are to serve everyone and to educate as you serve. Most professions generate such research perspectives in the same way, yet they vary in the extent to which their everyday practice and research is related to the intellectual apparatus of basic research, carried on by the more traditional university line departments. Part of that intellectual apparatus is research methodology. It seems clear that librarianship has borrowed liberally and creatively from the variety of methods developed by the social sciences. The incorporation of social science theories, concepts, and ideas into library science, however, has not seemed to me to have gone very far. Perhaps it is the tradition of polemical reassertion of library ideology mixed with a constricting pragmatism that prevents a cumulating body of theory. I mean here particularly the reliance on local surveys to match ALA standards.

Yet it seems imperative and possible to move in this direction, for the two formulations of the problems mentioned above suggest a translation of user studies into broad sociological concepts, furnishing thereby an abundant and continuing resource of ideas and empirical generalizations. To illustrate, the problem of making and keeping an adult audience for books is an example of the generic question as to how any habit, taste, or preference is maintained as a voluntary choice in a competitive and pluralistic society. The social process of creating and sustaining buttermilk-drinkers, bowlers, Republican voters, Beethoven-lovers, and book-readers is similar and in some cases identical.

While there is no single or definitive answer to the generic question of how tastes are formed and maintained, the processes of socialization and the processes of persuasion are the two most obvious and probably critical involved in creating and securing an audience for anything. That is, many tastes and preferences are either directly or indirectly created in the early school years; surely reading is one of these. So it is an important part of any research program on general reading to explore the array and relative strength of the influences determining skill and motivation to read all through the early years, especially at critical transition points in a child's development. Similarly, the preservation of reading as an adult habit requires the same kind of treatment. There are important clues that reading, like many other minority tastes in American life, depends upon some degree of social support for the activity, over and above the intrinsic satisfaction that the act of reading gives. Informal social support from family and friends, and more formal efforts at persuasion and influence, as well as the whole study of socialization have a rich research tradition in modern psychology and sociology.

An analogous translation can be made with the librarian's concern for the diffusion of information and its use among specialized groups. This formulation of the problem derives from one of the most important structural facts of modern industrialized societies, namely, the traditional professions (law and medicine), many of the maturing professions (architecture, teaching, social work, nursing, librarianship), many occupations even further removed from the professional niche (such as city planner, computer programmer, traffic engineer), and finally even occupations as farmer, skilled machine craftsmen, and sports instructors—all are increasingly dependent on basic research done in traditional departments of universities, special research institutions, and industrial and governmental laboratories. The physical, life, earth, and behavioral sciences transmit their research results through a dense tangle of special interest groups and occupational specialities via a communications network including formal conferences and meetings, journals of every type and level, and a variety of informal channels ranging from letters to corridor chats.

There are several social-science areas dealing directly with these problems, all of which can contribute basic intellectual resources for library science. The sociology of science, a rapidly growing subspecialty in the field, is an important one, the modern counterparts of communications research is another, and the interdisciplinary field of organization theory is still a third.

At this point, the obvious solution to both the curriculum problem and the research problem involved in studying library users would be to have those students interested in public libraries and work with children and young people take those social-science courses that deal with the processes of socialization and persuasion. Those students interested in special libraries and research libraries can be directed into courses in the sociology of science, organizational theory, and so forth. This is, I suppose, what is done now insofar as the social sciences enter the library-school curriculum at all. And if such practices were extended, all to the good.

But suppose we reverse the questions and ask about the communications patterns in a general audience and its relation to their decisions. Conversely, suppose we ask how to create and maintain interests for specialized fields. Such an orientation seems difficult to carry through, especially when we examine the implicit premise of the two questions. For studies of specialized audiences the touchstone has been the logic of *efficiency*: knowledge of communications patterns and assessments of information services to specialists, evaluated by the yardstick of efficiency. This is possible because there are objective criteria of assessing the

effect of various measures on productivity of the specialized audience, as measured by quantitative counts of articles or books or products produced or by individual or group judgments as to the usefulness of various bibliographic tools or other publications.

In contrast, a general audience can only report what it likes, how much of what kind of things it reads, and where it gets them. Since there is no consensus as to desired effects of general reading and no way of assessing whatever effects do occur, the question as to efficiency hardly seems appropriate. The only way the efficiency criterion has been used with respect to general audiences is with the ability of a library or any other agency to produce readers or circulation. Sheer amount of use and the degree of success in winning the non-reader become, therefore, the major services that tend to be measured quantitatively. The empirical studies of catalog use and reference service are among the weakest in all library research. Yet there may be gains in reversing the questions, especially if we shift associative gears somewhat. General audiences may not be a scattered and random aggregate of isolated individuals—the implicit assumption about them. There is, in fact, impressive evidence that such "general" audiences are constantly being moved in the direction of organization and specialization. Just a few items to show this pervasive tendency.

First, is the now-established finding (still new to some, however) that people come in groups: family, neighborhood, friendship, work, religious, ethnic, and so on. One of the elements of these groups is a division of function; some people sharpen the pencils and some people write with them. Another element is that some people initiate and sanction group activities, while others follow and support group action. The discovery of "opinion leadership" as a characteristic of large statistical aggregates of people bound together by community or ethnic ties provides a microstructure from which larger organized groupings emerge. And they emerge from the natural coagulative tendency for likes to seek out each other to share and to defend their interests. The process might begin and only go as far as, say, the Tall Girl Clubs that exist in practically all major metropolitan areas—they simply sponsor activities that will attract tall men and lobby among clothing and shoe manufacturers regarding the tall girl's special problems. In the field of reading we find comparably the Joyce Society, the Baker Street Irregulars, the now almost extinct but lamentably unstudied Browning Societies which once filled the landscape, or the countless bookreview clubs formed by literate housewives. I wonder, incidentally, if these clubs have disappeared over the years or is it simply their relative invisibility to me, compared to my youth, when my mother would be all in a panic when it was her turn to give her book report. (It was not clear then, or now, whether it was the intellectual task of the book review or the social task of serving an elegant tea that caused the panic, or maintained the group.)

Such "natural" groupings are sometimes strengthened, sometimes initiated, by the possibility of commercial advantage. The obvious case is the systematic development of special-interest book clubs—the emphasis is rarely put on the word *club* as meaning an association. Bowker lists about one hundred of them, all captured by the familiar wisdom that when he is properly identified, it is a more predictable strategy to sell one man ten books than ten men one book. Finally and most puzzling is the more vaporous structuring of literature subpublics of various types.[2] Little is known of their boundaries, internal differentiation, and overlap.

The same approach, that is, seeing the group structure within the general audience, is applicable to young people as well as adults. For example, everyone has talked for years about the reading ladder. Get children on simple things, and gradually there will be a development of taste. This is, as far as I can see, empirically unsupported and will probably remain so long as teachers and librarians tear up every year, in the name of efficiency, all the records they should have been keeping for longitudinal studies. Not only is the structuring of book choices among young people important, but also the social influences around them guiding the extent and nature of their reading. A pilot project Sara Fenwick and I are carrying out in a Chicago public school suggests that for sixth-graders reading patterns are very diverse but clearly linked to their immediate world. We had group interviews with five average youngsters, then later that week a group interview with their fathers, then an interview with the mothers, another session with the children and a final group interview with their current teacher, their librarian, and their teacher of the previous year. Taking this entire population as an interrelated system we found interesting areas of misperception—differing expectations as to who should be doing what about reading and learning. Mothers differed with the fathers; parents with teachers; and the children

appeared immensely more knowledgeable about the attempted control procedures the adults used than I had supposed.

In short, it seems propitious to explore, once more, the structure of reading audiences, beginning perhaps with a study to describe the variety of reading habits. The admirable start made years ago by Ruth Strang, in her *Explorations in Reading Patterns,*[3] might very well be tried again with new tools and new concepts.

With respect to specialized audiences, the reversal of the traditional library-research question would produce, I believe, several different research directions. One is toward the level of specialized systems as a whole. Specifically, an important limitation of many user studies is that they have been generally restricted in scope, dealing largely with one specialized audience at a time. This makes good sense methodologically and is the right approach if the unit under study is the individual user. But if the scope of the inquiry is extended under the directive of the kind of question asked of general audiences, then the perspective would see specialized audiences themselves as subunits in a larger institutional sector. For example, in the field of public primary and secondary education there are literally hundreds of specialized audiences who have some share in the operation and decision-making of a city or a state's educational system. An even larger number of specialized sub-audiences comprises the health sector. Combined with the fact that increasing numbers of occupations are being guided by the findings of basic science, the increasing interrelations among and between specialized groups make it important to look at the diffusion patterns of larger systems, including their network of information centers, libraries, and whatever other dissemination channels there are.

The methodology for such extensive studies is still in its infancy, but one point seems clear; as the design of such communications-systems studies increases in scope, the likelihood that individual users will be the basic unit of inquiry will lessen.

A second direction of study of specialized audiences emerges when we now take as problematical the motivation of specialists, and ask not only what are they doing and what do they need, but what kinds of motivations—individual and socially prescribed—are involved. Such inquiries are especially important when focused on the mutual expectations of specialist and librarian. It is more than likely that there are mutual misperceptions and misunderstandings as to who should be doing what about the control of information dissemination. Moreover, there is likely to be in specialized fields a counterpart of a common librarian-patron difficulty in the general audience field. It is the familiar complaint that people hardly ever ask the question they really want to ask, but it takes the skills of the reference librarian in what might be called an information interview to bring out the real problem and then to prescribe the solution. Even on this level, the same is probably true for librarians dealing with specialists, but to a lesser extent, for they are often housed together in the same organization, and the reference librarian himself is likely to be somewhat of an expert on the particular specialty. A more important difficulty is the degree of disagreement as to the subject classification schemes and basic categories involved, as well as the social control over the use of various categories.

Such disagreements will probably become more serious as advanced information technology continues to reshuffle task allocations back and forth between the specialist and those in charge of packaging information and moving it from one place to another and from one person to another. For instance, this is the influential opinion of Alvin Weinberg:

> The later steps of the information transfer process, such as retrieval, are strongly affected by the attitudes and practices of the originators of scientific information. The working scientist must therefore share many of the burdens that have been traditionally carried by the professional documentalist. The technical community must devote a larger share than heretofore of its time and resources to the discriminating management of the ever-increasing technical record. Doing less will lead to fragmented and ineffective science and technology.[4]

And in almost direct contradiction is the advice of the recent report, *Toward the Library of the 21st Century:*

> The library itself will help the user find and organize textual material relevant to the subject he is studying. . . we know that certain advances already made or now envisioned in science hold promise of alleviating burdens of information usage in all activities that draw upon resources of the library.[5]

There are already some studies of specialized information moving in the direction of combining psychological-motivational variables with sociological level variables focused on the structure of the work group within which research is carried out.[6] It should be no surprise to learn that these kinds of studies originate outside the library world and indeed often outside the university community.

These examples indicate that, while the traditional presumptions lying behind the study of general or specific audiences for information are still not exhausted, reversing them produces some different and useful research suggestions. Such a reversal also makes it more difficult to design a curriculum. If general and specialized audiences should be examined from both sets of presumptions, and if, as is clearly the case, types of libraries do not coincide very well with the distinction between general versus specific, then one cannot simply send public and school librarians off to one set of social-science courses and special and academic-research librarians off to another set. There is no easy answer to this. One choice is to send all library students to a carefully and individually chosen set of courses in sociology, psychology, economics, and so on. The risks here are that they will not be absorbed in the routine research and teaching assistantships and important informal relationships in either their library school or the social-science departments. Moreover, these departments are oriented toward producing their own products and furthering their own research interests; this is likely to create, albeit inadvertently, even further exclusionary practices toward our visiting library students.

A second choice is to increase the number of specialists (social science or otherwise) on library-school faculties. The difficulty here, administrative and intellectual, is the potential isolation of the visiting faculty member rather than the student, and his inability to get library students interested in his research, which is tied to his parent discipline.

A third choice is to demand higher entrance requirements for students. Like all complex problems, experimentation with combinations of all three choices will have to be employed and will vary from school to school and from time to time. But if something is not done to reconnect the study of use and users to their intellectual roots in the social sciences, then the spasmodic and noncumulative kind of library research will continue.

The amount and organization of research on library use suffers the same difficulties as does teaching. This is neither a new problem nor is it restricted to library schools. Research productivity of all types of professional school faculties tends to be lower than it is for the line departments. The teaching demands involved in producing practitioners is in part responsible, but I suspect that the resistance of practicing professionals

TABLE 2
Comparative Origin of Use Studies

	"Library Science Dissertations"			"Bibliography of Use Studies"		
	General	Specialized		General	Specialized	
"Inside"	39%	11%	50%	17%	4%	21%
"Outside"	28%	22%	50%	12%	67%	79%
	67%	33%	100% = 36	29%	71%	100% = 351

acts as a brake to university-based research, especially in the newer areas of research on use and users. As evidence for this Table 2 shows the distribution of use studies among library science Ph.D. dissertations (1925-63)[7] compared to use studies carried on in other settings. These latter are taken from the extensive bibliography on use studies compiled by Richard A. Davis and C. A. Bailey.[8]

From both the annotated list of library-science dissertations and the annotated Davis bibliography, only empirical studies dealing with the use or users of the library were selected. There was no serious difficulty in assigning any of the titles to one of the cells. The results here are illustrative only and should not be misconstrued as defining either the degree of productivity of library schools in general or the quality or content of their research.[9]

From the marginal percentages it is clear that high-level library-school research has been directed toward problems inside rather than outside the library (50 per cent of the empirical dissertations on use), and far more concerned with the general rather than the specialized audience (67 books and libraries). In contrast, the field as a whole, representing researchers far beyond the walls of library schools, shows a considerably different distribution with the emphasis clearly on the specialized

audience outside the library—the typical "use" study. If the curriculum and the research direction of the modern library school are to be at least responsive to the problems of its cousins, documentalists and information retrievers, then library-school research priorities should change.

A more compelling reason for a renewed interest in the study of users, however, is the change in the ways knowledge is created and communicated. I can think of no more dramatic way of underlining the rapidity and depth of these changes than to quote the following excerpt from the autobiography of Leonard Woolf who was writing about his experiences at the time of World War I. In less than one lifetime these words seem ironically outdated.

> I have often irritated people by saying that an intelligent person can become what is called an "authority" on most "questions," "problems," or "subjects," by intensive study for two or three months. They thought me arrogant for saying so, or if not arrogant, not serious. But it is true. The number and volume of relevant facts on any subject are not many or great and the number of good and important books on it are few. If you have a nose for relevant facts and the trails which lead to them—this is essential and half the battle—and if you know how to work with the laborious pertinacity of a mole and a beaver, you can acquire in a few months all the knowledge necessary for a thorough understanding of the subject.[10]

FOOTNOTES

[1] I am indebted to Carol Woolpy for her help in organizing and tabulating the quantitative parts of this paper.

[2] I recall here the insightful identification of this phenomenon by David Riesman in an article on reading in which he described the *New Yorker* cartoon about the young man who replied to the question whether he had read a current bestseller with the words, "Not personally."

[3] Ruth Strang, *Explorations in Reading Patterns* (Chicago: University of Chicago Press, 1942).

[4] Alvin Weinberg, "Scientific Communication," *International Science and Technology*, April, 1963, p. 65.

[5] Bolt, Beranek, and Newman, Inc., *Toward the Library of the 21st Century* (Cambridge, Mass.: Council on Library Resources, 1964), pp. 1, 10.

[6] See, e.g., the recent work, John A. Postley *et. al.*, *Report on a Study of Behavioral Factors in Information Systems* (Los Angeles: Hughes Dynamics, n.d.); and the older investigations; Herbert A. Shepard, "The Value of a University Research Group," *American Sociological Review*, XIX (1954), 456-62.

[7] *Library Science Dissertations: 1925-60—an Annotated Bibliography of Doctoral Studies* (Washington, D.C.: Bureau of Educational Research and Development, Library Services Branch, U.S. Office of Education, 1963). Information about library science dissertations for 1960-63 was obtained from *Library Literature, Dissertation Abstracts,* and the *Library Quarterly.*

[8]*Bibliography of Use Studies* (Philadelphia: Graduate School of Library Science, Drexel Institute of Technology, 1964).
[9]Since they represent a more serious research commitment, Ph.D. dissertations rather than M.A. theses were selected. The Davis bibliography occasionally reports studies in several forms—different research reports, multiple publication, and so forth. Insofar as possible these have been removed, but even with further excision the results do not change appreciably.
[10]Leonard Woolf, *Beginning Again* (London: Hogarth Press,1964), p. 185.

Information Needs and Uses

by William J. Paisley

This conceptual design, extracted from Paisley's review article, is one of the few efforts to construct a framework around which to orient research in one salient area of concern to library discipline. Because he sees, and clearly states the utility of theory, he has exploited the opportunity provided by reviewing the literature to do far more. Paisley's analysis, by detailing the present state-of-the-art and characterizing the limits and gaps in present knowledge, makes it possible for research in the future to contribute additively to the intellectual development and comprehension of information need and use. In this way, genuine meaning and significance is given to otherwise isolated and disparate study. Other areas of librarianship await the same sophisticated theoretical treatment.

INTRODUCTION

Information science meets behavioral science in the study of information needs and uses. At first, the meeting of these fields was inconclusive. Until the mid-1960s, there were only a few substantial studies of information needs and uses. Since about 1963, however, a significant literature has grown rapidly.

There is evidence now of a productive *entente* between the two fields. When information scientists see reliable, valid, and nontrivial data on users' behavior, they begin to use behavioral criteria in evaluating information system performance. When behavioral scientists glimpse the full complexity of dissemination, documentation, storage, and retrieval processes, they offer fewer naive solutions to "the information problem."

This mutual education and accommodation will undoubtedly continue. Information science and behavioral science need each other. Big Science needs them both.

. . . . .

Studying Information Needs and Uses

Until now, the most predictable and justified complaint against user studies has been defective methodology. Both previous authors of this chapter (Menzel, 11; Herner, 6) and the present reviewer (17) have expressed concern over the field's failure to adopt the sound methods of its own best work. Mistakes of the 1950s are repeated in the 1960s. Inconclusive studies are conducted to fill gaps left by previous inconclusive studies.

Although methodological defects still appear in the 1967 literature, it may now be time to object more strenuously to poor conceptualization. By and large, we now know how studies *should* be conducted. When a mail questionnaire comes back with 30% response, the investigators probably understand the doubtful validity of their data.

Shallow conceptualization is something else again. Even small projects can demonstrate awareness of the complex systems that affect the flow of information. Shallow conceptualization implies a failure to consider these factors:

1. The full array of information sources that are available.
2. The uses to which information will be put.
3. The background, motivation, professional orientation, and other individual characteristics of the user.
4. The social, political, economic, and other systems that powerfully affect the user and his work.
5. The consequences of information use—e.g., productivity.

As a result, in many studies, it is hard to glimpse a real scientist or technologist at work, under constraints and pressures, creating products, drawing upon the elaborate communication network that connects him with sources of necessary knowledge.

No study can treat all five factors at once, although the best (e.g., Pelz & Andrews, 20) come close. And some topics, such as "relevance,"

SOURCE: Reprinted from William J. Paisley, "Information Needs and Uses," *Annual Review of Information Science and Technology*, ed. Carlos A. Cuadra (Vol. 3; Chicago: Encyclopaedia Britannica, 1968), Chap. 1, pp. 1-6 and 23-30, by permission of the publisher.

should be taken to the social-psychological laboratory for the sake of experimental rigor. But we have seen too many field studies in which shallow conceptualization leaves the investigator without validity checks, without qualifying variables, and without the ability to reject alternative interpretations of his findings.

Conceptual poverty is independent of methodological richness. There is an example in this year's literature of a major methodologically sophisticated study (North American Aviation, 15) that received weak analysis because of a "conceptualization gap." The investigators carefully considered which variables should be included but backed away from the issue of how each variable should be treated. As a result, in spite of a large sample of 1,500 interviews with defense industry personnel (paralleling the excellent study of DOD personnel conducted by Auerbach Corporation, 4), the NAA analysis offers little insight beyond the two-variable case.

The specific difficulty arose in the investigators' desire to bring all of their variables into linear multiple regressions against such dependent variables as "first source of information sought." Their 55 *qualitative* variables had to be quantified somehow, and the chosen course was that of assigning numbers *by fiat*. For example, the respondent's highest earned degree was given these scale values: none, 0; associate's, 2; bachelor's, 4; master's, 6; professional (Ed.D., LL.B., engineer), 7; and doctorate, 8. Similarly, field of training was "scaled": behavioral and social sciences, 1; biological and medical sciences, 2; agriculture and agricultural engineering, 3; and so on through other engineering specialties to chemistry, 10; earth sciences, 11; physical sciences, 12; and mathematical sciences, 13. One searches in vain for a conceptual or even empirical justification of this particular order. Not surprisingly, the only strong independent predictors are those with a priori order, such as age. Such cavalier treatment of the conceptual dimensions of variables would disqualify a minor study; it seriously weakens the NAA study, which otherwise ranks among the year's best.

To summarize this discussion, the study of information needs/uses has matured methodologically (in most projects, most of the time), but we now urgently need theories of information-processing behavior that will generate propositions concerning channel selection; amount of seeking; effects on productivity of information quality, quantity, currency, and diversity; the role of motivational and personality factors, etc. The following *systematic* review of recent research will identify variables that any comprehensive theory must accommodate.

A CONCEPTUAL FRAMEWORK: THE SCIENTIST WITHIN SYSTEMS (WITHIN SYSTEMS)

We cannot interpret data on information needs and uses without recognizing that the scientist/technologist stands at the center of many *systems* that touch every aspect of his work. An understanding of these systems is essential if we are to improve information transfer. Computer-based storage and retrieval systems that are not integrated into these social, political, and economic systems will be expensive, unused novelties.

Certain systems are especially relevant to information use. For example, the scientist's work team and colleagues are primary information sources. Other systems close to him (e.g., his religious group) may not impinge on his working habits and information use; these systems we can overlook until later evidence tells us otherwise.

Systems affecting the scientist form a set of *almost*-concentric circles. Perhaps the largest circle should be known as *(1) the scientist within his culture*. However little control we have over it, we should not underestimate the cultural system, both as a tradition and as an ambient spirit. As Price observes, "Now that we have some feeling for what was possible (and what not) for these people [ancient Greek, Chinese, Babylonian, Mayan, Egyptian], we can see clearly that Western culture must somewhere have taken a different turn that made the scientific tradition much more productive than in all these other cases. We are now living in a high scientific technology, in which the material repercussions of science shape our daily lives and the destinies of nations . . ." (22, p. 3).

It is the cultural system that awards Nobel prizes, emphasizes priority of discovery, establishes great private foundations, and supports universities. The effect of our culture on science's information system is so pervasive as to be overlooked. However, we need only think of changes that would occur if, for example, the "priority" fetish gave way to an insistence on repeated success in replication. The system's glut of letters and hasty reports would vanish, monographic treatments would be favored over journal articles, and scientists would rely even more on informal channels to discuss findings that they could not yet certify for publication.

Somewhat more transitory is *(2) the scientist within a political system.* Three contemporary political factors powerfully affect the American scientist. One is a persistent scientific nationalism in many fields that causes the scientist largely to ignore foreign research. A second is the present strength of scientific federalism; the money begins in Washington. A third is the role of the Department of Defense. Leonardo spent many years designing weapons and fortifications for Cesare Borgia; in the United States, more scientists are hired by the military establishment than by, for example, pollution-control or food-research agencies.

With the promise, or at least the chimera, of DOD support for projects they would like to do, scientists are drawn to available funds, frustrated by security restrictions, distressed by moral issues. On the whole, their information systems have gained from the alliance: the Defense Documentation Center is a quick and cheap supplier of reports that would otherwise be buried in obscure journals or not available at all.

A system that is both within and beyond political systems and the culture, but smaller in number of people affected, is *(3) the scientist within a membership group.* When the scientist answers "what do you do?" by saying "I'm a psychologist," he is locating himself within a professional membership system. Other systems may command greater loyalty, but the membership system probably controls the "official" information channels of his field. The information system of the American Psychological Association, ably studied by Garvey and Griffith (1, 2, 3), is a strong example. The membership system may govern the scientist's appearance on its convention programs, may appoint him to the editorial board of its journals, etc.

System *(4)* is *the scientist within a reference group,* which includes other scientists with similar specialization, similar training, excellence of work, or other characteristics. Whereas the scientist might not attempt to save every paper or reprint received from others in his *membership* group, he might maintain a file for his *reference* group. Reference-group identification for our scientist above might be "social psychologist studying human information-processing behavior." A reference group need not be contained within a membership group; the reference group of scientists studying human information-processing is drawn from several membership groups. A reference group may

control a journal or two, but it rarely controls an entire information system.

A subsystem of *(4)* is *(5) the scientist within an invisible college.* "Invisible college" (or group of scientists—usually fewer than 100—who know each other and share information directly) has had elite connotations ever since Price rediscovered the term and linked it with "affluent scientific commuter" (21, p. 62). Probably every scientist has his invisible college in a functional sense, however. It only happens that certain colleges are closer to sources of funds, rewards, and power. If these colleges seem better trained and more productive, we cannot yet specify the direction of causality.

The invisible college "selects its own society, then shuts the door." The scientist may save papers and reprints from everyone in his reference group, but he does not correspond with everyone, nor arrange meetings in distant cities, nor plan joint projects, nor co-author books with them. What the invisible college gains in direct access, it loses in formal information exchange. Invisible colleges rarely control even a journal, and, according to anecdotal evidence, their efforts to operate information-exchange groups are undermined by each scientist's conviction that he is already in touch with the others who count.

While scientists in an invisible college share the same status level and are geographically dispersed, the system that we shall call *(6) the scientist within a formal organization* integrates several status levels at the same location. This system emphasizes roles, lines of responsibility, and products, rather than people themselves. Both in the facilities it provides and in the policies it sets, the scientist's formal organization (i.e., his employing organization) opens or blocks channels of information to him.

A subsystem of *(6)* is *(7) the scientist within a work team.* This is a most important information system. It is tuned to the scientist's problems. It documents the history of its projects in an informal and idiomatic way. Knowing what he does *not* need to be told, the scientist's work team can provide him with rich, nonredundant information through conversation.

In this regress of social and psychological systems, we come to *(8) the scientist within his own head.* This is the system of motivation, of intelligence and creativity, of cognitive structure, of perceived relevance of information inputs and uses of information outputs. Ultimately, all other systems support this one.

Two other, rather depersonalized systems cut across these eight. That is, we must also consider *(9) the scientist within a legal/economic system,* but it is hard to identify the people who speak for this system and look after it. This is the system of patents, copyrights, industrial secrecy, competitive research and development, etc.—all profoundly affecting the flow of information. In addition, the economic system determines the quality and quantity of information that other systems, such as the membership group and the formal organization, can afford to buy.

The obvious omission thus far has been *(10) the scientist within a formal information system*— libraries, technical information centers, etc. There is information transfer that transcends the other systems. There were libraries before the Scientific Revolution, and science would have journals and reviews if membership groups did not publish their own. In most fields of science, the formal information system is actually a marketplace of competing information systems. It takes Olympian perspective to see that each information system finds a unique function and audience, so that— much like commercial air service—a network coalesces from competitive elements.

The scientist is found within many other systems, but these ten serve to organize most of the literature that has appeared on his information needs and uses.

. . . . .

CONCLUSION

The literature on information needs and uses in science and technology is growing in size and maturing in quality. We are moving toward strong guidelines for information system design and evaluation. More adequate theories of information-processing behavior will follow.

Recognition of the Need for Use Studies

Each year brings more statements from information-system planning committees, task groups, etc., on the importance of these studies. For example, from the "COSATI Report" (Carter, 5, p. 109): "The centralized agency responsible for developing a national information system(s) should . . . (conduct) research in user needs, including experimentation with new methods for better serving user needs, as an important part of its total research program." The National Research Council's Committee on Information in the

Behavioral Sciences states as its first recommendation (14, p. 57): "Continuing studies in each behavioral science discipline of information flow from scientist to scientist, between scientists within a discipline and those outside it, and between scientists in different countries, in order to determine information needs and requirements in each discipline and for the sciences as a whole."

Of course, this point of view is not universal. In the Murdock-Liston "theme paper" for the 1968 ASIS convention (13), behavioral factors are virtually ignored. In so many other papers, system performance is evaluated as though successful interface with users can be taken for granted, once the computer or a panel of judges conjures up numbers for "recall" and "precision."

Behavioral factors can be incorporated in information system planning two ways. First, they can be studied after the fact, to explain why the system is not working very well. Second, behavioral data can become the system's foundation, and the proposed first story of hardware and second story of software can be tested to see if they stand on the given foundation.

A Stronger Role for Theory

Purely descriptive study of any set of behaviors has its point of diminishing return. Eventually (certainly not yet) we shall have sufficiently precise knowledge of how much information flows, to whom, through which channels, for what purpose, etc. The scattered findings cannot be combined in a coherent overview, however, without abstract concepts to replace the tired labels of current research, such as "basic" versus "applied," "scientist" versus "technologist," and "formal" versus "informal."

We need what Merton (12) calls "theories of the middle range." That is, we need concepts and theorems that are neither too close to information-use data nor too far removed into systems theory and cybernetics. In Merton's words, "To concentrate entirely on special theories is to run the risk of emerging with unconnected *ad hoc* speculations consistent with a limited range of observations and inconsistent among themselves. To concentrate entirely on the master conceptual scheme for deriving all subsidiary theories is to run the risk of producing twentieth-century . . . equivalents of the large philosophical systems of the past, with all their varied suggestiveness all their archetectonic splendor, and all their scientific sterility." (12, p. 10)

For any field of inquiry, "the middle range" is not self-evident; it has to be approached through successive approximations. Certain researchers in this field (Menzel, Pelz & Andrews, and several others) come close to what the reviewer sees as "the middle range."

Our challenge is to form testable middle-range hypotheses from such observations as:

> The mode of information transfer in technology is primarily oral. Even in his oral communication, however, the technologist is a different creature. Scientists working at the frontier of a particular specialty know each other and associate together in what Derek Price has called invisible colleges. They keep track of one another's work through visits, seminars, and small invitational conferences, supplemented by informal exchange of written material long before it reaches archival publication. Technologists, on the other hand, keep abreast of their field by close association with co-workers in their own organization. They are limited in forming invisible colleges by the imposition of organizational barriers. (Marquis & Allen, 10, p. 1053)

In any field of inquiry, researchers begin with typologies, however crude, and hope to transform those typologies into scalar dimensions with the help of theory. The study of information needs and uses is still in its typological phase, because we lack middle-range concepts that would specify how the types in a typology relate to each other. The progress that can be observed now is a refinement of typologies, with greater specificity of information needs, kinds, channels, etc. (an example in 1967 is Orr, 16). It has been the experience of other fields that some refined typologies strike almost accidently upon underlying conceptual dimensions that establish order. This field would advance more quickly if such concepts as "perceived utility," "perceived costs," "uncertainty," and "psychological distance" could supplant the *ad hoc* typologies with which we have begun.

Toward a More Eclectic Methodology

Mail questionnaires, diaries, and structured personal interviews have provided most of the data we now have on information needs and uses. Each of these methods has its shortcomings, yet each has proved its value. Beyond the standard set of methods in this field—as recently summarized, for example, by Parker & Paisley (19)—we should understand the advantages of an eclectic methodology, a "multiple operationism" (cf. Webb, et al.,

24). A multimethod approach has internal checks against biases introduced by methods themselves.

In the 1967 literature there is a report of "User's Conferences" (Hyslop & Chafe, 7) in which users of the American Society for Metals Documentation Service were convened "to offer their most critical opinions and evaluations of the service, its deficiencies and needed improvements." In other words, instead of collecting independent opinions and synthesizing them statistically, a synthesis was sought in open exchange.

Another example of a not-quite-conventional method is Parker's combination (18) of a secondary analysis of previously collected questionnaire data (from Libbey & Zaltman, 9) with tape-recorded depth interviews of essentially the same population. The two methods jointly comprised the first phase of continuing behavioral research in the development of the Stanford Physics Information Retrieval System.

A third example of extraordinary interest is not a study at all. It is a Nobel Laureate's memoir of two years' pursuit of the molecular structure of DNA (Watson, 23). Information scientists will find that Watson's low-key account of conversations, letters, and international meetings presents a different picture of information use from what the questionnaires tell us. Conversations among half a dozen people in London and Cambridge provided most of the pieces for the DNA puzzle, yet one long-forgotten journal article and a few handbook references filled in pieces that conversation alone could never supply. Conversation provided alternative concepts and models. The journal article and the handbook references, together with fresh X-ray crystallographs, provided data for choosing among the alternatives. Each information channel was essential, but scores of hours were spent in conversation for each hour of reading.

Dependence of Eclectic Methodology on Strong Theory

As long as the field has almost no theory, we are upset by discrepancies (e.g., in lab Y it is the engineers and not the scientists who are more literature-dependent). As theory is strengthened, we will welcome both consistent and discrepant findings. Each contributes to the growth of knowledge in its own way, as suggested in this table of outcomes:

	No Theory	*Strong Theory*
Consistent Findings	Needed confirmation	Additional precision or generality
Discrepant Findings	Confusion	"Broken paradigm" Impetus toward better theory

"Broken paradigm" comes from Kuhn's account of the progress of science (8)—that a good paradigm (or theory) permits a test that "breaks" it and forces scientists to propose a better paradigm in its place.

As of 1967, researchers in this field had not yet succeeded in breaking their first paradigm. That's a measure of how far we have to go.

FOOTNOTES

[1] AMERICAN PSYCHOLOGICAL ASSOCIATION. PROJECT ON SCIENTIFIC INFORMATION EXCHANGE IN PSYCHOLOGY. Reports. Washington, D.C., Vol. 1, Overview Report and Reports 1-9, December 1963; Vol. 2, Reports 10-15, December 1965.

[2] AMERICAN PSYCHOLOGICAL ASSOCIATION. PROJECT ON SCIENTIFIC INFORMATION EXCHANGE IN PSYCHOLOGY. Report 16: Innovations in scientific communication in psychology. Washington, D.C., December 1966. (APA-PSIEP-16) (PB-174651).

[3] AMERICAN PSYCHOLOGICAL ASSOCIATION. PROJECT ON SCIENTIFIC INFORMATION EXCHANGE IN PSYCHOLOGY. Report 17: The use of scientific information in the undergraduate teaching of psychology. Washington, D.C., March 1967, 38 p. (APA-PSIEP-17) (PB-174652).

[4] AUERBACH CORPORATION. DOD user needs study, Phase I. Final Technical Report. Philadelphia, Pa., May 1965, 2 vols. (1151-TR-3).

[5] CARTER, LAUNOR; CANTLEY, GORDON; ROWELL, JOHN T.; SCHULTZ, LOUISE; SEIDEN, HERBERT R.; WALLACE, EVERETT; WATSON, RICHARD; WYLLYS, RONALD E. National document-handling systems for science and technology. Wiley, New York, 1967, 344 p. (Information Science Series).

[6] HERNER, SAUL; HERNER, MARY. Information needs and uses. In: Cuadra, Carlos A., ed. Annual Review of Information Science and Technology. Interscience, New York, 1967, Vol. 2, p. 1-34.

[7] HYSLOP, MARJORIE R.; CHAFE, H. DAVID. User appraisal of an information system and services through a program of joint applied research. In: Schecter, George, ed. Information retrieval—a critical view. Thompson, Washington, D.C., 1967, p. 151-176.

[8] KUHN, THOMAS S. The structure of scientific revolutions. University of Chicago Press, Chicago, 1962.

[9] LIBBEY, MILES A.; ZALTMAN, GERALD. The role and distribution of written informal communication in theoretical high energy physics. American Institute of Physics, New York, 25 August 1967, 75 p. (AIP report no. AIP/SDD-1, rev.; USAEC report no. NYO-3732-1, rev.).

[10] MARQUIS, DONALD G.; ALLEN, THOMAS J. Communication pattenrs in applied technology. American Psychologist, 21 (November 1966) 1052-1060.

[11] MENZEL, HERBERT. Information needs and uses in science and technology. In: Cuadra, Carlos A., ed. Annual Review of Information Science and Technology. Interscience, New York, 1966, Vol. 1, p. 41-69.

[12] MERTON, ROBERT. Social theory and social structure. Free Press, Glencoe, Ill.; 1967.

[13] MURDOCK, JOHN W.; LISTON, DAVID M., JR. A general model of information transfer: Theme paper, 1968 Annual [American Society for Information Science] Convention. American Documentation, 18 (October 1967) 197-208.

[14] NATIONAL RESEARCH COUNCIL. COMMITTEE ON INFORMATION IN THE BEHAVIORAL SCIENCES. Communication systems and resources in the behavioral sciences. National Academy of Sciences, Washington, D.C., 1967.

[15] NORTH AMERICAN AVIATION. AUTONETICS DIVISION. DOD user needs study, Phase II. Final technical report. Anaheim, Calif., November 1966, 3 vols. (C6-2442/030).

[16] ORR, RICHARD H. Information sources for biomedical research. Institute for Advancement of Medical Communication, Philadelphia, Pa., November 1967.

[17] PAISLEY, WILLIAM J. The flow of (behavioral) science information: A review of the research literature. Stanford Institute for Communication Research, Stanford, Calif., 1965.

[18] PARKER, EDWIN B. Stanford physics information retrieval system (SPIRES), Annual report. Stanford Institute for Communication Research, Stanford, Calif., December 1967.

[19] PARKER, EDWIN B.; PAISLEY, WILLIAM J. Research for psychologists at the interface of the scientist and his information system. American Psychologist, 21 (November 1966) 1061-1071.

[20] PELZ, DONALD C.; ANDREWS, FRANK M. Scientists in organizations: Productive climates for research and development. Wiley, New York, 1966.

[21] PRICE, DEREK J. DE SOLLA. Little science, big science. Columbia University Press, New York, 1963.

[22] PRICE, DEREK J. DE SOLLA. Science since Babylon. Yale University Press, New Haven, 1961.

[23] WATSON, JAMES D. The double helix: discovery of the structure of DNA. The Atlantic Monthly (January 1968) 77-99, (February 1968) 92-117.

[24] WEBB, EUGENE J.; CAMPBELL, DONALD T.; SCHWARTZ, RICHARD D.; SECHREST, LEE. Unobtrusive measures: Nonreactive measurement in the social sciences. Rand McNally, Chicago, 1966.

IV

METHODOLOGY

Articles chosen for this section deal with some of the more important techniques, but go beyond method to explore the purpose and significance of the methods they treat. Methods considerations are treated also in the next section, *Research in Action,* while in the appendix there are a sample interview schedule, special scales and a mail questionnaire as illustrations of specific methodological instruments.

If the reader has assumed that because the volume treats method in only one section rather than as its entire theme, it is unimportant; he has come to the wrong conclusion. Understanding of the nature and utility of the several techniques of research is basic to the apparatus of the scholar. Particular techniques are then mastered in depth as one is engaged upon a problem requiring their use. Keeping abreast of new methods and of re-finements in longer standing methods will sometimes be a determinant of whether one perceives correctly whether or not a study can be done, or if it can be done, the level of sophistication of the research strategy. For just as creativity is critical to research design, so careful workmanship determines effectiveness in data collection. The ability to gen-eralize from a sample, for instance, is a function of sample design and execution. Even the more unconventional, unstructured and experimental approaches inevitably rely upon systematic and organized procedures.

While there are many specialized data collecting devices and approaches such as psychological tests, observation techniques, specially constructed scales, the most fre-quently used methods for collecting information about attitudes and behavior are the questionnaire and the personal interview. Since the mail questionnaire serves librarian-ship as probably by far the most pervasive data-gathering instrument, some limited ob-servations on its use seem warranted.

There are ample "do's and don'ts" of questionnaire construction to be found in re-search methods texts. Yet, the experience as respondent to many which come to one's desk, suggest they are little heeded. Pretesting the questionnaire would eliminate many typical kinds of blunders. For beginners, the construction of coding and analysis meth-ods, even to the point of determining the tabular form of eventual presentation, in advance of the mailing, will save many fruitless man hours at a later stage.

A critical factor in the use of the mail questionnaire, and one reason why personal de-livery of a questionnaire through the use of an interviewer is often preferable, is the bias introduced by the non-respondents. This problem, when it goes unheeded, calls into question the reliability and generalizability of the findings. The researcher must assess the extent and the nature of the non-respondent bias, if any exists. For, if some distinc-tive characteristic is common to those who do not cooperate in the study, the final sample will no longer be representative. One measure of response may often be seen in the relevance which the respondent sees in the instrument to his own interests. This is most easily achieved in studies of users and of professionals. Where the purpose, the utility and the evidence of the study is identified for the respondent as congruent with his own interest, one formidable barrier to cooperation is removed.

Studies of library users or of the general public are subject to a special kind of bias. This is the tendency for people to give normative answers regarding their attitudes toward libraries. As a culture symbol to which virtually all pay lip service without necessarily any genuine commitment, the value of such stereotypal response may be nil. There are also clear problems in dealing with issues upon which respondents may not have given much prior thought. Generalized response to questions treating interest in library services or need for improved financial support bear little relationship to how the respondent would in fact respond if the matter were the basis for a genuine political choice, as in a bond election, and correlations based upon such lines of analysis may well be naive and ill-conceived. Similarly, many individuals will distort their true reading habits and interests in responding to questions in order to convey a picture of themselves which they conceive to be more discriminating or in better taste. For some groups in the culture who are non-book or library oriented, or who may be alienated from the culture, standardized approaches such as the questionnaire simply are not workable at all.

A basic limit of research methodology in librarianship has been the absence of standardization in measurement instruments. One consequence is the ad hoc nature of research, without the replication and reinforcing value of additive and cumulative intelligence which derives from such standardized questions and scales. To the extent that the Orr group (reflected in the last selection in the section) is working toward a standardized measurement instrument, a research effort in itself, this activity is noteworthy.

The Personal Document in Sociology

by Robert Angell

Social research concerns itself with the design of instruments fashioned to test the hypotheses advanced in the study, and as a consequence, frequently overlooks or disdains already existing documentation. And, perhaps this is why Angell's now classic piece is one of a very few on the topic in the social science literature. In this essay, the author depicts the personal document as a fruitful rich source and by doing so, suggests that access to extraordinary and unusual personal records can serve as an alternative to certain types of field effort.

In another critique in this series under the auspices of the Committee on Appraisal Herbert Blumer has admirably indicated the contribution to sociological method of the pioneering use of human documents by Thomas and Znaniecki in *The Polish Peasant in Europe and America.*[1] It is the aim of this critique to appraise the developments of the past two decades in the use, by sociologists, of those human documents which may be called personal documents.

Blumer catalogues the human documents employed by Thomas and Znaniecki as (1) letters, (2) life histories (autobiographies alone are discussed), (3) Polish newspaper accounts, chiefly in the form of reportorial letters from local correspondents, (4) records of Polish church parishes in this country, and of Polish-American societies, (5) records of social agencies, and (6) court records.[2] He then goes on to indicate that the last four as compared with the first two are "more formal and reflective, less intimate, personal, and naive."[3] One judges that Blumer would not consider newspaper accounts and records of parishes, social agencies and courts as *personal* documents at all. This raises the whole question as to just what the types of documents are, the use of which should bring a study within the scope of the present critique.

For our purposes a personal document is defined as one which reveals a participant's view of experiences in which he has been involved. It is not absolutely essential that the individual whose conception of a situation is set forth should have written the document himself. A carful transcription of an interview may be regarded as a personal document provided it is not intermixed with the interviewer's own interpretation. Nor is it requisite that the individual himself be the focus of the experiences related in the document. That focus may be a group with whose activities he is thoroughly familiar, like his family, for instance, or it may be a social problem like race relations.[4]

The aim in collecting personal documents is to obtain detailed evidence as to how social situations appear to the actors in them and what meanings various factors have for the participants. It is of course true that not only is an individual unreliable in reporting a group's interpretation of a situation, but he is never wholly aware even of his own motives. Nevertheless, it is of great significance to know how participants interpret the situations in which they are involved, for it is on the basis of such interpretations, however fallacious, that they tend to act. It is difficult to see how the sociologist can arrive at generalizations unless he grasps the objectives toward which men are striving and how various elements of situations are interpreted with respect to the attainment of those objectives.

This critique is addressed not so much to the concrete results of studies made during the past two decades as to the methods employed. We are particularly interested in improvements in the personal document method or new applications of it. As a preliminary step it is necessary to understand the nature of scientific method generally. Only then can we determine whether or not advances have been made with respect to the specific method in which we are interested.

Science begins with selective perception. The analytic scientist does not approach objects and

SOURCE: Reprinted from Robert Angell, "A Critical Review of the Development of the Personal Document Method in Sociology 1920-1940," *The Use of Personal Documents in History, Anthropology and Sociology,* ed. Louis Gottschalk, Clyde Kluckhohn, and Robert Angell (New York: Social Science Research Council, 1945), Chap. 2, "The Personal Document in Sociology," pp. 177-185, by permission of the publisher.

events by attempting to grasp their crude entirety but rather approaches them with a certain type of interest, from a certain point of view. The criteria by which he selects aspects for investigation are determined by his way of conceiving the field. In the early stages of the development of any science its concepts are likely to be simple and the criteria may be of a common-sense sort. At later stages the concepts are highly systematized so that the criteria are very theoretical.

The verified statements which scientists make about phenomena in terms of some conceptual scheme are scientific facts. Such facts are thus not unrelated to theory. They are propositions about the aspects of phenomena which are relevant to a particular conceptual scheme, a scheme which in turn flows from previous theory. Some conceptual schemes bring into focus properties of objects and situations whose values in particular instances can be quantitatively measured. The facts in such cases are stated in numerical terms and can be manipulated mathematically. But such statement is by no means indispensable to science, for many important relationships have been discovered among non-measurable variables. Darwin's monumental labors which issued in the theory of natural selection constitute a case in point. In both instances the ultimate goal is the establishment of analytic laws.

A scientist can work either with or without an hypothesis, but except in the earliest stages of investigation the former is more usual. An hypothesis is a tentative statement of relationship among facts. It derives from previous scientific experience that suggests the possibility of the relationship stated. It is tested by analyzing the field of pertinent phenomena to determine whether or not the facts are such as would be expected by inference from the hypothesis. If the hypothesis is thus verified it is added to the organum of theory of the particular science. It then becomes a starting point for new deductions which in turn can be formulated as hypotheses and tested.

The discovery of new uniformities always involves both induction and deduction. If one starts from a set of facts, inductively, one must somehow arrive at a generalization. This is accomplished by imagining various possibilities that can be inferred from known principles of the science and seeing whether the facts accord with them. It would be impossible to investigate all the possibilities of uniformity in a complicated set of facts, so the scientist investigates those which seem

likely by inference from known generalizations. If one starts contrariwise with the principle and tries to deduce a new corollary, that corollary still has to be tested by empirical evidence. The bridge between phenomena and theory has to be built no matter from which side it is first projected.

Thus far we have been concerned with the nature of analytic sciences. There are also historical sciences. These are devoted primarily to the study of concrete phenomena, and are concerned with discovering their causes and consequences. Parsons has suggested that not only history and anthropology, but geology and meterology, have tended to fall into this category.[5] Such sciences draw upon analytic sciences whenever the latter illuminate the problems of the concrete phenomena under consideration. Various theoretical systems may be called upon. Thus, "for the historical sciences theoretical concepts are means to understanding concrete historical phenomena; while for the analytical sciences concrete historical phenomena are means, 'cases,' in terms of which the validity of theoretical systems may be tested."[6]

Though most competent sociologists would undoubtedly say that sociology aims to be an analytic rather than an historical science, the subject is too immature for us to be certain of its ultimate orientations. It seems unwise, therefore, to adopt for the purposes of this critique any dogmatic definition of what constitutes sociological research. We shall take the position that sociology is what sociologists do and shall examine studies of any kind, carried on by recognized sociologists, which have made use of personal documents.

Various Uses of Personal Documents. With some such conception of scientific method as that sketched above in mind, we may now ask: At what points in the scientific process may personal documents be useful? The answer to this question that is outlined in the paragraphs which follow has been arrived at both inductively and deductively; that is, the answer flows both from the studies that have been examined for this critique and from theoretical considerations.

1. Personal documents may be employed as a means of securing conceptual "hunches." By immersing oneself in documents which are thorough and full of insight one may secure leads to the identity of the most fruitful angle of approach to a given problem, that is the angle which will bring into focus those aspects of the phenomena that are particularly significant from a theoretical standpoint. This getting of new "slants" is a relatively

rare occurrence because it takes an unusually curious and independent mind to break away from the traditional modes of conception. But nothing is more necessary to scientific progress. The Darwins and Einsteins are all the more precious because they are few.

New conceptual "hunches" are few because they spring from breadth of grasp and flexibility of mind—a rare combination. When a person develops such a hunch it is probably a product of his whole scientific and personal experience rather than any particular segment of it. Therefore we should hardly expect to be able to say positively: "This came from studying personal documents." Even though the individual himself thinks that it did, he could hardly prove it. For our purposes it is enough if we can be satisfied that personal documents played some part in the development of his conceptual innovation.

2. Personal documents may suggest new hypotheses to the investigator who is thinking in terms of an established conceptual scheme. Confronted by the facts which his concepts lead him to see in the material of a document, the scientist will first determine whether the occurrence and arrangement of these facts could have been predicted from established laws. If not, and this is the almost universal case in sociology, he will try to formulate tentative generalizations which the data seem to support and which can be tested by further research. These tentative formulations are almost always influenced by pre-existing theory in the particular field. Thus they are both inductive and deductive.

Hypotheses derived from a few personal documents are peculiarly likely to prove false because of the possibilities of bias or lack of objectivity in the persons whose experiences are drawn upon. This is a point about which much has been said, and it is well to emphasize it. However, it is unlikely that all of a great many documents dealing with a certain set of phenomena would be biased in the same way, so that there is not much danger of the falsity remaining undiscovered if the hypotheses are submitted to a careful process of verification.

It should be clearer in the case of hypotheses than of conceptual "hunches" whether or not they were developed from the scrutiny of personal documents. If a critic has access to all the original documents studied by the investigator himself, he can pretty well determine the answer to this question. Even when he does not have such access, he can make some kind of judgment if the investigator publishes sample documents. But the critic is obviously at a loss to judge if no documents are given.

3. A less scientific use of personal documents than that sketched in (2) is the selection from them of the facts which seem important in terms of common sense and the formulation of rough hypotheses from these facts. This procedure might be termed crude or naive empiricism. Thus, one could study the relationship between decrease in income and family disorganization. The weakness in such studies is that all the thought that may have gone into building up conceptual schemes is wasted. Just because phenomena are very complex and have to be dealt with in terms of aspects, naive empiricism never succeeds in discovering true uniformities, but only various degrees of correlation among variables. It lacks the subtlety of analysis which an adequate theory couched in terms of a sophisticated conceptual system makes possible. The perception has not been sufficiently selective in the first place.

4. The next step in the scientific process is the verification of hypotheses and, indirectly, the validation of the conceptual schemes in terms of which they are formulated. Here also personal documents can be of service.

A good hypothesis must be capable of being tested; that is, the investigator must be able to infer from it consequences which can be compared with the results of observation.[7] This tests the hypothesis. If it meets this test successfully in every one of a large number of trials, it is verified.

The simplest use of personal documents in this connection is to verify an hypothesis by testing it with the same documents from the study of which it originated. This is not merely circular reasoning because it is a very difficult task to formulate an hypothesis from a number of human documents, and there is great likelihood that when it is checked against the original material it will be found wanting. Even if the hypothesis meets this test, it is rash to assume that it has been verified. There are two reasons for going beyond the original documents and testing it with new data.

First, the sample of cases originally canvassed may not be a random sample of the universe of cases to which the hypothesis applies. It may be that the latter holds true for this particular group of cases but would be found not to hold true for the whole population to which it supposedly is appropriate.

A second reason for going beyond verification in

terms of the documents from which the hypothesis was originally drawn is that thus one tends to state the hypothesis in more precise terms. One of the chief weaknesses which Blumer discovered in *The Polish Peasant*—the inability to put hypotheses to a crucial test[8]—may derive from this lack of precision. If Thomas and Znaniecki had had to think about how other investigators could use their hypotheses they might have refined their concepts, or stated the limitations of application of their hypotheses, or both. These procedures are not made necessary when an hypothesis is tested on materials with which the investigator is already familiar, because he naturally tends to notice the situations in which the hypothesis appears to be verified and to overlook those in which it does not. His assumptions as to the limits of application of the hypothesis remain unstated and perhaps even unformulated in his own mind.

The number of cases, original or new, required for verification of an hypothesis depends upon its character. A simple generalization in a complex field would have to be submitted to a large number of tests. For instance, the hypothesis that broken homes produce delinquent children obviously neglects many other factors of probable significance. To cite the cases of a dozen families would be no verification at all. On the other hand, if a complex hypothesis is put forward to cover perhaps an equally complex situation it may be verified by a relatively small number of cases. For instance, let us suppose the following hypothesis: an adolescent boy who has enjoyed high social status among his associates, who loses that status because of some public condemnation of his parents, and who finds no understanding of his predicatment from other members of his family, will become a serious behavior problem. If this were true of the first ten appropriate cases one could find, there would be strong evidence of verification. It would indicate that in all probability, the most important variables had been controlled and there would be little likelihood that the consistent results were due to unknown factors.

Verification of an hypothesis and demonstration that it has been verified are not the same thing. In the experimental sciences there is usually little difficulty at this point because the experimenter can describe in objective and mensurative terms exactly how the experiment was set up and what the results were. One has merely to trust his honesty and his ability to handle the requisite instruments accurately. And one experiment is crucial when all significant variables are controlled. But when personal documents constitute the evidence, there is no short way of describing the situation under which verification has been obtained, particularly when a large number of documents are necessary because of lack of control over variables. The investigator may be satisfied that he has verified an hypothesis, but he cannot convince others of it unless he presents all the evidence, or at least enough of it so that others may see the character of the inductive check which he claims to have made. This is almost certainly another reason for the weakness with respect to verification which Blumer found in *The Polish Peasant*. Perhaps the difficulty was in part in the demonstration process rather than in the verification process. The hypotheses of Thomas and Znaniecki were relatively so simple that the number of tests had to be large. But they had many documents, and it is conceivable that the hypotheses were actually checked inductively enough times to convince the authors. For practical reasons, however, they could not have presented the evidence for their verification even if they had had it.

There is probably no such thing as a decisive test of the usefulness of a concept. Only the accumulation of research results over long periods can indicate whether certain "slants," or approaches to reality are productive of significant theory. Human documents will certainly play their part in this gradual accumulation of scientific experience, but no one study or group of studies can be expected to be conclusive.

5. A further possible use of personal documents is to supply the facts to which the theories of various sciences may be applied so as to obtain an historical understanding of a person, a group, or an institution. The immediate object is not to build up scientific theory, as in preceding uses, but to secure greater understanding of why a particular social unit has developed as it has. Wherever there are practical problems to be met, wherever administrative decisions have to be taken, there is the need to bring together the contributions of one or several sciences and to focus them on the evolution of the unit in question so that that evolution may be explained. Such explanation gives a basis for predicting how the unit will probably react in the future to conditions similar to those which it has met in the past. One comes to understand what interpretations are likely to be put upon new situations by the person or group concerned. It is even possible to become so familiar with the dynamic interaction of factors in particular cases as to be able to predict with more accuracy than is

attained by the mere application of established theories. And, paradoxical as it may seem, the investigator may be at a loss to reduce this predictive ability, based on acquaintance with the essential orientations of particular cases, to any general formulas. Hence the body of scientific knowledge is not immediately enriched thereby, though in the long run such work is productive of important new hunches.

Again it is apparent that the personal documents employed must be fully presented. Without a grasp of all the conditions incident to action, one is not in a position to judge whether a particular theory is properly applicable to a situation. It is not enough that the investigator thinks it is. The critic must be able to satisfy himself on the point by inspection of the record.

6. The five uses already sketched seem to exhaust the *scientific* value of personal documents, but they also have an expositional value. The results of scientific investigation must be communicated if they are to be influential. Scientific truth known only to its discoverer is not fully functional. We have already alluded to this in discussing the demonstration of verification of an hypothesis. In that case it was pointed out that the personal documents are themselves the evidence that the generalization has been successfully tested. Documents are also serviceable, however, in illustrating concepts and established principles that are being used in an analysis. Meanings can be made clear by clothing scientific abstractions in the garments of reality.

A less specific use of personal documents but of the same general expository nature is to give readers broad acquaintance with the area to be studied. Several documents of some length may often serve as an introduction to the subject to be analyzed. They give the reader some orientation, what we call a "feel" for the scientific analysis to come. Such documents indicate in a broad way the type of situation with which the investigator was faced when he started work. In that sense they enable the reader to follow the various steps of the investigation intelligently.

Classification of Studies. Having before us the

points at which personal documents may make scientific contributions, we might seem to be in a position immediately to consider the use of such documents in various studies. But acquaintance with the studies themselves suggests the wisdom of classifying them first. They are so different from one another that our ultimate purpose will be better served by placing them in broad categories within which questions of method can be more appropriately discussed.

It is obvious that any particular investigator is likely to make more than one use of personal documents, so that we cannot employ the above six-fold classification in dealing with the studies here to be analyzed. Examination of them has suggested a three-fold division, which is not clear-cut in all respects but seems to furnish a practicable basis of procedure.

There seem to be three types of interest which lead sociologists to undertake work in which personal documents are useful. One interest is that of the investigator who wants to understand the development of a particular person, group, or institution, or class of them. The primary aim in this case is not to obtain new generalizations but to grasp the nature of particular social units or types by study of their past and present tendencies. Scientific laws are brought to bear at any point where they can help to explain the development. In addition the investigator may so familiarize himself with the peculiar concatenation of factors in the particular instance that he can make accurate predictions of future behavior. This is an essentially historical approach. A second type of interest is that in a body of theory rather than a social unit. Here the aim is to improve the theoretical system. Scholars with this approach are bent upon formulating analytical generalizations in terms of a conceptual scheme. A third interest is that in research method itself. Investigators who want to advance sociology as a scientific discipline are quite naturally led to test the efficacy of various methods of research, including that through personal documents. In such cases the study is not focused on obtaining new substantive results, but on appraising methodological tools.

FOOTNOTES

[1] Herbert Blumer, *An appraisal of Thomas and Znaniecki's 'The Polish peasant in Europe and America'* ("Critiques of research in the social sciences," I; New York, Social Science Research Council, 1939), p. 29.
[2] *Ibid.*, pp. 29, 47.
[3] *Ibid.*, p. 47.

[4] In one sense this definition is a broader one than that used by Allport who states: "The personal document may be defined as *any self-revealing record that intentionally or unintentionally yields information regarding the structure, dynamics, and functioning of the author's mental life.*" Hence Allport is not concerned with documents that are focused on the life of groups or on particular social problems. See Gordon W. Allport, *The use of personal documents in psychological science* (New York, Social Science Research Council, 1942), p. xii.

[5] Talcott Parsons, *The structure of social action* (New York, 1937), p. 598.

[6] *Loc. cit.*

[7] See W. Stanley Jevons, *The principles of science* (2nd edition; London and New York, 1887), p. 511.

[8] *Op. cit.,* pp. 38, 46-47, 75, 80.

Statistical Techniques

by Irwin D. J. Bross

The contribution of this chapter from a widely-used volume is as orientation to and explication of the several ways in which statistics are employed in research undertakings; as such it makes an excellent survey piece and introduction. Yet, there is no attempt to go into the subtleties or nuances of the process. The selection is included because the author sorts out so effectively the point and the purpose of statistical application without being bogged down and losing his objective in technical methodological treatment. He depicts statistics as an active relevant resource, rather than as dry, stale ritual. Seen thus, the work will not serve as substitute for greater immersion at the point of a particular investigation, but does help the reader better appreciate the utility and contribution of statistical methodology.

TOOLS OF THE TRADE

A carpenter needs to know about the nature of his materials and the principles of construction, but to build an actual table he also needs hammers, saws, and other tools. In the same way, if we want to make an actual decision we will need specific statistical tools as well as general principles. While I do not intend to go into the technical side of Statistical Decision in this book, I would like to provide enough information about the statistical tools to allow an interested reader to pursue the subject further. Therefore in this chapter I will list the principal types of tools and indicate their uses.

In the last fifty years statistical methodologies have proliferated at a prodigious rate, and important new tools are continually being developed. There are, today, so many special tools, and these devices are so varied in character, that it is no easy matter to decide which, if any, of the existing methodologies are appropriate for a given problem. The concepts of Statistical Decision serve to integrate the various special techniques and therefore the decision point of view makes the choice of an appropriate tool somewhat easier.

Most practical decision problems will be much more complex than the little examples which I have presented; they will be decision chains with many links. Each link will be a distinct problem and consequently many different statistical techniques may be required to handle the practical problem (just as a carpenter would not expect to use only one tool in building a table).

I shall confine the discussion of tools to those devices used in the construction of the Prediction System of the Decision-Maker. As we have already noted, the fabrication of an advanced prediction system has two phases—model-making and data-gathering. Successful prediction usually requires an inter-play between these two phases, but for purposes of exposition I will consider the two separately.

First, I will consider the techniques which deal with the evaluation of data. I have previously emphasized that it pays to scrutinize critically the procedures used in collecting the original data. The quality of the data which fuels the Decision-Maker often determines whether the mechanism is successful or not. The determination of the quality of the data will involve different techniques for classification data than for measurement data.

CLASSIFICATION

It may seem obvious to you that when classifications are used the very first step would be to see if the classifications are any good (i.e., unbiased, repeatable, and relevant). It may also be evident to you that if the classifications are inadequate it is rather futile to collect great quantities of this defective data. Yet strangely enough, there are many investigators who never try to check up on their methods of classification.

At the very least the individual who makes the classifications should be able to agree with *himself*. It often comes as a shock to investigators that,

SOURCE: Reprinted with permission of The Macmillan Company from *Design for Decision* by Irwin D. J. Bross. © by The Free Press, a Corporation 1957.

when this question of self-agreement is examined, the results indicate that the investigator does not even agree with himself. As an example of the use of statistical techniques to answer questions about self-agreement, I want to consider the following (rather common) situation in medical research. It is customary to use X-ray films to determine the severity of diseases such as tuberculosis. A doctor will examine a series of X-ray plates and classify them by degree of severity as (say) mild, moderate, or severe.

To check up on the classification system the doctor might read a series of plates and then, perhaps a month later when the original classifications were forgotten, read the same series of plates a second time. This little experiment can be presented as a *contingency table* (Figure 14.01). The name contingency table arises because all possible contingencies or outcomes are given in the table.

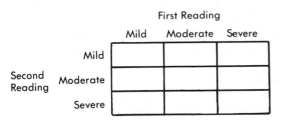
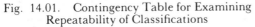

Fig. 14.01.   Contingency Table for Examining Repeatability of Classifications

The tally shown in Figure 14.01 would correspond to an X-ray plate which was read as mild the first and as moderate the second time. Each plate in the series can be tallied in some cell of the table. If the doctor always agreed with himself, all the tallies would fall in the main diagonal of the table (i.e., mild-mild, moderate-moderate, etc.). Such perfect agreement is rarely encountered in actual experiments, however, and ordinarily there will be tallies in most of the cells of the table. Various statistical techniques have been developed for further analysis of contingency tables and in particular for measuring the degree of agreement. Often, however, a glance at the contingency table will suffice to indicate that the method of classification is in need of improvement.

Not only should the investigator agree with himself, but it is also desirable that he should agree with his fellow experts. The agreement between two doctors might be studied by having them read

(independently) the same series of plates. A contingency table which would display the results of this further experiment could then be constructed.

Agreement as measured by the two previous experiments is closely associated with the concept of repeatability. But repeatability is not the only criterion for judging the quality of data. Suppose that the patients in the X-ray series are brought in for an intensive medical examination. Then these patients might be classified as mild, moderate, or severe on the basis of this further study and this second classification might be considered to be more reliable. If this examination classification is taken as the standard, it would be possible to compare the X-ray classification with this standard. It might be found that the X-ray readings were biased in the sense that the X-ray classifications were consistently more severe than the examination classification, or the bias might be in the other direction. It might also be possible that the X-ray classifications were irrelevant for the purposes of the investigation. The statistical techniques for testing relevance will be discussed later.

I do not want to give the impression that the contingency table is the only statistical technique for dealing with classifications, but it will serve as a point of entry to the literature.

MEASUREMENTS

It has been emphasized in this book that *quantification,* the replacement of words by numbers, is a key step in science. The advantages to be derived from quantification are not inherent in the numbers *themselves.* The use of numbers and measurements does *not* automatically improve matters—the measurement must prove its worth by the standards which have already been applied to classifications.

This point deserves some emphasis because of an increasing tendency of some scientists to use numbers and statistical techniques as sheer window dressing, as a device for adding a tone of scientific respectability to trivial papers.

Numerical methods are a tool and, like any other tool, they can be used frivolously. A buzz saw is also a fascinating tool, but the utility of a buzz saw is not intrinsic. A person can use a buzz saw to slice worth-while timber into waste ends and sawdust. The mere fact that a person is running a buzz saw does not mean that he is a good builder. The mere fact that an individual uses numerical analysis or statistical techniques does not make him a good scientist.

It will be necessary, when working with measurements, to study the quality of these measurements. The first step is to examine the repeatability of the measurements. If the measurements are approximately normally distributed, the variance (or standard deviation) of repeated observations can be used as a measure of repeatability.

Frequently a measurement is obtained by a series of operations. Measurements in chemistry, for example, are often obtained by an elaborate process involving pipetting, titrating, weighing, and other operations. We can think of the actual variation in the final measurement as composed of contributions from a number of different sources of variation. Some of the operations in the process may introduce large experimental errors, while the contributions of the other operations may be negligible. An improvement in the measurement process (i.e., a reduction in variation) may follow if the operations with large experimental errors can be improved. It is of interest, therefore, to determine which operations are major sources of variation.

The statistical techniques applicable to this problem fall under the heading of *components of variance* which is, in turn, a part of *analysis of variance*. With the aid of these methodologies, the contributions of the various sources of variation can be assessed numerically.

Questions concerning bias and relevance are also elucidated by the methods of analysis of variance. The information thus obtained may be used to improve and standardize measurement processes.

RECORDING AND STORING OF DATA

Every field seems to present peculiar problems in the recording and storing of data. Most of the discussion of this topic will be found in the field of application rather than in the statistical literature. Lately, the development of the electronic brains has led to wider interest in problems of recording, storage, and recovery of information. Current research may lead to a systematic body of knowledge on these questions which will go beyond the "cut and try" procedures currently in use.

There is one device which deserves special mention in connection with recording and storing procedures. It is usually worthwhile to make a preliminary study ("dry run" or "pilot trial") as a test of procedures before any large scale collection of data is set into motion.

The collection of data may be divided into three categories—experimentation, surveys, and systematic observation. The distinction is somewhat arbitrary and experimentation is distinguished from other methods of collection mainly by the degree of *control* which is exercised.

EXPERIMENTATION

There are a number of diverse statistical techniques which fall under the heading of *design of experiments*. These techniques are often simple extensions of common sense. Suppose, for example, that you were in the shoe business and that a new compound had been developed for making soles which was supposed to be far superior to materials currently used. You might want to test the new compound by making up a batch of shoes which differed only in the composition of the soles and then giving these shoes to various people with the understanding that after a fixed length of time the shoes would be brought back and rated as to amount of wear and other characteristics. Obviously different people will give different usage to the shoes. How can this factor be controlled?

A common-sense way of meeting this problem would be to make up pairs of shoes, one of which had the old sole, while the other had the new sole. This pairing process would lead to a better comparison of the two materials. It would also be common sense to put the old sole on the right shoe half of the time and on the left shoe the other half of the time. This would control inequalities in wear which might occur between right and left shoes.

In the *design of experiments* the devices for control of sources of variability are extended to much more complex situations. For example, suppose that we wanted to test three or four new compositions to see which one made the best soles. If you like puzzles you might try to figure out a design for this new experiment which would control the variation due to the different amounts of wear for the different people.

The development of techniques for efficient and well-controlled schemes for collecting data is one of the most important contributions of modern statistics.

SAMPLING SURVEYS

In principle the collection of data by a survey, such as a public opinion survey, is closely allied to the collection of data in laboratory experimentation, but in practice the problems encountered are so dissimilar that it is convenient to treat the two procedures separately. Earlier I remarked on the care that must be taken in drawing the sample. The sampling problem is treated in detail under the heading *sampling survey techniques*.

Sampling is not the only problem in a survey, and sometimes it is a relatively minor problem. It may be more important to choose the questions in the survey with great care and to control the methods of asking these questions. There are a great many other problems associated with the survey method, but unfortunately in a good proportion of surveys these problems are either ignored or treated with distain. As a consequence the survey method has a rather checkered record of performance.

I do not want to give the impression that a sampling survey is not a useful instrument—I only want to emphasize that it is a tricky one. Surveys have been useful to the government (estimation of population and resources), to business (consumer reactions), and to science.

SUMMARIZATION OF DATA

The traditional statistical techniques have been developed in connection with the problems of summarization of data. From the standpoint of Statistical Decision, however, it is somewhat pointless to summarize data without taking into account the *use* which will be made of the summaries. There has been much wasted work in connection with summarization (particularly on the topic of *index numbers*) because of failure to realize that the *use* of summaries must be considered.

Elementary statistics texts tend to go into tedious detail concerning summarization and to spend much time on averages, medians, rates, ratios, indices, index numbers, and so on. This sort of text gives the reader the impression that statistics consists of endless and very dull repetitions of arithmetic processes.

In the early days of statistics there was little more to the subject than the details of summarization, but things have changed. There are much more important topics which deserve attention now.

MODELS

The first step in solving a decision problem is to try to set up some sort of model—a verbal model is better than nothing. This process of setting up a

model is equivalent to formulating the problem in a clear-cut fashion.

When a mathematical model is used, the process of formulation may require not only mathematical methodologies but also techniques from the subject-matter field. In an engineering problem, for example, methodologies from physics and chemistry may be needed.

The *theory of probability* will be a basic instrument in the formulation of a model. *Frequency distributions* will also play a role. If probability event chains are involved, then the theory of *stochastic processes* may be useful. All of the above topics are branches of *mathematical statistics*.

In order to formulate a model for a prediction system we usually take three steps:

(1) Determination of the factors which are *relevant* for prediction.
(2) Determination of the actual *relationship* of factors to the phenomena to be predicted.
(3) Construction of a prediction system based on this relationship.

The statistical techniques associated with relevance can be divided into three types. This division is based on the nature of the data. The factor which we wish to predict may be either a classification or a measurement, and the factor which we would like to use for prediction may also be either a classification or a measurement. The situations to be considered are:

(1) Class vs. class
(2) Class vs. measurement
(3) Measurement vs. measurement.

CLASS VS. CLASS

Much medico-sociological data will fall in this category and, in general, class vs. class data will be found in subject fields in which adequate measurements are still in the developmental stage.

Let us suppose that we are interested in a specific disease, and we think that there may be a relationship between housing conditions and this particular disease. We may, in the first stages of a study, choose a sample and classify every individual in the sample in two ways. First, the person may or may not have the disease under study. Second, the person may live in a house which is substandard or he may be adequately housed. After the information is collected it may be presented in what is called a two-by-two contingency table such as the one in Fig. 14.02.

Number of Individuals in Categories

Health Status	Housing	
	Substandard	Adequate
Diseased	75	50
Not Diseased	1250	1790

Fig. 14.02.

The numbers in this table (which I have manu-factured) indicate that the proportion of diseased people is higher among those who are living in substandard housing than among those with adequate housing. But we must remember that we are dealing with a sample. If, instead of considering housing, I had divided the sample into two parts by flipping a coin for each individual and assigning him to category A if the coin were heads and to category B if the coin were tails, then I would not expect the proportion of diseased people in category A to be *exactly* equal to the proportion of diseased people in category B. But it would obviously be silly to regard my flipping a coin as relevant to the disease under study merely because there was some difference between category A and category B.

In order to guard against meaningless association, we would make a *chi-square test* (or use some related technique). First we set up the simplest model: Housing is irrelevant insofar as the risk of a given disease is concerned. The chi-square test allows us to determine whether the simplest model can account for our observations. To perform the significance test we would substitute the numbers in Figure 14.02 into the formula for chi-square. We would then go to the chi-square tables which can be found in almost all statistical textbooks. If our calculated number turns out to be larger than the appropriate number in the table (and if the sampling is unbiased, etc.), we reject the hypothesis that housing is irrelevant. As I have emphasized previously, this type of statistical technique may lead us to assert erroneously that the disease under study is associated with housing, but mistakes of this nature should be infrequent.

The *chi-square test* can also be used in more complex contingency tables. There are also some alternative tests which can be used in special contingency tables. The other tests are necessary because if the numbers in the cells of a two-by-two table are very small there are some objections to the use of the chi-square test.

CLASS VS. MEASUREMENT

The commonest data of this type involve measurements made on individuals in various classes. In agriculture, for example, we may be interested in the yield (say in bushels per acre) of three different varieties of wheat. Ordinarily the varieties would be planted on a number of small plots, say ten plots for each variety, so that the experimental results would consist of thirty numbers. We would want to know whether the variety was relevant to the yield. The factor to be used for prediction would be the variety, a classification, and the factor to be predicted would be the yield, a measurement.

The reverse situation, in which the factor for prediction is a measurement and the factor predicted is a classification, is less common and the techniques applicable here go by various names. The statistical literature generally refers to such techniques as *discriminant functions*. In the fields of application there are different nomenclatures. In medicine, for example, the techniques go under the title of *diagnostic parameters*.

Now let us return to the problem of the three varieties of wheat. When the average yields for each of the varieties are calculated, they will not be exactly the same. We would not want, however, to jump to the conclusion that the true yields of the three varieties are different because there is always a possibility that our results are merely manifestations of experimental error.

As in the class vs. class example we start by setting up a model which postulates that variety is irrelevant insofar as yield is concerned. We then apply *analysis of variance* to test this model. The test itself is called the *F-test* (in honor of R. A. Fisher). If this test is significant, we regard the variety of the wheat as relevant to the yield. As usual, we run a specified risk of erroneously concluding that variety is relevant.

MEASUREMENT VS. MEASUREMENT

A classic example of this situation is the study of the heights of parents and the heights of their children. The common method for presenting such data is a scatter diagram. In the scatter diagram the average height of the parents is plotted against the horizontal axis of a graph and the height of the child is plotted against the vertical axis. Each parent-child pair is represented by a point on this graph. Since the points are scattered over the graph, the name scatter diagram is quite appropriate.

If the height of the parents is irrelevant insofar as the height of the child is concerned, then it can be shown that a line parallel to the horizontal axis of the graph will fit the points as well as any other curve. The statistical techniques for testing the relevance of the height of the parents are *regression* or *correlation analysis*.

RELEVANCE AND RELATION

The statistical techniques for testing relevance are designed to avoid wild goose chases. If a factor, Z, turns out to be relevant to the quantity we wish to predict, Y, then we proceed to investigate the matter further. We would try to discover the actual relationship between Z and Y. But we would not want to go on to this next step until we had some evidence that Z was relevant. If Z is irrelevant, the additional study would not be likely to advance us toward our goal of predicting Y.

The tests for relevance may tell us that it may be worthwhile to pursue our study of Z, but in order to use Z for actual prediction it will be necessary to find a workable relationship. This relationship may be expressed verbally, but it is usually more useful to try to describe the relationship in the symbolic language (i.e., as a mathematical relationship). In general, it is not an easy matter to discover a workable relationship, and it usually takes creative effort on the part of the investigator.

In the housing vs. disease example we might be satisfied with the *estimation* of the proportion diseased in both housing situations. This information might be used for prediction and action. It might tell us, if the disease happened to be tuber-

culosis, where we should send the mobile X-ray units in order to locate cases of T.B.

When the yields of the different varieties of wheat are estimated, this information may lead us to recommend a particular variety of wheat to the farmers in the adjacent area. On the other hand, we may feel that the experiment was too small and we might want more information before taking action. If relevance had been demonstrated it might then be worth while to go ahead with more comprehensive experimentation.

The determination of the relationship between parental height and child height would be the next step in the measurement vs. measurement example. We might see if a straight line (but not a horizontal line) provided a good fit to the points on the scatter diagram. In this particular case, and in other scientific work, we may not be interested in prediction per se; we may be interested in learning more about the phenomena without thinking in terms of immediate application.

MULTIPLE FACTORS

In most practical situations the problem is more complex and involves not merely a predictor and a quantity to be predicted but many different factors. The contingency table approach, analysis of variance, and regression analysis can be extended to deal with these more complex situations. More advanced techniques, *multiple and partial regression,* and *multivariate analysis,* and others, may be pressed into service. The consideration of several factors simultaneously may tell us much more than the separate consideration of each factor.

As an example of simultaneous consideration of factors, we might consider the work on intelligence quotients (IQ). The early work on the performance of Negroes and whites on IQ tests gave ammunition to the racists because of the poor showing of the Negroes. Many other factors besides race enter the picture, however. For example, there is a relationship between IQ and economic status. Since Negroes have a lower average economic status it would seem, at first glance, quite hopeless to try to disentangle racial and economic factors. Some progress in this direction can be made through the use of *partial regression*, however, and the results of this further study were highly disappointing to the racists.

The first studies indicated that, if the race of an individual were known, we could do a better job of predicting his IQ than if we did not have the information about race. What the further studies showed was that if we knew the race *and* the economic status of the individual our prediction would not be materially better than if we knew *only* the economic status. According to the racist model our predictions should be much improved by including information about skin color, so the results are hardly in accord with the racist model.

There are many "facts" which are widely accepted but which turn out to be fiction when investigated statistically. Statistical techniques furnish protection against prejudices and superstitions, and a wider understanding of the principles of Statistical Decision might lessen the influence that biases currently exert on choice of action.

RELATIONSHIPS INVOLVING TIME

There are various specialized relationships which have corresponding specialized statistical techniques. Time, for example, is often an important factor in the prediction of phenomena, and techniques appropriate to dynamic situations have been developed. Under the broad heading *time series* there are many methodologies. In the past, numerous attempts have been made to analyze time series into components such as trends, seasonal variations, cyclic variations, and so on. In engineering applications this type of analysis of time series has been an effective instrument, but the application of similar techniques to economic problems has led to improved forecasting only in isolated cases. Such devices as *correlograms* and *periodograms* have had some success, but this particular statistical pathway has to be posted with a sign: "Danger, proceed at your own risk."

Another type of problem in which time plays a major role is in the prediction of population growth. The particular population studied may be a human one, or it may be an animal or microorganism population. There is an extensive literature on *growth curves.*

In industrial situations, time enters the problem of control of manufacturing processes. *Control charts* and *quality control* are statistical techniques which have been developed to meet industrial needs, but their application extends to other fields.

OTHER TECHNIQUES

It should be realized that I cannot give a complete listing of statistical techniques in a short chapter. There are many techniques which have been developed to meet rather special situations in the various fields of application. For example, *bioassay* is important in medical experimentation, and *factor analysis* has been used mainly in psychology. There are so many techniques nowadays that they crowd the three-year graduate course in statistics which leads to the Ph.D. degree. This does not mean, however, that there are statistical techniques which apply to all, or even most, decision problems. For many practical problems the statistical methodologies are rudimentary or nonexistent, and it is necessary to develop new methods for dealing with these decision problems. The job of developing statistical methodologies to fit practical problems is part of the function of a statistical consultant. It keeps him on his toes and makes his life interesting.

SUMMARY

This chapter has essayed a quick survey of the more important statistical techniques. Mention is made of the position these methodologies occupy in Statistical Decision. It is emphasized that, although there is an extensive body of techniques, the field is rapidly growing, and in many practical decision problems new tools will have to be forged to meet the needs.

Dimensions of the Depth Interview[1]

by Raymond L. Gorden

This essay is included because it details clearly the nuances, complexities and subtleties of a very potent research instrument. Written from his own experience, Gorden's article offers aid in the choice and in the use of the tool. The potential of this instrument is powerful and yet it is necessary to point out that nothing can be more dangerous and more misleading than the employment of this technique by one unskilled or cavalier in its use who may draw naive or incorrect conclusions out of keeping with the genuine facts of the matter studied.

What is the "depth interview"? The term is put in quotes because it is more often used with mysterious overtones than as a scientific word with a clearly delineated referent. The term has grown in popularity in motivation research, market research, and studies of human relations in industry and of other areas of pure and applied social science. The principal aim of the social scientist in interviewing is valid and reliable information, not therapy or motivation; however, this is not to deny that many interviews are conducted with more than one aim.

The success of depth interviewing will, in the long run, depend upon having (*a*) a frame of reference which provides a theoretical bridge between the type of information needed and the techniques to be used in obtaining it; (*b*) interviewers trained in the skills and sensitivities needed to detect which dimension they are dealing with at a given moment as the interview progresses; and (*c*) interviewers trained in the skills and techniques applicable to each dimension. Toward this end, a theoretical frame of reference is presented for distinguishing significantly different dimensions of depth.

DEFINITIONS

The definition of any type of interview might be in terms of the techniques or the observable operations. Thus the interviewer in the depth interview could be said to be "permissive," "reflective," "non-directive," or to be following the principle of "minimal activity."

A second and basically different definition of the depth interview is in terms of the types of in-

formation needed. The latter must be translated into social-psychological categories sufficiently abstract to be widely applicable. This has advantage over the first type of definition: first, it avoids the assumption that the specific techniques to be used have already been discovered and developed; second, it defines the goal as clearly as possible befor the issues of apparently contradictory techniques and tactics must be faced. These two reasons are logically related to a third: that the effectiveness of various interviewing techniques cannot be teste until a criterion of success is developed.

Not every failure to obtain valid and reliable information is due to the fact that the informatio is too deep. It may be due to the interviewer's failure to communicate his wishes clearly to the respondent. However, here we are primarily concerned with barriers to communication and are assuming that the interviewer has been successful in communicating the question.

The "depth" of any item of information depends upon its meaning for the respondent, which in turn, depends upon how he perceives the relationship between the information and the total social context in which it is given. What is in one social situation a mere "objective fact," as, for example, the respondent's age, may be a devastating threat in another.

How, then, is any kind of information deeper than another if it depends upon the situation? This is a particularly important question in view of the fact that the "deep" information is presumed to be accessible to the interviewer under certain conditions, and his hope for success depends upon his manipulating the respondent's de

SOURCE: Raymond L. Gorden, "Dimensions of the Depth Interview," *American Journal of Sociology*, 62 (Sept., 1956) pp. 158–164. Reprinted from *American Journal of Sociology* by permission of The University of Chicago Press. Copyright 1956 by the University of Chicago Press.

inition of the situation in such a way as to make what would ordinarily be deep information come to the surface. The word "ordinarily" is important as recognizing the norms regarding what should be communicated to whom under what conditions, as well as how the communication is to be carried out. The further the interviewer varies his techniques and tactics from the prevailing norms of social conversation, the deeper the information he obtains.

DEGREE OF EGO-THREAT

The respondent tends to withhold any information which he fears may threaten his self-esteem. There may be merely very mild hesitancy or complete repression. Three broad categories may be defined on the basis of the degree or kind of secrecy.

The strongest tendency to withhold information is often referred to as "repression." The respondent not only refuses to admit the information to the interviewer but also hides it from himself, to preserve his self-esteem and escape a guilty conscience. He is perfectly honest when he says that he does not know or that he has forgotten. This dimension has primarily occupied the psychiatrist, psychoanalyst, and clinical psychologist.

A less intense threat to self-esteem is found when the respondent, though he consciously possesses the information, hesitates to admit it to the interviewer because he anticipates that the latter will disapprove. Often the respondent is torn between the temptation to withhold the information and the yearning for catharsis. If he is made to feel confident that the interviewer will not condemn him, he may welcome the opportunity to "tell all."

Quite commonly, a victim of a community disaster suffers strong feelings of guilt over his "cowardly" behavior in the panic. His need for catharsis is evident in his expression; he may freely admit that he has not told his family or any of his friends about his behavior. Also it is common for the respondent to say at the end of the interview that he feels much better "since having a chance to talk."

Sometimes the respondent indulges in some shrewd interviewing of the interviewer to discover the latter's attitudes. For example, the respondent who would like to confess socially disapproved norms of sex behavior may first try to discover the interviewer's probable reaction by mentioning a case similar to his own and may even try to pro-

voke the interviewer into condemning it. If the interviewer condemns the hypothetical case, the respondent will not tell about himself. Confession is easiest if the interviewer is a stranger whom the respondent never expects to see again,[2] but in any case a generally accepting and sympathetic attitude toward the respondent as a person goes far to elicit candid responses.

A less intense threat to the respondent's self-esteem exists if the respondent is willing to give information to the interviewer but fears losing status if the information goes any further. This respondent must be assured that his anonymity will be respected. This is not always easy to do. The respondent may fear that the interviewer will be unable to conceal the source of the information, even with the best of intentions. Indeed, the higher the respondent's status, the more difficult to give information describing his role in the community without revealing his identity.

This was clearly demonstrated in the contrast between the attitude of the officials in a disaster-struck town and that of the average citizen toward having interviews tape-recorded. It was extremely rare to have an ordinary citizen object to the tape-recorder, but objections from officials were quite common. It appears that the higher the social status, the greater the possible discrepancy between the person's actual behavior and that expected of him. If the leaders had sufficient opportunity to rehearse the role expected of them under crisis conditions, it would be no crisis for them. Also, as the group becomes smaller, assuming that the group itself will not be anonymous, the less chance there is of keeping any particular individual anonymous.

Not only must the interviewer assure the respondent of anonymity at the beginning of the interview, but he also must be sensitive to any need for further reassurance as the interview progresses.

DEGREES OF FORGETTING

Almost as frequent a barrier to candor is the respondent's inability to recall certain types of information. Simple facts which are not ego-involved, such as the date of first going to work at a factory, cannot be accurately determined in a superficial interview. This was discovered when respondents' replies were checked against company records.[3]

It is difficult for an interviewer to predict which items of information will be difficult for a given respondent to recall. Only after a great deal of experience in interviewing a particular type of respondent for a specific type of information, will he acquire moderate skill in predicting degrees of difficulty. Not infrequently the respondent gives a spontaneous and sincere reply, only to contradict himself later when recall was somehow stimulated.

Several specific techniques have been developed to stimulate the recall of forgotten material, one of the best of which is given by Merton.[4] He points out that it is possible to create a mood of "retrospective introspection" in which the respondent imaginatively transports himself backward in time to an actual experience. Then, by certain types of probing to encourage a network of associations, the interviewer can help the respondent to recall specific details and experiences.

The memory dimension of the depth interview is a much more frequent obstacle to obtaining the needed information than is suspected by the inexperienced interviewer, and the techniques which are used to penetrate it are quite different in principle from those needed to penetrate ego-involvement. To complicate the interviewer's task further, the respondent does not say "I have forgotten" but usually continues talking, filling in the gaps in his memory with whatever his imagination suggests.

DEGREES OF GENERALIZATION

Specification may be conceived to be at one pole of a continuum and *generalization* at the opposite pole. In this scheme the term "generalization" designates information relatively free of time, place, or specific events and situations. In certain types of interviewing problems it is relatively simple to elicit a generalized statement but difficult to obtain concrete details of the events leading to the generalization.

There are at least four basic reasons why it is necessary to encourage the respondent to be specific. First, he may make errors in generalizing. Even though generalized information is what is needed for a particular study, the generalizations which the respondent has on the top of his mind may not fit the concrete experiences from which they have supposedly been drawn. This is an especially acute problem in interviewing victims of community disasters. It was not unusual for a local norm to be expressed as a myth which crystallized soon after the crisis was over. These generalized statements might have been about the

behavior of women as contrasted to that of men or about the "miraculous" way in which the rescue and first-aid work was carried out, for which the factual basis could not be found. In some cases the generalizations were merely projections of the norms as individuals tried to assess the buzzing confusion.

Second, a respondent is frequently unable to generalize. This may be because the concepts or categories relevant to the interviewer's problem have no direct clear meaning for him, a situation familiar to the anthropologists, who have learned, for example, that a direct generalized question about the kinship structure or the value system of a primitive tribe will not elicit meaningful answers. Unfortunately, this problem is not peculiar to studies of primitive societies but is found very frequently in any study of contemporary communities which attempts to reach an analytical level. For example, if an interviewer were to ask a twelve-year-old boy in a slum area of Chicago, "What is the most common way that conflicts between you and your parents are resolved?" there would be little chance of his being able to give a general answer.

Third, it is often found that a respondent uses evasive generalizations to conceal the real situation. In this case the respondent's inability or unwillingness to give concrete examples throws doubt upon the accuracy of the generalization.

Fourth, it is sometimes necessary for the interviewer to obtain generalized information indirectly by means of specific examples where the general category has a negative value. For example, if the question "Is there discrimination against Negroes in this restaurant?" is put to a white waitress who has recently arrived from the South, she might report that there is none, since nothing "bad" goes on in the restaurant, or she may realize that, since the interviewer is interested in discrimination, he would probably consider the existing relationships as "discrimination." Also, since she considers this to be only a Yankee's point of view, she is not going to give any facts which can be used by the interviewer to draw his own "biased conclusions."

There are certain similarities between the evasive generalization and the value-laden generalization, but in the former the respondent's use of the generalized form is a symptom of his resistance while in the latter it is caused by the interviewer's use of the generalized rather than the specific form of the question.

It should also be noted that no statement has

been made as to whether the general or the specific information is the more difficult to secure. This varies from one situation to another. Thus (a) the generalized information is more difficult to obtain when it calls for more abstract intellectual categories rather than for information on attitudes (this is also true if the respondent is expected to classify concrete events into categories not already in his mind); (b) on the other hand, the specific information is more difficult to obtain when the concrete event was either so ambiguous, confusing, or emotion-provoking that the respondent never had a clear perception of the event or so complex that he had only a general picture of it, or when the process of abstraction by the respondent was so automatic that he could not report the specific perceptions leading to the generalization.

DEGREE OF SUBJECTIVITY OF EXPERIENCE

Both subjective and objective materials constitute social facts. By our definition, a fact is "objective" if it can be readily observed and agreed upon by independent observers. From the standpoint of interviewing, the most significant difference between subjective and objective material is that the latter is less likely to be distorted or inhibited by highly active interviewing methods. For example, it is possible that the "third degree" could be used to learn whether the respondent had buried the body in the swamp or had thrown it into the river. On the other hand, it is highly unlikely that the same degree of activity could be used to obtain the sequence of definitions of the situation in a crisis. This is not to imply that subjective information can never be obtained by vigorous methods. Some conditions under which activity is appropriate in the interview have been demonstrated by Richardson.[5]

The subjective dimension constitutes a commoner problem for the clinical psychologist and psychiatrist, who are more interested in unique experiences, than it does for the sociologist, who is primarily concerned with more widely shared experiences.

It should be noted that experiences cannot be dichotomized into the purely unique and the shared but that, in actuality, they fall along a continuum and are a matter of degree. For example, the schizophrenic may use many words esoterically; yet, if they were completely unique, never being shared by other schizophrenics or used consistently by one, the therapist could never understand them.

CONSCIOUS VERSUS UNCONSCIOUS EXPERIENCE

Here the term "unconscious experience" refers to behavior which the respondent cannot report because he was not conscious of it at the time and not because of a fading memory, ego-threat, or the uniqueness of the experience. For this reason the answers to the following would be difficult to obtain: "What is the difference between the way you speak to a Negro and the way you speak to a Caucasian?" "When do you use the prepositions 'of' and 'at' after a verb in the English language?" "Which sock do you usually put on first in the morning?"

There are at least three types of unconscious behavior. The most common is simply custom. The degree to which it is unconscious is indicated by Sapir.[6] Next, there is the unconscious behavior which Blumer calls "circular reaction," which is the immediate, unwitting response of one person to the subliminal cues furnished by another.[7] Finally, there is the unconscious behavior found under conditions of acute emotional stress in crises. This differs from circular reaction, in that no interaction with other people is needed.

Disasters provoke many examples of unconscious behavior. For example, persons fleeing from their homes to escape an explosion frequently take the longest route in order to leave by the rear door which they habitually use. Perhaps more to the point: a man rescued several people from a burning building but had no recollection of the acts which were clearly observed by several others; a crowd at an air show obeyed the master of ceremonies' suggestion to extinguish all cigarettes and refrain from starting automobiles when an airplane crashed into the grandstand and parking area, yet many who obeyed the order could not report what made them do so.

Details of these types of behavior are very difficult to obtain from the respondent. However, it was not uncommon for respondents to say that they had never been aware of certain aspects of their behavior during the crisis until after the interview had been under way for some time.

DEGREE OF TRAUMA

Here "trauma" is used to denote an acute unpleasantness associated with an experience. The unpleasant feeling is often brought to consciousness when the respondent is reporting the experience. It is not due to his embarrassment or his fear of losing status or of embarrassing the interviewer; it is because reporting the experience forces him to relive the original emotions.

Here there is no chance of the respondent's obtaining release from a guilty conscience by "confessing his sins," because he has no sins. A comparison of the length of the interviews with disaster victims having traumatic experiences, such as having members of the family killed, with the length of interviews with people who suffered no loss shows that the former tended to give either extremely long or extremely short interviews. In the prolonged interviews there was a tendency to talk repeatedly of the most traumatic portion of the experience. For example, a woman whose daughter, who was standing beside her at the air show, was killed when an airplane crashed into the crowd, repeatedly referred to the horrors of seeing her daughter mutilated. However, a respondent who had had a similar experience would not mention that a member of his family had been killed; this information had to be obtained from other sources.

We make no pretense of explaining why one respondent dilates on the "gory details" while another adroitly avoids the subject. It is possible that the respondent has a need for catharsis after a traumatic experience just as he does when he has feelings of guilt. A permissive attitude in the interviewer might encourage the respondent to talk, particularly if he cannot forget or repress the ordeal. The respondent's repressing a traumatic experience may have some relationship to the length of time after the event. However, it is not sidereal time which is relevant but social-psychological time calibrated by certain local events. Most significant of the latter seemed to be the funerals.

Contrary to expectations, in a community disaster it was easy to induce the respondent to talk before the funerals about the death of friends and members of the immediate family. However, after the funerals his attitude changed markedly. The funeral as a community event seemed to symbolize the establishment of a new social equilibrium: it marked the end of the past horror and the opening of a new chapter in the history of the individual and the community. The individual respondent's attitude seemed to be "'Let's not discuss the dead." Somehow the disaster victims seemed to be more dead after the funerals than before.

DEGREE OF ETIQUETTE

Here we refer to the respondent's perception of the etiquette between himself and the interviewer with respect to particular types of information. Communication is given its form by taboos, secrets, avoidances, "white lies," what Simmel referred to as "vital lies," and etiquette; and certain symbols and attitudes circulate only in restricted channels or between people in certain social relationships. The respondent must perceive his relationship with the interviewer as one permitting the communication desired. The respondent may have the information clearly in mind but feel that it would be impolite to divulge it, a state of affairs corroborated by the fact that many of the most clear-cut examples are unprintable.

The etiquette barrier can be broken down by using an interviewer in a more appropriate role. Sometimes it is not enough to select the correct interviewer, but, in addition, special techniques must be used to define the situation as one permitting a breach of the usual etiquette.

CHRONOLOGICAL ASPECT

"Chronological aspect" refers to the relationship between the time an experience occurred and the time from which the respondent is actually or imaginatively viewing it. Of the many logically possible aspects which might occur in the interview, we will mention the two most frequently encountered.

First is the "introspective past," which refers to information about an event which the respondent is reporting from the same point in time as the event. In effect, he speaks about the past in the present tense, trying thus to relive the original experience in every detail. Merton refers to this as "retrospective introspection." Here we are seeking the person's original subjective experience without distortions due to hindsight.

In a disaster people have great difficulty in correctly defining a crisis, and their definitions often progress through several stages. The individual tries to make sense out of what happened by seeing the original experience in the light of information obtained after the event. This general tendency constitutes an interviewing problem because if we wish to understand why the respondent acted as he did, we must discover how he defined the situation immediately before and during his action.

Second is the "retrospective past," which refers to information about a past event which the respondent is reporting from the vantage point of the present. Here the perspective is quite different because the respondent has the advantage of having had time to rearrange his own personal experiences in relation to one another and he also has the advantage of much new information from other people involved in the same situation. One of the most difficult tasks of the interviewer is to separate the data in the retrospective past from those in the introspective past. In general, it is easier to obtain information in the retrospective past.

CONCLUSIONS

The foregoing scheme should be useful in three ways. First, it should help the interviewer by sensitizing him to some of the complexities of the depth interview and allowing him to apply his techniques and skills more critically. It might also make him more alert for new insights, techniques, or tactics.

Second, the scheme should help the student of the interview as a process by furnishing what Merton would call a "theory of the middle range" which has been derived inductively and is at a high enough level of abstraction to be applicable to many instances of a certain class. It should not only help locate some of the basic problems but also give some hint of the possible limitations of generalizations based upon the study of one type of interview. It presents the interview as a dynamic process in which there is a constantly shifting relationship between the type of information sought and its meaning.

Finally, the scheme may be useful in developing a realistic design of research by calling attention to some of the problems of collecting valid and reliable data. Although the scheme was developed in the course of the writer's experience in interviewing, it may throw light upon the over-all strategy and the relative desirability of using questionnaires, observation, projective techniques, or interviewing in gathering the data.

FOOTNOTES

[1] Many of the ideas presented in this paper were gained while the writer was acting as assistant field supervisor of the Disaster Study Project at the National Opinion Research Center, University of Chicago.

[2] The writer agrees with Stephen A. Richardson that if the interviewer remains in a community and it is evident that he is talking to many people, he may be suspected of passing on highly confidential information and lose public confidence.

[3] B. V. Moore, "The Interview in Industrial Research," *Social Forces,* VII (1929), 445–52.

[4] Robert K. Merton, "The Focused Interview," *American Journal of Sociology*, LI (May, 1946), 541.

[5] Stephen A. Richardson, "The Use of Leading Questions in Non-schedule Interviews" (unpublished paper).

[6] Edward Sapir, "The Unconscious Patterning of Behavior in Society," in E. S. Dummer (ed.), *The Unconscious: A Symposium* (New York: A. A. Knopf, 1927), pp. 114–42.

[7] Herbert Blumer, "Collective Behavior," in Robert E. Park (ed.), *An Outline of the Principles of Sociology* (New York: Barnes & Noble, 1946), p. 224.

The Methodology of Participant Observation

by Severyn Bruyn

Some of the most fruitful insights into the nature of organizations and human events have been offered by those who have exploited this research method most imaginatively. Seldom has this yet been the case in librarianship where there is little tradition either of detached scholarly analysis on the part of individuals conducting research in practice or involvement in the life of the community served. There is potential in this method for both the researcher and the practitioner. Without involvement in the culture, no genuine insight into the core issues facing librarianship is likely to come from research. Conversely, it is only by detachment and analysis of the library and its program, that those who practice may come to perceive where and how to influence change in the goals and in the nature of the library effort. Attaining a desirable degree of involvement requires that researchers become less fearful about losing their objectivity and that librarians in practice come to understand that one is not any the less humane or caring if he becomes analytic about client, community or service arrangements.

In the search for meaning and understanding in human relationships a significant number of sociologists in the classical tradition, as well as in contemporary research, have recognized the importance of participant observation in methodology. The place of this technique in the methodology of social sciences has yet to be thoroughly examined. It still remains a questionable technique for some social scientists largely because it raises some of the most fundamental questions about epistemology and challenges the traditions of science.

This article proposes to confront these questions and challenges in the light of larger perspectives involved in the pursuit of knowledge. To accomplish this purpose we shall review the conclusions of past researchers regarding the social role of the participant observer, then examine questions of epistemology, the challenges the role presents to the scientific perspectives and standards of research, and finally the potential that exists for developing new perspectives for research.

THE SOCIAL ROLE

Certain summary statements can be made regarding the role of the participant observer on the basis of research findings already reported. This should serve to orient our analysis of the methodological foundations of this approach.

1. *The participant observer shares in the life activities and sentiments of people in face-to-face relationships.*

Florence Kluckhohn has thus succinctly described the role as:

... conscious and systematic sharing, in so far as circumstances permit, in the life activities, and on occasion, in the interests and affects of a group of persons.[1]

While the traditional role of the scientist is that of a neutral observer who remains unmoved and unchanged in his examination of phenomena, the role of the participant observer requires sharing the sentiments of people in social situations, and thus he himself is changed as well as changing to some degree the situation in which he is a participant. However, researchers have found that although he becomes changed through his participation, it is important that part of him remain unchanged and detached. Although "sharing" the experience, he is not entirely of it.

2. *The role of the participant observer requires both detachment and personal involvement.*

In a research report by Morris and Charlotte Schwartz, the involvement of the researcher is recognized and qualified:

The issue is not whether he will become emotionally involved, but rather the nature of the involvement. The involvement, whether it is closer to one end of the

SOURCE: Reprinted from Severyn Bruyn, "The Methodology of Participant Observation," *Human Organization*, 22 (Fall 1963), pp. 224–235, by permission of The Society for Applied Anthropology.

172

continuum (sympathetic identification) or the other end (projective distortion), is very little a function of an observer's role. Rather, it is primarily a function of his experience, awareness, and personality constellation and the way these become integrated with a particular situation . . . Sympathetic identification includes empathic communication and imaginative participation in the life of the observed through identification and role taking. In this type of involvement the observer is both detached and affectively participating; he feels no need to moralize or judge the interaction; his attitude is one of interested curiosity and matter-of-fact inquiry directed toward understanding the observed.[2]

In seeking to share something of the experience of the observed the researcher must not only become personally involved, he must also acquire the role which can function within the culture of the observed. There is no standard role which he can assume, but the requirements for the selection of the role are evident.

3. *The researcher acquires a social role which is determined by the requirements of the research design and the framework of the culture.*

Some of the types of roles which researchers have considered include: general and specific, active and passive, complementary, and others designated but not fully described. In the Schwartz report on field observation in a mental hospital they note:

The role of the participant observer may be either formal or informal, concealed or revealed; the observer may spend a great deal of time or very little time in the research situation; the participant observer may be an integral part of the social structure or largely peripheral to it.[3]

Active and passive roles are selected for description in their report.

Florence Kluckhohn makes the distinction between general, specific, and complementary roles. In her study of a Mexican village she took the role of a local storekeeper (a role complementary to her customers) and thus came to understand reflectively the lives of the villagers. Her role as a housewife she conceived as a general role similar to that of most women in the village. Other examples of general roles (i.e. identical with a significant portion of persons studied) would be the researcher's role as prisoner in studying prison socialization,[4] or the role of an air force recruit which a researcher undertook in studying a military program.[5]

4. *The scientific interests of the participant observer are interdependent with the cultural framework of the people being studied.*

In his scientific role the participant observer is seeking to apprehend, register, interpret, and conceptualize the social facts and meanings which he finds in a prescribed area of study. He is interested in the people as they are, not as he thinks they ought to be from some standard of his own; he is interested in the uniformities of their culture, in their existent, predictable state of being. To achieve these ends he finds his cultural role an indispensable part of the process.

He finds that only by coming to know people personally can he achieve his scientific aims. In his cultural role he becomes involved, but his procedures, his hypotheses, his experimental design, his social role remain objectively recorded. They are not so rigidly fixed that they cannot be changed. As with all experimental work if he finds that any one of these elements is not broadly enough conceived to encompass the data, he refocuses, reformulates his project in whatever way he finds advisable. He assumes he can do this without ignoring the interests of the people he is observing or the standards of his own research.

The scientific role and the cultural role of the researcher are interdependent and complementary.[6] The personal lives of the people he is studying are of great importance to him in both roles. It may be assumed that without this primary interest in them as persons in his active role as participant observer his study and findings become subject to distortion. His skill in reporting his findings objectively and the means he takes to insure this are also of primary interest to him. He assumes that one dimension makes the other possible. (He also assumes that no wholly "neutral" relation can exist in personal relations; such attempts often result in being impersonal, which is in effect becoming personal in a negative way.) He believes that valuing his subjects as persons increases the likelihood that he will come to understand them in their true state. The two roles not only coexist and complement one another, in some ways they can be seen as two reflections of the same social process as the researcher becomes a natural part of the life of the people he studies.

5. *The social role of the researcher is a natural part of the cultural life of the observed.*

The role of the researcher coincides with the role of the observed in the sense that both reflect the basic social process necessary to live in society. In his description of scientific methodology Cooley has stated:

The human mind participates in social processes in a way that it does not in any other processes. It is itself a sample, a phase, of those processes, and is capable, under favorable circumstances, of so far identifying itself with the general movement of a group as to achieve a remarkably just anticipation of what the group will do. Prediction of this sort is largely intuitive rather than intellectual; . . . [7]

The elements that go into participant observer research are a reflection of the universal process of role-taking in socialization from childhood through adulthood. In his description of a self, G. H. Meade describes the fundamental character of learning as role-taking whose end is the complete self which

reflects the unity and structure of the social process as a whole.[8]

Without disregarding the tensions and disharmonies inherent in the social process (which Meade neglected to explore), the aim of the participant observer is to take part in the socialization process just as the other participants do, to the point where his own inner experience can reflect the unity and structure of the whole.

The participant observer has usually been conceived as one who is an outsider and seeks to take part in a culture unlike his own. It is now apparent that the elements that go to comprise the participant observer technique *are fundamental to the social act* (in the Meadean sense) and therefore are to some degree a part of all social research. This explains why a discussion of participant observation must go to the heart of general methodology in the social sciences. The role of the participant observer is in process of refinement, out of the natural social process, just as the role of the physical scientist was refined out of the natural experiments made by ordinary people interested in the world about them.

EPISTEMOLOGICAL BACKGROUNDS

A. Naturalism and Idealism

The technique of any researcher evolves from philosophic traditions and is founded in certain epistemological beliefs about the origin of knowledge. Broadly speaking, two major traditions which lay behind the development of the social sciences have been naturalism and idealism. Both philosophies have undergone considerable change and development since their modern origin in the seventeenth century.

The formulator of the modern variant of naturalism (having had earlier roots) was Thomas Hobbes, who conceived all of nature as basically materialistic. He believed that all men's actions, thoughts, and feelings could be reduced to their true state as small particles of matter in motion. A later naturalistic interpretation can be illustrated in Jeremy Bentham's official philosophy that all man's actions could be determined and understood on the basis of weighing (literally as would a physicist) the gains and losses people felt existed between pleasureful and painful consequences. A still later development was seen in Karl Marx who raised the particle theory of Hobbes and the physiological theory of Bentham to a broader base in economic determinism. The changing economic forces became the mechanism through which all of culture was determined. Still later, neopositivists broadened the position further to include man's *general behavior* (not simply economic) as the foundation for understanding and predicting man's actions. Throughout this development, however, the deterministic-mechanistic image of man was retained and it was assumed that all behavioral phenomena could be quantified.[9] The foundations of modern science have been built from this philosophy.

The modern expression of idealism took form with Berkeley, an English clergyman, who radically held that the external world had no real existence outside of the mental processes themselves. It was clear to him that physical properties could not be known outside the mind, therefore the mind itself was the source of all knowledge. Later developments such as German idealism (as in Kant and Hegel) accepted physical reality but insisted on the supremacy of the mind as a source and creator of knowledge. A still more recent variety, called personal idealism, focuses upon personality as the source of knowledge.

The modern conceptions of idealism base the source of knowledge in experience itself with its many dimensions. Thus, it has broadened to a position which, while emphasizing the importance of certain qualities of the mind to produce knowledge independent of external factors, does not ignore their place in the experience of man. In various ways modern approaches to these early divergent philosophies are interpenetrating as philosophy continues to explore the foundation upon which sciences can build systems of knowledge.[10]

B. The Empirical, Rational, and Intuitive Sources

Empiricism[11] and rationalism are epistemological traditions which have grown to be commonly accepted among social scientists. In various ways they have both been associated with previously described philosophies. Empiricism, however, in the narrower usage (associated only with building knowledge from sense data) has largely been associated with naturalism. Rationalism assumes that knowledge may be found or created through the association and dissociation of concepts, that truth may be revealed in the structure of thought. The dispute about which of these sources is more important is no longer serious; it is widely recognized that while different research activities emphasize one or the other, in all experience there is a common interplay, and both are basic to the development of scientific knowledge.

The intuitive capacity of the mind, however, has been less accepted as a legitimate source of scientific knowledge. Nevertheless, the participant observer finds it an important part of his work. Without ignoring the rational process or the importance of his record of sense observations, he must recognize an additional source—the nonrational, nonsensible, affective experience of the observed, as reflected in his own experience. He assumes that there exists in human feelings a capacity to reveal knowledge which is independent of (as well as interdependent with) the rational-empirical sources of knowledge.

The veracity or proof of this position is no more possible outside of itself than is the proof of the rational or empirical traditions outside themselves. These are the initial assumptions that must be made about the nature of knowledge. However, the necessity for persuasion or validation remains for social scientists and usually develops through a combination of trusted traditions bearing witness to its own value to the human enterprise. For example, one important justifying authority in science today is pragmatism whose major test would be a method's capacity to void knowledge which stands the test of time. Another would be its demonstrated ability to predict or anticipate human action. The participant observer technique has already begun to demonstrate this productiveness, but this should increase still further as the technique becomes increasingly utilized and procedures for its application systematically developed.

In order to clarify and underline the importance of this intuitive epistemological position for the observer, it is necessary to examine in some detail the kinds of data which researchers encounter in their efforts to understand human relationships.

SCIENTIFIC DATA

Social scientific data are symbolic in the sense that all culture is symbolic. A brief review of the basic types of symbols existing in culture should provide a closer look at the subject matter (and the conceptual tools) of the participant observer.

The Sign

George Herbert Meade, Ernst Cassirer, Suzanne Langer, Talcott Parsons, Leslie White and many others have made an important distinction between sign and the symbol which marks the beginning of culture. A sign is any human expression which communicates a message to another in a particularized situation in which the parties are involved. Examples would be the gesture to wave goodbye, or to verbalize "go," or "come here," or to cry for help. The sign is an early development in communication expressed (as Meade illustrates) in the bark of the wolf to the pack or the cluck of a hen to the chickens.[12] The development of language has been traced from the original cry of an organism (sign of need) to a call (a sign expressed to specific individuals) to the word and the differentiation of sentence structures.[13] Anthropologically the graphic expression of this development can be seen from pictographs (illustrations of specific events or things) to ideograms (pictorial symbol of an idea) to phonetic expressions (symbols representing speech sounds). Symbols always stand in place of something or referent. Words may be understood as symbols insofar as they stand for that which is apprehended and are understood by people without making reference to a particular object in their immediate environment. The symbol involves a capacity to abstract and recall; their references become removed from the immediate environment.

Denotative Symbols

The denotative symbol begins where the sign leaves off. These symbols *stand* for observable objects such as chairs or tables. Initially they were in the form of signs directing attention to particular objects, such as the moon, the sun, or Fido the dog. But soon a broader image becomes necessary to communicate not simply the uniqueness of a particular object, but the meaning of objects of a similar nature. The elementary processes of abstraction enter into forming the symbol.

The process is more complex than it would seem to indicate. To know the idea of a table requires considerable previous learning at the tactile or sense reactive level. That is, the learner must have had a sense of surface, an impression of solidity, of dimension, etc., before the elements can come together to form something new, a general image which has a central figure and peripheral possibilities of form which allows judgment as to whether different objects meet primary or secondary requirements.

Denotative symbols are the data with which the strict empiricist is primarily concerned. He is interested in defining operationally the visible world about him. He does this to maintain precison and clarity in his work. However, there is considerably more complexity and indefiniteness than technicians would always admit. A simple reference to a piece of furniture like a sofa has such diverse reflections in our language as davenport, settee, couch, divan, dais, ottoman, daybed, etc., all having their own central images overlapping to some extent. In fact, like the active participant observer, he must make certain inferences that the references he makes are the same among different researchers, *on the basis of verbal agreement.*

Abstract Symbols

As degrees of generality continue to be formulated, the image becomes entirely removed from visibility in the outside world. A symbolic fundament is built out of common experience, parts of which (ideas, concepts) begin serving as the source of reference in themselves. For example, the idea of "society" is a highly abstract symbol around which focuses much of sociological theory. Its level of generality is clearly higher than any of its constituent parts, such as "institution," and still more removed a more denotative component, the "primary group." The theorist assumes, like the operationalist, that there is something common about symbolic development in people which allows agreement in meaning, and if standard procedures are followed, knowledge can be developed at each level of inquiry.

Levy-Bruhl once claimed that primitives could not abstract, that they were prelogical and tended to participate personally in the objects about them without the capacity to differentiate themselved from the inanimate objects. This unconditional description of primitive mentality has since been qualified by recognizing at least an elementary logic in all human culture. The primitive does distinguish between subject and object, but he refuses to believe that

all reality lies in our external perception of it. There is an internal side and there are effects, constraints, from subject to object and from object to subject.[14]

The primitive's failure to develop his logic, to deny the existence of beings in inanimate objects has been a major basis for the claim to civilized man's superiority. However, in civilized man's efforts to overcome the indistinctiveness and emotional projections of the primitive life, he has become subject to error in denying the other reality, the "sensuous forms" (as Cassirer would describe it aesthetically) of the inner perspective as a source of truth.

Northrop makes the distinction between the theoretic component (highly developed in Western civilization) and the aesthetic component (developed in the East). It is difficult, he says, for the Western man to realize or understand Eastern culture because of his irresponsible habit of abstracting everything from experiences. It is difficult for him to appreciate and know a thing for what it is, to know it emotionally, to empathize with it, and consider this an end in itself.[15] As William James would have said, it involves the difference between knowledge about a thing and knowledge of it. The Western scientist is quite capable of developing the former, but quite unprepared to understand the latter.

Emotive Symbols

Like the denotative symbol, "emotive" symbols begin as signs. Their origin however is to inner needs and feelings rather than indications of external objects. Expressions of pain or surprise, or the child's call for "mommy" are such signs.

In secondary levels of learning these signs, the cry, or call, become emotional conditions which are understood without reference to specific persons. Just as the image of the chair persists through time in the mind of the learner, similarly the emotion of pride or anger takes on a persistence, is talked about, conveyed to others, has a life of its own independent of immediate needs. Thus the tribe develops a feeling of loyalty over a period of time. Ceremonial dancers cultivate religious devotion. The significant feature of the emotive symbol lay in its capacity to persist through time and be shared. It may be evoked by an outside reference; just as the sight of a chair may evoke the idea of one, so the sight of an enemy may evoke the fear or anger; but the inner condition develops an independence which is transmitted among participants and retained over a period of time.

Charles Cooley describes how our language has already given us the data by the mere fact that man has needed to record these states of being:

Under the leading of words we interpret our observation, both external and introspective, according to patterns that have been found helpful by our predecessors. When we have come to use understandingly such words as "kindly," "resolute," "proud," "humble," "angry," "fearful," "lonesome," "sad," and the like, words recalling motions of the mind as well as the body, it shows that we have not only kept a record of our inner life, but have worked up the data into definite conceptions which we can pass on to others by the aid of the common symbol.[16]

Symbols of Sentiment

Emotive symbols move into another stage in which (like abstract symbols) it is not possible to refer to an immediate external cause or reference. Such may be called spiritual symbols or symbols of sentiment representing the spirit of man which has become more deeply set in experience, less moved by outside stimuli, having its own level and pace of development. The expressions of modern man which indicate such conditions, types of anxiety, suffering, joy, are not altogether unknown to primitive man. However, like abstract forms, these symbols are less developed and encountered less frequently.[17]

The primitive's emotional experiences are more particularized in the sense of pain or pleasure, and have some real, if not imaginary, reference to a cause he considers outside himself. Creative suffering perceived as an end in itself, the inner peace in the culture of the mystics, the Buddhistic state of Nirvana, the persistent anxiety of the mobile man in mass society, persist through the daily emotional reactions and changing external stimuli. They vary in their independence from or dependence upon the emotional and physiological needs of the individual and his place in society. Like conceptual development, these symbols (and the conditions they represent) grow more from the association of other like symbols of the inner life than the emotive or denotative symbols to which they are ultimately connected.[18]

Ideological and Substantive Symbols

As these various symbols combine with each other and with the human need for purpose and direction, we can designate other variations on these basic themes. Combinations of emotive and abstract symbols create ideological symbols such as "communism" or "Christianity." Adding denotative references, we find substantive symbols such as the flag or the cross, which represent considerable rational development and deeply felt human interests.

The position of the symbol in the culture of the observed is fundamental to the interpretation made by the participant observer. Robert Redfield describes the various ways an observer may approach this problem by illustrating his efforts to comprehend the inner world of the Mayan villagers of Chan Kom. One approach came to him as several of the villagers traveled with him to the sea coast and expressed amazement at how people could live without maize. Then he began to see the vital position of this symbol in the village life:

So I began to form another way of conceiving parts as related to one another in a system of activity and thought. This third system is neither chainlike or maplike. It is radial: maize is a center and other things are grouped around it, connected to it in different ways, some by a series of useful activities, some by connections of symbolic significance. The mind goes out from maize to agriculture, from maize to social life, from maize to religion. Maize is always the center of things.[19]

The participant observer must comprehend all these basic symbolic forms as he may find them in his area of study. He recognizes that by his acquaintanceship with symbols of sentiment and emotion in a particular setting he is more likely to adequately conceptualize the meaning and significance of events in the lives of those he is observing.

BASIC PERSPECTIVES

Any description of the basic perspectives of men in the pursuit of knowledge necessarily includes only selective abstractions of what in reality merges in varying degrees according to the type of research. Such descriptive statements, in the tradition of the Weberian ideal type, are formulated for the purpose of gaining some further insight into the nature of the participant observer process of research.

Different types of research have indicated two basic perspectives, an inner and outer. The latter assumes that the study of man's *behavior* or conduct is adequate to produce knowledge about social life. The inner perspective assumes that understanding can only be achieved by actively participating in the life of the observed and gaining insight by means of introspection. There is no disjunction between these perspectives in reality as all research involves something of both. However, as one comes to analyze them and the types of research that tend to associate with them, other perspectives reveal themselves as important to understand.

Determinism and Cultural Freedom

As the participant observer enters into the common life of those whom he is studying he must act within a cultural framework which recognizes a measure of personal freedom, to which responsibility and obligation are attached. The amount and kind of free choice that is recognized varies from culture to culture and such differences become a part of the social role of the researcher.

The frame of reference of freedom which the participant observer assumes would seem to challenge the perspective of scientific determinism which research has inherited from the natural sciences. The dilemma must be resolved at the working level where the participant observer accepts the definition of freedom perceived by his fellow participants yet also comes to perceive the determining factors in their background.

Social sciences still utilize the perspective of determinism as the basis for interpreting social life; some scientists hold to it as the only correct perspective possible.[20] There should be no need for conflict between the determinism of science and the culture of the observed. There is a rational basis for the researcher to genuinely understand and accept the concept of cultural freedom.

The research design arising from scientific determinism, does not generally account for the fact that all factors or variables are to some extent determinants or causes in themselves. Which is cause and which effect depends upon the perspective of the observer. In the cultural framework, the participant observer simply enters into the inner perspective of the determinant, in this case the people themselves, and sees them as determining (causing) the effects about them. From their perspective of personal responsibility and free will, it is legitimately assumed that freedom exists to the extent that knowledge about and power over existential conditions is demonstrable. The two perspectives coexist, have validity, and actually depend upon the position one takes to his subject.

The Causal and Telic Principles

The participant observer seeks to know and become part of the purposes and interests of people. He assumes that all people have aims and that they have some latent or manifest knowledge about means to achieve these aims. The importance of understanding the purposive aspects of social phenomena has been stressed from Durkheim to modern functionalism, but the importance of this perspective to the participant observer requires it be restated.

Without ignoring causality, in fact being quite aware of causes and effects, he nevertheless comes to act toward people and react toward events within a purposive framework which comes to infuse and pervade his descriptions. The interests and valuations of people become a central pivot around which he guides his conduct and interprets the social setting in which he works.

Analysis and Synthesis

As the participant observer records, interprets, and explains social phenomena, he analyses it; he takes apart the events and looks at them separately. However there are two important ways in which contrasting features must be noted by the participant observer. First, he seeks to find some identity with the observed without analyzing them. Analysis at certain stages may prove to be a barrier to his understanding. The researcher seeks a certain kind of communion with the observed and in any efforts to comment descriptively about the situation keeps himself outside it.

There is no place for either rational or emotional comments at the point of intuitive contact. Cooley stresses this point with regard to reflective emotions:

> Sympathy in the sense of compassion is a specific emotion or sentiment, and has nothing necessarily in common with sympathy in the sense of communion. It might be thought, perhaps, that compassion was one form of sharing feeling; but this appears not to be the case. The sharing of painful feeling may precede and cause compassion, but is not the same with it. When I feel sorry for a man in disgrace, it is, no doubt, in most cases, because I have imaginatively partaken of his humiliation; but my compassion for him is not the thing that is shared, but is something additional, a comment on the shared feeling. I may imagine how a suffering man feels—sympathize with him in that sense—and be moved not to pity but to disgust, contempt, or perhaps admiration. Our feeling makes all sorts of comments on the imagined feeling of others.[21]

Secondly, the tendency of the participant observer is to seek the essence of the life of the observed, to sum up, to find a central unifying principle. The documents of many anthropologists are evidence of this inclination. Ruth Benedict's descriptions of the two Indian cultures as

Appolonian and Dionysian and Opler's culture themes are cases in point.

Of course there are limitations in stressing either mode of interpretation without some reference to the other. The difficulties in synthetic descriptions lie in the tendency to oversimplify (and thereby misunderstand) the nature of the culture. The difficulties of analysis lie in the failure to see the whole, and thereby the significance of the parts. All researchers inescapably apply both modes but the conditions under which they work causes one or the other to be emphasized.

Types of Concepts: Operational and Sensitizing

All scientific research involves the conceptualization of data. The types of concepts employed differ with the kinds of research design. The operational concept is most frequently used in quantitative research. It is defined as a statement of the specific procedures or operations used to identify and measure a phenomenon under study. Another kind of concept more frequently used in research has been described by Herbert Blumer as the "sensitizing concept." Blumer raises the question of how these concepts can be formulated and communicated. He notes that rather than formal definitions,

> It is accomplished instead by exposition which yields a meaningful picture, abetted by apt illustrations which enable one to grasp the reference in terms of one's own experience.[22]

This statement describes the character of much of participant observer research.

Contrary to the opinion of some operationalists, sensitizing concepts are not all necessarily on the road to becoming definitive, as though they were ideal. Such a position would deny the reality which they represent. By operationalizing a concept, its meaning becomes changed. Although it is true that all data are subject to measurement, it is also true that when this is done its distinctive character and meaning are lost. By defining an emotion or sentiment, for example, as that which is measured by certain visceral responses cannot convey the true meaning of that feeling. Sensitizing concepts therefore have a right to their own existence without changing their expression by way of enumeration.

	Inner Perspective	Outer Perspective
Epistemological Background	Idealism Intuitive imagination	Natural materialism Logical empiricism
Explanatory Principle	Teleology	Causality
Acting Framework	Cultural Freedom	Scientific Determinism
Methods and Techniques	Participant Observation Personal Documents	Statistics
Aims	Sensitive understanding of human values, institutions; anticipation of new directions	Adequate measurement and prediction of human behavior
Mode of Study	Synthetic emphasis	Analytic emphasis
Concepts	Sensitizing	Operational

Merging Reality

Anyone accustomed to the discipline of research knows that these types are only abstractions of what in reality tend to merge together in various ways. The ways in which this dichotomy of perspectives (illustrated in the diagram above) does not fit reality is as important to understand as the abstraction itself.

A complete statement of how these divergent perspectives have crossed in history and in the configuration of actual research projects would involve a lengthy dissertation. However, a few basic points will illustrate the crossings: 1) The participant observer is sometimes a part of a larger quantitative study and may enumerate his data to contribute solely to the larger quantitative study. 2) A functional (telic) analysis of social phenomena may very well also be quantitative in nature. 3) The history of idealism as an epistemological theory has also included theories of determinism. 4) Sociological analysis need not be cast in a deterministic framework.[23] 5) The participant observer (as has been noted) is aided by his senses and reason as well as by intuition; the logical empiricist is aided by intuition.[24] 6) Max Weber's concept of bureaucracy involved a process of synthesis (putting together of significant elements) as well as analysis, as does most of theoretical work.

With these and other exceptions which could be noted, the ideal type still stands on the basis of the emphasis which is given to each perspective. That is, the use of the participant observer to simply quantify data, while useful in some cases, is not the general role he assumes; while quantitative methods are used in functional analysis, the functional interpretations must be made on the basis of participant observation which characterizes the work of researchers who study their own culture;[25] while at times idealism has included deterministic perspectives, its emphasis in history has been on freedom; while the rational-empirical-intuitive capacities are interdependent, one or another is more evident in different research designs; much of highly abstract theoretical formulation involves intuitive observation.[26]

SCIENTIFIC STANDARDS

The standards of objectivity, control, reliability and validity are still important concerns for the participant observer. These guides to research require reexamination in the light of what they mean today.

Objectivity

Objectivity is an ideal, a state which is always in process of becoming. It is never fully achieved by any investigator in any final sense. It is a condition of reporting without prejudice, but it need not be a report without feeling or sentiment. There are two ways in which the participant observer assumes that feeling and objectivity may coexist.

First, it is possible for the investigator to have a feeling of respect for his subjects and remain open and unprejudiced in apprehending and reporting about their way of life. Second, it is possible for the sentiments of people being studied to be conveyed in the report without prejudicing the accuracy or correctness of the report itself.

Maurice Stein describes a "dramatic theory" developing among some sociological circles which focuses the problem of the participant observer.

> From a dramatic standpoint, the central problem of the community sociologist is to achieve an objective perspective that encompasses the partial perspectives held by various groups in the community in such a fashion as to call attention to hidden processes without losing sight of the meanings of the various partial perspectives. The playwright seeks to present his characters sympathetically without going so far as to allow the sympathy they evoke to swallow the larger meanings that emerge when they are viewed within the context of the entire plot and action of the play. The play suffers as much when the context is allowed to override full presentation of diverse characters. The playwright seeks a profound balance and it is similar to the balance sought by the community sociologist.
> Dramatic sensibility then consists of the capacity to encompass multiple interpretations of a social world within a larger context which distinguishes objective structures without obliterating subjective meanings.[27]

Participant observer methodology broadens the limits of the scientific framework to permit ideas for social and cultural studies which would not ordinarily be entertained.

Reliability and Validity

The participant observer does not need to defend the reliability or validity of his data (in the traditional sense) in certain stages of his work. This point has been sufficiently discussed in the research on personal documents.[28] As research proceeds, however, the accuracy of the denotative references of the subject's statements adds to the objectivity of the research. A description of the connection between the inner and the outer world of the subject is fundamental to a complete report.

The participant observer technique in some ways has already proven itself to be more reliable than other methods available. In the article previously quoted, Florence Kluckhohn describes how the direct interview and the questionnaire create special or unnatural situations. The subject may not know how to respond to formal methods, may unconsciously or purposely err, or may have a faulty memory. In contrast, the participant observer is there in the social setting which the interviewer may be seeking to learn about, and has the opportunity to record what actually happens. He is in a position to evaluate any rationalizations which the subject may make to a questionnaire or a formal interview.

Guides to Adequate Research

Rules which are appropriate for the participant observer to follow in his research are generally applicable to all research. Nevertheless, through practical experience, there is developing a know-how, and a set of principles which guide the observer around the pitfalls which are peculiar to his kind of work. A few of these guides can be summarized in the following directives.

1) *Examine all Significant Rules Existing in Counter-Position in a Circumscribed Social Setting*

The inclination of observers is to so identify with a particular segment of the population being studied that their work is hindered or their reporting is obstructed. Two pitfalls are in evidence here. First, the tendency of "over-rapport" in which too close a contact with the observed does not allow an investigation into certain questions without serious breach of the relationship.[29]

Second, the tendency to report sympathetically the plight of the subject under study. For example, studies of the juvenile delinquent in his natural setting have tended in some cases to romanticize his role. Examining only the symbolic meaning of "cop" in the life of the young slum dweller may shut out or overshadow the meaning of "brat" or "cop-killer" for the police officer. The participant observer should include both subject and object in contra-position to convey objectively the social context.

2) *Relate the Research Problem to a Larger Social Context*

In the field of industrial relations the role of the laborer needs not only to be examined with reference to the counter-position of manager, but ideally the two powers need relating to the community and the economic system in the context of the whole society. There are limits to any research problem, to be sure, but accurate references to the nature of the larger context adds to the objectivity of the report.

3) *Examine and Describe the Participant Observer's Own Status in the Social System*

A participant observer can very well make use of the findings and guides developed in the sociology of knowledge as a bridge from the biases inherent in his social position to a point of objectivity. Merton's paradigm is a good beginning guide.[30]

The stages of his acceptance into the community is vital to the kind of data he will receive.[31] The kind of image which those around him have of him provides a basis for their response to him. By examining and reporting these facts carefully, the research may avoid this easy pitfall.

4) *Observe the Subjects Under Contrasting Social and Isolated Settings*

Misconceptions have been avoided and insight added when this directive is followed. Howard Becker reports an experience in studying medical students:

> Thus, students in their clinical years may express deeply "idealistic" sentiments about medicine when alone with the observer, but behave and talk in a very "cynical" way when surrounded by fellow students. An alternative to judging one or the other of these situations as more reliable is to view each datum as valuable in itself, but with respect to different conclusions. In the example above, we might conclude that group norms may not sanction their expression.[32]

5) *Evaluate the Information as Any Personal Document*[33]

6) *Indicate the Proportion or Segment of the Group Which Expresses the Norms or Conduct Being Recorded*

7) *Carefully Specify the Procedures Used so that Other Investigators may Follow and Check the Findings From the Same (and from Different) Social Positions in the Setting Under Study*

8) *Examine Indexes of Distortion in Reporting and Evaluate the Data With Reference to Them*[34]

NEW PERSPECTIVES

The study of participant observation stimulates new perspectives. Just as the social scientist has consciously transposed and developed his techniques and methodology from the physical and organic sciences, so he may become conscious of the possibilities in other disciplines, including the humanities and the arts. He is far from alone in his pursuit of the meaning and objective character of culture and social conduct. He has a special opportunity to produce new blends, new research which will cast the social scene into a more human (and therefore a more realistic) form.[35]

Given the separate academic disciplines existing in their own right, there is still room for considerable fruitful exchange among them. For example, the fact that the subject matter of the social sciences and literature is so similar, makes it unusual that so little attention has been given to studying and comparing the approaches of each. The social scientific descriptions of latent and manifest functions, of social incongruities and dysfunctions in institutional settings, have long been a part of the devices of literary expression.

In the rhetorical allusion, in satire and irony, in the metaphor, the analogy and allegory, in the parable, and many other age-old artistic and literary modes may be found important instruments of inquiry and analysis, yet unexamined in the methods of sociological studies. The employment of such literary devices need not distort or misrepresent the essential purpose of sociological reporting. As techniques to convey social meaning (derived from empirical studies) they can be as useful and vital as have been the modes of logic or statistical analysis to scientific research.

Such literary devices need not be conceived as masked instruments of ideological or moral doctrine. They should rather be seen as tools of the intellectual craftsman to be used well or badly according to his training and experience. In a rather thorough analysis of the use of allegory in modern literature, Edwin Honig summarizes its instrumental character:

In one of its aspects allegory is a rhetorical instrument used by strategists of all sorts in their struggle to gain power or to maintain a system of beliefs. (Such usage and the motives lurking behind it have recently had the close study of critics as part of the semantic problem of symbolic action.) In addition to serving the expression of ideological aims, allegory is a fundamental device of hypothetical construction. In this broad way allegory is part of the creative process, observable in all literature generally, where the formulation of vital beliefs seem essential to maximum expressiveness.

The literary allegory does not oppose a realistic account of the universe. Its very power lies in its giving proof to the physical and ethical realities of life objectively conceived.[36]

Some of these literary mechanisms, have been built into the structure of language from its very beginnings.[37] With language so basic to social life, sociologists are coming to see their fundamental place in their work. Anthropologists have already recognized their importance in the study of primitive society. Robert Redfield describes the necessity of the ethnographer and the sociologist to make use of such devices in making their descriptions of community life.

In the portraitures accomplished by art, exaggerations, distortions and substitutions of one sort or another play important parts. Caricature and satire are special forms of portraiture. Each describes the whole by overemphasizing something felt to be significantly true of the whole. Metaphor and analogy offer different and parallel images for understanding the whole, as does the parable: a narrative standing for a human something other than itself. And in the more nearly scientific portraiture of communities metaphors and analogies play a useful part. No one expects Professor Fortes to produce the tangible warp and woof of Tallensi social structure; the words bring forward a metaphor which helps us to understand Tallensi life, and, indeed, the concept of social structure itself.[38]

There is no longer a necessity to justify the use of these rhetorical figures. The need now is for their study, and more critical use as part of the methodology of the social sciences.

The parable has its own place in the record of man's search for knowledge. It has often been employed by charismatic founders of religious movements in an effort to convey meanings which they believe have not yet been grasped by their followers. The function of the parable is to set a moral or spiritual truth aside, from the usual affections of the self so that it can be grasped more objectively or at least on another level of experience. It is usually a short fictitious narrative which is intentionally obscured so that it requires some reflective thought before it is grasped. It is not a device for hidden persuasion; it requires voluntary effort to see the meaning. It functions to establish or verify a new experience, a new understanding of an old principle, or a new state of mind. Students of theology have much to contribute to the sociologist in their studies of this medium of communication. Sociologists can utilize such knowledge in their analysis of the diffusion of the religious movement throughout the society.

Such studies have various applications to the

field of sociology. They can increase our understanding of the social character of language; they can cast light on the field of communication and studies of socialization; they can act as an enhancement (as well as a self-corrective)[39] of professional descriptions of social life.

The field of art has its own contributions to make. A study of the state of the aesthetic observer viewing an art object cannot help but add insight into the role of the participant observer as he observes the actors in his social setting. In a provocative discussion of aesthetic experience, Cassirer comes to Aristotle's theory of catharsis and interprets how, through tragic poetry, a person takes on new attitudes toward his emotions.

> The soul experiences the emotions of pity and fear, but instead of being disturbed and disquieted by them it is brought to a state of rest and peace. At first sight this would seem to be a contradiction. For what Aristotle looks upon as the effect of tragedy is a synthesis of two moments which in real life, in our practical existence, exclude each other. The highest intensification of our emotional life is thought of as at the same time giving us a sense of repose. We live through all our passions feeling their full ravages and highest intensity. But what we leave behind when passing the threshold of art is the hard pressure, the compulsion of our emotions; and he is able to transfer this mastery to the spectators. In his work we are not swayed and carried away by our emotions. Aesthetic freedom is not the absence of passions, not stoic apathy, but just the contrary. It means that our emotional life acquires its greatest strength, and that in this very strength it changes its form. For here we no longer live in the immediate reality of things but in a world of pure sensuous forms. In this world all our feelings undergo a sort of transubstantiation with respect to their essence and their character. The passions themselves are relieved of their material burden. We feel their form and their life but not their encumbrance. The calmness of the work of art is, paradoxically, a dynamic, not a static calmness.[40]

Cassirer quotes Hamlet in speaking of the function of dramatic art which might as well be interpreted as the function of the participant observer in recording and interpreting his observations of a particular culture.

> The purpose of playing, [as Hamlet explains] both at the first and now, was and is, to hold, as 'twere, the mirror up to nature; to show virtue her own feature, scorn her own image, and the very age and body of the time his form and pressure.

But the image of a passion is not the passion itself. The poet represents a passion but does not infect us with this passion. At a Shakespeare play we are not infected with the ambition of Macbeth, with the cruelty of Richard III, or with the jealousy of Othello. We are not at the mercy of these emotions; we look through them; we seem to penetrate into their very nature and essence . . . It is not the degree of intensification and illumination which is the measure of the excellence of art.

The cultural organization of people may be viewed in many ways other than its symbolic character, which has been of principal use in this article. It can be viewed as an aesthetic creation and described from the models of art criticism. For example, culture, like any art object, has many dimensions: its material product, its expression, its form, its function in the social order. If the sociologist were to begin by analysing the *form* which culture assumes, by using a model in art criticism, he would guide his study through the principles of harmony, balance, centrality, and development, and pursue his analysis by way of their derivatives —recurrence, similarity, gradation, variation, hierarchy, and progression, all of which can be aesthetically perceived and reported in an empirical study of a cultural system.[41]

The technique of participant observation is basic to the methodology of the social sciences. It presents real dilemmas for the researcher who identifies his field solely with the physical sciences. In this article the congruities and incongruities of these dilemmas have been sketched and judged in in the light of the scholarly pursuit of knowledge. This pursuit is conceived as a creative one in which new techniques, new perspectives are continually being formulated. The methods of the social sciences cannot remain static; in full regard of the standards of research which are its heritage, it must move on in its probe of the character, the drama, and the meaning of human enterprise.

FOOTNOTES

[1] Florence Kluckholn, "The Participant-Observer Technique in Small Communities," *American Journal of Sociology*, XLVI (November, 1940), 331.

[2] Morris S. Schwartz and Charlotte G. Schwartz, "Problems in Participant Observation," *American Journal of Sociology*, LX (January, 1955), 350.

[3] *Ibid.*, 344.

[4]Hans Reimer, "Socialization in the Prison Community," *American Prison Association Proceedings*, 1937, 151-155.

[5]Mortimer A. Sullivan, Jr., Stuart A. Queen, and Ralph C. Patrick, Jr., "Participant Observation in a Military Program," *American Sociological Review*, XXIII (December, 1958), 660–667.

[6]The problems and conflicts which can arise between these roles (not the subject of discussion here) are reported elsewhere. See: William Foote Whyte, *Street Corner Society*, The University of Chicago Press, 1955, pp. 279-358; Arthur J. Vidich, "Freedom and Responsibility in Research," *Human Organization*, XIX (Spring, 1960, Number 1), 3-4.

[7]Charles Cooley, *Sociological Theory and Social Research*, Henry Holt & Co., 1930, p. 308.

[8]Anselm Strauss (Ed.), *The Social Psychology of George Herbert Meade*, The University of Chicago Press, 1956, p. 221.

[9]Recent conceptions of naturalism broaden its form to cut across the stream of Western thought, including some modern strains of idealism. See: Vergilus Ferme, "Varieties of Naturalism," *A History of Philosophical Systems*, The Philosophy Library, 1950, pp. 429–440.

[10]For a modern system of metaphysics which links the traditions of idealism and naturalism see: D. W. Gotshalk, *Metaphysics in Modern Times*, University of Chicago Press, 1940.

[11]The term empiricism has developed varied meanings which can be described on a continuum from rigidly defined procedures for obtaining sense data with no inferences of a "subjective" kind, to the acquisition of knowledge on the basis of experience, which stands in contrast to the normative or ethical field of knowledge. The usage in this article refers to the former end of the continuum.

[12]George Herbert Meade, *op. cit.*, p. 213.

[13]G. Revesz, *The Origins and Prehistory of Language*, Longmans Green and Co., 1956.

[14]Paul Radin, *The World of Primitive Man*, Henry Schaman, Inc., 1953, p. 49.

[15]Filmer Stuart Cuckow Northrop, *Meeting of East and the West*, The Macmillan Co., 1946.

[16]Charles Cooley, *op. cit.*, p. 299.

[17]An example of primitive suffering which appears from the report to exist at this level of symbolization may be found in: Knud Rasmussen, *Observations on the Intellectual Culture of the Caribou Eskimo*, Copenhagen, 1930, pp. 52–55. Quoted in Paul Radin, *op. cit.*, pp. 76–78.

[18]This rough classification of symbols could obviously bear further analysis, but remains in this form only to indicate the kinds of cultural data the participant observer must learn to apprehend and interpret.

[19]Robert Redfield, *The Little Community*, The University of Chicago Press, 1955, p. 22.

[20]Donald R. Taft, *Criminology*, Macmillan, 1956, pp. 343–346.

[21]Charles Cooley, *op. cit.*, footnote, p. 102.

[22]Herbert Blumer, "What is Wrong with Social Theory?," *American Sociological Review*, XIX (February, 1954), No. 1, 9.

[23]McIver's concept of *"dynamic assessment"* illustrates an effort to overcome the deterministic perspective. Robert M. McIver, *Social Causation*, Ginn and Co., Boston, 1942, pp. 292–293.

[24]From his logical perspective, any discovery not evident in operational procedure would be defined as "rational processess" operating at the subliminal level of consciousness.

[25]Arthur J. Vidich, "Participant Observation and the Collection and Interpretation of Data", *American Journal of Sociology*, LX (January, 1955), 385.

[26]Contrariwise, participant observation has contributed to the breakdown of Weber's concept into more predictable parts. Alvin W. Gouldner, *Patterns of Industrial Bureaucracy*, The Free Press, 1954.

[27]Maurice R. Stein, *The Eclipse of Community*, Princeton University Press, 1960, p. 325.

[28]"It should be pointed out, also, that the validity and value of the personal document are not dependent upon its objectivity and veracity. It is not expected that the delinquent will necessarily describe his life situations objectively. On the contrary, it is desired that his story will reflect his own personal attitudes and interpretations, for it is just these personal factors which are so important in the study and treatment of the case. Thus, rationalizations, fabrications, prejudices exaggerations, are quite as valuable as objective descriptions, provided of course, that these reactions be properly identified and classified." Clifford Shaw, *The Jack-Roller*, Albert Saifer Publications, Philadelphia, Pennsylvania, 1930, pp. 2–3.

[29]S. M. Miller, "The Participant Observer and Over-Rapport," *American Sociological Review*, XVII (February, 1952), 97–99.

[30]Robert Merton, *Social Theory and Social Structure*, The Free Press, 1949, pp. 217–245.

[31]Robert W. James, "A Note on Phases of the Community Role of the Participant-Observer," *American Sociological Review*, XXVI, (June, 1961), pp. 446–450.

[32]Howard S. Becker, "Problems of Inference and Proof in Participant Observation", *American Sociological Review*, XXIII (December, 1958), p. 655.

[33]Louis Gottschalk, Clyde Kluckhohn, and Robert Angell, *The Use of Personal Documents in History, Anthropology and Sociology*, New York Social Science Research Council, 1945, pp. 15–27, 38–47, Reference in Howard S. Becker, *op. cit.*, p. 654.

[34]Morris S. Schwartz and Charlotte G. Schwartz, *op. cit.*, p. 347.

[35]This does not call for a super-discipline or new eclecticism among the social sciences. Like other disciplines they are circumscribed in their search for knowledge. The physical sciences do not wrestle with purpose in their data; the biological sciences do not reckon with sentiment; art, literature and drama do not characteristically pursue knowledge systematically, building propositions into a coherent theory of life. The social scientists in their turn do not search out the uniqueness of an event as an end in itself as does the poet or the artist. The social scientists cannot derive moral truths out of their studies as would the theologian or a playwright.

[36] Edwin Honig, *Dark Conceit*, Walker-dePerry, Inc., 1959, pp. 179–180.

[37] Susanne K. Langer, *Philosophy in a New Key*, Mentor Books, 1942, pp. 111–115.

[38] Robert Redfield, *op. cit.*, p. 162.

[39] It is worthwhile to examine the use of metaphors, similes, a set of images, in any sociological analysis as they affect the total meaning conveyed to the reader. Caroline Spurgeon sets an example by her study of the substructure of Shakespeare's tragedies. By the use of various literary figures the reader is unwittingly led to conclusions by way of various literary devices. For example in Hamlet are various images of disease (ulcer, cancer), a motif which suggests that the Prince is not to blame, but the whole state of Denmark is diseased. Caroline Spurgeon, *Shakespear's Imagery and What It Tells Us*, Cambridge, 1935.

[40] Ernst Cassirer, *An Essay on Man*, Doubleday and Co., Inc., 1956, p. 190.

[41] D. W. Gotshalk, *Art and The Social Order*, The University of Chicago Press, 1947, p. 114. This text presents a most unusual model for art criticism.

Development of Methodologic Tools for Planning and Managing Library Services

by Richard H. Orr, Vern M. Pings, Irwin H. Pizer and Edwin E. Olson

The basic premises which underlie one of only a very limited number of systematic efforts to develop reliable measures in the library field are developed here. Subsequent articles cover the specific method in detail.* Because it focuses upon service capability, the measurement tool holds out promise of having a potentially profound influence on the policy process in libraries. By shifting attention from such traditional criteria as collection size or strength to measures more nearly related to purpose, it opens for analysis whether there is discrepancy and to what degree, between what librarianship professes to do and what the reality of library service is. Seen thus, it opens up an avenue seldom traveled heretofore in library scholarship or practice.

This is the first in a series of reports on a continuing project aimed at developing a number of methodologic tools that will be useful to those responsible for individual libraries and for local, regional, and national library systems—methods that can be used to obtain the kinds of data urgently needed to realize the opportunities that new support programs and recent technologic advances offer for improving library services. Our chief reason for reporting the project's results seriatim is to make these tools available as soon as they are ready for practical application or for further development by others. This first report describes the overall project and sets forth the basic concepts underlying the entire effort. It represents an attempt to provide a common introduction for all later reports and, thereby, to obviate the need for repeating, in each report, certain background information essential for understanding and evaluating any of the project's results.

PURPOSE AND GOALS

Substantive work on the project began in July 1966, when the National Library of Medicine awarded the Institute for Advancement of Medical Communication a contract "to develop methods for collecting objective data suitable for planning and guiding local, regional, and national programs to improve biomedical libraries and the biomedical information complex." This succinct statement of purpose requires some amplification to make the unusual nature of the project completely clear. Unlike most studies in which the purpose is to collect data and test hypotheses, and methods are only the means to these ends, the emphasis is completely reversed in this project—it is methods, rather than data, that are of primary interest.

Initial Goals

Although our general objective is limited to developing methods that can be used by others, rather than attempting to obtain data that are valuable per se, this is still too broad an aim to serve as a realistic goal for any project limited by practical constraints on time and manpower. Therefore, to focus the effort, five specific aims, or "tasks," were established as initial goals: (1) to develop a method of measuring quantitatively a

*For a description of the method, see Richard H. Orr and Others, "Development of Methodologic Tools for Planning and Managing Library Services: II. Measuring a Library's Capability for Providing Documents," *Bulletin of the Medical Library Association,* 56 (Jul., 1968), pp. 241-267; and Richard H. Orr and Others, "Development of Methodologic Tools for Planning and Managing Library Services: III. Standardized Inventories of Library Services," *Bulletin of the Medical Library Association*, 56 (Oct., 1968), pp. 380-403.

SOURCE: Reprinted from Richard H. Orr, Vern M. Pings, Irwin H. Pizer, and Edwin E. Olson, "Development of Methodologic Tools for Planning and Managing Library Services: I. Project Goals and Approach," *Bulletin of the Medical Library Association*, 56 (Jul., 1968), pp. 235–240, by permission of the publisher. The original publication bore the following note: "This work was supported in part by U. S. Public Health Service Contract PH 43-66-540 from the National Library of Medicine."

library's capability for providing the documents its users may need; (2) to develop a standard procedure for making an "inventory" of all the services a library offers its individual users; (3) to develop a method for identifying, enumerating, and characterizing the user population that constitutes a library's primary responsibility; (4) to assess the feasibility of measuring quantitatively a library's capabilities for providing certain types of "reference service"; and (5) to evaluate alternative methods for measuring utilization of a library's services. These tasks were further sharpened by concentrating on academic libraries serving biomedical populations. Although the initial goals have been broadened and a number of new tasks have been added as work progressed, the five original tasks suggest the general scope of the project—at least of the part that is concerned with individual libraries, as contrasted with systems of libraries.

General Desiderata

Some of the above task statements make explicit certain specific requirements of the particular tool to be developed; for example, that the method should provide quantitative data. However, if the overall purpose of the project was to be served, it was highly desirable that all the methods developed should have certain general characteristics. The more important of these general desiderata can be summarized as follows: First, the data obtained by any method should be sufficiently reliable—that is, reproducible—to provide a sound basis for planning and management decisions. Second, the methods should have prima facie validity to users and nonlibrarian administrators, as well as to librarians. Third, they should be practical—costs should be reasonable, and execution should not seriously interfere with a library's regular operations, nor be burdensome to its clientele. Fourth, they should be widely applicable to libraries, regardless of differences in size, location, environment, or details of internal operations. Fifth, a library's capabilities for calling upon the resources of the "library system" should be assessed, as well as its ability to meet demands solely from its own resources. Sixth, the methods should be suitable for application by a library's own staff, rather than being useful only in the hands of outside "experts." Finally, they should be valuable for assessing changes in a given library over a period of time, and for comparing different libraries. These seven desiderata, which have influenced work on

all project tasks, can be epitomized as reproducibility, "face" validity, practicality, wide applicability, "library system" orientation, suitability for self-assessment, and comparability. Collectively, these general requirments constitute an idealistic and very stringent set of conditions; and in the course of work on a given task, it was usually necessary to accept some kind of a compromise on one or more of the desiderata if others were to be met at all. Where compromises were necessary, reproducibility, validity, and practicality generally received a higher priority than other requirements.

PROJECT STAFF AND WORK STRATEGY

From its inception the project has been a team effort. Thus far, in addition to the principal collaborators (the present authors), a total of sixteen other professionals from a variety of disciplines, including six graduate librarians, have worked full or part-time on one or more of the project tasks; their specific contributions will be acknowledged in later reports. To coordinate this team effort, the principal collaborators meet at roughly monthly intervals. Between meetings, the activities of project staff working in Philadelphia, Detroit, and Syracuse are coordinated by telephone and correspondence.

The Wayne State University College of Medicine Library and the Upstate Medical Center Library of the State University of New York serve as "laboratories" for the initial tests of all methods under development. When a given method works satisfactorily in these libraries, and the goal set for the particular task is to develop the method to the point where it is ready for general application, the method is then field-tested in other libraries. Since our aim is to develop methods, rather than to obtain data on any representative sample of biomedical libraries, these field tests are conducted in libraries selected for heterogeneity and for accessibility to the project staff. To date, more than a dozen biomedical libraries throughout the country have cooperated in formal field tests of one or more methods. Without the wholehearted, active cooperation of these libraries, and the considerable time and effort they contribute, this project would not be feasible. In later reports, the libraries that have cooperated in field testing a particular method will be identified.

CONCEPTUAL FRAMEWORK

All work on the project is structured by five basic concepts, which underlie our whole approach to the development of methodologic tools of the kind specified by the task statements and general desiderata. These concepts evolved from the "user viewpoint" that we have tried to maintain throughout the project, and from employing some of the techniques of systems analysis in thinking about library services.

The Library as a "Black-Box"

From the user's point of view, a library is a "black-box." What goes on inside the box, that is, how it operates, is not his concern; he is concerned only with its output—the services it can provide. Likewise, from a systems viewpoint, the primary consideration when assessing its effectiveness is how well its users' needs are served, rather than its mode of operation. Whether a library's operations are carried out by people or by machines and people in some combination, its effectiveness can be assessed by looking only at its output—the services it provides to users—without concern for *how* it goes about providing these services. This concept, which may appear trivial, turns out to be essential in thinking about how one might go about measuring, objectively and quantitatively, the effectiveness of a particular kind of service.

TABLE 1
LIBRARY FUNCTIONS AS SEEN BY USERS

I. Providing Documents

II. Providing Citations

III. Providing Answers

IV. Providing Work Space and Facilities

V. Providing Instruction and Consultation

VI. Adjunct Functions

Without it, one can easily be overwhelmed by the complexity and diversity of operations within different libraries; and the task will then seem impossible.

A Functional Classification of Library Services

The outline in Table 1 covers the *general* functions that any user might reasonably expect a library to perform, now or in the immediate future. This list of functions suggests a simple classification of library services based on what the user receives. Details of this classification will be covered in a later report devoted to a standardized method for making an inventory of the services a library offers. Very briefly, in this classification,

"document services" include all the means a library may employ to provide a user with the specific document he wants, given that he already has an adequate bibliographic description (citation) for this document. By "document" we mean a discrete unit of recorded information, regardless of its type or form; it can be a journal article, book, reprint, technical report, etc., or a facsimile copy of any of these types of documents. "Citation services" include all ways of providing him with bibliographic descriptions of some or all documents relating to a particular subject and of providing him with a correct citation for a specific document, given that he has only an incomplete or inaccurate bibliographic description of it. "Answer services" provide the specific information required to answer a question he has—as contrasted with referring him to a document that may contain the answer. "Facility services" include provision of space equipped for the user to "work" in the library. Here, "work" is defined very broadly to cover any user activity that the given library is intended to support; thus, in addition to providing space for using library materials, facilities for a variety of other activities may be furnished. "Instruction and consultation services" cover all the ways that library staff, individually and collectively, plays the role of teacher or advisor. The category of "adjunct services" includes certain less common services, such as editing, translating, providing nonprint media, etc.

One major advantage of classifying library services by the "user function" served, rather than in the usual way, is clarity and precision. Current terminology relating to user services is vague and confusing. As one example, the term "reference services" is a catchall covering a host of miscellaneous services—instructing users about indexes, providing answers to questions ranging from "where can I find . . ." to "what is the melting point of . . .," providing citations for documents relating to a given subject, referring users to other libraries or to subject authorities, etc. Almost every library offers something called "reference services," but what these services actually provide to users varies widely. The term "information services" is likewise unsatisfactory because it is sometimes used to subsume all services provided by libraries, sometimes to denote provision of the specific information required to answer a question and at other times to refer generically to all organizational entities that provide documents, citations or answers, such as libraries, abstracting services, data analysis centers, etc.

Another important advantage of functional terminology is that the "do-it-yourself," or self-service, aspects of libraries can be accommodated in the same schema as services that library staff perform on request (staff-mediated services). For example, maintaining open stacks, from which a user can obtain whatever document he needs, is seen as a way of serving the same *general* function that is performed when the staff delivers a document to him.

The User's Criteria for Assessing Library Services

A user assesses a library by its effectiveness as a means he can employ to meet a given need and by what it costs him to meet the need in this way. In his judgement of the effectiveness of a particular service, two criteria are important: (1) the quality of the service relative to that of some other means he employs to serve the same function or to that of some ideal service, and (2) the time that elapses between his turning to the library and the fulfillment on his need. His idea of the "cost" of using the library is more complex—it includes: (1) his personal time, or that of any agent he may employ; (2) the physical-psychological effort required of him; and (3) any expenses or charges paid from his own pocket or from funds for which he has more or less direct responsibility. Since the time required to meet a given need is measurable, for any service where it is also possible to devise some objective measure of quality, one can assess effectiveness in user terms. A similar direct approach to assessing user cost does not seem feasible; however, as we will show later, there are indirect ways to assess a user's perception of the cost-effectiveness of a given service.

The Central Role of the User's "Primary Library"

At local, regional, national, and international levels, there exists a multitude of organizational entities upon which a user may call to meet his needs for documents, citations, answers, and other services. The library maintained by his own institution is only one of these entities; but this library large or small, should have a unique role in the total "system" that has evolved to make available the world's information resources. Today it is widely recognized that everyone should have a "primary physician" to whom he turns for all his health needs, and who acts as his personal agent in acquiring from the world's resources for medical care whatever services he requires. The critical im-

portance of the analogous concept of a "primary library" is not yet widely recognized. However, at least until the day when everyone has his own computer "terminal" connected with global "information networks" and "data banks," we believe that the most feasible way to promote effective utilization of information resources is by implementing the primary library concept. Figure 1 depicts this concept; here the broken arrows indicate the flow paths that usually prevail today, and the solid arrows show the pattern that can, and should, exist.

Most members of the biomedical community are affiliated with some institution that maintains a library. We feel it is both reasonable and highly desirable that each biomedical user regard the library in his own institution as his primary library, and that he should not be required to deal directly with the many different service entities that may be able to help him but, rather, should be able to turn to his primary library for *any* need that can be met from the store of formally recorded information. In systems terminology, the primary library should be his interface with the total communication complex and should insure optimal coupling between him and the system as a whole.

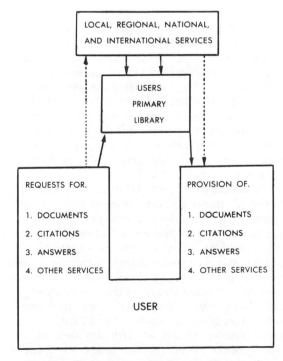

Fig. 1.   The primary library as the user's interface with the "system."

The full implications of this concept may not be immediately apparent. If the primary library concept is really accepted and implemented in practice, it means important changes in the philosophy and values of librarianship, at least as it is usually practiced. Traditionally, the main responsibility of the librarian has been to acquire and organize an appropriate collection of documents and to assist his user population in realizing the value of this collection. Any responsibility for making other resources available to users was strictly secondary, and actively helping users to exploit the world's resources more fully had a relatively low priority on funds and manpower. In the primary library concept, the librarian's *sole* responsibility is to make it possible for his clientele to tap the total store of recorded information as effectively and efficiently as possible within whatever practical constraints are imposed on him—the previous distinction between "own" and "other" resources disappears. The methods developed in this project attempt to accommodate this concept which, although it may not be stated explicitly, underlies all current plans for regional and national library networks and systems.

The Dynamic, Competitive Nature of the Information Complex

Users—whether students, teachers, practitioners, or researchers—usually have a choice among several alternative means, or "mechanisms," for meeting their needs for documents, citations, answers, and other services. These alternatives are symbolized by the three channels in Figure 2; here "formal mechanisms" are all organizational entities supported to serve such needs, and "informal mechanisms" cover all means of meeting needs without recourse to any organized service, e.g., by asking a colleague.

We assume that a user's information-seeking behavior is rational, and that, when alternative mechanisms exist, the user will choose the one he perceives as having the best cost-effectiveness ratio. Any particular library, and libraries in general, are utilized only when other means for meeting a given need are perceived as having a poorer cost-effectiveness ratio than the library. A user's estimate of the relative cost-effectiveness of alternatives may not be very good—it may be biased by habit, incomplete knowledge, and attitudes based on inadequate trials—but, good or bad, this estimate determines the decision on which means he employs. Demand on those mechanisms that are per-

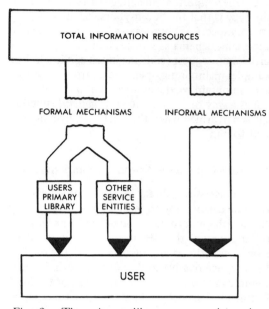

Fig. 2.   The primary library as one channel in a "competitive" system.

ceived as having better cost-effectiveness will tend to increase at the expense of demand on other mechanisms. At any given time, therefore, the proportion of the total needs of any type that are filled by a primary library reflects its user population's current perception of the relative cost-effectiveness of alternative mechanisms in the competitive system, and this proportion will change whenever this perception changes.

Viewing a library as "competing" with other formal mechanisms, and with informal mechanisms as well, has important implications for the development of methods for assessing library services. It rules out, as misleading, the use of certain types of data from library records that are sometimes used to assess performance, for example, the percentage of document requests that a library can fill from its own collection, and data regarding a library's "dependence" on interlibrary loans. A low percentage of unfilled requests and little dependence on interlibrary loans may only indicate that most of the library's clientele are not requesting documents they know are not in its collection; rather, they are using alternative means to obtain these documents (e.g., going to other libraries), or perhaps doing without. Measures of a library's capability for meeting all the requests that would be made *if users had no alternatives* are desirable to assess its performance in the realistic context of a dynamic system.

This concept is also useful in considering methods for measuring utilization of library services. Seen in this light, statistics on the frequency with which a typical user calls on the library to serve any given function tell only part of the story. If the aim is to have a yardstick useful in setting goals for a particular library's improvement, judging progress, or studying the factors influencing its utilization, unless one can assume that all *extra*-library factors remain constant, such statistics are inadequate in themselves. Measures of a library's utilization *relative* to the utilization of competitive mechanisms are also needed, since use of its services may be affected by changes in factors beyond its control.

We claim no originality for this concept, nor for the first four. They are presented here with little or no attempt to defend them by logic or by citing "authorities." Collectively, they represent the major tenets and assumptions of our conceptual approach in working toward the project's objective. We hope that making these tenets and assumptions explicit will help others to understand the why's of decisions made in the course of the work and to judge whether the resulting methods are compatible with their own conceptual framework.

V

RESEARCH IN ACTION

This section has a three-fold purpose. Reading these accounts should quickly disabuse the reader of the notion that research is a static process, or that it proceeds in a mechanical or sequential style, as so many textbooks seem to imply. For as the accounts here portray, the various stages are interlocking, interactive and at each phase new insights and findings constantly force review and reassessment of basic assumptions and hypotheses. Unforeseen constraints and unanticipated insights inevitably condition the research in both limited and more fundamental ways. The realities of this process become apparent in the cases detailed here.

Another purpose is to convey the sense of excitement, the drama and the intellectual satisfactions of the research role. Short of hearing a passionate and articulate spokesman describe his commitment and immersion in research, no better way of transmitting the sense of research exists than the type of personalized accounts drawn from actual studies such as are included here. All too frequently, the human side of the process remains undocumented. But, the conduct of his study as seen by the scholar himself orients one far more clearly to the nature of his role. (See also *Sociologists at Work,* detailed in the appendix.)

This section also supplements the section on methodology in important ways. Here in the context of actual study, important methodological considerations are revealed—problems of sampling, questionnaire construction, of access and establishing rapport with study subjects, and of interviewing. And in these personal observations, out of the experience of a number of sensitive social scientists, generalizable insights, cues and guidelines governing research working style are drawn. Since research case histories are virtually non-existent in librarianship, the editors hope that these selections will provoke like contributions from library scholars.

Great Books and Small Groups:
An Informal History of a National Survey

by James A. Davis

Seldom is the story told of a large national field survey and particularly is it unusual for such a piece to combine humor with truth. In this essay, the corner of the tent is raised, one is drawn behind the scenes and he shares with the study director secrets and confidences to which outsiders are seldom privy. But, the reader should not let Davis' candor mislead him. For, this is not simply an exposé of the difference between what the research methods textbooks say and how research actually happens, although these differences do come through. What is clear is that research abstraction must finally be brought down to matters of samples and questionnaires and the other mundane tasks which relate to them. Still more importantly, this is a report of how theory and method are brought together in imaginative ways to carry out a piece of first-rate research.

In the process, one learns how the skilled researcher brings to bear his past experience in working out a new empirical problem and in casting a practical problem in conceptual terms. Also illustrated is how, as the study proceeds, the investigator adapts his strategy and even introduces new elements into his analysis after the data have been accumulated. The evolution of this particular project may in some ways be typical of those which begin with considerable ambiguity and thereby allow latitude to the investigator as he proceeds; not every unstructured project necessarily has such happy consequences. Above all this piece conveys clearly the scholar's sense of satisfaction that derives from employing his own intellect with success in discovering something useful about the world which no one has ever known before.

This is, within the narrow limits imposed by perceptual defense and criminal libel, my recollection of how National Opinion Research Center Survey No. 408, the Great Books study, proceeded from its inception in the summer of 1957 to the publication of a book in 1961. Although I tend to view the chronicle as the struggle of a brave study director against time, money, clients, winter weather, Texas Great Books groups, and NORC's business staff, these events may better be viewed as a reasonably typical case study of how modern social research proceeds in a large nonprofit research organization.

This brings us to the subject of money. I think it may be stated as a matter of indisputable fact that there is no money available in the contemporary United States for unrestricted support of large-scale social research. On occasion, a professor whose work is fashionable or whose years of loyal back-scratching on professional committees is deemed worthy of a reward will receive the munificent unrestricted sum of $1,000 or $2,000, most of which he passes on to subsidize graduate students, but private donors prefer to see their names on university dormitories; the association of sociology and socialism is graven in the minds of congressmen; and foundations have (let us face it) retreated from social research. No one is going to give NORC or similar private institutions the wherewithal to pursue their own research interests at $50,000 per interest. The citizens of Michigan do subsidize the Survey Research Center, and its senior staff members have sabbaticals and swimming pools and who knows what else; but the private, nonprofit research center is in there hustling in the market place along with Ford, General Dynamics, and Joe's Drugstore.

Thus is born "the client," typically a large foundation or a government agency with a particular research question which it feels is worth the ex-

SOURCE: "Great Books and Small Groups: An Informal History of a National Survey" by James A. Davis, Chapter 9 of SOCIOLOGISTS AT WORK, edited by Phillip E. Hammond, ©1964 by Basic Books, Inc., Publishers, New York. The original publication bore the following note: "James A. Davis, *Great Books and Small Groups* (Glencoe, Ill.: The Free Press, 1961)."

orbitant costs and personal frustrations involved in commissioning research. And with the birth of the client comes the eternal triangle of client, organization, and study director. It is the operation of this triangle which is the key process in the poignant histories of surveys.

Let me begin, however, with a few kind words for clients. As a matter of fact, the client for this study, a foundation executive in one of the many progeny spawned by the Ford Foundation, is a fine guy, and at least prior to his reading of this document, I consider him my friend. But, as we know from introductory sociology, personalities and roles are two different matters. Rolewise, to be a client is somewhat like being a sugar daddy responsible to a board of directors. It is an extraordinarily expensive business, the satisfactions are occasional and fleeting, there is the distinct impression that one is being ruthlessly exploited, and all of this has to be justified at the annual meeting.

At the same time, those in the humanistic studies who are so enraged at the funds they see flowing into social research might momentarily consider how it would be receive an enormous commission, most of which disappeared into $25 checks to unknown ladies in New Jersey and a mysterious maw called "overhead," and to have the Medici Fund tell you that you could paint anything you liked as long as it matched the rug in their private audience room.

All of this would work out cozily, as it does in business, were it not for the motivations of study directors. There are, I would guess, no more than a hundred people in the country today leading the lives of noisy desperation characteristic of study directors, but they fall into two types. Historically, relatively few study directors in market research and in nonprofit organizations came from graduate study in sociology or social psychology, a Ph.D. in sociology being no more necessary for competence in this area than a degree in electrical engineering. Among NORC's senior study directors, for instance are non-Ph.D.'s trained in history, anthropology, and undergraduate liberal arts. Into this occupation, however, like locusts, have come the Ph.D.'s. They tend to be ambitious, steely-nerved young men who have worked out the implication of the following propositions: (1) academic success is contingent on research publication, regardless of the topic; (2) young men seldom get research grants on their own; (3) people come to research centers and give them the wherewithal to do large-scale studies.

While the two types of study directors appear indistinguishable to the naked eye, they vary considerably in their view of research and of their jobs. The "old-line" staff tend to identify with the research organization and to gain their rewards from pride in craftsmanship and budget-manship, reputed client satisfaction, and the feeling that they have contributed to the success of the organization. The new men, however, while often willing to deliver a thorough and honest piece of work for the sponsor, find their major satisfactions in milking the research for journal articles or publications to throw into the potlatch of academia, whence cometh their eventual reward: a research professorship.

I am, in truth, accentuating differences that are far from polar, for most people in research work find their major rewards from intellectual challenge (as well as salaries superior to teaching), and "applied" research is generally more challenging intellectually. That is what I said: applied work is usually more challenging—because there are more definite standards of accomplishment. In social-science theoretical work, the feeling that it "sounds right" or has the requisite polysyllabic mumbo jumbo is the typical yardstick; in "pure" empirical research, if *any* significant correlations can be wrung out, the material is generally publishable; but in applied research, there are rather precise questions at issue and the failure to answer them is painfully apparent. In addition, applied research in government agencies, the larger commercial firms, and centers like NORC is characterized by superior probability sampling, larger samples, better interviewing, more careful control of coding and tabulations, and informal monitoring of the work by colleagues who are specialists in the same area. One wonders why the Ph.D.'s have continual intellectual dissatisfaction in their jobs.

The root of the problem, I think, lies in the difference between generality and specificity. Clients commission research because they are interested in something specific: who has health insurance, whether enough people are training for careers in biochemistry, how much scholarship money is available to graduate students, to what extent people near airports are bothered by jet noise, and so on. Sociology is, however, the enemy of the specific. Even though the facts of social life in modern America are less well documented than the facts of marine life at the bottom of the ocean, the academic sociologist (the ultimate judge, employer, or journal editor whom our young Ph.D.

wants to impress) has a phobia against research which "merely" describes. This is "nose-counting," "dust-bowl empiricism," "trivia," and so forth and is not part of the grand scheme for building the science of sociology. That the history of natural science is in the reverse order—theories having been developed to explain facts, rather than facts gathered to ornament theories—weighs little against the pressure of intellectual tradition. Therefore, the academically oriented study director is faced with a dilemma. If he completes his research in such a fashion as to satisfy the sponsors, it will lack academic glamour. If, on the other hand, he completes a piece suitable for academic publication, it will probably tell the sponsor nothing about the questions which led to the research.

If one has attained sufficient eminence, one proceeds to conduct the study as one pleases, considering the client lucky to have his problem studied by an important person, even if in the process the client's problem disappears. For younger people and the struggling research organization, this is a dangerous tactic, and the natural strategy is to attempt both tasks: a specific descriptive report "for the client" and a high-brow article or monograph for the study director's self-aggrandizement. Thus, as well as a description of who gets scholarships comes a test of the theory of relative deprivation among graduate students; along with the descriptive materials on whether poor boys go on to college comes a paper on status crystallization and career choice; along with the statistics on what doctors prescribe brand-X drugs comes a paper on sociometric aspects of innovation; and so on.

It must be made clear to the reader, however, that these theoretical forays have little or no connection with the specific research questions. As currently developed, sociological and social-psychological theories are almost useless in predicting a dependent variable, either because they are stated so abstractly and vaguely that it is impossible to translate them into research operations or, if stated in usable terms, they are often wrong or account for only a negligible portion of the variance when compared with the "trivial" things such as age, sex, education, and marital status. I, personally, hold great hopes for the theories now being developed under the general rubric of "dissonance" and for much of George Homans' work, and I have to admit that a little exposure to theory suggests some interesting intellectual problems for research; but my reluctant conclusion is that in 90 per cent (plus or minus 20 per cent) of the research work, "theory" is dragged in only as a status symbol or to improve the eventual merchandising of the results.

Considered, then, as roles, social research is typically conducted by (1) a study director, who may be willing to do what he is paid for, but is more interested in wresting an academic article from the remains, (2) a sponsor, who stokes the fires with money and hopes vaguely that the evasive, fast-talking young man will complete within his lifetime a report bearing vaguely on the topic, and (3) a research organization, beset with financial woes and firmly aware of the fact that the study director (who gets no profits when a study makes money and pays no refund when he runs it into the red) is capable of spending the organization into the poorhouse without shedding a tear and in the process alienating the client beyond the point at which he can be persuaded to pony up the deficit.

Let us now see how these three archetypal characters proceeded to produce NORC Survey 408.

I did not have much to do with the Great Books study until it was about six weeks old. During the early summer of 1957, I was away from Chicago doing field work in Ohio for a community study directed by Peter Rossi. Why? Because I had been hired by NORC in the summer of 1957 to direct a study of physicians, which never took place. In order to keep me busy, I had been sent into darkest Ohio as gunbearer for Mr. Rossi, who was stalking community leaders there.

The infant Great Books study had been ushered into the world by Clyde Hart, NORC's director at that time, and the staff at the Fund for Adult Education, my role being that of pediatrician rather than obstetrician.

Had I been in Chicago for every moment of the initial negotiations, I would probably have little more to add to this chronicle than I can from my observation post in a commercial hotel in "Mediana," Ohio. Indeed, the exact origins of this survey, as for many, are a mystery. My hearsay version goes as follows.

The Fund for Adult Education, a subsidiary of the Ford Foundation, had since 1951 been supporting diverse activities in the area of adult education by grants to ongoing study-discussion programs, continuing educational centers, educational-television experiments, and so on. The fund was oriented to action, not research, and had commissioned little or no professional research prior to the Great Books study.

I am told that it came to pass that from within

the parent Ford Foundation came word that the time had arrived for the Fund for Adult Education to render an accounting of its stewardship and that the conventional medium for such an accounting was "research." The Fund for Adult Education, not unexpectedly, proceeded to commission a number of studies, of which Great Books was one.

Now, if the Fund for Adult Education was bemused to find itself bank-rolling a statistical survey, the object of the inquiry—the Great Books Foundation—was flabbergasted. The foundation, an independent, nonprofit corporation with headquarters in Chicago (which has no connection with Great Books of Western World, a commercial publishing venture), coordinates the national program of Great Books, using a small professional staff and a large number of volunteers. As intellectual types, the personnel of Great Books stand somewhere to the right of Jacques Barzun and Arthur Schlesinger, Jr., in their opinion of sociological surveys; but it is amazing how persuasive a large foundation with a history of generosity can be, so eventually the foundation was persuaded to cooperate. I think it would be fair to say that, while the foundation did provide the requisite liaison to complete the study, its stance was of one about to be photographed with a midget on his lap at a congressional hearing.

At this point, the following parties are involved: NORC, a research organization fully aware that evaluation studies usually make the client look bad; the Fund for Adult Education, an action organization already persuaded of the merits of Great Books, but hopeful of gaining concrete evidence of these merits; and the Great Books Foundation, already persuaded of the merits of its program, but quite doubtful that surveys can measure them.

Here ensued a number of conferences in Chicago and New York, during which the basic framework of the study was established. The only firm agreement prior to that time had been that the study was to be concerned with participants rather than the operations of the foundation and that we were interested in "the effects" of participation in Great Books.

For those of you who have not had the opportunity to read *Great Books and Small Groups,* the Great Books program in 1957 was roughly as follows. In 1957-1958, it consisted of some 1,960 discussion groups dispersed through the United States, with some additional groups in Canada and overseas. Each group meets every other week from September to June, and at each meeting the members discuss a specific selection which they have read before the meeting (e.g., Milton, *Areopagitica;* Tolstoy, *The Death of Ivan Ilyich*; Rousseau, *The Social Contract*). The readings are organized into blocks of one year each and, in theory, should be read in sequence. The groups vary in size (from around five to around thirty-five, with an average of eleven in our sample); in sponsorship (most are affiliated with public libraries, but a number are sponsored by churches, business firms, and individuals); and in leadership (some have a single leader, most have two leaders, a few rotate the leadership each meeting). The leaders are not formally trained teachers, but a number have had brief training courses conducted by the foundation. The members do not pay any tuition or get any certificate for completing the program. In fact, no one can complete the program, as additional years of reading are always available. Members are encouraged to buy the inexpensive readings from the foundation but are not required to do so.

It was this program which was to be evaluated, to the end of discovering whether the effects on the participants were such as to justify the continuation or expansion of Fund for Adult Education support. As a separate operation, the Fund for Adult Education commissioned a management-consultant firm to assess the organization of the foundation, market potential for Great Books, and similar internal affairs.

The design of such research falls naturally into two parts, which can be thought of as sampling, in the sense of deciding which people are to be studied and in what numbers; and questionnaire construction, in the sense of deciding what measures to use on the sampled respondents.

Of the two, sampling presented the fewest problems. It so happened that this is one social-science situation for which there is a clear-cut textbook sample design. According to the course I teach in research methods, one should collect a large number of people, arrange for a random subgroup to participate in Great Books, prevent the remainder from participating in the program, and measure both groups on the dependent variables before and after the experiment. (Technically, if you have done it perfectly, you do not need to measure both groups before.) It also so happened that, as usual, the textbook design was out of the question. Such an experimental study would be "possible," although there would be an enormous number of difficulties—making sure that the controls do not get Great Books or equivalent experience, establishing community programs which mask the mechanics of the sample design, and so forth. The major obstacle turned out to be time. We began active work on the study in the late summer of 1957 and had to deliver a report by fall 1958. It would have been plainly impractical (as well as quite expensive) to get a field experiment organized in two months before the 1957-1958 Great Books year got under way and results of a spring-1958 follow-up assessed by fall 1958. In addition, we all agreed that if the program's effects were as expected, some of them might not show up until after several years of exposure to the program.

It was this idea of long-term effects which enabled us to find a compromise design. If it is correct that, unlike indoctrination movies or television debates, the effects of Great Books require a long, long time for their appearance, then beginning participants should make a reasonably good "control group," particularly if the field work could be hurried so that first-year members were reached before they had attended more than one or two meetings. Because, in addition, both beginning and advanced-year members are equally self-selected, this design even has the advantage over a control group of nonmembers in that the latter would necessarily be suspected of less motivation or interest in joining Great Books.

The great problem with this design—and a problem which remained one of the main issues of the research—is that, as compared with a true experiment, the design left open the possibility that advanced-year members differ systematically from beginners, and it would be their other differences which produced any differences in the dependent variables. For example, almost necessarily, advanced-year members are older than beginners, and if age were related to the dependent variables, spurious differences would emerge. While this problem would give nightmares to an experimental purist, by and large it did not bother me too much. I knew that we were going to have sufficient cases so that by cross-tabulations we could control for any differences in gross variables such as age, sex, education, occupation, and so forth. A major pitfall, however, was the problem of retention. Nobody really knew the dropout rates in Great Books, but from all that is known of volunteer organizations, they had to be high. Furthermore, it made plain common sense that retention in the program would be correlated with the dependent variables, for people who were not getting the "effects," whatever they may be, would be prime candidates for dropping out, as in any educational institution. Even worse, there was no way of controlling for dropouts in a sample limited to current members, since we would have to introduce as statistical controls events that had not happened yet. The best we could do was to introduce some questions about intention to continue and use these for controls in comparing beginning and advanced members.

Looking back now, I wonder why we let it go at that. We could have interviewed some ex-members without too much difficulty, but I do not remember that this was seriously raised as a possibility. Perhaps at that time I already had the germ of the idea of a second study to determine actual dropouts; perhaps I did not. At any rate, I am glad now we let it go; for without the continuing problem of attrition, the study would have begun and ended as another evaluation project.

The net result of all of this was a decision to sample from existing discussion groups, stratified to oversample the advanced-year groups wherein lay the pay dirt, if any. At this point, another vital, but not deliberate, decision was made. The Great Book Foundation has no individual membership rolls but merely a rather loose file of group registrations. Given the lack of coercive structure for the program, a number of groups exist without the official blessing of the foundation; and at least in 1957, rather than groups' petitioning Great Books for the right to exist, functionaries of the foundation continually scanned press clippings to find their groups, which were then sent registration materials. If a file of individuals had existed, I do not know whether we would have used it; but having no choice, we sampled groups—a very important decision, as it turned out.

The final crucial decision was an economic one. Because of the money to be saved, we decided to raise the case base by asking entire groups to fill out a self-administered questionnaire at their meeting, gambling that the members would be literate and thus capable of filling out a questionnaire and hopefully sophisticated enough to cooperate with a research project. We also had the naïve hope that the foundation would put a little heat on the groups to increase cooperation.

In sum, while from an abstract point of view we should have had a sample of individuals both in and out of the Great Books program, because of a series of unwitting decisions based on practical exigencies we ended up with a sample of discussion groups within the program. We began with the Great Books, but the Small Groups got into the study by default.

While limitations of time and budget usually provide enough restrictions so that sample designs for national surveys amount to choosing among a number of restricted possibilities, when it comes to writing a questionnaire, the sky is the limit; or rather, one's guess as to how lengthy a document the respondents will complete without rebellion is the only boundary. Within this area—and it is amazing how much respondents will actually do for you if approached correctly—we had all of Western culture from which to pick items. It is precisely the major advantage and the major problem of surveys that an enormous amount of information can be collected, the marginal increment in cost for an additional item being very small when compared with the fixed costs of sampling and contacting respondents. At the same time, *the* intellectual challenge in survey analysis is in ordering and synthesizing the diverse information—in this schedule ranging from father's occupation to the respondent's opinion as to whether the course of history is capricious, purposive, or mechanistic. (In case you are curious, 25 per cent thought it capricious, 48 per cent thought it purposive, 13 per cent thought it mechanistic, and 13 per cent were "no answer.")

A certain amount of disagreement arose among the parties: the Fund for Adult Education backing two horses, the Great Books Foundation a third, and the study director a dark fourth horse. The first horse was "community participation," a matter of considerable interest to the Fund for Adult Education, which was convinced that participation in Great Books should and maybe even did lead people to become more active in community affairs. The general idea was that after reading, say, the Greek philosophers on the nature of the good society, the Great Books members would be impelled to remodel Toledo, Ohio, and Minneapolis, Minnesota. The idea met with polite skepticism on the part of Great Books and me.

The Great Books Foundation maintained, and with some justice, I think, that their program did not have any purposes at all, at least in the sense of the sort of thing that can be listed and translated into surveys. With the naïveté of a young man who had read all the texts on evaluation research, I kept hounding the foundation to list— 1, 2, 3—the purposes of their program so that they might at least be tried on charges of their own devising. In the face of such pressures for over simplification, all the foundation staff could come up with was the denial that participants were expected to become more active, passive, liberal,

conservative, or anything that directional. Rather, they were expected to become more sophisticated, more critical in their thinking, broader in their approach, and so on, whether or not they chose to favor the left, right, center, or to refrain from community life. In this the participants in the actual survey agreed, the bulk opting for the response, "The Great Books provide an intellectual understanding (of specific social and community problems), but few or no keys to plans for action," as opposed to "Great Books provide both an understanding of the problems and a key to plans of action" or "Great Books are not applicable to specific social and community problems." While the foundation opposed the community-participation stress on the basis of intellectual ideology, I was against it on the practical grounds that I doubted we would get any effects. To begin with, I thought that Great Books members were typically fugitives from community life, rather than involved. I was dead wrong, but more on that later. In addition, from all that I knew of the literature, I was sure that class, sex, political preference, for example, played such an important part in community participation that exposure to a reading discussion program could not make much difference. I was perfectly willing to let the facts speak, but I was not going out of my way to disappoint somebody who had given me $40,000 to do research.

At this point, the inevitable answer occurred: to stress both purely intellectual and also community participation materials. However, this led to a knotty problem of measurement. In assessing community and political involvement, we felt we were on safe grounds, for there is rich experience in survey measurement of such phenomena, and the content is heavily behavioral and hence fairly easy to translate into questions. In the measurement of such things as "critical thinking," "tolerance of ambiguity," "intellectual sophistication," that way madness lies. I was toying with pulling out existing tests of critical thinking and similar measures, and the Great Books Foundation had in desperation proposed that the respondents be given essay examinations which the foundation staff would evaluate, when the Fund for Adult Education split into two spokesmen, with the entrance of the late Carl Hovland, then a consultant to the fund. Hovland, as a psychologist, was highly concerned about the details of testing: whether the tests could be given under standard conditions, timed, collusion prevented, motivation maintained, and so forth. The answer, of course, is that they could not, or at least could not to the satisfaction of a testing specialist. Hovland felt that we might get away with it but that the results could never be sold to a really hostile critic who was oriented to psychological measurement.

The compromise decision actually became a sellout of the Great Books Foundation's position, for on the basis of Hovland's technical doubts, critical thinking and open-mindedness essentially disappeared, except in the form of some very simple attitude and opinion items in which, for example, the respondents were asked to name "any particular authors or schools which you once disliked, but now find more acceptable." Rather, we began to search for some sugar-coated test-oid materials to get at more superficial things. We actually found two good ones, a set of cartoon items (e.g., a gentleman in a nightshirt nailing a paper on a door, to denote Martin Luther posting his theses; a child in diapers composing at the piano, to denote the young Mozart, etc.), which had originally appeared in *Life* magazine, and a marvelous poetry test,[1] developed in the early 1920's by M. R. Trabue and Allan Abbott. Trabue and Abbott presented the original version of a well-known poem, along with versions systematically deformed in aesthetic content, and the respondent was asked to pick the one liked best. We never did find a complete set of the poetry-test items, even by long-distance calls to Prof. Trabue, by then a sprightly emeritus, but we got enough to go into print. In addition, we packed in voluminous materials on reading quality and musical taste and picked a number of items on philosophical points from the work of Charles Morris.

Note what was happening here. What should have been a series of technical measures of cognitive functioning became a set of crude information measures along with considerable materials on aesthetics and ideologies. Part of the shift can be explained by Hovland's technical qualms, part by the inability of the Great Books Foundation to come up with neat objectives for which nice tests exist, but a good proportion came from the wily maneuvers of the study director.

What was I up to? Viewed from the perspective of getting some academic yardage out of the study, Great Books appeared to have three possibilities, of which I picked the wrong one. The first possibility would have been to conduct an evaluation study of such methodological luster that it would attract attention despite the offbeat character of the sample and the stigma of "Adult Education." I knew in my bones that because of the

design limitation and the fuzziness of the measures, this one could not make it. Now, get me right. I felt all along that we could deliver useful and valid information to the client on the effects of Great Books (and I think we did), but I doubted that we could get out a study which would be cited as technically outstanding or particularly convincing to a *resistant* reader. This meant that while for report purposes the materials had to yield an evaluation study, for academic purposes I had to find an analytical theme such that the whole sample could be treated as a single group and differences in exposure to Great Books (our analogue of experimental and control groups) ignored.

Looking back now, I think there were actually two possibilities. It turned out that Great Books members are phenomenally active and involved in local community affairs and that we had the makings of a detailed study of community involvement among young, educated, middle-class Americans. Actually, Vickie Beale, who was on the staff, managed to get a good Ph.D. thesis on this theme, but for some reason I did not pick that tack. The third possibility was a detailed analysis of the members' intellectual lives, their tastes, ideologies, philosophical positions, and so forth. I had done a Ph.D. thesis on taste and status symbols, and I have always been fascinated by the writings of Russell Lynes, David Riesman, Eric Larrabee, etc. In the back of my mind, I envisioned the development—from data, mind you—of typologies of kinds of intellectual stances and styles within the Great Books members.

My own proclivities here were reinforced by a marvelous but misleading field experience. Because of the timing of the program, there was no way to see a Great Books group in action before the questionnaire was completed. (My record is still perfect. I have never actually seen a Great Books discussion, despite several years of almost full-time work on this project.) However, in the summer of 1957 Great Books was running a summer program at Aspen, Colorado, which I arranged to visit. While my strongest memory is of the magnificient train ride through the Rockies—a revelation to a midwestern boy—professionally I came away with two hunches. The first was that Great Books tends to attract a social type which can perhaps be described as "isolated intellectuals." It seemed to me that at Aspen a large number of the people I met were extraordinarily well read, very serious, and given to the construction of home-made philosophical systems, without being hooked into the orbit of academic intellectuals or professional creative artists. I do not mean they were screwballs, but they did seem to be the sort of people whose opinions on whether the course of history was purposive might be interesting. Apparently the people who attended that summer conference were quite unrepresentative of the Great Books membership, for the actual survey showed the Great Books participants to be a pretty clean-cut group of PTA joiners and *Time* readers, not much given to the construction of homemade philosophical systems.

I came away with one other impression which did have a pay-off, although indirect. While I have never seen a legal, in-season Great Books discussion, I did watch a number of the sessions in Aspen and tried to make some guesses about the group dynamics beneath the surface of the discussions. It seemed to me that what was going on was a sort of political process in which people would advance ideas, allies would rally to them, and enemies would muster forces against them and that the course of the discussions was heavily influenced by latent attractions and antagonisms among the participants. Mulling this over later in Chicago, I decided to insert some sociometric questions to see whether a member's isolation or acceptance by others in the discussion group affected his reactions to the program. In the back of my mind was the idea that perhaps the discussions worked best when there were fairly "even sides" in the ideological and interpersonal teams. However, the Great Books Foundation vetoed these questions on the grounds that it might produce complaints if members were asked to name their friends and enemies.

The key items in the final study—a series of questions about functional roles in the groups— were actually devised as a substitute. The items asked each member to rate himself and others in the group in terms of such roles as "joking and kidding," "making tactful comments," "providing 'fuel' for the discussion," and others. The logical structure of the items was suggested by the work of Robert Freed Bales. I have never had a course in small groups, but Bales's influence is very strong at Harvard, where I did my graduate work, and a sort of Balesian, functional approach to roles and group dynamics, absorbed by osmosis during graduate-school days, was the only one I knew.

This is the intellectual history of the questionnaire, a lengthy document bearing the stamp of the Fund for Adult Education's interest in community participation, some vestigial traces of the foundation's interest in "critical thinking," a lot of my own penchant for materials on aesthetics and ideologies, and a good bit of information on functional roles, inserted as a substitute for the excised sociometric items.

Were I to recount in detail the field work, coding, key-punching, and card-cleaning which took up the next ten months, this essay would become a book about a book. Let me merely say that with the superb help of Grace Lieberman, Mary Booth, Ursula Gebhard, Joe Zelan, and a charming group of Antioch College cooperators we came into the possession of schedules from over 90 per cent of the sampled groups and coded the data from the 1,909 individual respondents onto some dozen decks of IBM cards.

I am also going to gloss over the first report, a bulky, 256-page, single-spaced mimeographed document completed in August 1958. It consisted of (1) a description of the Great Books participants, (2) analyses of the members' reported effects of participation in the program, (3) comparisons between beginning and advanced members in terms of dependent variables, and (4) data on role structures and social correlates of role performance. Vickie Beale, who had joined the project staff in the spring of 1958, analyzed the materials on community participation; Ursula Gebhard had done most of the role analysis, and I did the rest.

Because the report was done under great pressure, the entire analysis and writing being concentrated in a period of about three months, the document was overly long and underly organized. In essence, however, we showed (1) strong differences in knowledge between beginners and advanced-year members, (2) slight differences in attitudes, consistent with the idea of increased tolerance or open-mindedness, and (3) few differences in behavior. Taken together, I feel that the material pretty well showed that exposure to Great Books does add to the intellectual depth and perspective of the members but does not produce striking or consistent effects on behavior, which is, after all, just what the results should be if the program does what its organizers think it does. We also found that, rather than being socially marginal, the Great Books members were highly educated, highly involved in their communities, and *less* upwardly mobile than comparable college graduates. While this may be a comfort to the friends of Great Books, it "did in" my plans for analyzing their intellectual lives. If the members had turned out to have a considerable proportion of homely philosophers, upwardly mobile people, or members of strange cults, the results might have been quite "marketable" because academic sociologists gobble up materials on strange cults and deviate people; but since the participants turned out to be quite typical suburban types, without being statistically representative of suburban types, it would be hard to justify detailed analysis of their tastes and ideologies.

The Fund for Adult Education received the report and must have been clairvoyant, for they gave Great Books a large-scale grant about a month before they saw the results, such being the crucial role that social research plays in decision-making in modern America.

The project was far from over in fall 1958. During the preceding winter and spring, while coding and key-punching were going on, I had been brooding about the dropout problem and came up with an idea. It occurred to me that if we could collect data in 1958 to determine which of our respondents had actually dropped out of the program during the year, we could subtract them from the tables and make comparisons only among members who were "destined" to continue. The following dummy table illustrates the idea.

PER CENT HIGH ON DEPENDENT VARIABLE

1957 STATUS	1958 STATUS		
	Dropped	Continued	Total
Advanced Year	$45_{(200)}$	$70_{(300)}$	$60_{(500)}$
Beginning Year	$10_{(200)}$	$60_{(300)}$	$40_{(500)}$

In this hypothetical example, 60 per cent of the advanced members are high on the item, in contrast to 40 per cent of the beginners. This would suggest that exposure to Great Books has a positive effect. However, it is seen that the item is strongly associated with retention, and when the beginners who continued are compared with advanced-year members, there is no difference, each group having a percentage of 60. Thus, the original difference can be explained because of selective attrition. Such a design, of course, could not catch spurious differences due to "historical trends," such as a decrease over the years in the proportion of new members possessing the trait in question, but it looked as if it would help a lot in solving the problems raised by dropouts. In addition, the data-collection problems were minimal, as no new sample had to be drawn and no information collected beyond continuation status.

In the summer of 1958, we proposed such a project to the Fund for Adult Education, and although they had not yet seen any pay-off from the initial grant, they were kind enough to support a follow-up that year. Ursula Gebhard superintended this operation, as by then I was working on another study, a survey of the financial problems of arts and science graduate students.

Because the follow-up data were simple, we were able by February 1959 to submit an edited version of the original report with dropout controls introduced into the key tabulations. (By the way, they did not greatly change the results, but I felt much more confident with these materials to support our findings.) This report, *A Study of Participants in the Great Books Program,* was printed and distributed by the Fund for Adult Education, and although it has never received any attention outside of those immediately concerned with Great Books and not much among those who are concerned, I think it is a reasonably good non-experimental evaluation study.

Enough budget money remained to support the substantive analysis of factors associated with retention in Great Books. Thus, *Great Books and Small Groups* has its operational origins in the evaluation study completed in February 1958, but its intellectual roots lie elsewhere—a substantive root reaching to Harvard University and a methodological one to Columbia.

Substantively, the major idea in the new study came from viewing the data, not as "why some people quit Great Books," but as "why some small-scale social systems lose the commitment of their members." The research problem is clearly structural-functional and comes simply because that was how I was indoctrinated at Harvard. My courses with Talcott Parsons and my informal contacts with the students working with Freed Bales had steeped me in the tradition of viewing social behavior as functional or dysfunctional for a given social system. In particular, I had been much impressed with an article, "The Functional Prerequisites of a Society" by Aberle, Cohen, Davis, Levy, and Sutton (*Ethics,* IX [1950], 100-111). I was not actually so much impressed with the content, which is highly speculative, as with the marvelous euphony of the names, and I remember that Parsons once mentioned in class that the paper had been done while the authors were graduate students at Harvard. It had never occurred to me that graduate students could make actual contributions to sociology, and the knowledge that Aberle, Cohen, Davis, Levy, and Sutton had made them served to buck up my spirits in many dark hours in Cambridge.

George Homans was involved, too. While I was

at Harvard, I had few contacts with him, and my strong attraction to Homansian theory has come in the last few years. In rereading *The Human Group* while preparing a lecture, I came across his astringent remark, "If we turn to history for help, it is astonishing how few societies have failed to survive . . . [but] small groups are breaking up every day. . . ." Thus was born the idea of studying the functional prerequisities for the survival of small groups. To be absolutely candid, there is also a less cerebral aspect to all this. My own work and interests diverge considerably from that of my graduate-student friends and the intellectual climate of the Harvard department, and I think in the back of my mind was the hope that such a study would show "them" that I was not a naïve empiricist but was capable of wrestling with the highbrow problems of sociological theory with a big T.

The methodological contribution of the book comes from a statistical technique for "contextual analysis" which Joe Spaeth, Carolyn Huson, and I worked out during 1958 and 1959. Joe was a senior assistant in the Graduate Student Finances study, and Carolyn was the research assistant on the Great Books continuation, Vickie Beale and Ursula Gebhard having moved on to Grinnell College and San Francisco, respectively. The statistical technique is fairly complicated, and I am going to have to assume that the reader is familiar with it, as a detailed explanation runs to ten or twelve pages. In essence, the contribution lies not in the idea, which can be traced to Paul Lazarsfeld and Patricia Kendall at Columbia University, but in spelling out in a mathematical form the logical possibilities which can occur. What is new here is the idea that there are specific "kinds" of "structural effects."

The "influential" in the flow of influence here is Peter Blau, a Columbia Ph.D., now of the department of sociology at Chicago. As of 1959, I was quite unaware of "contextual analysis," although some had rubbed off on me from Jim Coleman when he was in Chicago, and I had read but not fully appreciated Lazarsfeld and Kendall's discussion in their classic article, "Problems of Survey Analysis." However, the longer I was around Chicago, the more I heard my graduate assistants talking about "structural effects," as discussed by Peter Blau in his courses. One day, Joe Spaeth came back from a Blau lecture and started talking about structural effects. I remember asking Joe what they really were. He tried to explain them to me in Blau's formulation, but I did not understand it. When I do not understand something statistical, I try to work it out with dummy data, and I remember sitting around with Joe, trying various examples in order to pinpoint the idea. The result was that it occurred to both of us that there were probably several kinds of structural effects, and we instantly got the idea of trying to systematize them.

The trick lay in how to systematize them. I have never had any mathematics training beyond college algebra, and I try, without much success, to teach myself by reading on my own. At that time, I was reading E. F. Beach's *Economic Models,* so linear and nonlinear functions were on my mind. It was only a short step from there to seeing that when the contextual attribute is expressed as a proportion, its variation could be treated as quantitative and the contextual effect could be described as a mathematical function.

There were two different versions. In the first, the contextual effects were treated as deviations from a regression line. This version was sent off to *Sociometry,* which was quite unenthusiastic, one reader saying that structural effects were very important but we did not really understand them, the other reader saying that although we probably understood structural effects, they were not worth analyzing.

Although Joe and I were quite discouraged by this, we picked up the idea every so often and in spring of 1959 came up with the version which finally appeared in print. Carolyn Huson did most of the work on the section regarding tests of significance, so the final paper was authored by Davis, Spaeth, and Huson. An interesting case of independent invention soon turned up. At the fall-1959 meetings of the American Sociological Association, I read the paper and learned that two study directors at the Bureau of Applied Social Research at Columbia, David Caplowitz and Wagner Thielens, Jr., had worked out a similar scheme, which, however, they had dropped to work on something else. Apparently it was an idea which would come to light inevitably, once the problem was seen. I was convinced that this version would "sell," so I sent it off to *The American Sociological Review*, which accepted it and printed it without unseemly haste in April 1961.

The rest was just hard work. During the spring and summer of 1959, the statistical technique was applied to data on dropouts from the fall-1958 follow-up. Carolyn Huson analyzed the material on group leadership and its effects; Herbert Hamilton, an advanced graduate student, came on the project and analyzed the individual level differences; and Ursula Gebhard's scholarly master's thesis on correlates of role performance was reworked in my "breezy" prose as background for the materials on the relationship between role structure and retention. It was immediately clear that the strongest effect in the data was that membership retention increased considerably in groups where a high percentage of the members had some role (i.e., were named by people in their group as active in some phase of the discussion), but it did not make much difference what the role was. The functional theories which suggest that role content is important did not pan out at all, but they had led us to find the important variable; and, for that matter, my idea of balance of power never paid off either.

The work was complex and tricky. The actual data never quite fitted any of the theoretical models, and the tabulations for partial relationships when the same characteristic has to be held constant twice (at the group level and at the individual level) were nasty; but, once it became clear that role systems were the key to the whole thing, the parts fell into place, and a final report was completed in November 1959.

The report was submitted to The University of Chicago Press, which turned it down because they said it did not have any sales potential, and to The Free Press, which also said that it would not sell but agreed to print it, apparently just for the fun of it. During the 1959–1960 academic year, I was tied up with the final report of the Graduate Student Finances study (a story which would make quite a chronicle itself, but which chronicle could not be sent through the United States mails), so I reorganized and rewrote the report in the summer of 1960, delivering the manuscript to Jeremiah Kaplan of The Free Press and a waiting world in the fall of 1960. The Free Press was delivered of the completed volume in the fall of 1961, a little over four years after my visit to Aspen.

Were I to draw morals from this history, they would be these.

(1) I think the chronicle of *Great Books and Small Groups* illustrates the tremendous importance of technical methodological developments in the substantive development of social science. It is commonly believed that research technology is a mere servant of substantive or theoretical interests. Actually, research technology makes a direct contribution to the content of the field in the same way that the invention of the microscope or radiotelescope shaped the content of physical science, or perhaps more exactly in the same way

that Whorfians claim language shapes our thinking. We can ask of the data only questions that can be translated into specific research operations, and until such translations exist, the research questions remain purely ruminative. Thus, the existence of a national research center makes it both possible and inevitable that comparative studies of groups will take place. Thus, the statistics of correlation and partial correlation give meaning to the vague concepts of "cause," "intervening factors," "spurious relationships," and such, and thus, the development of techniques for contextual analysis focuses our attention on "social climates." The history of content in social science is the history of fad, fashion, and momentary preoccupations, but the history of research methods is one of cumulative developments which have enabled us to ask increasingly precise and sophisticated questions about human behavior. In this sense, I believe progress in social science is mostly in the ability to ask questions, not in the ability to foresee the answers.

Second, I think that this chronicle illustrates the ways in which survey analysis is much akin to artistic creation. There are so many questions which might be asked, so many correlations which can be run, so many ways in which the findings can be organized, and so few rules or precedents for making these choices that a thousand different studies could come out of the same data. Beyond his technical responsibility for guaranteeing accuracy and honest statistical calculations, the real job of the study director is to select and integrate. Of all the findings, only some should be selected for presentation, but which ones? Is this particular finding so unimportant that it should be left out as confusing to the reader, or so important that it must be reported even though it will make the results appear terribly complicated? Should we emphasize the smashing difference which is, however, "obvious," or should we give play to the puzzling surprise, even though it produces only a small difference? The 101 (an IBM machine used for cross tabulations) takes independent variables in batches of four; and having listed the seven obvious columns for cross tabulations, which "unobvious" one do you choose as a gamble for the eighth? How much attention shall we give to the client's areas of success and how much his areas of failure? How much of the data shall we present in the report: so much that no one will read it, or so little that the reader cannot check our conclusions against the evidence? In multivariate analyses, one can produce a large range in percentages either by dividing a very few variables into fine categories (e.g., cutting income by thousands of dollars versus dividing it at the median) or by taking a larger number of items and dichotomizing them. Which is preferable? Statistics books will not help you, for the answers must come from the study director's experience and his intellectual taste, his ability to simplify but not gloss over, to be cautious without pettifoggery, to synthesize without distorting the facts, to interpret but not project his prejudices on the data. These, I submit, are ultimately aesthetic decisions, and the process of making these decisions is much like aesthetic creation.

But all this should not be construed as support for the fallacious idea that "you can prove anything with statistics." Short of deliberate falsification, statistical data are remarkably resistant, as anyone who has desperately tried to save a pet hypothesis knows. It is almost impossible for two competent study directors to arrive at *contradictory* conclusions from the same data, but it is almost inevitable that they will differ considerably in their emphases, organization, and selection.

Thus, if survey analysis is an art, it is not an art like sculpture or painting, in which one can make almost anything out of the raw materials. Rather, it is an art very much like architecture, in which it is possible to show disciplined creativity by producing elegant structures while working with raw materials, characterized by limited engineering properties and for clients with definite goals and finite budgets.

Balance between discipline and creativity is very difficult in social science. By and large, the fashionable people in sociology are "action painters" who dribble their thoughts on the canvas of the journals, unrestrained by systematic evidence, while at the opposite pole there are hordes of "engineers" who grind out academic development housing according to the mechanical formulas of elementary statistics texts. It is not easy to steer between these courses, and I am not claiming that I did so in this study, but my opinion is that the fun lies in trying to do so.

There is a lot of misery in surveys, most of the time and money going into monotonous clerical and statistical routines, with interruptions only for squabbles with the client, budget crises, petty machinations for a place in the academic sun, and social case work with neurotic graduate students. And nobody ever reads the final report. Those few moments, however, when a new set of tables comes up from the machine room and questions begin to be answered; when relationships actually hold under controls; when the pile of tables on the desk suddenly meshes to yield a coherent chapter; when in a flash you see a neat test for an interpretation; when you realize you have found out something about something important that nobody ever knew before—these are the moments that justify research.

FOOTNOTES

[1] M. R. Trabue and Allan Abbott, "A Measure of the Ability to Judge Poetry," *Teacher's College Record*, XXII (1921).

The Image of the Federal Service:
The Problem and the Study

by Franklin P. Kilpatrick, Milton C. Cummings, Jr., and M. Kent Jennings

In effect, this is sort of a research manual, spawned by a large investigation and offering technical detail useful in understanding of interviewing, sampling, coding, punching and tabulating and other detail elements of survey research. It is workmanlike, thorough, and it presents method in its pure form seen through the eyes of the architect of the study. The process is detailed from problem to issues through to instruments and on to strategy and techniques of the study. This selection also demonstrates how the academic scholar matches his capacities with those of the commercial organization, with each side reinforcing the other in the sequence.

THE PROBLEM

The distribution of human effort, skills, and talent among the various enterprises in a society is a significant clue to both the nature and the probable lines of development of that society. It is a matter for grave public concern when any major enterprise essential to social welfare and progress fails to receive its necessary share of these resources. For some time there has been presumptive evidence that the United States government is facing serious difficulties in attracting the numbers of able people it needs to carry out its crucial functions, both at home and abroad.

Many complex considerations are involved in the distribution of people among different occupations. Of basic importance are the kinds, cost, and availability of formal and informal education and job training; the social and geographical mobility of the population; the size of the society; and the stage and rate of scientific and technological development. In most societies with respect to some activities, and in some societies with respect to most activities, coercion, whether of circumstance or law, is a determinant. But in a highly developed, free social order which has high mobility and broadly based opportunity for education and training, individual choice is also an important factor—and becomes increasingly important the higher one goes on the scale of ability and training. Today in the United States the factor of choice is the paramount consideration in the competition for the most able people.

Whenever an individual chooses a specific job and a specific employer, whether for the first time or later, he is the possessor of certain occupationally related abilities; of a complex set of occupational values; of ideas and attitudes concerning perceived characteristics of employing organizations; and of stereotypes or images concerning the kind of people who work for certain categories of employing organizations. Although the process is seldom as orderly as description makes it sound, choice involves a complex blending of the individual's perceptions of the situation—the requirements of the job, his own capacities and skills, the characteristics of the employing organization, the kinds of people with whom he would be identified —with his pattern of occupational values, that is, the kinds of things he hopes both to attain and to avoid in his job.

This study has been designed to assess (1) the patterning of occupational values among a wide variety of key groups in American society and (2) the images these same groups of people have of the United States government as an employer and of federal public servants in their occupational roles. The primary purpose of this book is to examine the competitive position of the federal government as an employer; to provide information that may be useful in modifying federal personnel organization, policy, and procedures; and to suggest means for improved communication concerning these matters.

To measure the appeal of government employment, it is necessary to learn what people want in a job. One can determine what people picture federal employment as providing, but whether or not this appeals to them depends on their basic occupational values. What kinds of things, for example, is a college student looking for as he contemplates taking his first long-term job? How do the features of a job that he may prize compare with the characteristics he sees in federal employment? What is the comparable relationship between the occupational values and perceptions of federal employment of other men and women who will be in the job markets of the 1960's?

Our study has attempted to answer these and many related questions by eliciting from people the image they perceive when federal employment is mentioned—and by exploring the extent to which that image attracts or repels them in relation to the variety of human desires, hopes, intentions, and ambitions which, subtly interwoven, may be said to constitute individual and group patterns of occupational values. To that end, structured personal interviews with employed adults in both federal and nonfederal enterprises and with high school and college students were conducted in all regions of the continental United States.[1]

The Federal Personnel Problem

To suggest that the federal government should at all times have priority claims on the best of the country's human resources would reflect a distorted view of government's relationship to the other institutions of our pluralistic society. And probably the various operating segments of the society can never reach agreement on what an ideally balanced distribution of skills and talent would or should be. It is clear, however, that the rapid pace of technological and social change has for some time been changing the needs of the government relative to other institutions. A full-scale assessment of the federal government in this regard would have to take into detailed account its present size, personnel composition, and multitudinous functions, as well as possible future trends in each respect. The following brief summary of these matters, however, reveals in broad perspective the major elements in this changing pattern.

The sheer size of the federal establishment, apart from any other consideration, means that a serious malfunction in any part of the government is bound to have an impact throughout the country and the world. In 1963 the administrative expenditures budget was approximately $93 billion, and the civilian federal work force included more than 2.5 million people. Both figures are almost certain to increase. The trend has been upward most of the time since 1910, when the annual expenditure was $694 million and civilian federal employees numbered 389,000; the many scientific, technological, and social developments of recent years would seem to indicate continuing trends in the same direction.

The functions of the central government penetrate all aspects of our domestic economy. Decisions made and procedures followed at the federal level have strong, and often decisive, influence on such matters as the pattern of employment, the amount and kind of scientific research, and the rate and direction of technological development. In its activities overseas, the federal service has assumed responsibilities which involve freedom, and possibly survival, both for ourselves and for a great number of the world's peoples. Thus the United States government can no longer afford to be without the highest capacities for innovation, leadership, judgment, and management in all parts and at all levels of the administrative establishment. The game cannot be played with a second team.

This is not to say that there are not large numbers of highly qualified and devoted public servants in all branches and at all levels of the federal service at the present time. The depression of the 1930's and the exigencies of World War II and, to a lesser extent, of the Korean war drew large numbers of very able people into the federal service, a great many of whom now staff a high proportion of the key positions. These emergencies helped to alleviate the personnel problem, but at the same time tended to obscure the basic, long-run nature of the problem. No longer can we rely on such crises as recruiting measures for able public servants in the numbers that are currently needed. A variety of recent testimony and evidence adds up to a consensus that almost all federal personnel areas which require a high order of training and talent are facing supply problems ranging from difficult to dangerously acute.

Beginning with the Franklin D. Roosevelt administration, every President has experienced increasing staffing difficulties at many levels, in both political and technical fields. During the 1960 hearings of the Senate Subcommittee on National Policy Machinery, which were concerned with personnel aspects of the government's operations in the field of national security policy, a wide variety of experts testified. Their testimony was remarkable for its unanimity on a point which was emphasized by Senator Henry Jackson: "The fact is, we have encountered disturbing difficulties in securing first-rate talent at the very time when the national security calls for the country's 'best brains' to man key posts at home and abroad."[2]

Something of the nature and magnitude of the problem is also suggested by the recent unprecedented upsurge of federal contracting with private or quasi-private organizations for a wide variety of research, development, and other high-level non-production activities. Undoubtedly the reasons behind this growth are many and complex, but one prime reason appears to be the inability of the federal government to hire and retain the numbers and kinds of people needed to perform such services within the federal establishment. John Corson, then a management consultant with McKinsey and Company, testified in 1960 before the National Policy Machinery Subcommittee as follows: "I think most nonprofit corporations that have been set up to perform essentially complementary functions for Government were established as a means of attracting talent that the Government could not obtain through its normal mechanisms."[3]

To a considerable extent, the urgency of the problem is rooted in the relative composition of the federal and the private work forces, and the rapid change occurring in both. The federal work force, because of the nature of the tasks assigned to it, has historically had a much higher proportion of managerial, professional, technical, and scientific personnel than the nonfederal work force. A 1960 analysis revealed that scientific and engineering tasks were performed by one in every fifty of the nonfederal work force and by one in fourteen of all federal employees. Considering only the people directly employed by the federal government—thus excluding large numbers in the private sphere who are performing scientific and engineering work under contract to the government—one finds that the federal establishment, compared with the general work force, employs twice the percentage of engineers and three and a half times the percentage of professional scientists.[4] Similar considerations apply to managerial and other professional and technical areas.

Technological change is shifting the nature of our manpower needs at a rapid and accelerating rate from production to service, and to ever higher demands for expertise and flexibility. Private industry, the universities and colleges, and the professions are more and more competing for the same kinds of highly trained people that are needed by the government. Since these people are also increasingly in short supply, the government is finding it difficult to meet the competition. Augmenting the federal problem is evidence that government service at all levels is an area of employment which will grow faster than the average rate for the nation, and that the government's rapidly expanding need will be greatest for trained professional and technical employees, and least for semiskilled and unskilled workers.[5]

Agreement on the nature and the urgency of the problem is fairly general, despite a disturbing scarcity of concrete information concerning the types, amounts, and locations of federal personnel shortages. The "pilot" analysis and projection published by the Program Planning Division of the U.S. Civil Service Commission in 1960 for the period 1958 to 1963 covered only physical scientists, psychologists, engineers, and medical officers (see footnote 4). Some other projections have been made since then, but have not been published in detail. In 1963 the chief of the Program Planning Division commented, "If these [1963] projections are anywhere near the mark, they indicate that not even minimum Federal staffing needs in engineering and the physical sciences will be met."[6] That the situation is comparable for the government's management needs is indicated by a 1960 statement of the chairman of the Civil Service Commission:

> For all agencies, an average of 38 percent of top career executives will be eligible to retire in five years, and 66½ percent in ten years. This does not count the normal losses from death, disability, and resignation. In the face of the urgency of public issues before our administrative agencies, the Civil Service Commission is alarmed and needs help in getting fuller recognition of the threat to effective government that the situation presents.[7]

Something of the magnitude of the need is suggested by the estimate that if the federal government does no more than retain its present size (and, as noted earlier, that seems unlikely in view of the long-time trend toward increasingly broad and complex federal responsibilities at home and abroad), more than 300,000 people must be recruited to the federal public service every year. Progress, and perhaps even survival, demand that there be included in this 300,000 a proper share of the best in human resources that our society has to offer. Yet, according to the Civil Service Commission:

The reputation of the public service generally . . . is not high enough so that it serves as a positive attraction to people. Any picture of civil service examining procedures as a means of choosing a few of the best from clamoring hordes of officeseekers is as old fashioned as the rolltop desk and the frock-coated dispenser of patronage. Our whole employment system must compete in attractiveness with those of private employers.[8]

Images and Values

The implication of the phrase "compete in attractiveness" is the core of this research. Of what does "occupational attractiveness" consist? It is often thought to connote primarily such matters as rate of pay, opportunity for promotion, retirement benefits, protection from firing and layoffs, and the like. But this assumes that knowledge about rate of pay, promotion opportunity, and other job characteristics is communicated in an undistorted fashion and in turn will give rise to undistorted perceptions among people in the potential work force. In actuality, communication and perception never achieve such perfection. The difficulty of putting job attributes into precise language, the varying nature, and often lack, of communication channels, and the selecting and modifying aspects of human experience and perception all intervene.

The result is that people usually perceive occupations and employing organizations, not precisely and realistically, but in terms of vaguely generalized cultural pre-judgments, which not only are undiscriminating in application, uncertain as to origin, and resistant to modification, but also tend to be self-perpetuating and self-enhancing by virtue of their selecting and modifying effect on current experience and perception. This is the pattern of stereotypes which, in the vocabulary of this study, add up to the *images* the individual has of kinds of employment and employing organizations. Thus, one of the keys to "attractiveness" is not what *is,* but *how it is perceived.*

Another frequent assumption is that occupational attributes are attractive or unattractive in the same way and in the same degree to most people throughout our society. But the fact is that an occupation's appeal is a function of the individual's perception *in relation to the goals he is striving to attain.* Whether the goals are many or few, immediate or long range, trivial or worthwhile, they are always complex in their patterning of intensity, saliency, and rate of change. Even though the patterns of human striving are rooted in a fairly common biology, their elaboration is a function of learning. They emerge as a compound

of the successes and failures and the social prescriptions and expectations to which an individual has been and is exposed as a member of a given family, a given social group, and a given society at a certain time in history.

Thus, the goals or values any individual wants to realize through his occupation are likely to be a patterned blend: some are unique to himself; some are common to members of various cultural groups of which he is, has been, or aspires to be a part; some are common to most members of his society; and some few are common to almost all human beings—and would be in any society at any period. Although particular groups of people in a society tend to share the same values, the amount and kind of variation among individuals and among groups is great.

Therefore, even if it were theoretically possible for everyone in a society to have the same image of federal employment, we would still expect it to vary widely in attractiveness among different elements of the population. And if the variations are not known or understood, efforts to enhance the appeal of an occupation or of an employing organization may miss their target. If we propose, for example, that higher pay will attract certain people to a certain kind of employment, we are *assuming* that these people have a set of occupational values in which such economic considerations are of sufficient concern to influence relative attractiveness and, thereby, choice. Such assumptions could, however, be erroneous.

THE STUDY

Our purpose here is to review briefly the methods employed in the study and the reasons for selecting them. We believe that such a frame of reference will help the reader in assessing the findings and the uses we have made of them.[9]

Within the context of the available resources of theory, method, time, and personnel, the over-all objectives of any research study dictate, or should dictate, the design of the research. Since we wished to explore (1) the patterning of occupational values among key groups of people in American society, and (2) how these same groups perceived both the United States government as an employer and the federal public servant in his occupational role, we established the following six major objectives:

1. *To learn what images people have of the federal government as an employer.* What occupational values are seen as being fulfilled or not ful-

filled by the government in its role of an employing enterprise?

2. *To learn what images people have of federal public servants.* Do people have generalized "pictures in their heads" concerning the qualities and traits of federal employees? How do they perceive these civil servants in terms of character, ability, and occupational values?

3. *To discover which occupational values are of concern to people and which are of basic importance.* What occupational aims, immediate and long range, are people trying to realize? What are they striving for in their jobs and what are they trying to avoid?

4. *To ascertain the patterns of these images and occupational values among the general public and among federal employees, as well as among a variety of subgroupings of these two populations by occupation, education, age, sex, and other differentiations.* Ideally, we would want to learn these things for all groups which are significant to the productivity and future welfare of our society, but for practical reasons we have concentrated on certain groups which are of special relevance to the personnel problems of the federal government.

5. *To be able to compare the findings for any one group selected for study with those for any other such group, and with the employed public in general.* Only through such comparative analysis can we approach a worthwhile understanding of the factors that go into the occupational decision patterns of given groups.

6. *To provide a base line of data, concerning these images and values, for trend analysis in future research.* A single study, such as this one, is only a snapshot of what *is* at a given point in time. It provides few clues to the direction in which things are moving. But it can be so designed as to offer a reliable comparative base. To provide an adequate base line, a study must be repeatable so that comparable data can be obtained at two or more points in time. This meant not only that the methods we used must be susceptible of fairly exact repetition but also that they and the basic data they yielded must be described with sufficient detail and clarity to enable future researchers to replicate our work on later samples.

GENERAL DESIGN

The nature of these objectives in combination suggested that the basic instrument to be used should be a standardized personal interview questionnaire. In such a questionnaire the wording and the order of the questions, the methods of recording responses, and the set of instructions under which the interviewers operate are all prescribed. Without as nearly perfect standardization as possible, neither comparative analysis nor trend analysis would be practicable or reliable, for we would not know whether differences in our results were due to differences in questions and procedure, or to actual differences in images and values.

Once we had decided to rely on standardized personal interviews (rather than on "depth techniques" or mail questionnaires) the objectives of the study told us specific things about the necessary content and form of the questionnaire. Certain broad decisions concerning the composition of the questions were also possible at this point. We knew, for example, that the categorical question—that is, a question which does not permit free response but offers a range of prescribed alternatives—has certain marked advantages in securing information of the kind we needed, and in the considerable range of areas we had to cover. It takes relatively less interviewing time than the free-answer question; is easier to code and tabulate; is more susceptible to precise statistical treatment; and in some forms is an aid in obtaining information which people either cannot, or prefer not to, verbalize.

On the other hand, the categorical question has one great disadvantage; it limits the respondent to choosing his answer from a certain number of preformulated alternatives, and does not permit him to state his answer in his own way. Thus, it eliminates the possibility of learning what the respondent might want to say if he were not obliged to confine himself to a choice of replies. In effect, the categorical question presumes that all the important categories or classes of response are known, and that research need only show how people sort themselves out in their choices of predetermined alternatives.[10] In the area of images and values which we wished to investigate, it would have been foolhardy to presume that we knew enough to be sure of including all of the important areas and categories of questioning and response. But to use only open-end questions would be too time-consuming and would make the entire study liable to a lack of analytic precision.

Our solution was to blend open-end with categorical questions. This promised two advantages. First, if both kinds of questions are asked about the same general topic, it is possible to check the answers against one another. Internal consistency analysis of this kind helps to provide an estimate of the reliability of the responses, and of the degree of caution one must use in interpretation. Second, the dual approach affords the possibility of cross-checking for *concern* and *importance.* Open-end questions tend to yield responses which are *salient* to the individual—that is, the kinds of things that are of current concern to him in his day-to-day transactions with his environment. They can, and often do, miss entirely matters which are of basic *importance* to the individual but are not salient.

This distinction can be illustrated by considering the act of breathing. One is rarely "concerned" with breathing, but, if it is interfered with, it immediately assumes great "salience." In response to an open-end question, one would be unlikely to mention "continuing to breathe" as a value, but if one were asked categorically to rate the importance of breathing the rating would probably be very high. Similar considerations apply to occupational values. Security of employment, for example, may be of little concern to most people during an era of continued high demand for the kinds of skills they have to offer, but one should not therefore conclude that security is not important to them. The onset of an economic recession can alter the saliency of employment security very markedly.

Another imperative imposed by the nature of our objectives was that the questions should not be "time-bound." They must be worded in such a way that they could be asked in exactly the same form, and with the same meaning, five years, ten years, or even twenty years from now. Otherwise, the results of the study could not serve as an adequate basis for trend analysis through a repetition of the research, or parts of it, at subsequent points in time, because it would not be known whether observed differences were due to changes in values and images, or simply to alterations in question form or meaning. It is of course difficult to be sure that all topical aspects have been eliminated from a group of questions, but there are certain kinds of questions which are *unlikely* to change very much in meaning over a period of ten or twenty years.

The broad objectives of the study also pointed to some general prescriptions concerning the categories of people (here often termed "populations") to be interviewed, and the manner in which they should be selected. It was clear that we must have a sample of the general employed public, because data from its members concerning occupational values and images of the public service were necessary as a base line for comparison with other groups. This population was also necessary if we were to make generalized statements about the distribution of these values and images in American society. Similar considerations dictated the necessity for obtaining a general sample of civilians presently employed by the United States government.

In addition, since the federal personnel problem is basically a shortage, not of numbers, but of skills and talent, it was important to make separate analyses of certain high-level occupational groups— for instance, natural scientists, social scientists, engineers, and executives. However, no reasonably sized sample of the general employed public would yield enough interviewees in any of these categories to make separate analyses possible; consequently, we needed to draw supplementary subsamples in each of the desired categories.

Of equal importance to our purposes was an understanding of the values and images of young people still in school. Since the above samples would miss this population, it was apparent that we needed to draw special subsamples of such groups as high school students, college students, and graduate school students.

The basic question of the number of interviews to be conducted was resolved according to arbitrary considerations of available time and money in relation to the known approximate cost per interview. We came up with a limit of about 5,000 interviews, which left us with the question of how many groups, which groups, and how to allocate the total number of interviews among them. We decided to make the samples of the general employed public and of general federal employees large enough to support analysis of each of them by such breakdowns as age, sex, geographic region, amount of education, general type of occupation, income, and the like. The minimum number of cases which will permit breaking into such categories and still permit meaningful (though gross) analysis is approximately 1,000. This meant that, out of our total of some 5,000 interviews, we must allocate about 2,000 between our two general samples and distribute the rest among the smaller samples of each of the special subgroups. This imposed restrictions on the study: first, we would have to content ourselves with having too few cases in each of our special subgroups to support any very complex breakdowns by age, school grades, amount of education, and the like; second, we would be unable to obtain samples of all the special groups that ideally should be included, simply because there would not be enough interviews to go around.

It had been apparent from the outset that we must use properly drawn probability samples clearly specified as to the manner of drawing, and drawn in such a way that future investigators would find it possible to repeat our procedures and draw comparable samples. Unless sampling is performed according to proper probability procedures, one cannot safely generalize from the sample to the population from which it was drawn or safely make comparisons among various special populations; furthermore, the results of the study could not constitute a proper basis for subsequent repetition and comparative trend analysis. But if probability sampling procedures are carefully carried out, it is not only possible to generalize and compare but also to estimate statistically the probable degree of error involved.

DEVELOPMENT OF THE STUDY

In constructing the questionnaire we took into account that our total sample would include three different types of populations: people who are presently employed but not by the federal government; people presently employed by the federal government; and high school and college students who have not yet entered upon full-time employment. Three forms of the questionnaire were therefore prepared, but the differences among the three forms were kept to an absolute minimum. The questionnaire for the nonfederal employed public was developed first as the basic form; then the necessary modifications and additions to this form were made for federal employees and for students.

In developing the basic form, we carried out four successive developmental studies, performing interviewing and extensive analysis each time. Approximately 200 interviews, from one to four hours in length, were conducted during this stage. Finally, the questionnaire was subjected to a pilot study carried out at ten different locations in the United States by the staff of field interviewers who would conduct the final interviews (see following section).

Discussion of the specific content of the basic questionnaire will be confined to those aspects of purpose and procedure which are not immediately apparent from examining the questionnaire itself.[11] The first matter requiring comment is the use of self-anchoring scaling. Briefly, a self-anchoring scale is one in which each respondent is asked to describe—in terms of his own perceptions, goals, and values—the top and bottom, or anchoring points, of the dimension on which scale measurement is desired. The respondent is then asked to employ this self-defined continuum as a measuring device and as a basis for further questioning concerning his values and goals.[12]

The self-anchoring scaling device, as adapted to probe into occupational values, is so central to this study that a description of how it was used is in order. The first step in the procedure was to ask the following question: "First, I would like you to think of what really matters most to you in your own life. Tell me what kind of a way of earning a living would be ideal for you—that is, the very best way of doing it from your point of view. Maybe no occupation could fit your ideal. But just let yourself dream a bit and tell me the various things *about* an occupation which would make it *absolutely ideal* for you. I am not asking for the name of a specific occupation, but for the *kinds of things about* an occupation which would make it *absolutely ideal* for you."

After the interviewer had encouraged as detailed a response as possible and had recorded as nearly verbatim as possible everything that the respondent said, the next question was: "Now about the worst sort of occupation. What kinds of things *about* an occupation would make it the worst or least satisfying to you." Again, the interviewer encouraged elaboration and recorded the responses.

The respondent was then handed a card showing a ten-step ladder scale. The interviewer said: "Here is a picture of a ladder. Suppose we say at the *top* of the ladder is the *very best*, the absolutely ideal sort of occupation you have just described. At the *bottom* is the *very worst* sort of occupation. Where on this ladder would you put your present occupation, that is, what you are doing now?" In the same manner scale ratings were obtained for where the person felt he (or she) was occupationally five years ago and where he expected to be five years hence. Following this, his reasons for rating his present occupation as he did were explored.

Then came a key question concerning federal employment and the image of the federal service: "Suppose your work or occupation stayed the same but you worked for the federal government, that is, the United States government. How much better or worse would that be? Show me on the ladder, please." The interviewer recorded the step number pointed to by the respondent. In this way we obtained a numerical representation of the degree to which the person felt he would move up or down the scale, *in terms of his own occupational values,* if he were to continue in the same sort of work, but in the employ of the federal government.

To elicit the reasons for this numerical judgment and to explore the individual's image of federal employment, the next two questions were: "What things would be likely to be better?" and "What things would be likely to be worse?" Thus we obtained the individual's feelings about the federal government as an employer, in the context of continuing to perform the same sort of work.

The above questions were phrased for people presently employed in nonfederal enterprises. When federal employees were interviewed, occupational values and ratings of their own occupations were secured in the same fashion. Then they were asked how much better or worse would it be on the ladder rating if they continued to do the same sort of work but did it *outside* the government, and what things would be likely to be better or worse.

Another procedural matter also requires some comment: the fact that the purpose of an open-end question is not always apparent from simply reading the question. For example, all respondents were asked: "If you were to describe your general idea of a United States civil service employee, what sort of a person would that be?" Since of course there are all kinds of people working for the government, the only really logical answer is simply to say so, and perhaps express a little anger that such a stupid question has been asked. But the fact remains that, in varying degrees, most respondents did have evaluative pictures or stereotypes in their minds, and they expressed them in response to the question.

The purpose of the question was to learn the degree and content of stereotyping in various segments of the population, and to learn whether the stereotyped images are predominantly favorable, unfavorable, or neutral. Therefore, the individual who responded, "That is a stupid question, for there are all kinds and types of people in the civil service," supplied us with valuable information directly relevant to the objectives of the study. Similar considerations apply to almost all the open-end questions concerned with the nature, type of work, and motivations attributed to civil service employees.

A third matter requiring discussion is the scale sort we employed in Item 17 of the basic questionnaire. The fifty-five statements used in the scale sort are identical for all three questionnaires (see Appendix). This scale sort does not involve scaling in the technical sense of the term, but is simply a way of getting reliable numerical responses on a ten-interval agree-disagree scale to fifty-five separate statements in a very short amount of interviewing time. The statements are concerned with such matters as the importance of certain occupational values, with the evaluation of certain aspects of federal employees and federal employment, and with attitudes toward government and politics.

Each item was printed on a separate small card. In the actual interview situation, the interviewer shuffled the small cards in order to insure random presentation, thus eliminating possible order bias due to presenting the items in the same order time after time. The interviewer then said: "Please take the small cards and place each one in turn on the large card (the scale) according to how much you agree or disagree with the statement on it." When the interview was over, the interviewer recorded the number of the scale space (1 through 10) into which a given item had been sorted.

Another slightly modified version of the scaling procedure was used at a later point in the questionnaires, with thirty items on individual small cards. The large printed scale on which the cards were sorted was labeled "Extremely High" at the top and "Extremely Low" at the bottom. Each item, instead of involving just one dimension, involved two dimensions of judgment. The respondent was asked, first, to consider a specific category of people and, second, to rate them on a prescribed personal quality. For example: "Consider: People in the top-level jobs in the federal civil service. On the average, how would you rate them on *honesty?*" And, "Consider: People in the top-level jobs in private business. On the average, how would you rate them on *ability?*"

In this fashion respondents rated general civil servants, people in the top-level jobs in the federal civil service, and people in the top-level jobs in private business on ability, honesty, how well respected they are, their interest in serving the public, and their drive to get ahead.

THE CONDUCT OF THE STUDY

Interviewing

The standardized questionnaires were administered to 5,078 respondents in the continental United States. The personal interviews ranged in length from slightly less than one hour to as much as two and a half hours, averaging, as expected from pilot study results, about one hour and twenty minutes. They were conducted by the interviewing staff of a commercial research organization that specializes in "custom design" survey research, rather than in simple, routine, repetitive polling.[13]

The first phase of interviewing—for the nonfederal populations—began in April 1960 and was almost entirely completed in May, with a few remaining interviews done in June. The total of completed interviews obtained in this phase was 3,576, conducted by a force of approximately 100 of the most experienced and skilled personnel on the research firm's roster.[14]

The second phase involved 1,502 interviews with federal employees, conducted from the middle of November 1960, through January 1961, with a very small number carrying over into February. Again, about 100 interviewers were employed, about 60 of whom had worked with the first phase.[15]

Sampling

A carefully devised, up-to-date, national (continental United States), general purpose sample provided the basic framework for all the samples of the populations studied. Technically, this master sample may be described as a two-stage, stratified random sample in which each primary sampling unit (a county or a group of counties) has a known probability of selection. Within this general framework, probability samples of different categories of people were interviewed in the numbers shown in Table 1-1.[16]

An element in sampling which must not be overlooked in this discussion is the specification for each sample of the larger group or "universe" from which the sample is drawn. The essential parts of the numerous universe definitions used in this study must be repeated here in order to make clear what we are talking about when we refer, for example, to the "general employed public," to "natural scientists in business," and so on.

The universe from which the sample of the general employed public was drawn was defined as regularly employed persons, male and female, 18 to 60 years of age inclusive, either self-employed or working for someone else (35 hours per

TABLE 1-1. *Population Samples and Numbers of Interviews in Each*

Populations	Sample Size
Nonfederal and Federal Populations (total)	5,078
Nonfederal Populations (total)	3,576
General employed public	1,142
Students	
High school juniors and seniors	359
College seniors	404
College graduate students	383
Groups in education	
High school teachers	203
High school vocational counselors	80
College teachers[a] (total)	470
Natural scientists	121
Social scientists	106
Engineers	87
Humanities	56
Other	100
Groups in business	
Executives	287
Natural scientists	85
Social scientists	73
Engineers	90
Federal Populations (total)	1,502
General federal employees[b]	948
Special federal populations	
Executives	273
Natural scientists	92
Social Scientists	90
Engineers	99

[a]The sample of 470 college teachers was purposely drawn in an unbalanced fashion, to obtain approximately 100 each of natural scientists, social scientists, and engineers. Before tabulation of the total college teacher interviews, the sample was statistically adjusted to the known distribution of college teachers in the five categories shown in the table. Details are given in the *Source Book*, Chap. 3.

[b]The sampling of general federal employees resulted in an under-representation of Postal Field Service employees. Before tabulating, this under-representation was statistically adjusted. Details are given in the *Source Book*, Chap. 3.

week or more), exclusive of the federal government.

The universe for the samples of high school juniors and seniors, high school teachers and vocational counselors was defined as all such people in high schools—public, private, and parochial—in the continental United States. Schools teaching grades

10, 11, and 12 were included, whether they taught one or more other grades or no other grades.

The samples of college seniors, graduate students, general college teaching faculty, and college natural scientists, social scientists, and engineers were taken at 100 institutions of higher education drawn by probability procedures from a listing of all four-year degree-granting colleges and universities in the continental United States.[17] Conventional definitions of seniors, graduate students, and teaching faculty were used. College teachers of natural science, social science, and engineering were defined in terms of specific lists of subjects in each of the three areas.

The business respondents were drawn from a sample of business organizations selected by random procedures from a list of such organizations.[18] A business executive was defined as one whose duties are primarily administrative (supervising, planning, organizing, coordinating, reporting, delegating, etc.). In organizations of over twenty employees, only those personnel above the supervisor or foreman level were included in the executive population; in organizations with twenty employees or less, only those at the level of manager or vice president and above were included. A natural scientist in business was defined as a person in a business organization who has had more than four years of college with a major or graduate degree in one of the listed natural science disciplines, and no higher degree in any subject not on the list. Social scientists were defined in the same way, in terms of the listed social sciences. In the case of engineers, however, the definition required only a four-year degree in one of the listed engineering disciplines and no higher degree in another subject.

The universe for the sample of general federal employees was defined as all regularly employed federal civilian personnel (except CIA and FBI) in the continental United States working 35 hours or more per week. Federal executives were defined as GS 12 or above (or equivalent based on salary) whose duties are primarily administrative. Definitions of federal natural scientists, social scientists, and engineers were the same as the above definitions for their counterparts in business.

Preparation of the Code

Whenever more than a small number of questionnaires are used in a research project, it is impossible to analyze the results simply by examining the questionnaires. The information must be classified, tabulated, and manipulated, in order to extract its meaning. Therefore, once enough interviews to provide a good sample had been returned from the field and had been checked and edited for quality and completeness, work began at the Brookings Institution on the next phase in the research—the preparation of a code whereby relevant, discrete items of information in the completed interviews are identified and assigned numbers. Our task was to turn the questionnaire data into a number code so it could be punched on standard 80-column IBM cards for machine reading and manipulation.

The categorical questions in the questionnaire presented relatively few problems, since a large percentage of them had been precoded by numbers appearing on the questionnaire beside the categories. Those which were not precoded involved only the relatively simple problem of managing the coding procedure with care so that the rate of error was kept within an acceptable limit.

The free-response questions, however, presented a very specific problem. One of the main purposes of open-end questioning is to permit the emergence of new information; consequently, the codes for such questions must emerge from the responses themselves. Yet the responses alone do not dictate the categories. Any given code must strike a balance between the hypotheses to be tested and the answers contained in the interviews. In some cases, the proper code may be dictated almost entirely by the nature of the hypotheses; in other cases, the content of the answer plays a dominant role. In all cases, however, the underlying nature of the code is a function of the hypotheses to be tested. This is true simply because there are innumerable ways of coding any given answer, and the only basis for choosing among them is to make the decision in relation to the hypotheses which the resulting data must test.

For example, the responses to the questions on occupational values could have been coded for the *number* of values mentioned without regard to their content; for the *kinds of names used to describe* the values; for the *quality or nature* of the values; and in many other ways. How were we to decide among these possibilities? If one of the hypotheses in our research had been that "fullness of response to questions on occupational values is associated with level of education, age, and other factors," then we might have constructed a code based on the length of response, or on the number of different occupational values mentioned, without regard to the qualitative nature of the responses. But since that hypothesis was not a part of our study, such a code would have been irrelevant.

We did hypothesize, however, that the *kinds* of occupational values mentioned in response to open-end questions would be differentially patterned according to occupation, age, education, and other factors. This meant that we had to construct a code based on the different *kinds* of values described by the respondents, the dimension for categorization thus being the distinction in their qualitative nature. But we did not know completely in advance the nature of the values that would be mentioned by people as matters of concern. Therefore, we had to let the code emerge from an analysis of actual responses to the questions.

As illustration, here is a brief recounting of the procedure used in deriving the code of occupational values. First, we drew a sample of about 300 interviews for analysis, turning our attention to all the questions which were designed to elicit occupational values. For coding purposes, the responses to each question were broken down into individual statements which described a single occupational value. Each value mentioned was then entered on an index card in the respondent's own words as recorded by the interviewer. One respondent, for instance, answered the question about what would make an occupation absolutely ideal this way:

> Well, pleasant work; that is, not all kinds of noise and dirt. I want it to pay fairly well. There would have to be variation in work; not monotonous. I would want pleasant companions around me. A good place to eat at work would be important, as well as good working hours, and interesting work.

For this response seven different cards were filled out, as follows: (1) Pleasant work; that is, not all kinds of noise and dirt; (2) I want it to pay fairly well; (3) Variation in work, not monotonous; (4) I would want pleasant companions around me; (5) A good place to eat at work would be important; (6) Good working hours; (7) Interesting work.

From the eight occupational value questions on the 300 sample questionnaires, over 7,200 of these individual cards were prepared, each containing a statement about a discrete occupational value, using the same phrasing as in the recorded responses. The next step was to use the 7,200 cards to prepare a set of value categories and a set of coding instructions with concrete examples. Two people, both of whom were thoroughly acquainted with the aims of the study, independently sorted, com-

bined, and recombined the cards to obtain a set of categories. Then they compared and reviewed their results and resolved their differences in consultation with the third member of the study team. The final result was a fifty-category code, with which it was possible to classify virtually all of the responses to the free-answer questions concerning occupational values according to the same set of categories and according to identical criteria. The nature and variety of the values are illustrated by the following summary headings of the thirty-six that were mentioned most frequently.

1. Financial reward
2. Financial reward (qualified by an explicit statement that it is not of primary importance)
3. Social motives: interpersonal relations with supervisors
4. Social motives: passive relations (having co-workers and other people around one who are congenial)
5. Social motives: active relations (having a chance to work or deal with people in an active, positive sense as part of one's occupation)
6. Doing work that is worthwhile or useful (not specifying the way in which it is worthwhile or useful)
7. Doing work that is worthwhile or useful (in the sense of serving others—without specifying the exact nature of the contribution to others that is to be made)
8. Doing work that is worthwhile or useful to others (in the sense of making others happy or giving them pleasure)
9. Doing work that is worthwhile or useful to others (in the sense of contributing to their training, or to their mental, social, or physical development)
10. Doing work that provides a sense of achievement or accomplishment
11. Obtaining recognition from others for one's work
12. Doing work of a religious, spiritual, or ethical nature
13. Doing work that is interesting or enjoyable (not specifying a particular type of work)
14. Doing work of a specific type that is interesting or enjoyable
15. Having adequate time off for leisure or recreation
16. Doing work that affords security, stability, or fringe benefits

17. Doing work that contributes to one's self-development (through which one can develop one's own capacities, talents, or knowledge)
18. Doing work that calls for self-expression and creativity
19. Having freedom from restrictions affecting one's work (having control over the work or over the way one does it)
20. Avoiding work where there is excessive pressure or tension
21. Avoiding an excessive work load
22. Doing work that is challenging (overcoming obstacles, keeping goals ahead)
23. Having work with responsibility and authority (the power to make decisions)
24. Avoiding work with responsibility and authority (avoiding the necessity to make decisions)
25. Doing work that has prestige
26. Doing work that provides opportunities for self-advancement and progress
27. Doing work that fits one's capacities or training
28. Having the equipment, facilities, or the wherewithal to do the job
29. Avoiding work that is too hard
30. Having good general working conditions (including a satisfactory physical environment in which to work)
31. Working in a desirable location
32. Doing work that is routine and ordered
33. Doing work that is varied and not routine
34. Doing work that provides opportunities to travel
35. Doing mental work
36. Avoiding physical or manual work

The next step after the categories of occupational values had been decided upon was to create the coding instructions.[19] This involved setting down in words the nature and content of each category, along with concrete examples drawn from the actual questionnaires, so that a trained coder would be able to classify any response in the intended way. It was recognized, of course, that a certain amount of slippage from one category to another is inevitable, but great effort went into making the instructions so clear and unambiguous as to reduce such slippage to a small percentage of the total.

This same procedure was followed in creating the codes for all the open-end questions where the nature of the code was not completely dic-

tated by the nature of the hypotheses. In the entire operation, over 14,000 cards were prepared, sorted, and classified as a means of preparing the code and coding instructions. The result was a coding instruction booklet of more than 200 pages, the major portion of it devoted to the open-end question codes.

The actual coding operation—the reading of the responses and the assignment of code numbers to the responses—was carried out jointly by National Analysts, Inc., and the Brookings Institution. The important question arises, "How accurate was the coding?" The question cannot be answered with a single set of statistics, because two quite different considerations are involved. In the case of the categorical questions, which require no judgment in assigning a code number, the accuracy of the operation can be checked against an objective standard quite easily. Errors of this kind were kept well below 1 percent. For the open-end responses, the problem is entirely different. Both interpretation and judgment are involved, and there is no objective standard with which to compare the results in order to get an absolute measure of error. The appropriate measure for evaluating such coding, therefore, is the degree of agreement between two sets of coders who have each performed the entire coding and checking operation independently. Independent tests of intercoder agreement were performed on two samples of questionnaires for all of the open-end coding. Both samples showed an average of 93 percent agreement for all the codes combined, with agreement on individual questions being 82 percent or higher in all cases and in some instances reaching 100 percent.

Punching and Tabulating[20]

Once the coding operation was completed, the coded responses to all of the questions in all of the questionnaires were punched onto standard 80-column IBM cards; a complete verification of all keypunching was performed. As a beginning step, question-by-question tabulations of responses were performed on all the questions for each sample population separately. They showed, as was expected, that many of the free-response code categories were mentioned too infrequently to permit analysis by smaller subgroups (e.g., age, income, etc.), even if the analysis were confined to the two large general samples (nonfederal employed public and federal employees). Consequently, some of the codes were combined into more inclusive categories, and others which could not logically be combined to form larger categories were eliminated.

Following this, numerous further tabulations were performed. These were designed to permit analysis and comparison of the patterns of responses in a considerable number of subdivisions of the sample populations (for instance, by age, patterns of occupational values, attitudes toward federal civil servants, educational levels, geographic regions, occupations, and income levels). Since the number of subgroup tabulations that are *possible* in a study of this kind is almost astronomical, judgment and considerable restraint had to be exercised to avoid being drowned in a deluge of data, some of it of little or no value.

In general, we confined our cross-tabulations to those which offered a chance of providing enough cases in the various subcategories to make analysis statistically feasible, and which at the same time had a clear bearing on significant hypotheses. Consequently, we made only about twenty sets of subgroup tabulations for each of the two large samples, and two or three additional sets of breakdowns for each of the smaller samples. Even so, the result was approximately 5,000 complex tables containing over 1,000,000 items of information,

all of which had to be examined for analytic value, abstracted, summarized, and finally reduced to the basic number we believed were needed to reveal the significant results with force and clarity.[21]

The matters with which this book is concerned—the images that people have of the federal public service and how these images are distributed in various segments of American society; occupational values and how they are distributed in American society; and the relationships between these two sets of factors as they shed light on the appeal of federal employment—have been the subject of much prior discussion, published and unpublished, and of a certain amount of previous research. This material was highly instructive to us when we were exploring the dimensions of the problem to be investigated, formulating the plan for the research, and interpreting our findings. How the federal service and the American public's attitudes toward it have varied with social change through the years of the Republic's existence is the subject of Chapter 2. The other main stream of previous material that was helpful to us in formulating the present study—informal commentary on and more formal research into both the public service and occupational values—is briefly noted at the end of that chapter.

FOOTNOTES

[1] A brief discussion of the design and conduct of the study is presented in the concluding section of this chapter.

[2] *Organizing for National Security: Mobilizing Talent for Government Service*, Hearings Before the Subcommittee on National Policy Machinery, Senate Committee on Government Operations, 86th Cong., 2d sess. (May 1960), Part III, p. 413.

[3] *Ibid.*, p. 526.

[4] U.S. Civil Service Commission, *The Growing Demand for Scientific and Technical Manpower in the Federal Service* (mimeographed; October 1960), pp. 7–9.

[5] U.S. Department of Labor, *Manpower–Challenge of the 1960's* (1960), pp. 9 and 11.

[6] Harold H. Leich, "Scientific Manpower: Progress and Prospects," *Civil Service Journal*, Vol. 3 (April-June 1963), p. 24.

[7] Roger W. Jones, "The Federal Civil Service Today," *Public Personnel Review*, Vol. 21 (April 1960), p. 118.

[8] *A Report on How People Are Recruited, Examined, and Appointed in the Competitive Civil Service*, Prepared by the U.S. Civil Service Commission for the Sub-committee on Civil Service, House Committee on Post Office and Civil Service, 86th Cong., 1st sess. (April 1959), p. 61.

[9] A more detailed statement of the design and procedures is presented in Chaps. 2 and 3 of this book's companion volume by the same authors: *Source Book of a Study of Occupational Values and the Image of the Federal Service* (Brookings Institution, 1964), hereafter referred to as *Source Book*.

[10] Certain types of highly refined statistical analysis of categorical responses (factor analysis, latent structure analysis, etc.) can yield "new" information, such as common underlying variables, patterns that are differentially characteristic of the individual as opposed to what is being judged, and the like.

[11] The basic form of the questionnaire (for the nonfederal employed public) and the other forms for the federal and student populations, wherein they differ from the basic form, are shown in the Appendix. The basic form consists of twenty-two open-end questions; eighty-five items or statements which the respondent sorts onto a ten-step response scale; four self-anchoring scale ratings; six categorical questions; and forty brief classification questions concerning the status and background of the respondent.

[12] The theoretical basis and general areas of usefulness of the method are described in F. P. Kilpatrick and Hadley Cantril, "Self-Anchoring Scaling: A Measure of Individuals' Unique Reality Worlds," *Journal of Individual Psychology*, Vol. 16 November 1960), pp. 158–173.

[13] National Analysts, Inc., Philadelphia, Pa. The staff of about 500 trained interviewers is distributed throughout the

United States, for the most part located near 100 sampling points in the organization's master sample. The interviewers are part-time employees—preponderantly housewives with some college education—personally selected and trained either by local field supervisors or by central office staff. The firm's volume of research is such that most members of this corps are kept busy for a large share of their available time. On the average, they have had about five years of interviewing experience; they have also had extensive interview training, conducted both as a routine matter and as a means of acquainting them with novel assignments involving new or modified procedures.

[14] In accordance with standard practice, each interviewer had been provided with an instruction booklet pretested for clarity, accuracy, and completeness in the pilot study phase of the research. It described the general purpose of the study, told exactly how respondent selection procedures were to be carried out, and gave question-by-question instructions on how the questions were to be asked and the answers recorded. In addition, before the interviewing began the interviewers were assembled in small groups at various conveniently located points around the country and given two days of intensive training by central staff members. These sessions involved general instructions, practice interviewing, review of the practice interviews, and individual corrective instruction.

[15] Instruction booklets revised to accomodate the special problems of interviewing federal employees were provided, and once again, personal training sessions were held.

[16] The master sample was National Analysts, Inc., National General Purpose Sample, 1960. Details of the procedures for drawing each sample are given in the *Source Book*, Chap. 3, and are not repeated here. However, it should be mentioned that our sample of general federal employees was drawn in accordance with our master framework from a larger sample of federal employees made available to the Brookings Institution by the United States Civil Service Commission. This consisted of the names and installation addresses of 5,000 civilian federal employees in the continental United States drawn by a random sampling procedure from the St. Louis Central Registry. (CIA and FBI employees were excluded from the list.) Also, at all stages in the federal employee phase of our work, we had the active and inventive support of the Interagency Advisory Group, the Civil Service Commission, installation personnel officers, and the chief personnel officers of almost all the major departments and agencies in the federal government.

In addition, with rare exceptions, the schools, the colleges, the business organizations, and the federal installations permitted interviewing to be conducted on site and during school or working hours. This was a main factor in achieving a high proportion of satisfactorily completed interviews with the people selected by the sampling procedures. In none of th nineteen groups did the completion rate, as conventionally calculated, fall below 85 percent; for all but two of them the rates were over 90 percent, and in a number of instances 95 percent or higher.

[17] U.S. Office of Education, *Education Directory, 1958-1959: Part 3, Higher Education*, Theresa Birch Wilkins, editor (1960).

[18] *McKittrick Directory of Advertisers Classified, 1960* (1959).

[19] Both the creation of the codes and the preparation of the coding instructions were done by the Brookings Institution however, much invaluable help and advice were given by Mrs. Genevieve Timm, of National Analysts, Inc.

[20] The punching and machine tabulating were performed under contract by National Analysts, Inc.

[21] The basic tables are presented in the *Source Book*.

Field Work in Bureaucracy and the Process of Conceptual Refinement

by Peter M. Blau

This selection describes how one investigator first conceived and then carried out a significant quantitative study. In the course of the account are detailed his errors, problems, reconciliations. This piece offers the chronology and record of a thoughtful scholar's efforts as well as good pragmatic advice on method, particularly as it relates to comparative issues. There are important lessons here for the novice researcher on technique as well as theory, and shrewd insights into the nature of relationships during the course of such a research. Particularly interesting may be the discussion of the morality of the researcher and the suggestion that honesty is the only way to deal with human beings whom one studies simply because deceit inevitably fails.

FIELD WORK IN BUREAUCRACY

This epilogue is devoted to a discussion of some of the methodological problems encountered in conducting and analyzing the research reported in the preceding parts of the book. While I shall report on my own experiences and decisions in a particular study, using the personal pronoun for this purpose, the expectation is that these have some general methodological implications, just as I have attempted to use the data on a few cases to derive some general substantive principles about bureaucratic work groups. What I am going to present is a case study of the case-study method.

Problems of study design and field work will be dealt with in this chapter. Quite a different methodological problem will be taken up in the final chapter, namely, the problem of conceptual refinement: how did some of the ideas presented originate, develop, and become modified in the course of the research? Before turning to the discussion of the design and conduct of the field research, let me indicate what theoretical considerations prompted my decision to study bureaucratic groups of officials.

An interest in theories of social structure may take many forms, and mine was largely shaped by Merton's approach. Compare, for example, the ways in which Weber's and Durkheim's theories are utilized and extended in Parsons' *The Structure of Social Action*, on the one hand, and Merton's "Bureaucratic Structure and Personality" or "Social Structure and Anomie," on the other.[1] Parsons is concerned with the interrelations between broad institutional complexes and, specifically, between abstract analytical aspects of institutional systems. Merton, in contrast, focuses attention on the influences exerted by social structures on patterns of conduct; the core concept is that of structural constraints. To be sure, Merton also analyzes the way social regularities in behavior become institutionalized and modify the social structure. But, in either case, the emphasis is on the relationships between some elements of social structure and an observable pattern of conduct rather than directly on the relationships between various abstract elements of social structure, as it is in Parsons. Later writings reveal parallel differences. Thus, Parsons' abstract conception of functionalism contrasts sharply with Merton's functional paradigm, with its down-to-earth concepts and emphasis on observed consequences.[2] I was Merton's research assistant when he worked on his essay on functionalism, and the opportunity I had of working with him while he developed this new theoretical framework undoubtedly contributed to the great impression it made on me.

My interest in the study of bureaucracy emerged naturally as the result of these influences on my orientation. If one's concern is with the compelling force the social structure exerts upon human behavior, a logical place to study it is in a bureaucracy, where this force is so apparent and pronounced and yet often produces quite un-

SOURCE: Reprinted from *The Dynamics of Bureaucracy: A Study of Interpersonal Relations in Two Government Agencies* by Peter M. Blau by permission of The University of Chicago Press. Copyright 1955 by The University of Chicago.

expected results, as Merton's analysis of the subject suggests. Besides, the implicit functional analysis in Weber's theory of bureaucracy raised the intriguing possibility that new insights could be gained from explicitly applying Merton's revised functional framework to the subject. Finally, the threat posed by bureaucracy for democratic institutions supplied an additional incentive for studying it to one who, like many others, had been attracted to sociology by an interest in social reform.

Having become increasingly concerned with bridging the gap between abstract theory and systematic research, I looked for a way to do an empirical study of the theoretical problems of bureaucracy. A possible approach for this purpose was suggested by the studies of industrial work groups and, especially, by Arensberg, who exposed me to the quantitative method for observing social interaction that Chapple and he had developed.[3] This method could be utilized for the systematic empirical investigation of some aspects of bureaucractic structure.

I consequently planned to carry out a quantitative case study of work groups in a bureaucracy. This was my way of integrating social theory and social research. It would be an empirical study of work groups, in the manner of the research in the sociology of industry, but in contrast to these investigations it would be guided by Weber's theory of bureaucracy. I would attempt to collect quantitative data on bureaucratic work groups and to apply Merton's functional framework in the analysis of these data. But how does one go about conducting such a study? I did not find a general answer to this question and often groped in the dark as I had to deal with the specific problems I encountered. It is in the hope of throwing some light on this question that I want to describe what I did—how I designed the investigation, the steps entailed in carrying it out, the problems that arose in the field, and, last but not least, the blunders I made. For, if learning involves trial and error, learning of my errors may spare other researchers some similar trials.

Initial Design

In the spring of 1948 I wrote many lengthy memos outlining a multitude of problems about bureaucratic work groups that could be studied. As one reads these scores of pages, two basic themes stand out: first, how the formal organization influences the informal organization of work groups and how the latter, in turn, influences the performance of duties; and, second, a functional analysis of the informal organization which explores the distinctive functions of the informal group structure in a bureaucracy. My ideas ranged from broad problems to be explored to quite specific hypotheses. For example, I stated that the various forms the displacement of goal takes should be ascertained, and so should the specific processes through which it comes about; I suggested that a basic function of the informal organization in a bureaucracy is to mitigate bureaucratic impersonality; more specifically, I hypothesized that informal relations among colleagues serve the function of relieving tensions that arise in the contacts of officials with the public.

Some of the hypotheses advanced at this early stage were later abandoned; others were supported by empirical observations, but even these were often modified and refined in the course of research. This process of selection and modification indicates that no claim can be made that hypotheses have been subjected to a rigorous test in this case study. But the idea that research methods can neatly be classified into hypothesis-testing and insight-supplying ones is grossly misleading, since these are polar types that appear in actual investigations in various admixtures. The double aim is always to develop or refine theoretical insights which explain reality—for instance, group structures in bureaucracy—and to discriminate between the correct and the false explanatory principles. It is all too easy to obtain some impressionistic evidence for our broad theoretical speculations. Such evidence, therefore, helps us little in discriminating between diverse or even conflicting theoretical principles. My endeavor to stipulate hypotheses, some in advance of the empirical research and some in the course of it, and to collect at least some quantitative data served the purpose of furnishing a screening device for insights. The ideas that survived this screening test, while still only hypotheses, since a case study cannot validate general principles of bureaucratic structure, were more likely to be correct than were the original speculations. Moreover, the quantitative analysis of specific relations between variables often produced unexpected findings that challenged the imagination and led to refinements of theoretical conceptions.

The significance of a quantitative case study, then, is that it stimulates the kind of theoretical insights that can be derived only from quantitative analysis as well as the kind that results from close observation of an empirical situation, and that it provides more severe checks on these insights than does an impressionistic study and thus somewhat increases the probable validity of the conclusions. It is only in retrospect, however, that I have arrived at this general formulation. While I was preparing my study, I was concerned simply with exploiting pertinent theories and translating their insights into specific research problems. This helped me in deciding what kind of bureaucratic group would be most suitable for the study. It also was necessary to prepare a proposal for the Social Science Research Council, which later awarded me a predoctoral fellowship. Last, though not least, the extensive outline of problems and hypotheses became the basis for the development of the research procedures for my case study.

On Merton's suggestion, from whose criticism and advice I greatly benefited at this stage, I modified my plan and decided to compare groups in two bureaucracies—a public and a private one. I reformulated my hypotheses in terms of this comparison between government agency and large private firm, and spent much of the summer trying to obtain permission for study from one organization of each type. The immediate cause for abandoning this plan was that I was unable to obtain permission to do this research from any suitable private firm, but by the time I had to make this decision there were other reasons for it too. My experience in the first agency made me realize that I had so much more to learn about social patterns in government agencies that a comparison of groups in two government agencies that differ in some ways but are not too dissimilar might be most fruitful.

In the weeks before I started observation in the first government agency, I designed a detailed schedule of research procedures, which was completed after I entered the organization and had become acquainted wih the actual setup. I had earlier decided to use three basic methods—direct observation, interviewing, and analysis of official records—and to employ various quantitative as well as qualitative research techniques under each. Thus, I planned not only to observe whatever I could notice about the relations among colleagues in the office but also to obtain a systematic record of all their social interactions for a specified period; not only to interview selected members of the organization on specific issues but also to administer a semistructured interview to all members of the work groups intensively studied; not only to read the procedure manual but also to abstract some

quantitative information from it. I put each research problem I had outlined on a 5 × 8 slip, making several carbons, which were cross-classified by the various research procedures to be used to investigate this problem. For example, the slip that deals with contacts between different sections in the organization is classified under "written regulations," "interview with management representative," "active observation" (by which I meant that I would ask questions to clarify what I observed), "quantitative observation," "self-recording," and "interview with officials." The resulting file indicated the different substantive problems that might be studied with any given research procedure.

This schedule served as the basic guide for my study, but it was not intended to be rigid or fixed. As new ideas occurred to me in the course of observation, or new techniques for investigating a problem, I added them to the file. And when it became apparent that a certain problem could not be studied with a given procedure, or not at all in this situation, I modified the schedule accordingly. I repeatedly went over the file in the early phase of observation, revising it and abstracting lists of problems under the various research procedures, which I carried with me into the field. There I explored how well the various procedures would actually lend themselves to studying the different problems. The revised lists resulting from this exploration were regularly consulted by me and directed my research activities.

I found such a schedule of procedures, somewhat flexible yet exerting some control over the research process, very useful. To be sure, it is possible that I missed some exciting leads because I was too concerned with following a research schedule. It may also be that I failed to collect systematic data that I could have obtained because I was too easily intrigued by new possibilities and diverted from following the predesigned procedure. But, whatever the wisdom of my specific decisions, I think that the general principle of using such a research schedule in a case study is sound. In a bureaucratic field situation the needs of the organization and not those of the observer determine what occurs and thus what he can study at any given time. While some events occur regularly, enabling him to determine when to study them, others do not. A change in regulations is introduced, a conference is called, two officials have an argument, and the observer must be ready to turn his attention to these incidents, which may bear on some of his central research problems. The researcher who compulsively insists on following his predesigned plan will miss these rare opportunities. Conversely, the one who is seduced by every new lead will find that he has failed to collect information on the theoretical problems that had prompted his research. A research schedule that is recurrently revised but that is quite closely followed guards against these dangers. During the last weeks of observation I carefully went over my lists, and while my design was so ambitious that I could not possibly carry out all my plans, I was able to select the items for completion that I considered most important. At the very least, my research schedule prevented me from inadvertently forgetting to obtain some information that was essential in terms of my theoretical framework.

Chronology

While there is a rough chronological order in this chapter, it is often violated to present the development of an idea more fully. In the next chapter, moreover, each section presents the development of some conceptual problem from beginning to end. Since the sequence of our discussion does not coincide with the chronology of events in the actual research, it might be helpful to present this chronology briefly.

The federal agency of law enforcement, although it was presented in the second part of the book, was studied first. The observation period started on August 31, 1948, and lasted for about three months. After an initial period of observation and an examination of official records, a section of eighteen officials, which I later called Department Y, was selected for intensive study, but the investigation also encompassed several special groups, such as reviewers and stenographers. I observed officials in the office, accompanied them on their field visits, had lunch with them, even went to an American Legion party, held scores of informal interviews and hundreds of briefer conversations, and abstracted various data from official records. I took notes of my observations and interviews whenever I could, and if it was impossible to do so on the spot I did so as soon afterward as possible. In the evening I typed all my field notes in duplicate. Since my notes were written under time pressure and I relied much on my memory when I typed them up, I tried hard to finish typing each day's notes on the same day, but I was not always successful, even though I often worked a sixteen-hour day. Weekends were devoted to catching up on field notes, doing some cursory analysis of the data to get some feel of what I had found, and going over the procedure schedule to plan the work for the coming week. It was a full three months.

At the beginning of December, I took time off to conduct a preliminary analysis of my data, after which I briefly returned to the agency to complete my observation, particularly to seek to answer some of the questions the analysis had raised. Since this was around Christmas, I took advantage of the opportunity of attending the office Christmas party, even though I had stopped going regularly to the office for observation by then.

I worked further on the preliminary analysis, which served as the basis for preparing an interview schedule. In January and February I conducted interviews with the members of Department Y, and students from a methodology course at Columbia University conducted additional interviews with clerical personnel for me.

I started the study of the state employment agency on March 2, 1949, and followed the same general schedule. The period of observation lasted about three months. In May I interrupted the process of data collection for a week to begin the preliminary analysis, and then returned to the agency to complete my observations. In June I worked further on the preliminary analysis and prepared interview guides not only for the members of what I referred to as Department X, which had been intensively studied, but also for the members of two other departments, which I planned to use for comparative purposes. These interviews were conducted during July and August.

In the fall of 1949 I started to teach at Wayne University. My twelve-hour teaching load occupied me fully during the first semester, and while I was able to devote some time to the study subsequently, most of the work on it had to be done during vacations. Hence, it took me an entire year, from the beginning of 1950 to the beginning of 1951, to complete the basic analysis, and it was not until the fall of 1951 that the first draft of the manuscript was completed. On the basis of Merton's detailed and helpful criticisms of this manuscript, I made extensive revisions before I submitted the final draft of it as my dissertation to Columbia University in the spring of 1952. Afterward, I continued to make further revisions, and another three years elapsed before *The Dynamics of Bureaucracy* was finally published in the spring of 1955, seven years after I had started to work on it.

Entry and Orientation

An interviewing survey of a sample of New Yorkers can be conducted without official permission from anybody, but a field study of a bureaucracy cannot be carried out without the explicit permission of management. This poses special problems. While not all respondents selected for a sampling survey agree to be interviewed, and those who do are typically not representative of those who do not, there are known procedures for correcting for this self-selection bias. But the problem of self-selection is far more extreme in research on organizations, and it is not easily possible to correct for the bias it introduces. Suppose someone wants to study bureaucratic rigidities and fear of innovation. The very fact that management gives him permission to conduct his investigation in the organization indicates that it is not resistant to trying something new. It may well not be an accident that all the old established bureaucracies I approached refused permission for the study and that both organizations that gave permission were relatively young ones that had been founded during the New Deal. Perhaps self-selection makes it inevitable that the organizations we study are those in which bureaucratic rigidities are least pronounced.

The members of the organization know, of course, that management must have given permission to conduct the study, and this creates another problem. The observer cannot escape an initial identification with management, since the assumption is that management must have a direct interest in the study. In the federal agency, I was suspected of being a representative of the Hoover Commission, which at that time carried out investigations in various branches of the federal government. These suspicions compound the problem posed by the sheer presence of the observer, since people become self-conscious if somebody sits in a corner and watches them, even if he tries to do so unobtrusively. Ultimately, I overcame these difficulties, but not until blunders I committed because of my inexperience had first intensified them.

On my first day, the district commissioner introduced me to his top assistants, told me that one of them would serve as my guide during my period of orientation, and assigned an office to me where I could read in private the extensive rules and regulations that governed the agency's operations. During the first week, the official who acted as my guide explained the operating procedure to me in lengthy interviews and answered the questions I had after reading the books of rules and regulations. He also introduced me to the supervisors of the various departments, and I had occasion to interview them. During the second week, I further explored the operations of various departments, discovered the quantitative operational records that were kept and abstracted information from them, revised my research design by adapting it to the concrete circumstances in this agency. I still spent much time in the private office, and only supervisors and some selected officials had as yet met me; most agents had not, although they had undoubtedly noticed my presence.

This fairly thorough initial orientation was a good preparation for the observation period. The basic knowledge I acquired about the organization and its operations enabled me to translate my general research procedures into specific operational terms appropriate for this field situation, and it helped me to select a suitable department for intensive study. But spending two weeks on becoming oriented to the agency's operating procedures also had serious disadvantages.

At the very start of the intensive observation of Department Y, I was introduced to all its members by a senior official at a meeting and given an opportunity to explain the study briefly. I realized that an observer must explain at the outset who he is and what he wants to do. What I failed to realize is that what I defined as the beginning of the actual observation was not the beginning for these agents. I had been seen around for two weeks, and my failure explicitly to clarify my identity earlier had given rumors about me that much time to circulate. The private office and my preoccupation with becoming familiar with a complex bureaucratic structure had blinded me to the fact that I was already being observed by these agents, even though I had not yet started observing them.

I learned from this experience. Six months later, in the study of the state employment agency, I explained the study in a brief talk to the members of Department X the day I set foot in their local office. (It was possible to arrange the preceding one-week orientation in a different location.) It seemed to be easier to establish rapport here than in the federal agency, but whether this was due to the lecture or the experience I had acquired as an observer is a moot point. In any case, the lecture was far less effective than it could have been, as I found out when I gave another lecture at the end of the observation period in the employment agency. The object of this farewell lecture was to illustrate what such a study of social relations seeks to discover; I presented Whyte's analysis of the relationship between informal status in a gang and bowling score,[4] and some of my own preliminary findings on consultations among officials and their discussions about clients. This lecture was much more successful than the first one had been. Officials were interested, asked numerous questions, and made some revealing comments afterward. One interviewer said that there should have been a meeting in which I explained my study at the beginning, not just at the end; she apparently had entirely forgotten that there had been such a meeting. Another interviewer, who had not forgotten the earlier talk, commented how much more interesting the second one was and how much more relaxed I appeared when giving it.

In the first lecture, I described the objective of the study in general terms, covering such points as the importance of human relations and the need of firsthand knowledge of government agencies. In the second lecture, I illustrated the study's objective with concrete findings. It is evident from the reactions that the second topic would have been a better way to introduce the study than was the first. There are a number of reasons. A discussion of actual findings is much more interesting than a mere description of formal objectives, creating some interest at the outset in what the observer has to say and wants to do. Besides, the concrete examples of sociological analysis, judiciously chosen, demonstrate more effectively than hollow-sounding explicit disavowals that the observer is really not an efficiency expert who wants to check up on the work of officials. The evidence the observer furnishes of what he and other social scientists can do, finally, not only affirms his professional identity but also helps to command respect for his research and to motivate respondents to co-operate with it.

The Role of the Observer

After I had been introduced to the members of Department Y in the federal agency, I spent most of my time in the room where they and the members of another department were located. I took every opportunity to become acquainted with these agents, asking them about their work and going to lunch with little groups, and slowly began to establish some rapport. But I soon became impatient with the slow progress I was making and decided that I could use my time more economically, since I was sitting in this room and watching what was going on anyway, by making

the quantitative record of the social interaction among agents that I had planned. I proceeded to start this record of all social contacts in the department within a week from the day I had been introduced to its members. This was a serious mistake.

I had just begun to overcome the suspicion and resistance aroused by my entry, and now I employed a technique of observation that the agents found very objectionable and that increased their resistance to the study again. Of course, I explained that I simply wanted to get a systematic record of the social contacts among officials, but this did not meet the objections of the agents. Even those who apparently believed my explanations considered such a record ridiculous and emphasized that I could not gain an understanding of the agent's job by sitting in the office but must go into the field, where the most important work was being done. Others suspected that I really tried to check on how much time they wasted, as exemplified by the mocking comment one whispered to me when he left the room: "I'm going to the washroom; will be back in two minutes." The continual observation to which keeping such a record subjects respondents makes them self-conscious and is irritating. I evidently should have waited until my rapport was much better before using this technique (as I did, of course, in the second study). Why did I make the blunder of using it prematurely?

I think the answer is not simply that because of my lack of experience I did not know how much resistance this method of observing interaction would create in a group not yet fully reconciled to my presence, since common sense should have told me so if irrational factors had not prevented me from realizing it. I was a lone observer in the midst of an integrated group of officials, who were initially suspicious of and even somewhat hostile to me and my research. While they were part of the bureaucratic structure, my position was not anchored in it. The anxiety engendered by my insecure position was undoubtedly intensified by the pressure I felt to progress with my observations, since I was not sure whether I could achieve my research aims in the limited time available. It seems—and I use the tentative wording advisedly because I am reconstructing now mental processes of which I was not fully aware then—that I tried to cope with this anxiety by imposing a rigid structure on my research activities. This emotional reaction may have prompted my decision to turn so early from more exploratory observations to the precisely circumscribed and fairly routine task of recording interaction frequencies.[5]

The feelings of insecurity that the bureaucratic field situation tends to evoke in the observer, particularly the inexperienced one, are generally a major source of blunders. This is the fundamental pragmatic reason, quite aside from considerations of professional ethics, why the observer, in my opinion, should not resort to concealment and deception. It is difficult to simulate a role successfully over long periods of time, and, if concern over detection adds to the observer's other worries, he is not likely to be effective in discharging his research responsibilities. I explained quite openly what I was doing and the aims of my study to any respondent who was interested, the major exception being that I never called it a study of "bureaucracy." A few times I did try to conceal something, against my better judgment, and this typically turned out to be a mistake. For example, the negative reaction of agents to the recording of social interaction made me worry about how senior officials would react to my use of this technique. Once, when a managerial official passed my desk, I inadvertently placed my hand over the recording sheet, and another time, when the district commissioner stopped by my desk and asked me about the research, my concern over his reaction, which proved to be quite unjustified, led me to give a vague and confused answer—two silly blunders that resulted from unnecessary attempts to conceal my research activities.

Since I was at first suspected of concealing my true identity and pretending to be an outside observer while really being a representative of some government commission, my trump card in establishing rapport was that I actually was what I pretended to be and that chances were that this would become apparent in continuing social interaction. I could not have played this trump if I had in fact practiced deception, for doing so entailed permitting my natural behavior in social intercourse to reveal the kind of person I am. There is little doubt that my success in overcoming the strong initial resistance that some union members had to the study was due to the fact that they perceived my genuine sympathy with their viewpoint even though I never explicitly expressed my political opinions. As our informal discussions revealed my familiarity with university life and the sociological literature, my claim of being a social researcher was validated. But the most convincing evidence that I really was not part of the government service was supplied by me inadver-

tently, often by mistakes I made. When agents, apparently not believing that I was an outsider, came to me for advice on a problem in their cases, my genuine ignorance of the complex official regulations became quite apparent. When I talked too freely to interviewers in the state agency during working hours, having become used to this practice in the federal agency, a supervisor several times reprimanded me, politely but firmly, for interfering with their work. I had made a mistake in not being more careful, but these incidents turned out to be to my advantage, since they demonstrated to the interviewers that I was only a tolerated outsider and really not part of the management hierarchy.

As one would expect, I found some officials more easily approachable than others, more interested in the research, and more willing to furnish information. A few seemed quite eager to talk to me and volunteered sensitive information on topics that others were most reluctant to discuss at all; for example, they freely criticized agency procedure and even their colleagues. It is my impression that the best informants in the early weeks tended to be officials who occupied marginal positions in the work group or the organization. Being not fully integrated among colleagues or somewhat alienated from the bureaucratic system may have made these officials more critical of their social environment, less restrained by feelings of loyalty from sharing their criticism with an outsider, and more interested in the approval of the observer than were those who received much social support and approval within the organization.

The marginal position of the observer in the bureaucratic field situation complements the marginal position of these informants, and this entails a danger. The observer may be tempted to rely too much on officials who make themselves easily accessible to him at the outset. If he yields to this temptation, he will obtain a distorted picture of the organization and the group structure. Moreover, if he becomes identified with deviant individuals or cliques, his ability to establish rapport with the majority and his effectiveness as an impartial observer will be impeded.

It is not possible, however, to avoid entirely the self-selection of informants. The observer is no neutral machine who selects the persons he talks to purely at random and devotes exactly the same amount of time to each. He can hardly be expected to reject the overtures some officials make to him, not only because his insecure position creates a need for social acceptance, but also because his research responsibilities demand that he take advantage of such opportunities for obtaining information. Somewhat marginal officials proved to be an invaluable source of new insights, particularly about dysfunctions of various institutions and practices. Their incomplete integration in the existing social structure made them perceptive observers of it and its shortcomings, and their concern with commanding the observer's respect gave them incentives to share their most interesting observations with me. The solution for the problem of self-selection of informants is not to ignore this important source of information but to supplement it with quantitative data based on responses from the entire group or a representative sample.

An interest in earning the observer's respect may well be a major motivating force for supplying him with information and explanations. Respondents make a contribution to the research in exchange for the respect they win by doing so, provided they care about being respected by the observer. The most competent officials can command respect by demonstrating their superior knowledge and skills, but the less competent ones cannot, and this leads some of them to seek to earn the observer's respect by acting as second-hand participant observers and sharing their inside knowledge and insights with him. Respondents variously located in the social structure differ not only in *how* they impress the observer but also in *when* they tend to become good informants. During the later phases of the field work, my best informants were no longer largely officials who occupied marginal positions but included some of the most competent and highly respected ones.[6] I think what happened was that once I became accepted as a social scientist, my prestige rose, increasing the value of my approval and respect for respondents. As long as my respect was not worth much, only the marginal officials who commanded little respect in the organization were interested in earning it, but later, when my respect came to be worth more, other officials too became interested in earning it.

Finally, a few remarks are in order about the interviews administered subsequent to the observation period. When I asked officials on my last day in the office for interview appointments, many assumed the interview would take place during office hours, and some were reluctant to devote their own time to it. But group pressures soon came to operate in my favor.[7] As these po-

tential refusals, who had said that they wanted to think it over and that I should call them back, noticed that most of their colleagues made interview appointments with me, a few approached me and said they had decided they could make an appointment now, and most of the others readily made one when I called them. Only two of the thirty-eight respondents in the two departments intensively studied were not interviewed. (Even these never overtly refused but postponed appointments so often that I finally gave up.)

The question that evoked most resistance was that on party preference in the last election, notwithstanding my repeated assurance that answers were anonymous and confidential. That this was not due simply to distrust of me is indicated by the fact that one agent said he would be glad to tell me if I would only promise not to use his answer in the research. (I refused to make such a promise.) Since politics is a sensitive area in civil service, agents did not want my report to describe the political preferences of civil servants,[8] and this, rather than fear that I would identify individual responses, probably accounted for their reluctance to express their voting preferences. The anonymity of our research reports protects only the individual from exposure and not the groups he is identified with, for our monographs do reveal the characteristics of various groups—civil servants, Negroes, Jews, and others. When the group with which responses will be associated in the final report is apparent, persons identified with this group will not be moved by our assurance of anonymity to reveal characteristic they do not want to be attributed to their group.

Conclusions

William F. Whyte's experience in explaining his research to the people of Cornerville seems to have been quite different from mine when explaining the field study in a bureaucracy. Whyte reports:

> As I began hanging about Cornerville, I found that I needed an explanation for myself and my study . . .
> I began with a rather elaborate explanation. I was studying the social history of Cornerville—but I had a new angle. Instead of working from the past up to the present, I was seeking to get a thorough knowledge of present conditions and then work from the present to the past. I was quite pleased with this explanation at the time, but nobody else seemed to care for it. I gave the explanation on only two occasions, and each time, when I had finished, there was an awkward silence. No one, myself included, knew what to say.

While this explanation had at least the virtue of covering everything that I might eventually want to do in the district, it was apparently too involved to mean anything to Cornerville people.

I soon found that people were developing their own explanation about me: I was writing a book about Cornerville. This might seem entirely too vague an explanation, and yet it sufficed.[9]

While my field experience led to the conclusion that a rather full exposition of the results this type of social research can accomplish is preferable to an explanation in terms of some general remarks, Whyte came to the opposite conclusion. One possible reason for this difference is that college-educated officials might be interested in a discussion of social influences on behavior, while the poorly educated inhabitants of an Italian slum find such a discussion abstract and meaningless. More important, probably, were differences in the expectations that Whyte and I had of our respondents. Note that both of us started with a formal explanation of the aims of our research and that both had the experience that our respondents were not greatly interested in such a formal description of research objectives. But while Whyte, who was confronted with uneducated respondents, concluded that his explanation was too complex, I, who was confronted with educated respondents, concluded that my explanation was not sufficiently penetrating to stimulate curiosity. Perhaps the fundamental shortcoming of our formal explanations was that, although they were not dishonest, we thought of them as a screen for our diverse research concerns, and our resulting self-consciousness made them sound unconvincing. Neither a simple reference to writing a book nor a straightforward account of research results is likely to make an investigator ill at ease, but the talk he has self-consciously designed as a front for his role as a researcher may well do so, as shown by the awkward silences it often produces.

Feelings of insecurity are generally a major source of blunder in the field, and the field situation engenders feelings of anxiety and insecurity, particularly for the lone investigator who is not a member of a team from which he can derive social support. Attempts at concealment may further intensify such feelings and thus lead to blunders. That is one reason why honesty is the best policy in field research, and there are others. In a bureaucratic situation, the researcher is often suspected of being a spy of management or of an investigating agency. Disavowals cannot allay such suspicions. What can allay them are the clues that one inadvertently furnishes to others about his

social roles and self if he permits himself to act naturally in social intercourse. This important method for disproving false accusations is not available to the field worker who is afraid of interacting with respondents in a relaxed and natural manner because he wants to conceal some of his research aims.

It is therefore, by and large, in the interest of the field worker not to deceive his respondents. But even when outright deception can make important contributions to a particular investigation, it should not be practiced, in my opinion. Indeed, the very fact that deception may benefit the individual researcher requires that standards of professional ethics be invoked against it, if only to protect the good will of the public toward social research, on which our continuing ability to pursue it depends. This is a complex issue, which should not be oversimplified. Complete frankness toward respondents is incompatible with the requirements of scientific method. Proper research procedure, for example, demands that we conceal our hypotheses from the subjects of the inquiry and do not reveal to them the exact implications of various reactions to questions and tests. Neither must we allow our concern with the future good will of respondents to influence our decision about what findings to report and to induce us to suppress those they would not like. Although where to draw the line may not always be clear, there is a difference between lack of complete frankness and outright deception. Respondents can and should be told that they are under observation in an empirical study and what the objectives of the research are. To be sure, behavior that is freely expressed in public belongs, so to speak, in the public domain for the purpose of scientific observation too, but researchers are not entitled to record without explicit permission behavior that is confined to restricted circles. I believe that the practice of eliciting information from people under the pretense of being an intimate without informing them that they are under study deserves condemnation by the profession, and so does the practice of deceiving the public about the purpose of the research—for example, by claiming to be engaged in a scientific investigation while actually conducting market research to promote the private interests of a firm.

THE PROCESS OF CONCEPTUAL REFINEMENT

In this final chapter I wish to trace the development of some of the ideas about bureaucratic work groups that have been analyzed. One possible procedure for doing so would be to start with all ideas and hypotheses derived in advance from the theoretical literature and examine which ones were discarded, why they were, and which ones found their way into the book. Then one could investigate which other ideas originated at subsequent stages in the research, during the field observation, as the result of interviewing, or only later in the course of the analysis. But this procedure is actually not feasible. I wrote page after page of research problems and hypotheses before I went into the field, many of which were later discarded, as I have already mentioned, because there was no opportunity to investigate them, because others appeared more promising, or because no meaningful pattern could be discerned. For example, I analyzed at length the extensive statistical records in the federal agency to derive a measure of performance quality, but I could not construct a valid one and therefore did not even present that analysis. It would be tedious and hardly worthwhile to describe all the ideas I later discarded.

An alternative procedure, which I shall adopt, is to select a few of the main conceptual problems analyzed in the book and follow their history from the first spark of the idea through the modifications and refinements that occurred in the course of the research to the final analysis and interpretation of the data. For most of these problems, as we shall see, we can find an early trace, be it ever so faint, but the pre-field-work conception typically underwent fundamental changes as a result of the research experience. The field situation is rife with serendipity; new insights are gained, and they can often be corroborated with empirical evidence, yet these insights can typically be traced back to earlier theoretical conceptions and thus serve to refine them.

Consultation

One of the fundamental general principles that governed my study from its inception was that informal relations influence the performance of duties. As I explored the implications of this proposition in the summer of 1948, prior to the start of field observation, I specified the hypothesis that officials who have frequent informal contacts, for example, who regularly lunch together, will tend to ask one another for information they need rather than some other official whom they might be officially expected to ask. Here I seem to have predicted the existence of the consultation pattern that I later observed in the federal agency,

but what I predicted was actually only a small element of what I was to find. I had in mind simple requests for information and did not anticipate at all the extensive practice of giving advice on complex problems that prevailed among agents. Neither did I realize the important implications of the consultation pattern for the group structure.

During my period of orientation in the federal agency, I asked a supervisor whether agents sometimes co-operate with one another. I did not yet know the operating procedures well and wanted to find out whether their duties sometimes required agents to work together on a case. The supervisor's answer, however, was not in terms of what I had had in mind. He said: "They are not permitted to consult other agents. If they have a problem, they must take it up with me." Unexpectedly, I had obtained my first clue to the practice of consulting colleagues.

At the very beginning of the intensive observation in Department Y, I could not fail to notice that agents frequently discussed problems of their cases with other agents and asked their advice. I was immediately impressed by the significance of this pattern. Here was an officially prohibited practice that clearly had important implications for official operations and that provided the kind of link between informal work group and bureaucratic operations in which I was primarily interested. Besides, this practice offered an opportunity for analyzing an aspect of the content of the informal relations among officials that would supplement the analysis of the quantitative form of their social interaction I had already planned. Exactly a week after I had entered Department Y, I started a tally of all the consultations I could observe, recording on a matrix which agent asked which colleague for advice. Two weeks later when I went over my procedure schedule, I noted that I should ask sociometric and other questions about consultation in the interview as well as continue the record of consultations in the office.

A section on consultation was included in the preliminary analysis I did at the beginning of December, near the end of the field observation. In brief outline, I pointed out that agents who needed advice on difficult problems were put under cross-pressure by the requirement to consult only the supervisor and their reluctance to reveal their difficulties to him lest it affect his evaluation of them. The unofficial practice of consulting colleagues that resulted from this cross pressure served to cement the informal relations in the work group. I also suggested that the socia esteem for the consultant strengthened his position among colleagues and that one dysfunction of the pattern might be that it weakened the esteem for, and position of, the supervisor. This discussion of consultation was the central topic of my first report to the Social Science Research Council, which I prepared later that month.

The skeleton of the final analysis of the consultation pattern can already be discerned in this early exploration of it. Numerous specific elements were still to be added, of course. For example, there are no data on the actual network of consultation, and there is no discussion of the tendency to consult not only experts but often colleagues whose competence is not superior to one's own. Most important, however, is the fact that the two crucial insights for an understanding of this pattern are still missing. There is as yet neither a reference to the principle that the informal institution of unofficial consultation improves performance, even when no advice is obtained, nor a conceptualization of consultation as an exchange process.

The interviews furnished clues for these insights. Several agents explained that you often discuss your cases with colleagues not in order to ask their advice but because you want to share an interesting experience or because you want to have an opportunity for thinking out loud. At first I interpreted these statements as defensive reactions through which agents wanted to convince me that they really did not need advice as often as I had seen them discuss problems with colleagues. The fact that the most expert agent in the department made such a statement, however, was not compatible with this interpretation. As I tried to think of a better one, the expression "thinking out loud" gave me the idea of what I called "consultation in disguise." Analyzing a problem in the presence of a fellow-expert can be considered consultation in disguise, since the non-verbal communications from listener to speaker indicate to the latter whether he is on the right track and thus serve the same function as explicit requests for confirmation of one's judgment. Talking out loud reduces the anxiety engendered by difficult problems and thereby improves the ability to solve them.

This interpretation of a special case of consultation suggested a principle for explaining consultations in general. The experience of being able to obtain advice from colleagues tends to relieve anxiety over decision-making, and the experience of being consulted by colleagues tends to increase self-confidence, and through these two processes the pattern of consultation improves the ability of agents to make correct decisions on their own, without consulting anyone.[10]

The interview responses indicated that agents enjoyed being consulted, and the explanation that one agent volunteered, "It's flattering, I suppose," gave me the idea of conceptualizing consultations as an exchange of value. By asking a colleague for help with solving problems, an agent implicitly paid his respect to the other's superior competence in exchange for the advice he received. This crucial insight became the cornerstone of the analysis of consultation, although it was crudely formulated when I first had it in the winter of 1949 and was embedded in a discussion that required much subsequent refinement.

Two important implications of this principle were perceived by me only later in the course of the intensive analysis of my data. Taking a hint from Whyte's discussion of the relationship between incurring obligations and the status hierarchy in street-corner gangs,[11] I came to realize that the process of consultation may have been the basic mechanism through which informal status became differentiated among agents. Some agents acquired superior status in the group in exchange for helping others with their work, just as the gang leader's status entailed doing more favors for the other members than they did for him. Expert knowledge was necessary but not sufficient for achieving high status among colleagues. Those agents who possessed expert knowledge but did not freely give advice to others did not achieve high standing in the group.

Another implication of the concepts of exchange is that the marginal principle might be applied to the analysis of social processes. A simple inference I derived from the marginal principle was that, as experts are increasingly often consulted, the value (utility) of the respect implicit in being once more asked for advice declines and the value of the cost in time of giving another piece of advice increases. This can explain why popular consultants, although they enjoyed giving advice, did not like it when others consulted them very frequently. It also explains why agents often consulted partners on their own level of competence rather than superior experts; by doing so with their less serious problems, they protected the supply of advice that experts were willing to give them from becoming exhausted.

This is as far as I went in the first edition. But the concept of exchange can be exploited more fully to explain the pattern of consultation and the social differentiation among agents, as I have indicated in the sections that were added to chapters vii and viii for this revised edition.

SUPERVISORY AUTHORITY

The initial design of my study did not particularly focus on supervision. My interest in the subject was stimulated by a change in supervisor in Department Y that occurred about a month after the beginning of the field work in the federal agency. The old supervisor was a blunt first sergeant; the new one was a smooth operator.

In his first departmental meeting, the new supervisor explained his operating procedures to agents. His discussion was replete with references to his identification with the agents and the benefits they would derive from the efforts he would make in their behalf. He also expressed repeatedly his disidentification with management, to which he typically referred as "the brass hats in the front office." When he announced a minor change in procedure, for example, he added: "I don't want you to think that these are my bright ideas." These deliberate attempts to curry favor aroused my curiosity.

At the beginning of the next departmental meeting two weeks later, the supervisor, apparently trying to prove himself a regular fellow, explicitly told agents that he would overlook violations of a minor office rule. He explained that the assistant district commissioner had complained to him that his supervisory report indicated no tardiness in Department Y, whereas some of its members had been seen coming late to the office. The supervisor ended with the admonition: "We have to watch this from now on. Don't come in late more than once a month. If you do, sneak up the back stairs or something." Later in the meeting, he explained how he had persuaded the district commissioner to fly to Washington to try to have put into effect a prospective promotion for most agents earlier than had been planned.

The tactics of this new supervisor suggested to me an explanation of the processes through which supervisory authority becomes established. The essential principle is that the supervisor yields to group pressure, permits subordinates to violate some rules, and exerts efforts in their behalf, because these practices make them obligated to him. Their obligations to him and dependence on him for continuing to derive such benefits constrain subordinates to defer to his wishes and comply with his requests, thus extending his influence beyond the limits of his formal authority. The social agreement that tends to develop among the group of subordinates concerning their common obligations to the supervisor specifies and legitimates the range of his influence and thereby transforms it from power into socially validated authority over them. The new supervisor, who must initially establish his effective authority, is under special pressure to find ways to obligate subordinates to himself.

Most new supervisors do not operate as did the one I observed, yet these ideas, which I assume to be applicable to supervisors in general, would undoubtedly not have come to me had I not had an opportunity to watch this man or someone like him. I think that the self-conscious and manipulative attempts of this supervisor to create feelings of obligations among his subordinates only placed in high relief processes that occur usually in more subdued and subtle form. That new supervisors whose approach was matter of fact also made special efforts to win the good will of their subordinates is suggested by the only bit of quantitative evidence I was able to collect on this topic. All three supervisors who had been transferred at this time were more favorable in their evaluation of the work of subordinates in the new department than they had been in the old department. Indeed, the exaggerated claims of the supervisor I observed of how much he did for his subordinates were merely designed to further increase their obligations to him, which fundamentally rested on the things he actually did to benefit them. This important insight was supplied by an agent shortly after the new supervisor had been assigned to Department Y. This highly competent and conscientious official criticized the new supervisor in a discussion with me not for making false claims of helping agents, as I would have suspected, but for being actually too ready to help them get by in order to assure that they would help him out in turn. As my informant put it, "It's the proposition: you scratch my back, I scratch your back."

This agent suggested the principle that underlies my conception of the establishment of supervisory authority. It is the same principle that underlies my analysis of consultation as an exchange process. But I did not make the explicit connection between the two. I did not use the concept of exchange in the analysis of supervision, although it is implicit in the discussion, and I used the concept of obligations only in passing in the analysis of consultation. Nevertheless, it may well have been that the train of thought stimulated by such comments about the new supervisor and watching him operate led to my conception of social exchange, even though I explicitly used this conception not in this analysis but in that of consultation.

Statistical Records

I did not anticipate the investigation of statistical records of performance. This was not simply an oversight. I explicitly stated in a memo in the spring of 1948 that production records, which were a basic source of data in the famous study of work groups reported by Roethlisberger and Dickson,[12] would not be available for white-collar workers in public or private bureaucracies. My ignorance on this point reflected the state of the literature. There was no analysis of the use of quantitative performance records in white-collar offices in the literature, and the mere mention of their existence was so rare that I had not yet come across it.[13]

In my first week of orientation, I learned about the detailed and varied quantitative records on operations and on the performance of every agent that were kept in a federal agency. My interest was immediately aroused, and I started scrutinizing those records and abstracting information from them. But at that time I had no idea of analyzing the significance of the quantitative evaluation procedure for operations in the bureaucracy. My interest in them was confined to employing them as a source of information about the performance of officials.

My observation in Department Y made it evident that supervisors used the production measures extensively as standards in terms of which to criticize the performance of agents and as incentives to spur them to exert more effort. The supervisor would tell agents that they must turn in more cases; he would explain to them that they found legal violations in so small a proportion of their cases that the chances were that they overlooked some of them; or he might discuss measures of more specific aspects of operations to pinpoint shortcomings in performance. When the supervisor gave agents the periodic civil service efficiency rating, he would often justify it by referring to their performance record. Despite the complexity and variety of the measures, there were three factors that were primarily emphasized. This suggested, as I commented in my field notes in November, that production records constitute a control mechanism that is quite different from the prototype of bureaucratic control and more akin to the profit principle. The agent is judged

by a few objective, quantitative criteria of effective law enforcement, just as the salesman is judged by his sales.

I did not follow this line of thought further at the time, however, because my attention was drawn to the dysfunctions of this evaluation system. Agents complained about the use of statistical criteria to put pressure on them, and several explained to me that such pressure is most likely to lead to silly practices. For example, it would motivate agents to consider as legal violations bookkeeping mistakes they found in the firms they investigated, just to improve their statistical record of successful cases. This was a beautiful illustration of the displacement of goals in a form quite different from the one Merton had examined. Bureaucratic emphasis on statistical records of operations, designed as a means to improve performance, induced officials to view making a good showing on the record as an end-in-itself.

My field work in the federal agency, then, had alerted me to the significance of statistical records in a bureaucracy. I had already thought of them as a control device, although it had as yet not occurred to me that they could serve not only as a tool in the hands of the supervisor but also as a direct mechanism of control that partly substitutes for him. My attention had been particularly drawn to some dysfunctional consequences of such a quantitative system of evaluating performance. This was the background with which I began the observation in the employment agency, where I found simpler statistical records whose specific influences could be more readily ascertained.

At the beginning of the second week of observation in Department X of the state employment agency, an interviewer spontaneously asked me: "Were you told that we are working on production like in a factory? That's what we don't like. The main emphasis is on the number of placements." I had already noticed some strange practices. The desk assigned to me, because it happened to be unoccupied, directly faced that of one of the most competitive interviewers, and I had seen her keep slips of job openings on her desk and even push them under a pad to conceal them instead of putting them into the file box where they belonged. I attributed these practices at first to a desire to save the best jobs for her own clients, but it soon became apparent that such hoarding of job slips was primarily motivated by a concern with making many placements. In the following weeks I had opportunities to observe much competitive hoarding of and vying for job slips. Interviewers told me that the statistical performance records, which had been introduced in this department a little more than a year ago, were responsible for these competitive tendencies, and some supplied many illustrations of illicit practices encouraged by competition. The monthly statistical records, which were passed around to all members of the department, indicated how many interviews each official had held and how many referrals and how many placements he had made, both in raw numbers and in percentages.

This comparatively simple performance record invited quantitative analysis, particularly since the emphasis in the department on placing clients in jobs suggested that placements would constitute a fairly valid measure of performance, that is, production. At the end of the second month, I took time out to analyze these statistical records and the accumulated job slips from which they were derived. I saw that initials on the slips showed which interviewer had taken the job order over the phone from an employer and which one or ones had referred clients to that job. Since I had learned that the best opportunity for competitive hoarding of job orders occurred when they were first taken, before other interviewers even knew about them, I realized that the proportion of referrals made by an interviewer to jobs he himself had received over the phone would furnish a fairly reliable index of competitiveness. This was a fortunate discovery, for I could not possibly have obtained a reliable measure of competitive practices, which are concealed, either through observation or through interviewing. I analyzed the data and obtained the basic findings for two sections in the department: placement productivity and competitiveness were directly related in the generally more competitive section but not in the less competitive section, and the total productivity of the more competitive section was less than that of the less competitive one.

In this case I had derived quantitative findings while I was still in the field and before I had come to understand fully the pattern to which the data pertained. I had explored various dysfunctions of performance records but had as yet no clear ideas about their functions. My talks with officials during the last month of observation furnished two important clues that directed my attention to their functions. When I asked a supervisor whether he discusses the performance records with interviewers, he answered first, "Yes," and then corrected himself, saying he used to discuss performance, but since the records had been available, he just sent them around and let them speak for themselves. Another time, the interviewer with the best performance record explained to me how each month she compared her performance on every single index with that of her colleagues, and if she was behind on any one of them, even though ahead on others, she modified her practices in an attempt to catch up. If I remember correctly, these illustrations of the direct influence exerted by performance records were what helped me to place various pertinent other data I had obtained earlier into proper perspective.

In the preliminary analysis that I carried out the following summer, I conceived of the use of statistical records for evaluating performance as a bureaucratic mechanism of control that enables managerial officials far removed from operating employees to exercise a direct influence over operations. For the statistical records designed by management furnish each official as well as his superiors with precise knowledge of how his performance compares with that of others and thereby motivate him to improve his performance in order to receive a good rating. Their direct influence on performance greatly facilitates the supervisor's job. I went on to note that statistical records were introduced by management in Department X to correct some deficiencies in placement operations, how they influenced operations, and that they promoted competition. In conclusion, I presented the correlations between productivity and competition previously mentioned, but I still was not able to offer any interpretation for these findings.

At this point, I had developed a functional analysis of statistical performance records as a bureaucratic control mechanism, but I had no systematic evidence to support my interpretive scheme, and I had found some quantitative relationships between placement productivity and competitiveness, but I had no systematic interpretation for them. Evidently, there was a need for two kinds of complementation, and I endeavored to meet this need in the subsequent full-scale analysis.

The hypothesis that the performance records in Department X served the function of directing operations to further the objectives that management specified in the records implies that the she existence of these records should improve placement productivity as well as the other phases of operations included in the records. Of course, I had no way of telling what, say, the proportion of each interviewer's referrals that resulted in placements had been before any performance records were kept. As I pored over the various statistical data on operations in the employment agency, however, I discovered that quantitative records on the placement actitivies of various departments had been kept before the records on the performance of individual interviewers had been introduced. This made it possible to check whether the productivity in Department X had, indeed, increased when the records on individual performance were introduced. The findings supported the hypothesis.

I started my interpretation of the data on competitiveness and productivity by suggesting that the fact that there was a correlation between the two in one group but not in another might account for the greater competitiveness of the former group. Competitive hoarding was apparently an effective way of improving an interviewer's placement productivity only in the first group. This required an explanation of the difference in competitiveness between the two sections. I carefully searched my field notes and found three differences in the experience of these two groups that might be responsible: the members of the less competitive group had had more employment security when the records had been introduced, they were more professionally oriented toward their work, and their supervisor placed less emphasis on the statistical records than did the supervisor of the more competitive section.

How about the intriguing paradox that the competitive group was less productive than the other, but the competitive individual in it was more productive than others? A possible explanation finally occurred to me. Group cohesion makes it possible to discourage competitive tendencies, and it reduces status anxieties, which impede effective performance. Competitive striving is an alternative way of relieving status anxieties which is open to the individual in the noncohesive group. Since both group cohesion, which involves little competition, and individual competitiveness serve to lessen status anxieties, these apparently opposite factors have the same influence, that of improving placement operations. I even found some quantitative data that indirectly support this argument.

Organization and Functional Framework

The last case history of conceptual clarification that I wish to report pertains not to a specific problem but to the over-all organization of the analysis in terms of a functional framework. First, however, I wish to say a few words about the procedure I followed in the analysis.

After completing the collection of data in the summer of 1949, I outlined the various data to be quantitatively analyzed and the different areas for qualitative analysis. This was helpful when I started the analysis half a year later. As I completed each part of the quantitative analysis—for instance, that of the interview responses I had put on McBee cards—I wrote one or a few memos about it. My field notes had been filed in folders roughly arranged by topic. I had typed two copies for cross-filing, since I had found that most observations were pertinent for more than one topic. I read the notes in each folder and put my analysis of them into one or several memos. I moved back and forth between quantitative and qualitative analysis, trying to cover related problems consecutively, and sometimes writing memos integrating several previous ones. I analyzed all data on the federal agency before I started on those on the state agency. I ended up with over three hundred memos, organized in folders by topics. After several reorganizations, these folders became the chapters of the monograph. I had too much material, however, and a good part was later discarded as less interesting or less relevant to the main theme than the rest.[14]

The functional framework was a general guide throughout, although it was by no means prominent in every part of the analysis. It may be asked on what basis I decided to trace certain unanticipated consequences of a pattern, but this question is as difficult to answer as the question how one decides to investigate some patterns and not others. The functional paradigm and its specific applications in terms of Weber's theory to bureaucratic work groups made me sensitive to particular kinds of matters in the agencies observed. Generally, I did not try to remember to look for functions and dysfunctions while in the field, although once my attention had become centered on a given pattern, I did deliberately search for as many of its consequences as I could discover. Some connections, however, occurred to me only in the course of the analysis. I realized, for example, that the pressure created by statistical records might have the latent function of discouraging discrimination against Negroes only after I had completed the quantitative analysis, which showed that there was some discrimination at the reception desk but that interviewers did not give preference to whites in their referrals.[15]

It is not easy to say what non-rational or irrational factors unawares influenced my decisions to investigate the problems I did, but one might be mentioned. As I look over the topics in the book, it seems that illicit practices aroused my interest, perhaps not only because I was explicitly concerned with informal patterns but also because the illicit stimulates curiosity. I discuss illegitimate competitive practices, illegal discrimination, prohibited consultations, and offers of bribes. The strange thing is that I am quite wary of—biased against, if you will—the study of intrinsically interesting subject matters in which a journalistic fascination with the engrossing substantive issues easily diverts the analyst from focusing on problems of theoretical significance. I chose an unglamorous bureaucracy for study, not the United Nations or the Pentagon, and my analysis ignores the sensational facets of problems in favor of those aspects I consider of theoretical significance; for example, my discussion of bribe offers is concerned simply with the enforcement of group norms, not with the sensational issue of bribery. Notwithstanding this orientation of mine and my focus in the subsequent analysis, the allurement of the illicit may have drawn my attention to certain problems.

As I approached the end of my analysis, I began to wonder how to integrate the separate elements into a whole. To be sure, the functional framework gave a common theme to my discussion of different topics, but there were as yet no apparent direct connections between them. In the fall of 1950, before I had completed the memo-writing stage, I had an idea that helped me to make these connections.

It occurred to me that the concept of emergent need supplies a crucial link between the dysfunctions of some social patterns and the functions of others, at least in a bureaucracy. For if dysfunctions lessen adjustment and functions further it, as Merton specified, one would expect that the emergent need for adjustment created by dysfunctions of one pattern often gives rise to another that functions to meet this need. This is particularly likely to happen in a bureaucracy, in which officials on various levels are held responsible for maintaining the adjustment necessary to achieve precisely formulated objectives. Since social practices have multiple consequences, one instituted to meet a given organizational need may have unanticipated dysfunctions producing new

needs, in response to which still other readjustments may occur in the social structure, and so forth.

This reconceptualization of Merton's paradigm[16] gave me a framework for organizing the analysis and interrelating its various parts. The scheme was especially well suited for the investigation of bureaucratic organizations, which are, of course, much more integrated social structures, than, say, societies, and in which formally stipulated objectives provide more precise criteria for defining functions and dysfunctions than does the general concept of adjustment. Moreover, it centered attention on the dynamic processes of change in organizations, which are always in danger of being ignored by the investigator concerned, as I was, with ascertaining the interdependence between elements in a social structure.

The explicit application of the scheme enabled me to see connections between various segments of the analysis that I had not previously noticed. It became apparent that the statistical records in the employment agency furnished a focus for interrelating a large part of my material on this agency. Performance records had been introduced to meet existing problems of operations. They served this function, but they also engendered competition, which had the dysfunctions of interfering with the work of a group of specialists and of impeding placement service in general. The two emergent needs for adjustment were met, respectively, by practices of specialists that elicited the co-operation of regular interviewers, despite their competitive tendencies, and by co-operative norms that developed in one group of interviewers to stem competitive tendencies. Another dysfunction of production records was to motivate interviewers, in the interest of making many placements, to engage in practices that led to conflicts with clients. The need to relieve the consequent tensions was met through informal discussions among colleagues, which served to restore equanimity after conflict.

The good fit of the data on the employment agency to the scheme guided my decisions on how to present my material in the monograph. I had not been sure whether to discuss the data from both agencies that pertained to a particular problem together, or whether to present first one entire case and then the other. The latter course was now clearly indicated, since otherwise I could not trace the dynamic interrelations between elements in a given bureaucratic structure. While I applied the scheme also to the data from the federal agency, not all the problems I analyzed there could be connected in terms of it. The fact that my general conceptual framework could be best illustrated with the material from the employment agency prompted me to present it first, although it had been collected and analyzed second.

Historical Role of the Case Study

As I come to the end of this chapter and pause for a moment to hold a mirror up *to* it, just as I held a mirror up *in* it to the book as a whole, I realize that I cannot tell what stimulated my decisions to organize the discussion in certain ways. Why did I, for example, present my observations of the supervisor in departmental meetings first straight and only then start to indicate what ideas they gave me, while I explained from the very beginning what various observations meant to me in the other sections of the chapter? I do not know. Was it because the section on supervisory authority is shorter? The detailed outline that I made before I started writing does not indicate this difference. The decision to organize the section on the supervisor differently occurred to me while I was writing, and I cannot tell what suggested it. If I am unable to say what stimulated such a decision a few days ago, I could not possibly recollect the specific occasion that gave rise to an insight more than a decade ago. Fortunately, my field notes contained many comments that have enabled me now in some instances to trace how certain observations suggested some new ideas, but there are also many gaps between an idea and its later refinement. By and large, such a chronicle can describe the process of the development of research ideas only in broad outline, and this is what I have tried to do, with as much precision as I could muster.

In conclusion, I wish to discuss briefly a basic limitation of the case-study method for research on bureaucratic organization as well as its merits and the historical role it has played.

It has become a sterotype to say that a major limitation of a field study of an organization is that it is restricted to impressionistic information, which is a good source of insight but which cannot serve to test hypotheses. This is wrong. While an observer in the field may choose to confine himself to impressionistic evidence, just as an interviewer may, there is nothing inherent in the field method that forces him to do so. It is possible to

quantify many observed social patterns, quantitative information can be abstracted from records, and interviews can be conducted in which responses in quantitative form are obtained. Indeed, a major merit of the field method is that it is capable of yielding more reliable systematic data than do other methods, since the availability of a variety of data-gathering techniques makes it possible to use the most reliable one. Thus, instead of asking officials how many contacts they have with their supervisor, as would be done in an interviewing survey, the frequencies of their contacts can be directly observed in the field situation.

Another important advantage of the field study is that it furnishes opportunities for shuttling back and forth between analysis and data-collecting, as my description has illustrated. Interpretations of findings do not have to remain *ad hoc* when they occur in a preliminary analysis while the investigator is still in the field, since he can collect further data to test their validity. Significant insights are gained not so much through first impressions as by confronting initial ideas with conflicting empirical information in order to refine them, and a great merit of the field study is that it facilitates such confrontation between theoretical idea and empirical evidence. But the field study is usually a case study, and therein lies its basic limitation.

I pointed out in the first chapter that a case study has the shortcoming that its findings are not representative. True enough, but much social research is based on data that are not drawn from a representative sample, the extreme example being perhaps the experiment. I now think that the major limitation of the case study is that a comparison of a number of cases is necessary not merely for testing hypotheses but even for discriminating between promising and misleading insights. A study of a single case must concentrate on contrasting the elements within it. I developed my ideas by comparing various individuals in a department, several segments of an organization, or the two organizations I had investigated. This approach can clarify the internal structure of bureaucracy, but it cannot readily discover the principles that govern how the formal organization itself develops and changes. A comparison of the managerial hierarchies in fifty organizations would reveal differences and stimulate insights that never crossed my mind, and the quantitative analysis of the interrelations between their characteristics would supply still other data to challenge the imagination of the theoretically oriented re-searcher.

I believe that we are on the threshold of a new phase in the sociological investigation of formal organizations that will see a proliferation of interest in this field.[17] In the initial phase sociological concern with bureaucratic structure found expression in theoretical analyses, and while theoretical monographs that were not based on empirical research were the dominant feature in the early stages of other branches of sociology too, this phase lasted longer in this field than in most. Not only Weber's essay and Michels' but also Merton's discussions belong to this period.[18] The next phase introduced empirical case studies. There was much research on industrial work groups, and there were some sociologically oriented studies of bureaucracies, such as Selznick's and Gouldner's.[19] The trend has been increasingly toward including quantitative data and systematic comparisons of groups in the case studies of organizations, as illustrated in the investigations of Katz and Kahn and in *Union Democracy*.[20] The earlier theories of bureaucracy served as an inspiration for the best of these case studies. At the same time, their empirical data furnished insights to refine our theoretical understanding of formal organizations. Case studies have played an important role in the advancement of knowledge in this field (in the opinion of an obviously not unbiased observer). But their very contributions to the theory of the internal structure of bureaucracy provides the foundation for now advancing further and turning to the investigation of the principles that differentiate formal structure on the basis of systematic comparisons of organizations.

This is the new phase of organizational analysis that lies in the offing. Indications of it can be found in recent research of two kinds. On the one hand, the survey method has been adapted to the study of organizations, as in some investigations of universities and colleges.[21] On the other hand, demographic sources and other published material on organizations have been used in the study of such problems as the implications of organizational size for the expansion of the administrative apparatus and for the rate of managerial succession.[22] The use of such methods by the theoretically sophisticated investigator promises to spur the development of a general theory of formal organizations and, ultimately, an even more inclusive theory of social organization. The only scientific significance of various research methods lies in the contribution that they help make to systematic theory. The case study of bureaucratic organization, in my opinion, has made its contribution and will now increasingly yield to other methods in this field.

FOOTNOTES

[1] Talcott Parsons, *The Structure of Social Action* (New York: McGraw-Hill Book Co., 1937), and Robert K. Merton, *Social Theory and Social Structure* (rev. ed.; Glencoe, Ill.: Free Press, 1957), pp. 195–206, 131–60.

[2] See, for example, Talcott Parsons and Neil Smelser, *Economy and Society* (Glencoe, Ill.: Free Press, 1956), and Merton, *op. cit.*, pp. 19–84. See also Alvin W. Gouldner's comparison of these two conceptions of functionalism in L. Gross (ed.), *Symposium on Sociological Theory* (Evanston, Ill.: Row, Peterson & Co., 1959), pp. 242–48.

[3] E. D. Chapple, with Conrad M. Arensberg, "Measuring Human Relations," Genetic Psychology Monographs, XXII (1940), 3–147.

[4] William F. Whyte, *Street Corner Society* (rev. ed.; Chicago: University of Chicago Press, 1955), pp. 14–25.

[5] This is a routine task but not an easy one. Spending most of a working day watching and recording all social contacts of a group of twenty leaves one quite exhausted.

[6] To be sure, everyone is marginal in one respect or other. My impressionistic observation that early respondents tend to be marginal requires testing with systematic evidence.

[7] I had this experience in both agencies.

[8] Particularly in 1948, when Wallace was the presidential candidate of the Progressive party.

[9] Whyte, *op. cit.*, p. 300.

[10] I would have liked to obtain empirical evidence to confirm this conclusion, but only an experiment or a panel study could furnish the data necessary for this purpose. Although I do have data to show, for instance, that the most often consulted agents were the most expert decision-makers, this was, of course, largely due to the fact that experts were the most attractive consultants (mutual partnerships notwithstanding). Whether it was also partly due to the fact that being often consulted had improved their decision-making ability, as hypothesized, could be ascertained only by observing changes in their competence through time.

[11] William F. Whyte, *Street Corner Society* (rev. ed.; Chicago: University of Chicago Press, 1955), pp. 256–58.

[12] F. J. Roethlisberger and William J. Dickson, *Management and the Worker* (Cambridge, Mass.: Harvard University Press, 1939).

[13] One of the very rare references to it, as I discovered after I had completed the field work, is in Marshall E. Dimock, *The Executive in Action* (New York: Harper & Bros., 1945), pp. 128, 143–47.

[14]For example, two chapters on careers.

[15]It will be remembered that Harry Cohen's replication indicates that the effect of production records on equitable treatment of clients is contingent on the power and market structure in which the bureaucracy operates.

[16]Robert K. Merton, *Social Theory and Social Structure* (rev. ed.; Glencoe, Ill.: Free Press, 1957), pp. 50–54.

[17]A cursory examination of the contents of the two major sociological journals (*American Sociological Review* and *American Journal of Sociology*) indicates that the proportion of articles dealing with formal organizations of some kind has roughly doubled between 1940 and 1960, from less than 6 to 11 per cent.

[18]Max Weber, *Essays in Sociology* (New York: Oxford University Press, 1946), pp. 196–244; Robert Michels, *Political Parties* (Glencoe, Ill.: Free Press, 1949); and Merton, *op. cit.*, pp. 195–224.

[19]Philip Selznick, *TVA and the Grass Roots* (Berkeley: University of California Press, 1949), and Alvin W. Gouldner, *Patterns of Industrial Bureaucracy* (Glencoe, Ill.: Free Press, 1954).

[20]Daniel Katz and Robert L. Kahn, "Some Recent Findings in Human Relations Research in Industry," in G. E. Swanson *et al.* (eds.), *Readings in Social Psychology* (rev. ed.; New York: Henry Holt & Co., 1952), pp. 650–65, and Seymour M. Lipset *et al., Union Democracy* (Glencoe, Ill.: Free Press, 1956). See also Stanley E. Seashore, *Group Cohesiveness in the Industrial Work Group* (Ann Arbor: Institute for Social Research, University of Michigan, 1954).

[21]See, for example, Paul F. Lazarsfeld and Wagner Thielens, Jr., *The Academic Mind* (Glencoe, Ill.: Free Press, 1958), and James A. Davis *et al., Stipends and Spouses* (Chicago: University of Chicago Press, 1962).

[22]See, for example, Seymour Melman, "The Rise of Administrative Overhead in the Manufacturing Industries of the United States, 1899–1947," *Oxford Economic Papers*, III (1951), 62–112; Theodore R. Anderson and Seymour Warkov, "Organizational Size and Functional Complexity," *American Sociological Review*, XXVI (1961), 23–28; and Oscar Grusky, "Corporate Size, Bureaucratization, and Managerial Succession," *American Journal of Sociology*, LXVII (1961), 261–69.

Social Theory in Field Research

by Joseph Bensman and Arthur Vidich

Here is more evidence from field researchers of the dynamic element of the process. This is seen in the way in which the authors characterize the adaptation from extant theory and the application to the problem being studied. Thus, the investigator draws what is useful from the work of others, tries it, tests it, and if he finds it useful, employs it, but if not, sets it aside. Where extant theory is viable, it leads to a reformulation of the research problem in which the original theories may or may not stand up. When they do not, the theories to explain the phenomena are revoked and other classes of theory are constructed. The sense of this piece is the openness of research and the way in which mature scholars resist being committed to one or another school or type of methodology, and instead are committed to experiment and adaptation. Perhaps the telling phrase is the one which suggests that the researcher can fail and that research can therefore be a relatively risky intellectual pursuit. The reader will note that the research from which these notes are drawn is the subject of the debate in the later section on the Environment of Research.

In the last fifteen years a central concern of both sociology and anthropology has been the relationship between theory and research. One of the turning points in this discussion was Merton's comment on the position of sociological theory,[1] in which he calls for more attention to "theories of the middle range"—"theories intermediate to the minor working hypotheses evolved in abundance during the day-by-day routines of research, and the all-inclusive speculations comprising a master conceptual scheme from which it is hoped to derive a very large number of empirically observed uniformities of social behavior."[2] Other studies addressed to issues in the relationship between theory and research are represented in the work of Mills, Blumer, Becker, Abel, A. K. Davis, Becker and Boskoff, Znaniecki, Borgatta and Meyer, Coser and Rosenberg, and Goode and Hatt, to mention only a few. All these authors have criticized the hiatus between low-level theory dealing with factually exact minutiae and the world-sweeping generalizations of theorists who appear to fail to appreciate the time-consuming task of systematically gathering and interpreting data. In addition, the older classical theorists have been explicitly criticized for being more interested in probing specific problems than in developing theoretical systems, independent of specific cases. This has led to a movement to construct a general theory that can be independent of specific data, but for the most part the authors mentioned have joined the issue on the disparity between generalized theory and low-level theory.

Two methods have been developed to provide a link between empirical observations and higher theory:

1. Closed logical-deductive models which presuppose that *co-ordinates* can be established which will make possible linkages between the models and the open systems of the empirical world.[3] When the general dimensions of elements or units of systems have been specified, the investigator can develop complex models of systems based on the various combinations and relationships of the elements in them. It may be a personality system, a terminological system, a social system, a cultural system, a kinship system, a motivational system, etc. A fundamental method in the construction of such systems is the comparison of specific empirically open systems with the abstract, common elements necessary to any social system.

2. The "codification of theoretical perspectives,"[4] in which the researcher-theorist attempts to state systematically the relationship of existing theories to each other. Specific and discrete theories which have been used in the past on specific problems are examined, and the investigator attempts to discover the fundamental dimensions, implicit and explicit, of each, after which he compares them.[5] In making comparisons, the codifier discovers overlapping areas, convergences, different levels of generality and generalization, and different vectors of observation and perspective. He constructs paradigms and models of

---

SOURCE: Joseph Bensman and Arthur Vidich, "Social Theory in Field Research," *American Journal of Sociology*, 65 (May, 1960), pp. 577–584. Reprinted from *American Journal of Sociology* by permission of The University of Chicago Press. Copyright 1960 by the University of Chicago Press.

the various theories so as to offer a complete theoretical point of view which points to the data necessary to answer theoretical problems. The net product
is a heuristic model which serves as a basis for future
research.

Both these approaches to theory have been
offered as corrections of the unsystematic uses to
which theory has been put in the past. It is useful, however, to inquire what the older "unsystematic" and "specific" theory purports to do and
how it focuses on the relationship between theory
and research. Blumer has indicated that adherence
to unsystematic theories sensitizes the theorist
and the researcher who is familiar with a wide
range of theories to a plurality of possibilities—to
wide ranges of data.[6] Shils has specifically shown
how the older, unsystematic theorists have helped
him to locate and define one of the major problem
areas in modern society, and he provides a vivid
description of their part in the evolution of his
own research and his perspective on society.[7]
Blumer and Shils both show that the researcher-
theorist can probe and check his data against a
number of perspectives in theory and then discern
the theoretical possibilities of them.[8] The researcher discovers novel and previously unspeci-
fied relationships in his data. Unsystematic
theory, in this way, can lead to creative work.

To explore systematically one way in which unsystematic theories have been used, we will confine ourselves to specific research problems in
which we have recently been engaged:[9] How is a
small rural community related to the large-scale
mass society? How does the mass society affect
the public and inner life of the individuals of the
community? How does the mass society affect the
social structure of the town, particularly its class
structure and the character of its institutional
arrangements? What is the response of the small
town institutionally and individually, to the institutions and agencies of the mass society that affect
it?

EVOCATION OF THEORY FROM OBSERVATION

In response to the research organization's inquiry into possible sources of creativity among
members of the community,[10] the observer's
attention was directed to the locally owned and
operated telephone company, whose management
was considering a program of expansion. A newspaper's announcement of a proposed plan to install
a new telephone system, with underground cables,

dial phones, and an automatic central switchboard,
offered an example of creative activity in community life which seemed ideal for investigation.

It was discovered that the force behind the
drive for expansion was not the local operator but
the state telephone company. In fact, the elderly
local owner and policymaker would have preferred
to keep the installation as it was, since he had
neither the stamina nor the capital to undertake
the expansion. However, he could not resist the
expansion program because he was dependent on
the state company.

The local system was linked to the state system,
through connecting trunks and long-distance lines,
to all neighboring towns and the state and the nation at large. In addition, the local company's installations and finances bound it closely to the
state company, which provided it with an auditing
service, engineering consultants, advertising lay-
outs, etc. The responsibilities of the local company were for maintenance, collections, and
ownership. The state company was interested in
promoting the expansion program because it
found the local installation cumbersome and awkward; incoming calls could not be handled easily
or automatically, and much attention from outside specialists was required. All these irritants
could be removed, and service could be improved,
by modernization.

The state company did not want to buy the local
company. It appeared that it wanted to retain this
and other independents as "competing independent companies." The local owner could not
close down, though he might have liked to, because the state Public Service Commission would
not permit termination of a public service. Since
the company existed and since some improvements had to be made, the local company announced and undertook the expansion program.
Almost nothing about the expansion, however,
could be attributed to local action.

When the various external influences in the local
"spontaneous" action were noticed, the attention
of the authors was directed to an entirely different
range of problems from those which led to the
original inquiry. Not only were state agencies,
other bureaucracies, and a whole range of experts
decisive in the case of the telephone company but
similar connections and influences were at work in
politics, education, religion, and the cultural life of
the community. Local educational policy, religious affairs, public policy and politics—all were
intimately related to policy-determining groups far
removed from the town. The question then was:

How is it possible to comprehend and interpret the relationships between local and external action in a way that is true to the basic facts and elements observed? We turned our attention to various unsystematic and unsystematized theories developed in the past to handle similar data and problems: those of Redfield, Weber, Tönnies, Veblen, Merton, Lynd, Warner, Mills, Sapir, and Tumin. In each case we applied their perspectives to our data. In effect, we asked: "What in their theories would permit us to comprehend our data?"

In the case of each theory which our initial finding made salient, we had a directive for data which could be elicited by further field research. Thus, for example, Veblen's study of the country town makes the point that the political conservatism of rural life rests in the rural village because economically it dominates the surrounding agricultural area. We did not find this to correspond with our observations and could only account for the difference by noting that Veblen wrote in a day when rural banks were strong and apparently autonomous agencies. While many things in Veblen's study of the country town rang true, it did not provide us with a basis for further investigation of our particular problem. On the other hand, Sapir's analysis of spurious culture, which emphasizes the role of cultural imports, directed us to view all phases of the cultural life of the community as a successive series of imports made at different times since 1890. In short, existing theory gave our field work a focus, and we could conduct it along the lines thereby suggested.

Theories were helpful in opening our eyes to specific facts about our problem. For example, Sapir called our attention to the agencies of cultural penetration; Mills and Selznick, to the agencies of institutional penetration and organizational co-optation. In some instances a theorist's minor point became a central point to us, while his central point seemed irrelevant. In no case did we view any theory as offering us a solution to our problem, nor did we use any one theory exclusively to direct our observations. Research, for us, did not demonstrate, document, or annotate theory, but rather it exhausted the theories that came to our attention. Sapir's theory of the genuine culture was exhausted when nothing was found in the cultural life of the community that was indigenous to it—when everything cultural could be traced to an external source. In our procedure a theory was exhausted if and when it either yielded little follow-up data or if the data suggested by the theory were not forthcoming.

THE EXHAUSTING AND "DESTRUCTION" OF THEORIES

If a theoretical perspective does not yield the expected data, the question to be raised is: What facts and what theories are necessary to account for the gaps left by the specific theory? When one set of theories does not exhaust the potentialities of the data, other sets can be employed to point to and to explain the facts which remain unexplained. Thus for any initial statement of the field problem a whole series of theories may be successively applied, each yielding different orders of data and each perhaps being limited by the special perspectives and dimensions on which it is predicated.[11]

The relationships between theories and levels, orders and vectors of analysis, are not resolved a priori but rather on the basis of the contribution of each perspective to the solution of the research problem. The order achieved (if the research is successful) is not the logical order of concepts but the order of uniformities in the social structure of the community. The value of these unsystematic theories is not in their formal order but in their heuristic usefulness.

Each of the theories provides a set of questions asked of the data, and the data lead to the continuous destruction of unproductive theories whenever the theories no longer yield new data or fail to solve the original problem. The reverse is also true: the theory may lead to the evocation of new data by focusing observation and its assessment.

THE SUBSTITUTION OF THEORIES

However, it has been our experience that, when new data are evoked by a theory, they lead quite frequently to the reformulation of the research problem, sometimes in a way that leaves the original theories (in this case dealing with penetration external influences, etc.) inadequate. This is the case in which the data evoked by the observation forces such a radical shift in perspective that new theories must be called forth. For example, in tracing both the impact of the mass society on the community and the response of the community to agencies of the mass society, it was relatively easy to discover that different social and economic classes responded in different ways. Farmers as a class, for example, were the only group directly protected and aided by federal legislation, but not all farmers responded similarly to the benefits it brought them. A farmer's reaction to federal legislation had an important effect on his local class

position. Small businessmen had lost their monopoly of the local market to the large urban chains,
and they responded to the loss in a psychologically
and economically defensive manner. The connections of the professional class to the outside world
were almost exclusively cultural, but these enhanced their prestige in the local community, etc.
In examining the problem of penetration, we
could not look at the town as a unified whole but
had to examine how each class was related to the
outside world.

As a result of these observations it was necessary
to recast our problem as a consideration of class.
Class had to be considered, however, in terms not
only of the specific problem of mass society but
also of the general theories of class. In posing our
problem as a class problem, again a whole range of
new theories was evoked, including those of Warner,
Lynd, Kaufman, Hollingshead, Weber, and Marx.
However, again, theories of class were not considered *sui generis* but rather as pragmatic devices which would bring us to a solution to the
original problem; that is, the alternative data which
would be selected by different theories were considered initially only in terms necessary to solve the
problem of the relationship of the local class
structure to the mass society, using as many dimensions as theory would allow. The new focus
meant making an examination of all relevant class
data.

When the data had been re-examined and additional research had been conducted on class,
theory was used in an additional way. The conception of the class structure of the community
which we had developed in our research was criticized in the light of the class theories with which
we were working.

THEORIES IN THE CRITICISM
OF FIELD WORK

The procedure we followed was to take various
theories of class and to postulate them as hypoth-
etically fruitful and, then, to ask what would the
hypothetical yield of each be toward exhausting
the data then locally available. Some data that
should have been elicited by certain of the theories
were not present in the initial field work. The
question was then raised: Is this a deficiency of the
theory or of the field work? It was necessary to
reanalyze the data already gathered and to make
additional observations in order to make sure the
fault was not the researcher's in these theoretical
respects. This does not mean that all theories were
equally productive or, in fact, productive at all.

We found that the prestige associations reported
in Warner's work were not to be found in the
initial analysis of our data. We postulated Warner
as a critic of our analysis and then found that we
had to ask ourselves why our analysis had not revealed socially exclusive local groups based on
prestige. However, while Warner's system forced
us to find groups of the type he describes, the class
system we had discovered and described did not
appear in most other respects to fit his model.[12]
This does not prove or disprove the validity of
Warner's work, which might in other communities
be more meaningful; however, it did not cover the
whole range of our data. In the same way, the
theories of Hollingshead yielded valuable data, but
again the phenomena were not entirely the same.

Theories of class led to another refocusing of
the problem, this time in the area of politics.[13] It
became apparent that members of different classes
played different roles in local political life.
Accordingly, we considered the political theories
of Weber, Centers, Marx, V. O. Key, Mosca, Neumann, Michel, and Mills.

Each successive application of theory, derived in
each instance from stimulation given by the
immediately preceding investigation, caused us to
take into account new orders of data which in
turn forced us to select different types of theory.
Thus the method compelled us to consider not
only politics but the relationship between political
and non-political leadership, between the public
ideology of the town and the private lives of its
members, the role of religion in local life, and
modes of personal adjustment to the social system. Our original starting point turned out to be
merely a starting point for an examination of the
major institutional and psychological problems of
the community.

Thus successive modifications of our problem
followed from the interplay of new data and new
points of view. Only a portion of this process took
place during the field phase; some was a result of
the re-examination of field records, and some
occurred during the writing-up of the data.

Let us summarize the functions that unsystematic theory can serve and the conditions under
which it can be employed in research:

1. The specification of possible areas of field work as
   the researcher leans upon the educated perspective
   of his predecessors to guide him to important and
   significant areas of investigation.
2. The criticism of field work while doing it. Alternative perspectives in theory yield alternative perspectives in field observation.
3. The discovery of the limitations of one's original

statement of the problem; the continuous discovery of new data compels new formulations of the problem.

4. The discovery of the limitations of one's own theory by its continuous confrontation with empirical observation.
5. The discovery of new dimensions of the problem.
6. The reconstruction of one's problem, field work, and past theory into a further limited and discrete theory to handle the problem. Such a theory is not final or general but adequate only to the specific problem in the specific field. However, this type of theoretical solution, in turn, provides raw materials for other research posing new problems, and these new problems as they are studied by other investigators in other settings contribute to the continuous cultivation of new theories.

THE RELATIONSHIP BETWEEN HEURISTIC AND SYSTEMATIC THEORY

Heuristic theory as outlined above is operative at every level of research: the statement of the problem, the gathering of the field data, the analysis and evaluation of the findings, and the analyzing and reporting of the results. However, heuristic theory is highly limited in that it does not produce generalized findings valid beyond the statement of the specific original problem. The generalization of the findings after observation, analysis, and interpretation must depend on other types of theory. Theorists of systematic theory have assumed the function of generalization.

As an enterprise, systematic theory can integrate new research findings with established theory and findings, thus accomplishing a continuous evaluation and assessment of research and heuristic theory. However, this can be accomplished only if general systematic theory pays attention to the differences in the problems, in the levels of heuristic theories, and in the field situations in which the problem and the theory are specified. The attempt to seek the common features of all social systems or of a hypothetical "the social system" overlooks the specific validity and the specific character of most heuristic theory and all research. If systematic theory is at all possible as an aid to scientific research, it must reach out and establish its empirical co-ordinates to the empirical world. It can do this only if it takes into account the limited and specific character of heuristic theory.

THE CODIFICATION OF THEORY AND THE HEURISTIC APPROACH TO THEORY

There is relatively little difference between the theoretical enterprise that codifies theoretical perspectives and heuristic theory as described above. The major difference—and it is very important—is in the timing of the integration of the theoretical perspectives brought up for consideration. Codification of theory attempts to bring together and relate the various theoretical dimensions that can be brought to bear on a problem by the rigorous logical analysis of received theory in terms of the theories themselves. All these theories are considered in one analytical operation; ideally, the composite perspective derived from them is applied as a unit to a field situation.

Contrary to codified theory, heuristic theory allows past theory to remain as a residue of latent possibilities which the research worker can bring to bear on his specific field problem. He cannot know in advance exactly what orders of theory are relevant to his problem until he discovers its nature in the field and what resistances to his preconceptions emerge as his field work progresses. Totally new perspectives emerge as he discovers these resistances. New perspectives, new levels, new orders, and new dimensions of data become salient, regardless of what level of codification he has considered in the past; in the field, in the encounter with the world, the press of the data is manifold, continuous, and not easily amenable to preconceived selection. Moreover, the level of detail of data, the precision of analysis, and the concepts employed are functions of the merging perspectives of the field worker in the field. It can thus happen that whole areas, codified in the past, may prove worthless for coping with a specific problem, though the past codifications may be valuable for other problems. However, there is no level of codification sufficiently precise to be applicable when empirical data become the focus of attention.

To exhibit all possible dimensions of a problem in advance, codification would have to be extremely complex, cumbersome, and unworkable (e.g., in one problem the authors reached 256 formal logical possibilities of the data without ever reaching its substantive level, and, because of the complexity, one is, in effect, forced to work with heuristic concepts rather than with the full range of logically deducible possibilities. One deals with five or six major cells in a logical matrix and ignores a host of others which, for purposes of social science, are conceived of as logical but irrelevant. As a result, the researcher-theorist must continuously refine his theoretical analysis in terms of his problem and data.

LIMITATIONS OF HEURISTIC THEORY

Heuristic theory, as subjected to the rigors of specific substantive problems, has a number of limitations:

1. It cannot work if the research worker on a priori grounds is unwilling to entertain the possibility of using or seriously considering all or a variety of the available theories. Commitment to one school or theory means, in most instances, commitment to selected levels of data. These forms of commitment prevent the research worker from criticizing his findings from alternative points of view and may blind him to the exhausting of his own favored theoretical approach. In the heuristic approach there is no guaranty that such standards of open-mindedness will prevail or that self-criticism can and will be made. Science, then—particularly social science—must depend not only on self-criticism but on the criticism made by others, willingness to accept which then becomes the basis of social science.

2. The *ad hoc* rotation of theoretical perspectives does not in itself guarantee the exhaustion of the empirical data if it is only ritual eclecticism. The only purpose in considering many perspectives is to solve or to redefine the problem. The listing of the alternative possibilities of different theories is not a solution, since listings are not a structural relationship of data. The end objective of the procedure is not only to find what data are relevant to the problem but also to determine how they are functionally related. The only point that needs emphasis is that the functional relationships are products of the research-and not of a priori theorizing.

3. These procedures of exhaustion and rotation of perspectives are dependent on the contingencies of field work, the investigator's background, and his sensitivity to his data; hence there is no guaranty that their use will assure success. There is no immutable deductive procedure which automatically guarantees the production of new concepts,

theories, or findings. The research worker must face the possibility of failure in the knowledge that it may be due to the way in which he handled the problem.[14] Scientific inquiry means living an intellectually dangerous existence.

4. The method outlined here is amenable to not all types of research. Experimental studies assume that causes can be postulated in advance and that the problem in research is simply one of determining their conditions and efficiency. Large-scale surveys frequently telescope all the procedures of research described above into a single operation which does not and cannot allow for the continuous modification, substitution, and refinement of hypotheses and problems on the basis of field experience. The survey worker, in the absence of these intermediate checks on his thinking, may be forced to pose all at the same time a wide range of theoretically possible alternatives resulting from a priori formulations and hunches, hoping that one or more of his theoretical dimensions will be productive after the field work is done and analysis is completed. He frequently finds that a limited number of areas are highly productive, but, since in the beginning he had to consider on a priori grounds a variety of alternative areas, time and funds limit the depth to which he can analyze those variables which finally proved productive. This is the familiar phenomena of knowing better how to make a survey after it is done than at the beginning.

It is apparent from this discussion that in no case can the research worker feel that he has fully solved his problem. He must recognize that new levels of theory and new theories of which he may not have been aware at the time might have required new levels of data and further exhaustion of theory. At best, he can feel that he has advanced his problem along an infinite path so that his work need not be repeated. One must recognize that there is no final accumulation of knowledge and no final solution, in the usual meaning of these terms.[15]

FOOTNOTES

[1] Robert K. Merton, "The Position of Sociological Theory—Discussion," *American Sociological Review,* XIII (1949), 164–68, republished in substantially the same form in Robert K. Merton, *Social Theory and Social Structure* (rev. ed.; Glencoe, Ill.: Free Press, 1958), pp. 4–10.

[2] *Social Theory and Social Structure,* pp. 5–6.

[3] Edward Shils has described this process in a similar way as follows: "The role of general theory consists of a general systematic scrutiny of particular facts: then the theory is either disconfirmed by the facts and is replaced by one more adequate to them, or the hypothesis and corresponding theory are confirmed and the problem is settled" ("Primordial, Personal, Sacred, and Civil Ties: Some Particular Observations on the Relationships of Sociological Research and Theory," *British Journal of Sociology,* VIII, No. 2 [June, 1957], 130–45).

[4] Merton, *Social Theory and Social Structure*, p. 12. Also see James Olds, *The Growth and Structure of Motives* (Glencoe, Ill.: Free Press, 1956), pp. 21–22, on "the limited theory viewpoint" in which the position of H. G. Birch and M. E. Bitterman (in "Sensory Integration and Cognitive Theory," *Psychological Review*, LVIII [1951], 355–61) is used as an illustration.

[5] Best exemplified by Robin M. Williams, Jr., *The Reduction of Intergroup Tensions: A Survey of Research Problems of Ethnic, Racial, and Religious Group Relations* (Social Science Research Council Bull. 57 [New York: Social Science Research Council, 1947], esp. chap. iii. Similar studies are Merton, "The Sociology of Knowledge," in *Social Theory and Social Structure*, pp. 217–45; R. Sarbin, "Role Theory," in Gardner Lindzey (ed.), *Handbook of Social Psychology* (Cambridge, Mass.: Addison-Wesley Press, 1954), pp. 223–58.

[6] Herbert Blumer, "What Is Wrong with Social Theory?" *American Sociological Review*, XIX (1954), 3–10.

[7] Shils, *op. cit.*

[8] Shils's article (*ibid.*) is a case history of this procedure. He has shown how the interplay between his research experience and received theory has led him to discard, revamp, and reinterpret the different theorists with whom he has been concerned, accordingly as his experience with different sets of data has called forth and brought into perspective different elements and segments of the theorists with whom he has been concerned—mainly Tönnies, Cooley, Mayo, Schmalenbach, Lenin, Weber, Parsons and Sorel.

[9] The analysis of these problems is reported in the authors' *Small Town in Mass Society: Class, Power and Religion in a Rural Community* (Princeton, N.J.: Princeton University Press, 1958).

[10] Cornell Studies in Social Growth, sponsored by the Department of Child Development and Family Relationships, New York State College of Home Economics, Cornell University, with the aid of funds from the National Institute of Mental Health, the United States Public Health Service, and the Social Science Research Council. The present study, as well as the original one upon which this one draws, is an independent by-product of Cornell studies and does not represent the authorized viewpoint of the project.

[11] Similarly Robert Redfield, in *The Little Community* (Chicago: University of Chicago Press, 1955), takes five different societies, each studied from a different perspective, and demonstrates how the perspective limits the data.

[12] The ladies' book clubs, card-playing groups, men's clubs and associations, and "old American" families resemble groups found by Warner, but other classes in our study did not; e.g., "Old American" families, or what we called the "Old Aristocracy," occupied symbolically important positions but could not be called an "upper-upper" class.

[13] In our first work politics received only scant attention; only the role of the lawyer as an intermediary between local government and state agencies had been examined by us (Bensman and Vidich, *op. cit.*, chap. iv).

[14] John Dewey, *The Quest for Certainty: A Study of the Relation of Knowledge and Action* (New York: Minton, Balch & Co., 1929).

[15] The following studies point to a similar conclusion: Max Weber, "Science as a Vocation," in *Essays from Max Weber*, trans. and ed. H. H. Gerth and C. Wright Mills (New York: Oxford University Press, 1946), pp. 129–56; Homer G. Barnett, "Comment to Acculturation: An Exploratory Formulation," *American Anthropologist*, LVIII, No. 6 (December, 1954), 1000–1002; Robert Redfield, "The Art of Social Science," *American Journal of Sociology*, LIX, No. 3 (November, 1948), 181–90; Herbert Blumer, *An Appraisal of Thomas and Znaniecki's "The Polish Peasant in Europe and America"* (New York: Social Science Research Council, 1939); Dewey, *op. cit.*; Allen H. Barton and Paul F. Lazarsfeld, "Some Functions of Qualitative Analysis in Social Research," *Sociologica*, I (1955), 321–61; Maurice R. Stein, *The Eclipse of Community: An Interpretation of American Community Studies* (Princeton, N.J.: Princeton University Press, 1960); Barrington Moore, Jr., "The Strategy of Social Science," in his *Political Power and Social Theory* (Cambridge, Mass.: Harvard University Press, 1958), pp. 111–59; and C. Wright Mills, *The Sociological Imagination* (New York: Oxford University Press, 1959).

A Field Experience in Retrospect[1]

by Elliot Liebow

Here is participant observation in action. A unique experience is recorded, one which appears relevant, not only as to its insight into method, but as it focuses upon a cultural element so long outside the range of the library's concern. Liebow's account and his explanation of the difference which color makes offers insight that is meaningful in other contexts. As a piece of sociological evidence relating to a corner of society which has not been effectively considered, understood, or studied, this piece clearly relates to the scene in librarianship today and to a perspective very much needed in its research.

Robert read the book slowly and with feeling, pausing only occasionally to take a swig of gin and chase it quickly with some beer. Lonny listened quietly and watched with blinking eyes as Robert changed his voice for each of the characters, assuming a falsetto for Snow White. But my own interest started to wander, probably because I had already read the book and seen the movie.

Suddenly Robert raised his voice and startled me back into attention. I looked at Lonny—placid, eye-blinking Lonny—and at Ronald—a handkerchief around his head and a gold earring stuck in his left ear making him look like a story-book pirate—and wondered what the hell I was doing there with these two guys, drinking gin and beer and listening to *Snow White and the Seven Dwarfs.*

I thought back to the events leading up to this situation. From this perspective, everything looked normal and reasonable. I retrieved my can of beer, sat back and listened to the rest of the story. Robert gave it a damn fine reading.

[Field Note, April 1962]

BACKGROUND

When I came to the Child Rearing Study Project on January 1, 1962, this NIMH-supported study of "Child Rearing Practices Among Low Income Families in the District of Columbia" was well into its third year. My job was to collect field material on low-income adult males to complement the data already secured through family interviews.

From the very beginning I felt comfortable with the prospect of working with lower-class Negroes. I was born and raised in Washington, D.C. My father and mother were both Jewish immigrants from Eastern Europe—my mother from Latvia, my father from Russia. My father was a grocer and we lived in rooms above or behind the various stores which he operated. All were in predominantly Negro neighborhoods.

School and playground were white, but all of our customers and most of the neighbors were Negroes. Among them and their children I had many acquaintances, several playmates and a few friends. The color line, retraced daily at school and playground and home, was always there; but so were my day-by-day contacts with Negro men, women and children in the store, on the street, and occasionally in their houses; watching a crap game in Sam's place; witnessing the Devil being exorcised from a woman writhing on the floor of a storefront church from my seat in the back row; shooting crap for pennies in a dark hallway; sitting with Benton on the curb, poking aimlessly at debris, waiting for something interesting to happen. It was not until I was seventeen and enlisted in the Marine Corps that I began to move in an almost exclusively white world.

PREPARING FOR THE FIELD

I spent the first week in familiarizing myself with the project and with the work that had already been done. I had several informal discussions with Dr. Hylan Lewis, the director of the project, and gradually gained a feeling for the kind of material that was wanted. Importantly, he laid down no hard-and-fast ground rules on the assumption that the job could best be done if I were free to feel my way around for a few weeks and discover for myself the techniques that were most congenial to me. His one prescription was that the work be securely anchored in the purposes of the

SOURCE: From *Tally's Corner: A Study of Negro Streetcorner Men* by Elliot Liebow, by permission of Little, Brown and Co. Copyright © 1967 by Little, Brown & Company (Inc.). The original publication bore the following note: "This chapter, in slightly different form, was originally written for the Child Rearing Study of the Health and Welfare Council of the National Capital Area."

project, remembering, too, that "Everything is grist for our mill." As I think back on this now, I see a clear connection between his instructions and his fondness for the quotation, "The scientific method is doing one's darndest with his brains, no holds barred."

Having partially digested the project literature, I told the director that I was ready to get started. He suggested a neighborhood that might be "a good place to get your feet wet." His instructions were: "Go out there and make like an anthropologist."

"Out there" was not at all like the Indian village of Winisk on Hudson Bay in which I had done field work. I was not at all sure how one "makes like an anthropologist" in this kind of "out there." Somewhat wistfully, perhaps, I thought how much neater things would be if anthropologists, as they had done in the early thirties, limited themselves to the study of "wholes," a tribe, a village, or some other social unit with distinct boundaries and small enough to be encompassed in its entirety by direct observation.

When I thought about just what I was going to do, I kept in mind the job Richard Slobodin had done for the Child Rearing Study in the summer of 1960.[1] As part of the effort to get at community as well as family influences in child rearing, the director had assigned Slobodin to "make like an anthropologist" in a one-block enclave in northwest Washington. It seemed to me that I could use his work as a model and, in the course of a year, produce several such studies, each covering a strategic part of the world of the low-income male. I thought of doing a neighborhood study, then moving on say, to a construction laborers' union, then a bootleg joint, and perhaps rounding these out with a series of genealogies and life histories. I was going to give myself about a month or so of poking around town, getting the feel of things, before committing myself to any firm plan of action.

IN THE FIELD

In taking up the director's suggestion that this would be "a good place to get your feet wet," I went in so deep that I was completely submerged and my plan to do three or four separate studies, each with its own neat, clean boundaries, dropped forever out of sight. My initial excursions into the street—to poke around, get the feel of things, and to lay out the lines of my field work—seldom carried me more than a block or two from the corner where I started. From the very first weeks or even days, I found myself in the middle of things; the principle lines of my field work were laid out, almost without my being aware of it. For the next year or so, and intermittently thereafter, my base of operations was the corner Carryout across the street from my starting point.

The first time out, I had gone less than one short block when I noticed a commotion up the street. A man—Detective Wesley, I learned later—was dragging a kicking, screaming woman to a police call box. A small crowd had gathered on each of the four corners to watch. I approached two men and asked what the woman had done. Both were uncertain. The younger of the two said that he had heard two stories and proceeded to tell me both of them, concluding with the observation that he had known Detective Wesley for six or seven years and that he was "nobody to fool with."

I said that sometimes being a cop seems to do something to a man. This led to a discussion of policemen and each of us contributed personal experiences or anecdotes on the subject. After ten or fifteen minutes of this, the older man said goodbye and walked off. The younger man stayed on. Across the street from where we were standing was the Downtown Cafe. I suggested that we go in and have some coffee and he agreed. As we walked across the street he asked if I was a policeman. I told him no and explained that I was working on a study of family life in the city. There was no more discussion about who I was or why I was there. We sat at the bar for several hours talking over coffee.

I had not accomplished what I set out to do, but this was only the first day. And, anyway, when I wrote up this experience that evening, I felt that it presented a fairly good picture of this young man and that most of the material was to the point. Tomorrow, I decided, I would go back to my original plan—nothing had been lost.

But tomorrow never came. At nine the next morning, I headed down the same street. Four men were standing in a group in front of the Carry-out.

Three were winos, in their forties—all marked with old scars on face and neck, dressed shabbily, but sober. The fourth was a man of thirty-two or thirty-three, who looked as if he had just stepped out of a slick magazine advertisement. . . . One of the winos had a month-old puppy stuck in the front of his overcoat. Only the dog's head was exposed.

The group approached me and one of the older men said, "Isn't he a nice puppy?" I said yes, and began patting the dog. "He just bought him," one man said. "I wanted the female, too, to breed them," said the man holding the dog, "but that woman, she sold the female to her friend."

The puppy was whining. "Maybe it's hungry," said the older man, "let's get him some hamburger." "No man, he'll get worms from that stuff," said one of the others. I suggested milk and we all went into the Carry-out. I asked the waitress for a half pint of milk. The man asked for a saucer. "You can't feed him here," the waitress said, "the Health Department would close us up." She gave us a paper plate and the milk (paid for by me). We took the dog into a hallway next door. Everyone was pleased at how eagerly the puppy drank.

A man who had been in the Carry-out joined us in the hallway. "That's a shepherd, isn't he? Just what I want for my little boy." I said, "I wish I could get one for my little girl, but she's allergic to all animals, dust, and lots of things." "It's better that way," said one of the winos. "She'll outgrow it. But man, if you don't have that until you're full grown—man, look out." "Yes, that's right," the newcomer agreed. "I know a woman who got allergies after she was grown and she got bronica asthma with it."

The dog finished the milk. The owner put him back in his overcoat and I shook hands all around with the winos. We split up three ways. The winos went up the street, the well-dressed man down the street, and the newcomer—who turned out to be Tally Jackson—and I went into the Carry-out.

For more than four hours Tally and I lounged around in the Carry-out, talking, drinking coffee, watching people come in and go out, watching other hangers-on as they bantered with the waitresses, horsed around among themselves, or danced to the jukebox. Everyone knew Tally and some frequently sought out his attention. Tally sometimes participated in the banter but we were generally left undisturbed when we were talking. When I left at two o'clock, Tally and I were addressing each other by first names ("Elliot" was strange to him and we settled for "Ellix") and I was able to address the two waitresses by their first names without feeling uncomfortable. I had also learned to identify several other men by their first names or nicknames, had gotten hints on personal relationships, and had a biographical sketch (part of it untrue I learned later) of Tally.

Back on the street, I ended up at the Downtown Cafe, this time by way of the morning's now very drunk owner of the puppy, who was standing near the entrance. The puppy was our bond and we talked about him with an enthusiasm that perhaps neither of us felt. Later, the well-dressed man who had also been part of the puppy episode came in and joined me at the bar. Then, still drinking

beer at the bar stool, I met two other men in quick succession. The first man had to leave shortly for his night-shift busboy job at the restaurant. The other was a surly man in his middle thirties who initiated the contact by taking the stool next to me and asking what kind of work I did, adding that he had seen me around the day before, watching Detective Wesley drag that woman across the street.

I told him briefly what my job was.

"Well, if you hang around here you'll see it all. Anything can happen and it does happen here. It can get rough and you can get your head knocked in. You'll be okay though, if you know one or two of the right people."

"That's good to know," I told him, guessing (and hoping) that he was one of the "right people." He left me with the impression that he was being friendly and, in a left-handed sort of way, was offering me his protection.

By the end of the second day I had met nine men, learned the names of several more, and spent many hours in close public association with several men, at least two of whom were well known. And perhaps most important of all, in my own mind I had partly sloughed off that feeling of being a stranger and achieved that minimum sense of "belonging" which alone permits an ease of manner and mind so essential in building personal relationships.

Over the next three or four weeks, I made several excursions into other neighborhoods and followed up at the Downtown Cafe and the Carry-out shop on an irregular basis, getting to know some of the people better and many others for the first time. Frequently I ate breakfast and lunch at the Carry-out and began putting occasional dimes in the jukebox and in the pinball machine. Ted Moore, who worked at a liquor store nearby and whom I had first met in the Carry-out while he was waiting for the store to open, regularly alternated with me in buying coffee and doughnuts in the morning. At the Downtown Cafe the man who told me that I'd be okay if I knew "one or two of the right people" publicly identified me as his friend. ("Sure I know him," he told another man in my presence. "We had a long talk the other day. He's my friend and he's okay, man, he's okay. At first I thought he was a cop, but he's no cop. He's okay.")

All in all, I felt I was making steady progress. There was still plenty of suspicion and mistrust, however. At least two men who hung around the Carry-out—one of them the local numbers man—

had seen me dozens of times in close quarters, but they kept their distance and I kept mine. Once, accidentally, I caught the numbers man's eye as I walked in. We held the stare for three or four seconds and I nodded slightly but he wouldn't let go. I went on about my business, determined that I wasn't going to be stared down next time and that he'd get no more nods from me unless he nodded first. As it turned out, I didn't have long to wait.

One mid-February day, I walked into the Carry-out.

> . . . Tally was having a cup of coffee. "Look here," he said. "Where is this place?" Tally took out a sheet of paper from an envelope and handed it to me. It was a summons to appear as a witness for the defense in the case of the United States versus Lonny Reginald Small. A faint stamp indicated that Tally was to report to the United States District Court for the District of Columbia at 3rd and Pennsylvania Avenue, Northwest, at ten o'clock this morning. I read off the address. It was then 9:40. I suggested that Tally take a cab, but when Tally said he didn't have the money I offered to drive him down. He quickly accepted. On the way, Tally explained that Lonny was a friend of his. Lonny was being tried for murdering his wife last summer. "Lonny is a nice guy," he said. "He's one hundred percent."

Thus began a three-week odyssey into the world of Lonny Small, a young man of twenty-six who, according to the jury's subsequent verdict of "not guilty," had choked his wife to death accidentally. Upon his acquittal, Lonny was rearrested in the courthouse for a violation of probation (on a previous grand larceny conviction) in another jurisdiction. He waived extradition, was given a hearing, was released on an appearance bond, and after another hearing he was again placed on probation.

Almost imperceptibly, my association with Tally, and through him with Lonny, was projecting me into the role of a principal actor in Lonny's life. By being with Tally through the trial, I found that first Tally, then Lonny, were looking to me for leadership and, as in the question of waiving extradition, for decision making. Court officials, apparently taking their cues from Lonny, began looking to me as his spokesman.

The follow-up of Lonny, which took most of my time for at least the next two weeks, carried me into dozens of places and into contact with scores of people. Throughout this period I stayed in close touch with the project director, getting clearance for and weighing the possible consequences of my growing involvement with the authorities. I went to three different jails during this time, sat through one murder trial and two hearings in judges' chambers, testifying at one of them. I went to bondsmen's offices, to the United States Employment Service, to the Blessed Martin de Porres Hostel (for homeless men) and into several private homes. I met policemen, judges, lawyers, bondsmen, probation officers, and one of Lonny's former employers. I talked with his friends and at least one enemy, his mother-in-law, whose daughter he had killed. I met in council several times with various members of his extended family (who accepted me, through Tally, as Lonny's friend, no questions asked) in their houses, and drove around with them to the houses of other members of the family trying to raise money for Lonny's bond.

Meanwhile, back at the Carry-out, where Tally and I were meeting regularly at night and where I tried to stop in during the day whenever possible, people I had never seen, or others I had seen but never spoken to, began coming up to me and asking, "Is Lonny out yet?" or "Did you raise his bail yet?" or simply, "How's it going?" Bumdoodle, the numbers man, one of those who had not known Lonny, was especially solicitous of Lonny's welfare. He, too, began calling me by my first name and, although I kept no record of it, I think it was at this time that he dropped all subterfuge in taking numbers in my presence and soon began taking bets from me.

By the middle of March, Tally and I were close friends ("up tight") and I was to let him know if I wanted or needed "anything, anytime." By April, the number of men whom I had come to know fairly well and their acceptance of me had reached the point at which I was free to go to the rooms or apartments where they lived or hung out, at almost any time, needing neither an excuse nor an explanation for doing so. Like other friends, I was there to pass the time, to hang around, to find out "what's happening."

I switched my day around to coincide with the day worker's leisure hours: from four in the afternoon until late at night, according to what was going on. Alone, or with one, two or half a dozen others, I went to poolrooms, to bars, or to somebody's room or apartment. Much of the time we just hung around the Carry-out, playing the pinball machine or standing on the corner watching the world go by. Regularly at five, I met my five "drinking buddies" when they came off from work and we went into a hallway for an hour or so of good drinking and easy talk.

Friday afternoon to Sunday night was especially exciting and productive. I'd go to Nancy's "place" (apartment) where, at almost any hour, one could get liquor, listen to music, or engage in conversation. Or perhaps seven or eight of us would buy some beer and whiskey and go up to Tonk's apartment near the Carry-out where he lived with his wife. Occasionally, I'd pair up with one or two men and go to a party, a movie, or a crap game, which might be in almost any part of town. Sunday afternoon was an especially good time to pick up news or happenings of the preceding forty-eight hours. People were generally rested up from the night before, relaxed, and ready to fill one another in on events which involved the police, breakups of husband-wife relations and bed-and-board arrangements, drink-stimulated brawls, sex adventures, and parties they had witnessed, heard about, or participated in over Friday and Saturday.

By April most people seemed to be taking it for granted that I belonged in the area. At least two men did not trust me or like me, but by then I was too strongly entrenched for them to challenge successfully my right to be there, even had they chosen to do so. New people moved into the area and I found myself being regarded as an old-timer, sometimes being asked to corroborate events which predated my arrival.

Throughout this period, my field observations were focused on individuals: what they said, what they did, and the contexts in which they said them or did them. I sought them out and was sought out by them.

My field notes contain a record of what I saw when I looked at Tally, Richard, Sea Cat and the others. I have only a small notion—and one that I myself consider suspect—of what they saw when they looked at me.

Some things, however, are very clear. They saw, first of all, a white man. In my opinion, this brute fact of color, as they understood it in their experience and as I understood it in mine, irrevocably and absolutely relegated me to the status of outsider. I am not certain, but I have a hunch that they were more continuously aware of the color difference than I was. When four of us sat around a kitchen table, for example, I saw three Negroes; each of them saw two Negroes and a white man.

Sometimes, when the word "nigger" was being used easily and conversationally or when, standing on the corner with several men, one would have a few words with a white passerby and call him a "white mother-fucker," I used to play with the idea that maybe I wasn't as much of an outsider as I thought. Other events, and later readings of the

field materials, have disabused me of this particular touch of vanity.

Whenever the fact of my being white was openly introduced, it pointed up the distance between me and the other person, even when the intent of introducing it was, I believe, to narrow that distance.

. . . All of us left Tally's room together. Tally grabbed my arm and pulled me aside near the storefront church and said, "I want to talk to you." With no further introduction, he looked me straight in the eye and started talking.

"I'm a liar. I been lying to you all along now and I want to set it straight, even if it means we can't be friends no more. I only lied to you about one thing. Everything else I told you is gospel truth but I did lie about one thing and that makes me a liar. I know that some white people think that if you catch a man in a lie one time you can't never trust him after that. And even if you feel that way about it I still got to tell you. You remember when you first come around here, I told you. . . . Well, that was a lie. . . . I didn't think nothing of it at first, but then you and me started going around together and when we started getting real tight, my conscience started whomping me. I kept looking for a place to tell you but it never seemed right. Then tonight . . . I knew this was the right time. I knew you were going to find out and I didn't want you to find out from somebody else. . . ."

Once I was with Richard in his hometown. It was his first visit in five years. We arrived in the middle of the night and had to leave before daybreak because Richard was wanted by the local police. We were in his grandmother's house. Besides Richard, there were his grandmother, his aunt, and two unrelated men, both long-time friends of Richard.

The group was discussing the possibility of Richard's coming home to stay and weighing the probable consequences. In the middle of the discussion, Richard interrupted and nodded at me. "Now Ellix here is white, as you can see, but he's one of my best friends. Him and me are real tight. You can say anything you want, right to his face. He's real nice." "Well," said his Aunt Pearl, "I always did say there are some nice white people."

Whether or not there is more to these citations than "Some of my best friends are . . ." or "Yes, but you're different," the wall between us remained, or better, the chain-link fence, since despite the barriers we were able to look at each other, walk alongside each other, talk and occasionally touch fingers. When two people stand up close to the fence on either side, without touching it, they can look through the interstices and forget that they are looking through a fence.

The disadvantage of being white was offset in part by the fact that, as an outsider, I was not a competitor. Thus, in the matter of skin color, I saw myself nowhere in the spectrum of black-to light-skinned (or "bright"); I was completely out of it, with no vested interest. It could be that this made it possible for some people to speak freely to me about skin color.

> "You know, I'm the darkest one in my family. All my aunts, uncles, everybody is light-skinned and they were all down on me, except my grandmother. . . . She'd do anything for me, maybe because she saw everyone else against me. . . . All the time I was coming up, I kept hoping somebody would have a baby darker than me."

Looking at me, however, the people I came to know in the area probably saw more than a "white male adult." They saw or knew many other things as well, any one of which relegated me to outside status. Those with whom I was in regular contact knew, for example, that I was with them because it was my job to be with them, and they knew, according to their individual comprehension and my ability to communicate, just what my job was. They knew that I lived outside the area. They knew that I was a college graduate, or at least they associated an advanced education with the work I was doing. Moreover, it was apparent, certainly to me, that I was not fluent in their language. Thus, I was an outsider not only because of race, but also because of occupation, education, residence, and speech. The fact that I was Jewish came up only twice. Once, a man who worked but did not live in the area threw some Yiddish expressions at me because "I thought you looked Jewish." The other time was when I met a soldier in a local bootleg joint. We had been talking for some ten minutes or so when he asked me whether I was "Eyetalian." I told him I was Jewish. "That's just as good," he said. "I'm glad you're not white."

The fact that I was married and a father, and that I was bigger than average size—6' 1", 185 pounds—probably didn't matter much, except as they entered incidentally into my personal relationship with one or another individual. Since the people I spent most of my time with ranged in age from twenty to the middle forties, I would guess that my age (thirty-seven) was not significant in itself.

On several different counts I was an outsider[2] but I also was a participant in a full sense of the word. The people I was observing knew that I was observing them, yet they allowed me to partic- ipate in their activities and take part in their lives to a degree that continues to surprise me. Some "exploited" me, not as an outsider but rather as one who, as a rule, had more resources than they did. When one of them came up with the resources—money or a car, for example—he too was "exploited" in the same way. I usually tried to limit money or other favors to what I thought each would have gotten from another friend had he the same resources as I. I tried to meet requests as best I could without becoming conspicuous. I was not always on the giving end and learned somewhat too slowly to accept food or let myself be treated to drinks even though I knew this would work a hardship on the giver.

When in the field, I participated as fully and as whole-mindedly as I could, limited only by my own sense of personal and professional propriety and by what I assumed to be the boundaries of acceptable behavior as seen by those I was with.

Occasionally, when I wanted to record a physical description of say, a neighborhood, an apartment, or a social event, I tried to be an observer only. In practice, I found it impossible to keep all traces of participation out of a straight observer role.

One Saturday night, with my observer role clearly in mind, I went to a dance at the Capitol Arena where more than a thousand people were jammed together. I was the only white male, this was my first time at such an event, the music was so foreign to me that I picked out the wrong beat, and I was unable to identify several of the band instruments. I was, willy-nilly, an observer. But here are a few lines excerpted from the field observation:

> It was very hot, it was very noisy, it was very smelly, and it was all very exciting. It was impossible to remain simply an observer in a place like this, even for someone as phlegmatic as I. It was only a few minutes after Jackie Wilson started singing that I discovered that the noise wasn't nearly loud enough, the heat wasn't nearly hot enough, and the odor from more than a thousand closely packed people was not really strong enough at all. Like everyone else, I wanted more of everything.

Almost from the beginning, I adopted the dress and something of the speech of the people with whom I was in most frequent contact, as best I could without looking silly or feeling uncomfortable. I came close in dress (in warm weather, tee or sport shirt and khakis or other slacks) with almost no effort at all. My vocabulary and diction changed, but not radically. Cursing and using ungrammatical constructions at times—though they came easily—did not make any of my adaptations confusable with the speech of the street. Thus, while remaining conspicuous in speech and perhaps in dress, I had dulled some of the characteristics of my background. I probably made myself more accessible to others, and certainly more acceptable to myself. This last point was forcefully brought home to me one evening when, on my way to a professional meeting, I stopped off at the Carry-out in a suit and tie. My loss of ease made me clearly aware that the change in dress, speech, and general carriage was as important for its effect on me as it was for its effect on others.

In retrospect, it seems as if the degree to which one becomes a participant is as much a matter of perceiving oneself as a participant as it is of being accepted as a participant by others.

FOOTNOTES

[1] Richard Slobodin, " 'Upton Square': A Field Report and Commentary."

[2] From the outset, I had decided that I would never shoot crap, pool, or play cards for money, or bet money in any way (numbers excepted, since playing numbers is safely impersonal), and would meticulously avoid the slightest suspicion of a personal involvement with any woman. These self-imposed restrictions to some extent did underline my marginality. My explanation that I couldn't afford to chance a fight or bad feelings because of my job was usually accepted and I was generally excused from participating in these activities rather than excluded from them.

VI

THE ENVIRONMENT OF RESEARCH

This last section puts research into the settings which give it its point, its purpose and its significance, and in great measure, set the boundaries for what can be done. Here, the researcher is viewed in terms of his various relationships—with those who are studied; in the social research organization in which he works; against the broader setting from which his support derives; with the world of practical affairs where his contribution is ultimately tested and utilized; and in terms of his personal satisfactions and rewards in scholarship. The overall aim here is to assist the student reader sort out his own values in research, to evolve a working posture and personal philosophy which will permit him to follow his propensities, to resolve the ethical issues which his work may arouse, and thus to contribute in either long term or immediate ways to the development of the library field. For the professional practitioner, there will be enhanced understanding of the nature of research, of its requirements and of its potential contribution to the practice of librarianship. Particularly those who support, who agree to participate in and who ultimately must assess and translate results of library research into action, may expect to extend their awareness through the careful reading of these final selections.

A number of issues treated hereafter deserve particular discussion as they relate especially to library research. Each of these issues could profitably be elaborated in more extensive discussion than the brief treatment which follows. One is the question of disclosure. In applied investigations, it is usually understood from the outset that the library or libraries involved will be later identified in formal reports. This fact exerts subtle but nonetheless real influences upon the conduct and reporting of a study. An example is when state agencies commission a research person to analyze a problem. If the funding agency is perceived as being a party at interest to the outcome, more than nominal cooperation from those being studied is made more difficult unless respondents are assured that the investigator is free to report his findings as he sees them. The researcher must also be perceived as a non-partisan observer. Throughout the course of such study, the researcher may find himself under considerable pressure from the various interests with something to gain or lose by the investigation. He must understand what transpires in the process and take it into account without being distorted in his perception as a consequence. Another question can arise out of the form his reporting will take. The scholar is bound to respect confidences given with the understanding they would not be revealed. Yet, frequently the solution to problems may be impossible without candidate discussion and their thorough airing. The analyst may thus be caught in an ethical bind between his need to respect confidences and the basic purpose of the investigation. The result is to compromise, with less than full disclosure and analysis in reporting as its consequence. Conversely, candor may not always increase the prospect of a problem's solution. The researcher, in an applied situation, must understand fully the subtleties of the situation and the political implications of his reporting.

Not infrequently, libraries and librarians who are studied feel betrayed by the outcome of the research as reflected in the study report. The discomfort may result from the kind of situation personified in the Springdale case which follows. Perhaps more likely in libraries, however, is the disillusion which attends the investigator's departure from customary ways of viewing and conceiving the realities of library existence and experience. When reports raise unanticipated questions about the status quo, librarians feel their confidence may have been misplaced. Even though an investigator may explain his procedure fully at the outset, because he may be operating from other than traditional library premises and from a different professional or intellectual value orientation, a consequence is that his contribution may engender difference, indifference and even hostility. As the library comes more often to be the focus of social science research attention, the problem may grow more difficult. Yet, with enhanced research sophistication among librarians and the concomitant wider appreciation of the potential for libraries of such contributions, perhaps the climate of acceptance will be improved.

Fundamental questions about the role of the researcher in his relationship to a funding agency, both in terms of his latitude in prosecuting the research and in the expectations of the sponsors, deserve consideration. The researcher in librarianship is commonly cast in one of two fundamentally different roles. The first is an authority role. Under these terms, there is deference, not because of what he does and what he learns as a consequence, but rather because he is a presumed authority on the subject. The view of researcher as all-purpose wise man comes about for a number of reasons. Since quite commonly there is simply not enough money or time to give to a problem the serious study it requires, short cuts must be devised. The use-of-consultants syndrome in librarianship is deeply rooted. To differentiate the research contribution from the consultative contribution requires perception still uncommon in librarianship. This may be as true for the consumer of the service as for its purveyor. Moreover, as Millikan suggests, resort to expert counsel frequently yields the best results, or at least the sought for results, with greatest dispatch, economy and strain. Very often research is a strategic misnomer for engaging expertise to support decisions already formulated and which lack only the legitimacy of outside authority. When this is the case, policy makers require substantiating data or testimony less to understand the nature of a problem than to influence its support by those who assume financial control.

Another perception of the researcher is as "hired hand." Sponsors under these terms not only define the problem, but prescribe the method for its solution. Such a stance is reflected in the way in which professional committees design projects, solicit funds and only then seek someone competent to conduct the research. What is illustrated by such a process is the limited perception of a world of practice which fails to appreciate how much research preparation and sensitivity is necessary, both in the design and prosecution of first-rate work. When this happens, the researcher who can be interested in such an assignment will frequently be less competent than one who would not accept without prior involvement in its conception. The more sophisticated researcher who for some reason sincerely prefers to be engaged in such a project, finds himself exploring the means for recasting the research in order to permit him to gather information he may view as more relevant than the instigators of the study. Often the practical problem requires redefinition, since in its original conception it may not lend itself to mature investigation or analysis. If a project is only broadly defined in the beginning, as is frequently the case, there is opportunity to develop mutual understanding as the program proceeds. Millikan details, however, the formidable barriers and the concrete differences in goals and values which can make for a frustrating experience for all the parties at interest throughout the course of a project.

In a time when the very premises upon which every social institution rests are being called into question, it would seem appropriate to assess whether the fundamental nature of library research may not be out of phase with contemporary requirements. Academics can scarcely remain outside the fray, particularly when the subject of their scholarly concern is a professional discipline rooted in cultures in conflict and ferment— cities, universities and schools. Research, particularly in applied disciplines, calls now more dramatically than ever before, for a social conscience. The society and its institutions, including its libraries, dramatically requires the deployment of expertise and insight on the basic questions relating to their purpose, their goals and their programs. This is not to suggest that scholars study problems precisely as those in practice see them, but rather in ways which will help the institutions orient themselves to a changing world.

Library research has been for the most part pragmatically oriented, yet it appears to be so closely tied to professionally acceptable solutions, that it seldom contemplates alternatives which might cause pronounced upheaval in the existing order. Too infrequently perhaps is the stark or radical departure even deliberated or tested before it is set aside. Moreover, research, very much reflecting the pragmatic values of the field, seems overly committed to technical problems rather than the human, organizational or clientele issues. Policy makers get little help in planning the future from studies which merely describe a marginal status quo. The cues will yield themselves only if analysis is oriented to discovering new relationships rather than merely confirming the past to the present. For the present is a time when institutions lag behind the need which the culture is imposing upon them to change and the research arm of every profession can be meaningfully enlisted in its cause.

The basic research which has characterized librarianship has dealt with the library as a passive institution. The intelligence thus generated characterizes public attitudes and political relationships of institutions acting out passive roles rather than exploring the consequences of change. Research resources and energies might fruitfully be invested in following the action frontiers of the field. Not simply to evaluate or justify programs— but to seek insight where it is desperately needed. Inquiry into achieving political and public acceptance for expanded library roles in poverty areas, analysis of values and behavioral factors acting to influence cooperative effort among libraries, study of the organizational limits which restrict libraries from assuming more active service roles, the behavioral questions relating to the contributions which the library makes in clientele response terms, all would profit from behavioral research.

The Rossi reading draws into focus the issue of research organization in the university. Only recently have research centers come to be attached to library education programs. But, their existence does bring into question a number of related issues, which those who contemplate research careers in librarianship need to ponder. Teaching has traditionally enjoyed a higher status in the university than has research, particularly in disciplines where empirical research is still uncommon or viewed as something exotic or extra, and this has been the pattern in librarianship and still is for the most part. The classroom role also is typically subject to only the most limited outside control. Much of behavioral research, however, is sponsored research. It is therefore characterized by a high degree of external pressure, control and time constraint. The researcher, when he is not functioning as an individual addressing himself to problems which do not take him out of the office or laboratory, not only assumes responsibility for people and tasks, but is forced to become an entrepreneur. Such a role calls for capacities which the professorial culture has not typically assumed—fund raising, proposal preparation, persistence in soliciting support, reporting responsibilities, etc.. Ultimately, with projects of scale, the researcher becomes manager. He hires and trains staff, concerns himself with bookkeeping and financial operations and develops relationships within the university and with external support bodies. Research success then becomes more a matter of managerial skill and strategy than the innate capacity to perform as researcher.

One route open to the scholar short of the full entrepreneurial role is that of combining teaching with research. Under these terms, there is the prospect of status both ways, even though there is conflict inherent in balancing the two perspectives. For students who come into contact with such an individual, both in the classroom or as research assistants engaged upon project activities, there will be particular gratification as a consequence of the liveliness and vigor which immersion or interaction with ongoing intellectual pursuit brings.

A more fundamental problem is the way in which professional disciplines, librarianship included, must sort out the relative contribution made by those who teach compared to those who perform research.   To the extent that library education remains deeply rooted in the classroom and concentrates less of its intellectual energy upon research, the reward structure will remain skewed toward those who are oriented more toward the classroom.   In a time of change, this pattern is being called into question and it now seems clear that the prospects for a rewarding and fully productive career are open to researchers and scholars and that perhaps even the incentive arrangements to lure the most creative minds toward research are being extended.

Privacy and Behavioral Research

by Executive Office of the President, Office of Science and Technology

As a much studied culture, we are beginning to sense that too frequently the bounds of propriety have been over-stepped by zealous or cynical scholars. This report addresses itself to the zones where research may intrude, to the appropriateness of certain lines of effort, and to the consequences which follow. Implicit here is respect for human values, with the individuals being studied seen not as subjects, but as human beings, not as numbers, but as private persons fully entitled to dignity and self-respect. The key issues are seen as consent, confidentiality and anonymity. But, the questions are those of ethics and morality. Perhaps the heart of the matter is that these issues are not simply philosophical questions, but relate genuinely to the rights and the dignity of the human beings who deserve the protection of the scholar through a code as rigid as that which is followed by the medical fraternity with regard to their patients. For students of research, as for research practitioners, these are profound questions and they must be thought through and understood before one can proceed seriously in behavioral research where human beings are the case in point.

INTRODUCTION

Recent years have seen growing threats to the privacy of individuals. Wiretapping, electronic eavesdropping, the use of personality tests in employment, the use of the lie detector in security or criminal investigations, and the detailed scrutiny of the private lives of people receiving public welfare funds all involve invasions of privacy. While often the purpose is clear, the impact on the persons involved may be damaging. Our society has become more and more sensitive to the need to avoid such damage.

This concern has led to extensive discussion about the propriety of certain procedures in behavioral research by the Congress, by officials in the various agencies of the Government, by university officials, by the scientific community generally, and by leaders in professional societies in the behavioral sciences. The Panel has examined these issues and in this report proposes guidelines for those who are engaged in behavioral research or associated with its support and management.

The Panel has restricted its attention to issues of privacy arising in connection with those programs of data collection and study which are intimately associated with behavioral research. For example, it has not reviewed a number of the programs for data collection which are sponsored by the Federal Government such as the various censuses, health and welfare statistics, and financial information secured from business and industry. These programs may also encroach upon the privacy of individuals either through the burden of disclosure which they impose on respondents or through their availability for unintended purposes.

It is our opinion that the principles described in this report for protection of privacy in behavioral research should apply equally to such inquiries. When response is mandatory, as in the case of information that must be furnished to the Government, there is an even greater burden on the sponsoring agency to protect the individual against disclosure unless disclosure is specifically sanctioned by statute.

The Panel, moreover, has not reviewed in detail the wide variety of mechanical or electronic devices which make it possible to intrude into private lives. We have become acquainted with a few of the problems in that field, however, and are dismayed to observe the disregard for human values indicated by the advocacy or actual practice of eavesdropping, the use of lie detection devices without clear justification, and the frequent

SOURCE: Reprinted from Executive Office of the President, Office of Science and Technology, *Privacy and Behavioral Research* (Washington, D.C.: Government Printing Office, February, 1967), pp. iii-v and 1-30. The original publication bore the following note: "This report on 'Privacy and Behavioral Research' was prepared for the Office of Science and Technology by a distinguished panel. Because of its significance for the conduct of social science research, as well as the general public interest in problems of privacy, it is being released for publication. Donald F. Hornig, Director. Executive Office of the President, Office of Science and Technology, Washington, D.C. 20506."

willingness to institute surveillance procedures to handle the problems of a small proportion of our population at the risk of eroding the rights and the quality of life for the very large majority. We have not reviewed in detail the propriety of procedures involved in employment or social welfare activities. Enough examples have been brought to our attention, however, to make us feel that the examination of procedures in these spheres is needed also.

The attitudes of various segments of our society about proper procedures for the protection of privacy and the right to self-determination have been explored by the Panel. It has reviewed relevant research in the behavioral sciences and the administrative practices of universities and Government agencies. The Panel has also consulted with the scientific community through various professional societies and associations.

SUMMARY AND RECOMMENDATIONS

The right to privacy is the right of the individual to decide for himself how much he will share with others his thoughts, his feelings, and the facts of his personal life. It is a right that is essential to insure dignity and freedom of self-determination. In recent years, there has been a severe erosion of this right by the widespread and often callous use of various devices for eavesdropping, lie detection and secret observation in politics, in business, and in law enforcement. Indeed, modern electronic instruments for wiretapping and bugging have opened any human activity to the threat of illicit invasion of privacy. This unwholesome state of affairs has led to wide public concern over the methods of inquiry used by agencies of public employment, social welfare, and law enforcement.

Behavioral research, devoted as it is to the discovery of facts and principles underlying human activity of all types, comes naturally under scrutiny in any examination of possible threats to privacy. All of the social sciences, including economics, political science, anthropology, sociology, and psychology, take as a major object of study the behavior of individuals, communities, or other groups. In one context or another, investigators in all of these disciplines frequently need to seek information that is private to the men, women, and children who are the subjects of their study. In the vast majority of instances this information is freely given by those who consent to cooperate in the scientific process. But the very nature of behavioral research is such that there is a risk of

invasion of privacy if unusual care is not taken to secure the consent of research subjects, or if the data obtained are not given full confidentiality.

While the privacy problem in scientific research is small in comparison to that which exists in employment interviewing, social welfare screening, and law enforcement investigations, the opportunity for improper invasion is not negligible. About 35,000 behavioral scientists are engaged in research in the United States, 2,100 new Ph.D's are graduated each year, and the total number of students enrolled for advanced degrees in the behavioral sciences exceeds 40,000 at the present time.

It is probable that relatively few of the studies undertaken by these scientists raise serious questions of propriety in relation to privacy and human dignity. From a survey of articles published in professional journals and of research grant applications submitted to Government agencies, we have concluded that most scientists who conduct research in privacy-sensitive areas are aware of the ethical implications of their experimental designs and make arrangements to secure the consent of subjects and to protect the confidentiality of the data obtained from them.

It cannot be denied, however, that in a limited number of instances, behavioral scientists have not followed appropriate procedures to protect the rights of their subjects and in other cases the importance of privacy-invading considerations has not been as sophisticated or as affirmatively implemented as good practice demands. Because of this failure there has been pressure from some quarters, both within the Government and outside of it, to place arbitrary limits on the research methods which may be used. Behavioral scientists as a group do not question the importance of the right to privacy but are understandably concerned when suggestions are made that the detailed processes of science should be subjected to control by legislation or arbitrary administrative ruling. All scientists are opposed to restrictions which may curtail important research. At the same time they have an obligation to insure that all steps are taken to assure respect for the privacy and dignity of their subjects.

It is clear that there exists an important conflict between two values, both of which are strongly held in American society.

The individual has an inalienable right to dignity, self-respect, and freedom to determine his own thoughts and actions within the broad limits set by the requirements of society. The essential element in privacy and self-determination is the privilege of making one's own decision as to the extent to which one will reveal thoughts, feelings, and actions. When a person consents freely and fully to share himself with others—with a scientist, an employer, or credit investigator—there is no invasion of privacy, regardless of the quality or nature of the information revealed.

Behavioral science is representative of another value vigorously championed by most American citizens, the right to know anything that may be known or discovered about any part of the universe. Man is part of this universe, and the extent of the Federal Government's financial support of human behavioral research (on the order of $300 million in 1966) testifies to the importance placed on the study of human behavior by the American people. In the past, there have been conflicts between theological beliefs and the theoretical analyses of the physical sciences. These conflicts have largely subsided, but the behavioral sciences seem to have inherited the conflict that arises when strongly held beliefs or moral attitudes— whether theologically, economically, or politically based—are subjected to the free-ranging process of scientific inquiry. If society is to exercise its right to know, it must free its behavioral scientists as much as possible from unnecessary restraints. Yet behavioral scientists, in turn, must accept the constructive restraints that society imposes in order to establish that level of dignity, freedom, and personal fulfillment that men treasure virtually above all else in life.

The root of the conflict between the individual's right to privacy and society's right of discovery is the research process. Behavioral science seeks to assess and to measure many qualities of man's mind, feelings, and actions. In the absence of informed consent on the part of the subject, these measurements represent invasion of privacy. The scientist must therefore obtain the consent of his subject.

To obtain truly informed consent is often difficult. In the first place, the nature of the inquiry sometimes cannot be explained adequately because it involves complex variables that the nonscientist does not understand. Examples are the personality variables measured by questionnaires, and the qualities of cognitive processes measured by creativity tests. Secondly, the validity of an experiment is sometimes destroyed if the subject knows all the details of its conduct. Examples include drug testing, in which the effect of suggestion (placebo effect) must be avoided, and

studies of persuasability, in which the subjects remain ignorant of the influences that are being presented experimentally. Clearly, then, if behavioral research is to be effective, some modification of the traditional concept of informed consent is needed.

Such a change in no sense voids the general proposition that the performance of human behavioral research is the product of a partnership between the scientist and his subjects. Consent to participate in a study must be the norm before any subject embarks on the enterprise. Since consent must sometimes be given despite an admittedly inadequate understanding of the scientific purposes of the research procedures, the right to discontinue participation at any point must be stipulated in clear terms. In the meantime, when full information is not available to him and when no alternative procedures to minimize the privacy problem are available, the relationship between the subject and the scientist (as well as with the institution sponsoring the scientist) must be based upon trust. This places the scientist and the sponsoring institution under a fiduciary obligation to protect the privacy and dignity of the subject who entrusts himself to them. The scientist must agree to treat the subject fairly and with dignity, to cause him no inconvenience or discomfort unless the extent of the inconvenience and discomfort has been accepted by the subject in advance, to inform the subject as fully as possible of the purposes of the inquiry or experiment and to put into effect all procedures which will assure the confidentiality of whatever information is obtained.

Occasionally, even this degree of consent cannot be obtained. Naturalistic observations of group behavior must sometimes be made unbeknownst to the subjects. In such cases, as well as in all others, the scientist has the obligation to insure full confidentiality of the research records. Only by doing so, and by making certain that published reports contain no identifying reference to a given subject, can the invasion of privacy be minimized.

Basically then, the protection of privacy in research is assured first by securing the informed consent of the subject. When the subject cannot be completely informed, the consent must be based on trust in the scientist and in the institution sponsoring him. In any case the scientist and his sponsoring institution must insure privacy by the maintenance of confidentiality.

In the end, the fact must be accepted that human behavioral research will at times produce discomfort to some subjects, and will entail a partial invasion of their privacy. Neither the principle of privacy nor the need to discover new knowledge can supervene universally. As with other conflicting values in our society, there must be constant adjustment and compromise, with the decision as to which value is to govern in a given instance to be determined by a weighing of the costs and the gains—the cost in privacy, the gain in knowledge. The decision cannot be made solely by the investigator, who normally has a vested interest in his own research program, but must be a positive concern of his scientific peers and the institution which sponsors his work. Our society has grown strong on the principle of minimizing costs and maximizing gains and, when warmly held values are in conflict, there must be a thoughtful evaluation of the specific case. In particular, we do not believe that detailed governmental controls of research methods or instruments can substitute for the more effective procedures which are available and which carry less risk of damage to the scientific enterprise.

Greater attention must be given to the ethical aspects of human research. The increase in the number of scientists and in the volume of research increases the possibility that carelessness or recklessness will lead to abuses in the hurried search for useful findings. Furthermore, if standards are not carefully maintained, there could develop an atmosphere of disregard for privacy that would be altogether alien to the spirit of American society. These increased potentials both for damage and for fruitful outcomes from new knowledge are in no small part consequences of increased Federal support of behavioral science. While no one would suggest that ethical standards should be different for scientists supported by public and private funds, the Government has an especially strong obligation to support research only under conditions that give fullest protection to individual human dignity. Government must avow and maintain the highest standards for the guidance of all.

Three parties—the investigator, his institution, and the sponsoring agency—have responsibility for maintaining proper ethical standards with respect to Government-sponsored research. The investigator designs the research and is in the best position to evaluate the propriety of his procedures. He has, therefore, the ultimate responsibility for insuring that his research is both effective and ethical. The formalization of our ethics concerning privacy in connection with research is too re-

cent, and perhaps too incomplete, to permit the assumption that all investigators have a full understanding of the proper methods for protecting the rights of subjects. Furthermore, the investigator is first and foremost a scientist in search of new knowledge, and it would not be in accord with our understanding of human motivation to expect him always to be as vigilant for his subject's welfare as for the productiveness of his own research.

We conclude, therefore, that some responsibility also must be borne by the institution which employs the investigator. The employing institution is often a university or a Government laboratory which has available other scientists who can review the research plan. Such persons, drawn in part from disciplines other than the behavioral sciences, can present views that are colored neither by self-interest nor by the blindspots that may characterize the specific discipline of the investigator.

Finally, the sponsoring agency is obligated to make certain that both the investigator and his institution are fully aware of the importance of the ethical aspects of the research and that they have taken the necessary steps to discharge their responsibility to the human subjects involved. In the majority of instances, we believe that it is neither necessary nor desirable for an agency to exceed this level of responsibility.

Conclusions

From our examination of the relation of behavioral science research to the right of privacy, we have been led to the following conclusions:

1. While most current practices in the field pose no significant threat to the privacy of research subjects, a sufficient number of exceptions have been noted to warrant a sharp increase in attention to procedures that will assure protection of this right. The increasing scale of behavioral research itself is an additional reason for focusing attention on procedures.

2. Participation by subjects must be voluntary and based on informed consent to the extent that it is consistent with the objectives of the research. It is fully consistent with the protection of privacy that, in the absence of full information, consent be based on trust in the qualified investigator and the integrity of his institution.

3. The scientist has an obligation to insure that no permanent physical or psychological harm will ensue from the research procedures, and that tem-

porary discomfort or loss of privacy will be reme-
died in an appropriate way during the course of
the research or at its completion. To merit trust,
the scientist must design his research with a view
to protecting, to the fullest extent possible, the
privacy of the subjects. If intrusion on privacy
proves essential to the research, he should not
proceed with his proposed experiment until he and
his colleagues have considered all the relevant facts
and he has determined, with support from them,
that the benefits outweigh the costs.

4. The scientist has the same responsibility to
protect the privacy of the individual in published
reports and in research records as he has in the
conduct of the research itself.

5. The primary responsibility for the use of
ethical procedures must rest with the individual
investigator, but Government agencies that support behavioral research should satisfy themselves
that the institution which employs the investigator has effectively accepted its responsibility to
require that he meet ethical standards.

6. Legislation to assure appropriate recognition
of the rights of human subjects is neither necessary nor desirable if scientists and sponsoring institutions fully discharge their responsibilities in
accommodating to the claim of privacy. Because
of its relative inflexibility, legislation cannot meet
the challenge of the subtle and sensitive conflict
of values under consideration, nor can it aid in the
wise, individualized decisionmaking which is required to assure optimum protection of subjects
together with the fullest effectiveness of research.

Recommendations

These conclusions lead us to make the following
recommendations:

1. That Government agencies supporting research in their own laboratories or in outside institutions require those institutions to agree to
accept responsibility for the ethical propriety of
human research performed with the aid of Government funds.

2. That the methods used for institutional review be determined by the institutions themselves.
The greatest possible flexibility of methods should
be encouraged in order to build effective support
for the principle of institutional responsibility
within universities or other organizations. Institutions differ in their internal structures and
operating procedures, and no single, rigid formula
will work for all.

3. That investigators and institutions be noti-
fied of the importance of consent and confidentiality as ethical requirements in research design,
and that when either requirement cannot be met,
the reasons must be explained in the application
for funds.

4. That when research is undertaken directly,
or is purchased on specification by a Government
agency, responsibility for protection of privacy
lies with the agency. When independent research
is funded by the Government, however, responsibility lies primarily with the scientist and his institution, and research instruments or design
should not be subject to detailed review by
Government agencies with respect to protection
of privacy.

5. That universities and professional associations be encouraged to emphasize the ethical aspects of behavioral research. When a training grant
is made, a university should be requested to indicate its understanding that support of education
on the ethics of research is one of the purposes of
the grant.

THE NATURE OF PRIVACY

With the growth in our population, the complexity of our society, and the dependence of individuals upon one another for service and support, there is increasing need for people to live in
the presence of others. Yet the fundamental human claim to personal freedom and dignity remains. Privacy is the right to live one's life in
one's own way, to formulate and hold one's own
beliefs, and to express thoughts and share feelings
without fear of observation or publicity beyond
that which one seeks or acquiesces in.

The claim to privacy is fragile, but persistent;
it is as subtle and powerful as the need for personal dignity; it is a fundamental aspect of individual freedom and worth. The claim to privacy
is supported by our society, subject to limitations
only when there is risk of injury to others or to
society as a whole.

The usual examples of privacy are too gross
to convey fully its nuances and strength. One
thinks of the right to turn away the interviewer at
the door, to throw away the mailed questionnaire,
or to exclude outsiders from a meeting. One
thinks of privacy to make love, to reflect on financial success, to express pride in professional
achievements, and so on. There are more subtle
and personal forms, however. The insecure student may find himself an unwitting subject in an
experiment which threatens his self-esteem. A

newly literate representative of a primitive culture may discover descriptions of his society that he considers demeaning, outrageous, or false. The masterful husband who has coped effectively with his subordinates all day may need to play the role of a child in his relations with his wife at night. The lover should be free to talk baby talk to his inamorata without having it quoted at his office. The mother should be free to be short tempered with her children at the end of a hard day without having her conduct described to members of her club. The seemingly selfless minister should be free to play the role of an entrepreneur in a group of friends formed into an investment club. The tough-minded medical investigator should be free to join a colony of artists, to talk their language, and share their beliefs.

All such illustrations fall short, however, because they tend to suggest that privacy can be defined in terms of specified areas of human activity, and that these areas are so private that they are closed to investigations of their fundamental nature. Actually, what is private varies for each person and varies from day to day and setting to setting. Indeed, the very core of the concept is the right of each individual to determine for himself in each particular setting or compartment of his life how much of his many-faceted beliefs, attitudes, and behavior he chooses to disclose. Every person lives in several different worlds, and in each his mode of response may—indeed must— be different. The roles of father, husband, clerk, good neighbor, union leader, school board chairman, candidate for office, solicitor of funds for the local church, call for different responses. The right to privacy includes the freedom to live in each of these different roles without having his performance and aspirations in one context placed in another without permission. Thus, any general injunction against study of a specific area of behavior wholly misses the essence of privacy; it fails to protect some people from being revealed in ways that are most upsetting to them while shielding others who are quite willing to reveal information.

Our society must recognize and provide for man's requirement to possess thoughts, feelings, and impulses that are expressed only in a setting of solitude, or in the presence of chosen associates. We now know that everyone hates, everyone has sex desires, everyone is dependent, everyone is rebellious, everyone is ambitious, and so on. We might wish that our society were structured and our value system were designed in such a way that

acknowledgement of these feelings and their free expression in any setting would have no hazardous consequences for the individual. For the present, we can only accept the fact that every individual has these feelings and that, in some instances, he may not be able to acknowledge them even to himself. We must also recognize the great need to understand these areas of private life and to realize that their study is both legitimate and essential.

The claim of privacy as a legal right has developed slowly in Western history. The concept of privacy as a protection of individual dignity is implicit in the first amendment to the Constitution with its concern for freedom of speech and the concomitant liberty of silence; it is implicit, also, in the fourth amendment's safeguards against search; and it is implicit in the fifth amendment's mandate for due process and against self incrimination. The classic paper of Warren and Brandeis[1] advanced the principle that public disclosure of personal information is a wrong against the "inviolate personality." The same principle was expressed 25 years later by Pound[2] who identified the claim to private personality as the demand which the individual may make that his private affairs shall not be bared to the world. This new freedom of private "personality" is conceived in parallel with the concept of private property which the individual is free to share or to withhold.

The awareness of the nature of personality and its significance has developed not alone from legal or social philosophy. It has emerged in part, also, from the study of man. Through widening research into the nature and variety of human behavior we have begun to understand man's needs, capabilities, and limitations.

BEHAVIORAL RESEARCH

Science has made its contributions to human welfare by virtue of its freedom to inquire. The investigator pursuing knowledge, whether his subject is man or some other aspect of the natural world, must not feel constrained to limit his study to those things which have current social approval. Freedom of inquiry is a part of the general concept of intellectual freedom and has been built into the value structure of evern university.

Behavioral science is obligated to explore all aspects of human behavior to the degree that such inquiry contributes to improved understanding of the nature of man and his society. The study of human behavior is challenging and difficult. Wher the scientist seeks to develop a meaningful and consistent set of concepts about some aspect of man's relations to others, he uses and must be free to use every means at his disposal to gain knowledge. In his search for truth he is less likely to think of social consequences of his work than he is of scientific consequences. In fact, most scientists in any discipline take the position that the search for truth should seek to replace myths, prejudices and misconceptions, and hence they view with great suspicion any limitation on their endeavors.

The behavioral scientist often has a different view of the problem under discussion. Many, for example, would discount, because of lack of evidence, the existence of an inner private self that must remain inviolate. Despite their skepticism on this point, however, most would agree that many individuals suffer pain that is very real indeed when their privacy is invaded, and that behavioral scientists have a responsibility to avoid inflicting such pain.

A wide variety of research techniques has been developed for the study of human behavior. Experiments with small groups are frequently conducted in the laboratory where conditions of the group's interaction can be modified. Aspects of communication, problem solving, and leadership have been studied in this manner. Measures of attitudes, opinions and personality characteristics, and tests of competence in performing given tasks are often used in economic, sociological, psychological, and anthropological studies. In some circumstances, data are collected in such a fashion that the individual under study does not realize what he has revealed about himself or indeed that he has been studied at all.

Some techniques are specifically designed to provide the scientist with information which the subject would consider privileged and private. Still other techniques focus on the collection of data generally accepted as public, but then employ analyses or develop generalizations which reflect adversely on certain social groups and thus may constitute invasions of privacy. These techniques all seek to make data, whether private or public, available to the scientist in order that he can develop a more complete and accurate picture of the particular process under study.

Our society places a high value on the rights of the individual, among them the right to privacy. When the techniques and research methods of the behavioral scientist impinge on these rights, they

pose a crucial question for the scientist and for society.

The scientific community has not ignored these problems. They are discussed during the graduate education of behavioral scientists. Several professional societies have developed codes of ethical conduct with respect to the rights of the research subject. The issues have also been increasingly discussed by individuals, not necessarily behavioral scientists themselves, who work closely with scientists in the academic community or in Federal agencies that support research.

Privacy must be considered by the behavioral scientist in the context of the methods he uses in his research. This means that it cannot be discussed merely as a philosophical matter, or as an abstract right to be kept vaguely in mind, but must be considered as an additional variable which will affect experimental design and must be taken into account in all research.

In a research project the investigator who wants to study a person, a group, or an entire society or culture must respect the rights of that person or group. The experimental design must protect the right of privacy. Thus, in research, as in all other areas of human intercourse, privacy becomes simply one more dimension for concern as we seek to secure the fundamental right of the individual to a sense of dignity, self-determination, and freedom from arbitrary hurt by others.

What is normal and acceptable behavior in one social context (e.g., in private family interactions) may be acutely embarrassing if it is described or observed in some other social situation (e.g., at a cocktail party or in a scientific laboratory). A research procedure which includes asking a child to report his parent's disciplinary methods represents this kind of invasion. A mother's methods of punishing her child may be entirely acceptable to her, to her husband, her children, and her neighbors. Nevertheless, to have it described by her child to a teacher or to a research psychologist who can associate it with her may be acutely embarrassing. On the other hand, some of the more critical aspects of the behavior patterns of disturbed children could result from cruel home punishment. Research designed to reveal the nature of such home situations could also contribute to the welfare of children and society as a whole.

Some examples of research procedures that may harm the participant through a violation of his rights, with an explanation of why they are harmful, may help to define the area of our concern:

1. In a study designed to discover the causes of personality qualities in children it was necessary to secure measures of the children's personalities. One device that has been widely used is the so-called sociometric measure which assesses certain personality characteristics of a child on the basis of judgments about him by his classmates. A set of statements about the child's behavior was prepared. Examples are: "He usually suggests a good idea for a new game." "He always gets mad when we don't do what he wants." "He can read better than anyone else in the class." The children were instructed to fill in the name of the child best described by each of these statements. By tabulating the answers given by all children in a class, it was possible to find out the peer judgment about various qualities of personality.

The problem of confidentiality did not enter this situation because the results were never seen by the children, their parents, or the teacher. However, the "sociometric method" invades privacy in the sense that it forces children to think about certain qualities of behavior shown by one another and to reach firm conclusions about what is "best" or "worst." The normal processes by which reputation develops were replaced by an artificial intervention:

2. In a series of experiments designed to discover the effects of a student's feelings of success or of failure at a particular task, the experimenter artificially induced feelings of success and failure in different groups of subjects. In the failure experiment, a subject was asked to learn a rather complex motor task and the experimenter expressed surprise at how slowly the subject learned, compared his performance unfavorably with that of other students, and expressed sympathy with him for his clumsiness. The net result was to induce in the subject a feeling of inferiority and of self-derogation. By the end of the experimental session, some subjects were depressed, brooding, and angry, and had lost a measure of self-esteem.

It is routine for an experimenter to explain the state of affairs following such an experiment. The subject can normally recover his usual level of self-esteem, but it is the responsibility of the experimenter to make sure that this recovery occurs. It should be added that the body of research of which this example is a part has led to a substantial modification of educational policy in America. The research showed clearly that the lowering of self-esteem and failure reduce learning ability. Educationally, the principle has been applied to modify teachers' schoolroom behavior in such a way that unsatisfactory performance can be challenged by means that avoid injuring the student's self-esteem.

The preceding examples illustrate the areas of research in which good practice has developed, and where principles are fairly well established. As behavioral scientists examine new problem areas or develop new techniques, the old principles are not easily applied. Studies that are ingenious and fascinating may raise the most perplexing issues about propriety:

3. In a study designed to discover the relationship between level of anxiety and the need to be with someone, the investigator induced an anxiety state by deceiving his subjects. Without deception, he could not have obtained the levels of anxiety required to demonstrate this relationship. Is such deception warranted? How is consent to participate nullified by such deception?

4. In a study to discover the degree to which persons could be persuaded to inflict severe pain on others, subjects were led to believe that they were administering electric shocks of considerable magnitude to other subjects. Many subjects were persuaded to increase the level of shock to points where the apparent subjects (who actually did not receive a shock) writhed in simulated pain. What warrant does the investigator have for this form of deception? How does he insure that the self-revelation of the real subject is not demoralizing and that it produces no permanent damage to him?

5. In a study to discover how well a family can survive an extended stay in a fallout shelter, the investigator recorded all conversations during the interval, without the family's prior knowledge or consent. What, if any, sanctions are there for such intrusion on privacy?

Threats to the privacy of individual subjects do not pervade all aspects of the behavioral sciences. A review of the literature in these fields indicates that only a small percentage of studies involve any issue of privacy. Of those that do, only a small number appeared to disregard rights of the individual subjects or fail to accommodate to them. The number of reported studies involving research methods which could have affected the subjects adversely in terms of stress, deception, or social sanction appears to be very small. Research reports, however, do not always give adequate information about the steps that the investigator took to ensure that subjects were in fact protected.

Examination of research proposals under review by various Federal agencies indicates that only a small number of proposed studies raise questions of propriety. In almost every instance, the applicant includes in his proposal for support a defense of his reasons for collecting data which may be intrusive or invasive, and also describes the steps he will take to insure confidentiality or provide other means for protecting the individual subjects. The reviewing agencies have, in fact, rejected proposals because inadequate provision had been made by the investigator to protect the privacy of subjects.

While the percentage of studies with potential for invasion of privacy is small, it is not inconsequential. Today there are over 35,000 behavioral scientists in the United States—anthropologists, economists, political scientists, psychologists, and sociologists. In 1965, 2,100 new Ph.D's joined their ranks. In the same year more than 40,000 graduate students were preparing themselves for teaching, research, and service in the behavioral sciences. More than 100 journals publish articles reporting on the work of these scientists. About 5 percent of Federal funds for the support of research is used to support this segment of science.

But the problem cannot be fully defined by citing only numbers of scientists or dollars. The specialist in the behavioral sciences studies people. He asks questions, observes behavior, conducts experiments, analyzes background information, and searches files. Hardly a member of today's society has not come under some type of study—by a mail questionnaire, by a telephone call, by a doorstep or marketplace interview, or as a member of a community or national organization. One behavioral scientist might study only a handful of subjects, but another might study thousands, or an entire community, or all members of a large organization. Improper procedures, or inadequate protection of subjects in even a small proportion of all of these studies, could thus have an undesirable effect on a great many persons.

Enthusiasm for discovery of new data or for trying a new technique is probably highest among the more recent entrants to a field. Graduate students pose a special problem, for as they become acquainted with current research in a field, they begin to repeat experiments reported in the literature. The more controversial studies, involving procedures that are also controversial, are more attractive models for replication than those in the conventional mode. Likewise, the investigator, however mature, who is greatly concerned with mankind's current pressing problems is likely to study topics that relate to real and immediate social issues, and to use procedures that pose more of a threat to the integrity of his subjects. With the growing need to deal with social problems, we foresee an inevitable increase in conflicts between rights to privacy and freedom of inquiry.

THE CONFLICT OF VALUES

The values held by an individual or by a society are, and must be, in competition since no single value can be absolute. Even the right to life is supervened by a society seeking to protect itself from criminal behavior. Thus the conflict between the claim of the individual to his privacy and the needs of society to become better aware of human characteristics is no rare or isolated phenomenon.

In each instance of conflict, the decision must rest on the totality of all the relevant issues and the result will vary from one occasion to another, and from one setting to another depending on the context within which the issues arise and the process by which a conclusion is reached. No general rule can be formulated to apply in each situation; rather, persons desiring to uphold our society's diverse values must make judgments. The strength of our society lies in pluralism and diversity. The shifting tensions among our values and in the relative primacy accorded them provide strong assurance for the continuance of the diversity on which much of our freedom and our growth are built.

No real difficulty would be experienced in resolving these conflicts, as they arise in connection with research proposals, as if the values involved had measurable dimensions. One could then calculate the benefits and costs and decide whether to approve or disapprove a proposal. At first glance, such mensuration appears to be impossible, but in fact, millions of such comparisons are made daily by individuals, by families, by communities, and by agencies of industry and Government. There exist a multiplicity of methods and institutions for coming to such resolutions.

A city for example, must make decisions about the relative advantages of demolition of large numbers of deteriorated dwellings in its central parts, as opposed to substantial programs for their renovation. Welfare agencies make hard choices between the impact upon a family of providing direct funds for maintenance as against the deteriorating effect this has on the initiative of a potential wage earner. Social workers must choose between invading the privacy of a home to determine whether a male wage earner lives there as against risking that welfare funds may be spent in circumstances for which they are not intended.

Even the rights to bodily integrity and privacy of property, which are recognized within our system of law and accepted generally as inalienable, are not really absolute. Every highway that is built involves personal and social cost, especially for those who are displaced or diminished by the construction. Indeed, there is hardly a social act that does not involve some social or human cost. There is no escape from the fact that limits exist for every basic value. Failure to limit any single one inevitably circumscribes another. In summary, it is a logical impossibility to have freedom without limits or values without qualification.

The resolution of conflict between these strongly held values calls for all the resources of our institutions. Solutions cannot be legislated or imposed by decree. They must be worked out case by case. All who participate in this process, to be effective, must be perceptive of and sensitive to the respective strengths of the values that are in competition.

In the front rank of this decision-making process, as it applies to the problem of accommodating privacy and the study of human behavior, are the investigators who are actually involved in research. In the last analysis, whether the tension between privacy and behavioral research is simply a challenge, or becomes a problem, will depend very largely on the perception, the wisdom and ingenuity of the investigator. But the resolution of any conflict between behavioral research and privacy cannot be left to the investigator alone; his immediate interests are too strong and the range of his perspectives may often be too narrow.

The home institution and the financing agencies are also directly involved in research projects and should participate in the decision. In addition, the subject of research clearly has a stake in this contest of values. Therefore, to the fullest extent feasible, he should participate in the decision concerning his own role in any experiment.

Beyond these participants is the community at large which has a crucial concern not only for sound research but also for assuring the dignity which is protected by privacy. There is no precise formula by which the judgment of the community can be brought into the conflict-resolving process. Indeed the need for formal community participation probably arises only to the extent that the investigator, the home institution and the financing agencies fail to respond adequately to other values which the community cherishes fully as much as it does freedom of inquiry.

Prevailing community consensus, it should be noted, even if it could be measured quantitatively, is often at variance with long-run community ideals and ultimate values, and one of the elements of our concept is the right of the individual to hold out against a community consensus. For this reason, no matter how useful measurements of

community opinion may be in balancing a judgment, they cannot be the sole basis for resolving conflicts of values.

The decision concerning proposed behavioral research therefore must be a balancing process without arbitrariness, rigidity, or absolutes. If both privacy and the pursuit of knowledge are to be accorded their due, no choice between them can be made without considering the circumstances of a particular case.

In this balancing process many factors must be considered and weighed. One factor is the proposed research. Is it desirable? Has it been done before? If so, is it worth repeating? Is it well designed and strongly staffed? Has the privacy issue been taken into account? Is it possible to redesign the experiment so as to avoid offense to privacy and obtain the same knowledge?

In weighing the benefits expected from an experiment, the value of the knowledge it is hoped to obtain and the probability of obtaining it must be taken into account. This value judgment must be made both in terms of social utility and in terms of the likely contribution to our general understanding of human behavior. Although a stronger weight is given to knowledge which is expected to yield social benefits, our society attaches worth to pure knowledge, recognizing that pure knowledge often develops unexpected utility.

In practice, we deal with specific proposals, designed to answer specific questions through the use of specific research techniques. When a proposal involves a conflict between protection of privacy and pursuit of knowledge, a technical issue must be resolved at the outset. This issue is whether the investigator's experimental design minimizes the conflict or whether it can be reduced by redesigning the study. Since conflicts between privacy and the pursuit of knowledge can, in many cases, be reduced by the proper design of studies, it is essential that reviewers of research proposals examine this question first. Only after the research has been designed to assure that the knowledge will be obtained at minimum cost in terms of privacy, need the basic issues posed by conflicting values be examined.

If an invasion of privacy cannot be avoided, the extent and character of the invasion must be scrutinized. Is it actual or theoretical, real or technical? Is there potential harm to the subject? If so, is the harm substantial or insignificant, lasting or fleeting? Is the invasion minimal? For example surveillance (by one-way mirror, camera, or monitoring devices) challenges directly and fundamentally the claim to privacy when the focus is on an individual. The challenge is drastically reduced if the focus is not on an individual but on social interactions; for example, at a bus stop or a street light.

This brings us to a third major set of considerations: Consent; anonymity; and confidentiality. More will be said about these later, for each is crucial to the decisional process.

If the subject is fully informed and freely consents, without coercion, to participate in an experiment, the issue of privacy evaporates because it arises not through threatened violation of absolute rules for any particular area of behavior but through threatened frustration of the claim of a specific individual to make his own choice of whether to withhold or disclose and to disclose, if at all, at a time and place, and to an extent, of his own choosing. Consent is the exercise of that choice and satisfies the claim to privacy.

Anonymity and confidentiality are related. Anonymity refers to preventing the identity of the subject from ever being known to anyone. Anonymity merges into confidentiality when the research design permits the identity to be known at one point in time or to a limited number of investigators, but is otherwise protected from dissemination.

Clearly, the extent to which there is anonymity or confidentiality will affect a subject's willingness to give consent. If consent is not consistent with the research objective, anonymity and confidentiality will have a direct bearing on the character, extent, and probability of a privacy invasion. Thus, the threat to privacy inherent in behavioral research can often be greatly diminished by conscientious effort to achieve the fullest possible anonymity and confidentiality in the research design.

It should be noted, however, that even with full anonymity or "complete" confidentiality, research can still be intolerably offensive to human dignity and privacy in that it involves the risk of psychic or physical damage to a nonconsenting but anonymous subject.

The considerations we have discussed apply to research endeavors whatever the source of their support. We emphasize the two stages of the review of a proposal: First, appraisal of research design for efficiency in obtaining the desired information in the sense of its success in minimizing costs (including the invasions of privacy); second, weighing of the relation between the cost of the most efficient of the alternative research designs and the benefits it will yield in knowledge.

While the community at large has an important stake in the outcome of this balancing process, it cannot play an effective role in most of the review. Few laymen can be effective critics of a research design and few scientists are willing to submit to a review by laymen. Review of a research proposal only by scientists in the same field as the investigator, however, fails to assure adequate representation of the values of the whole community. How to solve this dilemma without making the review process arbitrary, capricious, or irrelevant is a difficult problem which will require continuing experimentation and study.

This discussion of the balancing and decisional process has emphasized that the claim to privacy is not an automatic barrier to research. Nor is every intrusion on privacy automatically unreasonable. A wise and discriminating society has found, and will continue to find, that many invasions of privacy are tolerable and necessary for the health of the community.

PRINCIPLES AND DESIRABLE PROCEDURES

As the behavioral scientist develops techniques and methods for the study of man he must, in much the same fashion as the medical scientist, develop safeguards to protect his subject's welfare. Development of these safeguards requires positive action. Concern for the subject's welfare and rights will not be achieved by general prohibition of the use of specific research techniques.

In our view, two main criteria should generally be met to insure the subject's well being and integrity: First, he must be allowed to decide whether he will participate in a given study; second, if he consents, the information which he provides must be treated as privileged and confidential.

The concept of free and informed consent has been proposed as a mechanism to deal with the possible invasion of a subject's privacy by behavioral science research. The psychological meaning of "free and informed consent," however, is considerably more ambiguous than either the legal or administrative meaning of the term.

Free consent may be compromised by the subject's external circumstances. Potential subjects in a condition of servitude or duress are not, in fact, free to refuse requests from those in authority. The gravest invasions of privacy are likely to occur among the weakest and most helpless segments of the population—children, the very poor, the very sick, those who do not speak the language, and minority groups.

In other situations the principle of free consent falls short for less obvious reasons. The subject may desire to please the experimenter, he may need to talk about very personal problems, or he may wish to place himself on exhibit. The number of individuals with these tendencies increases whenever willingness to participate is the primary criterion for obtaining experimental subjects. Requiring consent can thus pose a problem for the investigator without providing the desired protection of subjects.

It is a practical impossibility for most subjects of behavioral research to be fully informed about all the details of research methods and design before giving consent. In many cases the information is too technical for a subject to understand. Moreover, full disclosure of a research protocol to prospective subjects would often invalidate the research. The results of an experiment can be profoundly affected if subjects know what is expected of them and if disclosure of specific details creates a volunteer bias.

For example, in one study, a set of questions was presented to sixth-grade children to discover which of several types of reactions to other persons were most characteristic of each child. The investigator wished to compare these reactions with parents' reports about their main methods of child rearing. One type of child reaction was negativism. If the children had been asked to review the questions beforehand, the more negativistic children might have refused to reply, introducing an important bias into the sample population.

Much valuable information about the physiological bases of emotions has been obtained by a study of the "startle response." This is a reflex reaction to an unexpected stimulus such as a loud noise or flashing light. The response is entirely different if the person expects the stimulus. The research could never have had scientific value if the design had been fully disclosed in advance. Another example is that of testing the effectiveness of drugs. Expectancy of some kind of effect from a pill leads, by suggestion, to reports of drug influence. Therefore, it is necessary to compare the reaction to the test drug with that to a placebo. This must be done without the subject's knowledge and, preferably, without that of the experimenter if the effect of suggestion is to be ruled out.

Informed consent, attractive as it is as a basic principle for deciding issues of privacy, has serious limitations unless the meaning of "informed" is qualified. No subject in behavioral research need be coerced or deceived into volunteering. He can be provided with information sufficient to enable him to judge that his participation is worthwhile and desirable, if it is. He can be provided adequate assurance that his sharing of himself will be privileged and protected. He can be assured that steps have been taken to protect him from pain and distress. He can be told about the limits which will be placed upon access to the information he provides. He can be guaranteed adequate procedures for insuring confidentiality or anonymity of his responses. These assurances should be a normal part of any request for research subjects.

When the scientist gains the confidence of a group by living in their midst, as occurs in anthropological research, he must respect the privacy of both the individual and group in conducting his research and in reporting his findings. The scientist must act in such a way as to obtain an appropriate level of informed consent from the group and report his findings so as to assure confidentiality. It is axiomatic that field studies, whether foreign or domestic, should be conducted with the same concern for the protection of privacy as would obtain in the scientist's home setting.

In summary, a simplistic concept of consent will not prevent invasion of privacy but can cripple behavioral research. To apply it would immediately force volunteer bias in essentially all studies and would influence choice of problem, research designs, and possible strategies.

There is no obvious or easy way to interpret or apply the principle of informed consent in the study of large groups, subcultures, or entire societies. New ways must be devised to obtain free participation and to protect the right of such groups to privacy. This area of ethics is not as well delineated and has not received enough attention from professional societies and others concerned with research on groups. Anthropologists, sociologists, and political scientists face this issue most acutely.

The principle that underlies consent is that the subject must have enough information about the investigator and the research to form the basis for reasonable trust. This means that the subject comes voluntarily to the experimental situation, knowing the nature of his participation and confident that the investigator will respect his welfare. These guidelines can be followed even when an experiment involves children. It is necessary to establish relationships with the parents or other appropriate community surrogates of the child in order to assure that the commitment to volunteer is valid. Community surrogates may be the school board, school principal, or superintendent, or some other agency which is entrusted by statute or tradition with the well-being of children.

Protection of privacy includes the protection of information which the subject provides the experimenter. A substantial proportion of educational and social science research requires investigators to secure personal information from the subjects. The vast majority of adults are willing to provide information for research that they would otherwise withhold. Similarly, most parents consent readily to scientific study of their children. Most adults recognize the crucial importance of the study of human behavior. So long as the surrender of privacy for research purposes does not create unnecessary or preventable distress or discomfort, most people will consent to cooperate and will permit investigators access to information that they might otherwise hold private.

There are two general ways in which research may be discomforting to subjects.

First, the research procedure itself may impose stress. For example, a pressing inquiry into remembered emotional reactions to the death of a loved one may reawaken painful emotions. Or, in an experimental setting, the artificial inducement of frustration to permit the measurement of a subject's tolerance may lead to a painful reaction as the procedure reveals tendencies of which he was unaware. Not all experimental methods which produce discomfort invade privacy, nor are they necessarily improper. An experiment which compared the effects on psychomotor efficiency of different degrees of boredom induced by prolonged and repetitive mechanical operations doubtless produced considerable distress, but in no sense did this involve an invasion of privacy or other impropriety.

Second, research that involves the invasion of privacy has the potential for producing unexpected social consequences if information is revealed. Religious beliefs, ethical values, financial facts, sexual experiences, intellectual capacity and many other qualities of personality are examples in point. While under some circumstances revelations about such matters are unimportant, under others they can cause the subject to suffer embarrassment, damange to his reputation, ostracism, or loss of social status. The best insurance against such consequences is to prevent any information collected about a subject from leaving the hands of the investigator. This can be accomplished by making responses anonymous, by protecting confidentiality, and by proper coding of data.

The most important responsibility of the social scientist whose research involves any invasion of privacy is to make certain that all persons involved in the study understand the vital importance of treating all data confidentially while it is being collected and as long as it is retained.

Respondents may give private information freely because they have been assured by the investigator that it will be held confidential and treated anonymously. Under current laws, the investigator cannot give this assurance, for the courts and Federal agencies may very well gain access to the data. Research procedures have been developed, however, to assure the subject that he will remain unidentified. Many standard coding methods greatly increase confidentiality and investigators are obliged to use procedures that will insure the protection promised to the subject.

In some studies, it is necessary to maintain a record of the identity of the individual in order to permit follow-up studies at a later time. In such instances the respondent should be told that his name will be retained by the researcher and consent should be obtained to maintain the material over an extended period of time.

The concept of consent takes on a different meaning when the subjects used are "captive" groups such as military personnel, prisoners, welfare clients, and school children. Collection of data from these groups may involve overt or covert coercion. Moreover, research data on military personnel and prisoners often are stored and remain accessible. The use of data fields of this type in further studies is understandable and is often in the national interest. We have been informed, however, that stored research data have been used also for purely administrative purposes. In the absence of crucial national need, to breach the confidentiality of data obtained for research purposes is unwarranted and inexcusable.

In several important studies investigators have collected highly sensitive and confidential information. These data have increased our understanding of significant segments of our population. At present there is no legal protection for the investigator or his subjects when the questions asked deal with infractions of the law. Investigations of drug addiction, of homosexuality, and of prostitution are examples. In situations of this type, investigators are well advised to seek expressions of confidence from the entire community about the importance of their studies and of the absolute necessity of maintaining the confidentiality of their data.

The discussion thus far has suggested that free and informed consent is a generally attainable ideal which should be pursued in all research involving human subjects. Consent signals the subject's trust in the scientist and thus is fundamental. In some research, however, soliciting consent at all or informing the subject fully about the nature, risks and objectives of an experiment destroys the experimental purpose. There is no magical formula for resolving this obvious clash of values. At best, we can only offer some of the criteria which responsible resolution should take into account:

1. Experiments in which consent is not sought at all should be undertaken only when the results promise to have significant social value, when the potential for producing damage by invading privacy is minimal, and when the desired results can be obtained in no other way. Social value should be interpreted to include a likely contribution to scientific knowledge, as well as the resolution of a current social problem. A substitute for consent should be sought by consulting an appropriate public body or a group of the investigator's peers. They should be asked to examine the researcher's decision concerning the desirability and necessity of proceeding without the subject's consent.

2. Where consent is sought but it is difficult or impossible to inform the subject fully of the research design without invalidating the experiment, the investigator should provide all possible information. The subject should know enough about the study and the investigator to have a basis for trusting him.

3. Informed consent has little legal meaning when children are involved. Consent is normally obtained after providing adequate information to adults who serve as surrogates for the children. These may be parents, school principal, or the school board. Exceptions even to this form of consent are occasionally justified by the overriding social value of the experiment, the unavailability of other means of accomplishing its purpose, and reduction to a minimum of the impact on the subject's privacy.

Participation in an experiment may impose a burden of time and energy on the subject. An individual who volunteers for a research study cannot be expected to judge whether the information sought by the experimenter is necessary or the burden placed on himself is excessive. Therefore, obtaining information that is not directly relevant to the design of an experiment is an exploitation of the subject's trust in the investigator. Thus economy in research design and specificity of information are highly desirable to insure against an erosion of the rights of the test subject.

In experiments requiring deception or unannounced observations, the subjects cannot be fully informed of the nature of the study, the procedures employed, or the personal effects of the study. A well-known example of such a study involves a group of subjects sitting around a table estimating the length of a line. All subjects in the room save one are actually "stooges" for the experimenter and, on his instructions, give obviously wrong estimates of the line's length. The final judgment is made by the real subject in the case. This experiment is designed to clarify the effect of social pressures on the subject's judgment. After the experiment is completed the subject is told the purpose of the study and the fact of his deception. It is clear that an experiment of this sort may put a subject under stress and raise self-doubts. Judgments about the appropriateness of the invasions that result from manipulating subjects in this fashion must take into account the methods used by the experimenter to reduce the aftereffects of enforced revelation of matters about themselves. Training in experimental procedures must include discussion of the impact of such procedures on the subject and investigators must accept as a major responsibility the constant sensitivity to the effects of their experimental procedures on their subjects.

All participants in the research process share responsibility for setting and maintaining high standards for protecting the privacy of subjects. In the following section we set forth our views on the responsibilities of (1) the scientist, (2) his home institution, (3) the Federal Government, (4) scientific societies and associations, and (5) the editors of scientific journals.

The Individual Scientist

It is recommended that the scientist, as a routine procedure, ask himself the following questions to evaluate the protection he is offering to test subjects:

1. What procedure will be used for securing the consent of the subjects?
2. How fully can the research procedure be ex-

plained to the subject in advance of requesting his consent?

3. If some aspects of the research will not be explained, to what extent is this reservation necessary as a part of the research design?

4. Are other less invasive designs for research available which can produce equally valid findings?

5. To what extent will any unexplained aspect of the research create pain, embarrassment, discomfort, or invasion of privacy?

6. What procedures will be used for eliminating this discomfort at the close of the research?

7. What measures will be taken to insure anonymity of subjects and confidentiality of the information obtained from them?

8. Will the research findings warrant the degree of intrusion on a subject's time and privacy?

The need to face these questions will alert the investigator to the importance of the moral, ethical, and human issues inherent in his research design. It will also emphasize the necessity for conforming to high standards of conduct in relations with his subjects. Furthermore, the investigator's answers will be useful to the other parties or agents who must make judgments about the propriety of his research proposals.

The Scientist's Home Institution

Responsibility for monitoring the propriety of behavioral research must be shared by the entire community of colleagues of the investigator in his home institution. The investigator may be too deeply involved in his hoped-for outcomes, as may colleagues in his own discipline; responsibility for reviewing matters of propriety must therefore be shared with less concerned but well informed associates. When the investigator is a member of the faculty of a university, there will be scientists and scholars in his own and in unrelated fields who can provide independent judgments about the quality of his research and the appropriateness of the methods he plans to use. In Government agencies and laboratories and, in fact, in almost every institution, similar peer groups can be established.

The individual investigator must accept the obligation for consulting with appropriate colleagues and senior associates about his work. In addition, the institution itself must accept the responsibility for insuring that the work is done by methods which it is willing to defend, and by investigators whose judgment it is willing to defend. The universities, especially those which have sub-

stantial research programs, can provide patterns that will serve as models for other institutions that sponsor research.

Beyond this, the universities, as the chief educators of the next generation of research workers, must accept the obligation to imbue their students with the highest standards in the conduct of research.

A university sometimes finds it difficult to play the role that it would be willing to accept since the individual investigator often establishes his primary relationship with the financing agency. The financial implications of this independence of the investigator and of his relationships with the funding agency have already been referred to in the report of the Wooldridge Committee.[3] The same considerations that apply to fiscal responsibility apply to the propriety of research. When an agency of the Federal Government awards a grant to an investigator, it should assign to the institution where he works the continuing responsibility for insuring that the investigation is carried out in accordance with the highest standards of conduct.

The Public Health Service has recently moved to place this responsibility upon the sponsoring institution. The procedures instituted and the instructions issued should have the very desirable effect of increasing the responsible review of research proposals by institutions. A further benefit of the new procedures used by the Public Health Service is the decentralization of supervision and review from agencies in Washington to institutional representatives who can play a more effective role on a continuing basis.

Universities and other research institutions can use a variety of procedures to review research applications and continuing research. The institution should have the prerogative of setting up the monitoring machinery for insuring that the proposed procedures are acceptable.

Nearly a third of all federally supported research is conducted by staff scientists in various governmental agencies. In the behavioral sciences, these efforts cover the spectrum from tightly controlled laboratory studies of individual behavior to collection or analysis of mass statistics on social and economic processes. In most respects the content and conduct of research in Government laboratories is similar to that supported by contract or grant in corporate and university laboratories.

The organizational hierarchy ordinarily consists of a laboratory, institute, or office containing research divisions. Within these divisions are branches which are frequently divided into sections. Each subdivision has an increasingly specific goal or functional research objective and ultimately is oriented to a dominant discipline. Within this structure supervisory authority is delegated downward with increasing constraints. Specific experiments are normally proposed by individual scientists in the context of a section mission. The proposal is given its most thorough technical review by the section chief and the branch head. At higher levels, proposals are normally reviewed for conformance with mission, for reasonableness of resource requirements and for priority.

Among the responsibilities left to the scientific staff of the agencies have been the ethical considerations involved in the research. This does not mean that administrative rules about the protection of the test subjects have not been stated; in a significant number of agencies the concrete aspects of the problem have been stated in one form or another. In general, the requirements for review in Government laboratories tend to be more stringent than those imposed in universities.

In social research requiring studies of segments of the public, another mechanism of review is added. This is approval by the Office of Statistical Standards in the Bureau of the Budget of all forms and questionnaires involving 10 or more respondents. Inevitably, such approval requires review of the research program that proposes to use the specific survey. In effect, the Federal Reports Act places the Bureau of the Budget in the position of a research review group, with the task of evaluating a survey form which is only a means to a research end.

In general, the same principles for decentralizing the review and monitoring of research which have been recommended as appropriate for universities should also apply to Government laboratories. Only procedures which permit opportunity for day-to-day discussion and review of procedures are likely in the long range to have the effects we all desire.

Today's computer technology has revolutionized the collection, storing, collation, and retrieval of information. With a common identifying symbol we can achieve almost instant assembly of data from a large number of sources. It is becoming possible to put together very rapidly much that is known about a person, corporation, state, locality, or neighborhood. This development has given rise to data banks or information centers. The idea of centralization is not new but with pres-

ent technology it can be more extensively and efficiently applied. For many years there have been central bureaus for assembly of credit information, insurance examinations, and claims histories. Police departments have long been able, however laboriously, to obtain any criminal record of suspects or, conversely, to compile a list of suspects, based on past records.

Our concern is that data centers, if misused, can invade privacy. Information voluntarily provided by a respondent for one purpose and in itself harmless to him, when put together with other data given either voluntarily or under mandate in other connections, can react to his disadvantage. Beyond this, the possible use of such information in connection with nonjudicial processes such as security clearance or credit ratings, where standards of due processes are not maintained, constitutes an even more serious problem.

The panel does not like the idea of dossiers on our citizens, our business establishments, and our institutions. We recognize, however, the usefulness of data centers as important administrative tools in a variety of legitimate circumstances. In the establishment and operation of such centers, extreme care must be taken to protect the individual against disclosure of information that would be embarrassing or detrimental to him and particularly, in the event of a possible criminal proceeding, cause him unknowingly to testify against himself.

Apart from data centers for administrative uses, similar centers to serve essentially statistical purposes already exist or are being proposed. We believe that the integration and analysis of data from diverse sources and over time will bring new knowledge and understanding of our society. Nevertheless, centralization of statistical data presents the same potential threat to privacy as does centralization of administrative data, if information concerning an individual is accessible for any use other than general statistical compilation. Safeguards are necessary. We recommend that when data centers are established under the auspices of Federal, state, or local government, all information stored in them should be placed, by law, under the same restrictions on grounds of confidentiality as are placed on the data collected under the Federal census status.

Nongovernmental data centers present a more difficult problem. We do not know whether it is practicable to provide confidentiality by statute. In any event, we believe the same guidelines we have discussed elsewhere in this report should be applied to all data stored in such centers.

Federal Research Grant And Contract Procedures

Research conducted by Federal agencies aims at furthering their missions and increasing the productivity of American science generally. As Federal research programs have grown, the Government's responsibility to examine the burden on subjects and the degree of invasion of privacy has also increased. Burden on subjects has always been a matter of concern, but until recently, other protection has received little formalized considerations.

When funding agencies, whether private or governmental, review applications for research support, they consider the methods to be employed. We believe that the list of items considered in such reviews should be expanded to include evaluation of the burden on respondents, of the invasion of the privacy of the subjects, of the intrusion into personal lives, and the effects on the dignity of individuals.

Government agencies should be concerned lest any trend develop toward a society in which all persons are subjected to and expect personal scrutiny. The mere thought of a society which would consider deviant any person unwilling to expose all aspects of his thoughts and ideas and personality to an investigator is repugnant.

The maintenance of freedom from scrutiny, however, cannot be achieved by imposing detailed procedures on the scientist. Any attempt to insure that no questions are asked that are embarrassing or offensive to some person will so impede creative research that much Government investment in the behavioral sciences will be wasted, or worse, the knowledge which our society expects and needs will not be obtained.

There is already precedent for the use of highly personal questions in the programs of welfare departments, of the Internal Revenue Service, of the Census Bureau, and in civil rights programs. In these instances, questions which in many settings would be considered improper are not only permitted but are required to achieve important social goals. We would regret the development of any set of regulations which would bar absolutely the use of any specific form of question or type of study, because such prohibitions would adversely affect research.

Funding agencies should develop procedures which accommodate these responsibilities to their own needs. A single set of regulations or procedures is unlikely to be appropriate for all. Some procedures already in effect are worth commenting on because of the way in which they relate to the principles stated in this report.

The Public Health Service has recently formalized its grant procedures to provide that for projects dealing with human subjects, the investigator's plans must be reviewed by a committee of institutional associates before the research is begun. These procedures assure an independent determination of the rights and welfare of the subjects involved, the appropriateness of the methods used to secure informed consent, and the risks and potential benefits of the investigation. This set of procedures appears appropriate for review of research sponsored by that agency. It is particularly appropriate in that it decentralizes the responsibility for review and monitoring, and places responsibility with the sponsoring institution in a way that should have beneficial long-term effects.

The Public Health Service also requires that for research on subjects below college age, the grant application must describe the manner in which the rights and responsibilities of the parent or guardian are respected—that is, how the consent of the parent or guardian is obtained or why this consent is deemed unnecessary or undesirable. This is a laudable provision, but needs to be interpreted so that community surrogates other than parents may give consent. This regulation properly places the burden of proof on the individual investigator and his institution when consent is deemed unnecessary or undesirable.

The Office of Education has established an ad hoc committee of its own staff members to review questionnaires involved in behavioral research projects. The committee was charged to review all questionnaires "to prevent injuring public sensitivities in such matters as the challenging of established morals, the invasion of privacy, the extraction of self-demeaning or self-incriminating disclosure, and the unnecessary or offensive intrusion of inquiries regarding religion, sex, politics, etc." While the ostensible objectives of this set of procedures are defensible, there is serious question about their effectiveness. The arbitrary censoring of items because they are socially sensitive operates only to protect the agency from embarrassment. Without careful consideration of the effect on the value and validity of the research, such review may fail to protect the subject, invalidate the research, and seriously inhibit research relating to important social problems.

More is at stake here than the effectiveness of educational research. Censorship merely to avoid offense to public sensitivities is totally inimical to a free society. Indeed the history of human progress is one of challenging established points of view. More often than not, such views survive the challenge and become better understood. But when the widely held view cannot withstand the challenge, whether or not the challenge touches public sensitivities, society learns and thus advances.

In addition to review by the supporting agencies, all questionnaires used by or in connection with projects supported by the Federal Government are subject to approval under the Federal Reports Act when there are 10 or more respondents involved. Administration of this act is lodged in the Bureau of the Budget. However, the Bureau of the Budget should not have to examine each project in detail for protection of privacy since this responsibility should rest with the individual Government agency sponsoring the studies and any participating institution.

A significant proportion of Government support of research employs the contract mechanism in which an agency invites a research proposal. In such cases, one or more would-be contractors propose to undertake research to meet the specifications and objectives defined by the agency. Most requests for proposals do not require that the bidder for the contract specify how he proposes to protect the subjects. This omission should be corrected. The agency which solicits the proposal has an obligation also to specify the degree of protection of subjects which must be provided.

Responsibilities Of Scientific Societies And Associations

The scientific associations in the behavioral sciences are custodians of and spokesmen for the values of their scientific disciplines. The current mores of these groups are reflected both in the setting of ethical standards and in their requirements for the admission of new members and for retention of membership.

It is obvious that the Federal Government cannot and should not prescribe a set of moral principles. Likewise, we cannot expect each man to develop de novo his own set of ethical principles without the guidance of those who have already experienced the ethical conflicts that are involved in behavioral research. It is thus logical to expect

that these professional associations, established to provide for the welfare of the behavioral sciences, will accept responsibility for establishing ethical principles and guidelines for conduct of research as one of their major purposes. These associations can make explicit certain rules of conduct and can provide the stimulus which will make information about such rules an integral part of the education of new research workers.

In addition, we expect these societies to provide a bridge between the discipline and the general public. This requires that professional societies play an active role in informing and educating the community at large and making their professional knowledge available to it.

No mechanism within the behavioral sciences is as well equipped to carry out these essential functions as that which can be offered by the professional societies themselves.

It is apparent that much of the criticism and anxiety expressed about behavioral research springs from failure to appreciate the nature of these sciences. If the public is to feel secure about behavioral research and to feel free to participate in it, then it must gain a greater understanding of its objectives, methods, and values.

The Role Of Scientific Journals

Closely associated with the role of the professional societies is the role of the editors of scientific journals. In the process of preparing this report, a number of recently published articles describing experimental studies and surveys were examined. It was found, in a few instances, that the procedures reported placed an undue burden on the respondent. In some, unnecessary physical or psychic pain appears to have been produced. In others, the amount of questioning involved appears to have been far in excess of that required to achieve the outcome of the investigation. In several, broad-scale personality inventories with inappropriate questions were used when more specific devices would have been better. In some reports, the procedures used were not described sufficiently to permit judgment on these points.

We believe that editors of scientific journals should require that manuscripts discuss the question of the propriety of the methods employed. Each investigator should be required to describe the burden on the respondent and the distress produced in him. Where deception is employed, the report should include an explanation of the experiment given to the subject afterwards. Where the respondent, because of the methods employed, has come to see within himself undesirable characteristics, the report of the researcher should include evidence that this trauma was handled satisfactorily. At present, some editors discourage reviews of the propriety of methods employed on the ground that they are not relevant to the results of research. Editors can do a great deal to establish high standards for the protection of subjects in behavioral research.

MEMBERS OF THE PANEL

Dr. Kenneth E. Clark, Chairman, Dean, College of Arts and Sciences, University of Rochester, Rochester, N.Y.

Dr. Bernard Berelson, Vice President, Population Council, Inc., 230 Park Avenue, New York, N.Y.

Dr. Edward J. Bloustein, President, Bennington College, Bennington, Vt.

Dr. George E. Pake, Provost, Washington University, St. Louis, Mo.

Dr. Colin S. Pittendrigh, Dean, Graduate School, Princeton University, Princeton, N.J.

Mr. Oscar M. Ruebhausen, Debevoise, Plimpton,

Lyons & Gates, 320 Park Avenue, New York, N.Y.

Dr. Walter S. Salant, Senior Staff—Economics Studies Division, Brookings Institution, 1775 Massachusetts Avenue N. W., Washington, D.C.

Dr. Robert Sears, Dean, School of Humanities and Sciences, Stanford University, Palo Alto, Calif.

Dr. Benson R. Snyder, Psychiatrist-in-Chief, Medical Department, Massachusetts Institute of Technology, Cambridge, Mass.

Dr. Frederick P. Thieme, Vice President, University of Washington, Seattle, Wash.

Consultants

Dr. Lawrence N. Bloomberg, Assistant Chief, Office of Statistical Standards, Bureau of the Budget.

Dr. Colin M. MacLeod, Deputy Director, Office of Science and Technology (Now: Vice President for Medical Affairs, The Commonwealth Fund, 1 East 75th Street, New York, N.Y.).

Technical Assistant

Dr. Richard M. Michaels, Office of Science and Technology.

FOOTNOTES

[1] Warren and Brandeis, "The Right to Privacy," 4 Harvard Law Review 193 (1890).
[2] Pound, "Interests of Personality," 28 Harvard Law Review 343 (1915).
[3] "Biomedical Science and Its Administration." A study of the National Institutes of Health. Government Printing Office, February 1965.

Freedom and Responsibility in Research: The "Springdale" Case

Human Organization

The case which follows documents the ethical dilemma posed by the divided responsibility and loyalty of the scholar to abstract science and to the human community who are his study focus. Less significant perhaps is the matter of proprietary rights in field efforts conducted by teams. Perhaps the basic question ultimately is what the research is for. For whom, for what ends? How does it contribute without impairing personal dignity, individual self-respect? And can it? Such questions must ultimately come to be raised about similar issues as libraries tend to be more and more studied in more and more sophisticated ways. Given the limits and gaps, and unanswered questions contained in the account, this selection still helps to pinpoint personal value assumptions and is certain to engender the type of intellectual discourse which makes a seminar a lively forum.

A small upstate New York village has now been immortalized in anthropological literature under the name of "Springdale." The local newspaper reports that the experience has not been entirely a pleasing one. We pass on this account:

"The people of the Village [Springdale] waited quite awhile to get even with Art Vidich, who wrote a *Peyton Place*-type book about their town recently.

"The featured float of the annual Fourth of July parade followed an authentic copy of the jacket of the book, *Small Town in Mass Society*, done large-scale by Mrs. Beverly Robinson. Following the book cover came residents of [Springdale] riding masked in cars labeled with the fictitious names given them in the book.

"But the pay-off was the final scene, a manure-spreader filled with very rich barnyard fertilizer, over which was bending an effigy of 'The Author'."

The account suggests that a good time was had by all—on this particular occasion. Nevertheless, local observers report that the disturbance caused by the book in the village has not been entirely compensated for by even such a ceremony carried out in the best anthropological traditions. The book and its aftermath raise some serious questions which, so far as we know, have never been publicly discussed. We feel that it is high time that these issues be raised:

1. What obligation does the author of a community study have to the people of the community he studies, particularly when it comes to publication of his findings?

2. When the author is a member of a research team, what obligations does he have to the project director? And what obligations does the project director have to him?

Vidich spent two and a half years living in "Springdale" as field director of a Cornell project carried out in the Department of Child Development and Family Relations. The project was directed by Urie Bronfenbrenner, a social psychologist. As a result of this research experience, Vidich published several articles, but the official report in book form regarding the project did not materialize during his tenure at Cornell and is only getting into print at this writing. Some time after he left Cornell, Vidich began work on a book of his own, in collaboration with Joseph Bensman, who had had no previous association with the project.

The Vidich manuscript gave rise to considerable controversy between the author and the Springdale project director. In presenting the issues which arose between them, we are indebted to both Bronfenbrenner and Vidich for allowing us to examine their correspondence (from late 1955 to 1958) regarding the manuscript.

SOURCE: Reprinted from "Freedom and Responsibility in Research: The 'Springdale' Case," *Human Organization*, 17 (Summer, 1958), pp. 1-2; 17 (Winter, 1958-1959), pp. 2-7; and 18 (Summer, 1959), pp. 49-50, by permission of The Society for Applied Anthropology, and reprinted from Cornell Studies in Social Growth, "Principles of Professional Ethics," *American Psychologist*, 7 (Aug., 1952), pp. 452-455, by permission of The American Psychological Association.

The points of controversy were essentially these:

1. Should individuals be identified in the book?
2. If individuals were identified, what—if anything—should be done to avoid damage to them?
3. Did Vidich have a right to use—or should he be allowed to use—project data which he did not gather himself? Who "owns" project data?

Before Vidich came onto the scene, Springdale people had been assured, when their collaboration was sought, that no individuals would be identified in printed reports. While all of the Vidich characters are given fictitious names, they can easily be identified within Springdale. The author argues that, when there is only one mayor and a small number of village and town officials and school board members, it is impossible to discuss the dynamics of the community without identifying individuals. He further argues that what he has reported in the book is "public knowledge" within Springdale. Even if this be true, is there a difference between "public knowledge" which circulates from mouth to mouth in the village and the same stories which appear in print?

In addition to his objections regarding the anonymity pledge, Bronfenbrenner claimed that certain individuals were described in ways which could be damaging to them. On this he submitted a long bill of particulars. One example (p. 97):

> One member of invisible government, in agreement with the principal's educational policy, has remarked that "He's a little too inhuman—has never got into anything in the town. He's good for Springdale until he gets things straightened out. Then we'll have to get rid of him."

Bronfenbrenner took the position that Vidich had no right to—and should not be allowed to—use project data beyond that which he personally had gathered. When Vidich wrote that, while he did not agree with Bronfenbrenner's reasoning, "wherever possible I will delete the material you consider objectionable," Bronfenbrenner responded by writing that, in this case, he would not object to having other project data used in his book. However, a comparison of the book with Bronfenbrenner's written objections indicates that, in most cases, changes were not made.

Beyond the specific questions raised by Bronfenbrenner, there is the more amorphous question of the "tone" of a book describing a community. Vidich speaks throughout of the "invisible govern-ment." (For this reason, the characters in his book rode with masks in the Fourth of July celebration.) The words themselves suggest an illegitimate form of activity, a conspiracy to gain and hold power. While Vidich himself says in a footnote that this is not true, the use of such a phrase, and the tone of his treatment, presents the behavior in that light, and so it has been interpreted in Springdale.

The Springdale experience also raises a general problem regarding the relations of a staff member to the project director in a team project, especially when there is a long period between the initiation of the study and the publication of major research reports. The junior member of such a staff must naturally think about establishing his own professional reputation, which he can do primarily through publication. An article or two will help, but a book would help even more. Is he to be a co-author on a book which represents a major report of the study? In that case, he may have to wait some time for the appearance of the book, and, in the meantime, he has little in the way of credentials to offer as he seeks new teaching and research jobs. Furthermore, when his name does finally appear on such a book, many people naturally assume that the book is largely the creation of the project director. A junior member may feel that he does not, in this way, get adequate recognition. The project director, on the other hand, already owns an established academic reputation and so does not feel a strong compulsion to rush into print with the findings of the project. Furthermore, he has other involvements on the campus of his university, which is not true of the field director.

Is there some way in which the project director can promote opportunities so that the junior staff members win their own reputations—without encouraging each man to go off in a completely independent direction? It was hoped in the Springdale project that this could be accomplished. Experience so far indicates that the results have not met the expectations on either side of the controversy.

We will let the author have the next-to-last word on the controversy. Replying in the *Ithaca Journal* to a statement made by Bronfenbrenner, Vidich writes:

> "Strictly speaking, I take the position that in the interests of the pursuit of scientific truth, no one, including research organizations, has a right to lay claims of ownership of research data.

"That is a violation of the entire spirit of disinterested research."

Asked whether he was aware that there would be a reaction in Springdale, Vidich replied:

> I was aware that there would be a reaction in the town when the book was published. While writing the book, however, it did not occur to us to anticipate what these reactions might be, nor did it occur to us to use such anticipations of reactions as a basis for selecting the data or carrying out the analysis.
>
> One can't gear social science writing to the expected reactions of any audience, and, if one does, the writing quickly degenerates into dishonesty, all objectivity in the sense that one can speak of objectivity in the social sciences is lost.

We do not have any firm answers to the various problems raised by this case, but we are quite convinced that the Vidich answer will not serve. He seems to take the position that he has a responsibility only to science. Has the researcher no responsibility to the people whom he studies? We are not prepared to state what the nature of this responsibility should be but we find it strange indeed to hear a researcher argue that he assumes no responsibility at all.

We suggest that this is a field in which we all need to reflect upon our own experiences in an effort to clarify the responsibilities we should be prepared to assume. The editor would be glad to hear from our members on any of the points raised here. Perhaps in this way, to borrow a phrase from the motto of Cornell University, we shall arrive at a better understanding of "freedom and responsibility" in field research.

Human Organization, 17 (Summer, 1958), pp. 1–2.

ARTHUR VIDICH AND JOSEPH BENSMAN[1]

We are pleased to be invited to join in the discussion of the issues which the Editor opened up in the editorial in *Human Organization*, Volume 17, Number 2, pp. 1–2.

The editorial raises issues worthy of discussion both with reference to the specific problems connected with the publication of our book, *Small Town in Mass Society*, and more importantly, to the general problem of the role of the researcher vis-à-vis both the community he studies and the research organizations which study human groups, organizations, and societies.

We feel, however, that his phrasing of the issues was too narrow, in that it was limited to the social and public relations problems of social science investigation. It failed to consider any of the problems related to the purposes of inquiry and to the scientific problems which social inquiry presumes to state and solve. For example, his editorial gave attention exclusively to the social scientist's responsibilities to the community and the research organization, and to his personal problems, such as career aspirations, rewards, publications, and the gaining of publicity. While all of these things are important as far as the organization of the discipline is concerned, they are irrelevant; progress in a science is somehow related to important substantive problems and issues, and the activities which lead to progress in the solution of the problems posed. This he altogether failed to bring up in his discussion.

His implication that publication in general is related only to career opportunism and that, specifically, this was our motive, is an extraordinarily limited perspective. In our case, we would feel that there are a large number of factors bearing on the writing of a book. All of these cannot be taken up in a brief reply such as this and, especially, they cannot be treated within the range of possibilities suggested by the editorial. We had thought that our Springdale material offered us an opportunity to define some problems central to basic anthropological and sociological theory, in a way would lead to some understanding of the development of contemporary society. In doing our work, we believe that these problems were worthy of inquiry and analysis, in and of themselves. We are gratified that almost all reviewers of *Small Town in Mass Society* have granted that we selected important problems and that we made some progress in stating and analyzing them.

In order to describe how the research developed we would like to present a short history of our work in relation to the Springdale project and the emergence of our book.

Vidich was employed by Cornell Studies in Social Growth, College of Home Economics, Cornell University, as a resident field director. His major duties in the field included administration of field surveys and supervision of field workers who interviewed the town's residents and observed the community's organizations. As an institutional obligation, he fronted for the project in the town and was responsible for maintaining rapport with all community members. As a result of this work, several thousand interviews were completed and three or four hundred protocols on meetings of community organizations were filed. In addition to these duties, Vidich acted as a participant observer in the community. In this capacity, he was allowed to do field work on his own initiative, using informal methods of research not subject to the formal mechanism of data collection.

In the course of this field work, Vidich and Bensman, who had worked together before on other problems, had occasion to discuss various aspects of the social structure of the community. Out of these conversations, which in the beginning were sporadic and almost aimless, there emerged a number of problems which we felt worthy of further thought and fuller exploration. The results of our work on these problems, as with all of the work which Vidich did alone or with others, were presented, as a matter of course, to project colleagues and were offered for discussion. By the end of the third year, a series of self-contained, separate papers, which both commented on aspects of the Springdale community and had some bearing on specific theoretical or methodological issues, were written and presented to the director, the project staff, and the head of the department. These papers consisted of an analysis of the participant-observer technique, a comparison of participant observation with survey data (in collaboration with Gilbert Shapiro), an analysis of the problem of the validity of data in social science, and an analysis of the relationships between the town and mass society.[2] All of this work had been submitted for publication while Vidich was still an employee of the project and, in addition, upon the invitation of Professor John Dean, the work on participant observation was presented to the Cornell University Social Science Seminar. There were other papers which we, Vidich and Bensman, had completed in draft form; one was an analysis of the class structure of the town and the other was a monograph-length analysis of the political structure of the town. All of this material was presented to the project staff while Vidich was still an employee. The project expressed no particular interest in these writings, or in the ideas which they represented, because they did not fall within the scope of its research design and theoretical focus. A book had not been envisaged by us at this time, although it was understood by everyone concerned that the project was free to use the manuscripts and drafts and articles for the several volumes which the project had planned at that time.

When Vidich completed his three-year appointment, the joint work with Bensman continued. The monograph on politics was entirely rewritten. The analysis of the role of the rural community in mass society was rewritten for presentation at a professional meeting. Again, all of this material, as it was completed and as a matter of course, was forwarded to the project. During all this time, except for the articles on "Participant Observation" and "The Validity of Field Data," no objection to the work was presented to the authors and the objections to the articles were of a substantive nature.

Only when the authors thought that they had discovered a theme which could sustain a more extended and unified treatment, did the possibility of a book emerge. Their intention of doing a book was presented in conference to the project staff. There were no objections to this enterprise, and it was not only understood, but also specified, that all work was to be forwarded in manuscript form, as it was completed, to the project, which of course we did.

About a year and a half later, only after we had presented a manuscript, complete except for a few chapters, were any objections made. A project policy was then formulated:

> It is clear from your material that all of us must face a rather complex problem in terms of the identifiability of organizations and people within the Springdale community—a problem which cannot be avoided even with the care we are taking to disguise individuals and groups through deliberate alteration and recombination of important identifying characteristics. This problem is further accentuated by the fact that our research was sponsored by the New York State College of Home Economics. We have given the whole matter careful consideration and have agreed to the following procedure. Before any manuscripts are shown to outside representatives, such as publishers or their agents, we shall ask one or two persons within the college and possibly in Springdale, to read the manuscripts from the point of view of public relations. Although the final responsibility for deciding what we publish will rest with the project staff, the reactions of such readers would receive serious consideration and we would probably re-write and omit in accordance with their recommendations.

We did not accept this policy and said so. However, project members were given every opportunity to state their objections. We took such objections as were made under advisement and felt free to accept or reject them, doing so in relation to the necessity of treating the issues under consideration. We believed that it was impossible to discuss leadership without discussing leaders, politics without mentioning politicians, education without treatment of educators, and religion without ministers. In this sense, we violated the project policy of anonymity. At no point, however, did we gratuitously call attention to identifiable individuals beyond the necessity of treating the material and, when this was done, pseudonyms were used. In all cases, the decision of what material to accept and reject was our own.

The policy on the use of project material only emerged after the entire manuscript was completed:

> . . . your book should not utilize or make reference to any of the "official" data of the project such as survey results or observer and interviewer reports.

Previously, the project had let us use selected project data which did not fall within the purview of the project's central focus. When the project's permission to use their data was revoked, we went through the manuscript before typing a final draft and cut substantial portions of their data which we had used for illustrative purposes. These were observer's protocols which were used to illustrate the organizational operations of the political boards and the school board. We felt we were successful in these excisions in almost all cases, but we know that there are six quotations on pages 125, 151, 157, 161-163, 173-174, 182-186, and the two census-like tables on pages 17 and 18, which technically were the property of the project. If there is any feeling that we have not given due credit for the use of this data, we wish to do so now.

The particular fates of Vidich, Bensman, the project, the department, Cornell University, Springdale, etc. are of much less significance than the problems which the editorial raises for the future of scientific investigation in western society. Not that the Springdale example presents a new problem; on the contrary, negative reactions by organizations, individuals, and interest groups have been characteristic for the Lynds' study of *Middletown*, West's study of *Plainville*, Warner's study of *Yankee City*, Selznick's study of the *T.V.A.*, Hunter's study of *Community Power*, and Whyte's study of *Street Corner Society* in the latter case, Doc still suffers from the recognition he received in the book.

Historically, this problem has not appeared, or has appeared to a much lesser extent, in the anthropology of non-western society. This is beeause primitive populations have been less concerned, aware, and vocal in their response to the anthropological description of their societies. The life history, studies of native politics and organizations, etc., all invade the native's "privacy," subject his inner life to exposure, and strip him of the magic on which his existence rests. Because it was possible to do this with native society, sociologists and anthropologists have learned a great deal about social life which they could apply to western society. Now that so many primitives have become westernized and are aware of the implications of anthropological research, they, too, resent the invasion of privacy and descriptions of the inner structure of their society.

There is an interesting parallel between the license taken by anthropologists and that taken by sociologists who have studied crime, minority groups, caste groups, factory workers, prostitutes, psychopathic personalities, hoboes, taxi-dancers, beggars, marginal workers, slum dwellers, and other voiceless, powerless, unrespected, and disreputable groups. Negative reaction to community and organizational research is only heard when results describe articulate, powerful, and respected individuals and organizations.[3] We believe there would have been no objection to our study if it had been limited solely to the shack people.

We think all of the community and organizational studies mentioned above made important contributions. The problem is: *At what price should a contribution be made?*

One of the principal ideas of our book is that the public atmosphere of an organization or a community tends to be optimistic, positive, and geared to the public relations image of the community or the organization. The public mentality veils the dynamics and functional determinants of the group being studied. Any attempt in social analysis at presenting other than public relations rends the veil and must necessarily cause resentment. Moreover, any organization tends to represent a balance of divergent interests held in some kind of equilibrium by the power status of the parties involved.[4] A simple description of these factors, no matter how stated, will offend some of the groups in question.[5]

The only way to avoid such problems is not to deal with articulate groups who will publicly resist the attention which research gives to them, or to deal with the problems in such a way that they are inoffensive. Research of this type becomes banal, irrespective of its technical and methodological virtuosity.[6] We think this has always been the case and that the Springdale example presents nothing new.

What has changed since *Middletown* and *Street Corner Society* is the organization and financing of research. At the present time, research is carried on by large-scale organizations of a relatively permanent nature and it is financed by businesses, governments, foundations, research centers, and colleges which have vested interests apart from the research. The successful researcher in this setting is expected to be aware of, and to anticipate, these interests, regardless of whether a policy is ever explicitly made.

The researcher, working for a commerical firm, or even for a governmental agency, must develop an ethic of responsibility. He defines the problem on which he will work in a way which will be useful to his sponsors. He deals only with material which is salient to their defined needs and interests. He writes, edits, and censors his own material so that it will appear in a way which enhances the interests of his employers. There is no implication here of outright dishonesty. The researcher who did other than this would be violating his contractual obligation to his employers if he exposed them to an unfavorable limelight or to public attention which might cause embarrassment. This is only to be expected. If the researcher confines himself to research problems which are of immediate interest to these groups, and publishes only findings which are acceptable to his employers-sponsors-supporters, he meets his obligation.

If, however, as in our work, fundamental issues which are related to the basic problems of social sciences are raised, one cannot predict in advance the embarrassment which research may cause, including the embarrassment to oneself. If the social scientist wants to raise these kinds of issues, he has to risk the possibility of getting into these kinds of troubles. We foresaw this, as the research progressed, and there is no easy solution to the problem.

We think the social scientist can only answer the problem for himself, by asking himself what kind of research he wants to do. If he wants to do practical research which is important to some sponsoring body, he must accept the ethic of responsibility and give up the illusion of independent inquiry. If he wishes to do serious research on problems which are not practical (as practicality is now defined in modern society) he must almost certainly conclude that he must work outside the framework of large research organizations, large institutional grants, or research-servicing organizations. The choice he makes must then be a personal one and, in each case, he can preserve the ethical system he has selected.

However, if social science is to have some kind of independent problems and identity and, if a disinterested effort is to be made to solve these problems, a certain number of social scientists, presumably residing at universities, must be willing to resist the claims for planned, popular, practical research.[7]

ROBERT RISLEY[8]

I have just read the editorial in *Human Organization* on the Vidich incident and would like to congratulate the editor on the manner in which he has set forth the fundamental issues.

As he knows, from our earlier discussions of this problem, I find myself in an interesting dual role in this case. On the one hand, I live in "Springdale," the community in which the study was made, associate with the individuals about whom it was written, and, in fact, was one of those interviewed in the course of the sudy. On the other hand, in the course of directing graduate students in their thesis work and in research of my own, including particularly some work in the small business area, I find it necessary to obtain community cooperation and understanding in order to obtain participation. As a consequence, my comments on the editorial relate, in part, to the knowledge which I have of the reaction and attitudes of individuals in "Springdale" to the study and its impact and, in part, to the problems which it seems to me are inherent in this type of research activity in the social sciences.

It seems to me that, if we are to be able to conduct research within the world of reality in the social science area, there are two principles which we have to accept. The first of these is that it is essential that we arrive at a clear understanding with those with whom we are to work concerning the nature of the reports and the publications which are to grow out of the research and, in particular, concerning the degree to which the specific situations or individuals in it will be cloaked with anonymity.

It may well be, on occasion, that, at an early stage of a project, there is temptation to provide greater assurances concerning anonymity than are justified in view of any use of data in published form. Sometimes this is done in order to "get in," with the thought that, once in, matters can be resolved later. It seems to me that this is not appropriate and if, in a given situation, agreements cannot be arrived at which are satisfactory to the researcher and to those individuals within the situation which is to be studied, research opportunities must be sought elsewhere. As a related point to this issue, it should, likewise, be clearly understood what review rights, if any, those being studied will have of the material prior to publication.

The second principle is that, if an individual in charge of a project has arrived at some understanding on these points in a given situation, those working with him are bound by the understanding as much as he. Possibly the director should make clear to the individuals who are planning to become involved in the project, the circumstances under which it is being undertaken. It seems to me clear, however, that the basic understanding arrived at by the director and the group being studied must be binding on all involved. Anything less than this provides no real standard of ethics which will be acceptable and will result in developing an unwillingness to permit research into lives and affairs of individuals, organizations, or communities.

As a corollary of this point, it seems to me that individuals who are hired to work on a project are not free to use data obtained from the project for their own purposes. Essentially, my position would be that the material accumulated by individuals assigned to the project belongs to the project. Consequently, no use should be made of data which a staff member of a project obtains, except in a situation in which the staff member has received authorization for its use from the individual heading the project.

I realize that my line of reasoning obviously will cause problems for junior members on the projects and might well be viewed as interfering with the freedom of a researcher. As the editor so well points out, however, "this freedom like other freedoms is balanced by responsibility." It seems to me, however, without the acceptance of some such mode of operation as I have suggested, there is no guarantee of this responsibility being exercised. What I am suggesting here seems to me to be consistent with the kind of ethics involved in other professions. Unless some such standard of ethics is generally accepted and acknowledged by those in the social science research area, access to individuals and groups for study will be severely limited.

Unfortunately, a violation of such ethics reflects, not only upon the individual concerned, but broadly upon the whole field of such research and upon individuals engaged in it. In the Vidich incident, I know that the feelings and distrust aroused will be generalized to a point where the feelings of the individuals and community involved

are such that I suspect it would be many, many years before any type of social research undertaken by anyone could be conducted in this community. Further, the indictment in this particular incident has been, not only against Vidich as such, but against all the others involved in the study and, in at least the minds of some, against the academic profession and the university.

RAYMOND E. RIES[9]

It seems clear that social scientists are as culpable as other human beings in their failure to carry out in practice the implications of their theoretical positions. For many years now, American social science has been insistent upon a sharp distinction between the spheres of science and value. In the area of public policy, it has claimed that the knowledge of the economist or sociologist is instrumental only, that it can in no way determine the ends or values which the community or its individuals should choose. The social scientist may clarify alternatives in action, he may point out the consequences of intended actions, but it is only as a citizen that he can decide which course to take. With a heavy hand, the textbooks in social science point out repeatedly that objectivity requires the elimination of bias, prejudice, and values of the investigator. And it is more apparent today, than it was generally forty years ago, that science has come to a grinding halt at the threshold of questions of the meaning and values of human life and conduct.

But the intellectual heritage within which science and values were perceived as exclusive has not been entirely accepted by American social science. Perhaps the tragic implications of this view were muted by the characteristic optimism of the American. While it was accepted that scientific objectivity required the exclusion of judgments of value, scientific objectivity became transformed into a value and meaning in itself. Somehow scientific objectivity became an object of faith and a road to salvation. When Lundberg posed the question: "Can Science Save Us?," his answer was "yes." But such a question is quite beyond science. As Max Weber pointed out forty years ago, science in itself is useful but meaningless in the sense that it can give no answer to the question, "What shall we do and how shall we live?".

Activities conducted in the name of science can be morally reprehensible, but the pursuit of objectivity in no way tells us this. The dramatic illustration of this fact was found in the Nazi medical experiments. Less dramatic and, therefore, apparently less reprehensible, is the deliberate misinforming of subjects in the "experimental situation," which some social scientists like to employ. One should include the field research situation, in which, the informant is made a victim of his trust in the researcher. Analogous situations appear in "theoretical" writings. I am reminded of an innocent statement of R. K. Merton, in his discussion of latent functions performed by the political boss:

> Examined for a moment apart from any "moral" considerations, the political apparatus of the boss . . . performs these functions (economic regulation, help to the destitute, etc.) with a minimum of inefficiency.

Indeed, such a statement could remain morally neutral only for a moment. Vidich's justification for the community study publication, which exposed the privacy of persons and utilized some data gathered by a cooperative effort—namely, that it was done in name of science—likewise only holds for a moment. Science can provide no statement of meaning or value, in terms of which ends (in this instance publication), may be chosen. My reaction to Vidich's situation is generalized to a rejection of the principle that pursuit of scientific objectivity is a value to which questions of moral responsibility are subordinate.

In this world, there are few, if any, men who can live an ethic of absolute ends. However, men, and only men, are morally responsible for their actions. Neither the corporation, the state, nor any collectivity, including scientific institutions, can substitute for the integrity of the individual. As sociologists are fond of reminding us, these are, after all, mere abstractions, and the tradition of western civilization has been decisive here. The social scientist has to face the fact that he is morally responsible for his scientific activities and that his science and its objectivity is not evidence of sainthood.

This is nothing more than what Max Weber said forty years ago. To affirm that the vocation of a social scientist can be understood a "God's calling" is a mere pretense. At the same time, "value free" social science is, in itself, meaningless. A meaningful social science is one in which we recognize the value implications of our own behavior.

HOWARD S. BECKER[10]

In a certain sense, the three questions the editor raises can be regarded as irrelevant to the issue of junior staff-project director relations. In this sense, at least: although the questions are important, what does matter is that there should be a clear agreement on them between staff and director at the time of hiring. Troubles arise precisely when these questions are left up in the air and each party makes certain assumptions, which may not be true, about what their rights and obligations are. If Vidich and Bronfenbrenner had stated beforehand the positions they now take, Vidich might not have wanted the job and Bronfenbrenner might not have hired him. If they had stated their positions and worked out an acceptable compromise, they would each now be bound by it. All issues of what data would be available to what people, who would have publication rights, etc., should, in my view, be made very explicit at the time of hiring. In addition to these "standard" issues, there should be an imaginative and frank exploration of ideas about such questions as the researcher's obligations to those he studies, the balance to be observed between "scientific objectivity" and "avoiding damage to respondents," etc. This exploration should culminate in an explicit agreement as to the line which all project personnel will take with regard to these issues.

Now, of course, some of these questions require other kinds of answers than simple agreement between project director and staff because an entire project might agree on standards and procedures we would argue to be wrong. For instance, I agree that the researcher has some obligation to those he studies. This obligation is contained in the commitments he made to these people at the time of the study. If he promised, explicitly or implicitly, not to identify them, no appeal to "objectivity" can release him from his obligation to honor that promise. He is required to observe it, first, by the obligation he assumed with the promise and, second, by his obligation not to give social science a bad name (which obligation he assumes when he identifies himself to those he studies as a social scientist). If a man wishes to identify the objects of his study, all right; but he must not get his material by taking on obligations which he will not honor. He can state his intentions to the people he studies and can identify himself as a journalist, or a man who wants to write a book, and thus be free to publish whatever he pleases.

All I have said so far, really, is that people ought to be explicit about the bargains they make—with their employees, employers, and research subjects—and then stick by them; and that they must recognize the obligations they implicitly assume toward these people and toward their own colleagues. It seems to me that the Society (possibly in collaboration with other scientific societies in sociology, anthropology, and related fields) could make a great contribution by initiating some formal discussion on the kinds of bargains which social scientists can honorably make with one another and with their objects of study. I do not have in mind anything like writing a "standard contract" for all project directors to make with their employees for, obviously, there is great variety possible, depending on the people involved. But at least we could spell out the points which ought to be covered in such agreements and try to make it standard practice for these things to be discussed openly. I believe that, in the hiring situation, the project director often does not think of these points and the junior staff person is afraid to bring them up.

Human Organization, 17 (Winter, 1958–1959), pp. 2–7.

EARL H. BELL[11]

I read with great interest the editorial, "Freedom and Responsibility in Research: The Springdale Case." The problem relative to responsibility of authors to the community is one which always pushes itself into focus when I start writing a report. Personally, I have come to the conclusion that responsibility to the community does *not* conflict with responsibility to science. As a matter of fact, I have found frequently that attempting to state material coolly and objectively, rather than in terms of personalities and anecdotes, sharpens my understanding of sociological processes.

After writing the first draft of the Haskell County, Kansas Study, I took the manuscript to the community and went over it with my major informants. In many ways, this was the most productive part of the field work. It enabled the informants, for the first time, to understand what I was attempting to accomplish. This broader understanding brought to mind many things which they had not told me, largely because I did not have the knowledge of the culture and social system to formulate some significant questions. They also pointed out numerous errors of both fact and interpretation and thus saved me personal embarrassment and scientific error.

Douglas Haring also involved key informants in the review and criticism of draft copies of articles

growing out of his field work in the Ryukyu Islands. He reports experiences similar to mine.

Ralph Linton used to say that we never would know the great errors in ethnological studies because non-literate people were not able to "talk back."

In summary, it seems evident to me that conscientiously fulfilling our responsibility to the community need not weaken our scientific integrity. Indeed, it may improve the scientific quality of our final product.

URIE BRONFENBRENNER[12]

In their comments on your editorial on "Freedom and Responsibility in Research," Vidich and Bensman state that a policy regarding "The identifiability of people and organizations within the Springdale community" was not formulated until after Vidich had left the employ of the project and had submitted a manuscript of his book.

Ironically enough, the Springdale project is probably the only social research endeavor which went to the trouble of developing an explicit code of professional ethics prior to the initiation of major field operations. The following is a reprint of an article from *The American Psychologist*, Volume 7, Number 8 (August 1952), which presents this code in full. Although the code does not refer to publication specifically, the general implications are obvious. The implications were made explicit in frequent statements to residents of the community.

Vidich joined the staff in the fall of 1951, was shown copies of this code, and participated as a staff member in a training program for field workers in which the principles were a major focus of attention. What is even more important, residents of the community were informed on numerous occasions that no material would be published which might identify particular individuals or groups.

The principles had been developed prior to the hiring of a field director (Vidich) precisely for the reasons stressed by Becker in his comments on this same issue:

> . . . What does matter is that there should be a clear agreement . . . between staff and director at the time of hiring. Troubles arise precisely when these things are left up in the air, and each party makes assumptions which may not be true about what their obligations and responsibilities are.[13]

A number of the principles bear directly on the

issues raised by Professor Whyte in his editorial. The code is included in its entirety since it may be of interest as one model for the ethical conduct of social researchers.

Human Organization, 18 (Summer, 1959), pp. 49–50.

PRINCIPLES OF PROFESSIONAL ETHICS CORNELL STUDIES IN SOCIAL GROWTH

The "Principles of Professional Ethics" were developed by the members of the staff of Cornell Studies in Social Growth, a long-range program of team research sponsored by the Department of Child Development and Family Relationships in the College of Home Economics at Cornell University. Miss Doris Kells, a clinical psychologist, had the major responsibility for collating ideas and preparing drafts for staff discussion. The code represents an attempt to anticipate the ethical problems likely to arise in a community study (The Springdale Project) involving extensive interviewing and observation by specially trained graduate students working under faculty supervision. The present preliminary draft was drawn up before the most intensive phase of field operations had begun. Since that time, experience has underscored two important considerations.

1. A code of professional ethics defeats its purpose if it is treated as a set of rules to be followed without question. It is effective only to the degree that it provokes genuine consideration—and even conflict—in the mind of the individual research worker, who has a value commitment not only to professional ethics but also to scientific investigation. These two sets of values are not always harmoniously matched, so that the researcher must weigh possible scientific gains against the risks involved. Thus it is manifestly impossible to conduct meaningful social research which does not in some degree invade the privacy and security of other human beings. Therefore the responsible scientific investigator cannot avoid the conflictful question of whether the invasion which he proposes to undertake is really justified by the potential gain in scientific knowledge.

2. This leads to a second and even more difficult dilemma, namely, that the social and psychological consequences of a particular research procedure often cannot be forseen. Thus the only safe way to avoid violating principles of professional ethics is to refrain from doing social research altogether. It follows that the scientist, having tried earnestly to recognize and weigh the social consequences of his scientific activity, must always be ready to accept responsibility for and discontinue in midpassage procedures which prove more damaging than was originally anticipated and considered justifiable.

These two considerations, while they seem in their immediate consequences to be delimiting for scientific progress, may in the long run, through establishing more viable experimenter-subject relationships and sensitizing the investigator to hitherto unrecognized variables in the experimental situation, enrich rather than impoverish our scientific insights and experimental designs.

—Urie Bronfenbrenner

Preamble: A code of ethical procedures for research operations serves a twofold purpose. The first is to safeguard the integrity and welfare of those who serve as subjects for or who may be affected by the research study. The second is to give proper and necessary recognition in the research design to the variables introduced by the presence of the research worker in the field and the consequent awareness of community members that they are under study. We are operating then on a double premise: (1) The integrity and well-being of those studied are to be vouchsafed and respected in recognition of ethical human values. (2) The ethical values implicit in any research operation and their consequent procedural expressions must be made explicit and incorporated into the research design in the interests of sound scientific method, for otherwise they would represent unknown or uncontrolled variables. Only by taking into account the ethical import of research activities can the effects of the research upon those being studied be reckoned.

It will be noted that this document contains not only a section devoted to *General Principles and Ethics in the Field but also a section on Relationships among Research Workers (staff and trainees)*. Here again the reason is twofold: (1) To take cognizance of ethical human values in the intragroup research operations. (2) To help insure the carrying out of the research design since the ethical values governing intragroup research relationships will tend to be reflected in the research relationships established with the community and also in the handling of data (e.g., matters of confidentiality).

I. General Principles

A. Professional ethics in research activities are a matter of first priority.

1. Progress in learning to establish adequate field relations and to apply ethical principles has first priority in evaluating trainees' continuation in the program and staff members' operations in the field.

2. Responsibility for the welfare of persons under study is a continuing one for all research workers (trainees and staff).

B. The social scientist views people as individuals, not as subjects to be exploited. Specifically, he takes every precaution to preserve the security and privacy of the individuals and groups under study.

1. Each technique developed for field use is carefully considered in terms of its potential for provoking anxiety or invading privacy. The research intent is to reduce maximally such threats.

2. The research worker in the practice of his profession shows regard for the social codes and moral expectations of the persons with whom he works.

3. To the maximum degree possible, the free consent of persons[14] involved is secured at each stage of research activity.

a. In requesting verbal consent, persons are given as direct and explicit an account as possible of research objectives and purposes. In requesting consent the investigator does not attempt to evoke or capitalize on feelings of obligation or desires to please.

b. Consent can be secured only in relation to those experiences the consequences of which the person is in a position to appreciate; that is, consent to an unknown experience is not regarded as true consent.

4. The basic criterion for the investigator's interest in and inclusion of all data is that they have relevance to the problem under investigation.

a. Any material given to the investigator in his role as research worker is suitable for inclusion in research records. Material offered or secured in any other context is not suitable for the records. Examples of material not suitable are: (1) material given to the investigator on the assumption that he is a personal friend or counsellor, rather than a research worker; (2) material given with the specific request that it be kept off-the-record (i.e., not recorded or communicated to anyone else).

5. All data from the field are regarded as confidential and every precaution is taken to insure the anonymity of individuals and groups save as such knowledge is essential to the work of persons specifically charged with responsibility for those data.

a. Information secured about persons involved in research is used primarily for research purposes. With proper regard for anonymity it may also be used for training and instructional purposes. Information that can be *identified with* community, specific groups, or individuals is used *only* for research purposes including training. With proper regard for anonymity it may also be used for other instruction (e.g., university classes).

b. Staff and trainees have access only to those files containing data essential to their work.

c. Permission to use field data for special research problems (e.g., theses, term reports, etc.) is granted by the staff as a whole. Permission is contingent upon the worker's ability to comply with the principles of professional ethics here outlined. In each instance the worker shall be instructed in his responsibility for maintaining the confidentiality of the material with which he works.

d. Trainees are evaluated and screened with regard to their ability to be entrusted with confidential data before identifiable group or individual material is used for training purposes and before trainees go into the field.

e. Professional colleagues shall not be told the name of the community(ies) under study save as it is essential for their own work, and regard for anonymity shall be maintained in conveying information regarding research procedures, data, hypotheses, etc.

f. Research workers have the responsibility for informing and indoctrinating family members in the professional ethics of field operations.

(1) Family discussion of individuals or groups under study is to be kept at a minimum.

(2) Family participation in community affairs is to be carefully planned to enhance rather than inhibit research relationships.

g. Personal information about research subjects, whether or not these subjects are identified by name, is not an appropriate topic for discussion at social affairs, informal gatherings, conversations with friends, etc. Discussion of the purpose of the study, the research design, or any generalized findings do not, of course, come under this heading.

h. Field activities and data are not suitable topics for entertaining staff members, colleagues, visitors, students, etc. In like manner, persons or community are not exhibited as a curiosity to visitors, friends, etc.

II. Ethics in the Field

A. Role and responsibilities of field worker are clearly specified before the field worker goes into the field (campus, community, etc.) and changes in the conception of the job or of the field worker's responsibilities are a matter for staff decision.

1. Whenever the field worker finds that circumstances require his adopting a role not covered by previous specifications, it is his responsibility to bring this to the attention of the appropriate supervisor or staff group for discussion and decision.

B. In this project, the research design limits the role of the research worker to that of scientific investigator. He is not an agent for change, a therapist, or specialist who can serve as a resource person. There are two reasons for this policy: (1) To reduce the number of complicating variables by designing the research procedures to have minimal effect on the lives of the community members. (2) To keep at a minimum any activities by staff members which may evoke feelings of conflict or anxiety.

C. It is the field worker's responsibility to keep his field role in the dimension of scientific investigator.

D. Every reasonable effort shall be made to convey to the persons under study, the nature and limits of the job of the field worker.

III. Relationships Among Research Workers (Staff and Trainees)

A. No research member is asked to undertake any activity which is not in harmony with his personal ethics and beliefs.

B. Any reflections upon the personality or actions of a field worker by a person involved in the research studies are considered to be a private matter. Wherever this is of vital concern to the research project, the matter should be discussed with a staff member. If the incident is to be made a part of the field report, it should be done only after discussion and agreement with the field worker concerned.

C. The responsibility of staff member to trainee is that of training him in research activities.[15] The training program in all its aspects is to be job-oriented.

D. It is staff responsibility to keep clear explicitly (in training) and implicitly (in office relations, etc.) the nature of the job and responsibilities of the staff and the nature of the job and responsibilities of the trainee.

E. It is staff responsibility to keep well-structured in the minds of the trainees their status-in-training and their responsibilities in the research project.

1. It is staff responsibility to convey to the trainee at the beginning of and throughout his training, the opportunities, limits, and trial nature of his participation in the research program.

2. It is staff responsibility to conduct planned evaluation conferences with trainees sufficiently frequently to provide them with a realistic awareness of their progress and status-in-training.

F. The basis for evaluation-selection of trainees for assistantships or other jobs on the project is their performance on the job.

G. In the event of evaluation-selection of trainee for assistantship or other job for which he has not had a previous trial, personal factors are considered in so far as they are pertinent to the job to be filled and have been evidenced in the trainee's performance during training.

1. Pertinent information known to a staff member by virtue of his activities and relationships outside of the research staff is not a proper subject for discussion with other staff members, but may properly influence the individual decision of that staff member in regard to the trainee's job qualifications.

H. It is staff responsibility to convey to the trainee, by precept and example, the professional ethics implicit and explicit in this document.

1. The area of professional ethics shall be included as an integral part of the training program.

American Psychologist, 7 (Aug., 1952), pp. 452-455.

FOOTNOTES

[1] Dr. Vidich is Assistant Professor of Anthropology at the University of Connecticut, Storrs, Connecticut.

Joseph Bensman is Manager of Consumer Research, William Esty & Co., Inc. and Lecturer in Social Sciences at Brooklyn College.

[2] Published as "The Validity of Field Data," *Human Organization*, XIII, No. 1 (Spring, 1954), 20–27; "Participant Observation and the Collection and Interpretation of Data," *American Journal of Sociology*, LX, No. 4 (Jan. 1955), 354–360; "A Comparison of Participant Observation and Survey Data," *American Sociological Review*, XX, No. 1 (Feb. 1955),

28–33; "Methodological Problems in the Observation of Husband-Wife Interaction," *Marriage and Family Living*, XVIII, No. 3, 234–239.

[3]C. Wright Mills, "The Professional Ideology of the Social Pathologists," *American Journal of Sociology*, XLIV, No. 2 (1939), 415–435.

[4]William Foote Whyte, *Street Corner Society*, University of Chicago Press (enlarged ed.), Chicago, 1954. See especially, Chap. VI, Section 6, "The Nature of Political Obligations."

[5]See the authors' "Validity of Field Data," *op. cit.*

[6]It is ironical that the very acceptance of research by all kinds of public agencies, businesses, managements, professions, unions, bureaucracies, churches, and other established and respected institutions tends to vitiate the power of research to deal with social issues for their own sake.

[7]Bernard Rosenberg, *The Values of Veblen*, Public Affairs Press, Washington, D.C., 1956, especially Chap. I for similar structures.

[8]Dr. Risley is Acting Dean of the New York State School of Industrial and Labor Relations, Cornell University, Ithaca, New York.

[9]Dr. Ries is Assistant Professor of Sociology of Colgate University in Hamilton, New York.

[10]Dr. Becker is Research Associate on the staff of Community Studies, Inc., a non-profit social science research organization located in Kansas City, Missouri.

[11]Dr. Bell is in the Department of Sociology and Anthropology at Syracuse University.

[12]Dr. Bronfenbrenner is in the Department of Child Development and Family Relationships, Cornell University, Ithaca, New York.

[13]Howard S. Becker, " 'Freedom and Responsibility in Research': A comment," *Human Organization*, XVII, No. 4 (Winter 1958–1959), 6.

[14]Throughout this document "persons" refers to all those who serve as research subjects; e.g., residents of the community under study, persons being tested, college students used in pre-field trials, etc.

[15]The functions of academic advisor, teacher of a subject-matter field, or personal counsellor, if they occur between staff member and trainee, are in the context of the staff member's role as member of the faculty or as personal acquaintance.

Inquiry and Policy: The Relation of Knowledge to Action

by Max F. Millikan

Here are both sides of the coin beautifully and logically explicated. On the one side is the operator's perspective—subject to the pressures of decision making and limited in his tolerance for the intellectual game which the researcher seems to be engaged upon. On the other—the angry scholar, sensitive of his prerogatives, reluctant to be manipulated or to be viewed to have sold out, and self-conscious about his professional standing if he gets his hands too dirty in applied work. Millikan identifies the problem as essentially that of polarity, with communication breakdown as the fundamental constraint. He details how the decision maker employs facts, while the researcher restructures concepts, and the need for policy to rely upon prediction in a time when social science is too frequently limited in its capacity to deliver predictors. Expectations and views of the role on both sides are seen to be distorted and at fault, with discourse and mutual understanding the route to better relations. Particularly germane to library research is the discussion about differences in the end value sought between men of action and men of knowledge. Also apt is the characterization of clashes in interest and utility most common at early stages of a science where the capacity of a scholarship to deliver anything more than intellectual approaches is limited. Here in essence lies the disappointment of library practice in the product of library research. Millikan's key words may very well be patience and discourse.

People do research for two reasons: first, because it is interesting, and second, because it may be useful. The relations of researchers with men of action are sometimes complicated by the fact that useful knowledge is not always interesting, or interesting knowledge necessarily useful. Thus, although researchers and decision-makers enjoy flirting with each other, if they are to make a serious and congenial marriage both parties must recognize—more than they usually do—the kinds of circumstances in which usefulness and interest coincide.

In the natural sciences a *modus vivendi* has been evolved over the past few generations which, although it does not avoid occasional domestic conflict, at least permits the necessary degree of cooperation on matters of importance. The engineer knows that he needs the natural scientist and has a pretty good idea of how to use him; the natural scientist in turn has learned something about which of his discoveries have action implications, and how these implications can be elaborated usefully for the operator.

In the social sciences, on the other hand, attempts to effect such a union have too frequently resulted in frustration and disillusion. Recently, and especially since World War II, there has been a growing feeling among both operators and social scientists that the growing body of social science knowledge should be applied to the solution of some of the pressing policy problems of our time. The remaining question is that of how it is to be applied. In certain fields this has been done with some success. Economic theory has proved relevant to the problem of controlling economic fluctuations in the more advanced countries. The work of students of the psychology of learning has influenced educational policy. Business enterprises have improved the productivity and satisfactions of their employees and sharpened the effectiveness of their advertising with the help of social science research. But in other areas the efforts of operators to use social scientists have been much less rewarding.

The contributions of social science to the solution of the great international problems of our time have not been notable. In the United States, at least, this has not been for want of trying. Here, the government has financed a variety of social science research projects designed in one way or another to illuminate foreign policy, and the great American foundations have supported a great deal of work directed to the same end. Yet the results to date have been disappointing to both the operators and the researchers.

The disappointment of those who have commissioned the research shows itself in a number of ways. They feel in the first place that much of what has been done is either useless or irrelevant to the problems they are struggling with. The work is obviously painstaking and thorough, a great deal of material has been surveyed, elaborate classifications have been developed, and a great many facts have been assembled. But there is a frustrated and irritated feeling that, when one has waded through a fat research report, one is no nearer to the answers he is seeking than when he began. When projects are formulated there seems to be agreement as to the problems to be explored; yet, when the results emerge, the problems the social scientist has been grappling with appear to be quite different from those the operator is interested in. The "conclusions" of such projects, in particular, often emerge as conclusions not as to what should be done—and how—but as to ways of describing in technical language a state of affairs with which journalists and diplomats have long felt they were familiar. This leads to a feeling that the social scientist stubbornly rejects the operator's real problems for some relatively unimportant or narrow aspect of a general issue, one which happens to interest him or to which his disciplinary tools happen to apply, leaving the central problem posed but unresolved.

All this is complicated by the operator's impression that the researcher is playing with complex intellectual machinery for its own sake. There seems an unnecessary amount of special language, a wearisome spinning-out of definitions, subtle distinctions, and elaborate classifications, and a ponderous amassing of documentation. Finally, if relevant conclusions do ultimately appear, they turn out to be things one knew in advance. The whole process appears to be a peculiarly complicated way of saying the obvious.

Similarly, and as often, the social science researcher emerges from the experiment angry and resentful at its failure. He probably undertook an applied research assignment with grave misgivings in the first place. There is a tradition in the aca-

demic world that to undertake research on behalf of a customer, particularly for pay, is to sell one's soul to the devil. The scientist is apt to have a strong conviction that applied research cannot be "fundamental," that there is something inherently contradictory in the advance of knowledge and the service of practical ends, and that to work for a policy-maker is therefore somehow to prejudice one's professional standing. Allied with this (particularly among social scientists) is a set of moral qualms concerning the ethics of placing scientific analysis in the service of persons who wish, for whatever purposes, to manipulate human beings. It may be recognized that the essence of social action is the manipulation of human behavior; nevertheless, there is a feeling that the scientific objectivity of an observer cannot help but be compromised by his involvement in a manipulative problem.

The recent history of social science is the history of a struggle on the part of social scientists to make their work more positive and less normative, to eliminate from the analysis of human behavior the influence of the value judgments of the researcher. Undoubtedly the clearer separation of social observation from judgments about social goals has been important to scientific advance. The researcher pressed to work on policy problems is plagued by the fear that this will plunge him back into the confusion between norms and observed reality from which he has been struggling so hard for decades to free himself.

These varied initial doubts are often compounded by the researcher's experience as an applied project proceeds. The researcher may face a growing conviction either that the operator has asked the wrong questions, that the questions are too vaguely or too narrowly formulated, or that as formulated they are incapable of being clearly answered. He becomes convinced that the concepts and categories in terms of which the operator has posed his problem are neither meaningful nor useful. If he accepts these categories and tries to frame his research around them, he feels intellectually frustrated. If he devotes himself to an attempt to restate the problem in more meaningful terms, he finds he has lost the operator's attention.

In either case, he submits his report only to find that his customer, though he appeared to be most eager to get it, makes little or no use of it. In many cases there is evidence that his reports have not even been carefully read; in many others they seem to have had little or no effect on the operational decisions subsequently taken. Not uncommonly, the researcher concludes in restrospect that his initial doubts about the wisdom of engaging in applied research were fully confirmed, and he withdraws once more into academic isolation.

In this essay I would like to analyze some of the reasons for this state of affairs. In a sense, they can all be described as failures of communication between researchers and policy-makers. But the roots of these failures do not lie merely in the semantic problems associated with the use of different terminology. Rather, they can be traced to a series of misconceptions on the part of both researchers and operators as to the relation of knowledge to action in the field of human affairs. Action specialists seriously misconstrue the kinds of help they can expect to get from social scientists, and social scientists have a variety of misapprehensions as to what the policy-making process involves. I would like to outline some of these sources of misunderstanding, examine how certain of them are to be explained by the nature and present state of the social sciences, and conclude with a few observations on whether, if some of the gross misunderstandings were eliminated, policy-makers and social scientists might expect to benefit from further collaborative attempts.

The operators, on the one hand, commit their elementary error in an inductive fallacy—the assumption that the solution of any problem will be advanced by the simple collection of fact. This is easiest to observe in governmental circles, where research is considered as identical with "intelligence." The military conception of intelligence as the collection of facts about the disposition of enemy forces (unquestionably an important kind of knowledge for one charged with responsibility for military action) has been uncritically extended to the whole spectrum of governmental policy. Roger Hilsman, in his interesting interview study of the views of the role of research and intelligence held by policy-makers in the U. S. government, has thoroughly documented the pervasiveness of the notion among operators that, if only they were supplied with more raw facts of almost any kind, they could make much wiser decisions on the issues that confront them.[1]

The operator who holds this view of the utility of new facts may find himself disenchanted with research on one of two grounds. In the first case, the social scientist may refuse to pander to this taste for new facts and concern himself instead with restructuring the concepts in terms of which previously known facts are to be interpreted. In this event the operator clearly does not get what he originally expected. Furthermore, what he does get fails to persuade him that he expected the wrong thing. I shall deal further with the reasons for this conviction.

In the second case, the researcher, frequently against his own better judgment, tries to be responsive to this expressed demand for new "factual information" and assembles a handbook containing a large amount of such material. The operator gets what he expected, but finds to his frustration that it gives him very little help in solving his problems. For example, a request for a report on the nature of the leadership of a foreign country may elicit a vast amount of data on the social origins, pattern of incomes, religious beliefs, and past affiliations of all key members of the foreign élite—information that leaves the operator in no better position than before to estimate the probability, for instance, that this élite will be susceptible to Communist blandishments. Indeed, some interesting experimental psychological work has been done by Alex Bavelas and Howard Perlmutter, at the Center for International Studies, which suggests that an individual's capacity for making sound judgment about a complex situation may be seriously impaired by supplying him with a lot of information which he believes should be relevant but whose influence on the situation is not clear to him. The relation between observational data and concept in the natural sciences is so generally understood that no operator would think of expecting an applied research project in the physical sciences merely to come up with a mass of observational data that might conceivably be relevant to the problem at hand, nor would he expect to make much use of such data if indeed it was assembled. Yet precisely this conviction is common among operators with respect to social science research.

A somewhat different misconception, logically incompatible with that just described but frequently held by the same people, is that the usefulness of social science research can be tested by its ability to predict complex social behavior in some detail. Whereas the obsession with the illuminating power of fact expects too little of social science research, the test of prediction expects too much. Here the analogy with physical science research, instead of being imperfect, is carried too far. In the natural sciences it is reasonable to assign a research team of scientists and engineers the task of designing an instrument that will with fair certainty achieve certain specified physical results. One can ask for a weapon of specified weight which will have specified explosive power, or a transmitter of so many kilowatts capable of sending a message a given distance to a known type of receiver, and then test the utility of the results against the requested criteria of performance.

One cannot, however, expect a social science research group to design a diplomatic initiative that can be expected with confidence to produce a desired response or to indicate the content of an information program that will with some certainty produce a specified change in the attitudes of those who hear it. Even abstracting from the philosophical question of whether a completely deterministic explanation of human behavior will ever be possible, it is clear that social science has not yet reached the stage where its formal models can often yield even a statistical prediction of a complex social event.

Our best formal models are still partial; they explicitly exclude consideration of some of the factors at work in any actual situation. The relative weight of the factors explicitly analyzed can seldom be measured, and their combined influence seldom computed. Prediction of a sort is, of course, a necessary component of policy-making. Any decision to act must be based upon a judgment that the net consequences of the preferred course of action will be more favorable than those of some alternative. But in social situations such a judgment can seldom be effectively made by "scientific" procedures. If the policy-maker simply desires advice as to what he should do, he had better rely on the intuition of a man of wide experience and demonstrated understanding rather than on the intellectual skills and techniques of the social scientist. The human brain is an extraordinary instrument, only a small portion of whose analytic powers can be reduced to communicable logic. A net predictive judgment in most human situations can be made more safely by the successful journalist, novelist, diplomat, or businessman than by any social science research team.

If the contribution of the social scientist to policy is neither the collection of facts nor the making of predictions, what is it? First, we must recognize that every practical judgment is based upon a structure of concepts and assumptions that is largely implicit and poorly understood. One of the functions of science is to make these implicit concepts and assumptions explicit, to test their generality, and to set forth more precisely the cir-

cumstances in which they are valid. Thus, although social science cannot often predict, it can make very important contributions to effective prediction. Social science cannot replace intuition and experience, but it can greatly enrich them, clarify them, and make them more general. Each of the social sciences concentrates on the relations between certain limited aspects of human behavior. Social science research on a problem can illuminate the variety of forces at work, can place limits on the range of possible outcomes, can force implicit, partial judgments into explicit form in which they can be systematically examined and their applicability tested, and can explore the internal consistency of a variety of intuitive expectations. Most policy judgments involve an implicit appraisal of resources, of motivations, of organizational and administrative possibilities, of political interests, and the like. Economic, psychological, political, and sociological analysis can expose these judgments to systematic scrutiny. Their combination into an estimate of the situation as a whole will almost always require a process that goes beyond the limits of "scientific" analysis, but such analysis can enormously strengthen the validity of the intuitive process.

If this picture of how the policy-maker can use social science research is correct, the operator must approach social science research with very different expectations from those he normally has. The operator's normal impulse is to ask for the conclusions of a social science research project and to regard the argument as none of his concern. But the payoff for him will usually be precisely in the argument rather than in the conclusions. The purpose of social science research should be to deepen, broaden, and extend the policy-maker's capacity for judgment—not to provide him with answers. Thus, the test of effectiveness will lie not in whether the research leads to a new and unfamiliar conclusion but in whether it clarifies and makes explicit the logical basis for a conclusion already perceived or suspected.

In one respect particularly the intuitive process may be misleading. A great many contradictory things can, by a skillful impressionistic presentation of a case, be made to appear obvious. There is a reasonable, "commonsense" interpretation of almost every form of individual and social behavior. Whatever regularities a study reports, a number of people are likely to feel that no study was required to reach this "obvious" conclusion. This would be equally likely if the findings of the study were precisely the opposite. When Samuel

Stouffer's exhaustive study of the attitudes of the American soldier appeared after the war, it was greeted by widespread lay criticism that its findings were apparent before the work was begun and that the whole enterprise was, accordingly, a waste of time and money. To meet this criticism, Paul Lazarsfeld, in a review, began by citing a series of soldier attitudes so described as to leave the reader feeling that these were precisely the attitudes any of us would expect. He then went on to say:

"But why, since they are so obvious, is so much money and energy given to establish such findings? Would it not be wiser to take them for granted and proceed directly to a more sophisticated type of analysis? This might be so except for one interesting *point* about the list. *Every one of these statements* is the direct opposite of what actually was found."[2] It is the task of a social science study to determine which of the contradictory but intuitively obvious conclusions about a situation is in fact true and in what circumstances it may be expected to obtain. The operator can gain from such a study a more sophisticated understanding of the assumptions he implicitly makes and the circumstances he envisions when he states a similar conclusion himself.

An effective marriage of knowledge and action is seriously inhibited in the modern world by an exaggerated emphasis on the virtues of the division of labor. Decision-making and the pursuit of systematic knowledge have come to be regarded as separable activities, and it is supposed to be inefficient for the researcher to concern himself with policy decisions or for the policy-maker to probe too deeply into research techniques. The policy-maker is supposed to recognize what it is he needs to know and to be able to levy a clear requirement on the researcher to supply the missing knowledge. The researcher, using techniques which it is his business and nobody else's to understand, is in turn supposed to answer the questions put to him. In fact, of course, the relations between knowledge and action are infinitely more complex and reciprocal than this image would suggest and cannot be adequately mastered unless each kind of specialist develops an extensive knowledge of the other's mental processess. Indeed, the most important task for both policy-makers and researchers is a better and more communicable definition of the problem to be solved.

To some extent this is true of the relation between knowledge and action in any field. It is much more true, however, of social and political problems than it is of physical and engineering ones. The man who wants a plastic material to do a specified job need not be a chemist to order or to use a research study designed to provide him with it. But a man who wants help on a social or political policy may well benefit more from an understanding of how research bearing on that policy is designed and conducted than from any conclusions such research may reach.

The dominant American theory and practice of administration in both government and industry contributes to this excessive division of labor between specialists in action and specialists in knowledge. In government there is a long-standing tradition of sharp separation of research and intelligence from policy-making and execution. The analyst in a research or intelligence organization is virtually prohibited from speculating about policy alternatives or even from intimate intellectual contact with policy-makers. Organizational procedures, based on the flase premise that the operator knows what it is that he needs from research, call for the formulation on paper of research "requirements" by operating organizations, the setting of these requirements by various intermediaries, and their ultimate delivery by courier to the research group. This group, in turn, is supposed to "fill" these requirements by its own occult means and to mail the "answers" back to the operators. These procedures are based on the notion that there are recognized gaps in the factual knowledge of the operator, that he can define these gaps with precision on paper, and that when the gaps are filled by research, as requested, the operator's problem will be clarified. This procedure virtually forecloses any opportunities for a fruitful attack on the really central problem—the joint reformulation of the policy problem by both researcher and operator. In private industry, this gulf between knowledge and action is sometimes bridged more effectively, but usually only over the bitter opposition of the efficiency-minded expert in business administration.

In summary then, the operator's misconceptions of the relationship between social science knowledge and action are of three sorts. First, he frequently has an exaggerated notion of the degree to which the solution of his problems can be effected by the collection of additional factual information. Second, he tends to expect prediction in situations in which this is clearly beyond the capabilities of present-day social science. Third, he too easily assumes that the conclusions of a research project will assist him when the important factor is actually the process of analysis underlying those conclusions. These misconceptions are supported and maintained by a mechanical and inappropriate application to both research and policy of the principle of division of labor.

The researcher's conception of the relation between knowledge and action is likewise plagued by a number of false perspectives. Like the operator, the researcher tends to have an exaggerated faith in the division of labor and, derived from this, an idealized image of the policy-maker. If the function of the man of action is, by definition, to act, then what he must want is conclusions, not analysis. Here again is an emphasis—this time from the researcher—on the answer rather than on the process of thinking by which the answer is supported. This leads to a research product consisting either of conclusions regarded as obvious by the operator in advance of research or of recommendations which are not persuasive because they are inadequately supported. The situation reflects a tendency on the part of the researcher to underestimate the intellectual content of the policy-making process. Any policy position is, of course, arrived at in the context of an implicit or explicit appraisal of the nature of the forces at work and of the way they can be influenced by a variety of policy instruments. Because the policy-maker usually does not articulate in social science terminology, his judgments about the variables he is trying to manipulate, the researcher often assumes that the man of action is guided to effective decision-making by some intuitive process beyond the reach of rational argument.

This misconception is frequently associated with another—inconsistent with it—that the operator knows what he wants from research and that his questions are therefore to be taken at face value. Here, the researcher overestimates the capacity of most policy-makers to make explicit the conceptual framework in which they define their operational problems. The researcher who wants to be genuinely useful has an obligation to force his customer to rethink in a fundamental way why he wants research done and the uses to which he will put it if he gets it. Unfortunately, it would seem clear that the policy-maker seldom has a realistic notion of what to expect from research, and that he cannot arrive at a sensible expectation without the help of the social scientist. Yet time and again projects are begun with only the most cursory mutual consideration of just how they are expected to be used. The subsequent result is apt to be bitter disenchantment on both sides, conversely, the most valuable product of many applied research projects considered successful has been a new conception in the mind of the operator of how the problems with which he is confronted are to be defined.

The researcher frequently, although he recognizes the inadequacy of the statement of the problem he has been given, is inhibited by the difficulties of communication from insisting on being provided with a better one. Instead he goes off to his library or his laboratory and makes his independent attempt to describe what he is planning to do in the language of his own discipline.

Here another difficulty arises. His first impulse will be to discard, sometimes without realizing it, those aspects of the problem which do not interest him. He can defend this on the ground that there is no point in his doing research on problems which are inherently not researchable. The higher his standards of scientific research, the narrower will be his selection of problems and the greater the eventual frustration of the customer with the result.

The clash of interest and utility is likely to be most marked in the early stages of a science, which are characterized by a great deal of attention to careful classification, to precise definition, and to the establishment of useful tautologies—that is, to the elaboration of all the logical consequences of a few simple assumptions. Scientific progress at this stage is likely to be gauged not by the number of practically applicable conclusions that emerge but rather by the degree to which a precise language of communication with fellow researchers is established and a set of fundamental categories of phenomena laid down. The early stages are therefore likely to consist of the construction of an elaborate intellectual tool whose cutting edge for shaping practical problems is small and weak.

What the researcher may justifiably regard as a major intellectual achievement in bringing order out of chaos may well strike the operator, who is uninterested in the machinery for its own sake, as a scholastic exercise of little relevance. To establish the proposition that business leaders tend to have a high level of achievement motivation, or that caste inhibits social mobility, or that social overhead capital has a high capital-output ratio may be scientifically significant but of little help to the policy-maker who has asked for an estimate of the "vigor" of the private sector in the Turkish economy or of the probability of "class conflict" in India or of whether China's economic development plan "will work."

There is as yet no general science of human behavior. We have only the beginnings of a number of separate social science disciplines, each of which has directed its attention to exploring the relations between certain limited and carefully defined aspects of behavior. Thus the social scientist who values precision and the establishment of repeatable and communicable results must carve the problem he has been given down to researchable size. The policy-maker must pass a judgment on a complex situation as a whole, being careful to take into consideration everything that may importantly affect the actual outcome. These legitimate—but different—responsibilities may produce a genuine conflict between utility and scientific interest as criteria for problem selection. Unless this conflict is clearly recognized, its sources understood, and an explicit effort made to resolve it by both the researcher and his customer, applied research will almost certainly be disappointing to both.

Certain other characteristics of the stage in which the social sciences presently find themselves further limit the utility to the policy-maker of much social science research, especially in the analysis of the relations between states. In many countries there is a vast amount of social science research going forward on the structure and characteristics of foreign societies from which the policy-maker feels he should be able to benefit. He finds, however, when he examines this research, that it has a strong static bias. The questions asked tend to take the form: "What is society like? What is the character of its institutions? What are the attitudes of various elements of its population? What is the structure of its economy?" rather than the form: "In what directions is the society evolving? How rapidly and in what directions are institutions, attitudes, and structure changing? And where is this process of change likely to lead?"

From the standpoint of scientific development this bias is thoroughly understandable. Dynamics always more complicated than statics; rates of change are harder to measure and analyze than states of affairs. Beyond this, there is logic in the need to know where we are before we ask where we are going. Also, the empirical study of social change requires a series of observations made according to a consistent plan over a period of years many times the duration of the typical project.

On the other hand, from a policy point of view the most important characteristic of our times is that societies are changing in almost all their fundamental dimensions at a rate unprecedented in history. All our most crucial international policy problems require an appraisal not of states of affairs but of patterns of evolution. Economic development, newly emergent nationalism, trends in the character of Communist society, the political implications of changing weapons technology—these are all questions which cannot even be posed in other than dynamic terms. If the social scientist is to help the policy-maker deal with these situations at all, he must find ways of introducing process explicitly into both his analytic frameworks and his empirical observations. The social sciences are moving toward the formulation of dynamic theories and their empirical testing, but at this stage realistic dynamic analysis can be undertaken only at considerable cost in rigor and precision.

There is the further difficulty of the requirement, in the analysis of most policy alternatives, that a number of factors lying within the focus of interest of a variety of social science disciplines be considered simultaneously. This has led to attempts, particularly in applied research, to tackle problems in an interdisciplinary way, normally by assembling a team of research workers trained in different disciplines. This is not the place to go into all the difficulties and obstacles to effective interdisciplinary team research, but one problem in particular has received inadequate emphasis. The most critical policy issues of our time are those relating to the interaction of complex national states. The international behavior of states, however, is conditioned in important ways by their own internal dynamics. National states, especially the more recently created ones, are not, of course, homogeneous entities possessing a common will but are themselves collections of interacting communities and groups. Thus research on the behavior of larger social units such as nations requires research in turn on the behavior and interactions of smaller units such as provinces, business communities, castes, and even families and individuals. The relation of macro- to micro-studies poses a serious dilemma for applied research. To study intensively all the thousands or millions of micro-units that make up the macro-units is obviously a task beyond the resources of any academic community. On the other hand, the two or three villages or business firms or newspapers or professions that one can afford to look at in detail may be unrepresentative and may tell one very little about how the multitude of micro-forces in a national society aggregate to produce a national or international result.

The different social sciences have developed different capabilities for handling different levels of social aggregation. By and large, psychology and anthropology are most confident and most at home in applying a microscope to individuals or small groups. Political science, on the other hand, has traditionally taken as its province the study of national and international institutions and organization. Economics, similarly, has concentrated a good deal of its attention on national aggregates, though it is the one social science discipline that, more than any other, has mastered the problem of integrating the analysis of the behavior of individuals in small economic units with the study of national and international aggregates. But systematic interdisciplinary research is complicated by the fact that each discipline is most at home in the study of a different kind of social unit. We do not yet have even an embryonic science of social change that offers a framework for integrating the kinds of work carried on by different social scientists. We are moving in the right direction. Political science has been increasingly concerning itself with the intensive study of the political behavior of individuals and small groups. Psychologists and anthropologists are more frequently asking, with the help of sociologists, how representative the phenomena revealed by their micro-studies are in the larger populations with which the political scientist deals. But the bridges between micro- and macro-studies need much more strengthening before they will bear the weight policy analysis places on them.

The final problem relates to the scientific respectability of an explicit analysis of values and goals as a subject for scholarly inquiry. As already mentioned, many social scientists are still powerfully influenced by the conviction that their work cannot be "objective" unless they avoid all analysis of normative propositions. They do not, of course, deny that policy propositions inevitably rest upon value assumptions. But here, too, they exaggerate the possibilities of a division of labor. Let the scientist concern himself only with the world as it is, and let the policy-maker or someone else worry about the directions in which we should be trying to push it. The trouble is, of course, that there is an inherent interdependence between the concepts we use to interpret events and those we use to articulate our values.

Three kinds of elements must be appraised in any policy analysis: goals, environment, and in-struments. The policy-maker must sort out carefully the various ends the policy is designed to pursue as well as the costs that are acceptable in terms of other values foregone. He must understand the forces at work in the world which are beyond his control and the directions in which they are likely to carry the environment, whatever he does. Finally, he must appraise the capabilities and limitations of the various policy instruments available to him to influence the environment in what he believes to be desirable directions. The social scientist tends to regard his tools as applicable only to the second of these three elements. But rational analysis of the first and third requires at least as great intellectual subtlety and precision. More important, these three elements cannot be examined in isolation, since each can be defined only in terms of the other two. A study of what is happening in Soviet society will be useful to the policy-maker only if it is written in the light both of what he would like to have happen there and of the instruments he can use to affect what happens. Equally, he cannot even state his goals or enumerate his instruments with clarity except in terms of an implicit or explicit theory of Soviet evolution. The division of labor among different analysts according to the distinction between normative and positive propositions cannot be carried very far without depriving social science of most of its operational utility.

We can summarize this discussion of the relation between utility and scientific interest by conceiving of a spectrum of types of approaches to the understanding of social behavior. At one end lie the net judgments about very complex real situations which the policy-maker confronted with the great issues of our time must make. No scientist can be wholly happy with the necessity to make such judgments, since in the present state of our knowledge they must inevitably rest much more largely on intuition, partially articulated insights, and informed common sense than on precisely defined propositions emerging from a clear theoretical model and supported by documented empirical evidence. At the other end of the spectrum lie rigorous scientific conclusions, unambiguously communicable in a language developed for precise communication and capable of demonstration by repeatable experiment or by reference to incontrovertible evidence. In the present state of social science the propositions at this scientific end of the spectrum necessarily relate to exceedingly simple and hence operationally unimportant phenomena controlled to exclude all but a few variables capable of treatment by the tools of a single discipline. This is, of course, a caricature. There are problems in the analysis of which the scientist can move quite a distance toward the practical end of the spectrum with relatively little loss of rigor and others in which the practitioner can get direct help from investigations conducted according to the strict rules of scientific inquiry. But these are the exceptions. There thus remains in social science considerable conflict between the canons of utility and those of scientific interest.

I have already suggested my reasons for believing that the policy-maker can broaden his insights and deepen his intuition by learning more of what is going on at the scientific end of the spectrum, if the policy-maker learns to share some of the perspectives and motivations of the social scientist. If he has the intellectual curiosity and persistence to learn some of the uses and limitations of social science tools, he can substantially improve the wisdom of his own practical judgments. But he will be continually disappointed if he expects rigorous scientific inquiry to yield conclusions directly and mechanically applicable to the fuzzy problems he confronts.

What of the social scientist? Does he stand to benefit from wrestling with the insoluble problems of the policy-maker, inextricably enmeshed as they are in a value context, or will such an activity threaten to compromise his scientific integrity and prevent him from making the fundamental contributions to communicable human knowledge which are his central responsibility? Much depends on how he approaches his task, and how self-consciously aware he is of what he is doing. If he confuses the distinction between a wise judgment and a communicable scientific truth he is likely to make little progress toward either. If, however, he devotes the bulk of his attention to his central scientific objective, uncompromisingly maintaining the highest scholarly criteria in these activities, his work can benefit greatly from an occasional concern with the muddy normative problems of policy. The rules of scientific method do not tell us what it is important to work on. The ultimate objective of social science is a scientific explanation of human behavior in all its complexity. An occasional effort to assist the statesman serves to emphasize not only our ignorance of social forces but also the extent to which our knowledge is intuitive and imprecise. The effort to sort it out, to give it precision, and to make it communicable, even where this effort is largely doomed to failure, can enormously stimulate the selection of promising areas for scientific inquiry. The principle of the division of labor is indeed a powerful one, but only if each of the specialists—in this case specialists in action and specialists in knowledge—devotes some effort to trying to understand both intuitively and logically the total human problem to which his specialty can make a contribution.

FOOTNOTES

[1] Roger Hilsman, *Strategic Intelligence and National Decisions* (Glencoe, Illinois: Free Press, 1956). The author's findings are summarized in an article, "Intelligence and Policy Making in Foreign Affairs," *World Politics,* Vol. V., No. 1, October 1952.

[2] Paul F. Lazarsfeld, "The American Soldier—An Expository Review," *Public Opinion Quarterly*, Summer 1949, p. 380.

Researchers, Scholars and Policy Makers: The Politics of Large Scale Research

by Peter H. Rossi

This selection provides an uncommon portrait of the academic milieu, for it identifies the internecine conflicts inherent between those who play variable roles in academia. But more than this, Rossi details the context of research in the university and explains why it is as it is, drawing upon recent and not so recent university and intellectual history for his explanations. The detailed critique of the tensions and problems faced by those who would conduct research in an academic setting offers a cool and precise analytical appraisal of the scene. By-product values of this reading are insights into where and how behavioral research happens in the present culture, as well as who supports it and why. Especially for the untutored, this is a quick and sensitive guided tour over the contemporary academic social science research terrain.

INTRODUCTION

The campus of a major university was once marked by definite borders, on the one side of which were the distinctively academic buildings—dormitories, classrooms, libraries, laboratories and administrative buildings—and on the other side, the motley architecture of the town. Nowadays the physical boundaries of the university have blurred as academic activities have taken over the nearby town structures to house a proliferation of "centers," "institutes," "bureaus" and "laboratories." Some of the new organizations, like the Argonne National Laboratory or M.I.T.'s Lincoln Laboratories, are located at some distance from the campus; others cluster close by in old townhouses or in large Victorian homes; and some, such as Brookhaven, are located, like the theology of community churches, close to no particular position. The concept of a campus on which all academic activities take place within the distance that can be spanned easily on foot by students and professors has given way to a more diffuse spatial pattern in which classrooms, dormitories and libraries are still at the center[1] but in which the periphery occupied by institutes and centers is vaguely defined and discontinuous. To walk from one end of the installation to the other is often a task beyond the capabilities of an academic procession.

The physical marginality of the new academic organizations reflects their academic marginality. Traditional university tables of organization lose their branching symmetry in attempts to place them in their proper places in chains of command, and university officials sometimes ignore them in the planning of university expansion, perhaps in the hope that if ignored they will vanish. Academic departments or schools to which the research centers may be attached are somewhat at a loss to deal with them, for the personnel of the centers and institutes are hard to assimilate into the rank and privilege systems of academia. The personnel of the centers are not quite sure of their identity, for on the one hand they are members of the university community, while on the other their major commitments are not to the teaching and training functions which are at the center of the university's activities.

The first research center to evolve within the structure of the university was the library, occurring at a stage so deep in the beginnings of the institution that we usually do not classify the library as a center for research. In the modern sen[se] of organizations devoted primarily to research an[d] organized separately from departments, centers were first established by the natural sciences, wit[h] the astronomical observatories representing the first of the structures to be physically separated from the central campus.[2] In the empirical branches of the social sciences, which have only

SOURCE: Peter H. Rossi, "Researchers, Scholars and Policy Makers: The Politics of Large Scale Research," *Daedalus*, (Fall, 1964), pp. 1142-1161. Reprinted by permission of DAEDALUS, Journal of the American Academy of Arts & Sc[iences], Boston. Fall 1964, "The Contemporary University."

recently developed strong research programs, the precedents for research centers are now being established. Social science research centers are connected with almost every one of the major universities, the density varying from the proliferation on the Berkeley campus, on which it seems as if every full professor has his own center, to the sparser distribution at Johns Hopkins, where there are only one or two presently in existence.

The major concern of this paper will be with some of the organizational consequences of the development of research centers within the university environment. Properly to deal with this topic would require a breadth of knowledge which has yet to develop about how such centers are organized in a wide variety of fields.[3] I will be concerned primarily with the newer social science research centers, bringing in such information on other types of centers as is available in the very sparse literature on the organization of academic research, from direct knowledge of the few such research centers I have been able to visit and from the excellent survey of social research centers conducted by P. F. Lazarsfeld.[4]

Because social science research centers have been established in any great numbers only in the last two decades, there has been a great deal of diversity in their organizational forms as universities and departments experimented with different arrangements. The experimentation, as I will indicate later, is an index of some tension between the research centers and the more traditional departments. To highlight this tension, I will deal with this topic as an analysis of political processes. More specifically, I will deal with the way in which the organization of research has affected the relationships among three roles—the *social researcher*, the *scholar* (or academic man) and the *policy maker* (officials of foundations and agencies which provide support for research). It should be clear that I will be using the term "politics" in a very broad sense to cover the processes by which power and resources are distributed in the system of relationships in which these three roles take part. Under this broadened definition, the study of politics then becomes the study of decision-making so that there is a politics of business enterprises or of university administration and, more relevant to our present case, a politics of research.

The essential nature of the American university[5] is being affected by these organizational developments, a topic to which the final section of this paper will be devoted. Universities may be more properly entitled "multiversities" as Clark

Kerr claims: certainly the extraordinary diversity of activities which are now put within one large organizational framework must necessarily affect the nature of teaching, research and the administration of our foremost institutions.

WHY RESEARCH CENTERS EVOLVED

The major missions of the first-rank university include both training and research. Since the establishment of graduate study in America and its diffusion to the major centers during the early part of this century, training has come to include both undergraduate and graduate instruction, and research has included both scholarly and laboratory activities.

There is no doubt that the amalgamation of training and research in the professorial role is an alloy at the same time beneficial to both activities, while tension-producing. Professors are supposed to be both scholars and teachers, with the proper mix variously defined from department to department and from university to university. University officials measure the worth of their institutions by two major outputs—neophyte scholars and the end-products of scholarship: books, articles, monographs and patents. University business managers have to handle both instructional and, increasingly, research accounts, each type with its own peculiar logic. Even buildings and grounds departments are baffled by the different space and maintenance requirements of research and teaching activities.

The tensions between the somewhat contradictory activities of teaching and research have several sources. Within the professorial role the tensions are produced partly by the different phasings of the two activities: teaching demands that a set schedule of classes, seminars, etc., be met, while research has variable and unpredictable time demands. In addition, the two activities compete for time: the proper nurture of undergraduate and graduate students can absorb the full-time attention of an instructor, but so can his scholarly activities.

Within the organization of the university at the departmental level, the tensions are produced by other mechanisms. The allocation of authority within a department need only be extremely rudimentary as far as teaching goes. The basic unit of activity is the course, for which a professor is responsible and which is conducted essentially without supervision. The division of labor within a department centers around the curriculum in which responsibility for courses is allocated among department members. I venture that more friendships among colleagues in departments have floundered on the rock of curriculum revision than over any other cause. But once a curriculum has been fixed upon, instructors go their own way relatively unsupervised by their department chairmen or by other administrative officials.

In contrast, research activity which involves more than the minimum division of labor between a scholar and his acolyte graduate students produces continual organizational tensions. Decisions have to be made continually, responsibilities for particular activities have to be allocated to different persons, men have to pace their work to the paces of others. There are strong strains to produce a bureaucratic organization for research activities in which there is a much more clear line of authority than is necessary for the teaching activities of a department.

The evolution of research centers can be seen as one attempt to solve by segregation the tensions between teaching and research: research institutes were to be the proper place for research and the departments to remain the proper place for teaching. To be sure, there are other reasons for the establishment of research centers, some of which will be touched upon later in this paper. The important point to be made in this context is that the organizational needs of teaching and research are different and lead to different types of organization.

Not all research activities lead to the establishment of centers and institutes. Research and scholarship in the more humanistic fields typically have not led to the establishment of centers and institutes, and those established have not been very long-lived.[6] The major reason for this difference between the humanities and other fields lies in the fact that the humanist scholar evolved his research organization so long ago that we no longer recognize it as such but have incorporated it into the heart of the structure of the university. A central building on every campus is its library, and the division of labor into "library science" and scholarship constitutes the basic organizational structure of research in the humanities.[7] The scholar in the humanities is essentially a solitary worker using the facilities provided by a library surrounded by a few graduate students, each working with him but not with each other.[8] The division of labor involved in research in the humanities is a primitive one in which each scholar has at best one or two persons of considerably lesser skills working with him, and in which there is a relatively minor amount of direct collaboration among colleagues.

The example of the humanities underscores the organizational imperatives that give rise to research centers in other fields. Research centers arose when research activities demanded collaboration among colleagues that went beyond the traditional organizational pattern of scholarship as presently exemplified in the humanities.

RESEARCH CENTERS IN THE SOCIAL SCIENCES

In the social sciences a good illustration of the organizational impetus toward the establishment of research centers is provided by the development of sample surveys in the last two decades. One of the major research developments in the empirical social sciences has been the set of techniques which has enabled social scientists to gather their own data on a broad enough scale to make statements about significant segments of large scale societies at relatively reasonable costs. Sample surveys have become a basic research tool in sociology and social psychology,[9] are a major tool in psychology, and are increasingly important in political science and economics.

Properly accomplished, a sample survey is a large scale enterprise involving a fairly elaborate division of labor and using a considerable amount of resources. This is best exemplified in the two major academic survey centers, the Survey Research Center at the University of Michigan and the National Opinion Research Center at the University of Chicago, as well as the survey activities of the Bureau of the Census or some of the better commercial firms. It takes a combination of skills, ordinarily not residing in a single person, to conduct a large sample survey properly. Even smaller surveys (involving perhaps the sampling of a small city or neighborhood) can be carried out by a single person only in an inefficient manner.

Not all survey research is carried out within the context of large research centers. Each year scores of surveys are conducted by single individuals or by small groups of researchers: a sample of articles in professional journals or of Ph.D. theses would provide ample evidence that it is possible for individuals and small research groups to conduct such surveys by themselves. However, there is a severe limitation to such research. In the light of current technical standards, one can discern that such surveys are often rather poorly designed and executed and, at best, severely limited in their coverage.[10]

Properly to conduct a survey, one needs to assemble at a minimum the following skills: (1) sampling; (2) questionnaire construction (an art perhaps rather than a skill); (3) interviewing; (4) data processing; and (5) statistical analysis. All of these would be needed to conduct a survey of an area larger than a small city or neighborhood.[11] To sample survey a population to which one ordinarily wants to generalize implies skills at a high enough level to require specialization. Furthermore, a large scale sample survey is expensive. Properly conducted national surveys (or for that matter, regional, state, or metropolitan surveys) collecting about 2,500 interviews of about an hour's length can cost anywhere between $50,000 and $125,000.[12] Surveys of special populations (for example, chiropodists or college students) can cost more or less depending on the existence of reliable sampling frames for the populations in question.

Survey research did not develop initially within universities but was grafted onto them after it had passed through the critical periods of infancy. The National Opinion Research Center is still an independent corporation affiliated with the University of Chicago. Michigan's Survey Research Center was set up initially by a group of researchers who had worked together in a survey organization run by the Department of Agriculture during the Forties. This is not to deny the contributions that academic men have made to survey research, but merely to state the historical fact that surveys were being made long before survey research centers became accepted parts of university organization. There are undoubtedly many reasons why survey research did not develop inside the groves of academe, but among the most important reasons is the organizational setup of academic departments. Essentially, an academic department is a collection of scholars whose work is only minimally integrated in a division of labor sense. Professors are required to teach courses, and these courses are supposed to be organized in some sort of rational way. In American universities, departments do not engage in common scholarly enterprises in which a research task is broken down into components, each member of a department taking one component as his contribution.[13] Indeed, when an academician refers to the independence of the academic life,[14] he is usually referring to the fact that once he has met his teaching obligations (over which he has often a great deal of control) he is free to pursue his own intellectual interests within the limits set by local production standards and the amount of

research funds he is able to obtain. Indeed, so pleasurable is the lack of a defined division of labor that any attempt to engage in large scale research enterprises has led to the grafting onto university structures of organizational entities in which such a division of labor is possible rather than imposing such a division of labor upon existing departmental structures.

Large scale research in the social sciences is no exception to this generalization. Large scale survey research in the universities is conducted by institutes and centers whose organizational principles involve a hierarchy of command and a distinct division of labor. Indeed, the larger the scale of research, the steeper the hierarchy and the more elaborate the division of labor. Thus the two university-affiliated centers which conduct national surveys (Michigan's Survey Research Center and Chicago's National Opinion Research Center) have more complex structures than that of the Bureau of Applied Social Research at Columbia or the Institute for Social Research at North Carolina, the scope of whose work is more restricted in scale.

Characteristically, institutes and centers have "directors" while departments have "chairmen," expressing in the titles of their chief administrative officers the greater authority of the one as compared with the other. Because of his greater authority the director's role is more critical to the proper functioning of a research center than a chairman's role is to the prosperity of a department. A research center functions best when its director provides both intellectual and administrative leadership.[15] It may have been the pious hope of university administrators as they allowed and in some cases fostered the establishment of research centers that the departmental organization and the institute organization could be integrated very closely. Indeed, the ideal pattern in some ideal sense might be one in which the personnel of a department and the personnel of an institute would be one and the same, and that while teaching courses, sociologists, for example, would run themselves along departmental organizational lines, and while doing research they would run themselves according to institute lines. In fact, this has never occurred. Rather, either the department has restructured itself along the hierarchial lines of the center (as was the case for Columbia's department of sociology) or the center never developed a good division of labor (as was the case for North Carolina's institute) or the two structures remained side by side with some overlap of personnel (as in the case of the Survey Research Center and the National Opinion Research Center) but with considerable tension between the two.

The strains against the amalgamation of these two types of organization arise out of the relatively greater demands for precise timing and phasing of activities that result from an elaborate division of labor. As long as he meets his classes and writes books and articles, a professor has fulfilled the demands of his job. In contrast, a researcher working in the context of a research center has to pace his total activities so that they gear into the work of the sampling section, coding section, tabulating section, etc. Were the academic department organized along the lines of research centers, professors would soon chafe under their apparent loss of freedom. Even where professors have attempted to work within the context of a hierarchically organized research center, the collaboration has been short-lived, for the demands of directors to maintain the flow of work among the specialized components of the center have been viewed by the academician as an infringement on his prerogatives. Furthermore, a director must oversee the quality of research as it is being performed, while the individual scholar has the end product of his work judged by his colleagues located usually at some distance. In response to the difficulty of integrating departments and research institutes, the latter have developed separate staffs to the extent that their operations are on a large scale. Thus, within the institutes has developed a set of persons whose primary task is research, whose position within the academic community is ambiguous because they have only "courtesy" rank within the instructor-to-full-professor hierarchial order, and whose freedom to control their own activities is considerably less than those of departmental members.

However, not all social science research centers have taken the direction indicated above. Others have more or less deliberately remained paper organizations without a significant division of labor (except between clerical and professorial personnel) providing convenient sally ports from which the professors can emerge to gather funds from foundations and government agencies. Most university social research centers are of this sort, collections of individual professors surrounded by their project staffs (composed of advanced graduate students), providing secretarial services, but mainly serving as administrative rubrics for the purpose of obtaining research support. Other research centers have developed organizational structures analogous to libraries, with their functions mainly to provide services to the professors.[16] Some of the newer survey research centers— for example, that established at Berkeley— have developed as their mission the expediting of research initiated by faculty members. Computer centers are also constructed on the same lines, manned by technicians and designed to serve the faculty.

Where research centers have accommodated themselves to the traditional academic organizational scheme by becoming primarily administrative subunits of departments or service arms of departments, tensions between centers and departments are minimized. In either case there is little infringement on traditional academic prerogatives, and no challenge to the freedom of the professor. But, as in the case of research centers which have engaged in research on a large scale, an attempt has been made to develop an elaborate division of labor, and tensions have arisen. The ability to embark on research on a greater scale has been bought at the price of coming into conflict with traditional organizational principles of academic departments.

There is little doubt that being a professor is more prestigeful than being a researcher. Tenure— that mysterious state of grace into which a professor is elected by his colleagues and from which he can fall only by committing crimes of the most revolting character—has not generally been extended to the institute personnel except on the highest level. Researchers' salaries have been generally higher for persons of the same age and academic accomplishments, but professors can and often do supplement their salaries from outside sources. Drawing a balance, it appears as if the professor has the edge; he has the higher prestige, the greater security, the greater freedom, and sometimes, through his outside activities the greater income.

In fact, it now appears that there have grown up two distinct career lines—that of researcher and that of professor—with relatively little interchange between the two occupations. If one follows the researcher line, one ends up a second-class citizen in the university community; if one follows the professor line, one ends up a first-class citizen but restricted in the scope of the research in which one can engage. This accounts for much of the low quality of research reported in the professional social science journals. The individual scholar working on his own cannot command the kinds of skill that make for a first-rate piece of research.

This also accounts for the oft-noted tendency on the part of academicians to start up their own research centers to increase their scope and power while looking upon the similar activities of their colleagues as academic imperialism.

Although the full-time personnel of a research center may not have the same psychic and sometimes monetary rewards of the members of the professoriat, there are advantages to full-time membership which in time may outweigh disadvantages. At its best functioning, the research center can multiply by some factor the efforts of a researcher, raising his work productivity as well as its quality. More than one better-than-average social scientist has been raised to the level of first-rank social scientist because he has had at his command the facilities and organization that a large scale research center represents. The efficiency of a division of labor cannot be gainsaid. But there are more subtle advantages as well that stem from close contact with colleagues of varying interests and accomplishments on a day-to-day basis. When a social research center is working well, it is indeed an exciting locale for one's work. One can feel the excitement in the snatches of conversation at lunch or in the visits made by colleagues to each other's offices.

Although the community of social scientists does not yet have the extensive character reported by Holton in which collaboration in the writing of an article may be the joint work of as many as ten different individuals from several institutions and two or three countries,[17] social science research is beginning to take on more and more of a cooperative slant. I surmise that the advantages of collaboration and close contact will become more obvious when the social scientists have more in the way of specialization in knowledge. At the present time, there is hardly a subfield of sociology and social psychology in which a good social scientist could not pick up as much detailed knowledge as the prime experts in that subfield to write an acceptable proposal to a grant-giving agency. When almost everybody knows as much as everyone else (or could know it easily) the benefits of collaboration are not as obvious as in the case when knowledge from one subfield could materially advance progress of work in another.

THE FINANCING OF LARGE SCALE RESEARCH

Large scale research in any field is expensive whenever it requires an extensive division of labor (as is the case for most social science research) and/or large capital investments in equipment. Unlike research in the humanities, in which continuing support is provided by the capital investment represented by a library collection and by regular allocation provided in the university budgets, other types of research tend to be financed on a project-by-project basis.

In empirical social research the *ad hoc* nature of financial support has important implications for the kinds of research that can be conducted and the kinds of personnel who can be attracted to research centers. Surveys on any appreciable scale are quite expensive. Furthermore, such research has grown increasingly expensive as its technology becomes more complex and as survey researchers demand more and more precision from their data. In some lugubrious sense, it is a shame that probability sampling was developed to a degree that it could be applied to the sampling of human populations, for the greatest increase in cost of surveys stems from the adoption of this technique. To draw a probability sample is expensive, and to administer personal interviews to the sample once drawn is also quite costly, particularly relative to the costs of surveys conducted under the now largely abandoned quota sampling technique. For example, the best known of the National Opinion Research Center's studies, the 1947 study of the prestige of occupations, cost a little more than $9,000 to conduct. We are presently conducting another study on this topic for which we have received a grant of more than $150,000. While the prices of many things have gone up since 1947, few have increased as much as large scale surveys.[18]

What are the implications of such high costs for surveys? One of the important consequences is that few individual researchers can command enough in the way of resources to mount an extensive survey operation. The limited scope of researches reported in the professional journals in sociology and social psychology is one of the consequences. Incidentally, this further exacerbates the tensions between the research institutes and the departments. In departmental research courses, graduate students are being taught how to do research in ways which their teachers themselves are unable to follow. Professors eye with some envy the large project budgets of the research centers, which are put at the disposal of persons often junior to them in status.

The most important implication of the high cost of surveys is that there are only a limited number of sources from which sums on this scale can be obtained, and the purposes for which such funds are given are limited in a peculiar sense. Few of the sources from which funds flow into social research give grants of one hundred to two hundred thousand dollars lightly. The major foundations and government agencies from whom funds on this scale are usually obtained are reluctant to part with this much money without being quite convinced of the practical importance of the survey in question. Hence large scale survey research is generally "applied" social research; that is to say, the grantor is convinced that the results will have some immediate bearing on policy formation. The high cost of social research has meant a close tie with the machinery of policy making.[19]

Some specific examples may help to illustrate dramatically what this implies for large scale research. At NORC we have developed a fairly strong program of research into the related areas of manpower and higher education, support for which comes primarily from the National Science Foundation and the National Institutes of Health. One of our studies involves a longitudinal study of the June, 1961 graduating classes of American universities and colleges. In 1961 we sampled that year's crop of new Bachelors for the purpose of studying how this group found their niches in the occupational world. The interest of the sponsoring agencies, in this case the National Institutes of Health, the National Science Foundation and the Office of Education,[20] was quite clear and direct: they were concerned about the impact of federal scholarship and fellowship policies on postgraduate training and how such policies might be changed to channel more of the talented into postgraduate training leading into critical scientific and professional niches. Spread over a period of five years, the total sum allocated to this project is half a million dollars. Two of these agencies are supporting a replication of this study on June, 1964 graduates, and I predict that we may be conducting such studies on a periodic basis in the future. Another of our researches is concerned with the educational activities of adults, particularly measuring participation in such adult educational activities as formal courses, and on-the-job training. The sponsor in this case is the Carnegie Corporation, which has a strong interest in supporting adult education and whose staff feels that there is a definite lack of information on how much adult education is going on, who participates, and what is being learned.

These two cases are typical in the sense that the surveys in question are supposed to yield information of value to the sponsoring organizations. They are also typical in that the initiative for the studies came from the sponsors and they have taken a strong interest in their outcomes.[21] The consequence of this pattern of research support is that if one wants to study a particular subject, one has to find some foundation, agency or person with a direct interest in the outcome of the study and with some understanding of and concern with social research. Consider the following hypothetical example: Suppose one were interested in recruitment to the humanities, such as history, English literature, and the fine arts. Support probably could not be found for a study of recruitment into these fields because there is no source of funds which has a direct interest in this problem and which is *at the same time* appreciative of the value of research.

These remarks should not lead to the erroneous impression that all of the work of the large scale survey centers is applied. This is not the case. Each manages to get some projects sponsored which are of no particular applied interest whatsoever, although it must be admitted that this happens infrequently and usually involves research on a lesser scale.[22] At least as important is the process of broadening applied interests to cover research topics of considerable intensive interest but only indirectly related to each applied interest. For example, there are probably no funds available to study directly the supply of humanists mentioned earlier. NORC did get a considerable amount of money to study recruitment to the physical, biological and social sciences, engineering, medicine and education. However, we are *also* studying recruitment to the humanities because we were able to convince the clients that it was more expensive for technical reasons to restrict the research only to those who might go into the "hard science" fields. Similarly, although Carnegie is primarily interested in adult education, NORC was able to broaden the study out to include other uses of leisure time because it is more fruitful to study adult education in the context of a study of leisure time activities than by itself.

What I have just described might be called passive "robinhooding"—as some researcher facetiously named the broadening of objectives of a policy-oriented sponsor to include concerns which are of intrinsic interest but for which no funded (or vested) interest is likely to be found to supply support. There is also the active type of robinhooding, in which one starts out with an objective of some intrinsic interest and then fits it to the applied interest of some agency or foundation. NORC's study of the career plans and aspirations of the June, 1961 graduates grew in part out of a long standing interest in measuring the productivity of colleges and universities as affected by their organizational characteristics. Robinhooding in both its passive and active forms leads to considerable tension between the policy maker and the researcher. On the one hand it looks as if the researcher is hoodwinking the policy maker; on the other hand it can be viewed as a process of bargaining in which the research center agrees to do something in return for support to do something else in addition. Incidentally, it often turns out that in the end the policy maker is quite pleased with the results of the extended study, perhaps more than he would be if he were given only that which he wanted originally.

In the negotiations between the researcher and the policy maker, there is an important weapon in the hands of the researcher—his technical expertise often puts the policy maker at a disadvantage. In the end, technical considerations must override other considerations if research of any great scientific stature is to appear. Indeed, one of the major reasons why government agencies come to the universities rather than to the commercial firms is that we are more concerned with technical purity than are the latter. Incidentally, when the market researchers and the advertising agencies want to have something that literally will stand up in court, they also come to the academic research organizations.

Of course, this pattern of financing large scale social research means that there may be projects of considerable intrinsic merit which are not supported at some particular point in time because there are no sources of support committed to research in the areas in question. For example, when the first draft of this paper was written in 1963 there were apparently no sources of support for research on the impact of the Negro protest movement on both whites and Negroes, even though this was (and is) one of the most salient features of the public life of our nation in this decade. We had an unparalleled opportunity to study a social movement in the making, but government agencies are understandably reluctant to support such research; and private foundations, for reasons I cannot fathom, also showed little interest. It is my impression that this is an unusual case. Ordinarily, given the diversity of interests represented by the large foundations and government agencies, there

are usually some sources whose interests are close enough to a project to consider supporting it.

The financing of large scale social research has put a distinct advantage into the hands of those social scientists who have affiliated themselves to the social research institutes. Foundations and government agencies properly conceive of such organizations as having better capabilities to carry through such research, and more of a sense of responsibility to carry them through. But there are disadvantages as well. Large scale social research is likely to have an applied emphasis, and worthy research endeavors may go unsponsored because none of the sources of large funds have an interest in the topic to be studied.

IMPLICATIONS FOR THE CONTEMPORARY UNIVERSITY

The basic structure of American universities scarcely has had a chance to react and accommodate to the great development of research activities within the university in the past forty years, and virtually no time at all to adjust to the growth of social science research in the two decades since World War II. The final pattern of accommodation has probably not yet appeared, to judge at least by the fact that few university officials, researchers and professors in any institution are sure that they have found a proper pattern in the organizational arrangements worked out on their campuses.

Partly because the solutions are not yet in sight, the problems resulting from the broadening of the goals of universities to include research as well as teaching are very much visible. There can be little doubt that the teaching function of universities, especially of undergraduates, is carried out differently today than when research was carried out by professors primarily as an extracurricular activity. In the major universities fewer and fewer faculty members are much less frequently exclusively teachers. In my own department of fourteen members, only two members are entirely on the departmental budget. The "teaching load" is becoming an item over which bargains are made in order to entice new faculty members.[23] Only in the small liberal arts college is teaching considered an activity through which a faculty member can make his major contribution to the university community.

It is hard to judge whether research activities unduly intrude upon the teaching function or whether it enriches teaching.[24] Certainly the faculty member who is wrapped up in his research may not be able to spend the time necessary to prepare lectures which are of the highest quality, but his lectures may have the benefit of being more up to date and alive because his research is on the frontiers of the field in which he is teaching. Perhaps the most serious inroad upon the university arises out of the rise of research as an alternative to entering upon a career of academic statesmanship. Departmental chairmanships appear to be going begging and on occasion few candidates have appeared as contenders for deanships. The rewards arising out of research are greater and lead to national recognition, while the rewards for chairing a department are restricted in the usually highly egalitarian department and arise out of local rather than national acclaim.

The teaching of graduate students appears to me to have benefited considerably from the development of research in the university. No longer is the dissertation the sole research experience of the new Ph.D. Ordinarily he has participated as an apprentice on perhaps several research projects of his major mentors. He has also probably had some practice teaching as a teaching assistant under the general supervision of an experienced lecturer. Since graduate study is more and more the goal of new B.A.'s,[25] the experiences of new entrants into the scientific and technical occupations more and more include some period of close and intimate contact with a member of the faculty. The intimacy of contact between faculty and students has disappeared in this era of mass higher education, to be replaced by intimacy centered around research on the graduate level.

It is more difficult to discern the trends concerning the roles of professor and of researcher. On the one hand there are strong trends toward the amalgamation of the two roles, with research institutes becoming more intimately parts of the university community. On the other hand, the trend toward research activities on larger scales and involving larger sums produces a strain toward the development of quite separate research organizations. Professors are doing more research, and greater demand exists for persons who will do only research. Right now the researcher and his institute are located at the periphery of the campus in both geographical and social structural senses, while the traditional departments are located at the heart of the university. The converted buildings in which the institutes are housed will give way to more permanent structures built with their use specifically in mind, and second-class citizenship for the researcher will probably give way to some kind of status equal to that of the professor.

It is hard to predict the specific form that the status of researcher will take in the evolving university structure. Perhaps the recent rashes of appointments of persons to "research professorships" presages the future position.[26] Or it may be the case that research institutes will develop into entities like departments, with complements of tenure positions to bestow. Whatever specific organizational forms will arise in the future in response to tensions I have described in this paper, one expectation will certainly be upheld: the American university will be profoundly affected by massive changes in the definition of the professorial role and perhaps even in the definition of the goals of the university community. Scientific activity apparently flourishes in the academic climate. I hope that the ecology of the academic community can support without radical alteration the rise to dominance of the species of scientific researcher.

FOOTNOTES

[1] Classrooms and dormitories also mark the center of the spatial distribution of prestige, with research centers and institutes marking their importance to the university by how close they are to this center. When space is reallocated through the construction of new buildings, a fierce jockeying occurs with each striving to improve its prestige by minimizing its distance from the university center.

[2] As telescopes increased in size and power and as the atmosphere of urban centers became more and more an obstacle to good observation, the observatories changed from being a dome on one of the campus buildings to separate installations located where the atmosphere was clearer.

[3] A literature concerning research centers has just started to develop, stemming in part from the needs of foundations, government agencies and universities to understand the intellectual implications of this organization of scientific activity. See, for example, H. M. Vollmer, "A Preliminary Investigation and Analysis of the Role of Scientists in Research Organizations," Stanford Research Institute (1962).

[4] P. F. Lazarsfeld, "Observations on the Organization of Empirical Social Research in the U. S.," *Information*, Bulletin of the International Social Science Council, XXIX (December, 1961).

[5] Most colleges and universities remain unaffected by these developments which are characteristic primarily of the larger and more prestigeful. But the total system of higher education must necessarily be affected by changes which are

taking place at the head of the academic procession. It is extremely easy to lose sight of the fact that most American institutions of higher learning do not include research as a major goal. In 1963 there were close to 1,500 institutions which granted bachelor's degrees, of which about 1,000 were accredited institutions. But only 150 granted higher degrees, and the top 30 graduate schools turned out about two-thirds of the Ph.D.'s. The distribution of the production of academic knowledge follows the distribution of higher degrees granted, with the top 30 schools producing the greater part by far of scholarly books and articles. It is these 30 institutions to which I refer as the "major universities."

[6] When such "centers" have arisen (e.g., the Russian Research Center at Harvard), they have often taken the form of *ad hoc* departments designed to cover an area of study common to several disciplines.

[7] This is not true of many European universities, where professors are expected to acquire and maintain private collections of works in their fields, and where university libraries are poorly supported and have sparse collections.

[8] Indeed, when collaboration of an enduring sort does occur, it is hard to assimilate. I know of the case of two young historians who had worked as a team as graduate students and obtained, with great difficulty, appointments to the same department. Their historian colleagues developed so strong an antipathy to the pair that neither was reappointed even though their scholarly production was considerably greater than the average, and either alone would have been (and eventually was) a proud acquisition for separate major departments of history.

[9] For example, about one-third of the articles in the most recent two years of the major professional journals in sociology were based on surveys, outstripping by a good deal the employment of other methods.

[10] The limitation of coverage gives rise to bewilderingly contradictory findings in some areas of knowledge. Thus, the score or more of studies of child rearing conducted over the last two decades have produced results which can lead to no firm conclusions concerning what are the *facts* concerning how children are reared in this country.

[11] Institutionalized populations (e.g., students or soldiers) can be reached more easily, and hence surveys of such populations are favored by the social scientist working on his own.

[12] Of course, there are commercial firms who will collect data from a national "sample" and present you with a report for less than $10,000. But if you examine their procedures, it is evident that the sampling plan is either nonexistent or highly deficient, the quality of interviewing haphazard and suspect, the number of interviews small (perhaps less than 500), and the analysis sketchy. While I am convinced that for many purposes such an operation may be all that is necessary (for example, to prove that most housewives are women or that people do not look kindly on foods that smell of sulphur dioxide), where the precision of data to be gathered is critical, such surveys do a considerable disservice.

[13] In contrast many European universities have maintained a different internal rank system in which there is usually only one professor for each major field and under him (and at his disposal) a number of assistants whose research activities can be directed by him. In adopting the German model of universities, American universities introduced a fundamental modification by allowing the appointment of many professors within each field, a development perhaps fostered by the larger number of American universities and the competition among them for personnel.

[14] I recall many incidents in which men from the industrial and commercial world have been baffled by their inability to locate the lines of authority within a department. Neophyte book salesmen have been floored by the discovery that a department chairman has little to say about adoption of textbooks, and irate conservatives railing against the imprudent radicalism of a press statement have been unable to find a "boss" to complain to.

[15] Paradoxically, this means that a man makes the best director when he is in the prime of his intellectual powers, but academic statesmanship favors the mature older man past his intellectual prime.

[16] Amitai Etzioni has pointed out that hospitals are also service organizations in the same sense as are libraries. Doctors have not organized themselves along elaborate organizational lines but use their hospitals primarily as service units.

[17] Gerald Holton, "Scientific Research and Scholarship," *Daedalus*, Spring, 1962.

[18] Derek de Solla Price, *Big Science: Little Science* (New York: Columbia University Press, 1963), shows that the costs of research have been increasing exponentially in a wide variety of fields in response to a corresponding increase in the complexity of research endeavors.

[19] Recently, NORC was visited by Mr. Louis Moss, who is director of the Government Social Survey in Great Britain. The Government Social Survey is a survey research organization within the British government which conducts surveys at the request of other government agencies. I was not surprised to find a great similarity between the structures of our two organizations, but I was very much surprised to discover that we had conducted so many parallel studies, his organization on behalf of Her Majesty's government, and NORC on behalf of federal agencies and private foundations. We could find parallel studies on about two-thirds of ours and about one-half of his projects. This means that together with other survey research organizations connected with universities or functioning as commercial enterprises, NORC is serving the same function for the American policy maker as the Government Social Survey functions for England.

[20] Coordinating three federal agencies is an administrative feat so massively delicate that it is surprising that our federal government manages to exist at all.

[21] Indeed, in one case we had difficulty keeping the client out of our hair, so eager was he to receive the results.

[22] In recent years, the establishment of a Social Science Division within the National Science Foundation and behavioral research study sections within the National Institute of Mental Health has increased considerably the amount of funds available for basic social research.

[23] In a joint NORC-Bureau of the Census study of persons in critical occupations and professions, the probabilities of scientists in all fields designating teaching as their primary duty increases drastically with age. For example, nine out of ten biologists over 55 with the Ph.D. list teaching as a primary duty while only one out of every ten under 35 makes the same claim. Similar although not as dramatic contrasts can be made for other scientific fields.

[24] Harold Orlans makes the point that the best graduate students are assigned duties as research assistants while the poorer quality students are given jobs as teaching assistants, thereby laying the groundwork for sorting out the best into

research and the poorest into teaching. There is no evidence to support his argument in NORC's study of graduate students (Seymour Warkov's "Subsidies for Graduate Study," NORC Report #97 [1964]). Teaching assistants and research assistants are roughly of the same quality.

[25] A NORC study of the June, 1961 graduating classes of American universities and colleges indicates that one out of three seniors enters upon postgraduate studies immediately after completing the B.A. See James A. Davis, *Great Aspirations* (Chicago: The Aldine Press, 1964).

[26] The University of Chicago has evolved a new status—Professorial Lecturer—to be held by persons with primarily research appointments who are so senior in accomplishment that they cannot be left out of the academic rank system. However, this new status does not involve the critical issue of assimilation of researchers into the university, their participation as voting members in departmental decisions.

Reflections on My Work

by William Foote Whyte

The environment of research is simply the sum total of all the scholars committed to the quest and their behavior patterns in its pursuit. Whyte's brief self-portrait identifies the man and distills his sense of his own accomplishment and its relevance. It is interesting to note how even a role as practicing administrator is exploited by the committed scholar to extend his theoretical insight. But, perhaps what is most telling is the reliance which this researcher has always placed upon his subjects and his colleagues to give his work the sure and clear perspective which always comes through in his writings. Whyte's comments are particularly germane for those drawn to research in the context of an applied field. More and more, those most sensitive to the uses and applications of behavioral science see it and see themselves essentially linking up in ways leading to the improvement and betterment of the human condition. This account puts the case as well as it is documented anywhere in the literature with economy and humility.

I would characterize my style of research in the following ways:

(1) *Immersion in field work.* I began my research experience as a participant observer on the street corners and remained very deeply involved for three and a half years. I have never had such full immersion since that time: but from 1942 until 1954 I maintained a heavy personal involvement in field work, getting into the field myself for long periods on at least a two day a week basis. While, after my first study in industry, I found myself supervising the research of graduate students, I felt an urge to be involved in the field myself. It seemed to me that I could only make my best contribution if I was out there, observing some of the same phenomena that students were observing, interviewing some of the same people or people like them. I feel that whatever theorizing I have been able to do has grown as much out of the personal experience of confronting the phenomena in the field as it has out of intellectual processes in the office.

(2) *Utilization of administrative experience as participant observer.* Since 1955 I have no longer been in a position to spend substantial time myself in field work, but I have sought to maintain the excitement of personal involvement by regarding myself as a participant observer in administrative activities. First came my experience (1956–61) as director of the Social Science Research Center at Cornell University and then (since 1962) with Lawrence K. Williams of Cornell and José Matos Mar of San Marcos University in Peru I have been involved in a rather large-scale comparative and longitudinal study of rural communities, along with research in high schools and business organizations.

As director of the Social Science Research Center, my entire staff consisted of a half-time assistant director and a secretary. I had no authority over any of the professors in the social sciences and a very limited budget to use as bait for promoting activities that I found interesting. I recognized that I could only make a useful contribution to Cornell insofar as I was able to stimulate voluntary cooperation across departmental and college lines. To do the job, I had to think about what would work and what would not work, and as some activities I promoted seemed to succeed whereas others made little headway, I was naturally led to reflection about the underlying social processes.

My participant-observer-as-research-administrator role grew out of an attempt to resolve the problems of role conflict in research administration: personal involvement in research versus project administration.

My Social Science Research Center experience pointed the way toward an attempted resolution of this conflict. If it were possible to structure the research activities so that they would provide pay-offs for all concerned, then the organization would operate primarily in terms of voluntary

SOURCE: "Reflections on My Work" by William Foote Whyte is reprinted from the *American Behavioral Scientist*, Volume XII, Number 1 (September/October, 1968), pages 9–13, by permission of the Author and the Publisher, Sage Publications, Inc.

cooperation, and those with the chief administrative responsibilities would be relieved to a large extent from the tasks of detailed supervision, inspection, and policing of activities.

Furthermore, it occurred to me that if we did prove successful in reconciling the apparently irreconcilable, the conclusions to be drawn from our experience should have some scientific as well as practical value. To the extent that I could treat myself as a participant observer in the process of developing this new form of organization, I would be gathering data for analysis and report writing in the process of administration. One published article (1967) has already come largely out of this experience, and others are in process. I am finding this experience not only productive in data but in the stimulus it provides toward building new and better theories of organizational behavior and interorganizational relations. In fact, I am now in the process of developing a new theoretical framework for the analysis of organizational behavior, and this is evolving directly out of my research-administration experience.

(3) *Combination of research methods.* For almost the first twenty years, I was completely committed to the field methods of interviewing and observation. I had little use for questionnaires and no experience with them. While I did occasionally have responsibility for a student thesis in which a questionnaire was used, my first direct experience with the survey method came in my 1954-55 year of research on industrial relations with Creole Petroleum Corporation in Venezuela. While some of the problems I was studying seemed to lend themselves well to my usual interviewing-observational approach, the problem of worker attitudes and values regarding living in a company home versus owning one's own home clearly called for a survey approach, and so I began in this direction somewhat tentatively in Venezuela. In the course of my fourteen months in Peru (1961-62) while I continued research through interviewing and observation, I encountered further problems that seemed to demand the survey approach, or a combination of the two approaches. Here I was fortunate in being able to collaborate with Lawrence K. Williams, who had come to Cornell after extensive experience in the Survey Research Center at the University of Michigan. Since that time he and I have been collaborating on a series of studies in organizations and communities, utilizing survey methods combined with interviewing and ob-

servation. I have come to recognize that the two approaches are not competitive. As I have argued elsewhere (1965), each of the two has its own strengths and weaknesses, and to a high degree the strengths of one method complement the weaknesses of the other.

Beginning in late 1966 or early 1967, particularly through involvement in the Chancay Valley study directed by Dr. Matos, I have been discovering how economic and historical data can be integrated with survey data and also with data from anthropological-type interviewing and observation.

(4) *Flexibility.* While anyone likes to think that he himself is flexible while other people are rigid, I think I can show evidence of flexibility in the development of my research career. I began with an urban community study. Then for many years I carried out studies in industrial sociology. Now, while I have continued industrial organizational studies (in Peru), I have also focused attention on Peruvian high school students, and I am concentrating particularly upon development and change in rural communities in Peru. As I attempt to put it all together in Peru, I hope one day to be able to write a book about that nation, based as much as possible upon the fruits of research (my own and that of others) extending across a range from urban to rural, from organizations to communities.

I began in an Italian American slum district, learning enough Italian to be able to communicate with the older people. I am now deeply involved in Latin American studies, having developed enough Spanish to handle field work, teaching, or research supervision.

(5) *Collaboration with key informants.* The man I called "Doc" in *Street Corner Society* (1943d) was far more to me than an informant in the usual sense of the term.[1] Beginning as my chief guide into the intricacies of Cornerville, he came to be also a collaborator in the research. We spent many hours discussing what he and I were observing. Piece by piece, he read through the first draft of the book and gave me his detailed criticisms. With Ralph Orlandella, then a leader of another corner gang, I also established a collaborative relationship that contributed to the book and that we have been able to revive from time to time in the intervening years.

In my first union-management case study, I found international representative Sidney Garfield providing me with my most valuable data and interpretations on the change from conflict to cooperation. As I became fascinated with his accounts of his experiences in other union-management situations that I was not studying, I proposed that we collaborate on a series of articles on "The Collective Bargaining Process" (1950-51). While I did all the writing, I could not really say that this series was more mine than his, for he provided nearly all of the case material and a large part of the analysis also. These materials and the ideas they generated for me helped later to shape the section on bargaining in my textbook, *Men at Work* (1961). Richard Walton and Robert McKersie (1965) have made liberal use of these cases in their impressive effort to place bargaining in a behavioral science framework.

Early in my work in Peru I encountered Robert R. Braun, who was then serving as interim director of IPAE, the Peruvian management association, and developing his own business as a management consultant. A Peruvian citizen who had emigrated from Vienna 26 years earlier, Braun was tri-lingual (German, Spanish, and English). As accountant, factory manager, or consultant, Braun had worked with Peruvian, English, and U.S. management people, fitting in and yet always maintaining the detachment that produces insights.

Braun asked me a series of questions about the factory studies I hoped to carry out, then invited me to his home so that we could talk further. With few preliminaries, he then made me his offer, in something like these words:

> I am very much interested in what you are doing. Now, while I am making a comfortable living with my consulting, it doesn't take up all my time. I wish you would feel free to call on me at any time for anything you think I can do for you.

I was then five thousand miles and 25 years away from my beginnings in Cornerville, but Braun's words projected me momentarily into that settlement house, where Doc had made precisely the same offer. I accepted without hesitation. For the rest of my 14 months in Peru, I consulted Braun on every major move I made and on all the ideas that were emerging from the study. He became not only my chief cultural consultant but also my most valued critic of Bill Whyte in action. When I was to present something before a management group or to seek entree for a plant study, I would discuss my approach with Braun beforehand and then, if he had been present for the occasion, I would later get his feedback impressions of why the others had reacted to me as they did.

After I returned from Peru and Braun went to Geneva to become Secretary General of C.I.O.S.

(the international organization of scientific management), our collaboration continued by correspondence. It has so far led to two joint publications (1966 and forthcoming) with more in process.

From these and other similar experiences, I am inclined to generalize in this way. The researcher who treats all of those he meets in a field study as passive informants is missing some of the major values that can come out of field experience. Now, whenever I get involved in a new field study, I go in with the following assumption: I will soon encounter one or more people who are at least as smart as I am, who know far more about their organization than I do, who already have considerable insight into what is going on, who can be encouraged to develop further their analytical talents and observational skills, and who will enjoy working with me.

(6) *Efficiency in production*. I am not troubled by the well-known professorial "writing block." When I have some idea of what I want to say, I can get it said in a hurry. Even when my ideas are confused, I find the exercise of writing an essential step toward clarification.

I started writing, beyond required school exercises, at about the age of 11. When still in grade school, I wrote an endless continued story. As a senior in high school I was responsible for writing the weekly school page for the *Bronxville Press*, which meant delivering about 20 pages of typed copy to my editor every Sunday night.

Through the Cornerville period, I typed both field notes and drafts of the book. On my next study, I began dictating field notes. In 1948 I dictated the first draft of *Pattern for Industrial Peace* (1949). Since that time I have dictated nearly everything I have written, working from a detailed outline.

While I am a fairly fast (if somewhat erratic) touch typist, I estimate that I can dictate a first draft 1½ to 3 times as fast as I can type it. Revision of the dictated draft does indeed take more time than I need for a typed draft, but the difference is not great, so the net gain is enormous.

(7) *Concern with application*. From the beginning I have been concerned with the application of research knowledge to human problems. I attended the first meeting of the Society for Applied Anthropology in 1941 and have been active in that society ever since, serving as editor of *Human Organization* for six years. I am a charter member and also one-time president of another association with a strong

orientation toward the practical application of research knowledge: the Industrial Relations Research Association.

ON APPLIED RESEARCH

I have never accepted the presumed dichotomy between basic or "pure" research and applied research. It seems to me that whether research makes a basic contribution to knowledge depends not upon the motivation of the researcher but upon the potential generalizability of the research findings. Chester I. Barnard (1957) expressed this very well when he criticized a National Science Foundation report which sought to separate basic from applied projects.

> As one example, we have Karl Jansky's discovery of radio signals from outer space. Jansky, according to the report, was not engaged in basic research; he merely made a basic discovery. Here the confusion arises from labeling research according to the motives for which it is carried on; there is an element of snobbery involved which ought not to be encouraged. After all, Louis Pasteur made his great contributions to the foundations of bacteriology in trying to find solutions to the practical problems of the French silk and wine industries. The whole discussion demonstrates that the dichotomy between basic and applied research can be overemphasized.

While I would agree that important advances in knowledge can arise whether or not a given project involves any attempt to apply its research findings, it seems to me likely that our field would progress more rapidly if more people were willing to do applied research. If a man has an obligation to try to apply his research findings, the effort he must make to come to terms with the realities of the field situation is likely to prevent him from indulging in ivory tower theorizing, which sounds impressive but leads nowhere. In short, I regard application as a necessary testing ground for the knowledge we think we have acquired.

I think there has been an unfortunate trend toward snobbism in sociology during the last 20 to 30 years. It seems to be assumed that the man who does "pure" research and has no concern whatsoever with application wins high prestige from his professional colleagues, whereas the man who is concerned with applied research may be looked upon as something of a hack. Where were we when "the Great Society" burst upon us (before its side tracking by the Vietnam war) and seemed to promise government guided transformations of the quality of American life? When government

administrators, charged with the building of new and adventurous programs in the fields of housing, employment, training, and community development, called out for the guidance that they hoped behavioral scientists would be able to give them, we found that there were pitifully few among us who had anything practical to contribute.

I do not mean to give the impression that I have always been deeply involved in the application of research findings. Only once have I taken on a project where the application of research findings was the major objective (Whyte and Hamilton, 1965). Still, in nearly everything I have written I have had in the back of my mind the question: can this be put to some practical use? At least I have tried to make myself understandable to men of action, and I have always been interested in communicating with them. At this writing, as chairman of the Sub-Committee on Research of the National Advisory Committee of the Department of Labor, I am now working to link research to some of the training and human development problems of our explosive urban areas.

WHAT SOCIOLOGISTS HAVE INFLUENCED ME?

In the early stages of my research career, sociological influences were notable for their absence. In the *Street Corner Society* study, I was particularly influenced by social anthropologists Conrad M. Arensberg and Eliot D. Chapple, who in turn had got their start in the direction I was then pursuing with W. Lloyd Warner. I learned my research methods from them and also the conception of my field of study. For the first decade of my professional career, the only sociologist whose influence I can now testify to was Everett C. Hughes. He seemed to me then—as he still does now—a master at the sociological contest.

I should also mention certain influences-by-reaction: physiologist and part-time sociologist Lawrence J. Henderson and Louis Wirth. While I sat in on Henderson's famous seminar on Pareto, it was not that experience that influenced me. Henderson believed nearly all social scientists were soft headed sentimentalists, and in the Monday evening dinners of the Society of Fellows at Harvard, he was always ready to pounce on any words of mine that tended to confirm this impression of me and my colleagues. For years, as I wrote up my research, I could feel Henderson peering over my shoulder, ready to attack any confusion of value judgment with scientific evidence.

In my period at the University of Chicago, students had to consider not only which professors they were working for but also which they were working *against*. If you took your main work with Warner and Hughes, as I did, you had to be prepared to fight off Wirth in your field and thesis examinations. Wirth began his thesis questioning (on *Street Corner Society*) by asking me to define a slum district. If I defined it in terms of "social disorganization," this would throw into question my interpretation of my slum. But since everybody else defined it that way, how could I avoid those terms? Through what seemed an endless grilling, I stuck to a definition in terms of geography, population density, housing conditions, and such objective factors. This did not satisfy Wirth, of course, and he kept after me with a skill that I found both impressive and infuriating. Still, he probably did me good because, in writing *Street Corner Society*, I had not bothered to orient myself to the literature. In preparing for the exam, I wrote a long introductory statement, examining the literature on slums, and pointing out what my distinctive contributions were. That exercise, plus the stimulus of the exam, led to the publication of several articles (1943a, 1943b, 1943c) that oriented me to the field and furnished the footnotes that *Street Corner Society* lacked.

As I pushed ahead with industrial studies after finishing graduate work at Chicago, the main personal intellectual influences upon me still came from outside of sociology. I think particularly of Muzafer Sherif, the social psychologist, whose experiments in inter-group relations seem to me classics in the field. My industrial studies were more directly influenced by Leonard Sayles and George Strauss, both of whom received their interdisciplinary doctorate at Massachusetts Institute of Technology.

It is only in the third decade of my professional career, beginning in approximately 1956, that sociologists have come to have a major impact upon my thinking. I am indebted to George C. Homans, Peter Blau, and Alvin Gouldner for their development of exchange theory, which seems to me to set forth a main line of my future theoretical development. I consider Joan Woodward, the British sociologist (whom I have never met) a major influence in showing me systematic ways to examine the impact of technology upon organization structure and upon the organization of work activities.

MY BOOKS

I suppose the favorite among my books has to be *Street Corner Society*. I lived that study, and it still brings back vivid memories.

I suppose the book is particularly popular with students and with professors who want to introduce students to sociology because the book presents live characters and whole human situations. While I am not generally regarded as a theoretician, I like to think that certain aspects of *Street Corner Society* have stimulated generalizable research results in the works of other people. Muzafer Sherif and his students (e.g., Harvey, 1953) utilized the relationship I observed between bowling performance and rank in the informal group to develop their own line of social experiments. Scudder Mekeel (1943) claimed that my discussion of "The Social Role of the Settlement House" could be applied practically word for word to the relations between the Indian Bureau and the Indians.

In the field of industry, my favorite is *Money and Motivation* (1955). I did not live this book in the sense that I lived *Street Corner Society*, but it represents a milestone of quite a different sort. By the time I put together *Money and Motivation* I had done a number of case studies in industry and had become increasingly concerned about possibilities of generalization beyond a given case. From time to time over a ten-year period before publication of this book, I had been working on the problems of financial incentives and worker motivation. An earlier effort to put together a book in collaboration with Donald Roy, Melville Dalton, and Orvis Collins did not come off. Years later as I was reading another article by Roy dealing with incentives and motivation—in my bathtub—I suddenly saw how this new piece fitted into certain gaps, and the framework of the book quickly evolved in my mind. I certainly set forth there no grand scheme, but I feel that my collaborators and I were able to pull together apparently disparate fragments of data and put them into a coherent framework.

I have somewhat mixed feelings about *Street Corner Society*. It is not entirely pleasant for an author to have to admit that his best book was also his first book. Have I been going down hill since then? Perhaps, but I like to think that the book or books that I see now evolving out of my

Peruvian studies will one day stand at least on a par with *Street Corner Society*.

MY IMPACT ON SOCIOLOGY

Up to this point, I feel that I have had little impact upon the development of general theory in sociology. I have contributed more to methodology in writing about field methods and the role of the participant observer. Perhaps the publication of *Street Corner Society* helped to set off the boom in small group research. I have certainly played a role in shaping the field of industrial sociology or organizational behavior, through my writing and through the students who have worked with me.

Not so long ago I had the impression that many sociologists regarded my favorite research methods as obsolete—interesting things to do until you learn how to be more "scientific." Now I think I see the tide turning toward an appreciation of the distinctive values and limitations of various research methods.

It seems to me that the heyday of the questionnaire came in with the development of new data processing technology during World War II and the post-war years. The investigator could now process such enormous amounts of data in so many ways that many sociologists were overwhelmed with the wonder of it all. For years many sociologists seemed to assume that the only "hard" research was questionnaire research.

I feel that this heyday has now passed. As I review the research findings of several decades of questionnaire surveys on one of the most studied problems in industrial sociology, the man-boss relationship, I am oppressed and also depressed with how little has been learned by how many bright people and how many hardworking machines. Few correlations have held up from one study to the next. Why this should be the case is beyond the scope of this paper (see Whyte 1963 and 1965), but I believe that sociologists are increasingly recognizing that the questionnaire is not an all purpose instrument but has certain very serious limitations.

I now believe that the combination of research methods that is representative of my current work will come increasingly to be the pattern in our field. I think I can even see that almost forgotten figure, the participant observer, coming back into view. In my service on the Research Advisory Committee to the National Manpower Administration of the Department of Labor, I have been arguing that before-and-after measures of the effects of a given governmental program are not good enough. We need to know what went on within the program that may be presumed to account for the differences, if any, in our before-and-after measures. In other words, we need data on social processes, and questionnaires do not provide such data. Who is to provide such data? Somebody who is out in the field observing what is going on, perhaps even a participant observer.

I have been gratified to learn that the agency has managed to encourage some young sociologists to get into the field as participant observers in connection with one or another of the poverty programs. While the scientific results are not yet in, I was struck by the practical implications of a comment from an executive of the agency:

> When the research men do a questionnaire study, we have to wait six months to a year after the data are all in before they can carry out their analysis and tell us what they have found out. With the participant observer, it is quite different. By the time he comes out of the field—if not before—he can tell us a great deal about the nature of the program he is studying. He can point out to us problems of policies or procedures that we can do something about and that we never would have discovered through a questionnaire survey.

I also see a new emphasis upon systematic quantitative measures of observed behavior, from Eliot D. Chapple's interaction chronograph to other methods which are less precise but more readily usable in field studies.

I would like to think that the well-trained sociologist of the near future will be well grounded in interviewing and observation, experimental methods, and questionnaire surveys. Will it take longer to train our students in this broad range of methods? Not if we shift our emphasis from systematic coverage of the literature (which in large measure simply documents our ignorance) toward providing students the tools for finding things out for themselves.

REFERENCES

BARNARD, C. I. (1957) "A national science policy." Scientific Am. 45 (Nov.).

HARVEY, O. J. (1953) "An experimental approach to the study of status relations in informal groups." Am. Sociol. Rev. 18: 357-367.

MEKEEL, S. (1943) "Comparative notes on the social role of the Settlement House as contrasted with that of the United States Indian Service." Applied Anth. 3 (Dec.).

WALTON, R. and McKERSIE, R. (1965) A Behavioral Theory of Labor Negotiations: An Analysis of a Social Interaction System. New York: McGraw-Hill.

WHYTE, W. F. (1943a) "Social organization in the slums." Am. Sociol. Rev. 8 (Feb.).
——(1943b) "A slum sex code." Am. J. Sociol. (July).
——(1943c) "A challenge to political scientists." Am. Pol. Sci. Rev. 34 (Aug.).
——(1943d) Street Corner Society. Chicago: Univ. of Chicago Press.
——(1949) Pattern For Industrial Peace. New York: Harper.
——(1955) Money and Motivation. New York: Harper.
——(1961) Men at Work. Homewood, Ill.: Irwin-Dorsey.
——(1963) "Toward an integrated approach to research in organizational behavior." The 1963 Presidential Address of the Indust. Rel. Research Assoc.; in Proceedings of I.R.R.A., Reprint No. 155. Cornell Univ.: New York State School of Indust. and Labor Rel.
——(1965) "A field in search of a focus." Indust. and Labor Rel. Rev. 18, No. 3 (April).
——(1967) "Models for building and changing organizations." Human Organ. 26, No. 1/2 (Spr./Sum.).
——(forthcoming) "On Language and Culture." In Festschrift volume for Everett C. Hughes, edited by D. Reisman and R. Weiss.
——and BRAUN, R. (1966) "Heroes, homework, and industrial growth." Columbia J. World Business 1, No. 2 (Spring).
——and GARFIELD, S. (1950-51) "The collective bargaining process." Human Organ. 9, No. 2 and 10, No. 1.
——and HAMILTON, E. (1965) Action Research For Management. Homewood, Ill.: Richard Irwin.

FOOTNOTES

[1] My relations with "Doc" are discussed in detail in the appendix to *Street Corner Society* (1955 enlarged edition).

Appendices

Bibliographies

Sample Instruments

List of Contributors

Bibliography Of Social Science
Research Methodology

This annotated listing of standard works on research methods was prepared with the assistance of several specialists on one or another aspect of research methods and for the most part selection was based on actual experience in use of the work. The listing serves to familiarize the student with the literature of research methods as well as to provide starting points for further reading and study on one or another topic. In some areas, notably the textbooks, statistics and mathematics, the literature of the field is now so voluminous that it was necessary to be highly selective. On these topics, an effort was made to include works at varying levels of difficulty. It was also necessary in the section "Theory and Method in Selected Disciplines" to be highly selective and the volumes included are among those most frequently cited by scholars. They provide overviews of research in various research areas and orient the reader to the most advanced discussion of theory in the discipline represented.

For introductory research courses it is recommended that the student dip into appropriate chapters in several methods textbooks as a supplement to this Reader and to class discussion of these topics. Bibliographies in the works cited here will lead the student beyond the book literature while the most current discussion of theory and method will be found in the scholarly journals of the various social science disciplines.

I. Philosophy of Science

Cohen, Morris R., and Nagel, Ernest. *An Introduction to Logic and Scientific Method*. New York: Harcourt, Brace and World, 1934.

This now classic volume was originally written expressly for students of logic. A substantial portion of the book, however, is devoted to applied logic and the scientific method. Specific areas covered include hypotheses, experimental inquiry, probability and induction, measurement, and statistical methods.

Feigl, Herbert, and Brodbeck, May (eds.) *Readings in the Philosophy of Science*. New York: Appleton-Century-Crofts, 1953.

This comprehensive compilation of writings treats general philosophical questions, as well as problems within specific disciplines ranging from physics to the social sciences. Designed as a multipurpose text, the volume includes material that varies in level of treatment from fairly elementary to quite advanced.

Kaplan, Abraham. *The Conduct of Inquiry: Methodology for Behavioral Science*. San Francisco: Chandler Publishing Co., 1964.

A philosopher makes a critical and constructive assessment of behavioral science and its methodological problems, emphasizing those common to all social sciences. The topics covered range from the abstract—laws, explanation, and values—to the more specific—experiments, models, and statistics.

Kuhn, Thomas S. *The Structure of Scientific Revolutions*. Chicago: University of Chicago Press, 1962.

The author sketches his concept of science based on study of the history of research activity within the context of conditions existing at a given time, rather than as an accretion of isolated events. The resulting image of scientific development, the process by which theories emerge, and the response of the scientific community are elaborated.

Nagel, Ernest. *The Structure of Science: Problems in the Logic of Scientific Explanation*. New York: Harcourt, Brace and World, 1961.

The logic of scientific inquiry and its intellectual products are discussed in detail on an abstract level. The character of the scientific method is further examined in the context of a variety of disciplines, including the social sciences.

II. Theory Construction

Glaser, Barney G., and Strauss, Anselm L. *The Discovery of Grounded Theory: Strategies for Qualitative Research*. Chicago: Aldine Publishing Co., 1967.

In an effort to make theory more relevant, the authors discuss the process of generating theory by means of comparative analysis of data systematically obtained from social research. The authors contend that too much emphasis has been placed on verification of theory at the expense of discovery of theory.

Gross, Llewellyn (ed.) *Symposium on Sociological Theory*. New York: Harper and Row, 1959.

This volume represents an explicit attempt to advance the state of sociological theory and theorizing. Sociological theories and the process of constructing theories are examined in an effort to find underlying principles.

Mills, C. Wright. *The Sociological Imagination*. New York: Oxford University Press, 1959.

Writing in a polemical style, the author examines modern sociology in terms of its potentialities and finds it wanting on many points. The shortcomings are delineated and remedies proposed. A substantial portion of the book deals with the social sciences in general, providing guidelines for future development.

Zetterberg, Hans L. *On Theory and Verification in Sociology*. 3d ed. Totowa, N.J.: The Bedminster Press, 1966.

To stimulate greater reliance on theory as a source of research projects, the author discusses in detail the principles of sociological theory construction through the use of a system of propositions. Means of testing such theories are also considered.

III. Research Methods

Textbooks:

Blalock, Hubert M., Jr., and Blalock, Ann B. (eds.) *Methodology in Social Research*. New York: McGraw-Hill, 1968.

This text, intended for advanced graduate students, emphasizes the quantitative aspects of methodology. Measurement, design, and analysis are treated in detail by specialists in each area. Several of the chapters are nonmathematical and are appropriate for beginning graduate students.

Doby, John T. (ed.) *An Introduction to Social Research*. 2d ed. New York: Appleton-Century-Crofts, 1967.

Social research is presented as a special type of problem-solving activity. After a discussion of the logic and procedural rules for scientific problem-solving, the methods and techniques for carrying out these rules in actual research are given. This collection of papers is designed as a basic introductory text in logic and current research methods.

Festinger, Leon, and Katz, Daniel (eds.) *Research Methods in the Behavioral Sciences*. New York: Holt, Rinehart and Winston, 1953.

This graduate level textbook emphasizes modern research techniques that are particularly relevant to problems of social psychology research. Although the articles are somewhat advanced and specialized, they cover a wide range of topics and are applicable to social science research in general.

Goode, William J., and Hatt, Paul K. *Methods in Social Research*. New York: McGraw-Hill, 1952.

All phases of research methods are covered in this text designed for the undergraduate social science student. The more abstract concepts of research methodology are interspersed with accounts of actual research experiences in order to give an understanding of the research process as a whole.

Phillips, Bernard S. *Social Research: Strategy and Tactics*. New York: Macmillan, 1966.

Based on the premise that theory is the most important research tool, this text discusses the conventional research methods and their relation to theory. One research problem is developed at length and provides the background for an elaboration of the techniques of data collection and analysis, measurement, and modeling. Statistical procedures are emphasized.

Riley, Matilda White. *Sociological Research*. 2 vols. New York: Harcourt, Brace and World, 1963.

> Lengthy excerpts from well-known studies illustrate different research approaches and methods of analysis. A detailed commentary follows, in which each study is analyzed using a paradigm developed by the author; a number of other teaching aids are included. Volume II is a manual of field and laboratory exercises.

Selltiz, Claire, and Others. *Research Methods in Social Relations*. Rev. ed. New York: Holt, Rinehart and Winston, 1959.

> This popular text presents the standard research methods and a detailed description of the major steps in carrying out a research project, from formulation of the problem to writing the report and applying the results, noting the interrelationships of each step. Statistical techniques are touched on lightly.

Theory and Method in Selected Disciplines:

Charlesworth, James C. (ed.) *Contemporary Political Analysis*. New York: Free Press, 1967.

> This collection of seventeen articles deals with the more recent methodological approaches to the study of government—behavioral, communicational, decision-making, political development, mathematical-metrical, simulational, structural-functional, and systems.

Eulau, Heinz, Eldersveld, Samuel J., and Janowitz, Morris (eds.) *Political Behavior: A Reader in Theory and Research*. Glencoe, Ill.: Free Press, 1956.

> The contributions of empirical research to the political science discipline are emphasized. An explicit attempt is made to relate this type of research to the development of political theory and to demonstrate the wide applicability of the behavioral approach.

Faris, Robert E. L. (ed.) *Handbook of Modern Sociology*. Chicago: Rand McNally, 1964.

> This volume summarizes the major areas of research in modern sociology, concentrating on those in a developmental stage. Although most chapters are organized according to sociological topics, a number deal specifically with methodological developments.

Gage, N. L. (ed.) *Handbook of Research on Teaching*. Chicago: Rand McNally, 1963.

> Research dealing with the methods, instruments, and media of teaching, as well as the behavior of teachers, is summarized, critically analyzed, and integrated in this collection of papers. A substantial portion of the volume is devoted to methodologies in research on teaching.

Lindzey, Gardner (ed.) *Handbook of Social Psychology*. 2 vols. Reading, Mass.: Addison-Wesley, 1954.

> The first volume in this set deals with theory and methods of research. The section on methodology includes advanced articles covering a wide variety of procedures. The second volume is devoted to the substantive findings and applications of social psychology.

March, James G. (ed.) *Handbook of Organizations*. Chicago: Rand McNally, 1965.

> This comprehensive reference work covers the foundations, theories, and methodologies relating to organizational and interpersonal behavior. The present state of organizational research and organization theory is emphasized, with specific examples and applications.

Merton, Robert K., Broom, Leonard, and Cottrell, Leonard S., Jr. (eds.) *Sociology Today: Problems and Prospects*. New York: Basic Books, 1959.

Significant theoretical, empirical, and procedural problems which must be solved before others can be dealt with effectively are identified. Problems of methodology are treated generally within the context of a wide variety of specialized areas in sociology.

Sills, David L. (ed.) *International Encyclopedia of the Social Sciences.* New York: Macmillan and Free Press, 1968.

Summaries of the concepts, principles, theories, and methods that characterize current social science are set forth in this reference work. Emphasis is placed on the analytical and comparative aspects of the topic, rather than on historical and descriptive material. The articles were written by social scientists representing more than thirty countries.

Young, Roland (ed.) *Approaches to the Study of Politics.* Evanston, Ill.: Northwestern University Press, 1958.

The nature of politics and the methods by which it can be studied are explored by a number of scholars, including Floyd Hunter, Peter Rossi, Richard Snyder, and Talcott Parsons. The approaches discussed range from the more traditional to the new and experimental.

IV. Major Approaches

Historical:

Carr, Edward Hallett. *What Is History? The George Macaulay Trevelyan Lectures Delivered in the University of Cambridge, January-March 1961*. New York: Knopf, 1961.

In this series of lectures, the author presents his conception of history as "a constantly moving process, with the historian moving within it." The topics of facts, society, morality, causation, progress, and change are discussed in relation to the author's viewpoint.

Gottschalk, Louis. *Understanding History: A Primer of Historical Method.* New York: Knopf, 1950.

The author discusses practical problems that history graduate students are likely to encounter in writing history. Methods of historical research are emphasized. The nature and theory of history are also discussed at an introductory level.

Gray, Wood. *Historian's Handbook: A Key to the Study and Writing of History*. Boston: Houghton Mifflin, 1959.

This brief work is designed as an introduction to the study of history, a guide in the preparation of term papers and theses, and a reference manual for the practicing historian. Specific aids include extensive bibliographies of sources of information and examples of bibliographic form.

Hockett, Homer Carey. *The Critical Method in Historical Research and Writing.* New York: Macmillan, 1955.

After an introduction to the principles of historical criticism, this manual treats in detail the steps in writing a master's thesis in history. A brief survey of American historiography and an extensive classified bibliography also appear.

Lipset, Seymour Martin, and Hofstadter, Richard (eds.) *Sociology and History: Methods.* New York: Basic Books, 1968.

This volume is designed to show the desirability of an interplay between sociological methods and the historical perspective. Most of the papers either illustrate the application by historians of sociological methods to specific subject areas in history or else deal with sociological studies on historical topics.

Muller, Herbert J. *The Uses of the Past: Profiles of Former Societies.* New York: Oxford University Press, 1952.

In a series of studies of a wide variety of former societies, the author presents his view of history as a great tragic drama, in which the most significant development is the freedom to make history. An essay on the nature of history—its philosophy and meaning—is included.

Nevins, Allan. *The Gateway to History.* Rev. ed. Garden City, N.Y.: Anchor Doubleday, 1962.

The scope, objectives, and pleasures of history are presented in this book intended for the novice. Different approaches to history are reviewed critically. Problems encountered in writing history are discussed and illustrated with interesting anecdotes.

Social Science Research Council. *Theory and Practice in Historical Study: A Report of the Committee on Historiography.* Bulletin 54. New York: The Council, 1946.

These papers, several of which were written by Charles R. Beard, include the following: a survey of major movements of thought in American history, a case study of the treatment of "causality" in historical writing, a set of propositions in historiography, a glossary of terms, and a bibliography.

Survey:

Backstrom, Charles H., and Hursh, Gerald D. *Survey Research.* Evanston, Ill.: Northwestern University Press, 1963.

The techniques of survey research are explained in detail in this practical manual designed particularly for political science students who are conducting field studies. A model field survey is used to illustrate each step of the process.

Glock, Charles Y. (ed.) *Survey Research in the Social Sciences.* New York: Russell Sage Foundation, 1967.

A brief history and description of survey research is followed by essays describing the applications and potential uses of survey research in the fields of sociology, political science, psychology, economics, anthropology, education, social work, and public health and medicine.

Hyman, Herbert. *Survey Design and Analysis: Principles, Cases and Procedures.* New York: Free Press, 1955.

Detailed descriptions of several major case studies are interwoven with discussions of abstract principles of survey design and analysis, in order to approximate for the student the experience of relating general procedures to the context of a particular survey. The appendix contains sample instruments and a series of exercises.

Warren, Roland L. *Studying Your Community.* New York: Free Press, 1965.

This action-oriented working manual, designed for laymen interested in studying their own community, emphasizes the survey method. Each chapter explores the factual basis of one particular aspect of the community, such as housing, and provides question outlines, methods of appraisal, and sources of information.

Young, Pauline V. *Scientific Social Surveys and Research: An Introduction to the Background, Content, Methods, Principles, and Analysis of Social Studies.* 4th ed. Englewood Cliffs, N.J.: Prentice-Hall, 1966.

This book, originally published in 1939, has been kept up-to-date by successive revisions based on the author's further experience and readers' criticisms. Designed as an introductory text for social science students, the present volume includes many examples drawn from empirical studies and other teaching aids.

Case:

See relevant chapters in research methods textbooks and actual case studies.

Experimental:

Cochran, William G., and Cox, Gertrude M. *Experimental Designs.* 2d ed. New York: Wiley, 1957.

The authors, who are statisticians, describe the most useful research designs that have been developed. Besides plans and descriptions of the appropriate situation for each of the designs, the book contains brief reviews of the basic theory and an extensive set of worked examples of the analysis for each type. Knowledge of statistics is assumed.

Fairweather, George W. *Methods for Experimental Social Innovation.* New York: Wiley, 1967.

In an attempt to bring social science methods to bear upon current social problems, the author describes general experimental procedures in nonmathematical terms and demonstrates how they can be used to effect changes in ongoing social processes with a minimum of disruption. Step-by-step procedures for planning, implementing, and evaluating new social programs are given.

Kirk, Roger E. *Experimental Design: Procedures for the Behavioral Sciences.* Belmont, Calif.: Brooks/Cole Publishing Co., 1968.

A detailed treatment of the more complex research designs and techniques is presented for the reader who has little mathematical sophistication. Each design is introduced by a research problem; worked-out examples and a list of advantages and disadvantages are given for each design. Extensive references, a systematic nomenclature, and a glossary are added features.

Ray, William S. *An Introduction to Experimental Design.* New York: Macmillan, 1960.

This book was written for beginning graduate students in psychology. After a discussion of the ideas and principles of design and analysis, the standard designs used in actual practice are presented, along with a review of more elementary statistical topics.

Winer, B. J. *Statistical Principles in Experimental Design.* New York: McGraw-Hill, 1962.

The logical bases of principles underlying the construction of those experimental designs most useful in behavioral science research are emphasized. These standard designs are considered in detail and potential applications are indicated. The presentation is largely in mathematical terms.

Game Theory, Models, Operations Research, and Simulation:

Ando, Albert, Fisher, Franklin M., and Simon, Herbert A. *Essays on the Structure of Social Science Models.* Cambridge, Mass.: M.I.T. Press, 1963.

The primary concern of these essays is with the logical foundations for choosing a methodology, as opposed to the definition of criteria. The problems of causality and the analysis of dynamic social systems are discussed on an abstract mathematical level. Theorems relating to these problems are developed and examples of their application are given.

Churchman, C. West, Ackoff, Russell L., and Arnoff, E. Leonard. *Introduction to Operations Research.* New York: Wiley, 1957.

This text provides an introduction to the systems approach of solving problems and the construction, use, and testing of models which have proved useful in conducting operations research studies. Emphasis is placed on industrial applications. Some mathematical background is required.

Guetzkow, Harold (ed.) *Simulation in Social Science: Readings.* Englewood Cliffs, N.J.: Prentice-Hall, 1962.

Man, man-computer, and all-computer simulation is described in this book designed to acquaint laymen and students with the use of simulation as a technique for experimentation and teaching in the behavioral sciences. The papers report on applications of simulation in a wide variety of fields, including political science, sociology, and business.

Kemeny, John G., and Snell, J. Laurie. *Mathematical Models in the Social Sciences.* New York: Blaisdell Publishing Co., 1962.

This book is designed for a mathematics course, but may also serve as a text for advanced social science graduate students interested in theoretical work with a mathematical orientation. After a brief discussion of the nature of mathematical modeling, a series of mathematical techniques are presented and applied to social science problems.

Shubik, Martin (ed.) *Game Theory and Related Approaches to Social Behavior: Selections.* New York: Wiley, 1964.

The editor provides a comprehensive introduction to game theory and related methods for the study of social behavior. Other papers discuss the relevance of game theory to social analysis and its applications to bargaining, threats, and negotiations in different settings.

Shuchman, Abe (ed.) *Scientific Decision Making in Business: Readings in Operations Research for Nonmathematicians.* New York: Holt, Rinehart and Winston, 1963.

Written for the most part by practitioners in the fields of production, marketing, and finance, these papers describe the general nature, methodology, and techniques of operations research in nontechnical language. Business applications are stressed.

Zwicky, F., and Wilson, A. G. (eds.) *New Methods of Thought and Procedure.* New York: Springer-Verlag, 1967.

The papers in this volume discuss certain methods which have been developed recently: operations research, systems engineering, dynamic programming, game theory, and morphological research. A general review of each topic is followed by examples of specific applications in the social sciences.

V. Research Tools

Sampling:

Cochran, William G. *Sampling Techniques*. 2d ed. New York: Wiley, 1963.

Sampling theory as it has been developed for use in surveys is emphasized in this text. Illustrations of how the theory is applied in practice are provided, along with exercises for the student. A high degree of mathematical sophistication is required.

Hansen, Morris H., Hurwitz, William N., and Madow, William G. *Sample Survey Methods and Theory*. 2 vols. New York: Wiley, 1953.

These volumes provide a comprehensive presentation of sampling theory and practice. The principles and methods of sampling and their applications to various problems are given in Volume I. Volume II is devoted to theory and the derivations and proofs of the formulas used in the first volume. Cross-references are given. Knowledge of college algebra is assumed.

Kish, Leslie. *Survey Sampling*. New York: Wiley, 1965.

Sampling methods are treated in this book as tools to be applied in social science research. The theoretical background is supplied, but the emphasis is on providing a working knowledge of the practical procedures and supplying sets of rules. The book was designed as an intermediate textbook and can also serve as a reference book for practicing researchers.

McCarthy, Philip J. *Sampling*. Bulletin No. 15. Ithaca, N.Y.: New York School of Industrial and Labor Relations, Cornell University, 1951.

Sampling distributions, random sampling, stratified cluster sampling, systematic selection, and sampling error are briefly discussed. This paper also appears as Chapter Twenty in Marie Jahoda and Others, *Research Methods in Social Relations*, Part Two: *Selected Techniques*, New York: Dryden Press, 1951, pp. 644-680.

Interviewing:

Hyman, Herbert H. *Interviewing in Social Research*. Chicago: University of Chicago Press, 1954.

All aspects of interviewing as a method of inquiry in social research are treated, with special attention to sources of error and their control. This volume is based on a six-year study conducted by the National Opinion Research Center in the late 1940's.

Kahn, Robert L., and Cannell, Charles F. *The Dynamics of Interviewing: Theory, Technique, and Cases*. New York: Wiley, 1957.

The authors, who are psychologists, consider the interview as an information-getting technique which depends upon interaction between the respondent and the interviewer. An understanding of the psychological forces at work in the interview situation is provided by emphasizing the theory, with many illustrations from actual interviews.

Merton, Robert K., Fiske, Marjorie, and Kendall, Patricia L. *The Focused Interview: A Manual of Problems and Procedures*. Glencoe, Ill.: Free Press, 1956.

This manual discusses the problems encountered in conducting a "focused interview", which is defined as eliciting a report of what was involved in the experience of a particular situation. Emphasis is placed on the techniques of conducting the interview, particularly those procedures which clinical experience has shown to be ineffectual. A section on group interviewing is included.

Richardson, Stephen A., Dohrenwend, Barbara Snell, and Klein, David. *Interviewing: Its Forms and Functions.* New York: Basic Books, 1965.

The various approaches to interviewing are examined, and the methods and situations appropriate to each approach are set forth. In addition, the authors discuss the skills, role, and personal characteristics of the interviewer in terms of the type of interview to be conducted.

Questionnaire Construction:

Oppenheim, A. M. *Questionnaire Design and Attitude Measurement.* New York: Basic Books, 1966.

Problems of survey and questionnaire design are presented, along with guidelines for the wording of factual and attitudinal questions. The author also discusses attitude-scaling methods, projective techniques, and various measurement techniques, including the semantic differential.

Payne, Stanley L. *The Art of Asking Questions.* Princeton, N.J.: Princeton University Press, 1951.

The author provides general guidelines for the construction and wording of single questions to be used in questionnaires. Numerous examples drawn from research experience are used to illustrate common pitfalls. Question sequence and questionnaire design are not covered.

Mathematics:

Alker, Hayward R., Jr. *Mathematics and Politics.* New York: Macmillan, 1965.

The usefulness of the mathematical approach to concept formation, theory verification, measurement, strategy, causation, and other problems in political science is explored. Important statistical techniques are described at an elementary level and then discussed in terms of their applications in political analysis.

Coleman, James S. *Introduction to Mathematical Sociology.* New York: Free Press, 1964.

Multivariate analysis, the Poisson process, and other mathematical techniques relevant to conceptual elaboration in sociology are presented in detail. The major portion of the book treats continuous-time stochastic processes as a mathematical framework for the study of social and psychological processes. Knowledge of calculus is required.

Kemeny, John G., Snell, J. Laurie, and Thompson, Gerald L. *Introduction to Finite Mathematics.* 2d ed. Englewood Cliffs, N.J.: Prentice-Hall, 1966.

Mathematical topics applicable to the behavioral sciences are introduced with a minimum of explanatory material. Logical operations, set theory, probability, vectors, and matrices form the core of the book. Sections on linear programming and theory of games also appear, as well as more advanced illustrations of specific mathematical applications to social research. Knowledge of calculus is not required.

McGinnis, Robert. *Mathematical Foundations for Social Analysis.* Indianapolis: Bobbs-Merrill, 1965.

Contemporary mathematical topics—sets, relations, real numbers, matrices, functions, and convergence—are introduced. The author explains the mathematical reasoning underlying these concepts in great detail and comments on their relation to social science research. The presentation is directed particularly at practicing social scientists who are not mathematically trained.

Polya, G. *How to Solve It: A New Aspect of Mathematical Method.* 2d ed. Garden City, N.Y.: Doubleday Anchor, 1957.

The steps in the mental process of solving mathematical problems are stated and analyzed, in terms a beginner can understand. The author suggests that these methods be emphasized in mathematics courses and gives numerous examples using elementary problems. Illustrative student-teacher dialogues are given.

Theodore, Chris A. *Applied Mathematics: An Introduction.* Homewood, Ill.: Irwin, 1965.

Written expressly for students in business education, this text gives detailed explanations of basic mathematical topics and makes their relation to business management explicit. Boolean algebra, analytic geometry, linear programming, calculus, and probability are presented. Prerequisite is high school mathematics.

Wilder, Raymond L. *Introduction to the Foundations of Mathematics.* New York: Wiley, 1952.

This book, designed primarily for mathematics majors, describes the ideas and methods which form the basis of traditional mathematics and discusses the foundations of mathematics and the various schools of opinion now in existence. Although advanced mathematics is recommended for full appreciation, many portions of the book can be understood by the non-mathematician.

Statistics:

Blalock, Hubert M., Jr. *Social Statistics.* New York: McGraw-Hill, 1960.

The underlying logic of statistical inference is emphasized in this introductory text written primarily for sociology students preparing for research careers. Probability, factor analysis, and other basic statistical procedures are described and illustrated by examples drawn from the social sciences. College mathematics is not required.

Cooley, William W., and Lohnes, Paul R. *Multivariate Procedures for the Behavioral Sciences.* New York: Wiley, 1962.

Some of the more useful techniques of multivariate analysis are described and illustrative computed examples of each are given. General flow charts and listings of specific FORTRAN programs are provided for each type of analysis. Utility subroutines are also listed. Background in mathematics and statistics is required.

Feller, William. *An Introduction to Probability Theory and Its Applications.* 2d ed. New York: Wiley, 1957.

The author treats probability theory rigorously as a self-contained mathematical subject. Practical applications are presented, as well as exercises, in order to develop the reader's intuition. The volume is restricted to discrete sample spaces.

Freeman, Linton C. *Elementary Applied Statistics: For Students in Behavioral Science.* New York: Wiley, 1965.

A general overview of statistical applications is provided, with emphasis on understanding the logic of statistical relationships. Concepts are explained in detail with a minimum of symbolic notation. Summarizing distributions, describing associations, and testing hypotheses are the major subjects covered. High school mathematics is the only prerequisite.

Fruchter, Benjamin. *Introduction to Factor Analysis.* Princeton, N.J.: Van Nostrand, 1954.

Although this textbook provides a step-by-step introduction to factor analysis, a background in statistics and analytic geometry is recommended. After introducing the fundamentals of matrix theory, the more important methods of factor analysis are described in detail. The final chapter summarizes some of the studies taken from the extensive appended bibliography.

Guilford, J. P. *Fundamental Statistics in Psychology and Education.* 4th ed. New York: McGraw-Hill, 1965.

This revised edition describes statistical procedures, descriptive as well as inferential, and explains their use in psychological and educational research. Mathematical derivations and other aids are included to provide insight into the underlying reasoning. Sections on measurement and scaling are an added feature. Knowledge of calculus is not assumed.

Hays, William L. *Statistics.* New York: Holt, Rinehart and Winston, 1963.

Inferential statistics is emphasized in this text designed for graduate students in experimental psychology. The mathematical theory underlying inferential methods, particularly probability and distributions, is developed in detail with explanatory text. The techniques and their applications to simple psychological experiments are also presented in detail.

Mosteller, Frederick Rourke, Robert E. K., and Thomas, George B., Jr. *Probability and Statistics.* Reading, Mass.: Addison-Wesley, 1961.

This text was written specifically for students taking Continental Classroom's television course in probability and statistics. The theory of probability and its applications to statistical theory and practical problems are presented at an elementary level. Numerous worked-out examples and exercises are included.

Siegel, Sidney. *Nonparametric Statistics: For the Behavioral Sciences.* New York: McGraw-Hill, 1956.

The nonparametric techniques of hypothesis testing are presented in terms familiar to the behavioral scientist. Each of the various statistical tests is discussed according to the research design for which it is suited, and its function is indicated. Numerous examples with all the raw data are given. Introductory work in statistics, but not in calculus, is assumed.

Weiss, Robert S. *Statistics in Social Research: An Introduction.* New York: Wiley, 1968.

This text provides an introduction to quantitative research methods. The processes of sampling, data collection, tabulation, tests and measures, and reporting are covered in some detail; statistical techniques most useful in survey research are described and their application explained.

Zeisel, Hans. *Say It With Figures.* 5th ed. rev. New York: Harper and Row, 1968.

The logic behind mathematical concepts and operations commonly taken for granted is pointed out. Close attention is given to understanding and manipulation of data with illustrations drawn from social science research. Percentages, multidimensional tables, causal analysis, cross tabulation, reason analysis, and panel data analysis are covered.

Computer:

Borko, Harold (ed.) *Computer Applications in the Behavioral Sciences*. Englewood Cliffs, N.J.: Prentice-Hall, 1962.

The past and present role of computers, the fundamentals of computer language and programming, and the use of computers in statistical data processing are discussed. Emphasis is placed on recent applications involving numerical and nonnumerical simulations of human behavior.

Janda, Kenneth. *Data Processing: Applications to Political Research*. Evanston, Ill.: Northwestern University Press, 1965.

This "how-to-do-it" manual introduces political scientists to the techniques of processing quantitative and qualitative data. The applications of several simple computer programs are demonstrated. The appendix contains coding suggestions and complete instructions and printouts for the FORTRAN IV NUCROS computer program.

VI. Special Measurement Techniques

Bales, Robert F. *Interaction Process Analysis: A Method for the Study of Small Groups*. Cambridge, Mass.: Addison-Wesley Press, 1950.

A standard method of observing and analyzing interaction in small groups is developed by the author. A set of general purpose categories for describing behavior is derived from an explicit theoretical framework. Practical and methodological aspects of training observers in the use of the method are also presented.

Cronbach, Lee J. *Essentials of Psychological Testing*. 2d ed. New York: Harper, 1960.

The general principles of testing are presented. Tests are viewed from the practical perspective of use in clinical applications, as well as from the technical perspective of theoretical and mathematical analysis of problems of hypotheses and validation. Specific tests are reproduced in the text as an aid in teaching selection and evaluation.

Miller, Delbert C. *Handbook of Research Design and Social Measurement*. New York: David McKay Co., 1964.

This book is designed as a reference manual for social scientists. Guides setting forth step-by-step procedures in the design of research and statistical analysis are provided. More than fifty scales and indexes to measure social variables, selected on the basis of high reliability and validity, are reproduced in their entirety.

Osgood, Charles E., Suci, George J., and Tannenbaum, Percy H. *The Measurement of Meaning*. Urbana, Ill.: University of Illinois Press, 1957.

The authors deal with the nature and theory of meaning and describe a general objective technique for its measurement which they developed. The application of this instrument— the semantic differential—to a wide variety of problems in the social sciences is reported.

Pool, Ithiel de Sola (ed.) *Trends in Content Analysis*. Urbana, Ill.: University of Illinois Press, 1959.

These papers, stimulated by a work conference on content analysis sponsored by the Social Science Research Council, report on recent developments in the theory and use of content analysis. A central issue is the problem of inference. Research applications in a variety of social science disciplines are described.

Shaw, Marvin E., and Wright, Jack M. *Scales for the Measurement of Attitudes*. New York: McGraw-Hill, 1967.

The purpose of this book is to encourage use of existing attitude scales that have at least minimal reliability and validity for research studies and group therapy. Over 175 attitude scales, categorized by type of attitude measured, are reproduced in their entirety. Each scale is described and evaluated.

Stone, Philip J., and Others. *The General Inquirer: A Computer Approach to Content Analysis*. Cambridge, Mass.: M.I.T. Press, 1966.

The content analysis process is discussed in detail as background for the presentation of the General Inquirer system, which is a new technique for performing content analysis using the computer. The rationale, basic procedures, and applications of the method are presented in this volume. A separate user's manual is available, which provides the technical specifications and detailed instructions for using these programs.

Stouffer, Samuel A., and Others. *Measurement and Prediction*. Vol. IV. *Studies in Social Psychology in World War II*. Princeton, N.J.: Princeton University Press, 1950.

A theoretical and empirical analysis of problems of measurement in the social sciences is presented. The development of models of scales and procedures for testing their applicability to qualitative data are emphasized. In addition, two major case studies of prediction are described in detail.

Torgerson, Warren S. *Theory and Methods of Scaling*. New York: Wiley, 1958.

Methods of constructing scales for the measurement of psychological attributes are discussed. The underlying theory, procedure for collecting data, analysis, and evaluation, as well as detailed derivations, are given for each method. A high level of mathematical sophistication is assumed.

Webb, Eugene J., and Others. *Unobtrusive Measures: Nonreactive Research in the Social Sciences*. New York: Rand McNally, 1966.

Written in an entertaining style, this book compiles a wide variety of novel research methods, grouped according to the characteristics of the data collected, which may be used to supplement surveys employing interviews and questionnaires. A methodological framework for evaluating these methods is presented.

VII. Presentation of Results

Graves, Robert, and Hodge, Alan. *The Reader over your Shoulder: A Handbook for Writers of English Prose*. New York: Macmillan, 1943.

The authors discuss the development of English prose, considerations of style, and the principles of clear statement. A major portion of the book is devoted to detailed analyses of numerous short passages drawn from the writings of eminent people during the 1918–1941 period.

Strunk, William, Jr. *The Elements of Style.* Rev. ed. New York: Macmillan, 1959.

The author states eight rules of usage and ten principles of composition, followed by pithy comments and examples in each case. The book contains short sections on form and commonly misused words and expressions; a final chapter on style in its broader meaning, written by E. B. White, was added to this edition.

VIII. Other Related Works

Anderson, James G. *Research Design and Analysis in the Behavioral Sciences: An Annotated Bibliography.* University Park: New Mexico State University, July, 1967.

This bibliography, which includes articles as well as books, covers the field of behavioral research, with particular emphasis on relevant mathematical and statistical procedures. The latter topics are broken down into detailed categories. Brief annotations are provided.

de Jouvenel, Bertrand. *The Art of Conjecture.* Translated by Nikita Lary. New York: Basic Books, 1967.

The author analyzes in detail the process of making predictions and discusses methods in the social sciences, particularly in economics, sociology, and political science, which can be used to study the future. The title derives from the author's conception of conjecture as a work of art which is nonetheless well-reasoned and based on articulate constructs.

Hammond, Phillip E. *Sociologists at Work: Essays on the Craft of Social Research.* New York: Basic Books, 1964.

The individual experiences of a number of social scientists in performing a specific research project are described in their own words. The chronicles are organized around either the sequence of events in time or the sequence of ideas in the mind of the researcher. Apart from their enjoyable aspects, the essays provide insight into the context of discovery.

Helmer, Olaf. *Social Technology.* New York: Basic Books, 1966.

The need for a reappraisal of methodology in the social sciences is established and specific proposals for the modification of traditional procedures are offered. These proposals are designed to narrow the gap between the physical and the social sciences. The appendix contains studies illustrating the proposed procedures, including the so-called Delphi technique.

Kahn, Herman, and Wiener, Anthony J. *The Year 2000: A Framework for Speculation on the Next Thirty-Three Years.* New York: Macmillan, 1967.

This book, which is the first report of a long-term study undertaken by the Hudson Institute on the future, presents the basic methods and framework for making systematic conjectures about the future. With America as the focal point, statistical baselines are sketched and several possible future worlds are described by means of scenarios.

Krathwohl, David R. *How to Prepare a Research Proposal.* New York: Syracuse University Bookstore, 1966.

This booklet offers practical suggestions and general guidelines for the preparation of research proposals to funding agencies. The proposal format of the U.S. Office of Education is used as a typical model; detailed comments are made on each item in the proposal.

Bibliography Of Library Research

This highly selective listing of library research covers four broad areas—Library History; Information Need and Use; Political and Community Relationships; and Administrative and Organizational Aspects. The selections were deliberately oriented around a broad subject rather than the more usual arrangement by type of research in order to put the selections into a broader context. The investigations included here present research avenues, approaches and methods in library research. Each is recommended as of sufficient merit to warrant the time spent in reading and analysis.

I. Library History

Ditzion, Sidney. *Arsenals of a Democratic Culture: A Social History of the American Public Library Movement in New England and the Middle States from 1850 to 1900.* Chicago: American Library Association, 1947.

Ditzion, Sidney. "Social Reform, Education, and the Library, 1850-1900," *Library Quarterly*, 9 (Apr., 1939), pp. 156-184.

Holley, Edward G. *Charles Evans: American Bibliographer.* Urbana: University of Illinois Press, 1963.

MacLeod, David I. *Carnegie Libraries in Wisconsin.* Madison, Wis.: State Historical Society of Wisconsin, 1968.

Maddox, Lucy Jane. *Trends and Issues in American Librarianship as Reflected in the Papers and Proceedings of the American Library Association, 1876-1885.* Ann Arbor, Mich.: University Microfilms, 1958.

Marshall, John David (ed.) *An American Library History Reader: Contributions to Library Literature.* Hamden, Conn.: Shoe String Press, 1960.

Powell, Benjamin Edward. *The Development of Libraries in Southern State Universities to 1920.* Unpublished Ph.D. dissertation, University of Chicago, 1946.

Shera, Jesse H. *Foundations of the Public Library: The Origins of the Public Library Movement in New England, 1629-1855.* Chicago: University of Chicago Press, 1949.

Shores, Louis. *Origins of the American College Library, 1638-1800.* Hamden, Conn.: Shoe String Press, 1963.

Spencer, Gwladys. *The Chicago Public Library: Origins and Backgrounds.* Chicago: University of Chicago Press, 1943.

Williamson, William Landram. *William Frederick Poole and the Modern Library Movement.* New York: Columbia University Press, 1963.

II. Information Need and Use

Allen, Thomas J. *Managing the Flow of Scientific and Technological Information.* Unpublished Ph.D. dissertation, Massachusetts Institute of Technology, September, 1966.

Allen, Thomas J., and Gerstberger, Peter G. *Criteria for Selection of an Information Source.* Cambridge, Mass.: Alfred P. Sloan School of Management, Massachusetts Institute of Technology, September, 1967.

American Psychological Association. Project on Scientific Information Exchange in Psychology. *Reports.* Washington, D.C.: The Association, 1965-1966.

Auerbach Corporation. *DOD User Needs Study, Phase I.* Final Technical Report 1151-TR-3. 2 vols. Philadelphia: The Corporation, May, 1965.

Columbia University. Bureau of Applied Social Research. *Formal and Informal Satisfaction of the Information Requirements of Chemists.* Interim Report. New York: The University, August, 1966.

Johns Hopkins University. Center for Research in Scientific Communication. *Reports.* Baltimore: The University, 1967.

Menzel, Herbert, "The Information Needs of Current Scientific Research," *Library Quarterly*, 34 (Jan., 1964), pp. 4–19.

Menzel, Herbert, "Scientific Communication: Five Themes from Social Science Research," *American Psychologist*, 21 (Nov., 1966), pp. 999–1004.

North American Aviation, Inc. Autonetics Division. *DOD User-Needs Study, Phase II*. Final Technical Report. (C6-2442/030) 3 vols. Anaheim, Calif.: North American Aviation, November, 1966.

Pelz, Donald C., and Andrews, Frank M. *Scientists in Organizations: Productive Climates for Research and Development*. New York: Wiley, 1966.

Price, Derek J. de Solla. *Little Science, Big Science*. New York: Columbia University Press, 1963.

Rosenbloom, Richard S., and Wolek, Francis W. *Technology, Information and Organization: Information Transfer in Industrial R & D*. Boston: Harvard University, Graduate School of Business Administration, June, 1967.

III. Political and Community Relationships

Abrash, Barbara, and Milton, John. "LSCA: Issues and Forces," in *Social and Political Aspects of Librarianship*, edited by Mary Lee Bundy and Ruth Aronson. Albany, N.Y.: State University of New York at Albany, 1965, pp. 13–22.

Aronson, Ruth. "The Role of Interest Groups in the Formation of a Library," in *Social and Political Aspects of Librarianship*, edited by Mary Lee Bundy and Ruth Aronson. Albany, N.Y.: State University of New York at Albany, 1965, pp 31–41.

Berelson, Bernard. *The Library's Public: A Report of the Public Library Inquiry*. New York: Columbia University Press, 1949.

Blank, Blanche D., Immerman, Rita J., and Rydell, C. Peter. *New York City Libraries: A Comparative Study of a Small Sample*. New York: Urban Research Center, Hunter College, 1968.

Bundy, Mary Lee. *An Analysis of Voter Reaction to a Proposal to Form a Library District in LaSalle and Bureau Counties, Illinois*. Research Series No. 1. Springfield: Illinois State Library, December, 1960.

Fiske, Marjorie. *Book Selection and Censorship: A Study of School and Public Libraries in California*. Berkeley: University of California Press, 1959.

Garceau, Oliver. *The Public Library in the Political Process: A Report of the Public Library Inquiry*. New York: Columbia University Press, 1949.

Garrison, Guy G. *Seattle Voters and Their Public Library*. Research Series No. 2. Springfield: Illinois State Library, September, 1961.

International Research Associates, Inc. *Access to Public Libraries*. Chicago: American Library Association, 1963.

Koepp, Donald W. *Public Library Government: Seven Case Studies*. Berkeley: University of California Press, 1968.

Kroll, Morton. "Public Library Boards of Trustees," in *The Public Libraries of the Pacific Northwest*, edited by Morton Kroll. Seattle: University of Washington Press, 1960, pp. 134–231.

Lindahl, Ruth G., and Berner, William S. *Financing Public Library Expansion: Case Studies of Three Defeated Bond Issue Referendums*. Research Series No. 13. Springfield: Illinois State Library, 1968.

Monat, William R. *The Public Library and Its Community: A Study of the Impact of Library Services in Five Pennsylvania Cities*. Pennsylvania State Library Monograph Series No. 7. University Park: Institute of Public Administration, Pennsylvania State University, 1967.

Monypenny, Phillip. *The Library Functions of the States: Commentary on the Survey of Library Functions of the States*. Chicago: American Library Association, 1966.

IV. Administrative and Organizational Aspects

Abell, Millicent. "Aspects of Upward Communications in a Public Library," in *Social and Political Aspects of Librarianship*, edited by Mary Lee Bundy and Ruth Aronson. Albany, N.Y.: State University of New York at Albany, 1965, pp. 91–99.

Carpenter, Ray L. *The Public Library Executive: An Exploration of the Role of an Emerging Profession*. U. S. Office of Education, Project No. BR-6-8336, December, 1967.

Meier, Richard L. "Communications Overload: Proposals from the Study of a University Library," *Administrative Science Quarterly*, 7 (Mar., 1963), pp. 521–544.

Meier, Richard L. "Efficiency Criteria for the Operation of Large Libraries," *Library Quarterly*, 31 (July, 1961), pp. 215–234.

Orr, Richard H., and Others. "Development of Methodologic Tools for Planning and Managing Library Services: I. Project Goals and Approach; II. Measuring a Library's Capability for Providing Documents; III. Standardized Inventories of Library Services," *Bulletin of the Medical Library Association*, 56 (Jul., 1968), pp. 235–267, and 56 (Oct., 1968), pp. 380–403.

Wasserman, Paul. *Toward a Methodology for the Formulation of Objectives in Public Libraries: An Empirical Analysis*. Unpublished Ph.D. dissertation, University of Michigan, 1960.

Sample Instruments

Lawyers on Their Own: The Interview Schedule

Jerome E. Carlin

(The order in which questions were asked in the interview, as well as the wording of the questions, did not always conform exactly to the schedule as presented below. Furthermore, respondents were allowed and often encouraged to elaborate on matters to a greater extent than is indicated in the schedule. This was done particularly in the section on nature of practice, in order to determine what respondents were actually doing in their principal area of practice.)

I. *Background Data.*

1. Age.
2. Sex.
3. Place of birth.
4. Nationality background and generation.
5. Father's occupation.
6. Father's education: number of years in school.
7. Religious affiliation.
8. Undergraduate school; years attended, degree, grade average, job.
9. Law school; years attended, degree, grade average and rank, job.
10. Where and when admitted to the bar.

II. *Career Choice and Expectations.*

1. When did you decide to become a lawyer? What happened then?
2. Did you want to be a lawyer, or was it something you fell into?
3. What kind of lawyer did you expect to be, and what kind of work did you think you'd be doing as a lawyer? Has it turned out that way?

III. *Getting Started and Sequence of Jobs.*

1. How did you get your first job after law school? What was your position, kind of work done, why left, how long there, earnings?
2. What was your next position? Etc. [Up to, but not including, present position.]
3. What were the problems of getting started on your own? What help did you get? How did you get your first clients?

IV. *Organizational Participation.*

1. To which professional organizations do you belong—Chicago Bar Association, Illinois State Bar Association, American Bar Association, Cook County Bar Association, etc.?
2. [As to each] How often do you attend meetings; on a committee or hold office; more or less active than before?
3. What significance do such organizations have for the average lawyer? For you in your practice?
4. How representative are the large bar associations? Are they controlled by certain segments of the bar?
5. To what other organizations do you belong—religious, fraternal, political, civic, etc.?
6. [As to each] How often do you attend meetings; hold office; more or less active than before?
7. Has such participation been of any help in your practice?
8. To what organizations do you regularly contribute money?
9. Do you give free legal advice to any organizations?
10. Have religious or ethnic ties helped or hindered you in your career?
11. Do you consider yourself a (Polish, Italian, Jewish, Negro, etc.) lawyer? In what sense?

V. *Office Arrangements.*

1. How many other lawyers are there in this office with you? How many non-lawyers?
2. What is your relationship to your office-mates—employer, employee, space for service, share office space?
3. [If share space] Do you work closely with any of them? Refer matters to one another? Any specialization?
4. Do you regularly work with or are you

SOURCE: Reprinted from Jerome E. Carlin, *Lawyers on Their Own: A Study of Individual Practitioners in Chicago* (New Brunswick, N.J.: Rutgers University Press, 1962), Appendix B, "The Interview Schedule," pp. 217-223, by permission of the publisher.

associated with any other groups of lawyers or individual lawyers?

5. What office arrangements are there with respect to: office rental (total, your share), secretary, receptionist, etc., library (what's in it, what services subscribe to, advance sheets, what other libraries used and how often)?

6. What is your overhead cost per month?

7. Who keeps your books, what kinds do you have?

8. How much clients' money do you have on hand?

9. How large an office account do you maintain? Do you lend money to clients from it?

10. What is your income from the practice of law and other sources?   [Hand card with income categories]

VI. Nature of Practice and Clientele.

1. Are you a full- or part-time lawyer? (If part-time, explain.)

2. How would you characterize your practice—specialist or general practitioner, substantive matters dealt with?

3. Describe what you did yesterday (or Friday, if interview on Monday) from the time you came into your office until the time you went home.

4. How would you characterize your clientele—problems, class background, ethnic background, geographic location, etc.

5. Do you ever turn away clients, and if so, for what reasons?

6. Do you ever refer clients to other lawyers? What kinds of matters, to which lawyers, how often—do they refer clients to you?

7. How do you get your clients? What proportion do you get on referrals from other lawyers (referral fee), recommendations from other clients, brokers, police, bondsmen, etc?

8. Do you have any permanent clients? How many?

9. Do you employ any conscious strategy for getting business?

10. Is there a problem of competition from other lawyers in getting business? In which areas—divorce, personal injury, etc.—how serious, have you been hurt by it?

11. Is there a problem of competition from nonlawyers—trust companies, accountants, real estate brokers, etc.?

12. What proportion of your total fees come in from retainer clients, from contingent fees, flat fees, fees based on an hourly charge, in kind, etc.? What kinds of fees from which matters?

13. How much do you charge per hour? Do you follow the Chicago Bar Association minimum fee schedule?

14. What was your largest single fee in the last 12 months, and on what kind of matter?

15. What per cent of your time is taken up with trial work?

16. How is your time divided among these areas of practice?
[Hand card]
Personal injury
Divorce, adoption, etc.
Criminal
Collections
Will-probate-estate
Patent, trade-mark
Unfair competition
Income tax
Federal estate tax
Inheritance tax
Tax foreclosure
Labor
Real Estate
Business-corporate-commercial
Other (specify)

17. Within an average week, how many hours are you:
  • in your office
  • in court (which ones; how much time in the clerk's office, judge's chambers, court room)
  • in government bureaus (which ones)
  • at the Chicago Title and Trust Company
  • in banks and trust companies
  • in savings and loan associations
  • in mortgage houses
  • at police stations
  • in real estate offices
  • in life insurance company offices
  • at a law library (Chicago Bar Association, Law Institute, etc.)
  • in other lawyers' offices
  • other (specify)

18. Within an average week, how many hours are you doing the following:
    - reading legal material
    - writing, drafting, dictating legal memos, briefs, opinion letters, etc.
    - preparing legal documents—contracts, leases, wills, pleadings, etc.
    - negotiating (get examples of things done and with whom)
    - meeting with or talking to government officials (which ones, under what circumstances)
    - talking to clients
    - other (specify)
19. How many hours a week are you on the telephone?
20. How often are you out of town on business—in the last month, year, and how far away?
21. Do you see clients at night or on weekends? Other night or weekend work?
22. Here is a list of individuals and institutions with whom the lawyer tends to come in contact in the course of handling clients' problems. [Hand card]
    Courts
    Judges
    Masters
    Clerks
    Bondsmen
    Bailiffs
    Deputies
    Police
    Probation and parole officers
    Other city
        county
        state
        federal officials
    Doctors
    Nurses
    Hospital employees
    Banks
    Trust companies
    Savings and loan assn.
    Mortgage houses
    Abstract and title companies
    Real estate brokers and agents
    Insurance adjusters and agents
    Accountants
    Collection agencies
    Other lawyers
    Others (specify)
        a. With which ones do you come in contact most frequently?
        b. Which are most important in your practice?
        c. For which is it most important to do favors?
        d. From which is it most important to get favors?

VII. General.

1. Would you give me the first names of your four closest friends and their occupations?
2. First names of people you usually have lunch with, and their occupations?
3. First names of people whose opinions you value most and their occupations?
4. Whom do you go to when you have a legal problem you can't handle or if you get into difficulty in a case or matter? (Try to get some recent examples)
5. Do lawyers come to you for advice? How many in past month, which ones, on what kinds of problems?
6. In what sense is the practice of law a profession? Is there a clear distinction between the practice of law and the operation of a business? Do you consider yourself a lawyer or a businessman?
7. What are the main functions of the lawyer?
8. What are the most important differences between lawyers and doctors?
9. What makes a successful lawyer—ability, personality, contacts, other?
10. Who are the most successful lawyers in Chicago?
11. How successful do you think you have been in the practice of law?
12. Have you been satisfied in the practice of law?
13. Would you still be a lawyer if you had it to do all over again?
14. What do you expect to be doing five years from now (what would you like to be doing)?
15. If you were going to advise a young man just going into the practice of law, what would you tell him—in all frankness and seriousness? (Advise him to go on his own or into a firm?) Can you still make it today as an individual practitioner?
16. How important are political connections in the practice of law?
17. What gives you the biggest kick out of the practice of law?
18. What have you been reading recently?

Explorations in Role Analysis:
Scales and Original Instruments

Neal Gross, Ward S. Mason and Alexander W. McEachern

APPENDIX TABLE B–1. SUPERINTENDENTS' SAMPLE ONLY
($N = 105$)

a. LEVEL OF ASPIRATION
   (1) THE INSTRUMENT

How Desirous Are You of Doing the Following Things? (Check one box to the right of each item below.)	I would not want to . . .	I am not especially anxious to . . .	I have some desire to . . .	I would very much like to . . .	I am extremely anxious to . . .
Response scored as ⟶	(1)	(2)	(3)	(4)	(5)
1. Obtain a superintendency position in a larger school system.	18	42	22	17	6
2. Obtain a superintendency position which would carry more prestige.	23	40	28	12	2
3. Take every opportunity to advance my own career.	7	20	27	34	17
4. Obtain a superintendency position which would pay more money.	9	32	22	35	7
5. Obtain a superintendency position in a larger community.	12	39	28	20	6
6. Take a more important role in the activities of professional educational organizations.	4	26	47	22	6
7. Establish a good reputation among my professional colleagues.	2	6	12	49	36
8. Receive more recognition for my work from the citizens of my community.	2	19	37	37	10
9. Obtain a higher salary in my present position.	2	13	24	52	14
10. Eventually be superintendent in a city of a million or more.	78	23	3	1	0
11. Someday be president of the AASA.	61	37	3	4	0
12. Some day obtain a superintendency in a city of 300,000 or more.	55	38	9	2	1
13. Obtain a superintendency in a wealthy suburban community.	28	31	20	20	5

(1 = No answer)

(2) LEVEL OF ASPIRATION SCALE: A 3-item H-technique scale. A high score means high aspiration.

Reproducibility   = 99.1
Chance Reproducibility = 92.7   Error Ratio = .12

The Scale

Scale Score	Frequency	Percent	Response Pattern A B C	Frequency
3	22	21.0	+ + +	22
2	31	29.5	− + +	28
			+ − +	3
1	30	28.6	− − +	30
0	22	21.0	− − −	22

Definition of Contrived Items

Contrived Item	Original Item	Positive Response	Positive Marginal	
$a =$	1	4, 5	23	
	13	4, 5	25	2/3 pos. = 25
	5	4, 5	26	
$b =$	2	3, 4, 5	42	
	11	2, 3, 4, 5	44	2/3 pos. = 50
	4	3, 4, 5	64	
$c =$	6	3, 4, 5	75	
	3	3, 4, 5	78	2/3 pos. = 83
	9	3, 4, 5	90	

SOURCE: Reprinted from Neal Gross, Ward S. Mason, and Alexander W. McEachern, *Explorations in Role Analysis: Studies of the School Superintendency Role* (New York: Wiley, 1958), Appendix B, "Scales and Original Instruments," pp. 352-365, by permission of the publisher.

APPENDIX TABLE B–1 (Continued)

b. JOB SATISFACTION
   (1) THE INSTRUMENT

Please check the box on the right which best indicates your satisfaction or dissatisfaction with the corresponding aspect of your *present job*.	Very well satisfied	Fairly well satisfied	Fairly dissatisfied	Very dissatisfied
Response scored as $\longrightarrow$	(4)	(3)	(2)	(1)
1. Are you satisfied that you have been given enough authority by your school committee to do your job well?	69	31	2	3
2. How satisfied are you with your present job when you compare it to similar superintendencies in the state?	52	47	4	2
3. Are you satisfied with the progress you are making toward the goals which you set for yourself in your present position?	18	79	7	1
4. Are you satisfied that the people of your community give proper recognition to your work as superintendent?	33	65	5	2
5. How satisfied are you with your present salary?	11	71	18	5
6. How satisfied are you with your school committee?	55	39	8	3
7. How satisfied are you with your staff?	28	75	2	0
8. How satisfied are you with the amount of time which you must devote to your job?	17	56	29	3
9. How satisfied are you with the amount of interest shown by the community in its school system?	22	59	20	4
10. On the whole, are you satisfied that the school committee accepts you as a professional expert to the degree to which you feel you are entitled by reason of your position, training, and experience?	55	41	7	2
11. How satisfied are you with your present job when you consider the expectations you had when you took the job?	47	48	8	2
12. How satisfied are you with your present job in the light of your career expectations?	31	63	11	0

(2) JOB SATISFACTION SCALE: A 3-item *H*-technique scale. A high score means high satisfaction.

Reproducibility   = 99.4   Error Ratio = .08
Chance Reproducibility = 92.1

The Scale

Scale Score	Frequency	Percent	Response Pattern			Frequency
			A	B	C	
3	25	23.8	+	+	+	25
2	26	24.8	−	+	+	25
			+	−	+	1
1	31	29.5	−	−	+	30
			−	+	−	1
0	23	21.9	−	−	−	23

Definition of Contrived Items

Contrived Item	Original Item	Positive Response	Positive Marginal	
$a =$	7	4	28	
	12	4	31	2/3 pos. = 26
	4	4	33	
$b =$	11	4	47	
	2	4	52	2/3 pos. = 51
	10	4	55	
$c =$	1	4	69	
	9	3, 4	81	2/3 pos. = 81
	5	3, 4	82	

APPENDIX TABLE B–1 (Continued)

c. CAREER SATISFACTION
(1) THE INSTRUMENT

In answering the following questions please consider the *superintendency as a career* rather than your present job.

1. How much does the superintendency give you a chance to do the things at which you are best?

Code	Frequency	
4	52	A very good chance
3	42	A fairly good chance
2	10	Some chance
1	1	Very little

2. How does the superintendency compare with other types of work?

Code	Frequency	
4	6	It is the most satisfying career a man could follow.
3	66	It is one of the most satisfying careers.
2	32	It is as satisfying as most careers.
1	1	It is less satisfying than most careers.

3. Considering the superintendency as a whole, how well do you like it?

Code	Frequency	
4	83	I like it very much
3	20	I like it fairly well
2	2	I don't like it too well
1	0	I don't like it at all

4. Are there any features of the job of superintendent which you dislike?

Code	Frequency	
1	0	Very many
2	26	Quite a few
3	73	Only a couple
4	6	None

5. If you "had to do it over again" would you enter the field of the superintendency?

Code	Frequency	
4	45	Definitely yes
3	44	Probably yes
2	14	Probably no
1	2	Definitely no

6. Are you making progress toward the goals you had set for yourself in your occupational career?

Code	Frequency	
4	5	I have achieved my goals
3	75	I am making good progress toward my goals
2	24	I am making some progress toward my goals
1	0	I don't seem to be getting anywhere
0	1	No answer

7. Has the superintendency lived up to the expectations you had before you entered it?

Code	Frequency	
4	18	Yes, in all respects
3	83	In most ways
2	4	In only a few ways
1	0	Not at all

8. If a young friend of yours were entering the field of education would you advise him to aim for the superintendency?

Code	Frequency	
4	31	Definitely yes
3	62	Probably yes
2	10	Probably no
1	2	Definitely no

9. Do you feel that the work which you do as a superintendent is satisfying?

Code	Frequency	
4	64	Very satisfying
3	41	Fairly satisfying
2	0	Fairly dissatisfying
1	0	Very dissatisfying

10. How many features of the job of superintendent do you especially like?

Code	Frequency	
4	72	Very many
3	31	Quite a few
2	2	Some
1	0	Very few

APPENDIX TABLE B–1 (Continued)

11. In general do you feel that superintendents are given adequate recognition when compared to that received by other professionals such as lawyers and doctors?

Code	Frequency	
4	8	Yes definitely
3	44	In most respects
2	48	In some respects
1	5	Not at all

12. How much opportunity does the superintendency give you to follow your leisure time interests?

Code	Frequency	
4	1	Very adequate
3	36	Adequate
2	52	Inadequate
1	15	Very inadequate
0	1	No answer

(2) CAREER SATISFACTION SCALE: A 3-item *H*-technique scale. A high score means high satisfaction.

Reproducibility   = 98.4
Chance Reproducibility = 92.1   Error Ratio = .20

The Scale

Scale Score	Fre-quency	Percent	Response Pattern A B C	Fre-quency
3	19	18.1	+ + +	19
2	31	29.5	− + +	28
			+ − +	3
1	29	27.6	− − +	27
			− + −	2
0	26	24.8	− − −	26

Definition of Contrived Items

Con-trived Item	Original Item	Positive Response	Positive Marginal	
a =	7	4	18	
	8	4	31	2/3 pos. = 22
	12	3, 4	37	
b =	5	4	45	
	1	4	52	2/3 pos. = 49
	11	3, 4	52	
c =	10	4	72	
	2	3, 4	72	2/3 pos. = 77
	6	3, 4	80	

APPENDIX TABLE B-1 (Continued)

d. SUPERINTENDENT'S INITIATIVE:
   (1) THE INSTRUMENT

Please indicate your agreement or disagreement with each of the following statements by checking the appropriate box to the right.	Response Categories*			
	1	2	3	4
1. A superintendent should use his own judgment in interpreting school committee rules in specific cases. (I)	3	7	73	22
2. A superintendent should not "stick his neck out" by taking a definite position when a controversy arises about the interpretation of school committee rules. (L)	9	29	60	7
3. The only way a superintendent can keep out of "hot water" is to stick strictly to the letter of the rules adopted by the school committee. (L)	9	25	66	5
4. It is more important for a superintendent to abide by the spirit of school committee rules, than to stick to the letter of such rules. (I)	0	8	72	25
5. In most cases school committee rules should be adhered to, but there are always some exceptional cases in which the superintendent should exercise his own judgment. (I)	1	20	60	24
6. In deciding whether to give a literal interpretation to school committee rules, the "burden of proof" to show why this should not be done is always on the superintendent. (L)	13	62	30	0
7. It cannot be expected that school committee rules will deal justly with all specific cases if given a literal interpretation; the superintendent must use his own judgment. (I)	0	12	73	20
8. The superintendent is the executive officer of the school committee and as such has no discretionary power. (L)	2	14	68	21
9. Although legal responsibility for adopting rules and regulations which govern a school system rests with the school committee, the superintendent has a responsibility to interpret those rules in a way in which his professional training indicates will be best for the School System. (I)	0	8	69	28
10. School committee rules are absolutely binding on the superintendent. (L)	8	56	40	1
11. If school committee rules are to be given any free interpretation, the committee itself must do it, not the superintendent. (L)	7	32	63	3
12. School committee rules are only a framework within which the superintendent operates; day to day administrative decisions always demand that the superintendent use his own discretion. (I)	2	8	70	25

*Items marked (I) are "initiative items" and are coded from 4 = strongly agree to 1 = strongly disagree; items marked (L) are "legalistic items" and are coded from 1 = strongly agree to 4 = strongly disagree.

(2) SUPERINTENDENT'S INITIATIVE SCALE: A 3-item H-technique scale. A high score means high initiative.

Reproducibility = 98.4
Chance Reproducibility = 93.0   Error Ratio = .23

The Scale

Scale Score	Frequency	Percent	Response Pattern A B C	Frequency
3	15	14.3	+ + +	14
			+ + −	1
2	12	11.4	− + +	10
			+ − +	2
1	47	44.8	− − +	47
0	31	29.5	− − −	29
			+ − −	2

Definition of Contrived Items

Contrived Item	Original Item	Positive Response	Positive Marginal	
a =	7	4	20	
	8	4	21	2/3 pos. = 19
	5	4	24	
b =	12	4	25	
	9	4	28	2/3 pos. = 24
	10	3, 4	41	
c =	11	3, 4	66	
	2	3, 4	67	2/3 pos. = 73
	3	3, 4	71	

APPENDIX TABLE B–1 (Continued)

e. WORRY:

(1) THE INSTRUMENT

Please indicate your agreement or disagreement with each of the following statements by checking the appropriate box to the right.	Never	Occasionally	Fairly Often	Frequently
1. Do the problems associated with your job keep you awake at night?	27	72	4	2
2. Once you have made a decision do you find yourself worrying whether you made the right decision?	16	82	7	0
3. Are you nervous when you go to School Committee meetings?	53	46	4	2
4. Do you "take your job home with you" in the sense that you think about your job when you are doing other things?	7	61	26	11
5. Do you breathe a sigh of relief when you travel away from your community?	54	39	6	6
6. Do you worry about what an individual or group will do if you make a decision contrary to their wishes?	34	65	6	0

(2) WORRY SCALE: A 3-item H-technique scale. A high score means high worry.

Reproducibility   = 95.9   Error Ratio = .44
Chance Reproducibility = 90.7

The Scale						Definition of Contrived Items			
Scale Score	Frequency	Percent	Response Pattern A B C		Frequency	Contrived Item	Original Item	Positive Response	Positive Marginal
3	17	16.2	+ + +		17	$a =$	4	3, 4	37
2	27	25.7	− + +		20		5	2, 3, 4	51 } 2/2 pos. = 27
			+ − +		7	$b =$	3	2, 3, 4	52
1	31	29.5	− − +		28		6	2, 3, 4	71 } 2/2 pos. = 40
			− + −		3	$c =$	1	2, 3, 4	78
0	30	28.6	− − −		27		2	2, 3, 4	89 } 2/2 pos. = 72
			+ − −		3				

APPENDIX TABLE B–2.   SCHOOL BOARD SAMPLE ONLY
(N = 508)

SCHOOL BOARD MEMBER SATISFACTION
  (1) THE INSTRUMENT

The following statements refer to various aspects of the way groups function which we would like you to apply to your school committee. After each statement would you say which of the categories on the card best describes *your feeling* about the way your committee functions.	Very well satisfied	Fairly well satisfied	Fairly dissatisfied	Very dissatisfied	No Answer
Response scored as ⟶	(4)	(3)	(2)	(1)	(0)
1. The way individual school committee members fulfill the responsibilities of their office.	289	169	35	15	—
2. Goals or guiding principles of your school committee.	255	209	34	10	—
3. Persistence of the committee in doing a job.	306	155	39	8	—
4. The leadership in your committee.	266	166	44	27	5
5. The way decisions are reached.	268	167	50	23	—
6. Interest shown by other members.	321	161	19	7	—
7. Attempts to understand different points of view.	270	170	47	21	—
8. My own position on this committee.	287	186	23	11	1
9. The level of information about the schools and educational practices.	194	233	62	18	1
10. The way school committee meetings are conducted.	319	136	37	16	—

(2) SCHOOL BOARD MEMBER SATISFACTION SCALE: A 3-item H-technique scale. A high score means high satisfaction.

Reproducibility   = 98.0
Chance Reproducibility = 91.2   Error Ratio = .23

The Scale

Scale Score	Frequency	Percent	Response Pattern A B C	Frequency
3	123	24.2	+ + +	120
			+ + −	3
2	161	31.7	− + +	147
			+ − +	14
1	107	21.1	− − +	98
			− + −	9
0	117	23.0	− − −	113
			+ − −	4

*7 no answer responses coded as negative.

Definition of Contrived Items

Contrived Item	Original Item	Positive Response*	Positive Marginal
a =	9	4	194 ⎫ 2/2 pos. = 141
	2	4	255 ⎭
b =	4	4	266 ⎫
	7	4	270 ⎬ 2/3 pos. = 279
	8	4	287 ⎭
c =	10	4	319 ⎫
	6	4	321 ⎬ 2/3 pos. = 379
	5	3, 4	435 ⎭

APPENDIX TABLE B–3.   COMBINED SAMPLES
($N = 613$)

a. IDEAL DIVISION OF LABOR: A 3-item H-technique scale. A high score means more responsibility for the superintendent. (The questions on which these scales are based are found in Appendix A.)

The Scale for Combined Samples

Scale Score	Frequency	Percent	Response Pattern A B C	Frequency
			A B C	
3	123	21.6	+ + +	114
			+ + −	9
2	180	31.6	− + +	164
			+ − +	16
1	191	33.5	− − −	143
			− + −	48
0	76	13.3	− − −	74
			+ − −	2
	570	100.0		
	43		No ans.	

Reprod.   = 95.6
Ch. Reprod. = 92.0   E.R. = .55

Definition of Contrived Items

Contrived Item	Original Item	Positive Response	Positive Marginal
	8	4	146
$a =$	1	4	244 2/3 pos. = 141
	12	4	280
	3	4	389
$b =$	11	4	406 2/3 pos. = 335
	9	3, 4	442
	7	4	450
$c =$	13	3, 4	502 2/3 pos. = 437
	10	3, 4	536

Scale for Superintendent Sample Only

Scale Score	Frequency	Percent	Response Pattern A B C	Frequency
			A B C	
3	61	59.2	+ + +	61
2	37	35.9	− + +	34
			+ − +	3
1	5	4.9	− − +	3
			− + −	2
0	0	0.0	− − −	0
	103	100.0		
	2		No ans.	

Reprod.   = 98.4
Ch. Reprod. = 98.2   E.R. = .89

Scale for SB Sample Only

Scale Score	Frequency	Percent	Response Pattern A B C	Frequency
			A B C	
3	62	13.3	+ + +	53
			+ + −	9
2	143	30.6	− + +	130
			+ − +	13
1	186	39.8	− − +	140
			− + −	46
0	76	16.3	− − −	74
	467	100.0	+ − −	2
	41		No ans.	

Reprod.   = 95.0
Ch. Reprod. = 92.5   E.R. = .67

b. RATING OF SUPERINTENDENT ON PERSONAL CHARACTERISTICS:
   (1) THE INSTRUMENT

For each of the following characteristics would you please check the statement which most nearly applies to you (superintendent's version) applies to your superintendent (school board version).

1. Personal Appearance	S	SB	Code
A commanding personal appearance	3	66	5
An attractive personal appearance	33	217	4
About average in personal appearance	65	203	3
Do not make an especially good personal appearance	3	21	2
Make a poor personal appearance	0	1	1
No answer	1	0	0

2. Practicality	S	SB	Code
Exceptionally hard-headed and practical	2	40	5
Very practical	68	311	4
Fairly practical	35	142	3
Rather impractical	0	15	2
Very impractical	0	0	1

APPENDIX TABLE B–3 (Continued)

3. Clearness of Expression	S	SB	Code
Exceptional ability to express ideas clearly	6	125	5
Above average ability to express ideas clearly	59	206	4
Average ability to express ideas clearly	39	155	3
Do not express ideas clearly	1	20	2
Have great difficulty in expressing ideas clearly	0	2	1

4. Intelligence	S	SB	Code
A man of intellectual brilliance	1	39	5
A man of superior intelligence	44	272	4
A man of average intelligence	59	184	3
Usually intelligent, but not very bright in some things	1	12	2
Not very intelligent at all	0	0	1
No answer	0	1	0

5. Level of Information	S	SB	Code
Exceptionally well informed on modern educational practices	5	136	5
Very well informed on modern educational practices	62	280	4
Fairly well informed on modern educational practices	38	84	3
Not very well informed on modern educational practices	0	7	2
Very poorly informed on modern educational practices	0	0	1
No answer	0	1	0

6. Working with Other People	S	SB	Code
Work exceptionally well with other people	44	145	5
Work very well with other people	51	196	4
Get along with other people	10	84	3
Sometimes create friction when working with other people	0	80	2
Do not seem to be able to work with other people at all well	0	3	1

7. Tact	S	SB	Code
Shows unusual tact; always says just the right thing	1	37	5
Very tactful; rarely says the wrong thing	51	194	4
Usually tactful, but occasionally blunt	53	195	3
Shows tact, but sometimes offends others	0	71	2
Very blunt; constantly offending people	0	10	1
No answer	0	1	0

8. Business Sense	S	SB	Code
Shows extremely good business sense in financial matters	13	115	5
Excellent business sense in financial matters	46	178	4
Shows rather good business sense in financial matters	46	181	3
Not especially businesslike in financial matters	0	26	2
Shows poor business sense in financial matters	0	7	1
No answer	0	1	0

9. Persistence	S	SB	Code
Exceedingly persistent; voluntarily bends every energy to finish task	24	111	5
Unusually persistent; seldom deterred by difficulties	49	209	4
Fairly persistent, ordinarily finishes a task before leaving it	30	145	3
Tends to leave difficult tasks unfinished unless encouraged to continue	2	39	2
Easily deterred by obstacles, often gives up even if encouraged to continue	0	4	1

10. Sense of Values	S	SB	Code
Unfailingly keen insight in distinguishing the important from the unimportant	8	91	5
Generally distinguishes the important from the unimportant even when confusion might be easy	79	209	4
Distinguishes satisfactorily between the important and the unimportant	18	121	3
Occasionally confuses the important with the unimportant	0	36	2
Commonly neglects crucial issues through attention to the unimportant	0	6	1

APPENDIX TABLE B–3 (Continued)

(2) RATING SCALE FOR SUPERINTENDENT'S PERSONAL CHARACTERISTICS: A 3-item H-technique scale.
A high score means a high rating.

The Scale for Combined Samples

Scale Score	Fre-quency	Percent	Response Pattern			Fre-quency
			A	B	C	
3	150	24.5	+	+	+	146
			+	+	−	4
2	221	36.0	−	+	+	206
			+	−	+	15
1	131	21.4	−	−	+	104
			−	+	−	27
0	111	18.1	−	−	−	110
			+	−	−	1

Reprod.   = 97.4
Ch. Reprod. = 91.8   E.R. = .32

Definition of Contrived Items

Con-trived Item	Original Item	Positive Response	Positive Marginal	
$a =$	9	5	135	
	6	5	189	2/3 pos. = 166
	1	4, 5	319	
$b =$	8	4, 5	352	
	4	4, 5	356	2/3 pos. = 383
	3	4, 5	396	
$c =$	2	4, 5	421	
	10	4, 5	432	2/3 pos. = 471
	5	4, 5	483	

Scale for Superintendent Sample Only

Scale Score	Fre-quency	Percent	Response Pattern			Fre-quency
			A	B	C	
3	21	20.0	+	+	+	19
			+	+	−	2
2	42	40.0	−	+	+	35
			+	−	+	7
1	20	19.0	−	−	+	16
			−	+	−	4
0	22	21.0	−	−	−	22

Reprod.   = 95.9
Ch. Reprod. = 91.1   E.R. = .46

Scale for SB Sample Only

Scale Score	Fre-quency	Percent	Response Pattern			Fre-quency
			A	B	C	
3	129	25.4	+	+	+	127
			+	+	−	2
2	179	35.2	−	+	+	171
			+	−	+	8
1	111	21.9	−	−	+	88
			−	+	−	23
0	89	17.5	−	−	−	88
			+	−	−	1

Reprod.   = 97.8
Ch. Reprod. = 92.0   E.R. = .28

APPENDIX TABLE B–3 (Continued)

c. EDUCATIONAL PROGRESSIVISM
   (1) THE INSTRUMENT

How do you feel about these policies or programs?	Sample	Answer Categories*					
		1	2	3	4	NA	Other
1. Pupils are separated into "bright" and "slow" classes. (T)	S	17	29	46	8	1	4
	SB	117	214	140	30	4	3
2. In the first six grades pupils must meet specified academic standards in order to be promoted. (T)	S	6	47	26	16	0	
	SB	176	253	66	10	3	
3. A maximum class size of twenty-five in elementary schools. (P)	S	2	0	28	75	0	
	SB	7	24	158	318	1	
4. Sex education in high schools. (P)	S	11	23	55	15	1	
	SB	39	122	254	85	8	
5. A great deal of emphasis on a program of extracurricular activities. (P)	S	2	23	57	23	0	
	SB	13	157	228	109	1	
6. Some kind of psychological guidance facilities available to pupils through the schools. (P)	S	2	1	32	70	0	
	SB	1	9	229	267	1	
7. Numerical grading given on regular report cards in the first six grades. (T)	S	1	8	53	43	0	
	SB	80	188	189	40	11	
8. Different salaries for elementary and high school teachers. (T)	S	7	3	21	74	0	
	SB	39	121	235	111	2	
9. Teachers act as advisers in extracurricular activities. (P)	S	0	1	36	68	0	
	SB	1	11	265	229	2	
10. More emphasis is placed on developing individual interests of the pupils, rather than on teaching subject matter. (P)	S	2	10	48	44	1	
	SB	12	150	224	117	5	
11. More emphasis is placed on teaching subject matter, rather than on developing individual interests of the pupils. (T)	S	0	14	58	31	0	
	SB	12	155	223	113	5	
12. Teacher participation in policy formation. (P)	S	1	2	41	61	0	
	SB	6	53	279	169	1	
13. Pupils regularly form into lines on the way to and from classes. (T)	S	4	20	58	21	2	
	SB	96	250	131	24	7	
14. Use of schools as neighborhood centers. (P)	S	2	0	28	75	0	
	SB	8	37	210	252	1	
15. Extensive use of psychological and mental tests. (P)	S	1	3	56	44	1	
	SB	4	83	279	136	6	

*The original check list read: A = highly desirable, B = desirable, C = undesirable, D = highly undesirable.

The items were classified as "Progressive" or "Traditional" (indicated by P and T respectively following the items) on the basis of their categorization by five raters, faculty members at the Harvard Graduate School of Education. On the 75 categorizations (5 x 15 items) there was 96% agreement.

APPENDIX TABLE B–3 (Continued)

(2) EDUCATIONAL PROGRESSIVISM SCALE: A 3-item *H*-technique scale. A high score means high progressivism.

The Scale for Combined Samples

Scale Score	Frequency	Percent	Response Pattern A B C	Frequency
3	103	16.8	+ + +	102
			+ + −	1
2	164	26.8	− + +	142
			+ − +	22
1	224	36.5	− − +	202
			− + −	22
0	122	19.9	− − −	119
			+ − −	3

Reprod. = 97.4
Ch. Reprod. = 92.6   E.R. = .35

Definition of Contrived Items

Contrived Item	Original Item	Positive Response*	Positive Marginal	
a =	9	3, 4	118	
	17	4	161	2/3 pos. = 128
	15	4	185	
b =	19	4	230	
	20	3, 4	234	2/3 pos. = 243
	21	4	327	
c =	14	3, 4	325	
	13	4	337	2/4 pos. = 463
	10	4	393	
	18	3, 4	425	

Scale for Superintendent Sample Only

Scale Score	Frequency	Percent	Response Pattern A B C	Frequency
3	50	47.6	+ + +	49
			+ + −	1
2	33	31.4	− + +	26
			+ − +	7
1	18	17.1	− − +	15
			− + −	3
0	4	3.8	− − −	3
			+ − −	1

Reprod. = 96.2
Ch. Reprod. = 93.5   E.R. = .58

Scale for *SB* Sample Only

Scale Score	Frequency	Percent	Response Pattern A B C	Frequency
3	53	10.4	+ + +	53
2	131	25.8	− + +	116
			+ − +	15
1	206	40.6	− − +	187
			− + −	19
0	118	23.2	− − −	116
			+ − −	2

Reprod. = 97.4
Ch. Reprod. = 93.8   E.R. = .42

*No answer coded negative (traditional).

APPENDIX TABLE B–4.   OTHER INSTRUMENTS

a. Political-Economic Conservatism Scale*

Instructions for Superintendents and School Board Members: The best answer to each statement below is *your personal opinion.* We have tried to cover many different points of view. You may find yourself agreeing strongly with some of the statements, disagreeing just as strongly with others, and perhaps uncertain about others. Whether you agree or disagree with any statement, you can be sure that many other people feel just the same way that you do.

Mark each statement in the box at the right according to how much you agree or disagree with it. *Please mark every one.* Write in +1, +2, +3; or ⁻1, ⁻2, ⁻3; depending on how you feel in each case.

+1: I agree a little	⁻1: I disagree a little
+2: I agree pretty much	⁻2: I disagree pretty much
+3: I agree very much	⁻3: I disagree very much

1. When private enterprise does not do the job, it is up to the government to step in and meet the public's need for housing, water power, and the like. □
2. Men like Henry Ford or J. P. Morgan, who overcame all competition on the road to success, are models for all young people to admire and imitate. □
3. The government should own and operate all public utilities (railroad, gas, electricity, etc.). □
4. In general, full economic security is bad; most men wouldn't work if they didn't need the money for eating and living. □
5. The only way to do away with poverty is to make basic changes in our political and economic system. □
6. There should be some upper limit, such as $50,000 per year, on how much a person can earn. □
7. At this time, powerful "big business" is a greater danger than powerful "big unions" to our national welfare. □
8. We need more government controls over business practices and profits. □
9. Labor unions in large corporations should be given a larger part in deciding company policy. □
10. The government should develop a program of health insurance and medical care. □
11. America may not be perfect, but the American way has brought us about as close as human beings can get to a perfect society. □
12. Strong labor unions are necessary if the working man is to get greater security and a better standard of living. □

*We are indebted to Dr. Daniel J. Levinson for making this short form of the PEC Scale available to us.

b. Rating Scale of Superintendent's Functions

Question for Superintendents: What kind of job do you think you are doing in each of the following activities associated with your job? (Response categories: Excellent, Good, Fair, Poor.)

Question for School Board Members: Could you indicate how you feel about how the superintendent is carrying out these parts of his job? (Response categories: Excellent, Good Fair, Poor.)

Items

1. *Personnel Administration*: The selection of teachers and other school employees, salaries, assignments, promotions, and separations from service.
2. *Financial Administration*: Budgets, handling of funds, purchases, and accounting.
3. *School Plant Management*: Site selection, relations with architects and contractors, furniture and equipment, repairs, and custodial services.
4. *Instructional Direction*: Curriculum planning, methods of teaching, evaluation of activities, working with teachers, audio-visual materials, textbooks, and libraries.
5. *Pupil Services Supplementary to Instruction*: Transportation, health services, and school lunches.
6. *Public Relations*: Community contacts with organizations, newspapers, radio, reporting to the public.
7. *General Planning*: for the school program as a whole.

c. Motivation Categories

Question for the Superintendent: Could you indicate what you think are the chief reasons each member ran for election to the school committee?

Response Categories: He (or she):

1. Felt that someone had to see that school expenditures were increased.
2. Wanted certain friends to get in or to advance in the school system.
3. Felt that the school superintendent should be removed.
4. A certain group in the community felt that they should be represented on the school committee.
5. Felt that someone had to see that school expenditures were decreased.
6. Felt it to be his (her) civic duty.
7. Did not like the way his (her) children were being educated.
8. Disapproved of the way the schools were being run.
9. Was interested in getting some experience in politics.
10. Other (what?)

An Analysis of Voter Reaction to a Proposal to Form a Library District in Parts of LaSalle and Bureau Counties, Illinois: Questionnaire

Mary Lee Bundy

Confidential report to:
Office of Research
Graduate School of Library Science
University of Illinois
Urbana, Illinois

RURAL LIBRARY STUDY: ILLINOIS

In some rural areas, voters have elected to form tax supported library districts or county libraries. In other areas people have voted against such proposals. Some people favor increased tax support for public libraries while others oppose it.

This study is planned to find out more about how you and other people living in rural areas feel. Your opinions will be appreciated. (Please answer on a family basis.)

1. Were you familiar with the plan to form a library district?

   a. _____ yes

   b. _____ no

2. If yes, do you remember when you first heard about the library district?

   a. _____ at the beginning of the bookmobile project

   b. _____ around the time of the hearing

   c. _____ near the time of the voting

   d _____ other (please specify) _____

3. Were you in favor of forming the Illinois Valley District Library?

   a. _____ very strongly for   e. _____ mildly against

   b. _____ quite strongly for   f. _____ quite strongly against

   c. _____ mildly for   g. _____ very strongly against

   d. _____ neutral

4. What was the main reason for your choice? _____
   _____

5. Did you vote at the referendum on October 17?

   a. _____ yes

   b. _____ no

6. If you did not vote, why not?

   a. _____ not in the proposed district   d. _____ couldn't get to the polls

   b. _____ not interested   e. _____ not sure which way I wanted to vote

   c. _____ didn't know about it   f. _____ other (please specify) _____

Please continue on next page

SOURCE: Mary Lee Bundy, *An Analysis of Voter Reaction to a Proposal to Form a Library District in LaSalle and Bureau Counties, Illinois* (Springfield: Illinois State Library, December, 1960), Questionnaire, "Rural Library Study: Illinois," pp. 1–4.

These are some of the statements which were made in the newspapers and other places about the library district and library service. Please indicate the degree to which you agree or disagree with them.

		Strongly Agree	Agree	No Opinion	Disagree	Strongly Disagree
1.	The cost of the proposed library district would have been small compared to its benefits					
2.	The information supplied about the library district was often erroneous and inadequate.					
3.	The use made of the bookmobile service is evidence of the need.					
4.	A few people were trying to railroad everyone else into something they didn't want.					
5.	Voters placed a few cents above education for their children.					
6.	The library district would have taken control out of local hands where it belongs.					
7.	Adults need books to keep up with a modern and changing world.					
8.	The library district would have meant an additional tax which rural people cannot afford.					
9.	There was no guarantee of good service if the library district were voted in.					
10.	Our schools, and mass media, take care of our educational and recreational needs. Library service is not necessary.					
11.	Although it was understood in the beginning that the bookmobile was on a trial basis, they were really trying to buy votes with books.					
12.	Bookmobile service is unnecessary in this area since books can be obtained from the state library or from near-by libraries.					
13.	Our school libraries are insufficient to cover needs of school children. They need supplementary public library service.					

What was your understanding as to how much the tax would be _____

_____

_____

Please continue on next page

The questions in this section are asked to find out more about how people formed their opinions on this issue.

1. Do you recall reading any newspaper articles about the library district?

    a. _____ many   c. _____ none

    b. _____ a few

Were they mostly:

    a. _____ for   c. _____ against

    b. _____ neutral

2. Do you recall reading any newspaper articles about the bookmobile demonstration project?

    a. _____ many   c. _____ none

    b. _____ a few

3. Do you recall hearing about the referendum on the library district over the radio?

    a. _____ yes   b. _____ no

4. Do you recall receiving any circulars or cards through the mail on the library district?

    a. _____ yes   b. _____ no

If yes, about how many did you receive? _____

5. Did you receive any telephone calls about the library district?

    a. _____ yes   b. _____ no

If yes, did they urge:

    a. _____ support   c. _____ received

    b. _____ opposition   both kinds

6. Were you at any meeting where the library district was discussed?

    a. _____ many   c. _____ none

    b. _____ a few

7. Did you discuss the issue with friends?

    a. _____ a great deal

    b. _____ quite a bit

    c. _____ very little

    d. _____ none

8. Were you a member of any organization which took a stand on the library district?

    a. _____ yes   b. _____

If yes, did it:

    a. _____ favor the district

    b. _____ oppose the district

9. Were you connected in any other way with the referendum on the library district?

    a. _____ an original supporter of the demonstration project

    b. _____ signed the petition to form the library district

    c. _____ a member of the project steering committee

    d. _____ spoke for the district at a meeting

    e. _____ spoke against the district at a meeting

    f. _____ attended the hearing

    g. _____ other (please specify) _____

10. Was there any one thing in particular which happened or one thing you heard which helped you decide how you felt about this issue (please describe)

_____

_____

11. What do you think was the main reason this proposal was voted down?

_____

_____

12. Do you usually vote in local elections:

    a. _____ almost always   b. _____ quite often   c. _____ almost never

13. Do you think people tend to ask your advice about local affairs:

    a. _____ more than   b. _____ about the same   c. _____ less than they do other people

Please continue on next page

The questions in this section are planned to learn more about how people living in rural areas use libraries.

1. Does your community have a library?

    a. _____ yes   b. _____ no

    If yes, do you borrow books:

    a. _____ often   c. _____ seldom
    b. _____ occasionally d. _____ never

2. Are you a non-resident borrower with another library?

    a. _____ yes   b. _____ no

    If yes, do you borrow books:

    a. _____ often   c. _____ seldom
    b. _____ occasionally d. _____ never

3. Did you personally use the bookmobile demonstration service?

    a. _____ often   c. _____ seldom
    b. _____ occasionally d. _____ never

4. Did the children in your family use the bookmobile demonstration service?

    a. _____ often   c. _____ seldom
    b. _____ occasionally d. _____ never

5. In general do you think the bookmobile service was satisfactory?

    a. _____ yes   b. _____ no

    What would be your main criticism, if any: _____
    _____

6. How valuable have you found libraries to be?

    a. _____ of great value
    b. _____ of some value
    c. _____ of little or no value

7. Have you or any member of your family read any part of a book other than school books and the Bible during the past month?

    a. _____ yes   b. _____ no

How would you describe your interest and participation in local organizations?

Organization	Very Active	Often Participate	Seldom Participate	Don't Belong	Officer or Committee Member
P.T.A.					
Women's Club					
Farm Bureau					
Home Bureau					
Grange					
Farmers Union					
Drama Club					
Church					
Other (list)					

Number of children in family of school age _____
Last year of school you attended _____
Property owner _____; non-property owner _____
Farm _____ town _____ resident
Occupation _____

Number of years you have lived in the community _____
Approximate family income last year (Do not answer unless you wish to)
Under $3000 _____; $3000-5000 _____;
over $5000 _____

Any further comments you may care to make about the library district or libraries and reading generally:
_____
_____

List of Contributors